2004 COBRA GOOD CURRY GUIDE

PAT CHAPMAN

THE 2004 COBRA GOOD CURRY GUIDE

Joint Editor and Database Management:
Dominique Chapman (DBAC)

Design: Peter Ward

Text Editor: Amanda Gray

Statistics: Taylor Nelson, Sub Continent Publishing

Researchers: Sarika Azad, Jonelle Bester, Zubin Bhedwar, Aftab Bhatti, Helena Bennett, Shahnoor Chowdhury, Roopa Gulati, Khurram Nelson, Horshang Noria, Ajay Patel, Samson Sohail, Biren Parikh, Buela Samuel, Samson Sohail, Puja Vedi,

Good Curry Guide Frequent and Prolific Reporters:
Dave Bridges, The Wirral; N.K.Campbell, Edinburgh; Hilary Chapchal, Surrey; Bill Parkes-Davis, Tunbridge Wells, Kent; Ray & Ruby Elliot, Worcs; Tony Emmerson, Lancs; Justin Harper, Hemel; Tony and Monika Hetherington, Yorks; Andly Glazier, London; Tim & Katherine Morgan, Scotland, Steve Osborne, Bucks; Grahame and Melida Payne, Coventry; Professor Dirk Pilat, e-mail; Ralph Warrington, Hyde; Cheshire (GM); Jeanette Wickes, Kent,; Malcolm Wilkins, Gravesend, Kent; Mick Wright, Beds.
plus many hundreds of others, without whom
this Guide would not exist, and whose names appear on page 352

This eight edition first published in Great Britain in 2004
by The Curry Club, PO Box 7, Haslemere, Surrey, UK. GU27 1EP

Previous Editions of this Guide:
First edition 1984, Second: 1987, Third 1991,
Fourth: 1995, Fifth: 1998, Sixth: 1999, Seventh 2001

ISBN 0 9537735-1-5

Printed and bound in Great Britain by Lookers Printers, Poole, Dorset.

A CIP catalogue recommendation for this book is available from the British Library

CONTENTS

THE ENTRIES

County Index

See page 359 for Town Index

London

England

The Isles and Islands

Ireland

Scotland

Wales

Author's Notes

Sponsorship The continuing sponsorship of Cobra Beer, the *Guide*'s sole sponsor, enables the author to finance the considerable costs of operating and producing this *Guide,* which include: maintaining the restaurant database on computer; subscribing to a press-cutting service and other information suppliers; printing a detailed questionnaire and mailing it to all 8,000 restaurants twice a year; mail-shotting the 1,500-plus restaurants that are selected to appear in the *Guide*; telephoning many for verification of information; producing, supplying and mailing the selected restaurants (free of charge) their wall certificates and window stickers; printing and mailing restaurant report forms for interested parties; collating and recording the info received (some 5,000 reports per annum) and operating the Awards Ceremony.

Accuracy The contents of this *Guide* are as up-to-date and accurate as possible, but we cannot be held responsible for any changes regarding quality, price, menu details, decor, ownership, health offences or even closure, following our processing of the reports.

Connections Pat Chapman, the publishers of this *Guide* and the proprietors of The Curry Club wish to make it quite clear that they have absolutely no financial or ownership connections with any restaurants, including those mentioned in this *Guide*.

False representation Restaurant reports are welcomed from any bona-fide source. We do not pay for reports – they are sent in spontaneously and voluntarily. Our own research and restaurant testing is normally done anonymously, the bill is paid, and often no disclosure is made as to our presence. On some occasions, such as openings, we accept invitations to visit restaurants as 'guests of the house'. Under no circumstances do we tout for free hospitality, and anyone doing so in the name of The Curry Club is an impostor. We have heard of cases where people claiming to be members of The Curry Club, or *Good Curry Guide* 'inspectors', request payment and/or free meals in return for entry into this *Guide*. In such cases, we would recommend that restaurants threaten to call the police. We would also like to be informed of any such incidents and we will not hesitate to take action against people acting illegally in our name.

Discounts We invite all restaurants selected to appear in this *Guide* to participate in a discount scheme for members of The Curry Club. Those restaurants who agree to participate are indicated by the symbol © on their entry. The terms of this scheme are clearly spelled out to all parties. We cannot be held responsible if, at any time, the restaurant declines the offered discount. *See also page 626.*

Certificates & window stickers We send all restaurants appearing in this *Guide* a 2001 certificate, hand-signed by Pat Chapman, and a 2001 window sticker. These items are supplied free of charge. Some choose not to display them, others display them proudly and prominently. You may observe that our certificate is not displayed alone. There may well be a host of others, some bigger and flashier than ours, including the Dome Grading certificates issued by Peter and Colleen Groves, which are genuine, as are certificates issued by London's *Time Out,* Ronay, local council health departments and certain others. Unfortunately, some certificates are a pure sham. They are issued to any restaurant who cares to pay for them, in some cases with a promise of entry into a *Guide* which does not even exist. We reported last time on a scam by *Good Food Guide,* yet again, but this is not The *Good Food Guide*.

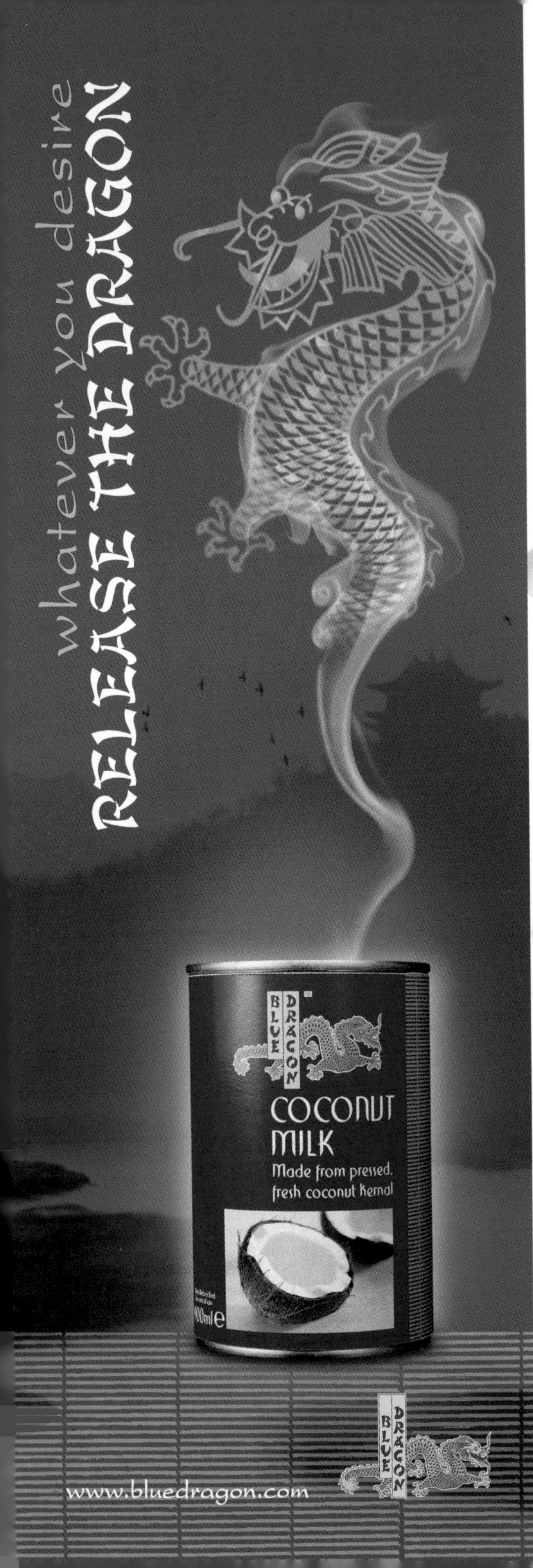

There is no *Guide* and this is the same outfit that were sued by the Consumers' Association some time ago and have now re-emerged at a different address. Masterchef returned after being exposed by BBC 'Food and Drink' in June. Certificates are on offer for £67.50 (£10 for extra copies) and £5 for window stickers. The *Asian Food Guide* was caught out on Radio 4. There are others on the bandwagon. Like Peter Groves, we would like to see this scam stopped.

But how do you know that the *Good Curry Guide* certificate you see is genuine? Earlier this year, we were sent a fax by one of the award-winning restaurants in the *Good Curry Guide*. It was a copy of a fax they had just received. Its heading in large type was *THE GOOD CURRY GUIDE*, with 'a new idea to make your restaurant more popular'. It told of a new website called *The Curry Guide*. Strange that, because we have registered *The Good Curry Guide.com* and *The Good Curry Guide.co.uk* as domain names and we've not been sending anyone any such faxes. It seems this fax is offering a *Good Curry Guide* certificate for a cost of £30. Funny that! We give our certificates free of charge. So who is this plagiarist?

It seems the person responsible is one Ian Cowan of Inc Software, Paisley, Scotland. We doubt that he will actually make any money but if even one restaurant is mug enough to hope to fool his customers with a dazzling *Good Curry Guide* certificate, it's bad news for the customer and for the industry, because I do not believe that Mr Cowan will stop at offering only entrants to our *Guide* the chance of a £30 certificate, He'll offer it to every UK restaurant. The problem is that selling a certificate is not illegal. And restaurateurs are anxious to impress their customers. In the last year you have flooded us with information on which certificates restaurants display. We'd like you to continue with this intelligence.

And, apparently, you've been telling your restaurants that you are aware of the scam, and prefer awards which are given free on merit.

About this Guide

The Good Curry Guide broke new ground when it was first published in 1984, by being the first restaurant guide to specialise only in the British curry. This, its eighth edition.. As usual, there there have been demotions and promotions since last time. We want continuity in each edition of the *Guide*, and because we do expect changes, we feel it is important that each restaurant completes our questionnaire. For one thing, it means the restaurant actually wants to be in the *Guide*. It also verifies its current name, address, telephone number, and above all, prices. Despite our earnest endeavours, not all restaurants reply, even if they did so last time. So if we have not received a reply from a restaurant that was in the previous edition, after it has been sent a form three times, should it be delisted? I believe it should if it cannot be bothered, for whatever reason, to talk to us. But curry restaurants are a peculiar trade; communications aren't always easy and normal rules don't apply.

A completed form from a restaurant does not guarantee entry to the Guide. We rely on various other sources of information. We can only visit a handful of restaurants each year, and do not have a team of paid inspectors. Most important to us are the opinions of the customers – you, the diners. We do not pay for such reports, though from time to time The Curry Club gives prizes for your efforts. The report itself can be a simple short note, though we have a special form (see final page) for all who want one. A report may deal with a single restaurant or several. Some reporters write to us only once, others write repeatedly. For this Guide, we received about 5,000 reports, yielding information on up to 50,000 restaurant visits. We read and record every report, although it is becoming increasingly difficult to reply to all of them. I would like, therefore, to thank all those who have taken the time to tell us where they have found the best, good, mediocre and even bad curries.

Of course reporting standards vary, and the The Wind of India, Puddlecome-on-the-Marsh may well be reported as the best in the world by an ardent, novice, local fan (and I want such opinions), but may not rate highly if compared with London's best. Nevertheless, it will be a competent curry house in that area, serving standard formula curry. Numerous entries in this *Guide* come into this category, and they are here because someone, maybe more than one person, has taken the trouble to write in and praise the place, and to exclude it would be wrong. We want to know what you know.

Answering the question 'Name your favourite curry restaurant(s)' may not always be as easy as it sounds. It is worth again quoting Sutton Coldfield's John Brockingham, a retired college lecturer: 'My favourite restaurants,' he wrote, 'range from opulent establishments like Rajdoot, Birmingham, where I might take the family on special occasions, to cheap and cheerful places like Erdington's Balti Express, where a meal costs £11 a head. I have a favourite posh curry restaurant, when I can afford it, and a favourite posh Balti. But I have a favourite plonk version of both, and a favourite takeaway, and then there's a favourite lucky dip. Some of my favourites are good enough to tempt me in whenever I'm in the district, but could not be nominated for the highest accolade.'

Of course we do not receive reports on every single establishment. On occasion a restaurant we normally receive good reports about gets damned. If this is the exception, we will probably still carry that restaurant. Some will have closed, and others should perhaps have been omitted. But none get into this *Guide* unless we have had at least one recent good report on it, preferably several. To get into the TOP 100 we need several detailed excellent reports, including at least one by one of our elite 60 or so regular reporters. As editors we visit a TOP 100 restaurant anonymously whenever we can, but it's impossible to go to them all within one year. We do our best to filter out 'good' reports on bad restaurants, particularly those written by their hopeful owners. This time we requested that restaurants selected for entry get their customers to write to us, and many did. This way, we have almost weeded out the few restaurants who previously sent us phoney reports, purportedly from adoring customers. However, even after twenty years in the editor's chair, it is possible that I've been conned and a 'bad' restaurant has slipped in. Equally, I'll guarantee that we've missed someone's favourite, and that there are a few *faux pas* too. Please let us know about these. No doubt, we'll continue to get irate letters from people who won't have bothered to read this section, telling us that, because this or that restaurant was awful when they visited, 'it casts doubt on the credibility of the entire *Guide*'. We certainly do not enter restaurants just because they ask us to. After over twenty years of bona-fide operations, you would imagine that curryhouse owners would clamour to be in the *Guide*. Indeed some do. As I have said in previous *Guides*, more than one restaurant has made veiled references to the benefits that would be made available to the editors if that restaurant were declared the UK's number one. The very idea is abhorrent. Besides, if one did accede to such bribery, word would soon get round risking the credibility of both author and publication. The book is paid for through book sales, ads and sponsorship, not through bribes.

So what's new in this edition? We've dropped our price check – it was out of date before we went to print Regular readers will know that we go alphabetically by county, then within that, by town and then restaurant. We are continuing with this system, since it is easier to see at a glance what alternative choices are nearby. We have also continue with the town index at the end of the book. At the start of each county's entry, we have also improved our thumbnail county maps, which help pinpoint the location of that particular county, along with a new feature, which lists adjacent counties, and a few statistics. It should make this *Guide* more informative and finding your way around it easier. And that, after all, is what this *Guide* is all about – finding good curries easily, and nothing else.

Welcome to the Eight Edition

Welcome to this, the eighth edition of the *Cobra Good Curry Guide,* whose history goes back to 1984, *see page* 4. Twenty years on, there is a quivering tension in the air among the up-market Indian restaurant sector about being given awards from another publication, the *Michelin Guide.* Being awarded the Michelin Star sounds like getting a like a war medal to me, and one has to ask why a perfectly sound Indian restaurateur goes overboard in the hope of receiving this accolade from a tyre company, whose inspectors don't know a Biriani from a Ding Bat. Perhaps, if such inspectors do not understand Indian food, they should omit it from their guides. When they do make an award Michelin give it to the wrong restaurants, Tamarind, whose chef left shortly after the award (*see page* 125) and to Zaika, whose food is eclectic to out it mildly, and who moved venue shortly after (*see page* 135). But if one gets it (or two in this case) why not more? Why not to more deserving restaurants like Chutney Mary SW10, Veerswamy W1, The Quilon SW1, The Bombay Brasserie SW7, La Porte des Indes W1, Sarkhel's SW18 and Café Spice Namaste E1 (apologies for any omissions).

Michelin seem to place their yardstick on the French dining experience; not surprising since Michelin is French. But Indian food isn't. They particularly look for presentation, service and the quality and matching of fine wines. And it almost certainly helps to be up-market, high price-tagged, with grandiose settings and in the big city. All those above-mentioned restaurants have all those criteria, bar one; they do not do French cuisine.

No one is more desperate to get the Michelin star than Iqbal Wahhab, an old friend of mine, best known for his ill-considered remarks. Few people who love curry will forget his 'all Bangladeshi waiters are miserable gits' remarks. Like Kilroy Silk it cost him his job. Wahhab still says stupid things. This was from the Financial Times in a recent piece by him on Chicken Tikka Masala: *'Mid-range restaurateurs come and see me, or Amin Ali of The Red Fort, or Cyrus Todiwalla of Café Spice, or Udit Sarkhel of Sarkhel's restaurant, on a daily basis to ask for our advice – and when we can, we oblige.'* The day one should ask Amin Ali for advice will be the day he stops going bankrupt (see page 125). And as for Cyrus and Udit, they were cheffing at the Taj Group while Wahhab was cutting his teeth on his GCSE maths. However, Iqbal is a survivor and master of spin, and his Cinnamon Club, set in spin-land Westminster, has got them all talking (*see page* 90). Of course, the *Cinnamon Club Cookbook* was an inevitable outcome and come out it did in late 2003. In its introduction, Wahhab mentions 'French' (cuisine) no less than eight times and 'Michelin' no less than four times. And to save you counting, it's 21 times in this piece.

Although Indian cuisine has been evolved to perfection over 3,500 years, Iqbal decided this wasn't good enough for him and he set about reinventing it. He made friends with Eric Chavot, a Michelin two-star chef from Knightsbridge's Capital Hotel. Chavot had no understanding of Indian food outside of his local takeaway (nothing new there then) but soon grasped what Wahhab wanted to achieve. Chavot believes each dish must be 'constructed on the plate', with ingredients piled up mini-tower style. Sauce must be placed over and/or under these ingredients, and each dish, he says, must have something crisp on top, an evolved bhaji, for example. And if no sauce, he employs the passée technique of drawing brown, green or red squiggly lines from squeezy bottles. As for the sauces, Chavot proposed inventing and

reducing them from scratch, to be cooked apart from the main ingredient, and only added on the plate, French-style. A hitherto unknown chef, Vivek Singh was brought from India and catapulted to stardom by spin-master Wahhab, his prime job to make Chavot's theories work. And so we have such fusion dishes as the Goan classic Pork Vindaloo, which now no longer gets a long marination and a slow-cook; it becomes Vindaloo of Pig's Cheeks, with a reduced sauce under/over it. Chicken Korma becomes 'a roulade of breast stuffed with spinach and apricot with an aromatic sauce'. Char-grilled sea bream gets 'pomegranate extract'. Loin of Rabbit comes with 'dried fruits in a mustard marinade', and Zucchini flower is 'stuffed with spiced corn and mushroom'. And to push away the curry house ritual even further, Wahhab made Cinnamon Club a popadom-free zone, with beer, if you must, served almost disdainfully from small bottles into fancy glasses. No sir, you are expected to open you wallet for some fine wine with prices ranging up nearly £1,000 a bottle.

It's clearly the stuff Michelin stars are made of. Says Wahhab: 'One day a friend of mine told me she shared a flat with a Michelin Guide inspector ... and that if I could convince her that Indian restaurants were being left behind by Michelin, she would take up my case with her friend. I took her to lunch at one of those restaurants I considered to be a worthy contender for a Michelin award. My friend soon showed me I was expecting too much. There was a mango chutney splat on the menu, one of the plates was chipped and my wine glass was refilled before hers.

These may be minor aberrations, but following these highly perceptive observations, this *Guide's* editors decided to approach every restaurant visit in reverse, so to speak. We decided that every place we visit already has five stars. It's then up to them to maintain them. Great food they may have and great service. But it is amazing how quickly the stars can be extinguished. One might argue that this is far too high a standard to set for any restaurant. After all, a restaurant is a moving living thing with so many variables, it simply cannot expect to uphold all its aspirations. Agreed it's hard, but it's not impossible. It all begins with care. Care from the owners, applied to staff, customers, settings and detail. An example of failure of care took place at Mint Leaf (*see page* 91). Chavot says it is necessary for the chef to go daily to market at 5 am to buy vegetables or meat. In fact if he does, he's an idiot; he won't be cooking at his best at 9.30pm, when diners most need his best. No, he should have selected the best suppliers, whose job it is to buy the best produce for the chef and deliver them to his venue before he starts work. And if the waiting staff dribble wine on that pristine expensive, starched white table cloth, or have BO, or smash that expensive huge thin-stemmed glass, isn't that a matter of training from the owners? And shouldn't the owners, or named chef be present on a frequent, if not permanent basis? Can you be sure that Ramsay, Jamie, Worrall Thomson, Blanc or Turner are there every night? But I can assure you that Sreeram of The Quilon, Vikram of The Bombay Brasserie, Mernosh of La Porte des Indes, Udit of Sarkhel's and Cyrus of Café Spice Namaste are there. That's their level of care and dedication.

I have dwelt a lot on Iqbal Wahhab and his Cinnamon Club, but he has set himself a rod for his own back, by assuming that he can can teach the industry, in which he himself has only been involved for just over a decade, how to run itself. It is not a bad aspiration to wish to run the best Indian restaurant in the land, if not the world. Does he achieve it? Our views are stated on page 90. But here's Cinnamon Club in summary: exterior interesting, reception good; cleanliness, good; toilet good; table settings good; cutlery, glasses and crockery, good, and expensive; service good, mostly French in black waistcoats and long white aprons, but a little hovering; food hardly Indian, in fact a definite French feel to it, indeed rather pretentious; presentation, very considered, almost too much so; wines, good list, very high price bracket; ambience, up-market; location as central in central London as you can get; clientele: stars, politicians, hangers-on, and black-suited young spenders. That is exactly what Iqbal wants, and I know it's exactly what Michelin want too. Is it what readers of this guide want at an Indian restaurant, or indeed the highly-trained chefs who work at the above mentioned restaurants? I quote from our entry on page 92 re Chef Sriram of The Quilon: *'Unlike others in town, Sriram proves that there is no need for flamboyance, spin or new wave, "Do not take a traditional dish and mess around with it", he says. In typical understated Taj style, he simply and quietly goes about his business of producing perfect Indian cooking'.* Sorry Iqbal, but no major award from us yet.

Applying our new rigorous methods, if we were Michelin we would have awarded Chutney Mary, The Quilon, The Bombay Brasserie, La Porte des Indes, and Veerswamy, Two stars and Sarkhel's,Café Spice Namaste and Coconut Lagoon, Kenilworth, Warks one star. As it is we have given them our own, far more relevant awards. *See page* 35.

We have great pleasure in breaking the capital city mould and making Madhu's of Southall, Middlesex our top-starred restaurant, the best in the UK. Southall??? Madhu's??? Oui monsieurs ... get your tails in there and see why. And we very nearly took our Top award further afield to Milton Keynes (*see page* 150).

We aren't Michelin, thank heavens. Our remit is Indian or curry, call it what you will and only Indian or curry. And the restaurants and our readers take our judgements very seriously indeed, as they should do. Indeed if it were not for the prolific and abundant views of our readers, this guide would not exist. And we dedicate and commend this *Guide* to them.

Winners All

Awards ceremonies have proliferated like everything else since *The Good Curry Guide* and *The Curry Club* jointly started the first ever *Restaurant Awards* ceremony in 1992. Perhaps we should start the *'Best of the Awards'* Ceremony, where all awards ceremonies are judged to find an overall winner. Meanwhile, here are a whole clutch of recent 2003 awards. Shyham S. Longanu, an Indian master chef at the Taj Mahal Intercontinental Hotel in Mumbai, won Tommy Miah's Edinburgh 2003 *International Indian Chef of the Year Contest.* Second came Chad Rahman owner of Mumtaj, St Albans, who is also twice and current winner of the *CIEH National Curry Chef of the Year.* Chutney Mary won the Indian restaurant of the year award at the *Tio Pepe Carlton London Restaurant Award* 2003. Red Fort won the *Best Indian Restaurant Award Time Out Eating & Drinking Awards,* then went into receivership. Aktar Islam, 24, restaurant manager at Lasan, St Paul's Square, Birmingham won the *Manager of Tomorrow Award of Excellence* from their Midlands Association of Restaurant Caterers and Hotels. Chef Munayam Khan was a recent winner at Hospitality Week's *Authentic Foods of the World* competition. Sous chef is Ashutosh Bhardwaj.

Gourmet India, sw, won the *London Home Delivery Challenge.* Head Chef is ex Chutney Mary's Murralli Dharan, who had had seven

Bengal Dynasty Tandoori Restaurant

Bengal Dynasty, Llandudno

Bengal Dynasty, Deeside

Bengal Dynasty Restaurants are recognised as the *"Best Restaurant in Wales"* by Good Curry Guide.

One of the *"Top 30 Restaurants in the UK"* by Real Curry Restaurant Guide 10 years in a row.

Visit us for finest traditional and contemporary Indian and Bangladeshi food prepared by our very experienced Chefs.

1 North Parade, Llandudno, North Wales, LL30 2LP
Tel: 01492 875928 Fax: 01492 878445

104a -106 Chester Road East, Shotton, Deeside, Flintshire. CH5 1QD
Tel: 01244 830455/822412 Fax: 01244 836181

At The Black Greyhound, Hall Lane, Wincham, Northwich CW9 6DG
Tel: 01606 351597 Fax: 01606 351397

Fully Licensed, Fully Air Conditioned, Disabled Access facilities.

Bengal Dynasty, On A559 Nr. Northwich at The Black Greyhound

years at after working at the Maurya Sheraton hotel Delhi. Glasgow won the *Kingfisher Curry Capital* title for the second year running. Shimla Pinks Manchester won Best Indian at the *Hi-Life Diners Club Award* for the fourth year running. Kingfisher Lager won a Silver Medal in the *Premium Lager Category* at the 2003 *International Beer Competition* sponsored by Booker Cash & Carry and organised by the Off License News. Kingfisher also is supporting the Bangladeshi film epic Hason Raja. The film depicts the life and times of the mighty Zemindar, born in the 1850's, who loses his father and brother at an early age and has to take over all family responsibilities. Cobra Beer's Karan Bilimoria was awarded the title of *Asian of the Year,* by the Asian Business Community. Then he won *Business of the Year* in the *Eastern Eye Asian Business Awards* 2003. And to top it all, for the third year running, Cobra won a Gold Medal at the Belgian-run 42nd annual *International Monde Selection Awards* against huge international competition. The only other British entry to win Gold was Johnny Walker Black and Gold label whiskey. Cobra also received the *International High Quality Trophy.* Cobra's new ingenious bottles have captured the market, and are universally available at just about all supermarkets, off licenses and Indian restaurants. Clever stuff. Shehzad Husain, former M & S curry consultant and curry author's highly successful book was a finalist in the *Entrepreneur of the Year Award,* part of the BDO Stoy Hayward's *Asian Women of Achievement Awards* 2003. Mrs Kaushy Patel of the Prashad Gujarati Cafe in Horton Grange Road, Bradford, won the *Yorkshire Forward's Chef of the Year Competition* at the *South Asian Food and Drink Exhibition* 2003. At the 11th *Booker Prize for Excellence Awards,* Best Ethnic Caterer sponsored by Natco went to Naim Munshi's Sultan of Lancaster Delhi's fabulous Bukhara Restaurant has been voted among the Top 20 restaurants in the world, according to a global survey by *'Restaurant'* magazine. Coming in at number 20 on the list, the restaurant is located in the five-star Maurya Sheraton hotel. When Bill Clinton ate there he was said to have wished for two stomachs. Topping *'Restaurant'* magazine's list was The French Laundry in California's Napa Valley, with London's Gordon Ramsay being the highest British entry at no 5.

Surveys Away

If it's not a plethora of awards ceremonies, it's surveys. Here's a summary of the recent crop:

Cashing Up

Cash topped off the list as the preferred method of payment for restaurant-goers, according to the annual *Alliance and Leicester Cash Usage Survey.* 57 per cent of Brits said they would rather dish out for their meals with cash, as it helps them control their finances. Debit and credit cards came in at a joint 18 per cent, which is a sharp contrast to the mere 2 per cent who opt to pay by cheque. Takeaways are a whole other story, with a phenomenal 87 per cent of people choosing to cash out, and a combined 6 percent preferring card and cheque as methods of payments.

Jubilee-ation. Long Live the Curry Queen

Microsoft Encarta's survey researches lifestyles, and asked about food history. 55% of those questioned thought that curry became part of the national diet in the reign of Elizabeth I. (nearly right – spicy stews were around in

Richard Ist's time, 300 years earlier. They'd dropped out by Lizzie's time.). 10% also thought she introduced the corgi, gin, roast beef and bananas. (Nearly right again, they reached England only 24 years after her death, being sold at Johnson's Herbalry in London.)

24 million Converts

A survey from the *Institute of Grocer Distributors (IGD)*, finds 25-34s form the main ethnic food consumer group, and that nearly three quarters of people over 65 have never eaten ethnic food It also revealed that 41% of Indian food consumers typically bought a takeaway meal and 21% ate in a restaurant. Budget meals generally account for the largest proportion of eating out, and this sector is expected to be accountable for 48% of projected sales in 2002. Average expenditure on cheap eats is £4-5 per head with teenagers being the largest takers for fast food and takeaways.Amazingly, the survey also finds that 3 in 10 people do not eat ethnic food market often, if at all. That's a remarkable 18 million people. It proves there is still a job for the *Curry Club* to do. When the *Curry Club* began in 1982, the figures were reversed, with only 3 in 10 people eating ethnic food. Even more remarkably this reveals that 40% of the nation (24 million people) have converted to ethnic food in 20 years. Says Pat Chapman *"my mission is to convert those 18 million people still in the wilderness".*

Staying in for an Indian

According to the MSI Marketing Presentation: *The Future of The UK Market For Eating-Out to* 2007, the Indian fast food industry was worth £312 million in 1998 and has been projected to be valued at £364 million in 2003. The belief is that the following factors affect the UK market for eating out: Modern Indian home delivery services focus on quality cooking and stylish packaging and are the latest players on the ethnic food scene. Vin Singh's Gourmet India, and Arjun and Andy Varma's Vamaji, both recently established home delivery services in south London delivery top-notch meals to a clientele with high expectations. Julien Cahn, owner of The Bombay Bicycle Club, opened his first sit in restaurant in Clapham way back in 1986. After increased demands for takeaway and home deliveries put too much pressure on the existing restaurant kitchen he made a move and branches out with retail outlets solely devoted to takeaway orders. Today, Cahn has a four-strong chain of successful Indian takeaway establishments based in Putney, Battersea, Wimbledon and Tooting. It's not only in the capital where home deliveries and takeaways have come of age. Charan Gill, MBE, and business partner, Gurmail Dhillon founded Glasgow's Harlequin Restaurant Group in 1984 providing locals in Glasgow with an affordable Indian masala option to burgers and pizzas. During the eighties Gill sensed a growing demand for 'armchair curries' and introduced a home delivery service from their first sit-in restaurant, Ashoka West End. Almost two decades later, home deliveries from the now fourteen-strong restaurant chain account for about 35% of Harlequin's £8m annual turnover. Gill chose not to located his restaurants in already saturated inner-city environs opting for smaller sites in lesser-known areas. One call centre for all restaurants, concise menus, and a central kitchen where meals are finished off on-site by a line cook has helped in standardisation and maintaining quality across their Ashoka Shak chain of restaurants.

Madhuban
Tandoori Restaurant
94, STATION ROAD, LISS, HANTS
01730 893363
Visit our restaurant
(see page 181)
Buy
our
Curry
Sauces
www.madhuban.co.uk

THE RAJ
TANDOORI RESTAURANT
& LOUNGE BAR
187 Main Road
Biggin Hill
Kent
TN16 0JR
For Reservations
and Takeaways
Tel 01959 572459
or 540217
also Sunday Buffets
See page 192.

TAMASHA
HOTEL & RESTAURANT
131, Widmore Road,
Bromley, Kent.
020 1460 3240
See page 193

SHAHI TANDOOR
GAS FIRED
CE
The Shahi Tandoor has been BSI inspected
& CE approved to conform with all the various
EEC gas supplies as wsll as LPG.
Charcoal fired Tandoor & kebab grills also available.
THE TANDOORI CLAY OVEN CO. LTD
164A DUKES ROAD, LONDON W3 0SL
Tel: +44 (0)208 896 2696 Fax: +44 (0)208 896 2686
www.tandoor.co.uk

THE COBRA BEER STORY

This is the story of one of the great beer brands. It starts in Bangalore. Travels to the UK. After that, it goes just about everywhere. On its journey, the beer and its originator battle against the odds. There are no shortcuts in the story. Cobra Beer isn't about short cuts. It is about not compromising. So, you will find everything in this story. Ingenuity. Passion. Vision. Everything. With just a little less gas.

Where better to begin the Cobra story than with the latest chapter? Our new bottle. It's mould-breaking. In fact, the mould got broken so often in the prototype stage that it's a little bit late. However, persistence is one of the Cobra values. The ingenious vision became reality. Phew, what a relief. A six-icon relief on the bottle that ingeniously tells the story of Cobra Beer. Perhaps it's time to start this story at the start.

THE GENERAL'S SON

Karan Bilimoria, the originator of Cobra Beer was born and brought in the Indian Army. His father was General Officer Commanding-in-Chief of the Central Indian Army, from the Gurkha regiment. Karan's first introduction to beer was in the army mess. It was a place to observe people and beer. He would hear frank opinions on food, wine and beer. It was market research before there was such a thing. It was here that he first began to think about a beer that would not be just another beer.

LEARNING LESSONS IN LAGER

Youth acquires enlightenment from seniority. Karan goes to Cambridge University to study Law. Karan qualifies as an accountant with Ernst and Young in London. Karan also studies British drinking and eating habits. After graduating he isn't going to be a lawyer. After qualifying he isn't going to be an accountant. He will use what he's picked up, in his goal to create a lager-beer so smooth it can perfectly accompany Indian cuisine and be enjoyed by both ale and lager drinkers alike. Before long, the entrepreneur is thinking big and thinking small. This beer will be available in both a double-sized 660ml bottle, favoured among the sharing and the thirsty, and a 330ml bottle.

2001, 2002, 2003
Awarded International High Quality Trophy for Three Gold Medals

CHARMING BEER

It's like it's always been there. But Cobra has only been here since 1989. It's as if the whole thing was created by magic. Out of thin air. Lured from the rice field. Just like that. However, a global beer brand can't be made out of nothing. If there's magic it must be the Cobra recipe. A unique blending of barley malt, yeast, maize, hops and rice and very importantly not as much gas as is often in a lot of other bottled lager-beers. The first brewing was carried out with the expert guidance of Indian brew master, Dr. Cariapa, one of the youngest ever Ph.Ds in brewing from the Czech Republic. Once again, Karan was prepared to look that little bit further in his quest for the beer in his vision. Hundreds of tasting and testing exercises later, the first Cobra Beer trickled out of Bangalore and Karan's dream to produce the finest ever Indian beer and make it a global brand had started to become a reality.

AGAINST ALL ODDS

In 1989 the scales the weigh every brand were heavily against Cobra. Forget the immediate challenge of bringing beer to the UK from India. Forget that Karan still student debts. A recession was raging in the UK. The beer market was the preserve of the giant beer brands. Against this, Karan and his business partner at the time, are piling 15 cases of Cobra at a time into the back of their 2CV and going cold calling on Indian restaurants, grocers and off-licences. Cobra's vision is to aspire and achieve against all odds. This looks like an aspiration too far. Until inspiration appears. From the generosity of the Indian restaurant industry, who stock Cobra and thanks to whose support Cobra is where it is today. Look very closely. The scale is moving.

FROM BANGALORE TO BEDFORD

The B on the building is for Bangalore. The city where Cobra was first brewed. However, Britain's thirst for Cobra is so great that by 1997 a UK home is a necessity. Cobra meets Charles Wells, the UK's largest independent brewer. They're famous for their ales and entrusted with UK licence by some of the world's most famous names in beer. Charles Wells brewers are in Bedford. So perhaps the B on the building ought to be for Bangalore and Bedford.

AROUND THE WORLD

Homecoming is usually the end of a story. In the case of Cobra, it's another start. The beer originally from Bangalore is being exported from the UK to India. And it isn't just going home. Over thirty other countries have tasted it. Perhaps Cobra should buy a liner. In fact, the Cobra team are beginning brewing all over the globe. They are out there right this minute. Looking, tasting and testing. They may be looking for their next brewing location near you. If you see Karan, ask him to buy you a Cobra. Then get him one back and then ask him to tell you about Cobra's next ingenious plan.

For further information see our website **www.cobrabeer.com**

COBRA BOTTLED BEER

INGENIOUS BECAUSE LESS GASEOUS

General Bilimoria
2000
MERLOT
Vin de Pays d'Oc
750ml
12%vol
General Bilimoria
2000
TERRET-SAUVIGNON
Vin de Pays d'Oc
750ml
General Bilimoria
SYRAH
PRODUIT DE FRANCE
General Bilimoria
MARSANNE-ROUSSANNE
PRODUIT DE FRANCE
750ml

Our Top Restaurants

Only one in every twelve of the nation's curry restaurants has achieved entry into this *Guide*, so they are all top restaurants and a cut above the norm. But, naturally, we are always asked to identify the best of the best, so to speak. And it is true that there is an élite number of really excellent restaurants including, by definition, those establishments about which we receive many consistently good reports. Since our 1992 edition we have listed them as our **TOP 100** restaurants. As usual, this year there has been quite a lot of change. There is the usual demotion from the list because of a decline in performance or closure. Fortunately, from the many you have brought to our attention, we have promoted 34 'new' entrants (indicated *). Some are indeed new, although some are long-established. One previous **TOP 100** Is returning after receiving many good reports this year. Once again we do not have an exact 100. This time the total is some 150. As ever, if there are yet others you feel we have missed, please report to us. For a restaurant to remain in our **TOP 100** list, we also need your views. There is a further, even more élite list, the cream of the cream, winners of our **SPECIAL AWARDS** all of whom attend the Guide's prestigious ceremony in London to receive their awards. For the record, previous winners of such an award are also indicated, since they all remain at the top of our **TOP 100.** At the request of the worldwide media, we commenced our **BEST IN THE UK AWARDS** in 1992, inour third edition of this *Guide.* Although our judgements at the time were nearly always received with some surprise, we are proud they have all stood the test of time. Each of these restaurants continue to thrive and deliver outstanding food and service. We hope to surprise you again this year by going outside London for the first time for our **BEST IN THE UK AWARD**, and by Awarding a unique and special **LIFETIME ACHIEVEMENT AWARD.** Here are the élite of the élite:

Our Ultimate Achievers:

BOMBAY BRASSERIE, SW 7, — **LIFETIME BEST RESTAURANT AWARD – 1982 to 2004.**

CHUTNEY MARY, SW10 — **BEST IN UK 1991-1994.** *Third Edition of this Guide.*
BOMBAY BRASSERIE, SW 7 — **BEST IN UK 1995-7.** *Fourth Edition .*
LA PORTE DES INDES, LONDON, W1 — **BEST INDIAN AND BEST IN UK 1998-1999.** *Fifth Edition.*
CHUTNEY MARY, SW10 — **BEST IN UK 1999-2000.** *Sixth Edition.*
THE QUILON, SW1 — **BEST IN UK 2001-3.** *Seventh Edition.*
MADHU'S, SOUTHALL, MIDDLESEX — **BEST IN UK 2004-5.** *This Edition.*

Our Award winners and Top 100 Restaurants:

KEY: **BOLD TYPE = CURRENT AWARD WINNER.**
* NEW TO OUR TOP 100.
† One of a group of restaurants.

London

E
* * Cafe Naz
* Café Spice Namaste (Best Chef 1992-5 / 1996-8 / Culinary Excellence 2001-3)
* Lahore Kebab House
* Shampan (Best Bangladeshi 2001-3)
* Tiffin Indian

EC1
* * City Café Lazeez
* *† **THE COCONUT LAGOON (BEST RESTAURANT GROUP 2004-5)**

	* Red Rose City
EC3	* Kasturi
N1	*† **MASALA ZONE (BEST NEW CONCEPT AWARD 2004-5)**
N3	Rani Vegetarian (Best Vegetarian 2001-3)
N16	† Rasa
	*† Rasa Travancore
N19	* Parsee
NW1	Diwana Bhel Poori House
	Great Nepalese (Best Nepalese 2001-3)
NW4	Prince of Ceylon (Best Sri Lankan 2001-3)
NW6	Geeta South Indian
	Vijay
SE1	Bengal Clipper
	*† **GEORGETOWN (BEST RESTAURANT GROUP 2004-5)** *See Kenilworth Warks.*
SE13	Spice of Life
SE23	Babur Brasserie
	Three Monkeys
SW1	* Cinnamon Club
	THE QUILON (BEST IN UK 2001-3) OUTSTANDING RESTAURANT AWARD 2004-5)
	Saloos
	† Woodlands
W3	Haandi PREVIOUS AWARD WINNER
SW5	Nizam
	Star of India
SW6	Blue Elephant Thai
	Nayab
SW7	**BOMBAY BRASSERIE (BEST IN UK 1995-7 / LIFETIME BEST RESTAURANT AWARD – 1982 TO 2004-5)**
	Café Lazeez
	Shezan Indian
SW10	**CHUTNEY MARY (BEST IN UK 1991-4 AND 1999-2000) OUTSTANDING RESTAURANT AWARD 2004-5)**
	* **PAINTED HERON (BEST CHEF AWARD**
	Vama The Indian Room
SW12	**TABAQ (BEST PAKISTANI 1998-99, 1999-2000 , 2001-3 & 2004-5)**
SW15	Ma Goa
SW17	Jaffna House
	Radha Krishna Bhavan
	Sree Krishna
SW18	* Calcutta Notebook
	SARKHEL'S (BEST NEWCOMER 1999-2000 / BEST INDIAN 2001-3 OUTSTANDING RESTAURANT AWARD 2004-5)
SW19	* Dalchini
W1	Anwars
	Café Lazeez
	Caravan Serai Afghan
	Chor Bizarre (Best North Indian 2001)
	* Chowki
	Gaylord
	LA PORTE DES INDES (BEST INDIAN AND BEST IN UK 1998-9 / OUTSTANDING RESTAURANT AWARD 2004-5)
	*† **MASALA ZONE (BEST NEW CONCEPT AWARD 2004-5)**
	Ragam South Indian
	† Rasa
	† Rasa Samudra
	Tamarind (Best Newcomer 1995-97 / Best Indian 1998-9 / Best Chef 1999-2000)
	Veeraswamy (Best newcomer 1998-9)
	† Woodlands
W2	Bombay Palace

	*** GINGER (BEST BANGLADESHI 2004-5)**
	Khans
	* Mandalay
W4	† Woodlands
W6	* Sagar
	Tandoori Nights
W8	Malabar
W8	Zaika (Most Innovative Chef 2001)
W13	Sigiri Sri Lankan (Best Sri Lankan,1998-99 & 1999-2000)
WC1	Malabar Junction (Best South Indian 1999-2000)
WC2	**INDIA CLUB (SPECIAL AWARD WINNER 1995-97)**
	* Mela
	Punjab (Best North Indian 1999-2000)

England

BERKSHIRE

Cookham	Malik's
Sunningdale	* Tiger's Pad
Theale	Café Blue Cobra (Best in the West 1995-7)
Windsor	* Spice Route

BUCKINGHAMSHIRE

Milton Keynes	**JAIPUR (BEST RESTAURANT OUTSIDE LONDON 1995-97, 1998-99, 1999-2000 , 2001-3 & 2004-5)**
Newport Pagnell	Mysore
Stony Stratford	* Moghul Palace

CHESHIRE

Chester	* Chutneyblu
Ellesmere Port	The Taj of Agra Fort (Best in the North 1998-9)
Northwich	*† Bengal Dynasty

DEVON

Ilfracombe	* Rajah
Plymouth	Kurbani Returns to TOP 100

ESSEX

Gants Hill	* Kanchans
Ilford	Curry Special
	Jalalabad

HAMPSHIRE

Fleet	Gurkha Square (Best Nepalese 1998-9)
Liss	Madhuban
Southsea	Golden Curry

HERTFORDSHIRE

Abbots Langley	Viceroy of India
St Albans	Mumtaj

KENT

Bromley	Tamasha (Best in the South 1998-99)
Folkestone	India
Welling	Tagore
Westerham	Rhondan at Pitts Cottage
	Tulsi

LANCASHIRE

Adlington	Sharju

LEICESTERSHIRE

Leicester	Curry Fever (Best in the Midlands 2001-3)
	Friends Tandoori

LINCOLNSHIRE

Boston	Star of India

MANCHESTER (GREATER)

Altrincham	* Barindar
Ashton-under-Lyne	* Indian Ocean
Manchester	Gaylord

Rochdale * La Tandoor

MERSEYSIDE

Liverpool Gulshan (BEST IN THE NORTH 1999-2000 AND 2001-3)

MIDDLESEX

Brentford * Pappadums

Southall BRILLIANT (BEST PUNJABI RESTAURANT 1998-9)

MADHU'S BRILLIANT (SPECIAL AWARDS 1991-2000 BEST RESTAURANT IN UK AWARD 2004-5)

* New Asian Tandoori Centre

Omi's

Wembley Chetna's Bhel Puri

Clay Oven

Curry Craze

† Woodlands

NORTHUMBERLAND

Berwick Magna

Corbridge The Valley (BEST IN THE NORTH 1995-7)

NOTTINGHAMSHIRE

Nottingham Chand

* Mogal-e-Azam

Saagar

OXFORDSHIRE

Oxford Aziz

SOMERSET

Bath (The) Eastern Eye

STAFFORDSHIRE

Kingsley Holt Thornbury Hall Rasoi

Leek * Bolaka Spice

Lichfield Eastern Eye

SUFFOLK

Woodbridge Royal Bengal

SURREY

Croydon Planet Spice

Epsom Le Raj

Oxted Gurkha Kitchen (BEST NEPALESE 1999-2000)

Woking Jaipur

SUSSEX

Worthing Ma'hann

TYNE & WEAR

Gateshead The Last Days of the Raj

Newcastle Sachins

Valley Junction 397 (MOST ORIGINAL 1999-2000)

VUJON (BEST IN THE NORTH EAST 2004-5)

WARWICKSHIRE

Kenilworth **† THE COCONUT LAGOON (BEST IN THE MIDLANDS 2002-3 and BEST RESTAURANT GROUP AWARD 2004-5)**

†* RAFFLES, MALAYSIAN (BEST RESTAURANT GROUP AWARD 2004-5)

Stratford on Avon **†* THE COCONUT LAGOON (BEST RESTAURANT GROUP 2004-5)**

†* GEORGETOWN, MALAYSIAN (BEST RESTAURANT GROUP AWARD 2004-5)

WEST MIDLANDS

Birmingham **†* THE COCONUT LAGOON (BEST RESTAURANT GROUP 2004-5)**

Maharajah (BEST IN THE MIDLANDS 1998-99 &1999-2000)

Adil 1 (BEST BALTI HOUSE 1999-2000)

Royal Naim (BEST BALTI HOUSE1995-98)

Coventry Monsoon

Solihull Rajnagar International

WILTSHIRE

Swindon Rafu's Tandoori

WORCESTERSHIRE

Worcester Monsoon

Spice Cuisine

NORTH YORKSHIRE

Skipton	† Aagrah (Best Restaurant Group, 1998-99 &1999-2000)
Tadcaster	† Aagrah (Best Restaurant Group, 1998-99 &1999-2000)
York	Jinnah

SOUTH YORKSHIRE

Doncaster	† Aagrah (Best Restaurant Group, 1998-99 &1999-2000)
Sheffield	Ashoka
	Nirmal's

WEST YORKSHIRE

Garforth	† Aagrah (Best Restaurant Group, 1998-99 &1999-2000)
Leeds	Darbar
	Polash
Pudsey	† Aagrah (Best Restaurant Group, 1998-99 &1999-2000)
Shipley	† Aagrah (Best Restaurant Group, 1998-99 &1999-2000)
Wakefield	† Aagrah (Best Restaurant Group, 1998-99 &1999-2000)

Scotland

FIFE

St Andrews	New Balaka Bangladeshi (Best in Scotland 1995-7 & Best Bangladeshi 1999-2000)

LOTHIAN

Edinburgh	Far Pavillion
	Lancers Brasserie
	Shamiana (Best chef 1998-99)
	Verandah
Leith	Britannia Spice (Best in Scotland 2001-3)
	Gulnar's Passage to India (Best in Scotland 1999-2000)

STRATHCLYDE

Glasgow	The Ashoka (Best in Scotland 1998-99)
	Ashoka at the Mill
	La Creme de la Creme
	Koh-i-noor
	Mister Singh's India
	Murphy's Pakora Bar

TAYSIDE

Dundee	*** DIL SEE (BEST IN SCOTLAND 2004-5)**

Wales

CLWYD

Colwyn Bay	**† BENGAL DYNASTY (BEST IN WALES 2004-5 – FOURTH TIME)**

GLAMORGAN

Cardiff	Jubraj 2 (Best in Wales 1999/2000)
Swansea	* Bonophul
	Moghul Brasserie

GWENT

Monmouth	Misbah

GWYNEDD

Llandudno †	**BENGAL DYNASTY (BEST IN WALES 2004-5 – FOURTH TIME)**

What price a curry?

We have removed the Price Check from most entries in the *Guide*, largely becuse prices so quickly go out of date. We have retained prices on Special dishes, but bear in mind that they do change. Alison Palmer of Woman magazine asked about curry prices at average (not up-market) restaurants in the UK for a piece she was writing in late 2003. These prices are from the following restaurants
1: Akash, London, w1; 2: Depa, London,wc1 3: Sussex; Seezan, Selsey, West Sussex; 4: Shamrat Indian Brasserie, Maidstone, Kent; 5: Madhuban, Liss, Hants; 6: Amer, Birmingham,West Midlands; 7: Spice of India, Northallerton, N. Yorks;. 8: Shanaz, Haslemere, Surrey; 9: Chilli Nights, Haslemere, Surrey.

	1	2	3	4	5	6	7	8	9
Chicken Tikka	2.30	2.30	2.65	2.50	2.75	2.50	2.10	3.50	3.25
Chicken Jalfrezi	5.20	4.75	0.00	4.50	5.95	0.00	5.40	6.50	000
Chicken Tikka Masala	5.50	5.50	6.25	5.95	6.10	4.50	5.50	6.50	6.50
Chicken Madras	4.30	3.95	4.10	3.95	5.60	3.40	3.50	5.50	5.25
Chicken Korma	4.50	3.95	4.25	3.95	5.60	3.40	3.50	5.50	5.25
Bombay Potatoes	2.30	2.30	2.25	2.20	2.60	2.80	1.80	2.95	2.85
Vegetable Curry	2.30	2.30	2.25	2.20	2.60	2.90	1.80	2.95	2.85
Plain Nan	1.10	1.40	1.50	1.20	1.60	0.70	1.25	1.90	1.85
Pullao Rice	1.60	1.60	1.90	1.75	1.85	1.50	1.50	2.50	2.35
Plain Rice	1.30	1.50	1.70	1.50	1.60	1.00	1.30	2.00	2.00

Tail Pieces, or is that up yours?

Meena Patak on *'The Entrepreneurs'* one of BBC TV's *'Big Dreams'* programmes said *" I taught the British how to eat curry. Before I did all they ate was hot, hot hot"*. Big dream indeed, Meena has only appeared on the curry scene in the last two decades, but yes I'll agree the Patak empire has grown considerably in that time. And some of that success is due to her plus her more reticent husband Kirit, not to mention her father and grandfather, who laid down the ground work in their Drummond Street shop, long before Meena could spell '*curry*'. The title of Big Head of the Year is vacant (having last been awarded to Cyrus). I'm reinstating it for Meena Patak.

Or should it go to Iqbal Wahhab of Cinnamon Club. Here he is in the Financial Times: *'Should we be proud, or should we be appalled, that the chicken tikka masala has become the cultural symbol of our times? A bit of both, I suspect. But either way, the question arises of why exactly the then Foreign Secretary Robin Cook settled on this particular made-up dish, concocted to soothe the sensitive British palate, when he was searching for the perfect metaphor to show how successful that other concoction - multiculturalism - had become? The progeny of this now tiresomely common dish has never been fully uncovered. When many years ago I set up Tandoori Magazine, I amused myself by creating curry myths and am touched that, to this day, many of these are earnestly quoted back at me. One of these legends concerned the chicken tikka masala. The story goes that one day, probably around the early Seventies, an Englishman walked into his local Kohi Noor or Taj Mahal and ordered himself a chicken tikka. When it arrived he was taken aback by the fact that tikka just meant "pieces". So he sent it back demanding that basic British right – sauce .Back in the kitchen, the chef was flummoxed. Sauce with chicken tikka? I'll show him. Looking through the unlikely constituents of his kitchen larder, he found a can of Campbell's tomato soup. He had heard that the English use this in their cooking, so into the pan it went, along with fenugreek, the aforementioned chicken and a dollop of cream for good measure. The customer was bowled over and wiped his bowl clean. How the staff laughed that night. And to this day they continue to laugh (and cry) as the nation's curryholics pour through their doors in search of a dish that is now on the Chef's Recommendations list - namely, the one we can charge*

THE NEW CURRY BIBLE
THE ULTIMATE MODERN CURRY HOUSE RECIPE BOOK
PAT CHAPMAN
THE NEW CURRY BIBLE
PAT CHAPMAN
CURRY CLUB
VEGETABLE AND DHAL CURRIES
Aloo Gobi Methi
Bhajee
Bindi Bhajee
Bombay Potato
GOOD NEWS.
PAT CHAPMAN'S CURRY BIBLE
has been reprinted after an absence of four years.
It has been retitled with a bright new cover.(although the content of the book is the same).
It is now called
THE NEW CURRY BIBLE.
ISBN 84358-0876-X
It is available in bookshops now. Or you can order your signed copy directly from The Curry Club.
Want to see more sumptuous pages like these?
ORDER NOW.
£19.99 plus £5.01 p&p.
by post from The Curry Club
PO Box 7, Haslmere, Surrey, GU 27, 1EP
01428 658327
www.patchapman.co.uk

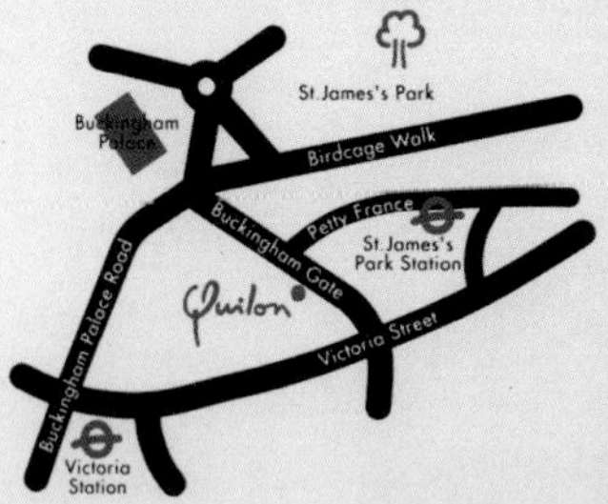

Passing the test of time

When did your love of Indian cooking begin? Chances are, if you're over 40, it's probably only over the last 15-20 years you've noticed that certain Indian restaurants have become more sophisticated, more adventurous, more stylish and, perhaps, more interested in you as a customer. There is a reason for this; The Bombay Brasserie has influenced many of the Indian restaurants that have opened over the last 20 years.

In the eighties the Indian restaurant business recognised that the British love of Indian cuisine was not receiving the respect it deserved. The wake-up call came from India herself, from one of its most successful companies, the Taj Group.

The Bombay Brasserie opened in late 1982 and was an immediate sensation. As Fay Maschler, doyen of restaurant critics noted: *'The Bombay Brasserie, known by its aficionados as the BB, changed the perception that Indian cooking was little more than meat and veg combination with an all-purpose sauce. Indian cuisine, which had developed over hundreds of years, influenced by so many external influences (not least the British Raj) was now of a new age.'*

Expansion followed quickly. The BB doubled the size of its celebrated conservatory a few years ago. Today, **The Bombay Brasserie** is a world class, international brand. Its premium chilled dishes are sold exclusively by Sainsbury's, and its home-made Chutneys by Harrods. Yet the restaurant has always resisted the temptation of creating a chain of Bombay Brasserie restaurants, set in the belief that there can only ever be one restaurant by that

The celebrated Bombay Brasserie Cobra Coffee. *Ingredients are strongly brewed black coffee, sugar, orange liqueur, orange peel and cream. Above, the sugar, is melted to a thick syrup. Middle: As sugar-work, it is enrobed snake-like around a glass. Dangerous stuff if it touches your hand. Next: the coffee is heated.*

name. Even when it decided to open a sister restaurant four years ago, again the logic was to be innovative and unique. The Quilon forged its own identity and has been acclaimed at a level that is entirely in keeping with Bombay Brasserie standards. Fay Maschler noted that it is *"confidently producing the most interesting and delicious southern Indian food in London."*

In 2001, The Cobra Good Curry Guide went further by voting The Quilon the best Indian restaurant in the whole of the UK, having already given the BB that accolade in 1995. The father of all that excellence among Indian restaurateurs, as a shining example of how imaginative, yet authentic Indian cuisine can be is **The Bombay Brasserie**

And it just gets better. The Cobra Good Curry Guide has just announced that **The Bombay Brasserie** has been awarded the industry's unique and only **LIFETIME ACHIEVEMENT AWARD**, recognising the completion of its first 21 years, an achievemnt it shares with the Guide itself.

Congratulations BB. Here's to the next 21

The celebrated Bombay Brasserie Cobra Coffee. *Top: In goes the liqueur. Next: The orange peel now resembles a cobra, and it decorates the glass. Finally, thick cream is dolloped on top. Below: Two customers are enjoying the fruits of this labour. Dominique left, Guide editor, and her identical twin sister Helena. Below right: Meanwhile Exec Chef Vikram Sing and Pat Chapman watch on.*

Share a point of view with maharajas and heads of state.

The Cuisine of the Subcontinent

It is a pleasant duty to enlarge this section in this edition. The average overseas tourist expects to find a gastronomic desert when they visit the UK, although many it seems, find intense relief that they can populate Macdonalds and its clones. Gourmets know better and head for culinary delights the like of which they can only dream of in their home countries. Despite our reputation for our boring, tasteless food, it is now several years since London has held the crown as the world's food capital. Since we put this in print in the previous *Guide*, we've been challenged frequently about the claim's voracity. London has at least one restaurant representing every nationality on earth. In this *Guide* I can only speak for 'Indian'cuisine. Before I set my case out below, and on the next nine pages, let me ask where else can you order, for example, Bengali, Chetinad, Coorg, Dum Pukht, Pakhtoon or Syrian Christian food. These specialities are Indian food styles which have come one the scene since our last *Guide* edition.

All the cuisines defined here, plus every one of the items in the A to Z of the menu which follows can be found in London, cooked to the highest, most authentic quality. No other city in the world comes anywhere close. Not New York, the former culinary capital, (curries are still dire in NY) not even India, where you can get good regional cuisine in the region you're in, but not that of all regions in any one city. Outside London, it is not so easy, but pink-sky-at-night, and the sun is rising on an optimistic dawn. Coconut Lagoon restaurants (see Kenilworth, Warwickshire) are in the vanguard of an Indian regional food revolution. Let's hope that it is just the beginning.

Afghani Afghanistan's location had always held the strategic key to India until this century, for it was through the solitary mountain passes that the invaders came and possessed India from as early as 3000 BC. Located between Iran (formerly Persia) and Pakistan (formerly NW India), it brought the cuisine of the Middle East to India – and that of India to the Middle East. Afghan food features Kebabs and Birianis, and skewered spiced lamb over charcoal. The only UK Afghan restaurants are Caravan Serai, London W1 and Afghan Kitchen, London N1. (*See Pashtoon*).

Balti In the high mountains of north Pakistan is the ancient state of Baltistan, sharing its border with China and India's Kashmir, and once on the Spice Route to China. These days, with Pakistan and India in a permanent state of war, the few roads connecting the two countries are permanently closed. Little may have been known about Balti food outside its indigenous area, had it not been for a small group of Pakistani Kashmiris, who settled in east Birmingham in the 1960s. There, they opened small cafés in the back streets, serving curries made aromatic with Kashmiri Garam Masala, and herbs, with plentiful coriander, in two-handled pots called the 'karahi' in India, but known here as the 'Balti pan'. Eating with no cutlery, using fingers and bread to scoop up the food, is the norm to the community, but a revelation to Birmingham's white population, who made Balti their own.

Bangladeshi Most of the standard curry houses in the UK are owned by Bangladeshis and nearly all of those serve standard formula curries (from mild to very hot). Bangladesh, formerly East Pakistan, is located at the mouth of the River Ganges. Before Partition, the area either side of the Ganges was Bengal. Today Bengal is the Indian state that shares its border with Bangladesh. Bangladesh is Muslim, so pork is forbidden. Unlike Hindu India, beef is eaten. The area enjoys prolific fresh and seawater fish – pomfret, boal, ruhi, hilsa and ayre, and tiger prawns – and specialises in vegetable dishes such as Shartkora and Niramish, some quite bitter, such as Shuktoni; Shatkora, a kind of grapefruit is an ingredient in meat/poultry dishes. Until recently, true Bangladeshi cuisine was nigh on impossible to find in the UK. Now more of our Bangladeshi restaurants are serving the delights of their own country.

Bengali The clear difference between Bangladesh and Bengal is religion. Bengalis are mainly Hindu, and this proscribes no beef. Many dishes are common to both, for example, Jhol (runny curry), Chorchori (Bengali style of curry) and Kalia, curry process (meat, poultry or fish) in which red-coloured ingredients are mandatory, especially red chillies, tomatoes and poppy seeds, and Rezala, a creamier curry than Korma (q.v.) in which green chillies are mandatory. Shingara is a short crust Bengali samosa. Potoler Dolma is the small wax gourd stuffed with a spicy filling. Begun Shorshe, fried aubergines in yogurt and mustard sauce. Calcutta is the city of culture and invented those wonderful, sticky sweets, such Gulab Jamun, Jalebi, Ras Malai and Ros Gulla. The one and only truly authentic Bengali restaurant has arrived. It is Calcutta Notebook.

Bombay Bombay curries are mellow and light and, although a favourite restaurant dish, Bombay Potato (*see page* 42) is not found as such in Bombay, but it is typical of Bombay tastes. Also in the glossary are Bombay Duck, no longer banned from the UK, Bombay Mix, re-invented under this name in Southall in the 1970s. Bhel Puri, also in the glossary, is Bombay's favourite kiosk food, most famously available at the city's Chowpatti beach and now found in the Bhel Puri houses in Drummond Street, Wembley, and other places around London. It is served cold and is delicious. Most of India's Parsees (q.v.), with their distinctive food, live in Bombay.

Burmese Burma, now renamed Myanmar, shares its boundaries with Bangladesh, India, China, Laos and Thailand. Its food is a combination of these styles. Rice is the staple and noodles are popular too. The curries are very hot and there are no religious objections to eating pork, beef or other meats. Duck and seafood are commonly eaten. The only UK Burmese restaurant is the Mandalay, London W2.

Chetinad A style of cooking from the southern Indian state of Tamil Nadu. A meat-eating community called Chetiyars, have been resident in the Madras area since the earliest times. Under the British, they became merchants and money lenders, owning large amounts of Burmese farmland. Fish Kozambhu – sour sauce tamarind & chillies. Chetinad dishes appear on menus all over the place but Coconut Lagoon restaurants (*see Kenilworth, Warks*) are owned by Chetiyars so are one of the few places to do them correctly.

Dum Pukht A cooking term meaning 'containing the steam'. The technique originated in ancient Persia deriving from the Persian word 'dampukht' or baked. A pot was filled with meat and spices. A tightly-fitting lid was sealed with chupatti dough. A hole was dug in the desert sands. and hot coals were placed in its bottom. Next the sealed pot was surrounded with hot coals, buried in the sand and left undisturbed to cook for a few hours. The magical moment comes when the lid is opened in front of the diners, releasing all those captured fragrances. This was the perfect vehicle for cooking Biriani. The contemporary exponent is Delhi master chef Imtiaz Qureshi. His modern versions use pastry as the lid, and of course the modern oven. Qureshi has not ventured to London, but we have the next best chef, Mohammed Rais. He also hails from Lucknow and he too claims ancestry back to the Nawab court and Qureshi is his uncle. Rais worked at the Red Fort (W1) from 1997, but moved to Darbar, SW6. *See also Kasturi,* EC3 *and Naresh Matta (Rias' former assistant at the Red Fort) now at Eriki.* NW3.

Goan Goa is on the west coast of India, about 400 miles south of Bombay. It was established in 1492 by the Portuguese who occupied it until 1962. It is now a state of India where Christianity prevails and there are no objections to eating pork or beef. The food of Goa is unique. Their most famous dish is Vindaloo, but it is not the dish from the standard curry house. The real thing is derived from the Portuguese dish Vino d'Alhos, traditionally pork marinated (the longer the better) in wine vinegar and garlic, then simmered until tender. To this the Goans added hot red chillies, creating a rich red curry gravy. Goa also has delicious seafood and fish dishes. There is only one true Goan restaurant in the UK, Ma Goa in London SW15, although Goan dishes do appear at the better Indian restaurants.

Gujarati Gujarat is a largely vegetarian coastal state, north of Bombay. The first British diplomat docked at the port of Surat in 1608, and the town was used as a British trading post, until Bombay was built in 1674. The soup-like dish, with gram flour dumplings, called Khadi, whose yellow gravy is made with turmeric, spices and yoghurt, may have been the very dish which gave curry its name. The food is India's least spicy. The Parsees, who lived in Gujarat for 500 years (*see below*), influenced the food, with subtleties of sour and sweet. Yoghurts and gram flour prevail. The famous Bhaji also originated here, as did the lesser known Dahi Vada, a gram flour dumpling in a tangy yoghurt sauce. Gujarati restaurants are prevalent in Leicester and Wembley, Middlesex, and they pop up elsewhere, too.

Kashmiri The once Mughal state, high in the northern mountains is now shared uncomfortably by Pakistan and India. Mutton is the key ingredient. A 15kg male sheep considered ideal. All parts are used. Leg for dhaphol, ribs for tabak maz, neck for roghan josh, entrails for methi maz, quorma soured with apricots, jakhni soured with curds. Gushtaba giant meatball, with curd gravy, is traditionally the final dish, though a semolina might follow. *See Chor Bizare, London,* W1.

Moghul The curry from the standard curry house is based on rich, creamy dishes developed by the Moghul emperors. No one was richer than the Moghuls, and it was during their time, four centuries ago, that Indian food was perfected. Authentically, this style of food should be subtly spiced. It can be found in an increasing number of 'haute cuisine' restaurants around the country, spelt variously Moghul, mogul, moglai, muglai mugal, mugul, etc.

Nawabi The Nawabs were the rich royals of the Lucknow area of India who lived over two centuries ago. Like the Moghuls before them, they perfected a style of cooking which was spicy and fragrant. Called Dum or Dum Pukt, it involves cooking the curry or Biriani in a round pot, whose lid is sealed into place with a ring of Chapatti dough. The resulting dish is opened in front of the diners, releasing all those captured fragrances, as found in some of the better UK curry restaurants.

Nepalese Beautiful Himalayan mountains, the world's only Hindu kingdom, home of Gurkas, sherpas, yak and yeti, Kumari the living virgin goddess-princess, Everest, and unique food. Some similarities to north Indian, with curry (tarkari), rice (bhat), and wheat breads (roti haru). Kukhura (chicken), Khasi (lamb), Dumba (mutton), Bhutwa (pork), Hach Ko (duck), Jhinge (prawn) and Maccha (fish) are cooked in the clay oven (chula) or curried. Specialities include Aloo Achar, potatoes in pickle sauce, Momo/Momocha, keema-filled dumplings, and Tama Bodi, bamboo shoots and black-eye beans, a dish showing Tibetan/Chinese roots. More examples will be found in the entries for Great Nepalese, NW1, Gurkha Kitchen, Oxted, Surrey and Gurkha Square, Fleet, Hants.

Pakistani Until independence in 1947, Pakistan formed the north-western group of Indian states. Located between Afghanistan and India, it contains the famous Khyber Pass. The people are predominantly meat-eaters, favouring lamb and chicken (being Muslim, they avoid pork). Charcoal cooking is the norm, and this area is the original home of the tandoor. Breads such as Chupatti, Nan and Paratha are the staple. Balti cooking originated in the northernmost part of Pakistan (*see earlier*). In general, Pakistani food is robustly spiced and savoury. The area called the Punjab was split by the formation of Pakistan, and it is the Punjabi tastes that formed the basis of the British curry house menu (*see Punjab, London* WC2). Bradford, Glasgow and Southall have sizeable Pakistani populations.

Parsee/Persian It is quite common to see Persian dishes listed on the standard curry house menu. Dishes such as Biriani and Pullao did indeed originate in Persia (now called Iran). Bombay's Parsees came from there, having fled from Persia centuries ago. In India, they originated dishes of their own, such as Dhansak and Patia. The real thing is a subtle cooked-together combination of meat and vegetables and/or fruit. True Persian food is hard to find in the UK, although it is served at the Old Delhi, London W1. There is one Parsee restaurant in the UK (Parsee N19) but south-west London's Bombay Brasserie and Chutney Mary both have Parsee chefs who cook decent Parsee dishes.

Pashtoon It refers to tribal people and their language from the rugged mountain passes of Afghanistan (q.v.) and Pakistan (q.v.) in the former North-West Frontier Province, whose name for themselves is Pathan, Pashtun, Phuktana or Pukhtun. Afghan food is pretty basic, especially at tribal level, involving hunting wild life then grilling it or slow-cooking it in pots. Grills, Kebabs, Koftas and Birianis are popular, spiced with the unique Afghan spice mix, Char Masala (four aromatic spices) and cooked mostly in their own juices. Visit Tagore, Welling Kent and Kasturi E3.

South Indian Until recently we could be forgiven for believing south Indian food to be all-vegetarian food from Kerala. Specialities include Dosas, huge, thin, crisp rice-lentil-flour pancakes, with a curry filling (Masala) and Idlis – steamed rice or lentil-flour dumplings accompanied with Sambar, a lentil-based curry, Rasam, hot soup and coconut chutney. Other rice-based items include Upuma and Uthappam (*see* p58). Many types of vegetables include, drumstick, mooli, snake gourd, doodi, bottle gourd, bitter gourd (karela). tindoora, and long beans. Vegetable curries using them include Avial, Thoran and many others. Restaurants specialising in this food are dotted around London. Tooting SW17 is a haven, though almost impossible to find outside. The first restaurant to bring south Indian meat, chicken and sea food dishes to the UK was Chutney Mary. But other restaurants have developed the theme as specialisations. The two best are Rasa Travanvore, N19 and Coconut Lagoon restaurants (*see Kenilworth, Warks*). Udipi food is to be found at Sagar, W6.

Sri Lankan Sri Lanka is the small, pearl-shaped island, formerly Ceylon, at the southern tip of India. Its cuisine is distinctive and generally chilli hot. They eat similar fare to that eaten in south India, i.e. vegetarian dishes, but they also enjoy very pungent meat, squid, chicken and duck curries. Good Sri Lankan restaurants include Palm Paradise, Southall, Middlesex, Prince of Ceylon, London NW4, and Sigiri, London W13.

The A to Z of the Curry Menu

To the first-timer, the Indian restaurant menu is a long and complex document. This glossary explains many of the standard, and some of the specialised, dishes and items that you are likely to encounter. See also The Cuisine of the Subcontinent. Spellings of vowel sounds will vary from restaurant to restaurant, reflecting the 15 languages and hundreds of dialects of the subcontinent. (See *Masala, Moglai, Papadam and Rhogan Josh Gosht for some examples.*) Our spelling here is as near as possible to the standard accepted way of spelling, when translating phonetically from the main languages to English.

A

Aam or Am Mango.

Achar or Achaar Pickle, such as lime, mango, aubergine, etc. *Achar Gohst* is meat curry, curried in a pickle base, *Achar Murgh* is the chicken version.

Afghani Curry Nuts and fruit are added for the standard curry house interpretation.

Aloo Potato.

B

Baigan or Begun *see* Brinjal.

Balti Balti originated centuries ago in north Pakistan's Mirpur, Kashmir and Skardu (Baltistan). It found its way to east Birmingham in the 1970s, where any combination of ingredients was curried in a two-handled pot known as the *karahi* (q.v.) elsewhere, but the Balti there. Served to the table still cooking, the art is to eat the food – which should be spicy, herby and aromatic – Indian-style, with the bread as the scoop in the right hand. In the 1990s, Balti spread rapidly all over the UK and beyond. The Balti found at the standard Bangladeshi curry house, however, owes its flavours more to Patak's acidic Balti paste than to Mirpur, and unless it is cooked in its pan and served cutlery-free, it will (correctly) never convince the Brummy purist that it is anything other than hype.

Barfi or Burfi Indian fudge-like sweet made from reduced condensed milk (*koya* or *khoa*), in various flavours.

Basmati The best long-grained rice.

Batera Football-sized puri (q.v.) becoming increasingly popular.

Battar Quail.

Bengal Curry A chicken or meat curry with chilli, sugar, potato cubes and halves of tomato.

Bhaji or Bhajee Dryish, pan-fried mild vegetable curry.

Bhajia Deep-fried fritter, usually with sliced onion, mixed with spiced gram flour batter, then deep-fried. Bhajia is the correct term, meaning fried. Bhaji or Bhajee is the anglicisation. For the real thing, visit Maru's Bhajia House, Wembley, Middlesex. *See also* Pakora.

Bhel Puri This is the delicious street food snack from Bombay. It is a cold combination of those crunchy squiggles you find in Bombay Mix (q.v.), the smallest of which is called *Sev*. To this is added small-diced cooked potato, puffed rice (*mamra*), coriander leaf, onion and chilli. It is laced with brown sweet and sour tamarind (*imli*) sauce, green coriander chutney (*dhania*) and red chilli/garlic sauce, and topped with crispy puri biscuit chippings. The result is an exquisite combination of crisp, chewy and soft textures with sweet, hot, savoury and sour tastes. Variations include differing amounts of ingredients, under various similar names, such as *Sev Batata Puri, Dahi* (yoghurt) *Batata Puri, Chat Aloo Papri* and *Batata Pava. Bhel* can be accompanied by Gol Goppas (q.v.). This delicious food is generally beyond the abilities of the average curry house, so is rarely found. Try it when you can (*see* London NW1's Drummond Street).

Bhoona or Bhuna Cooking process involving slowly frying out all the water content to produce a dry, usually mild curry.

Bindi A pulpy, rather sappy vegetable also known as okra or ladies fingers. Correct cooking of this dish is a good test of a chef's ability.

Biriani Traditionally, rice baked between layers of meat or vegetable filling, enhanced with saffron and aromatic spices, served topped with edible silver leaf (*vark*). The restaurant interpretation is a cooked rice, artificially coloured, with filling stir-fried in. It is usually heavily garnished and served with a vegetable curry sauce (*see* Pullao).

Bombay Duck A smallish fish native to the Bombay docks, known locally as *bommaloe macchi*. This was too hard for the British Raj to pronounce, so it became Bombay Duck. It is dried and appears on the table as a crispy deep-fried starter or accompaniment to a curry.

Bombay Mix An age-old traditional Indian snack nibble, called *muruku*, made from a savoury, gram-flour, spiced batter called *ompadi*, which is forced through a press straight into the deep-frier, to give different shapes and thicknesses of squiggly nibbles. Nuts, pulses, seeds and other ingredients are added. It should always be really crunchy and fresh. Re-invented by GK Noon, owner of Royal Sweets in Southall, under the catchy name Bombay Mix, it will keep you going at the bar.

Bombay Potato A popular invention of the curry house. Potatoes in curry sauce with onions and tomato.

Boti Kebab Marinated cubes of lamb cooked in a tandoor oven (*see* Tandoori).

Brinjal Aubergine, also called *baigan* or *began*. In *Baigan Burtha*, aubergine is smoked, spiced and mashed, in *Baigan Bhaji* it is chopped and curried by pan-frying.

CTM Chicken Tikka Masala. Invented by a British curry house chef (identity unknown) *c.* 1980, as a way to exploit his already popular Chicken Tikka by adding a creamy, pink, mild sauce made tasty by skilful blending of curry sauce, tomato purée, tandoori paste, cream, coconut, mango chutney and ground almonds. It is now ordered by 65% of all diners. Not only that, it appears in supermarket sandwiches, flavours crisps, is a pizza topping and even spices mayonnaise. If only that chef had copyrighted it, he'd be earning millions in royalties a year. *See* Makhani and Tikka.

Ceylon Curry At the curry house, this is usually cooked with coconut, lemon and chilli.

Chana A yellow lentil resembling, but not identical to, the split pea, used in Dhal (q.v.) and to make gram flour. *Kabli chana* is the chickpea. Both can be curried or dried and deep-fried as in Bombay Mix (q.v.). *See also* Paneer.

Chasni, Chicken A central Scotland Pakistani restaurant name for CTM (q.v.).

Chat or **Chaat** Literally means 'snack', though often a salad.

Chilli Fleshy members of the capsicum family, ranging in heat from zero (the bell pepper) to incendiary. All chillies start green and, if left long enough, eventually turn red, the one being no hotter than the other. The chilli normally used in Indian cooking is the narrow 7.5cm (3in) cayenne. The hottest in the world are Mexican habañeros, Caribbean Scotch bonnets and Bangladeshi nagas. People build up a tolerance to chillies, but they should never be inflicted upon the novice, not even in fun.

Chupatti A 15cm (6in) flat disc of unleavened bread, cooked dry on the tava (q.v.). It should always be served hot and pan-fresh. The spelling can vary – Chupati, Chapatti, etc.

Chutney The common ones are onion chutney, mango chutney and tandoori chutney. There are dozens of others that rarely appear on the standard menu. *See* Sambals.

Curry The only word in this glossary to have no direct translation into any of the subcontinent's 15 or so languages. The word was coined centuries ago by the British in India. Possible contenders for the origin of the word are: *Karahi* or *Karai* (Hindi) – the wok-like frying pan used all over India to prepare *masala* (spice mixtures); *Karhi* or *Khadi* – a soup-like dish made with spices, gram-flour dumplings and buttermilk; *Kari* – a spicy Tamil sauce; *Turkuri* – a seasoned sauce or stew; and *Kari Phulia* – Neem leaves, which are small and rather like bay leaves, used for flavouring. The Dutch, who were in India in the 17th century have their own derivation. They say it was used in Malaya for their Malay curries, and that it derived from the word *Lekker* meaning delicious, or in colloquial Dutch, *Lekkerie*.

Curry House *See* Formula Curries.

Dabba or **Dhaaba** The subcontinent's version of the transport café, it's a ubiquitous roadside eatery usually made of tin sheets and thatch or tarpaulin. Millions exist. If packed with truckers (their lorries parked all around) it's good. A limited menu offers dhals, spicy omelettes, mutton and vegetable curries, tea (chai) and soft drinks at truly low prices. Seating usually a charpoy or rope-strung cot in the open air in front of the eatery. Primitive kitchen fully visible. Vertical neon tubes are its night time symbol. Dabba dishes are appearing on some London chi-chi menus, at rather more expensive prices.

Dahi or **Dohi** Yoghurt, used as a chutney (*see* Raita) and in the cooking of some curries. Most curry houses make their own, and it is delicious as an accompaniment to curry, being less sharp than the shop-bought equivalent. Incidentally, Dahi, not water, is the best antidote if you eat something that's too hot for you.

DAHI VADA South Indian savoury gram-flour doughnut, deep-fried, cooled and dunked into cold, spicy yoghurt (*see* Vada).

DAL or DHAL LENTILS There are over sixty types of lentil in the subcontinent, all packed full of nutrients. The common restaurant types are *massor* (red, which cooks yellow), *moong* (green), *chana* (also used to make gram flour) and *urid* (black).

DEGCHI or DEKHCHII Brass or metal saucepan without handles.

DHANIA Coriander leaf or spice.

DHANSAK Traditional Parsee meat dish cooked in a purée of lentils, aubergine, tomato and spinach. Restaurants use dal and methi, and sometimes chilli and pineapple.

DOPIAZA Traditional meat dish. *Do* means two, *piaza* means onions. Onions appear twice in the cooking, first fried and second raw. They give the dish a sweetish taste.

DOSA South Indian pancake made from rice and *urid* (lentil) flour, which, when made into a batter, soon ferments to give a superb sour taste. *Masala Dosa* is a Dosa filled with mashed potato curry spiced with onion, chilli, turmeric and mustard seed.

DUM Cooking by steaming in a sealed pot, invented by the Royal Nawabs (*see* The Cuisine of the Subcontinent), e.g. *Aloo Dum*, steamed potatoes. Also called Dum Pukt or Pukht (pronounced 'pucked').

ELAICHI Cardamom. Can major in curries – for example, *Elaichi Murgh* is chicken curried with a predominance of green cardamom.

FOOGATH Lightly cooked vegetable dish found in the Malabar area of South India. Any vegetable such as gourds or plantain can be used.

FORMULA CURRIES Many of our 'Indian' (q.v.) restaurants operate to a formula which was pioneered in the late 1940s. In those days, a way had to be found to deliver a variety of curries, without an unreasonable delay, from order to table. Since all authentic Indian recipes require hours of cooking in individual pots, there was no guarantee that they would even be ordered. So cubed meat, chicken or potatoes, dal and some vegetables were lightly curried and chilled, and a large pot of thick curry gravy, a kind of master stock, was brewed to medium-heat strength. To this day, portion by portion, on demand, these ingredients are reheated by pan-frying them with further spices and flavourings. At its simplest, a Medium Chicken Curry, that benchmark of middle ground, is still on many menus, though sometimes disguised as Masala, and requires no more than a reheat of some gravy with some chicken. For instance, take a typical mixed order for two. Chicken Korma (fry a little turmeric, coriander and cumin, add six pieces of chicken, add a ladleful of curry gravy, plenty of creamed coconut, almonds maybe and a little cream – result, a mild dish, creamy-golden in colour), with Vegetable Dhansak (fry some cumin seeds, dry methi leaves (q.v.), chopped onions, a little sugar, tomato, red and green capsicum with the gravy, add dhal and some cooked veg – result, colourful, and still medium-strength). Meat Korma (as for the chicken, using meat), and Prawn Vindaloo (fry spices and chilli powder, add the gravy which at once goes red and piquant, then cooked peeled prawns, fresh tomato and potato, simmer and serve). Maybe also a Sag Paneer (fry cummin, some thawed creamed spinach and pre-made crumbled paneer together, add fresh coriander – done). One cook can knock all these up, simultaneously, in five pans, within minutes. Rice is pre-cooked, breads and tandoori items made to order by a different specialist. And, hey presto, your order for two! The menu can be very long, with a huge variety of dishes, sometimes numbered, sometimes heat-graded, mild, medium and hot, hotter, hottest, and any dish is available in meat, poultry, prawn, king prawn, and most vegetables, too. That's the formula of the standard curry house. Just because this is not authentic does not make it bad. It can be, and variously is, done well. This *Guide* is full of many such restaurants, about which we say 'a standard curry house, doing the formula well'.

GARAM MASALA Literally meaning hot (roasted) mixture (of pepper and aromatic spices), it originated in Kashmir and is added towards the end of cooking in certain north Indian curries. *See also* Masala.

GHEE Clarified butter or vegetable oil used in high-quality north Indian cooking.

GOBI Cauliflower.

GOL GOPPAS or PANI PURI are mouth-sized puffed-up crispy biscuits, served with *Jeera Pani* (water spiced predominantly with chilli, black salt and cumin water) and *Aloo Chaat* (potato curry) at Bhel Puri (q.v.) houses. To eat the correct way, gently puncture the top of the biscuit, pour in some *Jeera Pani*, and pop into the mouth in one. Chew and then add some *Aloo Chaat*.

Gosht Meat, usually refering to lamb or mutton.

Gulab Jaman An Indian dessert of cake-like texture. Balls of curd cheese paneer, or flour and milk-powder, are deep-fried to golden and served in light syrup.

Gurda Kidney. *Gurda Kebab* is marinated kidney, skewered and cooked in the tandoor.

H

Haleem A Muslim speciality found in Pakistan and Hyderabad (central India) where it is regarded as a delicacy to them but an acquired taste to everyone else. Pounded mutton is cooked with wheat, chillies, ginger, garam masala and onion tarkal to become a sort of gruel. A bread called Girda is traditionally eaten with Haleem. Found at Salloos SW1 and Lahori Kebab E1.

Halva Sweets made from syrup and vegetables or fruit. Served cold in small squares, it is translucent and comes in bright colours depending on the ingredients used. Orange – carrot; green – pistachio; red – mango, etc. Has a texture thicker than Turkish Delight. Sometimes garnished with edible silver leaf.

Handi or Haandi Is a traditional round-bellied, sometimes earthenware, sometimes metal, narrow-necked cooking pot used in many parts of India, and especially Gujarat. Pottery shards have dated it from 2500BC.

Hasina Kebab Pieces of chicken breast, lamb or beef marinated in a yoghurt and spice (often tandoori) mixture, then skewered and barbecued/baked, interspersed with onions, capsicum and tomato. Turkish in origin. *See* Shaslik.

I

Idli Rice- and lentil-flour steamed cake, about the size and shape of a hockey puck, served with a light but fiery curry sauce. South Indian in origin.

Imli Tamarind. A very sour, date-like fruit used in cooking or chutney which is of purée consistency, sweetened with sugar.

Indian In 1947, the subcontinent of India was partitioned. To cut a long story short, in Britain and the West we still generally erroneously refer to our curry restaurants as 'Indian'. In fact, over 85% are Bangladeshi, with only around 8% run by Indians and 8% run by Pakistanis. There is a smattering of Nepalese and Sri Lankan restaurants, and only a single Afghan and a single Burmese restaurant in Britain. *See* Formula Curries.

Jalebi An Indian dessert. Flour, milk-powder and yoghurt batter are squeezed through a narrow funnel into a deep-frier to produce golden, curly, crisp rings. Served in syrup.

Jal Frezi Sautéed or stir-fried meat or chicken dish, often with lightly cooked onion, garlic, ginger, green pepper and chilli.

Jeera Cumin or cummin seed or powder, hence *Jeera Chicken*, the signature dish at Madhu's Southall.

Jingri or Chingri Prawns of any size.

Kalia Traditional Bengali/Bangladeshi meat, poultry or fish dish in which red-coloured ingredients are mandatory, especially red chillies and tomatoes. *See* Rezala.

Karahi A two-handled Indian kitchen dish. Some restaurants reheat curries in small karahis and serve them straight to the table with the food sizzling inside. *See also* Curry and Balti.

Kashmir Chicken Whole chicken stuffed with minced meat. *See* Kurzi.

Kashmir Curry Often a medium curry to which is added cream and coconut and/or lychees, pineapple or banana.

Kebab Kebab means 'cooked meat' in ancient Turkish, traditionally cooked over charcoal, in a process over 4,000 years old. It was imported to India by the Muslims centuries ago. Shish, incidentally, means 'skewer'. *See* Boti, Hasina, Nargis, Shami and Sheek Kebab.

Keema Minced meat, e.g. as used in curry. *See also* Mattar.

Kofta Balls made from ground meat, poultry or fish/shellfish or vegetables, then deep-fried and simmered in a curry sauce.

Korma Probably derived from the Persian *Koresh*, a mild stew. The Moghuls made it very rich, using cream, yoghurt and ground almonds, fragranced with saffron and aromatic spices. But, traditionally, Kormas need not be mild. In Kashmir a popular dish is the *Mirchwangan Korma*, red in colour because it is full of Kashmiri chillies. To the curry house, Korma is terminology for the mildest curry, sometimes made sickly by the overuse of creamed coconut block, cream and nuts.

Kulcha Small leavened bread. Can be plain or stuffed, e.g. *Onion Kulcha.*

Kulfi Indian ice cream. Traditionally it comes cone-shaped in vanilla, pistachio or mango flavours.

Kurzi Leg of lamb or whole chicken given a long marination, then a spicy stuffing, e.g. rice and/or Keema (q.v.), then slowly baked until tender. This is served with 'all the trimmings'. It is many a curry house's Special, requiring 24 hours' notice (because of the long preparation) and a deposit to make sure you turn up to eat it). Often for two or four, it is good value. Also called Khurzi, Kasi, Kozi, Kushi, etc. *See also Murgh Masala.*

L

Lassi A refreshing drink made from yoghurt and crushed ice. The savoury version is *Lassi Namkeen* and the sweet version is *Lassi Meethi.*

M

Macci or Machli Fish. Today, fresh exotic fish from India and Bangladesh are readily available and, when a restaurant offers them, you have the chance of getting a truly authentic dish.

Madras You will not find a Madras Curry in Madras. It does not exist. But the people of the south eat hot curries, firing them up with as many as three different types of chilli – dry, powdered and fresh – added to the cooking at different stages. As the Brits got used to their early formula curries, they began to demand them hotter. With no time to add chillies in the traditional way, one of the pioneer curry house chefs simply added one teaspoon of extra-hot chilli powder to his standard sauce, along with tomato and ground almonds, and ingeniously called it 'Madras'. The name stuck. *See also* Chilli, Phal and Vindaloo.

Makhani A traditional dish. Tandoori chicken is cooked in butter ghee and tomato sauce. Some say this was the derivation of CTM (q.v.).

Malai Cream. So *Malai Sabzi Kofta,* for example, means vegetable balls in a creamy curry gravy. *See* Rasmalai.

Malaya The curries of Malaya are traditionally cooked with coconut, chilli and ginger. In the Indian restaurant, however, they are usually based on the Korma (q.v.), to which is added pineapple and/or other fruit.

Masala A mixture of spices which are cooked with a particular dish, e.g. *Garam Masala* (q.v.). It can be spelt a remarkable number of ways – Massala, Massalla, Masalam, Mosola, Moshola, Musala, etc.

Masala Dosa *See* Dosa.

Mattar Green peas. So *Mattar Paneer* is peas with Indian cheese, *Keema Mattar* is mince meat curry with peas, and so on.

Medium Curry *See* Formula Curries.

Methi Fenugreek, pronounced 'maytee'. Savoury spice. The seed is important in masalas. The leaves, fresh or dried, are used particularly in Punjabi dishes. At the curry house, the flavour of these leaves predominates in their *Dhansak.*

Moglai Cooking in the style of the Moghul emperors, whose chefs took Indian cookery to the heights of gourmet cuisine centuries ago. Few restaurateurs who offer Moglai dishes come anywhere near this excellence. Authentic Moglai dishes are expensive and time-consuming to prepare. Can also be variously spelt Muglai, Mhogulai, Moghlai, etc.

Mulligatawny A Tamil vegetable consommée (*molegoo* pepper, *tunny* water), adapted by the Raj to create the thick, meat-based British soup.

Murgh Chicken.

Murgh Masala or Murgh Massalam Whole chicken, marinated in yoghurt and spices for hours, then stuffed and roasted. *See* Kurzi.

N

Nan or Naan Pronounced 'narn', it is flat, leavened bread, usually made from plain white flour (*maida*) dough, but sometimes from wholemeal flour (*atta*). After the dough rises, it is rolled out and baked in the tandoor (q.v.). It is teardrop-shaped and about 20-25cm (8-10 inches) long. It must be served fresh and hot. As well as *Plain Nan,* there are many variations involving the addition of other ingredient(s). *Keema Nan* is stuffed with a thin layer of minced, spiced kebab meat. *Peshwari Nan* is stuffed with almonds and/or cashew nuts and/or raisins. Garlic, onion, pineapple, tomato, indeed anything, can be added. Double- or treble-sized *Karak,* Elephant or Family Nans are offered at Balti houses to share to scoop your food up with.

Nargis Kebab Indian scotch egg – spiced, minced meat around a hard-boiled egg.

Niramish A Bangladeshi mixed vegetable, often cooked without garlic, and spiced only with *Panch Phoran* – Indian Five Spice mixture.

Oothappam *See* Uthappam.

P

Paan Betel leaf folded, samosa-fashion, around a stuffing of aniseed, betel nut, sunflower seeds, lime paste, etc. and eaten in one mouthful, as a digestive after a meal. The leaf is bitter, the mouth-feel coarse and the taste acquired; but more acceptable (to Westerners) small spices and seeds (*supari*), sometimes sugar-coated in lurid colours, are often offered by the curry house after the meal.

Pakora The true pakora is a whole piece of vegetable, lightly coated in gram-flour batter and deep-fried, although at the curry house it is to all intents and purposes the same as the Bhajia (q.v.).

Palak *See* Sag

PANEER Cheese made from milk by separating the whey (liquid) from the curds (solids) which, when compressed, can be crumbled, chopped, fried, tandoori-baked and/or curried (*see* Mattar). In Bengali, Paneer is called *Chhana*, not to be confused with the lentil, Chana (q.v.).

PAPADAM or PAPAD Thin lentil-flour wafers. When cooked (deep-fried or baked) they expand to about 20cm (8 ins). They must be crackling crisp and warm when served. If not, send them back and deduct points from that restaurant. They come either plain or spiced, with lentils, pepper, garlic or chilli. There are many ways to spell papadam, using any combination of the vowels 'a', 'o' and 'u', and double 'p' and double 'd'. But, despite many people calling it so, it should never be referred to as a pampadom.

PARATHA Dough combined with ghee (q.v) thinly rolled out and folded over itself to create a layered disc, like puff pastry. Pan-fried to create a soft bread.

PASANDA Meat, usually lamb, which traditionally is thinly beaten, then cooked in a creamy curry gravy to which some chefs add red wine. The dish and wine were both true treats of Moghul emperor Jehangir who, though Muslim, blessed the wine to make it 'holy water' thus circumventing the rules of Islam. Then he and his court proceeded to drink themselves legless while enjoying this dish.

PATIA Restaurant curry with a thick, dark, red sweet and sour sauce. Based on a Parsee prawn or fish dish.

PATRA A Gujarati speciality, in which colcasia (*patra*) leaves are rolled in gram-flour paste, like a Swiss roll, then steamed, sliced and deep-fried.

PESHAWARI NAN *See* Nan.

PHAL The hottest curry, also known as a Bangalore Phal, invented by the British curry house restaurateurs.

PICKLE Pungent, hot, pickled vegetables essential to an Indian meal. The most common are lime, mango, brinjal and chilli. Though rarely seen at the restaurant, meat and game are made into traditional and very delicious Rajasthani pickles.

PODINA Mint. A fresh chutney, puréed from fresh mint, chilli and onion. Can also be spelt Pudina.

PRAWN BUTTERFLY Usually a large or giant king prawn, cut so that it opens out and flattens, butterfly-shaped, marinated in spices and immersed in gram-flour batter, then deep-fried. A curry house invention, whose name could also have derived from 'batter-fry'.

PRAWN PURI Prawns in a hot sauce served on a Puri (q.v.) bread. Although sometimes described as Prawn Puree it is not a purée.

PULLAO Ancient Persia invented *Pollou*, with rice and meat and/or vegetables, cooked together in a pan until tender. Following Muslim invasions it evolved into Turkey's *Pilav*, Greece's *Pilafi*, Spain's *Paella* and, of course, India's *Pullao*. In many curry houses, the ingredients are mixed after cooking, to save time. (*See* Biriani.) There are many other ways to spell it: *Pillau, Puloa, Pillar, Pilaw, Polaw*, etc.

PULLAO RICE The restaurant name for rice fried with aromatic spices, usually with rice grains coloured yellow and/or red and/or green.

PURI Unleavened wholemeal bread: rolled out flat to about 10cm (4 ins) in diameter, it puffs up when deep-fried, and should be served at once.

QUAS CHAWAL or KESAR CHAVAL Rice fried in ghee (q.v.), flavoured and coloured with saffron (*kesar*).

RAITA A cooling chutney of yoghurt on its own (*see also* Dhai) or vegetable, e.g. cucumber or mint (sometimes called Tandoori Sauce) to accompany papadoms, the starter or the main course.

RASGULLA Walnut-sized balls of paneer (q.v.), or semolina and cream cheese, cooked in syrup (literally meaning 'juicy balls'). They are white or pale gold in colour and served cold or warm. *See* Rasmalai.

RASHMI KEBAB Kebab of minced meat inside an egg net or omelette.

RASMALAI Rasgullas cooked in cream, served cold. Very rich, very sweet.

REZALA Bengali/Bangladeshi speciality. Lamb cooked in evaporated milk, rich and subtly spiced, it would be milder than Korma except that green chillies are mandatory. Traditionally no red- or orange-coloured ingredients should be used. *See* Kalia.

RHOGAN JOSH GOSHT Literally meaning 'lamb in red gravy'. Traditionally, in Kashmir, lamb is marinated in yoghurt, then cooked with ghee, aromatic spices and natural red colorants. It should be creamy but not hot. The curry house version omits the marinade and the aromatics, and uses tomato and red pepper to create a red appearance. There are many ways of spelling it – Rogon, Roghan, Rugon, Rugin, Rowgan, Ragan, etc, Just, Joosh, Juice, Jash, etc, Goosht, Goose, Gost, etc.

ROTI Indian bread of any type, rolled out into thin flat discs.

SABZI Vegetable.

SAG or SAAG Spinach, also called *Shak* in Bengali, *Palak* in the Punjab and *Rai*, although these are mustard leaves. *Lalshak* is delicious red spinach.

Sambal A Malayan term describing the chutneys accompanying a meal. Sometimes referred to on the Indian menu. Malays also refer to Sambal as a dish of various ingredients cooked in a hot sauce, e.g. prawn sambal.

Sambar A hot and spicy, runny, almost consommé-like south Indian vegetable curry made from lentils and exotic vegetables, such as the drumstick. In the Manchester/Merseyside area, the curry houses have a dish called *Samber*. It bears no resemblance to Sambar, except that lentils and a lot of chilli powder are added to meat, chicken or prawn curry.

Samosa Celebrated triangular, deep-fried meat or vegetable patties, supreme as starters or snacks.

Shami Kebab Round minced meat rissoles.

Shashlik Kebab Shashlik in Armenia means 'to grill'. Cubes of skewered lamb or chicken are marinated (in an oil, garlic and chilli mixture) then grilled. *See* Hasina.

Shatkora A Bangladeshi citrus fruit, the size of a grapefruit but sharper in flavour. Can be eaten fresh or used in cooking.

Sheek Kebab or Seekh Literally means (from Turkish *shish*) a skewer. Spiced minced meat, usually coloured lurid red at the curry house (from proprietary tandoori/kebab paste), is moulded onto the skewer, then baked in the tandoori and grilled.

Singara Bengali for Samosa (q.v.).

Standard Curry *See* Formula Curries.

T

Tandoori An ancient style of cooking, which originated in the rugged north-west frontier of India (now Pakistan). It gets its name from the cylindrical clay oven, the tandoor, with its opening at the top, fired with charcoal in its base. Originally the ingredients were chicken and lamb, marinated for many hours in a spiced yoghurt-based sauce, traditionally slightly reddened with red chilli, then skewered and baked in the tandoor. Now the curry house product also includes fish, prawns, paneer (q.v.) and vegetables. But its lurid red or orange colour is created by the unnecessary use of tartrazine food colouring in proprietary ready-to-use pastes. *See* Boti Kebab, Tikka, Nan Bread and Raita.

Tarka Dhal A tasty, spicy lentil dish, the Dhal being *massoor* (red) lentils, cooked to a purée, to which the Tarka (crispy, fried caramelized onion and/or garlic) is added as a garnish. This simple-sounding dish is a great test for the cook. It should taste very slightly burnt (from the Tarka), and be subtly, yet decisively, spiced, neither too thick nor too thin.

Tava A heavy steel, rimless, flattish frying pan, used to cook items such as Parathas.

Thali or Tali A round tray (*thali*) with a low rim, averaging about 34cm (12in) in diameter. It is a plate on which an entire meal is served. Dry items (rice, bread and even dry curries) are placed directly on the thali. Wet portions (curries, dhals, soups and sweets, etc) are placed in matching serving bowls (*tapelis*), and they too reside on the thali. They were made of gold for the Moghul emperors, silver for the Maharajas, and stainless steel for the rest of us. To be found at certain restaurants serving 'special' meals.

Tikka Literally, a small piece. For example, *Chicken Tikka* is a filetted chunk of chicken, marinated (*see* Tandoori), skewered and baked in the tandoor. Traditionally, the marinade is identical to Tandoori marinade, and cooks a naturally russet brown colour. Proprietary Tikka paste, as used in the curry house, is lurid orange or yellow because of the tartrazine it contains.

Tindaloo *see* Vindaloo.

U

Uppuma South Indian dish. Lightly fried semolina with onion and spices.

Uthappam A spicy south Indian pizza, made from rice flour and topped with onions, tomatoes and chilli.

Urid A type of lentil, its husk is black, and it comes whole, split or polished. Available as a dhal dish in some restaurants, e.g. *Maharani Dhal*.

Vada or Vadai Lentil-flour spicy doughnut, enjoyed in Gujarat and south India. *See* Dahi Vada.

Vark Edible silver or gold leaf, made today in Hyderabad, but a Moghul speciality, said to be an aphrodisiac.

Vindaloo A fiery dish from Goa. (*See page* 50). It now means the second hottest dish (two spoonfuls of chilli powder), usually with a chunk of potato (Aloo). Also sometimes called *Bindaloo* or *Tindaloo* (even hotter). *See also* Chilli, Madras and Phal.

Yakni Literally mutton, or a spicy meat-based stock.

Zaffron Saffron, also known as *Kesar* or *zafron*. The world's most expensive spice.

Zeera Alternatively called Jeera, which is cumin. *Zeera Gosht* is lamb cooked with cumin.

The 2004 COBRA GOOD CURRY GUIDE

THE ENTRIES

The Entries
An explanation of our method

There is no perfect system for laying out a nationwide restaurant Guide. Many Guides simply list their entries in town alphabetical order. The problem here is that there is no geographical relationship between each town. The method we have adopted in our Guides is to record the entries by county. We believe that most people understand the ancient British counties. We list them alphabetically. Unlike some Guides, we do not group the counties in National Regions (such as 'The Midlands' or the 'West Country', etc), since this too lacks logic. Counties are not without confusion. In some cases, their once sacrosanct borders have been altered by frequent local government tinkering. Greater Manchester is one example. When it was established as a 'Unitary Region' in 1965, it nibbled away parts of Cheshire and Lancashire. Many residents prefer to stick to these counties in their addresses, though we have adopted 'Greater Manchester' as a 'county' in this *Guide.* Other bodies, such as the Post Office, add to the confusion of recent years. Their postcodes are far from logical and do not follow county borders. BT also have their own system of geographical reference. It is because few people understand postcode logic, and even fewer understand phone codes, that we use the counties.

Starting on page 143, we cover the English counties. With the demise of Avon (which was in any case, not a county, but a Unitary Region), we now start with Bedfordshire. Within each county, we record the relevant towns alphabetically, and within each town, we record each restaurant alphabetically. In Bedfordshire, for example, the first town we record is Arlesey, and its first restaurant is Raj Villa, and so on. Following England, we then look at the Isles and Islands, then Scotland and finally Wales. Scotland has now replace Lothian with City authorities, though we retain it here for the time being.

We start with London, as is explained alongside. Before we are accused of London bias, it is worth giving our usual caveat: Of the 8,500 British curry restaurants on our nationwide database, nearly 20% of them are in London. Naturally, with such competition, many of the country's best are in the capital. Our coverage reflects this, with a strong London section.

CENTRAL LONDON

Area: British capital
Postcodes: E, EC, N, NW, SE, SW, W & WC
Population: 5,735,000

For the purpose of this Guide we define Central London as its 1870 postal districts, now known as postcodes. We run them alphabetically as follows: E, EC, N, NW, SE, SW, W and WC. Within each individual postcode, we run numerically, starting with E1 and ending with WC2. As with all postcode logic, this is not in any geographical order. For example, W5 Ealing, shares its borders with W13, West Ealing and W3, Acton. For 95 years these postcodes comprised all of London. In 1965 Greater London, (GL) was established. It includes these postcodes and expanded its borders, absorbing Middlesex and parts of Essex, Hertfordshire, Kent and Surrey (shown in black in the drawing below).

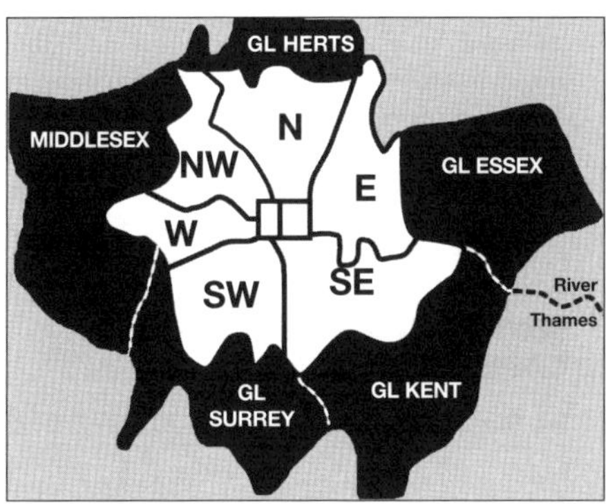

For GL (Greater London) towns/boroughs in these areas, please see the relevant county (Essex, Herts, Kent, Middlesex and Surrey) – see list on page 8.

London E

Area: East London
Postcodes: E1 to E18
Population: 1.050,000

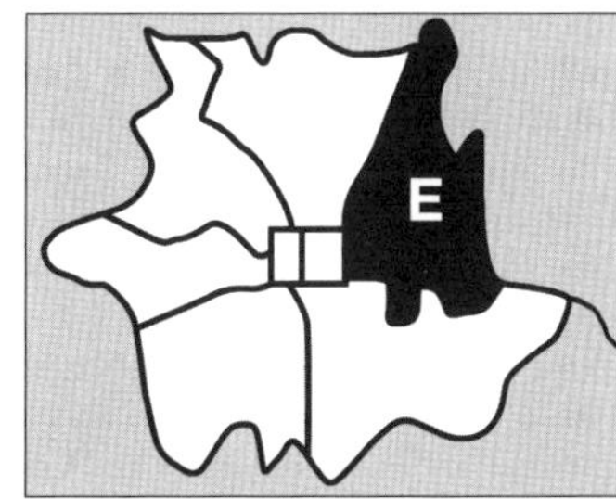

London E1

Brick Lane – Banglatown

Once predominantly Jewish, and bustling with tailors, salt-of-the-earth street markets and cab drivers, (to emphasise its roots you'll still find a 24 hr fresh-baked bagel shop at 159 where cabbies queue for sustenance) the long and narrow Brick Lane, has, since 1971, become home to the country's largest Bangladeshi community. Running north between Shoreditch and Aldgate East tube stations, it is now called Banglatown, indicating its proliferation of cheap and cheerful curry cafés, snack bars, restaurants and provisions shops, run by the thriving community. Some of these establishments have remained fairly spartan, and unlicensed (you can BYO). Others have redecorated and become licensed. We're not convinced that a Balti house is PC on the street, but there is one. But the curry-hungry can get breakfast from 8am here (Sweet & Spice, no 40). The late arrivals can get into Shampan until 2.30am. Many other on the Lane are open all day. Here are your favourites:

BENGAL CUISINE

12 Brick Lane, E1 0120 7377 8405

'Rashid has finished refurbishment from plate windows, new fittings, new staff dress.' says BF. *'Continues to provide best food on Brick Lane. Buy his privilege card and you get a 10% discount on all meals, and notes of functions, special evenings etc.'* BF. Those special evenings sound good, Bernard, let's hear more details about them. Bernard ate Jha, which he says is really hot. Delivery: 3-mile radius. Hours: 12 to 12 non stop, daily. Branch: Taja, 199a, Whitechapel Road, E1.

CAFE NAZ NEW TO OUR TOP 100

46-48 Brick Lane, E1 020 7247 0234

Fully licensed. Its decor broke Brick Lane away from tradition. It is bright and fun-like. Cafe Naz enjoys a very busy and lively buffet lunchtime trade. Above the main restaurant there is a large room, which can be used for private meetings and functions. The editors have been here several times recently and found the food very good indeed, including some authentic dishes. Some of the chefs are Indian and some Bangladeshi, which makes for a very interesting mix. Their recent Moghul Food Festival, spearheadded by Group Exec Chef Stephen Gomes and his brigade, proved this, and is he says, planning more to come. Gomes trained at Delhi's Oberoi, and is based at the Cafe Naz Cardiff branch. All round very happy reports with some saying best in Brick Lane, though as these pages show, opinions about everything vary. One previous regular complained about 'unsympathetic staff' when he felt unwell. BF. Despite this we welcome Cafe Naz to our **TOP 100**. Hours: 12 to 12 non stop, daily. Branches Cambridge, Chelmsford Essex and Cardiff.

CITY SPICE

138 Brick Lane, E1 020 7247 7012

Serving a good representation of Bangladeshi dishes (Salmon, Rui and Bekti feature amongst the fish dishes) it has a loyal following who are happy to retain it in the *Guide*.

LE TAJ

134 Brick Lane, E1 020 7247 4210

Opened in 1995, seats 40 diners. Authentic Bengali food on the stylish purple and cream menu. Biran Mass – a slice of boal fish marinated in a mixture of freshly ground herbs, then fried with onions. Singara – golden triangle of pastry filled with cottage cheese and spiced chicken, served with a chunky pineapple chutney. Shorisha Raja Chingri – grilled gholda king prawns in a chilli and fresh mustard marinade served sizzling. Lal Gootha – pumpkin and King Prawn dish, extremely popular in the fishing districts of Bangladesh. Beguner Borta – smoked aubergine pulp, muddled with green chillies, ginger and fresh lime. Pepe Bhajia – green papaya diced and tossed with light chillies and aromatic spices. Tomato Bhorta charcoal grilled tomatoes, puréed with a hint of spices, mustard oil and chillies. Set lunch: £7.27. Set dinner: from £15 to £22. Lunch to 2.30pm (not Saturdays). Dinner to 12 daily.

SHAFIQUES BENGAL BLUES CAFE BRASSERIE

94 Brick Lane, E1 020 7377 9123

Popular venue seating 80. Chicken and Lamb Haryali is the most popular dish. Snack menu available, including Chicken Tikka, Prawn Puri, Salmon Dhaka , Shobji Golati Kebab. Set lunch: £7.95, set dinner: £10.95. Hours: 12 to 12 non stop, daily.

SHAMPAN

PREVIOUS AWARD WINNER & TOP 100 ©

79 Brick Lane, E1 020 7375 0475

'If you want something unusual, THIS is the place to go,' says NP. *'Came one lunch time, on strength of Guide, very good indeed. I unimaginatively began with a meat spring roll, very nice. Can't remember the main course except that it was a Bangladeshi Chicken recipe involving a whole/half spring chicken – delicious. Impressed with food, although wasn't cheap.'* NP. Here's the fully licensed place for the night owls. Hours: 12AM to 2.30AM non stop, daily.

SHEBA

36 Brick Lane, E1 020 7247 7824

It just serves standard curries, without any claim to Bangladesh, but good and reliable. *'Still the best place in Brick Lane for formula curries,'* says NP. *'I've tried others – Nazrul and Nazrul II and while I can't remember much about them, I remember thinking they weren't nearly as good as Sheba. If you want cheap, enjoyable curry, Sheba is definitely the place to go. Prawn Puri and Chicken Bhuna – both very good, never been disappointed. Egg and Mushroom Curry is ideal to soak up the Friday night alcohol! Extremely reasonable prices. Place often packed with city workers, atmosphere often merry and smokey, service almost always polite and well-timed.'* NP. Lunch and dinner daily.

SWEET AND SPICY © U ANP

40 Brick Lane, E1 020 7247 1081

Being established in 1968, this makes it one of the Lane's oldest, and so is its decor. But never mind that. It's the cuisine you go for and it's Pakistani. Seats 40 diners in simple clean cafeteria style. Prices here are very good indeed, choose from the counter established favourites such as Seikh Kebab or Aloo Bora for 70p each. Chicken Karahi or Vindaloo or Korma for £3.75. Karahi Gosht or Madras Chappatis, Puris and Popadoms are all 30p each. A local favourite is the Kebab Roll from 85p to £1.90. Specials: Halwa Puri and Chana. Set lunch: £5, set dinner: £7. They deliver to your table. Sunday Buffet: £4.25. One of the few places where you can get curry breakfast in London. Hours: 8am to 10pm non stop, daily.

Elsewhere in E1

CAFE SPICE NAMASTE ©
PREVIOUS AWARD WINNER

16 Prescot Street, E1 020 7488 9242

Opened in 1995 by Cyrus Todiwala, Pervin Todiwala (Cyrus' wife) and Michael Gottlieb. Cyrus can really cook, specialising in Parsee and Goan cuisine, and a good dose of Innovative Indian. The former because he is Parsee, Goan because he was chef supreme in the holiday destination of Goa (Taj) where he cooked wonderful Portuguese-influenced curries. Innovative Indian because, well, he's Cyrus, though octopus and kangaroo can get up some noses, if you know what I mean. But do not get up and go; try some more traditional fare. Menu extracts: Papeta Na Pattice £3.95 – mashed potato cakes filled with green peas, grated coconut, chopped nuts, spices, rolled in semolina, fried, served on Parsee style hot tomato gravy. Leeli Chutney Ma Salmon – fillet of salmon in green chutney, skewered, chargrilled in the tandoor. Murgh Behroopia – half corn fed chicken cut into two, one leg marinated in the notorious peri-peri masala and other in Cafreal Masala. Tareli Machchi Nay Leeli Curry – tilapia fillets marinated in lime juice, garlic, cumin and coriander, pan fried, served with steamed rice, green coconut curry, small fried Papads. Parsee Dhansak – a lamb and lentil combination. All main course dishes at between £11 and £13. *'Encouraged by the GCG entry. Three of us opted out of the Brick Lane Halal and went 'up market.' [very sensible] 'Very different menu, place was packed at 8pm on a Tuesday night with patrons waiting at the bar for a table. Machli Kay Pakoda, being tilapia fillets was described as 'delicate.' My Wild Boar Chorizo £6.25 was excellent. Plentiful portions, Barbary Duck – subtle flavours, Masala Lamb Shank – correctly described as 'not spicy' despite green chillies. 5% Curry Club discount helped offset the 12.5% added service charge, but service was attentive. £100 for three, including drinks.'* CHC. *'Every bit as good as you recommended. I can still remember the Lamb Cutlets, perfectly spiced. Someone had Canadian Buffalo steak, which was also good. I didn't like the pudding – creme brulée style – don't think garam masala in a sweet pudding works. Other than that superb, £40 a head with wine, very reasonable.'* NP. *The small alfresco patio out back, with Indian snacks and cold beer, opened in time to take advantage of the hot summer of 2003 (remember that?). Delivery Service. Lunch – weekdays (frantic) and dinner daily to 10.30. Quietest time Saturdays. Closed Sundays. As a postscript, all who know him (and I've known him 24 years) know Cyrus is a bundle of energy, and one of his dreams has been to open an Asian cookery school. He has achieved that, and it got him the MBE. See Zen Satori London* N15.

©	Curry Club Discount	U	Unlicensed
V	Vegetarian	ANP	Alcohol not permitted
e-a-m-a-y-l	Eat as much as you like	BYO	Bring your own alcohol

EMPRESS TANDOORI

NEW ENTRANT 

141 Leman Street, E1 020 7702 1168

Owned by Mr Islam since 1992. Good Bangladeshi choices here, including the restaurant's most popular dishes: Skiandari Lamb – marinated and roasted. Cox's Bazar Crab – soft crabs cooked with ginger, garlic, coconut and fresh herbs, garnished with cucumber and lemon. Annan's Haash – succulent roasted breast of duck, cooked in aromatic spices, served with pineapple and cherry tomatoes, fairly hot. Takeaway: 10% discount. Minimum charge: £12. Delivery. Lunch to 3pm weekdays. Dinner to 11.30pm.

HALAL NEW ENTRANT

2-6 St Mark Street, E1 020 7481 1700

Established way back in 1939, making it the second oldest in London. '*Management know me as a regular now, and service remains very good as is the food. Dhansak has always been my favourite dish at the Halal. Still very reasonably priced being so close to the city and portions more than adequate.*' CC. Fully licensed. Hours: 12 to 12, Saturday and Sunday 12 to 10.30.

EASTERN SPICE NEW ENTRANT

12a Artillery Passage, Bishopsgate, E1 020 7247 0772

A full range of Tandooris, Baltis, Kebabs, Samosa. Bhajis and Curries are available at this well-established City curry house. 'We often drop in here for lunch, and very good it is too' HEG. Hours: 12-3/6-11.30. Closed Sat/Sun.

LAHORE KEBAB HOUSE

U BYO TOP 100

2 Umberton Street, E1 020 7488 2551

For anyone who has not been to either Pakistan or to Sparkbrook, the LKH is what it's all about. Despite Brum's claim to be the inventor of the currinary world, this gaff has been doing Balti, under what some say is its true name, Karahi – or Karrai (sic.) – since it opened in the seventies – serving darned good food, geared to Asian tastes, without compromising it for Westerners. At least that's what it used to be. But its relatively new-found glory as a lunchtime dive for the money boys and girls from the City has permeated into the evenings, and it's had an effect on management. The redec has now become old hat, and tatty even, much to the delight of LKH's aficionados and its Asian patrons, who were wary of such inventory as arty line drawings. Cutlery is still for wimps (though you no longer have to ask for it). But when in Rome, eat the correct way, please, using a piece of Roti to scoop up your curry, in your right hand only – too bad if you're left-handed. And expect limitations if you're a veggie. Halal mutton, chicken and quail are it, in the karahi, from the tandoor as tikkas or kebabs, or as steam roast (Choosa), with robust lentils and fragrant rice. Real veterans show their spurs by enjoying the celebrated, and very filling and satisfying, Paya (lamb's trotters), laced with the Hot Chilli Raita, followed by their gorgeous Kheer rice pudding. Service is swift and accurate, but don't expect pampering, and don't expect to pay more than a tenner, including tip, in cash, please – nothing fancy like credit cards. It has a different atmosphere at different times of the day, different again at the weekend, depending on who's eating when. *'The eight downstairs tables are communal, each seating 6 – 12. There are eight more tables upstairs. One wall is covered with mirrors. The restaurant is worn but clean. The main dishes are on display in a glass-fronted heater. I sat next to two businessmen and ordered Saffron Rice and Chicken Karahi. Almost but not quite – too hot. My Spinach and Potato offers a pleasant counter note, flavoured with nutmeg'* LB, Dallas. *'Service very good: they're used to large crowds with diners in and out very quickly. This place is my Mecca, my Garden of Eden, my Golden Temple. It's the best food anywhere.'* RCE. *'Please. please delist this restaurant from your Guide. It's already too busy, and we don't need you piling in more people.'* ANON. Hours: 12-12 non stop, daily.

PRIDE OF ASIA 

207 Mile End Rd, E1 020 7780 9321

A bog-standard, 65-seater owned and managed by Abdul Habiz. Chef Amir Uddin continues to provide all the favourites at prices made all the better with the Curry Club Discount. Delivery: £10 min, 3 mile radius. Lunch to 2.30pm. Dinner to midnight, daily.

TAJA

199a Whitechapel Road, E1 020 7247 3866

Taja, they tell us, translates as *'fresh'* which applies to the food. Specials: Mushroom Kebab, Mango and Coconut Curry and Goan Prawn Sag. This 80 seater can get busy at times. Ask about their loyalty club for instant savings, which will ensure you get your fill for under a tenner. Hours: 11AM to midnight, non stop, daily. Branch: I Brick Lane. E1

TIFFIN INDIAN TOP 100 ©

165 Cannon Street Road, E1 020 7702 3832

Since our last *Guide* (2001) owner Abul Kalam opened and closed a branch of Tiffin in Gillingham, Kent. They're just not ready for sophistication, he moaned. But his E1 branch clearly is and goes from strength to strength, according to its fans. It starts with the menu. *'Very dramatic and stylish glossy purple menu for the food, wine and other drinks are listed in an equally good looking orange and green menu.'* RL. Start with Tiffin Special, an absolute feast, including Murghi Tikka – chicken marinated in yogurt and spices cooked in a clay oven. Keema Chops – seasoned mince coated in finely mashed potato and breadcrumbs lightly fried. Sheek Kebab – finely minced meat mixed with onion, coriander and an assortment of rich exotic spices, skewered and cooked in a clay oven, all served with salad, at a reasonable £4. The vegetarian alternative is also equally tempting at £3.20, lightly spiced aubergine slices in batter; vegetables in a spicy sauce wrapped in filo pastry and fried. But do leave room for your main course, for example Tandoori Batak c£9 – duck breast marinated in curd and coriander or the Murgh Ur Saag £5.50 – chicken cooked in a dry sauce with spinach, onion and spices. And many more such delights. Minimum charge: £7, set lunch: £4.95. Lunch and dinner daily.

London E2

Bethnal Green

AL AMIN 

483 Cambridge Heath Road, E2 020 7739 9619

Abdul Noor's two-room 39-seater remains a popular standard curry house, with all the trimmings, including Balti. We've not had one bad report about this place; it pleases everyone. Reasonable prices. Delivery: £10 minimum, 2-mile radius. Lunch to 2.30pm. Dinner to midnight, daily.

London E4

Chingford, Highams Park

PURBANI

34 The Avenue, E4 020 8531 8804

Established 1983. Owner Tony Turu Miah's air conditioned 54-seater is a regular in the Guide, and has built up a good loyal following. Chicken

Tikka, Chicken and Prawn Bhoona with green salad and Special Pullao Rice for nigh on a tenner. Bamboo Shoot Bhajia is something different. Lunch to 2.30 and dinner to 11.30 daily.

London E14

Docklands, Dogs, Limehouse, Poplar

MEMSAHEB ON THAMES

65 Amsterdam Road, E14 020 7538 3008

Mridul Kanti Das, managing partner of Memsaheb, puts on regular food festivals, specialising in regional food with delights such as Machli Amritsar – boneless pieces of white Indian fish in a spicy batter which is deep-fried. Murghi Lababdar – minced chicken cooked in a thick spicy tomato sauce, garnished with fresh coriander. Punjabi Roghan – on the bone lamb cooked with medium hot spices with fresh tomatoes and fresh coriander. A popular place with several reporters in the area, who speak reverentially of the views (of the Dome across the Thames) and the staff curry, oh yes and *'the adorable staff!'* Lunch to 2.30 weekdays and dinner to 11.30 daily.

DOCKMASTERS

Dockmaster's House, West India Dock Gate, Hertsmere Road, E14 020 7345 0345

Formerly Tabla, which opened in early 2000 in a grand Georgian building near Canary Wharf. The House was built in 1807 for the Dockmaster. Now renamed. There are three elements. A 100-seat restaurant with a satisfying range of Indian regional dishes. Down in the extensive cellars, is now a 120-seat bar offering a range of spicy pub grub. Outside there is a garden large enough to accommodate 80 seats which serves summer barbecues of Indian kebabs, grills and tandooris on platters alongside pitchers of beer. Its opening masters have moved to grander things. Wahaab to Cinnamon Club, W1 and super-chef Yogesh Datta the to The Painted Heron, SW10 (*see entries*) and of course things are not quite the same now, but the reports we are still getting are happy enough. Lunch to-3pm. Dinner to-1030pm.

TALE OF INDIA

53 West India Dock Road, E14
020 7987 3418

Seats forty diners in air-conditioned comfort. Check out the interesting starters which include: Cauliflower Pakora, Iribeesi Baja – runner beans fried with onions and Fish Bora – salmon, mixed with fresh coriander and onions, lightly spiced and deep-fried with egg and breadcrumbs. Main courses are just as exciting: Shathkora Bhuna – chicken spiced and flavoured with shathkora, a sour citrus fruit, Rezalla – tikka cooked in sauce of yoghurt and green chilli and Dal Samber – vegetables and lentils lavishly flavoured with garlic and butter. Delivery: 3 miles, £10 minimum. Lunch to 2.30 weekdays and dinner to 11.30.

©	Curry Club Discount	**U**	Unlicensed
V	Vegetarian	**ANP**	Alcohol not permitted
e-a-m-a-y-l	Eat as much as you like	**BYO**	Bring your own alcohol

London E15

Stratford

SPICE INN

22 Romford Road, E15 020 8519 1399

'Dark interior, tasteful Indian drawings on walls. Swift and polite service, but lacks interpersonal skills. Mixed Kebab – sheik kebab, chicken and lamb tikka, reshmi kebab, all very well spiced and delicious, but lukewarm. Methi Gosht – best I've had since the untimely demise of the Shish Mahal in Dumbarton, but again warm. Nevertheless very, very good. £17 for food plus 2 pints Cobra.' DP.

London E18

Redbridge, S. Woodford, Woodford

MEGHNA GRILL 

219 Woodford High Road, E18 020 8504 0923

Siddiqur Rahman's long-established (1971), competent Bangladeshi curry house. It's one of those places which is always busy. Says it all really. For those who don't eat curry (they won't be reading this then) let them eat chips, as Marie Antoinette didn't say. But the Meghna serve them and Roast Chicken. But I'd plump for the Tikka Duck or Bangladeshi Fish-on-the-bone, myself. Half price Mondays if you book. Home delivery and takeaway.

THE ROSE 

65 Woodford High Road, E18 020 8989 8726

The Rose has been operated for 25 years by Messrs Miah and Hoque, who offer all the favourite tandooris and curries at sensible prices. The media often ask the editors for flock-wallpapered venues, presumably so that they can make disparaging remarks about curry. Well the flock went and the food got better. *'Food delicious, service exemplary, as ever'* says SSTC. *'Chef's Rallwa – chicken or lamb tikka with prawns, keema and spring onions in ginger sauce, very tasty. Generous portions and rice served in little china dishes (Villeroy and Bosch) with matching lids.'* SSTC. Be more adventurous and try the Garlic Mussels on Puri – mussels cooked in a garlic, red onion and white wine sauce, served on a puri. 20% discount on collected takeaways. Lunch to 2.30pm. Dinner to 11.30pm.

London EC

Area: The City of London
Postcodes: EC1 to EC4
Population: 145,000

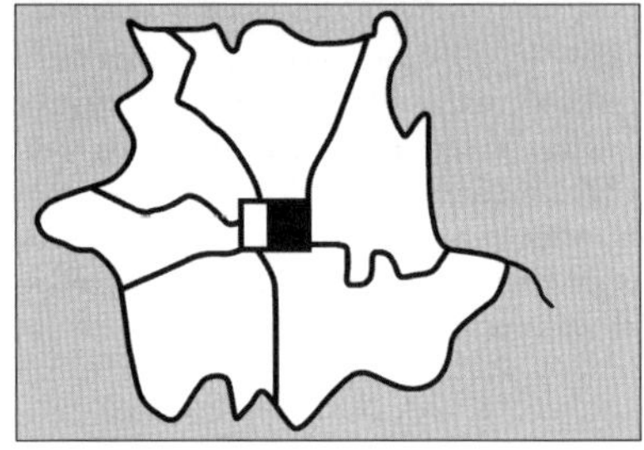

London EC1

Angel, Barbican, Clerkenwell, Farringdon, Old Street, Smithfield

CAFE GULSHAN NEW ENTRANT

33 Charterhouse Square, Barbican, EC1 020 7600 7277

'It is a large restaurant, a very pleasant building in an excellent location. We had been there twice before, not long after it opened. We were always happy enough with the food but something was missing. This time it was different from the moment we stepped through the door. We were welcomed immediately, shown to an upstairs table, (before we had always been ushered downstairs even though upstairs was not full), promptly handed menus and wine list and generally given the impression that the whole place was much more professional. Apparently the owner is the same but the whole staff has changed, with a 'proper chef', keen waiters and an ambitious manager who has already made changes and has plans for more. The menu has a few less common items, unfortunately no fish except the usual prawns and a crab dish. The food was very good, portions generous and prices very fair for central London. Very good to find an Indian restaurant with a better wine list and offering espresso coffee. Coffee is usually a dreadful let down in Indian restaurants. Unfortunately there wasn't a

single Indian dessert. Perhaps they will offer these in the future if the improvements continue as planned.' HC.

CITY CAFÉ LAZEEZ TOP 100

88 St John Street, EC1 020 7253 2224

The move into the City is exemplified by Café Lazeez, who were amongst the first to spot the gap in the market (few if any Indian restaurants, and plenty of fat city wallets) and established this branch in 2000. It seats 125 diners in three rooms. The menu is identical to the original Café Lazeez (*see* London SW7). Not expensive, (eg Set lunch ,£10) though service: 12.5%. The branch tell us the suits find Chicken Dum Korma their most popular dish. Hours: 11.30 to 4.45 and 5.00 to 10.30. No I don't understand the 15 minute closure. Saturday 5 to 11.30. Sunday closed. *See* Café Lazeez, London SW7 and W1.

COCONUT LAGOON NEW ENTRANT BEST RESTAURANT GROUP, 2004 TOP 100

7 – 21 Goswell Road, EC1 020 7253 4546

From the owners of the original Coconut Lagoon restaurants in Kenilworth and Stratford upon Avon, comes this new 160 seat branch, located in the former Nico restaurant. It's alongside a decent hotel, so check in, fill up and flop out in bed. The restaurant is decorated in the company style, displaying the bright colours so redolent of South India. For those who need a restaurant that can serve a decent dinner before curtain up at the Barbican theatre, this place is for you.

I was walking around the Barbican and couldn't believe my luck. Very large, decor is almost over the top, very colourful, masses of silk flowers, some arrangements with mock parrots in them, cane furniture, all very eye catching. The menu is Southern Indian, which made a very pleasant change and all the food comes plated on colourful plates. The main courses are good value as all come complete with the rice and vegetable the chef thinks appropriate. The food was very good and very attractively presented. There is a pretheatre menu for £12.95, particularly good value with a reasonable choice. We saw from the menu that its sister restaurant is one of the **TOP 100,** *this one certainly deserves to be and will no doubt become so. Service was excellent, all the waiters in Nehru style suits, all very friendly, helpful and professional. It is an upmarket Indian restaurant and the whole meal was a wonderful experience. Stuffed Roti for starter – served with a silver paper, frilled holder, like one end of a cracker, very attractive and practical. Wonderful Stuffed Pomfret with Prawns. One of the best Parathas I have ever had. Large piece of Halwa dessert, very good served with pretty slices of kiwi and cream.'* HC. This is another of those restaurants that will attract bad comments. I've seen one or two, quite spiteful actually (anon, of course on the web – see my comments in the Guide intro about web critics). So if it's two pints of vindaloo and some verbal abuse you look forward to giving, don't go to Coconut Lagoon and save yourself the effort of complaining to me about it. For discerning diners who enjoy excellence, albeit at a price, you'll be pleased to hear that we've awarded this and the owners' other restaurants our Award for the Best Group of Restaurants. See Coconut Lagoon, Kenilworth, Warwickshire for full menu details. Lunch-2.30. Dinner 5-11, daily. *See page 1.*

SEMA INDIAN BALTI U BYO ©

141 White Cross Street, EC1 020 7253 2927

Proprietor, Abdul Khalique Choudhury says he'll provide the glasses, you just BYO at his friendly 25 seater. He tells us Chicken Jalfrezi Balti £5.75 including a Nan bread is his most popular dish,probably because all Balti dishes come with a free Nan bread. Interesting starters : Liver Hazri £2, I can hear screeches of 'yuk' but liver curries very well. Semi Balti Soup £1.75. Main courses: Ginger Chicken, Chicken Tikka Pepper Balti and Nan around a fiver. Set lunch: £5.50, set dinner: £6.40. Delivery: 1 mile, £10 minimum Takeaway: 10% discount. Lunch to 2.30pm. Dinner to 11.30pm.

SMITHFIELD'S TANDOORI NEW ENTRANT

4 Lindsey Street, EC1 020 7606 3868

'The decor has had a complete facelift. The menu is fairly standard and the prices are on the low side for central London, but the portions are average and the cooking well above average. Had Tandoori King Prawns, a meal I haven't had for years. The prawns were gorgeous, well spiced, moist, small areas of burned tandoori patches, lots of sizzling onions. Full marks – they had several Indian sweets – I had Gulab Jamun, served warm, lovely. Danny made to feel welcome even though he wasn't eating. An

unplanned and unexpected Indian meal turned out to be a real pleasure. Service really good, particularly one waiter who really added to the evening. HC.

SONIA BALTI HOUSE NEW ENTRANT

1 Lever Street, EC1 020 7253 3398

Brisk takeaway trade. Service is very homely and friendly. Very tender and tasty Sheek Kebab £1.95, with a cool crisp salad and very yellow and garlicky yoghurt sauce. Lamb Taba Gosht £5.95 – rather tough lamb in well spiced and appetising, but thin gravy. Very doughy Garlic Nan £1.40.' RW. No credit cards. Takeaway: 10% discount. Delivery: £10 minimum. Hours: 5.30 to 12.

London EC2

Barbican, City, Liverpool Street, Moorgate

MEHEK NEW ENTRANT

45 London Wall, EC2 020 7588 5043

A pretty Indian girl, who takes coats etc, shares space with a comfortable leather sofa (for the takeaway customer) and a clutch of tables. An extremely long bar leads to more tables at the back. Throughout our visit, suited men, men and more men arrived. Some perched themselves on high stools, drank pints of beer and talked loudly while crunching on woven metal baskets piled high with Popadoms. We were swiftly seated and passed menus. However, all chutneys and no pickle, cachumber or raitha does make quite dull eating. From the short menu, we chose a starter of Bhalla Papria Chaat – light, fluffy buns of fermented and steamed rice flour, smothered in natural yoghurt and imli which were quite plain. I decided on a firm vegetarian favourite, Aloo Tikki. Three nicely shaped patties of spiced potato and green peas were delivered with salad and yoghurt dip. The main course Achari Gosht £12 – tender lamb, mildly spiced, was too sweet for us both. Madri Murgh £11.50, a new twist on CTM, this dish contained Vodka (and that's why I ordered it!). Side dishes of Jaipuri Bhindi £4.50, diagonal slices of okra, deep-fried in a very light batter of besan and sprinkled, too sparingly, in my opinion, with mango powder and kala namak. Though still a good dish. Our benchmark Dal Makhni was £4.50. I try this one everywhere I go. It was well cooked, creamy, not over salted, wonderful. While we ate, our waitress 'stalked' our table. I strongly object to this habit. She could have chatted to the coats girl, who wasn't doing anything, except for, of course, flirting with the floor manager. He took delight in showing off like a peacock in front of her reception desk. While, she in turn, giggled and fluttered her long, well mascared eye lashes at him in appreciation. In between his performances, he stood on the pavement outside, glancing left and right as if about to cross the road. In fact, he went no where, he just stood and smoked. The Sommelier was also at a loose end. He constantly returned to our table to fill our drinking receptacles, very annoying and quite rude. You should not overfill a glass, wine needs to breath. After a short rest and totally unlike our normal eating habits, we decided to indulge in a pudding. HC will be over the moon – real Indian sweets on offer. We shared Dudhi (marrow) Halwa. Service charge at 12.5% was added to our bill and the credit card slip was returned, closed – congrats! Food OK. Staff need training. Lunch and dinner.

RED ROSE CITY

NEW ENTRANT NEW TO OUR TOP 100

37 Crutched Friars EC2 020 7702 9739

Moin Uddin has six Red Rose restaurants out there in the sticks. (That's what the City guys and gals call any place not on the tube network – dangerous, lawless territory, best left to the yokels. They're strange these people, but not so strange as Crutched Friars as a street name? What the heck does it mean?). For those of us who read and write this *Guide*, all the Roses are the sort of places we yokels enjoy; well managed, competent, welcoming. This is a big investment for Moin, and the sheer grandure of the place shows that he's got the City investment curry bug, which is to go in there and cash in on those high-earners. Red Rose City probably will never have the atmosphere of those Rosy locals. The main restaurant is upstairs and it's large (150 seats) but spacious. One wag tells us she thinks the decor resembles an international hotel lobby. I guess she means it's impersonal; (you can't win Moin). But it's what's needed in the City. Who would believe they've employed a white chef to cook 'English food' for the wimps. He loves it, and is fast learning how to cook curry properly. Which brings me to the real menu. Firstly, (for the yokels) it ain't cheap, but we've seen worse. Our benchmark dish Dal Makhani – black lentils and kidney beans, cooked overnight on the Tandoor, served with a dash of cream is £3.30. (See Guide intro) Starters start at £3 for onion bhaji (sic) and go via Mussels cooked in Garlic sauce £5, Crab Khola Puri, Crab meat cooked in coconut cream, curry leaves and South Indian spices served with baby Naan. £6, Spiced Scallop served on fried Puri bread £7 ,to Lobster Khum, Chef's speciality, lobster meat cooked with mushroom, garlic, white wine and mild spices. Served with baby naan, £8.50. Main courses Murgh Makhoni (that's CTM to you and me) is £10. Editor DBAC's favourite is Duck Mirchi Wala, pieces of duck marinated overnight with herbs and then cooked with chillies and green peppers. Welcome to our **TOP 100.** Lunch -3pm . Dinner -11pm.,weekdays only.

London EC3

Aldgate, Fenchurch Street, Tower of London

KASTURI

NEW ENTRANT NEW TO OUR TOP 100

57 Aldgate High Street, EC3 020 7480 7402

Nur Monie's Tanjore, Welling, Kent has been in our **TOP 100** for ages. In late 2002 he teamed up with Bashir Ahmed (owner of five popular Kohinoor restaurants in Holland) to open their 80-seater Kasturi. It has the current look of blonde wood floor, bright lights, colourful walls and pot plants. Management tell us, Kasturi means *'the strong scented secretion found in rare musk deer, used in expensive perfumes'.* Phew! I don't know about that, but the scent of the tandoor is more likely to be encountered. Because Kasturi has an ace up its sleeve – Chef Rajandra Balmiki, head chef at The Tangore. He trained at the Delhi's Mauyra Sheraton Hotel, under chef Imtiaz Qureshi of Dum Pukht fame and former training chef, the highly respected C.P Rahman. Maurya has the best Tandoori restaurant in the world. What a background for Balmiki. Kasturi claims to specialise in Pakhtoon cuisine. It's a far cry from Delhi and Welling. It refers to the tribal people of Afghanistan from the rugged mountain passes in the former North-West Frontier Province, whose name for themselves is Pathan, Pashtun, Phuktana or Pukhtun. Afghan food is pretty basic (*see pages* 49 & 50), especially at tribal level, involving kebab-skewer cooking and slow-cooking in pots. Grills, Kebabs, Koftas and Birianis are popular, spiced with the unique Afghan spice mix, Char Masala (four aromatic spices) and cooked mostly in their own juices. Try the Kebab Ke Karishma, a selection of kebabs. It includes Chicken, Lamb and Minced meat kebabs. Served as a starter for two persons with special bread: £10.95. Kadak kebab Samarkand – minced lamb roll stuffed with cheese and grilled – £3.90. Then there's Mahi-e-Ghazni – whole pomfret fish marinated in fresh coriander and mint and roasted in the Tandoor £9.95, or Grilled Seabass – marinated in a sauce of yoghurt and olive oil with black and white pepper £10.95. Any of the Biryanis will 'blow you away'. HEG. Our benchmark Dal-Dera Ismail Khan – 'A harmonious combination of black dal and herbs, simmering on slow charcoal fire' (aka Dal Makhani) is just £3.50. Kasturi has attracted rave reviews from our reporters But such a menu and such a skilled Indian chef will of course bring adverse comments from what Monie calls *'those with their brains closed'.* He's prepared for it, and he offers them formula curries. [How sad.] We're prepared for it too, and have no hesitation in saying if it's formula that you want go to nearby Brick Lane and enjoy yourself. We welcome Kasturi into our **TOP 100**. Takeaway and Delivery. Hours: 11-11 weekdays. Dinner -11.30 Saturdays. Closed Sundays.

MATAB'S

76 Aldgate High Street, EC3 020 7481 4010

Owned by the personable Matab Choudhury, one of the prime movers and Chief Treasurer of the Bangladeshi Caterers Association, this restaurant in some way acts as a flagship and example to the 12,000 other restaurants which the BCA quotes as its membership. One is struck by the vibrant wall paintings and ceilings, with contrasting crisp white tablecloths, King's cutlery and wooden floor. The deft service provides all the old favourites that one has come to expect of the Bangladeshi formula curry venue. And it is a favourite haunt of many a city regular, of which VW-P and LD-W are two. Reports please.

PLANTERS INN

25 Great Tower Street, EC3 020 7621 1214

The original owners named this venue after Bangladesh's major industry, tea planting. Of the 138 tea estates in Bangladesh, 128 are in Sylhet. Now under new management with partners Vernon Menezes, a personable Goan, formerly of Zaika and Chor Bizarre Chef Joydeep Chatterjee, from Calcutta and formerly chef of Ophim and Pitts Cottage. The 64-seater, opposite the Tower of London, is uncluttered, with white walls, mirrors, polished wood, tiled floor and potted glossy palm trees which divide the tables. The restaurant gets busy at lunchtime with suited City folk grabbing a served-within-the-hour quick lunch before resuming their afternoon business. *'Different atmosphere in the evening. I like both, and I like the food. It's not your typical curry house.'* RCF.

RAJASTHAN

49 Monument Street, EC3 020 7626 1920

'Closest to my work, occasionally go at lunchtimes. Packed with city workers, so specialise in getting you in and out quickly. Good fast service, nice decor and food varies from OK to pretty good. Duck Pineapple, very nice, enjoyably unusual. Obviously priced to reflect that it's in the city, although not bad.' NP. Bhuna £9, silver pomfret, marinated, medium sauce. Air conditioned. Menu extracts: Tangri Kebab £3.50, marinated chicken drumstick, tandooried. Lamb Rezala £8 – lamb tikka, hot, tangy sauce, fresh green chillies, coconut and tomatoes. Roop Chanda – a Bangladeshi fish dish. Lunch to-3pm. Dinner to-11pm., daily.

London N

Area: North London
Postcodes: N1 to N22
Population: 1,250,000

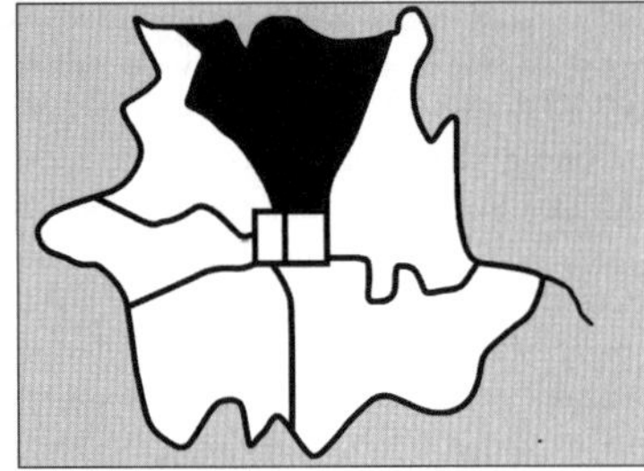

London N1

Islington, King's Cross, Shoreditch

AFGHAN KITCHEN

35 Islington Green, N1 020 7359 8019

There are only two Afghan restaurants in the UK (*see also page 49 and Caravan Serai,* W1). Afghani food is Muslim, big on Halal goat (here they use lamb) and goat's milk. Yoghurt always accompanies a meal. Try Dogh – Savoury Yoghurt with mint, and the Tourshis or chutneys. The food is less spicy than Indian, but the names are similar. Bread isn't Naan, it is Nane Lawash – thinner, glazed and basket-shaped. Qurma is Korma, etc, etc. *'Not knowing anything about Afghan food, four of us were delighted to find that it bore a close resemblance to Indian with the Murgh Kofta – chicken meat balls in sauce, Gosht Qurma, a type of meat Korma, Suzhi Gosht – meat with spinach spiced with Char Masasa (a four-spice version of India's Garam Masala), each £4.50 with the bread as the staple, chilli pickle to liven up the delicate spicing, house wine to wash to it all down.'* GR. Small menu. No credit cards. Average spend £9. Hours: 12pm-12am Tues.-Sat.

ANGEL CURRY CENTRE

Chapel Market, N1 020 7837 5727

'I'm actually quite surprised that of the numerous curry houses in Chapel Market, only one is currently in the Guide. The one we first tried is the Angel Curry Centre and it is the one we keep coming back to. Nothing fancy, just consistently excellent formula curries. It's very cheap, and made even cheaper by the BYO policy – there's a dodgy off-license next door selling cheap lager. The service is fast and polite. NP.

BALTI MANIA

391 Liverpool Road, N1 020 7697 0406

Seats 36 diners. Formerly a Fish&Chip shop, which explains the white tiles. *'Balti Mania tops the lot. Doesn't look much from the outside but it is one of Islington's best kept secrets. Karahi Chicken £4.20 is a special fave! Staff are wonderful which is an added bonus.'* SD. *'An unsung gem. Unbelievably reasonably priced with friendly and efficient staff. Offers an extended and delicious menu for such a small restaurant. My favourite – Patra £2.50, curried avri leaves. Don't be put off by the decor which is reminiscent of a public toilet – all white tiles – much much cleaner!. It is worth the 200 mile journey.'* MM Vegetable Thali £7.95, good value for six dishes plus Pops and Bread. Hours: 5.30-12.

CURRY RAJ

3 Penton Street, N1 020 7278 5080

'Please don't put this one in the Guide. It's already full of long term fans, and I don't want it fuller'. ANON. Tough. You should have given me your name. It's a popular curry house, doing the job right, at sensible prices.

INDIAN VEG BHEL POORI HOUSE V

92 Chapel Market, N1 020 7837 4607

'Although I have sung the praises of the excellent value eighteen buffet dishes e-a-m-a-y-l £2.95, I feel I must praise it again. I now lunch there once a week and the quality is always consistent. Occasionally there is a superb mashed potato and onion curry. Always a friendly welcome and my half lager is now brought automatically.' TN. *'All the dishes are superb, and I'm no veggie. The Bhel Puri is still my favourite though.'* ME. Hours: 12-11.30.

MASALA ZONE AWARD WINNER NEW ENTRANT TOP 100

80 Upper Street, N1 020 7359 3399

Its menu, and no-booking concept is explained in the entry for the pilot branch Masala Zone in Marshall Street W1. But unlike there, we've had a bit of complaint which may or may not be surprising. One would expect Islington to be 'in-the-know' about real Indian food as opposed to curry house formula. But maybe not. One reporter liked the diabetic dishes. But of late the reports have cheered up, so there's hope yet for Islington. Put it this way, you won't find better real Indian food at such prices (av £10) *See page 37*.

PARVEEN

6 Theberton Street, N1 020 7226 0504

Established 1977 and seating 60 diners on two floors. It's now an air-conditioned, contemporary restaurant, decorated in bright colours – turquoise, red, royal blue, canary yellow. Polished blonde wooden floor, spot lights and marbled bar. You'll find the curry formula done well here. Here are the views of some of Parveen's many friends: *'Great decor and food that tastes authentic!'* HN. *'Faruk and staff are so amazing, makes everyone feel special. Food lovely and decor fantastic.'* JO B. *'Great food and service.'* HM. *'By far the best Indian in Islington, highly recommended.'* CR. Rupchandra £8.95 and Lamb Pasanda £7.95 are regular favourites. Set dinner £33.95 for two. Hours: 12-3 and 6-12. *See overleaf.*

RAJ MONI NEW ENTRANT

279 Upper Street, N1 020 7354 1270

Small, about fifty covers, pleasantly decorated. *'Prompt service. Standard menu – Silsila Masala Chicken and Afgani Chicken new to me. Started with Rajmoni Special which was basically Chicken Chat – good portion, nicely spiced with tender chicken, OK, but nothing special. Main course – Chicken Tikka, good portion, 10 pieces, served on sizzler; Madras Curry Sauce – nice and hot; Plain Rice – generous portion, light and fluffy. Standard formula curry house.'* DB. Lunch and dinner daily. Delivery evenings only.

©	Curry Club Discount	**U**	Unlicensed
V	Vegetarian	**ANP**	Alcohol not permitted
e-a-m-a-y-l	Eat as much as you like	**BYO**	Bring your own alcohol

ZEN SATORI RESTAURANT AT THE ASIAN AND ORIENTAL SCHOOL OF CATERING

40 Hoxton Street, N1. 020 7613 9590

Cyrus Todiwala (*see Café Spice Namaste, E1*) was one of the three restaurateurs behind Hackney's recently opened £1m Asian and Oriental School of Catering. Courses with a time-span of anything from an afternoon to three years, are available in cooking, drink and service in ethnic cuisine. A demonstration and training area enables up to 80 students at any one time to observe and learn from top professional guest lecturers such as Terry Tan and Stephen Gomez (of Cafe Naz, E1). The School has already successfully placed several hundred people in employment and handles up to 800 students a year on a range of courses with a time-span of anything from an afternoon to three years. The School also has a fully operational restaurant, Zen Satori, located on the ground floor. Head chef Saviour Thomas has worked in a variety of London's leading Asian restaurants giving him a sound knowledge of several styles of cuisine. Zen Satori's menu changes frequently and offers many curry items such as South Indian Curry, Lemon Chicken, Daal Vegetables and Birianis. Thai dishes might include Green Chicken Curry, Sweet & Sour King Prawns, and Green Paw Paw Salad. Turkish, Malaysian and Vietnamese dishes will also appear, as they are introduced into the school's curriculum. The colourful restaurant is split into a 'fine-dining' area and casual section situated close to the bar area. The open kitchen enables diners to watch the fledgling chefs working tandoori ovens, flaming woks and hot grills. Manager Leon Zhang has an ever-changing team of young, enthusiastic floor staff, the school's students, who have reached a certain standard before beginning a spell in Zen Satori. Hoxton Street gained notoriety when a certain Jamie opened his own restaurant at no 15. Why go there when you can enjoy the output of youthful students, keen to impress their first real customers, at far more reasonable prices. Lunch Mon to Friday. Dinner, Tuesdays to Saturdays. Closed Sundays Hours differ, so ring to check.

London N2

East Finchley

MAJJOS 

1 Fortis Green, N2 020 8883 4357

Established in 1993 by Mrs Ashraf. Manager S Mogul. A shop with a seating area for just 10 diners, so you can enjoy some spicy dishes while shopping for your Indian groceries. Kashmiri, Pakistani and Indian food. Great prices: Meat curries £5.25 or £3.50. Veg curries £3.50 or £2.30 Hours: 10.30am-10.30pm (10pm on Sun.).

London N3

Finchley, Fortis Green

RANI VEGETARIAN

PREVIOUS AWARD WINNER TOP 100

7 Long Lane, N3 020 8349 4386

Jyoti Patni is front of house in this venue tastefully decorated in shades of turmeric and red, with Georgian chairs and glass-topped tables. Rani means Queen, and the term could as well refer to the cooks, Jyoti's wife and his mother, because their Gujarati vegetarian food cannot be bettered anywhere. The menu features mainly Gujarati items which are tasty enough to please all but the most obdurate non-veggie. India's most western state, Gujarat, is the home of mild, slightly sweet dishes, with a love of yoghurt and gram flour. The soup-like curry Khadi is one dish showing Gujarati adoration of both. The famous bhajia also originated in Gujarat, as did the lesser known Dahi Vada, a gram flour dumpling in a tangy yoghurt sauce. Kachoris – Spicy mashed potato and peas spicy ball, coated in batter and deep-fried. Bhel Puri are all there along with Gujarati curries e.g. Undui – five vegetable stew, and a Gujarati national dish. Traditionally the five vegetables are beans, aubergine, red pumpkin, sweet potato and a further vegetable. These are cooked in a sauce made from gram flour, asafoetida and yoghurt. It is often served with besan kofta balls in it. Another superb dish is Lasan Bateta, £3 – literally garlic potato, but it's not that simple – it is baby new potatoes, and the stuffing includes spices and red chilli.the whole is dipped in gram-flour batter, deep-fried and served in imli (sweet tamarind chutney). Wow!!! Innovations to prevent diner boredom make this restaurant different. How about pizzas (which are after all just Naan bread cooked in the oven) with Indo-Italian toppings, such as banana (plantain) methi with green chilli and mozzarella. Great stuff. And they are innovations retaining the ethos of Indian, rather than fusion food which does not. *'The menu has some cold starters which are "to die for". Rashia Vall, great. Rice and breads as good as usual.'* CT. Says the highly critical RL: *'Menu includes unusual and tasty dishes. Recommended to me by so many people. Aloo Shai Poori (crispy pooris, potatoes, onions with yoghurt) and Vall Papri (spicy beans and onions on pooris with tamarind and yoghurt), both a taste of heaven. This restaurant is pure quality. It's world class.'* RL. Thali £10, Set meal £13, min 2, Average Spend £15. Kid's menu. High chairs for the tinies. Sunday lunch 12.15-2.30. Dinner 6-10.30 daily.

London N7

Tufnell Park

BENGAL BALTI HOUSE 

6 Brecknock Road, N7 020 7609 7075

A popular haunt in the area owned by Ashik Ali since 1994. This air-conditioned restaurant seats 86 in two rooms, serves all the favourites, *'with friendly panache'.* HEG. Another reporter adores one of the waiters. Hmmm!! wonder who and whom? Hours: 12-2.30pm/6pm-12am (Sat. to 12.30am). Branch: Hillmarton Tandoori, Hillmarton Terrace, N7.

London N8

Crouch End, Hornsey, Turnpike Lane

MASALA DELI BAR NEW ENTRANT

59 Park Road, N8 020 8442 9222

Gujarati food, predominately vegetarian, e.g.: Kachori 60p – minced peas / split mung beans in pastry balls. Patra 50p, spiced gram flour wrapped in arvi leaves. Pani Puri £2.50, six small puffed puris filled with sprouted mung beans and potato, served with tamarind and date dressing (yum yum!). Roti Wraps £1.50, bread filled with a choice of sweet corn; potato and nut; shredded cabbage with carrot and lime. Light lunches include: Tuna Thali £6, plain rice served with spicy tuna, a vegetable dish or your choice, a roti and a juice drink. Falafel Meal £3, spicy lentil fritters served with salad and dressing in pitta bread. www.masala-uk.com. Hours: 11-9.30.

London N10

Muswell Hill

TASTE OF NAWAB 

93 Colney Hatch Lane, N10 020 8883 6429

Established in 1996 the comfortable air-conditioned Nawab has 'all the old favourites plus exciting dishes. Owner Abdul says it all. If you as customers are happy, then I'm happy. If I'm happy the waiters and the cooks are happy. And it seems Abdul's customers really are happy. Chef won the local area Curry Chef Award, *'All dishes are large, reasonably priced and tasty.Service great!'* SM. Delivery: £10 minimum, 3 miles. Hours: 12-2.30/6-12am. Sunday buffet 12-5.30, eat all you can.

London N11

Friern Barnet, New Southgate

BEJOY 

72 Bounds Green Road, N11 020 8888 1268

Established 1995, Abdul Sukur's restaurant seats 54, party room 16. Bangladeshi standards and side dishes cooked by chef M Rahman. Price check: Papadam 50p, CTM £6.30, Pullao Rice £1.60, Peshwari Nan £1.75. Delivery: £8 minimum, 2-mile radius. Hours: 12-2.30pm (Sat.-Thurs.)/6-12am. Sunday buffet £5.95 per person, 12-11pm. Branch: Sunderban, N4.

London N12

North Finchley, Woodside Park

FINCHLEY PAN CENTRE

15 Woodhouse Road, N12 020 8446 5497

A tiny, unlicensed Indian snack bar, frequented by Indians. Kebabs, samosas, veg rissoles, etc., very inexpensive. Friendly service. Cash please. Oh, and as for Pan or Paan, it's not a cooking vessel, it is a collection of edible ingredients, ranging from very bitter to very sweet wrapped in the paan or bright dark green paan or betel leaf. Paan is an acquired taste, used as an aid to digestion. The observant visitor to India will have noticed very busy street kiosks dispensing paan all hours. We only know of a few other Paan houses (in Asian communities such as Southall). *See page 58 for more about Paan.* Hours: 12-10pm (Fri., 3.30-10); closed Tues.

London N13

Broomfield Park, Palmers Green

DIPALI INDIAN 

82 Aldermans Hill, N13 020 8886 2221

The popular Dipali restaurant appeared in the first and subsequent *Guides* but suffered a huge fire tragedy. It came back last edition much to the delight of the locals. Specials: Murghi Shassle £5.50 – piece of spring chicken marinated in mint sauce, cooked with selected spices and topped with salad. Murghi Tamatar £3.95 – chicken cooked in fresh green chilli and coriander ginger, very spicy hot. Achar Murghi £4.75 – cooked with pickle, slightly hot. Sunday buffet 12-3.30pm. Delivery. Hours: 12-2.30/6-12.

London N14

Oakwood, Southgate

BEKASH 

6-8 Hampden Square, N14 020 8368 3206

Owned by Nazrul Miah (manager) and Harun Ali (chef), decorated in yellow, seats 55. Delivery. House wine £7.80. Price check: Papadam 50p, CTM £6.25, Pullao Rice £1.60. Hours: 5.30-11.30pm (Sat. to 12am).

London N16

Stoke Newington

RASA TOP 100 V

55 Church Street, N16 020 7249 0344

Shiva Das Sreedharan's and his wife Alison's first restaurant. He worked at a Delhi hotel before coming to England to manage a small restaurant. Believing he could do things better, he set up this restaurant in 1994 in this then unfashionable street serving then unfashionable south Indian vegetarian food. Thanks to enthusiasts like Das, we know that there is so much more to Keralan food than Maslala Dosas. Rasa chefs are expert vegetarian cooks. Cooking uses coconut, mustard, curry leaves, curds, chillies, lentils and rice. Exotic vegetables include plantains, drumsticks, gourds, sour mango, and beans. The differences between the cooking of the five Kerelan groups is intensely subtle, including the names of the similar dishes. But differences there are, so try it out. Ask managers Usha or Bhaskar or the staff for advice. Favourites include Nair Dosa – a Keralan speciality, usually eaten during festivals and celebrations. A rice and black gram flour pancake filled with a mixture of potatoes, beetroot, carrot, onions and ginger, served with sambar and fresh coconut chutney, £5. Chef Narayanan's signature dish is the Rasa Kayi, a mixed vegetable speciality from the Southern State of Karnataka. A spicy curry made of beans, carrots, cauliflower, potatoes and simmered in a sauce of garlic, ginger and fennel, £3.85. Cheera Curry is Paneer and spinach cooked with garlic, peppers and tomato in a creamy sauce, £2.50. For pudding, if you have room, try Banana Dosa, the Palakkad Iyer (Brahmin) speciality with a difference. These tiny pancakes are made from bananas, plain flour and cardamom. Lots of reports. Most love the food and are happy with the service. One or two complain of crowding; there are only fifteen tables. It's the problem of being popular. Sunday to Thursday: 6–10.45. Fri, Sat to 11.30. Saturday/Sunday Lunch: 12– 3.

RASA TRAVANCORE TOP 100

56 Church Street, N16 020 7249 1340

This recent Rasa is nearly opposite the original at 55 (*see above*). You can't miss it. The colour is the key. Das just loves pink – the hue that is blackcurrant yoghurt. It's the colour of his venue frontages, decor, menu and his web site. So why this new venue? We normally think of Kerala as a vegetarian state. In fact there have been passionate non-vegetarians – Muslims, Jews and Christians – living there side by side for centuries, each with a distinctive cooking style. As for the latter, St Thomas the Apostle landed in Kerala in AD50 and made many converts to Christianity. His language was Syriac Armenaic, his converts known as Syrian Christians. To this day they eat offal, chicken, duck, fish, shellfish, beef, and wild boar. Dishes with very unfamiliar names crowd the menu. A great introduction is the Travancore Feast, where you get a good selection of dishes for £20. Chicken Puffs, spicy chicken masala stuffed in puff pastry are frankly Anglo Indian Raj stuff, but they're great stuff, £3.50, and eat them with Meen Achar – Chicken pickle. More traditional Syrian Christian specialities include Kerala Fish fry, £3.95, kingfish marinated in a spicy paste made of ginger, green chillies and coriander, then shallow fried in the traditional fashion. Chicken Stew, £5.25, chicken cooked in fresh coconut milk, with finely chopped ginger, green chillies and flavoured with cinnamon, cardamom, cashewnut and raisins. Erachi Olathiathu, £6.95, cubes of lamb and dry cooked in turmeric water, then stir-fried in an open kadai with an abundance of black pepper, curry leaves, and finely sliced fresh coconut slivers. Tharavu roast, £6.95, duck cooked in a thick sauce with ginger, garlic, onion and coriander. Rasa in Sanskrit means amongst other things, taste, flavour, liking, pleasure, delight and essence. There is so much more. The venue is managed by Jinu and Mustafa. Let them and the staff guide you. Hours: as Rasa alongside. Branches: previous entry, and London NW1, and W1.

London N19

Archway, Tufnell Park, Upper Holloway

PARSEE NEW TO OUR TOP 100

34 Highgate Hill, N19 020 7272 9091

Dr CF has been a regular *Curry Club* member and a major *Guide* restaurant reporter since 1982. He still is, and his reportage consists of a phone call, often in the middle of his surgery session. *'Yep I've got a patient lying down now'*, he says. *'He likes curry too, so he won't mind'*, and he goes off into a high speed dialogue about this or that restaurant. Woe betide you if you don't keep up. Usually it was about medicinal drugs company reps hosting 30 or 40 local doctors on a jolly night out. Often they'd go to Indian restaurants. *'Most of them are Indian'*, says Dr CF *'and usually they'd hate the restaurant they were hosted at. Finally one day I said to myself, Cornell you really ought to buy your own.'* And he did! The Parsee was his brain child. It was set up in a failing curry house. Dr CF adores Cyrus Todiwalla's cooking, and being persuasive, he got Cyrus to become involved as chef consultant and supplier. Cyrus is a Parsee (*see page 50*). And his brainwave was to create the only authentic Parsee restaurant outside Bombay, sorry Mumbai, (where Cyrus and the largest Parsee population come from). Even there it's hard to find. I know of only six where Parsi food appears amongst other cuisines (such as Italian), though probably the best is the improbably named Strand Coffee House on Colaba. Authentic delights include Akoori on Toast £3.95, scrambled eggs on toast spiced with chilli and garlic. Papeta Na Pattis £3.95, mashed potato cakes filled with green peas, grated coconut, chopped nuts and spices, rolled in breadcrumbs and fried, served with green coconut chutney. Keema Pao £4.50, minced lamb flavoured with garam masala, served with a warm chilli roll. Laal Masala Na Chaamp £6.50/£13.95, chops marinated in red masala of red chillies, garlic, ginger, cummin and spices, chargrilled and served with Dhaan (rice) and Daar (lentils). Haran Na Kabab £4.50/£10.25, venison minced with fresh ginger, garlic, coriander and chillies, flavoured with mint and garam masala, formed over skewers and chargrilled. Patra Ni Machci £9.25, Pomfret, filetted and filled with green coconut chutney, wrapped in a banana leaf and steam baked. Sali Boti £9.95, lamb with chopped shallots, whole spices and pitted Hunza apricots, garnished with sali (straw potatoes). Khattu Mitthu Istew £3.75 /£7.25, green peas, carrots, cauliflower, whole baby shallots, baby potatoes, yam and sweet potato make this a delightful stew, served with Jeera Pullao if ordered as a main course. Hours: 12 to 3, Sunday only and 6 to 10.45, Sunday to 10. Welcome to our **TOP 100.**

We need you.

Tell us your views on the Curry restaurants you visit.

See page 365.

London NW

Area: North West London,
Postcodes: NW1 to NW11
Population: 680,000

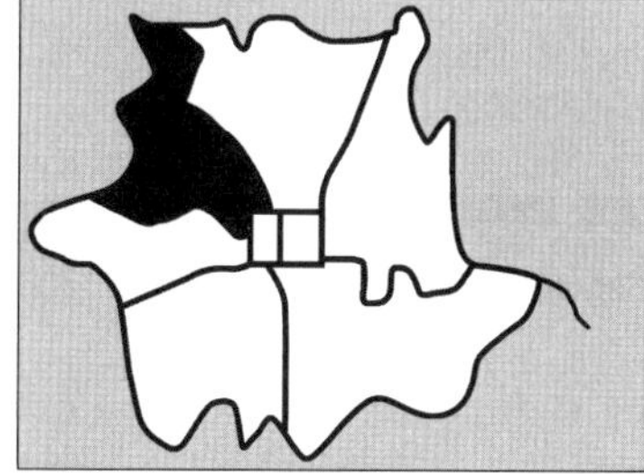

London NW1

Drummond Street, Euston

I am often asked where the best restaurants are. It's the reason for producing this Guide. Drummond Street is one such area. West of Euston Station, it will not win any beauty awards, and it lacks the ethnic glamour of Southall and Wembley, or the intensity of purpose of Brick Lane. Its assets are a concentrated selection of extremely good, mainly inexpensive Indian food vendors. There are greengrocers, a Halal butcher and ingredient stores, such as Viranis, where Pataks began trading in the 60s. It is open all hours for all things Indian including Cobra (useful for the nearby BYOs), a dozen or so takeaways and restaurants. Here in alphabetical order are your Drummond Street favourites:

AMBALA SWEET CENTRE

112 Drummond Street, NW1 020 7387 3521

Ambala started trading in 1965. It specialises in takeaway-only savoury snacks (Pakoras and Samosa, etc.), Indian sweets (Halva, Jalebi, Gulab Jamun, Barfi, etc.) and a few vegetarian curries such as chickpea. Established initially for Asians, it now has branches in Birmingham, Bradford, Derby, East Ham, Finchley, Glasgow, Leicester, Leyton, Luton, Manchester, Slough, Southall, Tooting and Wembley. All branches serve identical items at identical prices. The quality is first-class and the prices are always reasonable. Be prepared to queue, and pay cash. Open daily 10am-11pm.

CHUTNEYS V

134 Drummond Street, NW1 020 7387 6077

Good vegetarian food at good prices. Lunch and dinner daily.

DIWANA BHEL POORI HOUSE
TOP 100 V BYO

121 Drummond Street, NW1 020 7387 5556

It's a café-style, unlicensed, open all day, still very cheap, highly successful. 100-seat restaurant, divided into two ground-floor sections plus a further floor. The food is all vegetarian, with much vegan, and above all, it's all fabulous, and it's most certainly all authentic. Diwana pioneered Bombay pavement kiosk snack food in the UK and is undoubtedly still the best of its kind. It is one of DBAC s favourites, *'not to be visited for the decor, nor for a long and relaxing meal – sitting on the floor would be more comfortable than sitting on the bolted-down benches, so opt for chairs if you can. I have the same thing every time I visit, Papadam with Coconut Chutney, Rasam, a soup, whose chillies without fail give me attention-drawing hiccups, then a Dosa £3 to £4.60 depending on type, with more Coconut Chutney, with its mustard seed and chilli and Sambar. If Pat and I share, I try to get all the drumsticks before him. And of course I never miss out on one of their adorable Bhel Puris, their masthead and their most ordered dish.'* Bhel Puri, or Poori, is defined on *page* 50. Diwana offers several types – Batata Puri, Dahi Batata Puri, Chat Aloo Papri and Batata Pava, all £2.10. Bhel can be accompanied by Gol Goppas (*see page* 53). A super alternative starter is Dahi Vada (*see page* 52). By now you've spent £5 or £6, and you're probably full. But try to leave a little space for the Diwana's desserts. Their legendary Kulfi, perhaps, or *'the highlight of our meal, the Falooda – an Indian knickerbocker glory – probably the best in London. The quality of the food outweighs the numbness in your backside!'* DB. *'All first class. Reasonably priced.'* MW. *'Consistently good quality and low prices. Never changes.'* JR. *''On one of the hottest days in July, I needed lunch in Drummond Street. I chose Diwana because of the jug of water that is automatically provided. It was too hot for alcohol and lassis is too filling when there is serious eating to be done.'* BS. *'Will certainly go back, but not for buffet.'* NP. [told you, ED] *'The back of the bill has a questionnaire. I was pleased to tick excellent for everything.'* HC. Booking is hit and miss, and they won't even try on Fri. to Sun. so expect a queue (especially at peak hours). Great value and don't forget to BYO (no corkage charge). Off-license with chilled Cobra available at Viranis up the street. Thali from £4.00 to £6.00. E-a-m-a-y-l lunch to 2.30pm, £4.50. Hard to exceed £12 for a good veggie blow-out! It remains very high in our **TOP 100.** Hours: 12-11.

GUPTA CONFECTIONERS

100 Drummond Street, NW1 020 7380 1590

Overshadowed, perhaps by the nearby Ambala, Gupta is nonetheless a very good, long-established, less flashy vegetarian snack and sweet takeaway. Samosas and Pakoras, plus their unique, delightful, and often still-hot Pea Kebab, a Gujarati speciality, are freshly cooked in the kitchens behind. Their sweets achieve a lightness of touch, and seem to avoid the taste of tinned evaporated milk that sometimes spoils those made by others. Cash or cheque. Branch: Watford Way, Hendon, NW4.

RAVI KEBAB HALAL ANP

125 Drummond Street, NW1 020 7388 1780

Not the first on the street., but one of the longest stayers (opened 1978). As the name says this is a Pakistani meat venue. 'Kebab' tells you it's very much a meat place, Halal that there's no pandering to Western tastes, as one can tell by its local mostly Muslim patronage (so no alcohol permitted). Grilled and curried meats are all there at bargain prices. There are some vegetable and dhal dishes but this is no place for the veggie. *'One of my favourites. Cheap and cheerful. Food superb. Sheek Kebabs amongst the best anywhere.'* RE.

RAVI SHANKAR V

133 Drummond Street, NW1 020 7388 6458

Vegetarian restaurant similar to the Diwana which it followed into Drummond Street. Prices are still very reasonable and it is usually busy at peak hours. Recommended are the two Thali set dishes, the Mysore and the Shankar, and the Shrikand dessert. *'Every dish was excellent – flavoursome, spicy and delicious. Prices are extremely reasonable.'* MW Daily specials at under £4. Hours: 12pm-11pm. Branches: Chutneys, and Haandi, both on Drummond Street.

Elsewhere in NW

Camden Town, Chalk Farm, Marylebone, Regent's Park

CAFE INDIYA NEW ENTRANT

71 Regents Park Road, NW1 020 7722 5225

Seats 28 in two rooms. We hear of Goan Fish Curry with coconut milk, £7.95, and Chicken Xacutti £7.25, fairly hot. Sabziyon Ki Shaslick £5.95, fresh vegetables, marinated in a special tandoori sauce and grilled in the clay oven. Paneer Simla Mirch £3.25, medium spiced stir-fry of homemade cottage cheese, green peppers and fresh tomatoes. Service: 10%. Hours: 12-2.30 (Saturday only) and 5.30 Saturday 6.00) to 11.30. Sunday 12-11.30.

GREAT NEPALESE
BEST NEPALESE AWARD & TOP 100 ©

48 Eversholt Street, NW1 020 7388 6737

Started by Gopal P Manandhar in 1982, this Nepalese restaurant has stood the test of time, Chef is son Jeetendra, whose charming wife Mandira also adds her culinary expertise, especially with Nawari (an Nepalese ethnic group) food, for example the starter, Momo, or Momocha – steam-cooked meat-filled pastries, £3.50. Other Nepalese specialities include Masco Bara, black lentil pancakes with curry sauce £3.45, Kalezo Ra Chyow (chicken liver). Main courses include Dumba (mutton), Pork Bhutwa (the Nepalese have no proscriptions of either pork or alcohol) and Hach Ko (duck) curries. There is also a range of eleven Nepalese vegetable dishes. Add those to sixteen 'standard' curry house vegetable dishes and the vegetarian will be spoilt for choice. In addition, the Great does all the standard curries and tandooris, from Phal, 'very very hot', to Shahi Korma, 'very very mild', though why you'd go there for these is beyond me. Go for Nepalese food, and if virgin to it, ask the staff to explain. *'Second visit. On first occasion Jackie and I had imbibed a little too much. On this occasion we were sober enough to appreciate just how good it is. Packed full on Friday night, glad we had booked. Service polite. Tried Masco Bara and Vegetarian Mamocha – both perfectly cooked and generous. Shared a Vegetable Jalfrezi – full of fresh vegetables, very chilli hot. Dhal complemented perfectly. Well worth its* **TOP 100** *spot'* AG. Not sure where you imbibed, Andy, but if you need the hair of the dog, ask Ghopla for a shot of Coronation rum. Brewed in 1975 in Katmandu, its bottle is kukri-shaped, its contents lethal. Set Nepalese meal £13.50. Service 10%. Average spend: £15. Takeaway: 10% discount. Delivery: £12 minimum, 5-miles. Hours: 5.30-11.30. Sat. to 12.

RASA EXPRESS

327 Euston Road, NW1 020 7387 8974

Das' Rasa empire grows and grows. Liken Rasa Express to Holiday Inn Express as a simple, inexpensive, no fuss brand, and clearly the pilot (along with the W1 Rasa Express) for a franchise operation nationwide. It's fast food with just seven items on the menu at prices ranging from £1.50 to £2.95. In the latter category are Mysore Bonda – Potato balls laced with ginger, curry leaves, coriander cashew nuts and mustard seeds, dipped in besan batter and crisply fried. Fish Cutlet, spiced cassava and tuna breadcrumbed and Veg Samosa, all served with coconut chutney. Top of the bill (at £2.92, is the Rasa Lunch Box, two curries, a stir-fried vegetable dish, bread, rice and sweet of the day. Monday to Friday: 10-5 (likely to extend soon). Branches: *See Rasa London* N15 *for more information.*)

PUKKABAR NEW ENTRANT

40, Chalcot Road, NW1 020 7483 0077

Trevor Gulliver (of Fire Station, Putney and Waterloo and St John, Smithfield, fame) is on the move again, last time from SE26, this time from SW13. This move took place as we went to print so we can only tell what it was like before. The short menu included Tandoori Salmon for starters and Hara £3.95, deep-fried spinach and cheese balls. Barwan £3.95, eggplant [it's aubergine, Trevor – we're in England] stuffed with minced lamb and topped with cheese. Main courses: Lamb Chilli £5.95. Goan Prawn Coconut Curry £7.95. Takeaway: 10% discount. Delivery: 1-mile radius. . Hours: 12.30-2.30 (Sat & Sun -3.30)/6-10.30.

London NW3

Belsize Park, Hampstead, Finchley Road, Swiss Cottage

FLEET TANDOORI 

104 Fleet Road, NW3 020 7485 6402

'A good restaurant for those seeking a dependable, quiet and inexpensive meal. The Sunday buffet is a must for those who wish a cheap alternative to meat and two veg. An additional attraction is the Special on the menu – Pomfret Fish, which comes either tandoori or, for those with a rich palate, bathed in a curry sauce flavoured with a multitude of spices. Good prices enhanced by a 10% discount to Curry Club members at any time!' AD

ERIKI NEW ENTRANT

4 Northways Parade, Finchley Road, NW3
020 7722 0606

New to this industry, entrepreneur Sat Lally opened here in 2002 in a former Italian restaurant. It's a 75-seater with a modern Indian look (pink colours, cushions and carvings) and a huge bar. Lally has recruited serious talent here: Goan Godfrey Menezes from Chor Bazaar is manager, and the kitchens are run by two experienced chefs with gilt-edged curriculae vitae – Jude Pinto, also Goan, and formerly a specialist at Veeraswamy and Chutney Mary. And Naresh Matta who was for many years one of Amin Ali's Indian chefs at Jamdani and more latterly Red Fort, W1, working under Mohammed Rias. Like Rias, he got out before the crash, and the two bring the Eriki a mix of traditional Goan and Dum Pukht dishes *(see page 50)* plus some Indo-new-wave items. It's one to visit and one to watch, so let's hear about it from you please. Set menus from £17. Lunch and dinner daily.

London NW4

Hendon

PRINCE OF CEYLON FORMER BEST SRI LANKAN AWARD TOP 100 ©

39 Watford Way, NW4 020 8202 5967

Abdul Satter has been here since 1979, during which time it has grown to 150 seats split over five rooms. Manager Nelson presides over a kind of bamboo/coir jungle with yellow-ochre and brown linen, olive green leather seats, and a lot of natural dark wood – tables given privacy by carved wood screens. The Prince's standard menu of tandooris, kebabs, curries and all the business, all perfectly competently cooked, are not what you go there for. It is the Sri Lankan specials. And if these items are unfamiliar, ask the waiter's advice, but be patient if explanations are unclear at first. It is a rice (Buth) cuisine. Jaffna Thossai, soft pancake made of soaked and ground urid dal, served with coconut chutney. Devilled curries are there, including Squid curry. Fried Cabbage with onion £2.75. Coconut Chutney £1.50. Hoppers or Appas are rice and coconut-flour pancakes; String Hoppers, like string made of wheat or rice flour dough, but resembling vermicelli nests (10 for £3); or Pittu – ditto dumpling. These or straight rice are accompanied by pungent watery curries, in which coconut, turmeric, tamarind, curry leaves and chillies feature. But they can be mild, too. Look out for aromatic black curries and fragrant white ones. Fish dishes, such as Ambul Thial (a Sri Lankan national dish – a sour, spicy tuna fish dish) and the Ceylon Squid (Dhallo) curry are popular. And there are substantial curries such as Lumpri (chicken, meat and egg). Sambols, or relishes, include dried fish and chilli. Contented reports, for example, *'They usually don't do buffet takeaway, but kindly made an exception. I was told I could fill two containers for £8.50 from 15 dishes – great value for money, food first class (didn't enjoy my first encounter with bitter gourds). Considering quality of buffet, a la carte should be even better.'* BH. Average spend £13. Sunday buffet, noon-5pm, £8.50. Hours: 12-3/6-12, weekdays. 12pm-12am, Saturday and Sunday.

London NW5

Kentish Town

CHETNA 

56 Chetwynd Road, NW5 020 7482 2803

Established as the Indian Lancer in 1990, then Indian Brasserie in 1999 this 42-seater's owner Edward Graham has decorated in a minimalist style with very pale pink walls, redwood furniture with pinky red cushions, modern spot lighting and red carpets. His chef, Ramdas, was Gujarat region chef of the year 1993 and has held post as executive chef at the Sayji group of hotels in northern India. Ramdas' signature dishes include: Dover Sole Kaliwala, fresh dover sole, cooked with red chillies, yoghurt and curry leaves, spicy!, Chicken 65, dry-fried Hyderbadi style in a light batter, topped with fried green chillies and curry leaves, Phaldari Kofte Paneh Phoran and Chicken Malwari. The most popular dish ordered is Dum Pukht Gosht – a royal favourite. Set lunch: £2.95 to £4.95. Hours: 12-2.30 (Sunday 4) and 6-12 (Sunday -10). Closed Monday.

London NW6

Kilburn, South and West Hampstead

BENGAL SPICE

245 West End Lane, NW6 020 7794 5370

Established 1957. Fully licensed and air-conditioned. *'When your daughter graduates as a lawyer, leaves home and moves to London with her partner a dad experiences many emotional feelings – will she be safe in London, will she succeed, will she live near a good quality Indian restaurant? I am relieved to say that their new flat is near to the Bengal Spice. External and internal decor is in 'modern brasserie' style. On entering we were shown to our table, drinks served swiftly, fresh Popadoms, good selection of pickles. Shish Kebab, Onion Bhajia £1.95 and Meat Samosa £1.95 – proved to be excellent starters. CTM, CT Bhuna and C Jalfrezi £5.95 were served with Pullao Rice, Peshwari Nan £1.75 and chunky chips (sorry Pat but they were great) all generous portions and beautifully spiced. Highly satisfactory at £15 per person.'* AIE. Hours: 6-12, Friday and Saturday -12.30.

GEETA SOUTH INDIAN TOP 100

57 Willesden Lane, NW6 020 7624 1713

Try the mainly south Indian vegetarian food at which Geeta excels, and has done since the 70s, with never a decline in standard. Dosas, Idli, Sambar, Upamas Karela (bitter gourds), drumsticks (long pithy marrow which you suck to extract the tender flesh), Ravaiya – baby aubergine and plantains stuffed with a coconut spicy filling Rasam – and more. And with most of these around the £2 mark, and providing you keep off the carnivorous items, you'll fill up for less than a tenner, with drink. You can get standard meat and chicken curries, et al, and from the reports I get, the thoroughly devoted following adore it. It's all fine stuff, served in less than glamourous, but typically Indian surroundings, to a thoroughly devoted following. '*This and Vijay (below) are different and should not be missed.*' DMW. Hours: 12-2.30pm/6-10.30pm, Fri & Sat. to 12am.

KOVALAM NEW ENTRANT

12 Willesden Lane, NW6 020 7625 4761

Kovalam restaurant opened in 2001 in a former curry house. Kovalam is a rather good government-run (Ashoks group) beach hotel at the town of Trivandrum, just 30 miles north of India's southern most tip. Actually it's probably the best hotel in that chain. Coconut palms, temple elephants, white dotis, sea, sun and sand. Ah me!.Their restaurant is called Sea Shells and it serves a range of south Indian dishes, protein as well as vegetable. I digress; Trivandrum is a far cry from Willesden, but you'll get the picture from the pictures on the wall. And as at Sea Shells, the food is spot on. It offers south Indian dishes such as dosas, Idli, Sambar, Upamas and Vaadia (*see glossary page* 50) plus it does meat, fish and chicken dishes aux curry house, but with south Indian chefs. Lunch and dinner daily.

GOLDEN BENGAL ©

73, Fairfax Road, NW6 020 7372 4646

Owned and managed by Mr R Khan, since 1998. Delivery. Price check: Papadam 40p, CTM £5.45, Pullao Rice £1.60, House wine £6.95. Hours: 12-2.30pm/6-11.30pm (Sat. to 12am).

SURYA V 

59 Fortune Green Road, NW6 020 7435 7486

Mr (front of house) and Mrs Tiwari (chef) really pack 'em in at this tiny, 34-seat vegetarian, licensed restaurant – there's no room to move, almost literally – it's always full. The dish of the day (it changes daily) excites several of our regulars. We hear well of Gujarati dishes such as Patra and Kaddu Kari and inexpensive prices. Hours: 6-10.30pm, and Sun. lunch. Branch: Shree Ganesha, 4 The Promenade, Edgwarebury Lane, Edgware, Middlesex.

VIJAY TOP 100

49 Willesden Lane, NW6 020 7328 1087

Vijay was founded in 1966, and predated nearby Geeta (*see above*) by several years, so it can take the crown for being the earliest to provide south Indian food for NW6, and its menu contains all the vegetarian items listed in Geeta's entry, at much the same prices. Indeed my remarks are the same, since Vijay like Geeta does carnivorous dishes too. Vijay has its own clan of loyal regulars who know they'll get 'very nice tasty food.' B&WW. Prices are much the same, perhaps just a tad higher here, but again, even with the ridiculous 10% service charge (please get rid of it) you'll only spend a tenner if you stick to the scrumptious vegetarian delights. '*This and Geeta (above) are different and should not be missed.*' DMW. Hours: 12-2.45pm/6-10.45pm (Fri & Sat to 11.45pm).

London NW7

Mill Hill

DAYS OF THE RAJ 

123 The Broadway, NW7 020 8906 3477

Established in 1989 by S Miah, who tells us that he changes the wallpaper every six months to 'maintain standards'. M Miah manages the 100-

©	Curry Club Discount	U	Unlicensed
V	Vegetarian	ANP	Alcohol not permitted
e-a-m-a-y-l	Eat as much as you like	BYO	Bring your own alcohol

seater, whose extensive menu appears to be formula stuff from Kurma to Phal, etc. But a closer look provides a number of 'unique' dishes. What are Noorane, Sherajee, Kushboo, Dilkush and Bakhara curries, for example? Each available in chicken, lamb, beef, prawn, king prawn and vegetables (the menu explains their attributes), they are clearly house inventions. So is the dish Days of the Raj, gently cooked with pineapple, lychees and sultanas in a thick creamy sauce sprinkled with nuts. It sounds like a fruit salad but is, we're assured, *'really quite delicious, the chicken quite succulent, and mild enough for my boss who is a curry novice.'* GC. It is more than a 'safe-bet' curry house. It is very smart indeed and is a place to go for an enjoyable meal out. Service 10%. E-a-m-a-y-l lunch buffet daily £7. Delivery: £12 minimum, 3-mile radius. Hours: 12-2pm/5-11.30.

London NW9

Kingsbury

LAHORE KEBAB HOUSE
REENTRANT

248 Kingsbury Road, NW9 020 8424 8422

This branch of the celebrated London E1 original, never achieved the glory. So it was sold to H. Hameed as far back as 1994. No longer connected, it was permitted to keep the name and menu, and it has now built its own following. It's licensed, and the kebabs are good and the curries. For the menu *see the E1 Lahore Kebab House review.* No credit cards. 1pm to midnight, daily.

London NW10

Harlesden, Kensal Green, Willesden

ANN MARIE AT THE TASTE OF THE TAJ ©

4 Norbeck Parade, off Hanger Lane, Ealing, NW10 020 8991 5366

Ann Marie has sold up. It's not just the end of an era, it's the end of the world. It's worse than loosing Concorde. But grieving fans tell me she's kind of hanging in there. The fortunate will get an appearance, now and again– the new owners realise that without her, they're lost. So to help them I repeat myself about location, location, location. Anne Marie's Taste(or whoever's), which has been going since 1989, is in Ealing. It's also in NW10, which Ealing isn't (but it used to be W5). The North Circular Gyratory rebuild caused mayhem with Ann Marie's access, if you follow me, not to mention with her postcode. She says herself it's 'essential to phone and ask for directions, because the access to the front is now closed from the NCR'. So phone and go, and if you see the great lady, get her autograph and enjoy a welcoming taste experience. Delivery: £12 minimum. Hours: lunch weekdays only/6-12am.

London SE

Area: South East London
Postcodes SE1 to SE28
Population: 910,000

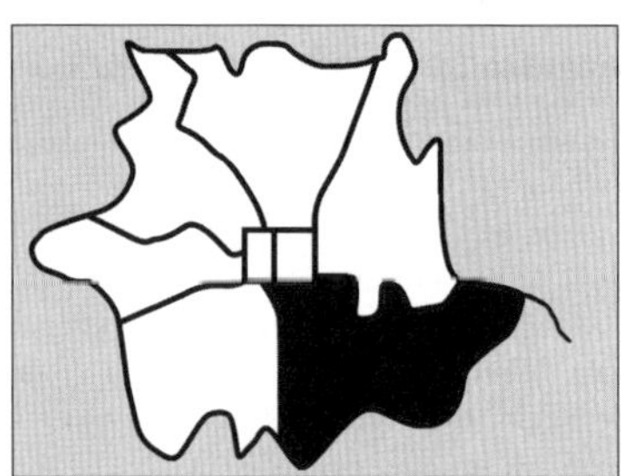

London SE1

Borough, Elephant & Castle, London Bridge, Old Kent Road, Southwark and Waterloo

BENGAL CLIPPER TOP 100

Cardamom Building,
31 Shad Thames, SE1 020 7357 9001

Finding it is the problem. It's a fair walk from the tube! Taxis will find it (it's behind Conran's). If you're driving, and you've squeezed through the narrow one-way streets, you'll then have to find a parking space (min. £4). Once inside, you'll find Kenneth Lynn's sophisticated and expensive interior. Chef Ram Das turns out curry house food, but the Bangladeshi dishes are the best bet. *'Tried twice, both on Times Newspaper 'eat-for-a-fiver' deals. On both occasion, service first class. Excellent atmosphere, with chap in corner playing the grand piano (8-11 Tues – Sat). Popadoms and Pickles carried a hefty cover charge per person, but variety was good. Limited menu for the offer as expected. Spiced Potato Croquettes – fresh, tasty and very spicy! Chickpea Curry – excellent and spiced to my taste – accompanied with Pullao Rice, had fun picking out the pits of bark! Portions small but adequate. I imagine it would be wall-breaking to pay full price, but quality, service and ambience would justify it!'* EG. You're right Emma; expect to pay more than usual here. Average £25-30. Lunch and dinner daily. Branches: Bengal Trader, E1, Bengal Mangrove, Halstead, Kent, and the original Bengal Lancer, Chislehurst, Kent.

BRIDGE TANDOORI

214 Tower Bridge Road, SE1 020 7375 7826

Fully licensed and air conditioned. *'Very busy on a Wednesday at 7.30pm. Decor is nothing special, bus stop outside the window did nothing for ambience – food was surprisingly good! Spicy Popadoms and Chutneys – excellent, served promptly. Very well cooked, full of flavour Tandoori Mixed Grill £8.95. After a 40 minute wait Non-Vegetarian Thali £12.95, excellent with Keema Nan £2.35, which seemed to be peshwari with keema added – not great, arrived. Colleague ate Bridge Special Chicken £7.95 and Special Mixed Fried Rice £2.95, very good, full of flavour. Excellent value for money – watch out for the slow, verging on rude service and the bus queue looking in through the window.'* DL. Sunday buffet: 12-6 – £7.95 per person. Hours: 12-3/6-12. Sunday 12-12.

CASTLE TANDOORI

200 Elephant & Castle Shopping Centre, SE1 020 7703 9130

Mr Uddin's Castle is a spirited place, and a regular entrant in our *Guide*. He once told us, and will tell you, if you care to be entertained by him, that he's outlived twenty-two Hoovers, two recessions, and several prime ministers, and served enough nan bread to stretch from Waterloo to Paris. No update on this yet; but I expect he's calculating anew. The menu is pretty much formula (135 items) but includes duck, lamb chops and trout in various guises. Reports tell of the value for money. We know of no longer hours in London (let us know if you know better). So, if you're an insomniac curryholic, or just a late-night reveller, note this place well. Hours: Lunch Mon.-Fri./6-1am daily (Fri. & Sat. to 2.30am).

SILKA NEW ENTRANT

6 Southwark Street, SE1 020 7378 6161

With the pedigree of cheffing at Tamarind, Chutney Mary, Three Monkeys and the Red Fort, Abdul Mushahid turned proprietor and opened his 80-seat Silka in 2003 in the basement of a Grade II listed building. Managed by A. Hannan, it is between London Bridge and Tate Modern. Luxury woods, lighting and decor lead the eye to Mushahid's window kitchen from where emanates cooking with Ayurvedic (low-fat, health-conscious) principles leading to to an original menu. *'Our tarters included Baked Lemon Sole wrapped in a banana leaf, Stir-fried Baby Squid, and Mixed Sprout Lentil Soup – a modern take on a traditional Indian staple. Interesting salads such as a lotus leaves coated with white sesame seeds and spiced gram flour batter is refreshingly innovative and served with a typically tangy tamarind chutney. Other gems include Wild Duck braised with delicate spices, Roasted Cauliflower marinated with cheese, yoghurt and cashew nuts and fiery Peri Peri Prawns. Try the tasting Ayurvedic platters. Potatoes cooked in a creamy sauce, and spiced vegetable and rice, served with tiger prawns is one example of the choice on offer. Side dishes include pan-fried fresh mustard leaves and the steadfast Indian favourite of simmered black lentils.'* RG. Lunch platter at £7.95. Dinner average £25. Take Out. Free Delivery. Valet Parking. Lunch and dinner daily.

THAMES TANDOORI

79 Waterloo Road, SE1 020 7928 3856

Kalkur Rahman established this one in 1985. Managed by Amirul Islam this air-conditioned 52-seater is still there under the railway bridge, and, yes, its neighbour, the fab-named Fishcotheque [it's a fish & chip shop for those new to this *Guide*] is still there. *'Fell out of Waterloo Station into this restaurant'*

[I can think of worse places to fall into, Bernard.] *'Confirm all your comments about the food and service. Only one small complaint – food a touch cool, in cooking sense. King Prawn Jalfrezi absolutely excellent.'* BF. *'Keeps a consistently high standard. Staff welcoming, food above average, very modest prices. Definitely in a higher league.'* HLC. *'On another occasion, had such a good meal, an unassuming restaurant, staff are pleasant and food is so good – deserves to be praised.'* HLC. *'We have been here many times, always enjoyable. Yesterday no exception, in fact, better than ever. Outwardly this restaurant seems very misleading, very ordinary, but food is miles better than the decor. £86 for four including drinks.'* HLC. Delivery: 2 miles, £20 minimum. Hours: 12-2.15 / 5.30-11.45.

TOWER TANDOORI

74 Tower Bridge Road, SE1 020 7237 2247

8 minutes walking distance from Tower Bridge. Tower Tandoori Specialities include: Shatay Chicken £6.45, three quarters of breast chicken marinated in special sauce then cooked in tender clay oven, served with separate mossala sauce and with green salad. Me Gori £6.75, a special biriani consisting of meat, prawn, king prawn and pullao rice, green salad on top, served with mixed vegetable curry. *'It was a delicious meal – especially the King Prawn Dopiaza £6.50. All prices were very favourable.'* NB.

London SE3

Blackheath Village

TASTE OF RAJ

9 Royal Parade, SE3 020 8344 2823

'Our first visit for some time, because we have become addicted to Spice of Life, SE13*! Continues to be very good indeed. Shared a wonderful and very filling Afgan Puri followed by a chilli-hot Sag Chana Dhansak, also very good with plenty of sag and chickpeas. Garlic Nan was light and fluffy and Tarka Dall full of mustard seed and garlic – good food and good value all round.'* AG.

London SE9

Eltham, Falconwood

CROWN TANDOORI TAKEAWAY ©

7, Lingfield Crescent, SE9 020 8294 1313

Owned and managed by Saiful Abedin, since January 1997. Set meal excellent value from £3.85 for Chicken Tikka and Nan to £7.50 for Onion Bhajia, Chicken Bhuna, Bombay Aloo, Pullao Rice and Nan. Complimentary Popadoms, Mint Sauce and Onion salad with all orders. Delivery: 3-mile radius. Hours: 5-11.30.

CURRY GARDEN ©

144 Westmount Road, SE9 020 8850 2250

Opened in 1992, taken over in 1999 by A Miah (manager), F Haque, S Miah and K Miah. Interesting menu additions: Koleze Puree £1.95 – chicken liver delicately prepared and served with pancake, Bahari Nan £1.65 – with green chilli and coriander. Delivery: 5-mile radius, £15 minimum, no delivery to high rise buildings. Hours: 5-10.30. (Sat. -11).

RUCHITA TAKEAWAY ©

31 Avery Hill Road, SE9 020 8850 1202

Unusually for a takeaway-only, Miss Salma, Mohammed Yousuf's and Chef A Mukid's Ruchita is licensed. It's been going since 1975, so they know what they're doing. Their Chicken Tikka is still easily their most popular dish (surprise, surprise). Delivery: £10, 3-mile radius. Hours: 5.30-12.

London SE13

Hither Green, Lee, Lewisham

BABU SAHEEB

406-408 High Street, SE13 020 8690 7667

Decorated with white ceiling, spot lights, light blue walls with chandeliers, blue carpet. Fully licensed: £2.95 pint lager, £6.95 bottle house wine. Service: 10% Buffet Dinner Nights: Sunday to Thursday £8.50 adult and £4.50 child under 12. Delivery: 3 miles, £2 charge. Hours: lunch by appointment and 6 to 12.30. Branch: Ladywell Tandoori, 81, Ladywell Road, Lewisham, SE13.

BENGAL BRASSERIE 

79 Springbank Road, SE13 020 8461 5240

This 60-seater restaurant, prettily decorated in pale shades of pink, is owned and managed by Syed Ahmed. CT describes chef M Chowdhury's efforts as *'a nice little menu, now containing a few originals'. 'The spinach in Lobster Saghee makes this a fine dish.'* ES. And others enjoy the Sea Thali – clever name. Most popular dish Sali Ana Roshi, chicken or meat with pineapple and honey, lightly spiced. Minimum charge £15. Parties of 20 diners, eat and drink as much as you like for £25 per diner! Service 10%. Cover charge £1. Delivery: 3-mile radius. Hours: 5.30-11.30 (12am on Sat.).

GREEN CABIN SRI LANKAN 

244 High Street, SE13 020 8852 6666

40 seater opened in 1996 by SE Jebarajan and serving Sri Lankan and South Indian food. I'd love a Sri Lankan to open near us; unfortunately middle England just isn't ready for it. Maybe SE13 isn't either, because the Green Cabin does the safe-bet Korma-through-Vindaloo range. Forget all that and go for the real stuff – you won't be disappointed. Meat Roll (diced lamb, onions, chillies and potato wrapped in a pancake, bread crumbed and deep-fried, served with spicy sauce), Potato Kulambu (deep-fried cubes of potato cooked in coconut milk with dry roasted chilli), Cabbage Mallung (shredded cabbage stir-fried with mustard seed, turmeric and spices), Kotthu Roti, soft and thin as a silk cloth rotti sliced into pieces and mixed with shredded chicken on a hot griddle and blended together). Delivery: 2-mile radius, £15 minimum, dinner only. Takeaway: 10% discount, £15 minimum. Hours: 12-3 /6-11; closed Mon.

SPICE OF LIFE TOP 100 ©

260 Lee High Road, SE13 020 8244 4770

Owner, Mahmud (Moody) Miah, head chef, has a multi-talented crew – Jilad Miah, head waiter and menumaster, Moshaid Miah, barman, music master and tandoori chef, Harris (Harry) Miah-head barman and decor coordinator. Their fully licensed, air-conditioned venue seats 58. *'Small, cosy restaurant which is hard to fault. Its special gourmet nights and daily blackboard specials lift it well above average.'* say C &GM. [Blackboard specials showing dish(es) of the day are still rare in the curry business. But it's such a simple way of varying the menu, and customers love that. It's one of my bones of contention, and we should go on nagging at the other curry restaurants until they all do it.] *'Friendly atmosphere, service excellent, food delicious and well presented.'* RL. *'This restaurant deserves – in my opinion – a place high in the* **TOP 100.** *Service is friendly and warm, they make a real effort to get to know you. Food is simply out of this world. It is quite small and does not do a delivery service, helps keep the quality high. Special vegetarian dishes – Garlic Chilli Vegetables – are outstanding, King Prawn Chilli Vegetables – absolutely superb. Nans fluffy and hot. Long may this restaurant continue to prosper!'* AG. *'Still going strong. Thursday evenings are Fish Specials, what ever is fresh at the market Moody's wife cooks – super dishes.'* G&CM Takeaway: 10% discount. Spice Club: save 20%. Lunch and dinner daily.

London SE22

East Dulwich

AL AMIN TANDOORI 

104b Forest Hill Road, SE22 020 8299 3962

Established in 1994 by Kabir Khan. Try Chicken Roll – spicy boneless chicken roll in thin pancake. Chuza Mossala – baby chicken with thick gravy. Set meal for one: £7.95 includes: CTM, Pullao Rice, Nan and 2 Pops. Delivery: 3 miles, min £15. Hours: 5.30-12.

©	Curry Club Discount	**U**	Unlicensed
V	Vegetarian	**ANP**	Alcohol not permitted
e-a-m-a-y-l	Eat as much as you like	**BYO**	Bring your own alcohol

Free home delivery
10% discount on collection
for orders over £10.00

Surma
Curry House

established 1976
finest indian cuisine

Buffet £6.95 (£3.95 for children)
Sunday buffet all day
12pm - 11am
020 8693 1779
020 8693 9169
42 Lordship Lane, East Dulwich, London SE22

SURMA

42 Lordship Lane, East Dulwich, SE22
020 8693 1779

Surma Curry House is what is says. It's one of those venues which delivers the goods exaclty as enjoyed by a wide range of regular customers. It's been around for years. *'We just love going here. We go with our parents and with our kids. What more could you ask for?'* AAR. Lunch and dinner, daily. Sunday 12-11.

London SE23

Forest Hill, Honor Oak

BABUR BRASSERIE TOP 100 ©

119 Brockley Rise, SE23 020 8291 2400

Babur established the Moghul Empire in 1483 through his courage and daring in capturing Delhi. This restaurant captured Forest Hill in 1985, though its ownership by the dynamic Rahman brothers did not occur until 1992. Quite simply, it's in our **TOP 100** because everything the Rahmans do, they do well. Enam Rahman's cooking is bright and fresh, while front of house is equally so, under the careful supervision of co-owner manager Emdad Rahman. Regulars get frequent mail-shots telling of festivals and al-fresco dining. Talking about outside, the front is really attractive, with white Mogul arches, each one enhanced by hanging baskets and floor tubs. The white decor continues inside, offset by 56 air-force-blue chairs. Dining is intimate in a screened area or in the conservatory. The menu is interesting with no formula stuff done here. The restaurant seats 56 and serves unusual delights such as Patra £2.25, avari leaves layered with a spicy chick pea paste, steamed, sliced and then deep-fried. Harrey Tikka £5.95, diced chicken marinated in green sauce of pureed coriander and mint, cooked in the tandoor. Shah Jahani £5.95, smoked river fish, marinated, cooked in tandoor. Shugati Masala £5.50, chicken in masala sauce of coconut and white poppy seeds. Dum Tori £2.50, courgettes with turmeric and mango. Aloo

see overleaf

see overleaf

©	Curry Club Discount	U	Unlicensed
V	Vegetarian	ANP	Alcohol not permitted
e-a-m-a-y-l	Eat as much as you like	BYO	Bring your own alcohol

Makhani £2.50, tiny whole round potatoes with rich masala sauce. Fully licensed. Sunday lunch: buffet £8.95 adult, children up to 7 years, free. Delivery: 6-12, closed Tuesday. Hours: 12-2.30 (not Friday) and 6-11.30 daily. Branch: Planet Spice, 88, Selsdon Park Road, Croydon, Surrey.

London SE24

Herne Hill

THREE MONKEYS TOP 100 ©

136 Herne Hill, SE24 020 7738 5500

Three Monkeys opened in a former bank building in 1998. This 110 seater is the concept of Mr Jan Peacock. Managed by Robert Pinto who trained at India's Oberoi and the elite Bombay Gymkhana Club, QE2 and Hilton. Its modern lines are graced by a remarkable entry bridge, which looks down onto the bar below. In the centre of the main dining area you can watch chefs in the open kitchen. Both floors, the bar and open kitchen are on view giving an airy spacious feel to the place. Since Udit Sarkhel (*see* SW18) was consultant chef, with Prem Singh as Exec Chef, what you get is perfect Indian food. The Starter Platter for two £9.95 includes a piece each of Zinga 65 – battered prawns with a chilli topping. Chicken Kebab. Aloo Tuk – crisply fried baby potatoes topped with yoghurt, spices and chutney and Medu Vada – lentil doughnuts served with coconut chutney. These are on the menu, along with many other delights and an average range of Tandoor specialities. Mains include a long list of great dishes, and yes there is CTM, if you really cannot risk anything else. £9.75. But do yourself a favour and be adventurous. Here are just a few examples: Dhaba Murg, a 'road-side-caff-style' chicken in a sauce of tomatoes, spices and fresh coriander. Handi Subz, mixed vegetables with peppers, tomatoes, ginger, spices, served in an earthen pot. Dum Ka Biryani, chicken, basmati rice & spices cooked in a dough-sealed pot (*see Dum Pukht page* 50) and served with your choice of Raita or Dal. £11.92. Two fishy favourites include Crab Malabari – crabmeat prepared with coconut, chopped curry leaves, mustard seeds, tomatoes and onions and finished with lemon juice. £7.25. Patrani Macchi, seasonal fish coated with mint, coriander and coconut and steamed in banana leaves...a traditional hard-to-find Parsee dish. £6.25. *'It's truly delicious. I'm a Parsee myself, and it's worth a journey.'* KB. Large Prawns Peri Peri, prawns marinated with Goan peri peri (chilli) masala, topped with onions, tomatoes and chillies. £18.25. They have a list of options for coeliacs (gluten allergy from wheat, which a lot of people have and are unaware they have it). Indian food should be cooked without wheat flour, apart from breads and samosa pastry, but it is reassuring that Three Monkeys have this level of care. Deli and Delivery. Lunch and dinner daily.

London SW

Area: South West London,
Postcodes: SW1 to SW20
Population: 705,000

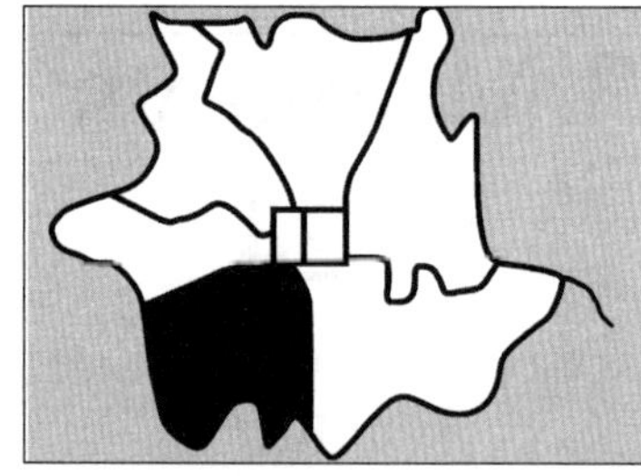

London SW1

Belgravia, Pimlico, St James's, Sloane Square, Victoria, Westminster

CINNAMON CLUB

NEW ENTRANT NEW TO OUR TOP 100

The Old Westminster Library, Great Smith Street, SW1 020 7222 2555

More has been written about Cinnamon Club and its *'totally new approach to Indian food'* than anything else, mostly no doubt by spin-master, Iqbal

Wahaab himself. We discuss this in the *Guide* intro *on page* 15. It opened after our last *Guide* came out so here it is, a new entrant. It is no ordinary curry house; no CTM or even Popadoms. *'On our first visit, we sat in the buzzing bar, I drank Gimlets – really good, 2nd best I've tasted – (best in Goa's Fort Aguada, by the pool). Pat had spritzers, while Iqbal drank Krug. Boy has he got expensive tastes! After a relaxing chat, we moved to the dining room, where a cleanly laid table, situated in the corner awaited us. We dined on fab food – I liked my duck curry, but I liked Iqbal's venison better, so I ate his! (I also ate half his starter – he is so generous!). Pat and I don't really eat puddings in Indian restaurants, (too full) but we were seduced by Iqbal's delectable selection and finished with fruit stuffed Samosas, home made sorbets and ice creams – delicious.'* DBAC. Chef Vivek Singh ex Jaipur Raj Vilas Hotel has the dubious accolade of cooking for President Clinton. He also has a brigade of 20 chefs. And he needs them. The menu literally changes daily, so this review gives you a flavour. Starters: Seafood Selection – Scallop, Salmon and King Prawn Kebab £8, Mussels with pickled Carrot and Beetroot £5.25. Green Moong Lentil and Basmati Kedgeree £5. Sandalwood flavoured Tandoori Chicken Breast £5.50. Potatoes stuffed with cottage cheese in a sweet and sour sauce £9. Hyderbadi-style aubergine steaks with coconut rice £9. The mains go in the same unusual direction: Fillet mullet with a Bengali style shrimp and vegetable broth £12.50. Mustard-flavoured tandoori king prawns with saffron kedgeree £16.50. Goan-spiced duck with curry leaf flavoured semolina £13. Calves liver with masala-mashed potatoes and stir-fried okra £13.50. Rack of lamb with a mint and onion sauce, peas pullao £17. Rajasthani spiced rack of 'Oisin' red deer with pickling sauce, pilau rice £31. A lot of diners have found Cinnamon Club not to their liking, as is to be expected. It's expensive, and as you'll read on *page* 15, it's different. One other difference ... apart from Brick Lane, and Tiffinbites (*see page* 16) this is the only restaurant to do Indian breakfast. Bombay spiced vegetables with cumin 'pao' £10. Spicy scrambled eggs on layered bread £11.00 and Uttapam, Rice pancake with choice of toppings, onion, green chilli, tomato or peppers. Served with coconut chutney and lentil broth £10. Or you can have Anglo Indian Kedgeree with smoked haddock and poached egg £13, or continental £12-£16. As we go to print, the first of Iqbal's proposed chain of bars (in Cockspur Street), has yet to open. This says the spin-master, will have four tandoors serving fast snacks all day, and will be nationwide. Further afield, also as we write, the opening of Cinnamon Club in downtown New York is also imminent. We award Cinnamon Club a **TOP 100** cachet. No higher award from us just now because we feel the innovation has veered a little too far away from Indian food. This may be inconsequential to Iqbal and Cinnamon's deep-pocketed owners, but you should listen to your friends. Hours: Breakfast 7.30-10am. Lunch 12-3pm, weekdays. Dinner 6-11, daily except Sunday which does lunch only, 12-3pm.

MINT LEAF — NEW ENTRANT

Suffolk Place, Pall Mall, SW1 020 7930 9020

People love it, they say. But what do they love? The trendy, black, sexy decor and lighting? It cost a fortune according to owners Dinu Bhattessa and Manju Karia. This couple, it seems, have not run an Indian restaurant before. They bored our companions (Indian vineyard-owner and wine exporter Kapil Grover and his wife and sales manager) for 90 minutes, virtually ignoring us. (they'd not heard of the *Good Curry Guide* evidently – not that we cared – we were just HUNGRY!). It was a Sunday night and there was our party of five and about eight other diners rattling around in this 4,000 sq ft 140-seater. The decor and barman-licensee Danny Smith is maybe more suited to a night club. His Tom-Cruise-Cocktail-performance failed to impress, as did serving drink that customers (me) didn't actually order, then arguing about it, rather than changing it. The food, when we eventually got to it? Average sort of Punjab, from chef KK Anand ex Cinnamon Club. Hours are supposed to be till midnight, however, at 11.45 arsy barman Smith announced that it was *'drinking up time!'* and that *'we are closing.'* We were quite shocked; we're not used to being thrown out of a restaurant, especially when the bill exceeded £250 for five. We wished the owners were there to witness just how the their staff applied the Mint Leaf code of practice: "a *style of service rooted in the finest Eastern traditions. You can be excused for thinking you have entered a different world. Welcome to Mint Leaf.*" We walked to our car, and belted up. Then, without noticing us, Mint's owners, emerged and locked up. It was not yet midnight. So it all stems from the top.

THE QUILON

TOP 100 PREVIOUS BEST IN UK AWARD

St James Court Hotel, 45 Buckingham Gate, SW1
020 7821 1899

Taj Hotels Group have owned London's unique Bombay Brasserie (sw7) and the elegant St James's Court Hotel for many years. But it took until 1999 to open an Indian restaurant here. Though within the complex, the restaurant is only accessible from the street. It is modern, with clean lines and sparkly mosaics running discreetly around the room and a splendid monkey mural on one wall. It's a modern, light and airy restaurant, seating 92 diners in two areas. The restaurant's name comes from Quilon, an unremarkable town on the coast road in the south of Kerala, not far from India's southern-most tip. This is the clue that the food is from the various states of south India. Indeed, the restaurant reflects what has been happening in Taj Hotels across India, where regional food of a high order is on their menus. In fact, Taj piloted this restaurant in Bangalore in 1988. Called Karavali, (meaning coastal food) it has become one of the city's favourites. Karavali owes its success to its original chef, Chef Aylur V Sriram. He originally trained with his father at the Hotel Sriram, and went on to work in some of India's top hotel restaurants. While at Karavali, the New Statesman described him as 'One of the top five chefs in India.' In 1999 he opened Quilon; his mission to recreate Karavali in London. Chef Sriram is a master; his spicing lyrical; his balance of flavour dreamlike; his menu a super choice of meat, fish and vegetable dishes. Unlike others in town, Sriram proves that there is no need for flamboyance, spin or new wave, *'Do not take a traditional dish and mess around with it,;* he says. In typical understated Taj style, he simply and quietly goes about his business of producing perfect Indian cooking. His reward is that he is now Quilon's General Manager as well as Chef. His small but perfectly balanced menu awaits you. It's an education. Here are some of the wonderful delights that you could sample. Starters: Partridge Masala £5.25, cooked in red chilli, ginger, garlic, fried onion flakes, tomatoes, lime juice and freshly ground roast masala of cardamom, cinnamon, aniseed and cloves – one of Pat's favourites, it's the red chilli that does it. Crab Cakes £5.95, crab meat sauteed with curry leaves, ginger, green chillies and cooked on a skillet until golden brown. Coorg Chicken, tangy preparation of sautéed chicken with roasted and ground coriander, peppercorns, mustard seeds, cinnamon, cumin seeds, laced with Coorg vinegar – I've eaten this dish many times and find it a must for those particular Coorg flavours. Masala Vada £4.95, crispy dumplings of yellow lentil, green chilli, fennel and curry leaves. Delicious main courses: Masala Fried Stuffed Squid (Quilon's most ordered dish) – squid, crispy fried and stuffed with spiced spinach, potatoes and drizzled with lemon and curry oil dressing. Mangalorean Chicken Curry (Kori Gassi), succulent pieces of chicken cooked in finely ground fresh coconut and roasted red chilli, peppercorns, cumin seeds, coriander seeds, tempered with chopped onion, fenugreek seeds and cumin seeds. Eat with a delicious Appam £1.95, soft-centred, lace-edged rice-pancake, (cooked on view in the restaurant) perfect for dipping into the rich masala sauce – I know its traditionally eaten with Istew, lamb or vegetable cooked Keralan-style, but hey! – let's break a few rules. Malabar Lamb Biryani £13.25, lamb marinated in traditional Malabar spices and cooked with basmati rice in a sealed pot, served with Pachadi (whole wheat layered bread cooked on skillet with pure ghee) and a lamb sauce. This dish is particularly delicious and outshines any other Biryani that you might have tried. Finish off with cooling and refreshing ice creams with traditional desserts of Bibinca or Dodal, unconventional to the western palate perhaps, but you will be converted – fabulous! In conclusion, a restaurant with management of this calibre means its quality remains rock-solid. It won our **BEST UK RESTAURANT** award last time, which means what it says. Though this award goes elsewhere this time, nothing will change our opinion. Hours: 12-2.30 and 6-11.

SALOOS TOP 100

62 Kinnerton Street, SW1 020 7235 4444

M Salahuddin's Saloos is a Pakistani institution. It's been around for decades and at the beginning it set a new standard of service, decor and, yes, expense. Even 15 years ago, it was easy to spend £100 for two there. The elegant Farizeh Salahuddin (daughter of the house – she can be heard out of hours on the answer machine) handles bookings with considerable aplomb. It's still much hallowed by my Pakistani and Indian friends, well-educated wealthy citizens, who ignore politics when it comes to conviviality. But I am beginning to wonder if it has become overtaken by so many really excellent newer venues. Being Pakistani, meat, meat and more meat predominates (*'A vegetarian-free heaven'* says RA who, like Bernard Shaw, despises vegetables). The faithful still adore it. *'Succulent, natural-coloured, divinely-flavoured offerings like Chicken Shashlik, Lamb chop and Shami Kebab are insurmountable'* HEG. Hard-to-find, acquired taste Haleem, (see glossary) is one speciality. But we get somewhat reserved reports about Salloos from occasional or first-time visitors these days. The place is an institution and is worth at least one visit. Remains in our **TOP 100**. Should it stay there? Reports please. Set lunches at £12 and £16, (2 & 3 courses). Cover charge £1.50. Service 12.5%. Hours: Mon.-Sat., 12-2.30/7-11.15.

SPICY WORLD NEW ENTRANT

76 Wilton Road, London SW1 020 7630 9951

Mohammed Uddin carefully runs this venue. Despite its expensive postcode, prices are normal. sunday e-a-m-a-y-l lunch at £5.95 is really good value. All your favourites are on the menu. Baltis, curries, specials, nothing is missing(RCF loves the Nargis Kebabs – kebab mince around an egg) . Hours: Lunch 1-3. Dinner -1130., daily. *See page 11.*

WOODLANDS TOP 100 V ©

37 Panton Street, SW1 020 7930 8200

Long-established (1985) licensed, vegetarian, south Indian 55-seat vegetarian restaurant, just off Haymarket. It is the tiniest of UK Woodlands. The big news is that they've opened a new fourth London branch in Chiswick, W4 (there are branches in India, Singapore and LA, each serving an identical menu. Bhel, Dosa, Idli, Vada, Samosa, Pakoda, Uthappams (*see page 52*). *'I particularly like southern Indian food, and find the menu so appealing, it makes choice difficult. We chose one exceptionally good-value set meal, Thali, £6.50, which was quite generous, with good variety, and the Paper Dosa, £3.95. Upma, £2.95, Lhassi, £1.25, and Channa, £3.75 are as good as ever. Also glad to have a choice of Indian desserts. Good value.'* HC. *'Enjoyed my lunchtime visit, indulging in the vegetarian buffet. Plenty of flavoursome dishes.'* RL Service 12.5%. Hours: 11-2.45/5.30-10.45. Branches: London W1, W4 & Wembley, Mddx.

London SW3

Chelsea, King's Road, Knightsbridge

HAANDI
PREVIOUS AWARD WINNER TOP 100

136 Brompton Road, SW3 020 7823 7373

A restaurant with bar and two entrances. One at the rear on Cheval Place is at street level, while the one on Brompton Road is down a generous staircase, leading to a bright, clean and tidy reception and the bar, which serves snacks, and on the left is the restaurant. The lemony-yellow decor, with inviting tables and chairs, give a cheerful sunshine welcome. *'We propped up the bar on high stools, and sipped glasses of red wine, which Ray (proprietor) had chosen for us – very good. We chatted about India, its food and his Kenyan connections (Ray has a highly regarded restaurant there). We enjoyed Kebabs and Tikkas – a chef speciality; you can see them cooking through a plate glass window, followed by Chicken Tikka Butter Masala £7.80, fantastic, not overly tomatoey, creamy, smoky, with a little chilli kick, Gosht-Ki-Haandi £8.10, one of Pat's favourites with Dal Dera Ismail Khan £4.10, creamy black lentils, rice and Pudina Nan £2.10, quite thin, not doughy, sprinkled with finely chopped mint – lovely*

©	Curry Club Discount	**U**	Unlicensed
V	Vegetarian	**ANP**	Alcohol not permitted
e-a-m-a-y-l	Eat as much as you like	**BYO**	Bring your own alcohol

(Pat liked it and he's not a bread fan!). All dishes cooked properly, presented carefully, served professionally and in generous portions. DBAC. Other diners think the same. *'Excellent menu, food and presentation with a warm welcome. A wonderful restaurant.'* RB *'Chakula Mzuri Sana is Kenyan for Good Food!'* NH. *'Absolutely gorgeous, good food, wine and service.'* JH. *'A great experience, not only the place was relaxing, the atmosphere and the staff really helpful. We had one of the best Indian meals we have ever come cross. We'll definitely go back.'* NM. *'I have become a regular. Absolutely amazing food, a great ambassador of Indian cuisine.'* AB. *'Absolutely love Haandi. Food so flavourful, spicy and delicious. Courteous staff are welcoming.'* CM. Menu Extracts: Khajy Til Rolls £5.20, vegetable roll with cashew nuts and mint. Bindya Prawns £12.20, crispy queen prawns. Diwani Haandi £6.50, mix of peas, corn, carrots and beans. Gosht Kabuli £8, lamb with chickpeas, lentils and fresh mint. Lunch Menus: from £7.95. Bar Hours: drinks served between 12-10.30, light meals and snacks available all day. Lunch -3. Dinner: 6-1130.

SHAHEEN OF KNIGHTSBRIDGE ©

225 Brompton Road, SW3   020 7581 5329

With Shaheen 150 yards from Harrods, if you are feeling a bit battered and worn, elbowing your way past the tourists, why not drop in at Shaheen to revive yourself and rest your feet! It's a long-standing restaurant, which understands its regulars and tourists equally well. *'Several years since I had been to the Shaheen but I remembered I had been pleased at the time. It was late of a Sunday, the only diners, but there were eight of us, didn't matter. Two staff – very friendly and helpful. Very happy with the meal. Decor plain and menu short. Prices very fair, considering location. All food very good and all chose something different, so had a good range. Full marks for having a dessert menu that wasn't the usual fancy ice-creams. Very pleasant Gajar Halva. £26 a head.'* HJC Lunch to-3pm. Dinner to-11.30, weekdays. Saturday and Sunday 12-11.30.

London SW4

Clapham

CLAPHAM TANDOORI 

10 Clapham Common S, SW4 020 7622 4470

Clapham's second oldest (1971), owned by Abdur Rhaman Choudhury. His restaurant seats 72 diners, and head chef Shiraze Ahamed serves well-liked curries and side dishes and has some Indo-French specials up his sleeve, £6.25-8.95. Sunday lunch e-a-m-a-i-l £5.95, children (under 12) £3.25. Delivery: 3-mile radius, £10 minimum. Hours: 12-2.30/6-12.

MAHARANI

117 Clapham High Street, SW4 020 7622 2530

The 104-seat Maharani was established in 1958, at which time there were under 200 curry houses in the whole of the UK. It was not only Clapham's first curry house, opened long before Cla'am became trendy ma'am, it was one of the first to open in a London suburb. It has always earned its keep by providing good, bog-standard, formula curries; indeed, owner SU Khan was one of the pioneers of the formula. Under the same ownership for all these years, Khan has kept up with the trends, though, and everything is as it should be. Hours: 12-2.30pm/6pm-12am; Sun. 12pm-12am.

London SW5

Earls Court

LOOF'S 

234 Old Brompton Road, SW5 020 7370 1188

Opened in 1999 by Lesley Cornell-Wash and Luthfur (Loof) Rahman. Formerly of Cafe Naz. Forget the curryhouse food, you must try the Bangladeshi dishes. Specials: Singara (triangle pastry filled with cottage cheese and spiced chicken, served with chunky pineapple chutney), Pepe Bhaji (green papaya diced and tossed with light chillies and spices). Aloo Chops (potato paté blended with coriander and dried chillies, served with tomato chutney). Leboor Gosht (with Bangladeshi limes), Lau Gootha (pumpkin and king prawns, served with Pullao Rice). Delivery available. Hours: 6pm-12am. Branch: Viceroy, 100, Middle Street, Yeovil, Somerset.

NIZAM TOP 100 

152 Old Brompton Road, SW5 020 7373 0024

The Nizam was the former ruler of Hyderabad. Until partition he was the richest man in the world, and his dining table seated 101 guests, yes, at one table! On it was a silver model railway which chugged around the table dispensing whisky et al to the guests. M Mian's 1989 vintage Nizam is rather smaller, seating 65 on several tables in two rooms. *'Attractive appearance and warm reception. The food was varied and excellent with a number of dishes new to me and my guests. Chicken and prawn main courses with excellent vegetables, especially the smoked aubergine. Service was superb throughout.'* RH. Service is exemplary, with smartly waistcoated waiters, exuding expertise. North West Frontier and Moghul cuisine is carefully executed by chef M Riaz. Specialities include smoky Baingan Bharta, (charcoal-grilled aubergine, its flesh then mashed to a purée), Prawn Piri Piri, (coconut milk and chilli). Cover charge £1. Takeaway 10% discount. Delivery: £12 mini. Hours: 12-2.30pm/6-11.45pm.

NOOR JAHAN

2a Bina Gardens, off Old Brompton Road, SW5 020 7375 6522

'Food, indeed very good. Chicken Tikka was succulent, the Goan fish curry taste and the Roghan Josh excellent. Nan is not huge and you need one each, but they are light, fluffy and served hot. Service left a lot to be desired, being rather rapid and a little condescending. However, we will certainly return.' Mr & Mrs P. Most people like the place, so we need reports please to decide whether to keep it in the Guide for next time. Lunch and dinner daily.

©	Curry Club Discount	U	Unlicensed
V	Vegetarian	ANP	Alcohol not permitted
e-a-m-a-y-l	Eat as much as you like	BYO	Bring your own alcohol

STAR OF INDIA TOP 100

154 Old Brompton Road, SW5 020 7373 2901

Reza and Azam Mahammad run this startling restaurant. I say startling because the decor is a dead-ringer of Michael Angelo's Sistine Chapel. Now to the food (with prices!). Starters include: Galouti Kebab £5.25, smooth mince lamb patties, served with onion and cumin relish. Samundri Ratan £5.95, Saffron infused chargrilled scallops served in a creamy sauce. Chenna Samosa £5.50, crispy parcels filled with a trio of goat, buffalo and cow's cheese, mixed with leeks, ginger and green peppercorns, served with a spiced tomato and chive chutney - interesting! Main courses: Murghabi Tawe Wale £13.50, escallops of mallard marinated with garlic, nutmeg, lemon and chilli oil, pan fried on an iron griddle. Raan Mussallam £19 (serves two), roasted leg of baby lamb marinated in a mixture of spices then cooked over a gentle flame in a rich onion and tomato gravy, flavoured with nutmeg and flambéed with rum. [now doesn't that sound scrumptious!] If you can spare room for a pudding, try either the Dum Malai Chikki £4.95, steamed milk pudding scented with nutmeg and cardamom, topped with caramelised jaggery and carom seeds, served chilled, or the Phalon Ka Muzaffar £4.75, home made seasonal fruit compote, served with cardamom ice cream, or have both! *'Having been before, I had a distant memory of Chocomosas being a highlight, and they were again. Got a seat by the open windows on a balmy mid-week evening. Pops - cold and Pickles - looked tired, slightly disappointing, how long had they been sitting on the table before we arrived? (Cover charge £1). Headed straight for the main courses - Laal Maas - a spicy lamb dish which came in a pungent sauce and although described as hot, had less of a kick than expected. Still, all the spicing was distinct and a side order of dhal - very tasty with good texture. Maggie's prawn dish was also well spiced and eagerly mopped up with the Naan. With wonderful (but pricey) chocomosas to finish off with - another good meal.'* AR. Lunch and dinner daily.

London SW6

Fulham, Parson's Green

BLUE ELEPHANT THAI TOP100

4 Fulham Broadway, SW6 020 7385 6595

Undoubtedly the UK's best Thai restaurant. The group, headed by Belgian Karl Steppe, and his Thai wife has branches worldwide, recently including a cookery school in Bangkok. London's Blue Elephant has always been the group's flagship. But to maintain its position, it has undergone a major refurbishment. The addition of the stunning new Blue Bar, based on the Royal Thai Barge, enhances the whole experience. The bar menu includes a salad of young sour mango, palm sugar and roast coconut. On entering this enchanted kingdom, allow yourself to be taken on a wonderful journey, tasting some of the finest Thai cuisine in the capital. Cross the delightful bridge stretching over a picturesque lily pond and enter the heart of lush jungle, exotic blooms and thatched Thai dining 'Houses'. Bundles of redolent orchids, freshly imported from Bangkok's famous floating market fill the light and airy interior. Specialist chefs prepare the finest in Royal Thai cuisine, ensuring each dish possesses the stamp of authenticity. Friendly and efficient staff are at hand to recommend and advise from the extensive menu that boasts a fabulous array of vegetarian dishes. The spectacular Sunday Brunch includes entertainment for children and unlimited servings for only £16.75! All this is why we rate it the best Thai restaurant in the country. Lunch and dinner daily. A *Guide* Award winning **TOP100** restaurant

DARBAR NEW ENTRANT

92 Waterford Road, SW6 020 7348 7373

When the'Fish' chain fishled out, this place came on the market giving Pravin Chawan, whose family run London's Diwan-e-Am, the opportunity to open his own restaurant. Darbar, (meaning royal court) is the outcome. His choice of chef shows the astrologers were smiling on Pravin. He got Mohammed Rais from the Red

Fort London W1. They must have been smiling on Rais too; he went before it went bust having been there since 1997. His speciality is Dum Pukht (*see page* 50). Starters include Galauti Kebab – the smoothest patties of minced lamb and spices. These are often cooked at your table to add to the drama. Teetar gilafi kebab – spiced roasted minced partridge. Monkfish tikka – chunks of monkfish smoked with ginger. For main course, the wallets love Dum ka lobster – lobster steamed in a delicate sauce of mace, cumin and saffron, £28. But the Dum Pukht cogniscenti go for any of Rais' Birianis cooked in a sealed pot: Avadhi gosht biryani – Rais' 300 year old family recipe of lamb and rice. Samudari biryani – scallops, squid, prawns and rice. Subz biryani – moist basmati rice, vegetables and spices. Desserts include Strawberry Shirkhand – yoghurt flavoured with fresh raspberry couli, £6. Not cheap, but this is Chelsea. Minimum spend £25 lunch and £40 dinner.

NAYAB TOP 100 

309 New Kings Rd (jnct'n Munster Road), SW6 020 7731 6993

Praveen Rai runs a very good upmarket restaurant. His menu is full of 'some dishes you won't recognise and some that you will. The former are Indian and Pakistani specials cooked by head chef Akeel Ghani. These include: Nihari Kohe Avadh, pot roast shank of lamb. Most popular dish ordered is Goan Galinha Xacutti (Sha-Coo-Tee), browned onion, fresh coconut. Meat Dhaba Wala Lamb cooked in bone marrow stock and mince (ask Rai to tell you about this). This is all dedicated stuff, and well spoken of by the regulars. For the if-you-must-brigade, Mr Rai offers 'old curry-house favourites' which include everything except Phal (he'll explain how it came to be *'invented by chefs as a revenge against the lager lout – and he'd never serve it or them!'*). So if you are chilli-addicted, as Praveen himself is, then choose the hotter specials. Set menus for two at £13 and £16 pp. Delivery: Hours: 12-2.30/6-11.45 (11.30 on Sun.).

©	Curry Club Discount	U	Unlicensed
V	Vegetarian	ANP	Alcohol not permitted
e-a-m-a-y-l	Eat as much as you like	BYO	Bring your own alcohol

London SW7

Kensington

BOMBAY BRASSERIE

LIFETIME BEST RESTAURANT AWARD

14 Courtfield Close, Courtfield Road, SW7
020 7370 4040

It's amazing really. The BB pioneered Indian regional cooking in this country, in fact the world. It hadn't even been done in India in 1982. It is now the 50-strong Taj Hotel Group's flagship venue, earning millions of profit each year. It is an icon. Yet it has recently had a panning from the critics. That's typical. They build you up then smack you down. Well this *Guide* has always told it as it is, and there have been niggles in our pages in previous editions; we don't just issue gushing reviews. But that's what friends are for. Staff turn round is minimal. Locals and regulars, of which there are very many greet the same staff faces year after year. So just how the same management and chefs, waiters and back room staff can be so different now, from a few years back, search me. Of course, they aren't. Of our many thousands of reports received each year, we typically get around 100 about the BB. It way out does any other venue. Despite seating a considerable 265, you are advised to book. Some nights they serve 400 guests, split between a stylish restaurant and conservatory. It's nothing to see Madonna on one table, Hugh Grant on another, and the odd politician on a third. [Did I say odd?] None of this phases the waiters. The kitchen is managed by the experienced hands of executive chef Vikram Sunderam. Vikram originally trained with the Taj Group in Mumbai and in Delhi and his career spans some of the best hotel restaurants in the world. He draws his culinary inspirations from his mother (from Maharashtra) and his strict vegetarian father (a Tamil Brahmin). He is also an authority on tandoor cooking, which uses clay ovens fired with charcoal. He is visiting professor of Indian Culinary Arts at Thames Valley University. He has been described by the British edition of India Today as one of the top ten Indian chefs working in the UK. And this is some of what he does: Samosa Chaat £6.25, vegetable samosas, served with chick peas, sweet yoghurt and a medley of chutneys. Aloo Tuk £6.25, crispy fried baby potatoes in jacket, topped with sweet yoghurt and imli (tamarind chutney). Sev Batata Puri £6.50, small biscuits like puris topped with cubed boiled potatoes, gramflour straws, sprouted lentil, coriander leaves and covered with a mix of mint, tamarind and chilli chutneys. And for mains: Chicken Tikka Makhani £15.25, chicken tikka immersed in a spiced butter sauce – fantastic CTM done the proper way. Lamb Chops with ginger and green herbs £17.75, French cut, English lamb cooked Indian style. Margi Ni Sali £15.25, chicken curry topped with straw potatoes. *'Pat and I enjoyed a candle-lit dinner for two, sitting in the conservatory. After finishing a bottle of well chilled champagne in the bar, we sampled an abundance of delicious starters and main dishes and enjoyed everything immensely, but we always do at the BB! We finished off in the bar with their unique Cobra coffee - if you haven't had it, you don't know what you are missing!! It's absolutely fabulous as is the whole BB experience.'* DBAC. *'A friend booked six of us after our annual 'Messiah from Scratch' at the Royal Albert Hall. The BB is the sort of restaurant in which to spend a whole evening, and our concert made us late, but it was still such a treat. Surroundings are lovely, menu different, wonderfully tempting, food fantastic. Usual grumble – service. Professional when it came but had to attract attention to order drinks, ditto food. But atmosphere made up for everything. First class restaurant whatever its cuisine. Not cheap but top quality never is. Haven't been since 1984, so pleased it has kept up high standard. Had an out-of-this-world lobster dish. All superb, generous, and individual. Most impressed, we all were. £72 per couple.'* HC. *'attended the London International Trade Fair at Olympia and stayed in a hotel near the BB. Booked a table for 12 and entertained my colleagues with a top-class Indian meal. On arrival we were warmly greeted as we drank glasses of Omar Khayyam. Shown to an excellent round table in the conservatory and served us Chef's Choice. What followed can only be described as a procession of exceptional food with a variety of dishes too numerous to remember or name, washed down with 6 bottles of fabulous white wine. All who dined, thought it was the best meal they had ever eaten and would return again on special occasions – or when the company was paying!! £735 for twelve.'* DL. Daily lunch buffet: £16.95. Min charge: £30.00. Service 12½%. Hours: 12-3/7.30-12. *See page* 40. Branch: Quilon, SW1.

CAFÉ LAZEEZ TOP 100

93 Old Brompton Road, SW7 020 7581 9993

Lazeez, meaning *'delicate and aromatic'*, describes itself as a 'new type of Indian restaurant'. It operates in true café mode, with nonstop opening hours. It has a striking frontage, with 26 good-weather seats outside. Inside are 130 seats, on two floors. Downstairs in stark, minimalist surroundings, is a short-menu café (which changes to full menu after 7pm). Upstairs is decorated with an illuminated, white, tented roof, and a full menu. Its owners are Pakistani, in the persons of the elegant Ms Sabiha Kasim and her brother Zahid. They were undoubtedly ahead of their time with their bar/new-wave concept. Despite criticism in earlier years about the evolved nature of some of their food, they've stuck to their guns. Suddenly, and at long last, we're getting the good reports we've always longed Lazeez to achieve. HC glows: *'Spicing different, and not necessarily Indian. A good place to take people who say they don't like Indian food. Succulent prawns, sizzling lamb chops, well-spiced vegetables, rich and creamy Korma, the Lamb Sag, not enough lamb, but good flavour, Saffron Rice fantastic, firm, fresh and spicy mushrooms, star dish, aubergine – superb – and the Nan, small, round, lightest and crispest I've had. Expensive, but first class. Overall, a wonderful meal.'* HC. That Korma is a good example. It's authentic, as done in the Pakistani heartlands where the meat is marinated in yoghurt to tenderise it, resulting in a mild, aromatic dish with subtle spicing, including a hint of garam masala, ergo Lazeez! *'It's a lively place. We like to enjoy the bar downstairs for an hour or so then go upstairs for our meal.'* Average snack price £6, meal price £30, inc. service and cover charge. Hours: 11-11. (10.30 Sun.). Branches: Café Lazeez London EC1 & W1.

DELHI BRASSERIE

134 Cromwell Road, SW7 020 7370 7617

Owner Mr A Jabber says 'shop out and pop in' (it's near Sainsbury's). A bright comfortable spacious 60-seater. Chef Ram Singh's food and service excellent. Hours: 12-11.30.

©	Curry Club Discount	U	Unlicensed
V	Vegetarian	ANP	Alcohol not permitted
e-a-m-a-y-l	Eat as much as you like	BYO	Bring your own alcohol

KHAN'S OF KENSINGTON

3 Harrington Road, SW7 020 7584 4114

60-seater, est. 1991 by Mr Khan (no relation to Khan's, W2). We have several good reports about this venue. It's a meat-eater's haven – scrumptious chops and tikka, tender lamb main courses, and all at a reasonable cost. Hours: 12-2.30/6-11.30; Sat. 12-12; Sun. 12.30-11.

MOTI MAHAL ©

3 Glendower Place, SW7 020 7584 8428

BA and T Rahman's 40-seater opened way back in 1956, and amazingly it pioneered curry in Kensington. Every one that tells about this place reports a great buzz and care and good value for money. All the formula dishes done perfectly. Useful hours: 12- 11.30.

SHEZAN INDIAN TOP 100

16 Cheval Place, Montpelier Street, SW7
020 7584 9316

This long-established (1966), very traditionally elegant 120-seat Pakistani restaurant, is in a residential street a block north of Old Brompton Road. The downstairs dining room, past the bar, is elegantly simple, with its downlighters, pewter plates, long-rolled napkins, traditional Pakistani chairs, all made theatrical by strategic lighting and candlelight. Chef Khan's food is as sophisticated as the service. It's traditional authentic Pakistani food done as it would have been for the royal courts. No innovation, no nonsense. Not even CTM (but its originator dish, Murgh Makhni) £12. The prices are Knightsbridge, but it's worth every penny just for regal service and care. Our favourite is still on: Choosa e Shezan – a chicken (whole poussin)-and-egg story described on the menu as *'a speciality of our dear old Khansama (cook)'*, and billed at a dear old £16! Set lunch £12.95. Minimum charge dinner £25. Service 10%. Cover charge £1.50. Takeaway 20% off. Shezan branches in New York and Washington DC. Lunch and dinner daily.

London SW8

South Lambeth, Vauxhall

BOMBAY BICYCLE CLUB DELIVERIES

28 Queenstown Road, SW8 020 7720 0500

See branch at SW12 for details.

London SW9

Brixton, Oval, Stockwell

OLD CALCUTTA 

64a Brixton Road, SW9 020 7582 1415

Old Calcutta and its predecessor (Oval Tandoori) have been in this Guide from the beginning. Owner Abdul Mazid says: *'we're situated at the Oval tube end of the road (the a23) an area sometimes described as a gourmet desert.'* But not for curry gourmets who love the formula. Delivery: 3 miles, £12 min. Hours: 12-2.30/6 -12.

London SW10

Chelsea, West Brompton

CHUTNEY MARY
AWARD WINNER AND TOP 100

535 Kings Road, SW10 020 7351 3113

Chutney Mary opened in 1991. Indian friends believed we'd gone bonkers, when in 1992 we made it our **TOP UK** restaurant. *'My dear, this isn't Indian food,'* they'd say rather patronisingly, *'try Salloos!'* In those days, CM billed itself as *'Anglo Indian'* – something we found a tad bemusing, since they only had a couple of ex Raj dishes on the menu, and narry an Anglo Indian chef in sight. What they did have was a brigade of six chefs each from a different region of India, each dispensing their own speciality dishes. OK, I hear you say, done it, seen it, at the Bombay Brasserie for a decade already; in fact at the time it was better there. Chutney Mary's spicing was decidedly bland, and the place half empty. But Chutney Mary had something the BB didn't have. Passionate owners with this one expensive-to-run baby to bring to adulthood. That was then. Soon those same owners had bought out their former partners. By 1999 when we again awarded CM the Top UK Restaurant Award, the Anglo aspect had gone and spicing had become definitive and accurate. CM was by now packed out and my Indian friends told me 'this is an exemplary Indian restaurant'. The owners next bought Veeraswamy (W1) and opened two revolutionary Masala Zones (W1 & N1). So with CM's first decade under the belt, it takes a brave decision to close for three months – risking loosing the goodwill of your regulars, of which there are many. But as we say, these are passionate owners, with the clearest vision I know. We held our breath. DBAC takes up the story: *'On a preview visit, Pat and I were treated to an exclusive dinner. The refurbishment left little trace of its pre-existence. The old colonial bar has gone, replaced by a bright and airy private dining room. Sparkling Indian mosaics (a glass ball is made, and then smashed, the pieces are then gathered to make the mosaics) take you down to the main restaurant, which is decorated with works of modern Indian art, concealed spot lights, and masses of candles held in clear crystal glass. The conservatory is still there, complete with tree and sparkling fairy lights. The water fountain has gone, but new pot plants decorate the perimeter of the encirclement. We start with Bombay Blush (Champagnoise with rose liqueur, decorated with purple orchids).'* DBAC. The wine list by Mathew Jukes is definitive, and would do justice in any restaurant. Nothing is over £55, not even Bollinger or a Grand Cru Bordeaux (Chateau La Dominique) DBAC's favourite. Least expensive is a reasonable £13. Chef Nagarajan Rubinath has taken the mantle from Hardeep Singh, and the menu is new too. Yet it retains all the former CM qualities. Starters include the magnificent Tokri Chaat, potato lattice basket with street food favourites and chutneys £6, or Konkan Prawns with asparagus, £8.50. Mains include four different Chicken Tikkas, £14, Duck with Apricots (a Parsee favourite – Jardaloo), fanned slices of pinky duck breast, drizzled with a spicy minced sauce with halved apricots, £16.50, and a fab Tandoori Crab £16.50. Mains come plated, which some don't like because it makes sharing hard. There is a good selection of sides and breads, including Black Urad Dal (Maharani) – [DBAC's favourite] dark, rich, creamy, aromatic spices, swirl of cream £4. But it's the presentation which is striking. Each dish has its own bespoke platter and food-layout. We wondered what the owners meant when they told us they were looking for new ways of presenting Indian food. Now we know, and it is unique in the Indian market. Suffice to say, the bold redec venture paid off. The place is more gorgeous than ever. Its regular clients are back, and loving it all the more. Presentation is outstanding. One way to try it all is to order the Tasting Menu of seven courses at £55 per head. Chutney Mary deserved its 1992 and 1999 Awards and it deserves it again. Nobody does it better. Hours: Lunch 12.30-2.30, Saturday and Sunday only. Dinner 6-11, daily except Sunday - 10.30 *See page 37.*

EXOTIKKA OF INDIA ©

35 Stadium Street, SW10 020 7376 7542

Someone had to think of the name! And it may as well be owners Hye and Hussain. Competent curries from chef A Kalam at this 40-seater. Set lunch £6.95. Hours: 6-11.30. (Sat. to 12am).

PAINTED HERON BEST CHEF AWARD AND NEW TO OUR TOP 100

112 Cheyne Walk, Chelsea, SW10 020 751 5232

It's between Albert and Battersea Bridges, on a corner site formerly occupied by The Bong Tree Thai restaurant. Parking is difficult, there are few single yellow lines. Perhaps a valet system should be investigated? We were shown to a prominent table in a completely empty restaurant, though, it nearly filled later. It is tastefully decorated, under the minimalist banner – white walls with modern prints. Tables are simply laid, white linen cloths, napkins, contemporary cutlery and a single wine balloon. Rounds of moulded glass contain coloured oil with wick to light each table inadequately. Chairs are painted black wood, seated with leather and comfortable. Lumber floors are polished and the large plate glass windows are dressed with wooden slatted blinds.

We perused the menu and sipped Shiraz (£17), over a large oval platter, generously piled high with fresh Popadom strips, accompanied by three chutneys – Beetroot, Coconut and Mango and Chickpea with Chilli. All hand-made and all fabulous. Staff are smilers - smart, clean and very willing. However, no Michelin star will be awarded. Wine was poured to Pat first and sparkling water was spilt. Plates were cleared from one diner, over the other. These are small etiquette indiscretions, easily correctable. The Painted Heron's young owner decided in 2003 to get into the Indian restaurant business. It wouldn't be my advice, but he's in property and owns the building, and he seems to have an instinct for it. His ace card is his choice of chef – Yogesh Datta. He's come from Tabla (E14) and he's Taj-trained, and it is amazing just how good Taj chefs are. In some respects he reminds one of Udit (*see Sarkell's* SW 18). Yogesh enjoys a challenge and he's very much hands-on. His menu, which changes every few days, has no long, meaningless narrations, just short, concise definitions, or perhaps the best explanation, honesty! And like Udit, Yogesh runs the kitchen with just two other chefs. It is not new wave, though it has an innovative signature. It is glorious Indian food, all carefully crafted and accurately spiced. For starters,we settled on 'Pheasant Breast with Green Chilli and Garlic' £7 a good piece of foul, carbon-tinged from the Tandoor – tender meat on a minuscule bone, accompanied by a salad flavoured with ajwan and ginger – delicious. We also had 'Chutney-stuffed Paneer Cheese Tikka' £5, an oblong of exquisite hand-made cheese, split into two, rather like a sandwich, stuffed with Podina (mint). As if that wasn't enough we couldn't resist Gol Goppa, a wheat-flour mini 'flying saucer', loaded with a spicy small potato cubes drizzled with imli and a trickle of natural yoghurt. Main courses were a quarrelsome choice, with so many delectable dishes. We agreed on 'Chicken stuffed with green chilli pickle in hot Rajasthani curry' £11, a very clever dish of chicken breast which Yogesh had lightly beaten, making it flat. Chilli pickle had been positioned and the chicken rolled in a cylinder then baked. The enrobing spicy, creamy sauce contained curry leaves with long slivers of lightly sauteed onion. Ingeniously innovative but very Indian in taste. 'Lamb Shank with aromatic spices' £11.50, was served in a impressive, round, shiny, white metal bowl with a wide flat rim. The portion was so large it could have generously fed two and was so tender it literally fell of the bone. I choose side dishes of 'Wild Mushroom Pullao' £2.50. Basmati rice, oval-plated, good flavour with tonnes of garlic and delicate slices of different fungi varieties. Since giving up wheat, I am now appreciating rice much more than before and can tell the good stuff from the dud! Simply described as 'Black Lentils' £3, urid dal, well cooked, creamy, with a whirl of fresh cream decorating it surface. Quite chilli hot, but with a full, rounded flavour, not raw. Pat requested a Mint Paratha. He thought it would harmonise his meal well and he was right. It was delivered in a basket, rolled very thinly and sprinkled with finely chopped, dried, mint leaves. Pat's words 'VERY nice.' Full to the gills, we resisted Gulab jamun with chocolate ice cream £4, or Coconut tarte with coconut ice cream and chocolate syrup £4. We are delighted to give Yogesh our **BEST CHEF AWARD.** He joins Cyrus, Mernosh, Udit and Atol (*see page* 29). Sort out the parking and service and it can only get better. Discretionary 12½% service charge. Hours: Lunch 12.30-2.30 weekdays. Dinner - 11.30 Mon to Sat. Sunday 12-10.30.

STICKLEBACKPINK

168, Ifield Road, SW10 020 7835 0874

Find Brompton cemetery and you've found Ifield Road. Sticklebackpink opened there in 2003. On the ground floor is the bar plus room for 20 diners, seated on chocolate-leather chairs which contrast nicely against against the white tablecloths and white-washed walls. Beaten metal fish sculptures gleam in the light. A spiral staircase, which leads down to the 50 seater basement where walls are softened with a graduated pale lime colour in two comfortable dining areas. Majibur Rahman co-owns (with Gary Froud) and heads the cheffing. He had worked at John Burton Race's L'Ortolan then Cafe Blue Cobra, Reading and owns Malik's in

Cookham. Rahman cooks traditional Bangladeshi dishes as well as creating his own modern interpretations. The Stickleback platter offers a selection of marinated meats and seafood roasted in the clay oven, £7.50. His signature dishes are Zeenok, £6.50, steamed mussels cooked with white wine, coriander and coconut (excellent) and Bengali Khashi, £12, slow-cooked chunks of goat meat simmered with lentils and beans. Average spend: £30 excluding drinks. Hours: 6.30-12, Tuesday to Sunday.

VAMA THE INDIAN ROOM

TOP 100 

438 Kings Road, SW10 020 7351 4118

Vama, meaning 'womanhood', was established in 1997 by brothers Andy and Arjun Varma. Stylishly decorated with ochre walls and teak chairs, hand-made crockery from Khurja, and a fossil-stone floor. It is quite obvious to see why the 110 seat Vama is so popular. The Varmas (different spelling) are charming men, who are very relaxed chatting to their many regular clients including Lloyd Webber, Rowan Atkinson and Curry Club member Sir John-Harvey Jones. He was the guest of honour at the launch of Vama-Ji, the brothers' new Indian cuisine delivery service. Cooked at their state-of-the-art, new Central Processing Unit in Battersea it delivers to homes and businesses within a 10 mile radius of Battersea, ring 020 7736 2300. Plans are afoot to roll-out the brand nationally over the next few years. The menu is identical to the restaurant. The cuisine is North West Frontier. This takes us from the Afghan border to the Punjab. Specials: Mahi (Salmon Tikka) Ajwaini £8.75. Tandoori Jhinga, Tiger prawns marinaded in yoghurt, chilli-oil and fennel, roasted on charcoal, £13.50, being the most popular dish ordered. Mains include duck, partridge or quails. We certainly rate Vama's and are delighted to keep it in our **TOP 100.** Good weather seating outside on the patio: four tables to choose from. Entertainments: cabaret and belly dancer. Service 12.5%. Cover charge £1. Hours: 12.30-3/6.30-11.30.

London SW11

Battersea

BATTERSEA VILLAGE RICKSHAW

15- Battersea Square, SW11 020 7924 2450

'Had very good meal, just after it opened a few years ago. Very pleasing to find it still really good, particularly welcoming atmosphere. Large buffet of special Bengali dishes, many diners choosing, certainly good value £15 a head. We were tempted by the menu. All food very good in quality, cooking and quantity. Small grumble: chicken served in very large chunks, a bit tough. A large plus, one of the best wine lists we have seen in Indian restaurant, superb bottle of French white wine (£31.90) a real treat. Outstandingly good, smiley, helpful service made the biggest difference, unfortunately all too rare.' HC. Hours: 7-12pm Monday-Saturday. Branches: SW8, SW12 and SW20.

London SW12

Balham

BOMBAY BICYCLE CLUB

95 Nightingale Lane, SW12 020 8673 6217

See previous entry. Great logo of a turbaned Raj-style waiter holding a serving dish while riding a penny farthing. Known to some as the BBC! *'Something wonderfully luxurious, elegant decor, massive vase of flowers dominates the room, charming staff, starched white tablecloths and napkins. In the winter, it's cosy and snug, in the summer the windows and doors are thrown open, the colonial ceiling fans whir, and it all looks extremely pretty.'* RL. Hours: 7-12 Monday to Saturday. Branches: SW8, SW11 and SW20.

NANGLO

88 Balham Hill Road, SW12 020 8673 4160

Fully licensed and air conditioned. One of the few Nepalese restaurants in the country actually serving authentic Nepalese food. Starters include (all £2.70): Shekpa Soup, noodles, chicken, lamb and spices. Tareko Chyau, mushrooms covered with spice lamb mince. Soaltee Alu, potato patty, lentils, onions, herbs, cooked on flat iron plate, served with sweet yoghurt. Main courses:

Khorsani Chicken or Lamb £5.70, fiery dish with fresh green chillies, ginger and spices. Nepalese Sam £7.70, noodles with chicken, lamb, vegetables, served with side sauce. Fewa Fish £8.50, spicy salmon, medium hot. Pahelo Pharsi £3.50 - pumpkin, tomato and onion. *'I am a retired Major - 6th Gurkha Rifles, who lived in Nepal for 5 years. The food we had was authentic Nepalese, very tasty, large portions. Service excellent. A clean, fresh and modern decor (no garish painting of Mount Everest! All staff Nepalese. Head chef is Anand Kumar Gurung who is cultural secretary of the Yeti Nepal Association in the UK.'* JT. Hours: 12-2.30/6-11.30, Friday and Saturday to 12, Sunday to 11.

TABAQ ©
BEST PAKISTANI AWARD 2004/5 TOP 100

47 Balham Hill, SW12 020 8673 7820

From the outside, it looks slightly like a cafe – the sort of place that serves lovely iced maderia cake with Earl Grey tea. However, inside it is a very comfortable, cosy restaurant, with pink linen table cloths and napkins and just 50 seats. Lovely stylish, traditionally hand-made embroidered wall-coverings hang all around the room, depicting scenes from Lahore. Little bottles of Perrier appear on every table, along with Tabaq's special menu which includes their famous, whole, marinated and stuffed baby lamb, apparently enough to feed fourteen people – lucky them!
Tabaq is owned by the brothers Ahmed. Mushtaq runs front-of-house. Manoor is head chef, and the culinary magic emanates from him and his brigade. But don't expect quick food from him. He cooks everything freshly, and a 30-minute wait is not uncommon. The menu is pure Lahori cuisine. Lahore, now in Pakistan, was once one of four major palace cities, resided in by rotation by the great Moghul emperors, rather in the way that QEII rotates round Buck Pal, Windsor, Sandringham and Balmoral. Agra, Delhi and Srinagar in Kashmir were the others, all linked by still-extant tree-lined trunk roads. Lahore is famous for its cuisine. *'After greetings were over with M and M, we settled down with Popadoms and the menu. Tabaq is a Pakistani restaurant, but the brothers are from Kenya, so the cooking is different from your average high street 'Indian'. After a quick glance down the starters, I stopped at Aubergine Pakora.*

That's the one for me, I thought. Four lovely, big slices of augerbine, covered in a spicy and very crispy batter were served with a delicate julienned salad and its own little pot of yoghurt dip - delicious. Pat plumped for Lamb Kebabs. I had given up eating kebabs (except for my own of course), because they are invariably disappointing, being fatty and chewy, with little bits of sinews getting taught between teeth and being an irritating distraction for the rest of the meal. My own kebabs are 'Katori' meaning 'silk' which melt in the mouth and that's because I go to the considerable effort to mince my own meat and pick out by hand (a tedious job) all the gristle etc which I dislike so much. However, Tabaq kebabs, were four perfectly shaped kebabs, served from a sizzler with salad, and they were very good indeed, being well ground with unwanted matter removed. For our mains, I chose Murghi Makhani - chicken slices in a saffron coloured, creamy, butter sauce. Not my usual choice, but I knew it would be properly cooked here and I intended to spice it up with chillies (much to the dismay of the chef). It was wonderful and worked really well with my tiny slices of fresh green chilli. Pat leapt upon Palak Lamb – one of his favourites, it was exceptionally good. Very tender chunks of lamb (no chewy pieces), well cooked with spinach, lovely. We chose Jeerawallah Aloo, Plain Rice, superb and hot Fenugreek Paratha, thinly rolled and fried in butter – fantastic Brandy and coffee finished a perfect meal.' DBAC. Hours: 12-2.45 /6-11.45; closed Sunday.

London SW14

Mortlake, Putney, Sheen

TASTE OF THE RAJ

130 Upper Richmond Road West, SW14
020 8876 8271

A typically well-managed Bangladeshi formula curry house, owned by the charming and personable Shawkat Ahmed, which has been operating for years and producing a highly popular formula at reasonable prices. Such venues form the backbone of this *Guide*, up and down the country, and are much-loved locals enjoyed weekly by their regulars. There is little more to say about such venues. Lunch and dinner daily.

London SW15

Putney

BANGLADESH CURRY MAHAL

NEW ENTRANT 

294 Upper Richmond Road, SW15 020 8788 7880

Even old hands (est 1971) can appear for the first time in this *Guide*. You've asked for this one, so here it is. Fully licensed. Air-conditioned. *'Delicious Shami Kebab £3.30 and Mulligatawny Soup £1.80. Hot and tasty, Lamb Sajhani £8.95, Mushroom Rice £2.95, Tarka Dall £3 and Keema Nan £2.25 – all beautifully served. Newly refurbished restaurant, making to very open and modern. Portions a little small.'* DAB. Specials: Chicken Cutlet £3.50. Duck Bhoona £5.90. Carrot Nan £2.10. Service charge: 10%. Hours: 1-2.30/6-12. Friday closed.

GHARANA NEW ENTRANT

4 Chelverton Road, SW15 020 8788 3182

'Spicy and Plain Popadoms with a Pickle Tray which included coconut. Thoroughly enjoyed Murgh Tikka Peshwari £5.95, a first for us. Pickle King Prawn £12.95 with Tarka Dal - wonderful roasted flavour, Mushroom Rice and Keema Nan. Portions just right, we were comfortably filled.' DAB. Menu extracts: Murgh Chilli Masala £4.95,chicken, fresh ginger, garlic and green pepper, medium hot. Achar Gosht £5.95, marinated lamb, pickle masala and green chilli, spicy. Knoju Pappaas £5.95, with smoky tamarind and coconut milk. Anardana All £2.95, saute potatoes cooked with pomegranate masala. Kulcha-e-Lasson £2.25, leavened bread stuffed with fresh garlic, onion and coriander. Lunch and dinner daily.

JUST INDIA NEW ENTRANT

193 Lower Richmond Road, SW15 020 8785 6004

Chef Vasaikar worked at Bombay's Oberoi then to the UK as deputy head chef of Chutney Mary and then head chef of Veeraswamy. He became chef-partner here. We'd written a glowing entry for this venue, then just before going to print we found he walked following a partner row. The area is not devoid of Indian talent, but just where Just India will end up depends on you, so reports please.

MA GOA TOP 100

244 Upper Richmond Road, SW15
020 8780 1767

Opened in 1993 by the Kapoor family. Deepak looks after the diners, while Sushma is the chef. In fact she's his mum, so easy on the Ma Goa gags! The restaurant seats 50 in a rustic atmosphere – wooden floors, whitewashed walls and Goan art. Goa is one of India's 24 states, not a country in its own right, as some think. It is on the western coast of India and, because it was Portuguese for nearly 500 years, it inherited different characteristics from the rest of India, including a small pork-eating, Christian population. Goan cooks were prized in the Raj (because they would handle beef and pork and could cook well). Until a few decades ago, Goan cooks were frequently to be found in merchant ships. In the 1960s Goa was 'discovered' by hippies, and more recently, it has been 'discovered' by holiday companies offering the cheap package at formerly beautiful, exclusive, caring hotels. Goan food is rarely found in Britain. And what of Sushma's food? As a regular visitor to Goa, I can vouch that it's as near to home-cooking as it gets. Goan food is unique, having that Portuguese influence – any meat goes and pork is the favourite, as is the chilli. Good examples at Ma Goa are Goa Sausage £4, (Chorizo) pork meat sausage with cinnamon, cloves, garlic, palm vinegar and red chilli, topped with spicy onion salsa, and Porco Vindaloo £8.65, this is the real thing, based on the Portuguese dish, Vinho d'alhos. In the Goan version, pork is marinated with palm (toddy) vinegar, garlic and roasted spices and plenty of red Goan chillies. It is then slow-cooked to achieve maximum penetration of flavours. Ma Goa serve it in traditional earthenware. Offal, beef, chicken and vegetable dishes prevail e.g. Sorpotel £4 starter,£7 main (lambs liver, kidney and pork in rich sauce with lime and coriander), Cha Cha's Beef Fry £8.25 (beef marinated in spices, then fried with onions, chilli and potato), Fish Caldin £8.75 (chunks of fish with coconut, palm vinegar, mustard seeds, kokum and curry leaves). The daily specials board makes this restaurant an adventure. Goan delights, with unique names such as Cafreal, Balachao, Assado, Temperado, Buffado, and Recheiado all appear at one time or another. Advice is forthcoming. *'If you ask for Goan heat, you'll get it hot! For loonies like Pat, look under side orders and accompaniments for Taliwi Mirch £1 (fried green chillies in mustard oil). There are even Goan puds, such as Bebinca, a heavily sugared egg layer-cake, with cashew nuts — fantastic but sickly!'* DBAC. But a word of caution. Please be patient. Sushma will not be hurried in the kitchen. Relax with their chilled Portuguese Vinho Verde wine, and nibble something while you wait for your order to be cooked. No complaints at all. This is typical. *'Deserves its place in the* **TOP 100** *and should be in the upper half. Had one of the best evenings we have ever had. Decor and general feel is not obviously Indian. Cosmopolitan waiting staff, definitely the sort of restaurant to enjoy the whole evening. Interesting food, good portions, well presented and fabulous. Faultless service and atmosphere. Mature clientele. Not cheap, but reasonable, superb for the value – £59 for two. Slight drawback, only one ladies loo – not enough for full restaurant.'* HC. *'Preferred the decor here to Sarkhel's, much more cosy and far less formal. I found the food excellent, but Sarkhel's had the edge; my son disagreed with me. Service was top notch and represented excellent value for money.'* CC. Service 12.5%. Takeaway: 10% discount. Hours: 12.30–2.30, Tuesday to Friday, Sat. to 3.30. Dinner 6-11. (10pm Sunday).

MUNAL 

393 Upper Richmond Road, SW15 020 8876 3083

Khem Ranamagar established his 65-seater in 1991. You'll find at least 100 of your favourites here. But this is Nepalese and the 'always-polite' crew would love you to try some of chef Bijaya Thapa's few Nepalese items on the menu, such as the starter Momo, £2.95, meat dumpling with tomato chutney. Or Sadheko Meat or chicken £2.95, marinated, cooked, served hot, mixed into a salad and quite spicy. Nepalese mains include Meat or Chicken Bhutuwa, £6.90, a dry-fried dish. *'This restaurant is where I took my wife on our first dinner date together,'* says RAC. *'A frosty evening but welcome was as warm as ever. Chicken Pakora and Dal Soup, served hot and spicy. Butter King Prawn (huge) Masala, Boiled Rice, Tarka Dal and Keema Nan. Only grumble, Dal was cold.' 'I just thought to tell you about my daughter's wedding reception. We agreed on a three course meal with a set menu for 45 people and champagne. The starter was Chicken Tikka, Prawns and Vegetable Samosa. The main course was a buffet style serve yourself affair. The choice was Chicken Tikka Masala, Lamb Bhutuwa and a beautiful Masala Fish Curry. Also Tarka Daal, Rice and a wide selection of Naan breads. Dessert was a wedding cake provided by us but fruit salad and coffee was available. The cost of this was £650 which included all drinks from the bar and seven bottles of champagne.'* DAB. Minimum charge £10. Delivery: £12 min, 3-mile radius. Hours: 12-2.30/6-11.30 (12 Sat & Sun).

London SW16

Norbury, Streatham, Streatham Hill

MIRCH MASALA BYO

1416 London Road, SW16 020 8679 1828

Est 1997, Mirch Masala, 'pepper mixture', is an offspring of the ever-popular Karahi King, where meat is king, cutlery is out (OK, limpets can have a knife and fork) and BYO is in, no corkage charge. This unlicensed café is pleasant, light and bright, air-conditioned and seats 70. Open kitchen, with unusual Kenyan-Asian specials by owner Raza Ali's brigade, who delight in bringing their own cooking straight to the horse's mouth – yours that is. Great theatre, enhanced by high decibel Bangra and lively diners. Cassava chips (mogo) can substitute for popadoms, Patra £2.50, Kebabs 70p. Wide selection of dechi (saucepan) or karahi dishes, kebabs and all the trimmings. Main course: Karahi Methi Gosht/Murgh £4.50 (lamb/chicken with fenugreek leaves) – can't imagine a Punjabi restaurant without this dish. Good veggie stuff, too. How about Karahi Valpapdi Baigan, £4, or Matoki, plantain curry. Set lunch: £5 for veg, £6 non-veg, served from 12-4. Credit cards accepted. Hours: 12-12 daily. Branch: Mirch Masala Takeaway Lavender Hill SW17.

SHAHEE BHEL POORI VEGAN 

1547 London Road, SW16 020 8679 6275

Lebas Miah's licensed 75-seater, opposite Norbury Station, serves Gujarati vegetarian and some south Indian dishes. As you can see on *page 50*, there is a wide range of goodies in this style of

©	Curry Club Discount	U	Unlicensed
V	Vegetarian	ANP	Alcohol not permitted
e-a-m-a-y-l	Eat as much as you like	BYO	Bring your own alcohol

cooking. Thalis and Dosas are still, we hear, the most popular dishes served. Specials include Chappati Chana (hot), chick peas marinated in a balanced blend of spices and sauce, served with green coriander. Bhel poori (cold), delicious mixture of Indian savouries blended with spices and exotic sauces which make this dish unique. Dahi Vada (Bhalle) (cold), spicy black-pea-flour fritters, with yoghurt and sweet and sour sauce, all £1.75. Rava Onion Dosa, a crispy onion vegetable pancake stuffed with delicately spiced potatoes, served with coconut chutney and Sambar, £4.10. Hours: 12-2.30./6-11. Sunday buffet.

SHAMYANA BYO ©

437 Streatham High Rd, SW16 020 8679 6162

Another good value Pakistani Punjabi caff, opened by Mohammed Tanveer in 1998. No frills. Seats a huge 130 in two rooms, black-and-white tiled floor, enormous menu, some 130 dishes, cooked in an open kitchen. Starters: Masala Fish (white fish in spicy sauce), Dhal Bhajia (spiced lentils deep-fried in chicken pea dough), Zeera Chicken Wings £2.50 (wings marinated in spicy sauce). Main courses: Masala Karella Gosht (lamb cubes cooked with bitter melon), Ginger Chicken, Lamb Biriani (chunks of lamb with stock flavouring the rice). Daily specials. Delivery: 3-mile radius, £14 min. Service 10%. 50 space car park at rear. Sunday buffet: 12-6pm, £5.50. Set lunch: £5. Service 10%. Hours: 12-12.

London SW17

Tooting

Upper Tooting Road (UTR) has reached a maturity, though with less street (pavement) trading than Southall. For years, the area has reflected the varied roots of its Asian population. In the half a mile, between Tooting Bec and Tooting Broadway tube stations, there are restaurants serving nearly every style of authentic food from the subcontinent. Nowhere else in the world has such variety cheek by jowl. South Indian restaurants include Sree Krishna, 192 UTR, Radha Krishna Bhavan, 86, and Kolam, 58. There are now more than one Sri Lankan outlets, the best of which is still Jaffna at the Broadway. Milan, 158 UTR and Gossip, 180 are two Gujarati vegetarian havens, and largely vegetarian Kenyan Asian food is to be found at Kadiri, 32 UTR, and Kastoori, 188, while at Masaladar, 121, you get this food plus Bhel Poori and meat curries alike. Handis, 164 and Lahore Karahi at the Broadway are Pakistan and fill the carnivore gap, Southall-style. As if that were not enough there are two formula Bangladeshi curry houses, the Peacock, 242, Calcutta Indian, 116, and Raja, 169. Veggy Indian sweet and snack takeaways include Ambala, 48, and Alaudin, 98, with Royal beyond UTR (north of Tooting Bec). The shops are getting better and more varied. Competition is rife with more and more excellent rivals opening, all displaying their wares on UTR itself, many until late, every day including Sundays. Sakoni, 204-208 UTR, is still the best Asian veg shop in London and there is no better Asian grocer than next-door Dadus, 210. There are several Sri Lankan grocers too. Utensils shops, sari boutiques and halal butchers have sprung up too. My prediction that parking would become impossible has come to pass. But with the tube so convenient, UTR is an all-day curryholic's theme park. Here's more detail:

HANDIS

164 Upper Tooting Road, SW17 020 8672 6037

A 60-seater Pakistani restaurant owned by Mrs S Sheikh and managed by Mr J Sheikh. Cooking is down one entire side. The Handi is a cooking pot, and dishes are served either in this or in the karahi. It's kebabs, tikkas, tandoori meat and chicken dishes in which this type of venue excels. There are a number of Punjabi-style vegetable dishes, such as Aloo Sag, and well cooked side dishes. One correspondent loves their chupattis. CT. Hours: 11-11.

JAFFNA HOUSE TOP 100

90 High Street, SW17 020 8672 7786

For those who must have meaty tandoori items and north-Indian curries, you've got your own side entrance and dining room, with food cooked by Aziz and Kannan. I've no idea how good it is; but do enjoy (and tell us about it, if you like). Where the serious palates boldly go (through the front door) is into K Sivalogarajah's and M Sivanandan's Tooting Broadway place, which built its name on its authentic, no compromise, chilli hot (as-it-should-be) Sri Lankan and south-Indian dishes with its particularly popular different Friday, Saturday and Sunday specials. Tastebud-tantalising stuff like Vadai – gram flour doughnut, drenched in home made yoghurt and sprinkled with garam and (if you are lucky) chopped fresh green chilli, Masala Dosa £1.50 – must be one of the cheapest in the country. Sri Lankan specials are delightful, with Pat's benchmark crab curry scoring really high because it was searingly hot, and used fresh crab. *'Wow!! this was the second* **TOP 100** *restaurant in 24 hours... lucky or what?!'* [Yes] *'and we didn't break £50! I have LOVED this restaurant/cafe for years, eight or nine at least. It remains magnificent value for wonderful food. Potato Bondas and Onion Bhajia simply the best, and this before we got to Mushroom Curry, Chana Curry, Coconut Rice – fragrant and so light, almost floated off the plate! Vegetable Kottho – substantial, full of fresh vegetables. Curries clearly freshly prepared, very chilli-hot, just beautiful. We were stuffed full, long before we finished the food... all for £9!! Wonderful!!!'* AG. *'We holidayed in Sri Lanka and were longing to try the food again. Starters were the best – delicious Masala Dosa and lovely spicy Devilled Chicken which was very reminiscent of the food we had sampled in Sri Lanka. Chicken and String Hoppers, but they came all mixed together, which made it taste a bit like vermicelli or chow mein – anyway I shall definitely try again.'* NP. Set lunch: £4 and £5, served from 12-3. Hours: 12-11pm.

KADIRI

32 Upper Tooting Road, SW17 020 8672 0710

A Kenyan Asian licensed restaurant, it does tandooris, kebabs, and regular curries and all the trimmings. If East African food is new to you, dip into Cassava chips (mogo) with imli as a good substitute for popadams, served with authentic imli, sweet and sour tamarind chutney. Fried fish Masala, Tali Hui Jinga, breadcrumbed, deep-fried prawns, and Tandoori King fish, that tasty fish so loved in south India, are three unusual starters. Jeera chicken or butter chicken are *'just like the Brilliant's'* (*see* Southall Middlesex) according to one scribe (AN), while another (BD) was *'smitten by the biriani.'*

KASTOORI PURE VEGETARIAN

188 Upper Tooting Road, SW17 020 8767 7027

The Thanki family hail from Kenya and specialise in both Gujarati and Kenyan vegetarian dishes. The former include Vegetable Samosas, Dahi Vadas, Kadhi (yoghurt and besan sauce, with dumplings), and Katia Wahd, a tomato-based curry. Karela Bharah is stuffed bitter gourd. The latter gives Cassava Chips, Chilli Banana, £4.50 (green banana stuffed with chillies and served with pickle), Kasodi, £4.50 (sweetcorn in a peanut and yoghurt-based sauce), and Matoki, plantain curry. Their Bhel Poori is a crunchy snip at £2.50, and this is one of the few places where you can experience Bhatura, giant puri bread, £1, which puffs up to balloon-size when deep-fried. Thali curry selection is extraordinary. Vegan dishes. Hours: 12.30-2.30 (Mon. & Tues. closed)/6-10.30, daily.

KOLAM BYO ©

58 Upper Tooting Road SW17 020 8767 2514

Established in 1982 by S Rajakumar. Seats 52 in one long thin dining room. The food is authentic South Indian, as they have it in Tamil Nadu, plus standard north Indian items. Service is very friendly, albeit at freeze-frame slowness. Mañana is far too fast, which reminds one greatly of India. Patience will reward you with a good inexpensive meal, and, as ever, go for the South Indian delights, which is what they know best. **BYO** is allowed: £1 corkage. Hours: 12-2.30, Tues.-Sun./6-11pm, daily (12pm on Sat.).

LAHORE KARAHI BYO

1 High Street, SW17 020 8767 2477

This Tooting Broadway Karahi-house has been open since late 1995. Stand at the counter and order your takeaway – if you plan to eat in, sit down and wait to be served, with the cooking on view. Typical Pakistani Kebab House menu. Starters include: Masala Fish, chunks of marinated fish, fried. Sheek Kebabs. Main courses: Chicken Jalfrezi. Veggies might try the Karahi Karela, bitter gourd, Methi Aloo or saag Paneer. Cash preferred. No credit cards. Unlicensed, no corkage. Average meal £10. Hours: 12-12.

MASALEDAR ANP

121 Upper Tooting Road, SW17 020 8767 7676

What lies behind the smart frontage with its smoky plate-glass window? 25 more seats than last time. Terracotta tiles on split-level floors. Plants in pots and trailing leaves. Smart up-lighters behind large halved karahis. You can sit outside watching all this through that window, at the five pavement tables. Service is slow, but they really do cook it fresh to order in the open kitchen. Many old favourites on the menu, all good. Starters include Bhel Poori, and Mandazi, samosa-shaped deep-fried bread with an African-Asian name, both £1.50. Mains: *'Rich, vivid Punjabi-type curries. Ginger Chicken and Methi Gosht very good. Cumin-flavoured Pilaw Rice (just like you get in Rusholme). Reasonable prices, thoroughly recommended.'* JR. Seek out the unusual: Dekchi Gosht, Halal mutton, on-the-bone, slow-cooked in a metal-waisted cooking utensil without handles. Strict Muslim rules apply and BYO is not permitted. Credit cards accepted. Hours: 12-12.

MILAN VEGETARIAN ©

158 Upper Tooting Road, SW17 020 8767 4347

Taj Mehta's vegetarian café is just the sort of place we like to recommend. It's unpretentious, unexpectedly licensed and air-conditioned. But for the vegetarian, what more could you ask for? If I were you, I'd ask for popadams and their adorable fresh home-made relishes. Next I'd ask for their fabulous Bhel Poori. I'd avoid the Masala Dosa (they do it better at Sree Krishna), and I'd go for its subtly-spiced Gujarati curries, made largely from besan flour and yoghurt, spiced with turmeric and curry leaves. If it's new to you, ask for help. The dish of the day is always a good option. And do try the fresh Rotla (millet bread). Leave some room for the terrific Indian sweets on display. And buy some fresh 'Bombay mix' items. For a complete filling meal, try the Thali – a good selection of vegetarian curries including something sweet for pudding – at £6 a real feast. *'Another good one'* SM. Minimum charge still a ridiculous £2. Average meal under £10. Takes no credit cards so cash preferred. Sunday lunch £5.75. Hours: 10-10.

PEACOCK TANDOORI 

242 Upper Tooting Road, SW17 020 8672 8770

When this 50-seater Bangladeshi curry house opened in 1988, Tooting's current crop of fine authentic restaurants didn't exist. But the Peacock has stood the test of time. Owned and managed by Mr Yogi Anand, [he's heard all the bear jokes.]it does the formula to a high standard. But look for the unusual, for example, Paneer Pakora (curd cheese, dipped in spiced gram batter and fried), Brinjal Pakora (sliced brinjal coated with batter and fried, served with salad) as starters. Mains: Sag Kamal Kakri £4.25 (lotus roots cooked with spinach and onion), Batair e Khas £7.65 (quails in mild curry sauce with fresh coriander). Weekend buffet £7 (under 12, half price). Service 10%. Takeaway: 10% discount. Hours: 6-12.

RADHA KRISHNA BHAVAN TOP 100

86 Tooting High Street, SW17 020 8682 0969

This restaurant was opened in 1999 by H.K.Haridas, an experienced Keralan restaurateur, following a partnership row at the Sree Krishna. Haridas got the head chef and set up this Krishna down the road. It specialises in South Indian Keralan cuisine, with dishes from the cities of Cochin, Malabar and Travancore. Have the Rasam (hot and spicy soup, with floating slivers of garlic, curry leaves and a red chilli! – this is a DBAC benchmark, which if she doesn't get hiccups, it's not hot enough for her!), Masala Dosa, Sambar and Coconut Chutney are as good as it gets. Some have that choice for starters and go on to curries. I don't know how they do it. I'm too full for it. But the curries are worth trying. You can stay vegetarian if you like. All their vegetable curries are spot on. Contrary to popular belief, meat, chicken and fish dishes are commonplace. Even the Chicken Korma (if you must) is given the South Indian touch – creamy, coconut with ground almond. But don't forget the wonderful Lamb Cutlets £4.50 (patties of spicy minced lamb, bread crumbed and fried, served with tomato sauce and salad), King Prawn Fry £7.90 (with ginger, garlic, spices and sliced coconut), Malabar Chicken £7.50 (with coconut, curry leaves, garlic and mustard), Spinach Vadai £3 (fried crunchy doughnut of channa dal, green chillies, onion, ginger, curry leaves and fresh spinach served with chutneys). And if you have any room left Banana Leaf Cake £4 – rice with sweet filling of coconut, banana and jaggery wrapped in banana leaf and steamed – divine. Min charge: £6. Service 10%. Licensed. Credit cards accepted. Hours: 12-3/6-11 (Fri. & Sat. to 12am).

SREE KRISHNA TOP 100 

192-194 Tooting High Street, SW17
020 8672 4250

This was the original Tooting Krishna restaurant. And now there are three (*see* Rhada above and Vijaya). Regular readers know it's a regular haunt of ours, involving a round-trip of 90 miles. Last time we asked whether Tooting can support all three Krishnas. It isn't that Sri Krishna has changed much, and maybe that's it's problem. We get complaints [I think from Krishna virgins] about it being tatty. But that's what it's all about. What do they think India's like? I don't want a Lawrence Lewellyn-Bowen make-over here. Tat isn't dirt, and Sree isn't dirty. Service, is just fine; accurate and pleasant, and they're used to full houses (120 seats). The menu offers all the same south Indian items as Rhada, and this Krishna cooks them just as competently and accurately. To me there's too much curry house food being dispensed. Blame the customers for demanding it, I suppose, but they should go the the Peacock, and leave the Krishna to do what they do best, which is anything South Indian, and preferably vegetarian. It's more satisfying than any carnivore realises. So read the caveat, and note we retain its **TOP 100** cachet. Service 10%. Credit cards accepted. Hours: 12-3/6-11; Sun.-Thurs. (12am on Fri. & Sat). *See page* 11.

VIJAYA KRISHNA 

114 Mitcham Road, SW17 020 8767 7688

The third Krishna in the trilogy opened in 1995 by Vijayan Mullath; he also manages front of house at his 40-seater and keeps a watchful eye on the kitchen, where he poached the sous chef from Sree Krishna at the time of the partnership row. His restaurant is decorated with scenes of South India. The Keralan specialities don't disappoint. Popular authentic dishes such as Masala Dosai, a light rice flour pancake, rolled over a firm, gently spiced potato curry, Avial, a fluid curry made with yoghurt and mixed vegetables, and Sambar, a runny lentil curry containing, if you are lucky, many drumsticks, with which you are to scrap the flesh off with your teeth – lovely says DBAC, who also enjoyed Kozhi Varutha Curry, chicken in garlic and coriander sauce, and Green Banana Bhajia are served. Delivery: 2-mile radius, £12 min. Service: 10%. Hours: 12-3/6-11 (Fri. & Sat. to 11.30).

London SW18

Earlsfield, Southfields, Wandsworth

CALCUTTA NOTEBOOK
NEW TO OUR TOP 100

201 Replingham Road, SW18 020 8870 1483

Opened late 2003 in the adjacent unit to Sarkhel's is the latest edition to their restaurant empire. But it is not Sarkhel's – it is quite separate, it has its own identity, entrance, waiters and bar. All that connects it to Sarkhel's is a serving hatch near the bar. It has been individually decorated with a style of its own, and is fairly compact, seating around 20 diners. Seating on wooden chairs, upholstered in rich chocolate brown leather or banquette. Unseen by the public, Sarkhel's kitchens have been enlarged, and serve both restaurants enabling Udit to pop his head around the kitchen door now and again with a smile and a wave. Calcutta Notebook serves Bengali food. Let Udit explain: *'It's my long-waiting dream, culminating three generations of Sarkhel culinary passion. My grandmother's classical East Bengali cuisine, my mother's frugal and wholesome West Bengali cooking, and my interpretation of both their magic comes to life as a very personal expression in my Calcutta Notebook.'* We already had reports. This one is our favourite. *'My ample size bears testimony to the fact that food is my passion. In a city that prides itself on hospitality, few restaurants can surpass the warmth of Calcutta Notebook.*

Distinguished by the outstanding cooking and lively turn it gives familiar dishes the cutting edge of traditional Bengali cooking. Comfortable and innovative, a true original. It was one of the most delightful personal dining experiences that I have had in London. While Curry has made its mark in UK and we have a Balti or Karahi at every street, it would actually be impossible to locate a Bengali restaurant. One has to be careful not to confuse with the Bangladeshi cuisine. I hope you take time to visit the place and would be delighted to know of your views on it.' AD. Happy to oblige, Avishek. This is deputy Ed's (DBAC) report on our first visit. *'We sat down and without asking, three plain Popadoms, sprinkled with freshly scraped coconut flesh, chilli powder, finely chopped green chilli and coriander leaves were served. A delicious original pointer to what was to come. The menu is a concise definition of Bengali food. We chose Mochar Chop, potato croquettes filled with tender chopped banana flowers, and Chicken Kobirahi, chicken fried in frilly egg batter and served with red onion chutney, both £3.75. We shared both dishes and enjoyed them very much especially the Chop. In fact, the banana flower stuffing was so delicious, you could be forgiven for thinking it minced meat! For mains I dithered between Panthar Jhol, goat on the bone, and Gol-barir Kosha Mangsho pot roasted, well marinated lamb with a piece of liver and potato, both £7.50 I eventually decided on the latter, accompanied by plain rice. My only criticism was that the potato was a little on the firm side for my taste, otherwise it was quite delicious. Pat chose one of his all-time favourites, crab in the form of Kakrar Jhal £8.95, chilli-hot blue swimming-crab and green onion stew.' The specimens arrived, concealed in a large lidded karahi. The body and legs were all intact and needed to be 'cracked'. Pat had no option but to go in with both hands. Quite a messy job eating a crab and time consuming. He spent a wonderful hour licking sauce from the shell and sucking the flesh from its claws. [this dish is not one to eat when you're trying to impress or entertain]. Side orders of Cholar Dal £3.50, split Bengal gram with five spices and sweet coconut, made a good change from my usual. It had a floury taste, with firm texture and the delicate chunks of fresh coconut gave it a wholesome feel. Veronica insisted that Pat tried the Luchi £1.95 – fried light and ballooned out Bengali bread. Made from white flour, they were so soft and delicate, perfect for mopping up the sauce from the crab.'* DBAC. It's another innovative idea, which simply makes us wish we lived in Wimbledon. Hours" 12-2.30 / 6-10.30. Cooked-to-order snack menu available 12-6. Welcome to our **TOP 100.**

SARKHEL'S TOP 100
OUTSTANDING RESTAURANT AWARD 2004/5

199 Replingham Road, SW18 020 8870 1483

When the country's top Indian chef gave up the top job and set up on his own in 1997, our hearts stopped. Udit Sarkhel was, for over a decade, Exec Chef at the BB, SW7. He wanted more freedom and was prepared to take the risk. He has a secret weapon; his delightful Chinese wife, Veronica, once managed the Taj Bombay's flagship restaurant, the Tanjore. They chose an unfashionable part of SW, in a tiny shop front on a yellow-lined, outside curve of a bend on a busy road. People in the industry tut-tutted, saying it was crazy and doomed. But they underestimated the couple's drive and sheer competence. Clearly, the venue had to cater for locals first, who would become regulars. Only after that could they hope to attract a wider clientele and the major critics. Within a year, their business was solid enough for them to get the two units next door doubling the seating to 72. As if that was not enough, the Sarkhel's next opened Dalchini, a unique Indian-Chinese restaurant in 2001 (*see* SW19), and in 2003 another unit alongside the original became available. Rather than expand Sarkhel's, they have opened an independent unit which they've called Calcutta Notebook. (*see previous entry*). We have had numerous good reports about Sarkhel's. We do get a few who are not au-fait with the Sarkhel style: *'First new place we visited on strength of Guide. Ironically, I was very impressed by everything but food! Lovely atmosphere, superb service. Friendly and helpful staff who recommended a starter instead of Popadom, something with chickpeas, very good. However, rest of food wasn't impressive as expected. Spinach Curry – creamy, excellent. I'll give it one more try.* NP. *'Outstanding in every respect but the decor which although extremely smart and tasteful, I found a trifle cold. Maybe it was because it was early evening and we were their first customers. However, the management were on hand and gave us an extra dish on the house for us to try, which was a very nice gesture.'* CC. *'Proving that Udit is a cookaholic, the regular menu is frequently augmented with one of his regular food festivals, examining the regions of India. We went for the Hyderabad festival. We ate lightly fried plain Popadoms with three small pots of Chutney – including chilled concoction of smoked aubergine and coconut –*

©	Curry Club Discount	**U**	Unlicensed
V	Vegetarian	**ANP**	Alcohol not permitted
e-a-m-a-y-l	Eat as much as you like	**BYO**	Bring your own alcohol

deliciously different. Pat always enjoys Udit's Chettinand Shrimps. More up my street are Shrikampuri Kebabs – two melt-in-the-mouth round patties of minced meat, stuffed with slices of boiled egg, served with onion rings, wedges of lemon and an ample pot of Podina Chutney – wonderful! You don't see 'billy-goat-gruff' on the menu often – but that's what we ate for main course, Goat Curry, on-the-bone, with another unusual curry, rabbit, served with scrubbed new potatoes and baby carrots, large joints of delicious juicy white meat, again on the bone smothered in a rich spicy sauce. We decided against rice, and ate Roti and Potato stuffed Paratha – fantastic.' DBAC. Essential to book. Continues with its **TOP AWARD** winning status. Hours: 12-2.30 / 6-10.30, Tuesday to Sunday. Closed Monday.

TANIM'S TAKEAWAY

232 Earlsfield Road, SW18 020 8877 1990

NP tells us *'The food is up to scratch, but beware of price shenanigans ie: automatically charging extra for chicken breast, when there is no other type of chicken available. When I protested, the charge was removed but it shouldn't have been on in the first place. The menu also lists various special deals 'for limited period', a very limited period since they generally seem to be unavailable on any day with a 'y' in it. You'll also notice from the menu that it claims a Master Chef award from the Curry Club.'* NP. We need to address this. Firstly we don't have anything to do with *Masterchef*, which sells their award to any restaurant which cares to buy it. – whereas ours is given free of charge. Secondly it isn't in the 2001 *Good Curry Guide* It isn't correct for any restaurant to associates itself with us except via us. It nearly got Tanim's the chop, and it will if the persist with their shenanigans] NP goes on *'I still rate it as the best formula curry house I know – most dishes are excellent and I've been through much of the menu. Portions range from generous to huge. Prices are high for a takeaway – £4 Chicken Korma, £5 Chicken Jalfrezi, but well worth it.'* NP. Chef's Specials include: Butter Chicken Tikka £4.95, Murghi Masala £4.95, diced tandoori chicken, minced meat, egg and tomato, medium spiced. Hours: 5.30-12.

London SW19

Wimbledon

AHMED

2 The Broadway, SW19 020 8946 6214

'Decent, cheap restaurant serving good formula curries. Popped in on off-chance. Condiments with Popadoms were different, including coconut and delicious tomato and raitha. A good start. Chicken Tandoori – very tasty. Mushroom Bhajee – good as was my girl friend's Chicken Korma. With a Nan, two beers came to £24 inc service. Polite and friendly service. NP.

DALCHINI NEW TO OUR TOP 100

147 Arthur Road, SW19 020 8947 5966

Almost opposite Wimbledon Park Underground station (so parking difficult) this is a Chinese restaurant, but it's no ordinary Chinese. Dalchini (meaning Chinese cinnamon) serves Indo-Chinese. If you've never experienced Bombay's most popular dining-out food, you must do it. Called Hakka Chinese cuisine, this is where you'll find it and it is Britain's only restaurant serving it. Hakka means 'Guest People.' As with everywhere else in the world, there have been Chinese living in India for over two millennia, but Indian civilisation predated that, so the new immigrants were guests. Cochin, that beautiful Keralan seaboard town means 'Chinatown', and uses its famous Chinese fishing nets to this day. Cochin was the major port for Indo-Chinese trade from Roman times and for centuries until the demise of the Silk route. Over time, these Chinese settlers, merged their Oriental style of cooking with Indian ingredients. Nothing personifies this marriage more than the husband and wife team of owners Udit and Veronica Sarkhel – him Indian, her – Hakka Chinese, raised in Bombay. So is her uncle, Johnny Chang, who is the super-smooth front of house manager (he managed Mumbai's top Chinese, China Garden until he came here). The three chefs are also from Bombay. Hakka, led by Steven Lee. At it's really impossible to recommend dishes; they are all so good. Everything has a light Indian spicing. To me this brings Chinese food to life. Ask Johnny or the staff for advice. They are happy to help. Or else just dive in. Dishes to savour include Spring Chicken Lollipops – cute name, in fact pretty little chops dusted with a Hakka spice mix, or Red Pumpkin Fritters (starters). Mains we like include Hakka Chilli Chicken cooked with five spice and green chillies, Prawn Manchurian cooked with coriander, ginger and garlic and Crispy Okra, smothered with hot garlic sauce; Hot Garlic Paneer Szechuan, or Moi-Yan aubergine, folded with minced chicken and shrimp. Because Indians don't eat beef, Hakkas created a range of goat dishes, translated at Dalchini into lamb. I suppose today's celeb chefs who believe in their arrogant fusion foods should come here to find out just how to mix Indian spices with soy. Dalchini is the only place in Britain which does it successfully. Welcome to a position high up on our **TOP 100** list. Lunch and dinner daily except closed Mondays.

HOUSE OF SPICE

Kingston Road, SW20 020 8542 4838

'Service is great – especially good to be able to say hello to the chefs in the open plan kitchen as you go in. Nice touches like oranges after the main meal, free liqueur and mints with the bill and friendly waiters welcoming the locals make it very enjoyable. My Murgh Green Masala, chicken in a spicy, coriander-laden sauce and Cara's Salmon Masala,c hunks of salmon in a tangy but mild red sauce. Worthy of a special mention are the beers – Cobra, Bangla, Goan Beer and Kama Sutra. Being innocent, I'm not sure if I spelt that right.' AR. [how many times have we heard that one, Andrew?!!]

London W

Area: West End
Postcode: W1
and West London W2 to W14
Population: 630,000

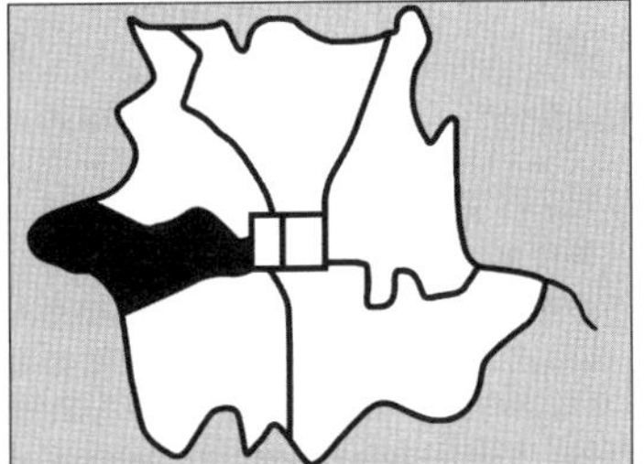

London W1

The West End

ANWARS TOP 100 BYO

64 Grafton Way, Tottenham Court Road, W1 020 7387 6664

Treat Anwars as the forerunner to the numerous successful Lahore Kebab Houses. It opened in 1962 as a 52-seater to serve local Asians, drawn to the area to buy spices next door at the then renowned Bombay Emporium, which later closed and went on to become BE International (Rajah brand), which is now owned by HP foods. Anwar's itself was taken over in 1985 by Muhammad Afzal Zahid. who keeps to the old ways. It serves gutsy, spicy Pakistani food. You walk in, make your choice from the dishes of the day (no menu as such) on display in the serving counter, pay – they do accept credit cards – then carry your tray to a formica table, jugs of water in place, and enjoy it. *'Everything, including bhajis and naan bread, is microwaved. Seekh kebabs, Karahi Gosht was really tasty. ambience and, more importantly, the food all remain unchanged. Set lunch, £6 for Chicken Curry, ladle of mixed vegetables, ladle of Chana, ladle of Sag Aloo over a mound of rice, with a Puri and a cup of tea.'* MW. The vegetarian version is £5. Unlicensed, **BYO** no charge. Hours: 12-11, daily.

BENARES

12 Berkeley Square, W1 020 7629 8886

We said in our last (2001) *Guide, 'there can be no doubt that Atul Kochar can cook – he excels himself executing classical Indian cuisine'.* That was before he got his much-hoped-for Michelin star along with Vineet Bhatia whose Zaika W8, we review later. I've no idea why chefs are so desperate to receive this accolade from a tyre company who, years ago happened to do a French dining guide. Whether Michelin know about French food or Gordon Ramsay, I neither know nor care, because they know diddly sqat about Indian food. If I were Michelin editor, I'd award stars to several other Indian chefs, before Atul and Vineet. Strangely, instead of withdrawing the Award from Tamarind after Atul left, the tyre men issued it again and it remains in

©	Curry Club Discount	U	Unlicensed
V	Vegetarian	ANP	Alcohol not permitted
e-a-m-a-y-l	Eat as much as you like	BYO	Bring your own alcohol

place. Atul developed the new M&S range of curries. I liked them so much I helped M&S on their way to getting the 2002 top Supermarket Award (Gold Q). Of course, Atul was lured by M&S because of his Michelin star, and to be fair he did a good job for M&S by persuading them to remove all chemicals and preservatives and to cook slowly in brat pans. (A major break-through for ready-meals but no big deal in the Indian kitchen.) Atul is Oberoi-trained and worked at their Delhi Hotel. He was poached by an Indian magnate who opened Tamarind in 1994. At first Atul was understaffed and produced timidly spiced dishes for an underwhelmed clientele. But we saw the talent and awarded Tamarind our **MOST PROMISING NEWCOMER AWARD** in its first year (1995), **BEST INDIAN** 1998 and **BEST CHEF** 2000. So little wonder the tyre men followed us. The problem is, we already had reservations. Is Atul a good exec (manager) rather than a brilliant hands-on chef? I'm really not sure. Now he's changed venue, how does it fare? Benares is named after India's holiest city (formerly Varanassi). Up stairs to an expensive, architect-designed bar (serving snacks) with three private dining rooms off. The main dining room has polished grey limestone flooring, textured and sculpted white walls, and interspersed with artifacts, and is undoubtedly expensive but unexceptional. The service was exceptional, though frequent *'how are you', 'how is the food', 'is everything fine'* could get a bit wearing. A basket of large and baby plain Popadoms with Chutneys were delivered to our table, de facto. The baby pops were stale. We approved of the home-made chutneys. For starters, we chose 'Bhalla Papri, £6.50, crispy pastry and lentil dumplings with mint, tamarind and yoghurt dressings. It looked good but the dumplings were stale and the chutneys insufficient. Aloo Tikki, £6.50, pan-fried potato cakes, consisted of four spiceless, rissoles on a spoonful of average chick pea curry. The plate was decorated with little dots of chilli sauce. I virtually licked them off, as it added much needed flavour. I have to tell you that we were both a little disappointed. My Tikki Main course Nalli Gosht – lamb shank with coriander and red chillies, £20, was delivered in its own beaten copper pot. It had been slowly cooked,was very tender, meat falling off the bone, lovely. Salis (potato straws) were generously sprinkled on top. Our other main was Kaali Aur Hari Mirch Ka Murgh – fry-style chicken curry with curry leaves, onions and black pepper, red and green chillies and cashew nuts,' £16. The chicken was succulent, smothered in a dryish sauce and decorated with deep-fried curry leaves and toasted cashew nuts. This garnish was not only disagreeable it was out of context, and if this is innovation Atul, you can keep it. Both dishes were blandly spiced, reminding us of Atul's early Tamarind days. But the worst dish was Dal Makani – DBAC's benchmark at a massive £7.50. *'Far from being creamy, the lentils were hard, undercooked, and lacked salt, spicing and cream. But to confuse us totally, the Roomali Roti £2.50, was good and the Boiled Rice, £3, was absolutely perfectly cooked, beautifully fragrant, and the best rice we've had for many a year.'* DBAC. To conclude on our experience, we both feel that Atul is being too timid. We expect the tyre men will disagree, and you are welcome to disagree as well. Reports please before Benares gets promoted. Service charge 12.5%. Hours: 12-3 weekdays and 5.30-10.30 Monday to Saturday.

CAFÉ LAZEEZ TOP 100

21 Dean Street, W1 020 7434 9393

See SW7 for menu details. This newer venture has outside tables, a bar/brasserie and a huge restaurant. *'Ignore the non-Indian snacks downstairs and upstairs perhaps avoid their pan-Indian inventions and pick some authentic Pakistani haute-cuisine'.* JGS. *'Really excellent.'* KB&SS. Hours, Brasserie: 12-1AM, daily. Restaurant: Lunch 11-3/5.30-11.45, Mon to Sat. Branches: SW7, & EC1.

CARAVAN SERAI AFGHAN TOP 100 BYO

50 Paddington Street, W1 020 7935 1208

Nayebkhail's 50 seat Afghani restaurant, est. 1975 starts with a very nice touch – free samosa with carrot and chilli pickle (Tourshou) given at the beginning while you examine the menu. Afghan food is spiced more lightly than Indian, but there are many similarities, which will appear more obvious once you have studied the menu. The Tanoor is the Tandoor, Quorma is Korma, Gosht is meat, Murch is chicken, Palaw is Pillao, and so on. Yoghurt and garlic, root vegetables and pulses are also popular. Even if you know none of this, the menu explains everything most clearly. Try the Logery – leg of lamb, flavoured with spices and saffron – or the Sekonia (skewered lamb, cooked in the tandoor). Ashaks are pastries, filled with a spicy leek and mince filling, with yoghurt. Kohi is roast lamb, spiced with blackcurrant and Char Masala (the Afghan four (char) spice version of Garam Masala). End with Carrot Kulfi or Coconut Halva. Licensed but **BYO** allowed: £2 corkage. 20% discount on takeaway. It remains in **TOP 100,** not just because Afghan restaurants are rare in the UK (the only other one being Afghan Kitchen N1), but because its food, ambience, service deserve it. Hours: 12-3/6-11.30.

CHOR BIZARRE

PREVIOUS AWARD WINNER AND TOP 100

16 Albemarle Street, W1 020 7629 8542

Delhi's Chor Bazaar is a kind of permanent cart-boot-sale, where you can buy anything at knock-down prices. Meaning 'thieves' market' it was originally the place where the villains pushed stolen goods. Entrepreneur Rohit Khattar, owner of Delhi's 32-room Hotel Broadway, hit on the idea to exploit this image. The hotel restaurant needed a revamp, and he cannily renamed it Chor Bizarre exploiting the linguistic twist from 'Bazaar' to 'Bizarre'. The spin told Delhi it was furnished from the real Chor Bazaar. No two chairs of tables were the same. It took Delhi by storm. Mr Khattar set his eyes on Mayfair. When Mahendra Kaul's 85-seat Gaylord site became available, in 1997, it was perfect. 'Antiquities' abound and one table, for example, is encased in an '18th-century four-poster bed' from Calcutta. Chefs Deepinder Sondhi and Manpreet Ahujas major on Kashmiri dishes which include: Goshtaba, a Kashmiri speciality of minced lamb balls cooked in a yoghurt gravy, Nadroo Yakhani, lotus stem in spiced yoghurt gravy. Gilauati Kabab, lamb kebab flavoured with saffron served with tomato and white radish salad and mint yoghurt chutney and Marz Wangun Korma, lamb cooked with Kashmiri chillies with cardamom and cloves, Haaq, spinach cooked with aniseed, Rajmah, red kidney beans and Chaaman, (lotus stem). A neat way to try these and other Kashmiri dishes is to order the Tarami £24. There are many other dishes on the menu from other Indian regions, and all are expertly cooked. For example Soups, Chaats, Tikka and Tandoori starters, and from Pakistan, Tak-a-Tak. After the chef starts frying the dish, he takes the two steel, flat-edged spatulas and rapidly bangs them one after the other on to the pan to chop, mash and mix the ingredients. The dish gets its name from the noise made – taka-taka-taka-taka. Try Kalaji Tak-a-Tak, chicken liver tossed on a high flame with coriander £6. Our benchmark Dal Makhni, thick black lentil flavoured with tomatoes and cream, immersed overnight on the tandoor. It clocks in at a hefty £6.50, but here it's masterly. The Tamil Nadu speciality, Chicken Chettinad, £ 13 (*see page* 50) is turning up on many a menu, usually cooked totally incorrectly. But here it's perfect, cooked in a hot sauce with a predominant flavour of pepper, aniseed and curry leaves. And if you want a good southern taster, the South Indian Tiffin £24, brings you (in typical office Tiffin carrier) Orange Rasam, Chicken Chettinad, Malabar Prawn Curry, Avial, Sambhar served with Rice and Malabari Parootha on a ceramic banana leaf platter. We like this report: *'We probably spent more time standing outside deciding whether or not we could afford to go in than actually eating! Once inside, it didn't disappoint. Bizarre is certainly the right word, the mismatch of chairs, tables, ornaments actually works well. Food, it has to be said, was fantastic. Started on the right track with bowl of mini pops and excellent pickles, left on table for us to devour. Maggie ordered the Maharani (Vegetarian) Thali consisting of Pakoras, Kurkuri Bhindi Nadroo, Wild Mushroom Mattar, Palak Makkai, Zeera Aloo, Dal Makhni, Cucumber Raita and Zafrani Pulao £22. I had the Maharajah (meat) Thali, with Gazab Ka Tikka, Sharabi Kababi, Tikka Masala, Mirchi Korma, Palak Makkai, Zeera Aloo, Dal Makhni and Cucumber Raita and Zafrani Pulao £24. As if this wasn't enough along came unadvertised mini Nan. Superbly fresh and nicely spiced. Exquisite Mango Kulfi. A really good meal. However, at £40 each, including service, it was baked beans on toast for the rest of the week.* AR. *'Had not been since it opened, wonderful to find it just as good, probably better. Fantastic decor,*

friendly service, cheerful and efficient. Absolutely superb food, well spiced, good initial ingredients in good portions. A first class lunch – lucky that my new office is in the same street! [Danny, do you need an excuse?] *£97 for two, very typical for lunch in Mayfair.'* DRC. Wines matched to each dish by Charles Metcalfe, available by the glass. Culture evenings: e.g. book readings, comedy evenings, creative writing workshops to theatre/movie festivals. Food festivals. Private room downstairs, seats 30. Service charge 12.5%. 12-3/6-11.30, Monday to Saturday. (6-1130, Saturday).

CHOWKI — NEW TO OUR TOP 100

2 Denman Street, W1 — 020 7439 1330

Chef Kuldip Singh and his gang opened Mela in 2000, and to prove their success Chowki opened in 2002, in a short street behind Eros, better known for its formula curry houses. But Chowki isn't one of those. Operating with 120 seats in three areas, it changes its menu monthly, with food from three different Indian regions at a time. And with the gang all being Taj-trained it's well within their capabilities to cook highly accurate dishes. For example it's Punjab, Sikkim and Keralan food one month, then Pakistan, Calcutta and Coorg another, and so on. The format is three starters and four mains from each region, all available a-la-carte, or priced at £10.95 for three mains and any four starters, and with lunch from £6, you can't complain (except you do, about the fifties formica decor mostly). It's cheap and cheerful. Welcome to our **TOP 100**. Busy at peak times but usefully open all day: 12-11.30 daily except Sunday to 10.30. Branches: Mela, WC2, Soho Spice, W1.

GAYLORD — TOP 100

79 Mortimer Street, W1 — 020 7580 3615

When it opened in 1963 it was not only Britain's first upmarket Indian restaurant, it also pioneered the Tandoori oven in Britain. The name is a play on the names of the original owners Gai and Lamba, who had opened one of Delhi's very first Indian restaurants called Kwality in 1948. By the 50's there were Kwalities all over India. But they were little more than caffs. Having made a fortune producing ice-cream, the pair decided to go upmarket, with their first Gaylord which opened in Delhi in 1958. Other branches followed soon after in Bombay, San Fransisco, Kowloon, Kobe Japan, Bahamas and Manchester. *'Our friends, Andrew and Diane, my husband Rob and me are regular curry eaters and we love to try somewhere we haven't been before. We enjoy excellent quality curries and the dining experience is very important as we make a night of it. So with the crew and our aims named let me tell you about the Gaylord. All four of us agreed that it was a wonderful curry with such different tastes. We started with tandoori fish, onion pakora, vegetable samosa and chicken chat. The starters were good quality with the chicken chat being made up into a salad, very interesting and quite spicy, but not too spicy. Chutneys were good with an especially hot green 'harassi like' substance the favourite of us all, though to be used with caution. Diane had to wait for her starter of samosa a bit longer than the rest of us because according to the waiter the chef had discarded the first lot because they were not up to standard!!! (A good sign I think) Main courses were superb, sag chicken – the best we have ever tasted! Chilli chicken tikka had an excellent char grilled flavour, chilli lamb was some of the tenderest lamb ever in a curry and my channa kabuli was stunning, very hot with lots of taste and small pieces of raw chilli...all excellent. The side dishes were good too, with Aloo Zerra being our favourite. The rice was good but nothing spectacular. Plain naan was good, stuffed paratha a little too greasy for my liking and the missi roti competent (Taste of Raj in Sandbach do a much better one). We were all very impressed with the food and will certainly return. Just a couple of notes of caution, I personally would describe the restaurant as 'faded' with a new carpet a definite requirement. The service charge is included automatically and while I understand that many people don't tip realistically, we do and use it to tell the restaurant that the experience has been good. The service was fine though there was a wait for the food, which you don't object to when you taste the quality and you realise that it has all been cooked from first principals and not the same sauce-base with different ingredients. That said, we did wait quite a while for one of the rounds of drinks, which I suggest is unnecessary, but we will put this down to an oversight. Overall 8/10 (I'm a hard woman to please!!!).* KW. And what's wrong with that Katherine? Despite the carpet and the wait, we'll keep it on our **TOP 100.** Service 15%. Cover charge: £1.20 – includes a Popadam and pickle. Delivery. Takeaway: 10% discount. Hours: 12-3/6-11.30 ; Sun. to 11.

GOPALS OF SOHO

12 Bateman Street, W1 020 7434 1621

Gopal, real name NT Pittal, earned his spurs building Amin Ali's part, by cooking superb food, first at the Lal Qila, then at the Red Fort. Feeling his career was going nowhere, he opened his own restaurant in 1990, and the accolades poured in. We got a dip for a few years, but now you like it again. Mr Pital jnr, Gopal's son, runs the place while Dad competently cooks classic Indian food to the standard menu, with the full range of starters from bhaji to kebabs, tandoori and curries, but a closer look reveals specials from Goa to Kashmir, Lucknow to Hyderabad: *'Father of a French student came over for a conference at OFSTED Headquarters. I rolled up to meet him at the appointed hour, to be faced with the prospect of an evening with not one, but six Inspectors, his colleagues coming along as well!!! I had done by homework the night before. I called up Gopal's on my mobile – I had stored the number – reserved a table and whistled up a couple of cabs. Gopal's was very good indeed, helpful with the menu, and very tasty indeed.'* JGR. Hours: 12-3/6-11.30

INDIAN YMCA CANTEEN

45 Fitzroy Street, W1 020 7387 0411

Like this place this entry hardly changes, though the acceptance of credit cards, a longer lunch time and non-resident access to dinner are new, as is the price rise – up by an inflationary 10 pence per curry. To find it, follow your nose north up Fitzroy Street – the large modern block on your right may already be permeating curry smells from its basement kitchen. Enter, and out of courtesy, please ask at reception, (manned by gentle young Indians) if it's OK to use the canteen. The canteen, on your right, is clean, with brown functional formica-topped tables. It's deserted 5 minutes before opening time, then as if the school bell's rung, it's suddenly packed full with Asians, many of whom are students, and this is their residence. (Like all YMCAs, residency is open to anyone, though officially this one is subtitled Indian Student Hostel.) All students of good curry, should visit here before they can graduate as aficionados. These are the rules: Be punctual, (opening and closing times and rules are as sharp as the Post Office); no bookings, no smoking, no license, no alcohol, so no **BYO,** and no nonsense! Unlike the Post Office, everything else works, and staff care. Take a plastic tray, join the always-busy queue at the stainless-steel servery. It's basic, and unsophisticated but authentic expertly spiced and cooked Indian school-dinner-style – food, like you get at streetside Dabbas the length and breadth of India. Chicken and fish curries £2, lamb curry £2.30, vegetable curries all £1.30 and lentils £1. Your choice handed to you in bowls. Top up with chupatties, tea or coffee, and pay at the till. It's absurdly cheap – hard to exceed a fiver, and it's remarkable that they now take credit cards. Then jostle for space at a shared formica table. The food may not be five-star but the company can be, when you share your table with talkative, friendly students. Men in white coats tidy up after you. *'Marvellous.'* MW. Set lunch £5 two courses, Sat. & Sun.. Hours: 12-2 daily, except Sunday 1230-1.30 and dinner 7-8, daily.

THE KERALA

15 Great Castle Street, W1 020 7580 2125

We criticised this one in our last *Guide.* Owned and run by David Tharakan, this 40-seater is decorated in a very Indian way, with artifacts hanging off the walls including golden umbrellas used by temple elephants. His wife Mille is in charge of the cooking. The food is pure south Indian, with a full list of protein and vegetable dishes. And for the most part it's reasonable, but it's not memorable. *'It was, I feel, very authentic, but not particularly good. We shared a Dosa – spicy potato in a wrap – fabulous! But Vardi – lentil cake in yoghurt is probably an acquired taste. Prawn Biriani was ridiculously hot, nice rice, fabulous Paratha. £33 for three courses including lager – very reasonable.'* MG. Hours: Lunch 12-3/5.30-11, daily.

LA PORTE DES INDES

AWARD WINNER & TOP 100 ©

32 Bryanston Street, W1 020 7224 0055

Owned by the Blue Elephant Group (*see* SW6) it opened in 1997, under the management of Sherin Modi Alexander with her husband, Mernosh Modi, in charge of cooking. Both Taj-trained they have really grown into the role. Their professionalism cannot be bettered. Once a ballroom which blossomed in the wartime 1940's, and lying derelict by the 1980's, owner Karl Steppe applied his Blue Elephant decor yardstick here, and went all-out with a £2.5m spend. Unlike others whose budget claims are greatly exaggerated, you can easily see how transforming this vast place cost all of that, particularly since its layout isn't an easy one to deal with. Features include a sandstone arch, a 40-foot waterfall, a sweeping staircase made of white marble with pink sandstone balustrades, imported especially from India's pink city, Jaipur. Airy, domed skylights enhance La Porte's daytime atmosphere, making it a different place in darkness. There is a forest of jungle plants, a wealth of Indian artifacts and antiques, and the range of eating rooms, including the tiny private dining rooms seating 12 and 24 respectively, and three more dining areas bringing the total seating up to 300. The lunch presentation of food on raised copper salvers is opulent and attractive, and you can e-a-m-a-y-l for £19.90. *'We've eaten lunch here many times and have not been disappointed'* RL. *'I love this restaurant. From the welcome at the door to the presentation of the bill.'* [the bill? You' cannot be serious Dominique] *'The food, is just superb. Murgh Makhani (CTM) is just how it is in India and just how it should be. Flavoursome chicken pieces from a whole chicken – not the usual chunks of tasteless chicken breast – are smothered in a delicious, creamy, delicately spiced crimson gravy. Potato-stuffed parathas are buttery and light. You will want to eat them even if you are full to bursting. Big, fat, juicy King prawns floating in a light, mustard seed, turmeric coloured, coconut milk sauce. The puddings will not disappoint. The frequently held themed food festivals are a remarkable eduction in Indian regional food.'* DBAC. *'Deservedly* **TOP 100**, *my all-time favourite restaurant.'* SO. We continue to remain impressed by La Porte. La Porte's ambience, decor, service, food is all as good as it gets. La Porte has become an Indian's Indian, with an ever-increasing clientèle from the subcontinent. We gave it our **BEST IN UK AWARD** in 1998. This Award has only gone to two other restaurants since we started our Awards a decade ago. This Award is a permanent accolade, and does justice to

Mernosh's fabulous food and Sherin's tight management. Average spend £46. Service discretionary. Cover charge £1.50. Hours: 12-2.30 Mon.-Fri (to 3pm Sun)/7-11.30 Mon.-Sat. (Sun. 6-10.30). Branches: Blue Elephant Thai, sw6, and others in Europe.

MASALA ZONE BEST NEW CONCEPT AWARD NEW TO OUR TOP 100

9 Marshall Street, W1 020 7287 9966

Let me tell you a story. Once upon a recent time some dumb politicians spent £1bn pounds of tax-payers' money on a dumb project to mark the millennium. They called it the Dome, and decided to fill it with things they found interesting in areas they called Zones, which they imagined that one quarter of the UK's population would visit in its one year's existence. They peopled their Dome with equally dumb managers, to whom they gave great powers. The managers invited great restaurants to tender to be in the Dome. Ranjit Mathrani, owner of Chutney Mary sw7, the first restaurant to get an **AWARD** for best restaurant in 1992, agreed to open an Indian restaurant, which the managers said would feed 2,000 diners a day. But as opening day drew closer, the managers imposed their powers on their operators. They stipulated decor schemes and menu items, and nominated food suppliers and then they stated that they would hire and fire the restaurant's labour. Ranjit pulled out. The Dome opened and did not live happily ever after and it doth remain the national joke. Fortunately for Ranjit, it was only the beginning of the story. Far from being a dead duck, he located the project in a permanent home, in the former Cranks restaurant in Soho. The name 'zone' also survived. Masala Zone was born in 2001. The concept is to serve real Indian food cooked by a fresh new wave of young Indian chefs at a price point of under a tenner, which will appeal to a new young wave of customers. It's a concept so simple that one is unaware, perhaps of just how brilliant it is. As you approach the interior is revealed behind full-length, full-width plate glass windows. There are 160 seats, some at street level, and the remainder a few steps down on a lower lever, overlooked by the higher level, giving the venue character. Chairs and tables are light and modern, on a wooden floor. Wall decor is inspirational, and deserves your attention. It was painted on a mud-like terracotta background by Indian tribal artists, who paint cartoon-like line-drawings in white with sticks. They'd never been outside their village, let alone to London. Doing what the tribe has done for centuries, they tell the history of mankind, in a series of episodes. The drawings carry humour, pathos and perception. And the artists were so awe-struck with the capital, that they added a new penultimate episode – scenes of London, including some things they'd not seen before – Buck House, some guardsmen, the Tower, and their favourite – a stretch limo. Their final episode is drawn around the restaurant's bar servery hatch and depicts mankind getting drunk and falling over. There's not much chance of that at Masala Zone, only soft drinks, wines and beers are sold, and customer turnround is fast. This is because service is fast, from young men and women, smartly dressed in spice-coloured smocks and the kitchens are fast too. But this is no criticism. It's fast if you need it, but if you want to dwell, we've never noticed pressure on you to leave, no matter how busy it gets. The actual cooking takes no shortcuts – curries are slow-cooked to maximise flavours in the large kitchens behind, which includes a completely separate vegan kitchen, with its utensils coded so that they never touch meat. There is a further kitchen in view, with a series of smallish warmers containing ready-cooked food, which are constantly refilled by the chefs behind. Cold food emanates from one side of the kitchen, hot on the right. You place your order, and it's immediately doled out to the waiter . This leads to what some reporters complain about as being chaos. This is because dishes arrive to your table as soon as the chefs issue it. Some things take longer than others, and your order may arrive mains first, starter last, in any order. Masala Zone has been likened to Wagamama. A few other aspects of Masala Zone already noted: price, queues, youth and fun may be likened to Wagamama But the resemblance is skin-deep. Service, rather than self-service is an obvious difference, as are comfortable chairs. Most importantly, Masala Zone's food is much more complex. Wagamama's id noodle nosh doshed out by non-skilled cooks. All Masala Zone food requires very high skill levels to cook. Snacks (or starters) include several types Bhel *(see page 52)* – Bombay street food at £2.50 a plate. Chicken Samosas £3.25, lightly spiced, finely minced chicken with green peas; Shikampuri Kebab £3.25, melt in the mouth, aromatically spiced, minced lamb croquettes. Malabar Seafood Bowl £6, prawns, calamari, fish kofta with flat noodles in a richly curried soup. Everything is available a la carte., but way-to-go is with the Thalis *(see page 58)* each of which feature a complete meal. The items do change weekly, but this is an example — snacks of Khandvi, Dhokla (a pancake of besan flour, spiced and rolled up like a swiss-roll and cut into slices, served chilled). Yoghurt Curry, Potato Curry, Dal, Aubergine and Plantain Curry, Rice and Chuppatis served with chutneys of Mango and Coriander. Add to that your choice of Achari Chicken Curry and it's £8.75 or Prawn Curry or Lamb Curry both £9.25. There is a vegetarian Thali £7.75, and a weekend children's Thali £4. Desserts: Caramel or Mango Kulfi, Shrikand with Fresh Fruit, Gulab Jamun with ice-cream, Caramelised Carrot with ice cream all priced at £2.50 each. Lunchtime treats also include spicy sandwiches. Spend between £7 and £15 plus drink. No reservations. No smoking. Service: 10%. Hours: 12-2.30/5,30-11. Sunday 12.30-10.30. (snacks only between 3-5). We are so delighted with the concept that we must give Masala Zone a special award. **BEST NEW CONCEPT AWARD** is it, and we hope to see Masala Zones nationwide as time goes by. Branch NI. *See page 37.*

PALMS OF GOA

12 Charlotte Street, W1 020 7636 1668

'After lubrication in the Bricklayers Arms round the corner, Palms of Goa is the usual destination. Rapidly becoming one of my favourite haunts. Lamb Xacutti is very good, as is the Goan Chicken and fish dishes. Not as authentic as Ma Goa, but very tasty. Good rice and breads, excellent attentive service and the best Tarka Dal I've had in a long while. Good value in the heart of London.' AR. *See next column.*

PALMS OF GOA

4 Meard Street, W1 020 7439 3509

'I'd enjoyed the Palms of Goa in Charlotte Street and so keen to try this new branch. Started with plain and spicy Popadoms and a choice of Chutney – onion salad, mint sauce and lime pickle – just 25p per person. Aloo Chana Chat – spicy, followed by Chicken Sag £5.95, Mushroom Bhaji £3.95 and Pullao Rice £1.95 – all lived up to my expectations from the original Palms, with good quality meat and vegetables served in tasty spicy sauces. Quantities were good, service attentive and decor pleasant and light.' MK. [Just a light lunch then, Mike.] Menu extracts: Onion Palak Bhajia £2.50, chopped onion and spinach in light spicy batter and deep-fried. Batata Wada £2.50, potatoes with green peas and chilli fried with gram flour. Chicken Liver Suuka £3.50. Pumpkin Curry £3.95, medium hot, coconut based, Mangalore style. Green Banana Bangi £3.95, mild. Lamb Xacutti £5.95, coconut, vinegar, garam masala, medium hot. Hours: 12-3/6-11. Sunday closed. *See previous entry.*

RV2 — NEW ENTRANT

69 Shaftesbury Avenue , W1 020 7287 7189

Five boys Tahir Kahn, Manjot Raytt, Zakaria Hussan, Shabaz Lais and Mo Lais were at school together. They now own Ware, Hert's RV1 restaurant. RV2 opened late in 2003. It's a smart and modern, two-level 160-seat corner (of Dean Street) site venue allegedly costing £2m. Who pays for this? Why you do. And the boys are clearly expecting the wallets to rendezvous with them. Take the wine list: Champagne from Mercier Brut £6.50 by the glass to Louis Roederer Cristal, 1985 at £995.00. Cheapest red a Côtes du Rhône, 2001 is £21.50 while Ch. Haut-Brion, 1er Cru Classé, Pessac-Léognan, 1990 is £750.00. Ex Tabla (E14) chef Bhuwan Bhatt (he worked under Yogesh who is now at the Painted Heron – SW1) is in charge of the kitchens. It means good food. From his small menu you can choose starters ranging from £7.50 for Makhmali Sheek – skewers of bakedspiced lamb mince, to £10 for Tandoori Tiger Prawns. RV 2 Special (serves two persons) at £25 and yields crisp crab cake, salmon tikka, marinated chicken and sheek kebab. Mains include Malai Murgh or Lamb Rogani at £10, through Raspberry Kofta £14.50, cottage cheese & potato stuffed with sweet cheese, raspberry & cashew nut sauce. Lamb shanks and Lobster, £18 and £25. Our benchmark Dal Makhani clocks in at a huge £7.50. Lunch and dinner daily.

RAGAM SOUTH INDIAN TOP 100 

57 Cleveland Street, W1 020 7636 9098

Established in 1984 this cosy restaurant seats 34 upstairs, 20 downstairs, and has a strong following. Chef Nair cooks standard curries and, being from Kerala, authentic south-Indian food. All the south Indian favourites are there. 'It remains in our **TOP 100** because you say it should. Don't forget the lunchtime 'quick meal' £5 for curry, rice and bread! Service, 10%, not included. Delivery: min £10, local area only. Hours: 12-3/6-11.30; Sat. 12-3; Sun. 6-11.

RAJ TANDOORI 

72 Berwick Street, W1 020 7437 2897

This old-hand opened in 1969. Abdon Noor serves Northern Indian food, all the usual curry favourites, plus some Bangladeshi specials including Ayer Bhuna (Bangladeshi fish) £8 and Satkora (Bangladeshi citrus fruit) Gosht £8. Seats an intimate 36. Air-conditioned. Takeaway: 10% discount. Hours: 12-2.30/5.30-12.

RASA TOP 100 V

6 Dering Street, W1 020 7629 1346

Opened in 1998, this is the second of three restaurants established by Shivadas (Das) Sreedharan and his wife Alison. As with the original Rasa (London N16), they specialise in southern-Indian vegetarian cooking from Kerala, south India's richest state. Superb cooking by Chef RS Binuraj and his team. Nibbles include Pappadavadai (paps dipped in batter and sesame seeds and deep-fried) and Acchappam – rice batter crisp made from a mould (acch). Starters include: Banana Boli £4.25 (ripe plantain dipped in besan flour and black sesame, fried, served with peanut and ginger sauce), Vadai Selection £4.25 (fermented lentil soft dumplings, deep-fried to give a crisp outside). Main course curries (all at £6.25) include Moru Kachiathu – sweet mangoes and green bananas cooked in yoghurt with green chillies, ginger and fresh curry leaves, Beet Cheera Pachadi – fresh beetroot and spinach in a yoghurt with roasted coconut, mustard seeds and curry leaves, and the house signature dish Rasa Kayi (minced vegetables, ginger, garlic and fennel seed). To experience several of these try the Travancore Feast £20, Tamarind, Lemon and Coconut Rice (with fresh coconut and black dhal) £3.75 each. During the evening all main courses are traditionally served on banana leaf. Prices are a bit higher than N16, but to be fair they've not changed since our last Guide. Like its sister restaurants, the place is very tiny with seating on two floors packed into the narrow rooms. It does two full sessions every night, plus a full week-day lunch trade. As if it needed it, Rasa's popularity was considerably boosted when one Mr Oliver used Das to cook his naked curry. Problem is, Jamie didn't do Keralan cooking justice, and there followed a spate of complaints on my desk about Rasa not being a curry house. Not all publicity is good publicity, and I'm sure Das would agree. But for the discerning, this and all the Rasas are very bright stars on the horizon. The discerning love them. So book and go early. Service 12.5%. Hours: 12-3/6-11. Sunday dinner only. Branches: Rasa 55 & 56 Church St, N16 Rasa Express NW1 & N16 and next entry.

RASA SAMUDRA NEW TO TOP 100

5 Charlotte Street, W1 020 7637 0222

Outside it has the same pink paintwork, with ice-cream yellow on the upper floor. Lovely hanging baskets burst with red flowers. Inside wooden carvings hang on pretty Wedgewood blue walls. The menu includes many of Rasa's signature vegetarian dishes (*see* entry above). But here Das uniquely specialises in Keralan fish and seafood (Samudra means *'of the sea'*) Special seafood starters: Rasam £5.95 (consommé with prawns, crab, mussels, squid and tomato), Crab thoran, £7.50 – fresh crabmeat stir-fried with coconut, mustard seeds and ginger. Main courses include: Meen Elayil

Pollichathu £9.95 (pomfret marinated in paste of Kanthari chillies, curry leaves, green pepper and fresh coconut slices), Crab Varuthathu, £12.50, crab dish cooked dry with ginger, curry leaves, chilli and mustard seeds, Konju Manga Curry £12.95 (king prawn, green mango and coconut sauce), and Varutharachameen curry, £10.50, tilapia fish in a sauce made with roasted coconut, red chillies, tomatoes and tamarind. Puddings: Pal Payasam £3.50 (spiced rice pudding, cashew nuts and raisins). Set menus: £22.50 vegetarian, £30 seafood. Add 12.5% service charge and expect to pay at least above average. *'Feeling flush. Lots of different types of funny-shaped Pops and numerous delicious chutneys are a meal in themselves including the remarkable Meen Achar (fish pickle) and Konju Achar (prawn pickle). Fantastic Fishy Broth to start (Rasam). My friend's main was also very good – fish steaks in a spicy tomatoey sauce. My crab a let down – would have been nice to have a bit more help from the waiters who seemed to enjoy my frustration at not being able to get any meat out rather than helping get it out for me! Made me leave the restaurant feeling as if I'd had a bad experience. Wine is expensive for what is on the list and took ages to grab someone's attention for the bill.'* AR. Hours: 12-3 /6-11. Sunday dinner only. Branches, see above. Welcome to our **TOP 100.**

RED FORT

77 Dean Street, Soho, W1 020 7437 2525

In 2000 fire gutted the place and Amin's insurers, Norwich Union were reluctant to pay up until Labour MP Keith Vaz (of Humaja brothers fame) invited Amin and the Norwich Union to the Foreign Office, after which Amin's claim was accepted and paid up. A fanciful £2m rebuild took place including a space-age, air-conditioned kitchen (minus ace-card Mohammed Rais, who by then had shrewdly taken his magic to Darbar, SW6. as had his sous chef Naresh Matta, now at Ekiri, NW3). So that's where to get your Dum Pukht (*see page* 50). The rebuild included a 'sexy' bar (Akbar which runs to 1AM deep in the vaults). It reopened in late 2002 to a fanfare of publicity, something Amin is adept at. Unexpectedly, within months, it again went into administration, then closed, then reopened just as we go to print. So how do we review it? Best to proceed with what we know. Exterior still modernised but recognisable. Inside, modernist Mughalist with sand-coloured walls, Indian trimmings, slate floor with red path, dotted with mosaics leading you to the back where water drizzles down the wall. Nearby, Tandoors are in view (behind glass). The drama continues in the toilets, where no expense has been spared. Dramatic lighting but we get complaints about it being hard to see menus and food. Service charge 12.5%. Table d'hote lunch and pre-theatre specials from £12 for 2 courses. Mon-Fri lunch to 2.30. Mon-Sat Dinner 5.45-11.30. Sun 6-10.30.

REGENT TANDOORI NEW ENTRANT

16 Denman Street, Piccadilly, W1 020 7434 1134

Long-established standard curry house waving the flag for the formula. Good for a fix at sensible prices. Lunch and dinner daily.

SOHO SPICE

124 Wardour Street, W1 020 7434 0808

Following the receivership of The Red Fort (see above) Amin's other Soho restaurant, Greek Street's Soho Spice followed suit. News from the receivers is that Soho Spice has been bought out of administration by chef Kuldeep Singh, Asraf Rahman and Dinesh Mody who jointly run Shaftesbury Avenue's Mela WC1 and Chowki W1.

TAMARIND AWARD WINNER

20 Queen Street, W1 020 7629 3561

So in 2001 it got its Michelin star. We are compelled to mention this because Michelin seems to overwhelm the industry. We agree Tamarind is an exceptional place, after all we've helped it on its way by giving it a succession of **AWARDS** since it opened in 1994, despite its faltering start. But there are equally, if not more deserving Indian restaurants, and it's this *Guide* in which you'll find them. Anyway, no sooner than he got his star, than Atul was up and away. (*see* Benares W1). Sous chef Alfred Prasad (ex Delhi Sheraton and Veeraswamy) took on the mantle of Head chef. Rajesh Suri (formerly with Red Fort and Veeraswamy) remains as General manager. To complete the clean sweep, the restaurant has been refurbished with bright, clean lines. Prasad has maintained the Tamarind tradition on the new menu, with old Tamarind favourites, but has put on new dishes as well. Here are some examples: starters include Saag Aloo Tikki, spiced potato cakes with a spinach filling, served with tamarind chutney, Tandoori Subzi, grilled broccoli and paneer in spicy marinade £5.95, Murgh ka Chat, smoked chicken salad with red onions and peppers in a spiced avocado dressing, £6.95. interesting mains include: Seafood Moilee, scallops, squid, mussels and kingfish in a mild coconut sauce, £16.50, Lamb Chettinad, cooked with Chettinad spices, £16.50 and Bhuna Achari Khargosh, rabbit cooked with pickling spices £15.50. Our benchmark dal Makhni, low-cooked black lentils, is £6. *'With a huge reputation to live up to as outlined in the Guide. I chose to meet a business associate for a 'working lunch.'* [Really David, those 'working lunches' always seem to take place at a luxurious Indian restaurant]. *'Booked in advance, warmly greeted, shown to table and offered Kingfisher and Popadoms as I waited – excellent. Each dish was fabulous, definitive spices and flavours that did not overpower. We complimented our meal with two bottles of Ellen Riesling – excellent value at £34 per bottle from an impressive wine list. Fabulous service, from booking to bill. Many will be put off by the prices but should not be. Whether impressing clients or celebrating a family occasion, a visit is highly recommended. £182.31 for two.'* DL. Tamarind retained its star, and remains a **TOP 100** restaurant in our book. Then it always was. Delivery: Hours: 12-3/6-11.30.

TASTE OF MUGHAL ©

29 Great Windmill Street, W1 020 7439 8044

Long-standing Piccadilly curryhouse, a much-needed venue for some who love it seats 50 diners. *'Never varies after all these years of visits.'* RW. Takeaway: 10% discount. Hours: 12-11.45.

TIFFINBITES

88, Wardour Street, W1 020 8747 4536

From knickers and bras to dabbas and bhajis; here's one to watch. Jamal Hirani and Jonathan Marks spent six years buying the former. Now they are selling the latter. Jamal's family sell Indian ingredients. His mum taught him to cook, and as a student in Brum he used Pat Chapman's Balti cookbook to stave of the pangs. Bored with lingerie and curryhouse snacks, the two men dreamed of opening a High Street fast-food operation, modelled on Pret A Manger, but selling Asian cuisine at home-cooked quality. They are not the first to have this aspiration, but there's something different about these two. First, they got good funding, then with their M&S training, they prepared a meticulous brief for their designers and suppliers. They brought in a Taj-trained chef, and developed their original menu. Then they applied all this to their first branch in early 2003. It's pretty, yet earthy with spice colours, tiles and spice jars to catch the eye. What's more it worked. Their plan is to have 50 branches in 5 years. Within a year they've already rolled out five at locations strategic enough to catch the busy worker at all times of day. Primarily a takeaway, you can alternatively eat in at a small number of tables. For spicy breakfast you can have Naan bread with light curries at £1.30 which can be washed down with coffee, chai, smoothies or lassi. Later in the day you can buy Chaat and Bhel £3.25, Kebabs, samosa and bhajis, £1.50 and a wide range of Indian sweets and hand-fried crisps. There are also several Wraps containing organic fillings c£3. Choice of three tiffin boxes (bespoke plastic trays) eg CTM, Veg Jalfrezi and Pilau Rice at £5. Hours here: Mon to Fri: 8am-10pm. Sat: 12-10. Sun – Closed. Branches: 122 Cannon Street, EC4, Mon to Fri: 7am-6pm. Weekends: Closed. 24 Moorfield, Moorgate, EC2, Mon to Fri: 6.30am-9.30pm. Weekends – Closed. Opening early 2004: Liverpool Street, Broadgate Circus and Birmingham Bull Ring. Delivery orders over £15, to all EC and W1. *See page* 16.

VEERASWAMY

PREVIOUS AWARD WINNER TOP 100

99 Regent Street, W1 020 7734 1401

Namita Panjabi and Ranjit Mathrani, owners of Chutney Mary (SW10), bought Britain's oldest Indian restaurant (founded 1926) in 1998. The entrance is on the aptly-named Swallow Street. Go up the stairs one floor, or take the lift. Enter to a discrete reception desk, and you'll swiftly be shown to one of the 130 seats in one of the dining areas, to your left or your right. The wine display is a work of art. The walls are painted in vibrant glowing earth colours: aubergine, saffron, garam masala, coriander leaf. Discrete artifacts and etched glass take it far away from its early days. The floors are polished expensive hardwood, the lighting is modern, the view to Regent Street dominant. A few carefully selected pictures of yore are displayed on a small wall area to remind us of the Veeraswamy heritage. As we go to print new chef, Gopal Kochak has brought in a new menu, reflecting his style, while maintaining the Veeraswamy ethos (high quality gourmet food as expected by the discerning Indian diner). His brigade of specialists from different Indian regions, continue to offer sophistically presented items from bhel, to dosas and lamb shank to lobster from Hyderabad, to Chowpatti beach, and Goa to Delhi. This is not to everyone's liking, since it's as far removed from a curry house as a caravan is from a palace. Dishes arrive plated, which is another concern to those who like to share. It's in the higher price range. Caveats issued, let me now tell you why this restaurant is so high in our estimation. Let's take price. It's not always out of reach. Try the two- course light lunches, Monday to Saturday which offer tandoori or grilled chicken, duck, prawns, fish and lamb, £11. Or on Sunday, it's a 3 course e-a-m-a-y-l, served at the table – no compromise on ingredients or quality for only £15. Take the kids – under 12, £7.00. A la carte is interesting, of course. *'After a busy evening, four of us hurried off to Veeraswamy for a late dinner. We sat by the window overlooking Regent Street and enjoyed its festive light display – it was a Christmas treat. Roasted, plain and spicy Popadoms were brought to us with delicious homemade chutneys. We enjoyed three types of Bhel. We all had different main courses, brought to us artistically served on large white plates, which I confess we surreptitiously shared, by passing forks around and hoping the waiters wouldn't see. We all ate dessert – fairy portions of everything. We were a bit late (last out I think) but they didn't press us.'* PLC. *'Menu is limited but perfectly balanced, excitingly different and wonderfully imaginative. £1.50 cover charge pays for some crisp triangular Popadoms and chutneys, while you study the exotic dishes on offer. Oyster Stir-fried with Chillies – wonderfully flavoured. Mussels cooked in Coconut Milk delicious, coconut sauce made a soup after the mussels had been devoured. We spooned it up unashamedly. Duck breast sliced and served with a tangy, fairly sweet and delicately spiced thick sauce. Achar Gosht – tender chunks of lamb perfectly cooked in light-coloured sauce, well spiced with black peppercorns – superbly flavoured. Aubergine side dish comprised of two whole small aubergines in a tamarind and peanut sauce – exquisite. Peshwari Nan relatively small but nicely nutty. Prices naturally high for location and excellence, but not outrageous. Portions modest but quite sufficient. Excellent service, as expected. A really superb meal.'* MW. One more thing: the wine list is an exemplary selection. Mr Mathrani is a connoisseur, and it shows. If ever there were a time to convert from beer to wine, this is it. Set dinner: 5.30-6.30pm and 10.30-11.30pm, £11 two courses, £13.95 three courses. Cover charge: £1.50 includes popadams and chutneys. Service 12½%. Hours: 12-2.30 (Sun. to 3pm) 5.30-11.30. (Sun. to 10.30). *See page* 37.

WOODLANDS TOP 100 V ©

77 Marylebone Lane, W1 020 7436 3862

A branch of Mr Sood's well-liked, small chain of southern Indian vegetarian restaurants. See SW1 branch for details.

YATRA

34 Dover Street, W1 020 7493 0200

Opened early in 2000 by Sonu Lalwani with his wife Liah. Yatra, meaning *'pilgrimage'*, or *'journey'*, is so called because the couple's concept is that their diners *'journey into India and beyond'*. Beyond might be their highly profitable basement Bollywood Bar. This runs on Thursday, Fridays and Saturdays 10pm-2am, during which hours it heaves with young Asians Bangra-ing the night away at £10 per head and £7 per cocktail. This popular Bar has a USP. It is a London waterhole for Bombay Bollywood movie stars. The restaurant is a separate operation. Few diners avail themselves entrance fee to Bollywood, at £5 if you've eaten, £10 if you haven't. The kitchens are manned by Oberoi-trained chef Krisnapal Negi, and we've tried his food. It's good. The menu is short, but our favourites include the Yatra Platter for two consisting of jumbo prawn, lamb chops, tandoori salmon, seekh kebab, malai kebab, paneer tikka and aloo tikki (per head) £17.00. Then there is Patrani Machli – salmon coated in a paste of fresh coriander leaf, ginger, green chillies and lime juice, wrapped and steamed in a banana leaf, £5.50. For mains, those with Raj connections will delight in Railway Lamb – a kind of spicy curry stew, the like of which is still dispensed at Indian stations. Lamb and baby potatoes are cooked with coconut, curry leaves, served with spinach seasoned in black cumin and garlic, £14.50. Average spend £40 (it is Mayfair!). Set lunch: £19, set dinner £23. Hours: Mon to Fri 12--3. Mon to Wed 6-11. Thu to Sat 6-11.30. Sunday 6-10:30.

London W2

Bayswater, Edgware Road, Paddington, Westbourne Grove

BOMBAY PALACE TOP 100 

2 Hyde Park, 50 Connaught Street, W2
020 7258 3507

In the late 1970s, Mr SS Chatwell was a successful Indian restaurateur in Ethiopia. Then a regime-change left him fearing for his life. He packed his bags and left for the USA. Luckily he'd packed his many bags full of dollars, and I mean FULL. I know because I met him in NY and he told me. It was not long before he opened Bombay Palace branches: Beverly Hills, Budapest, Houston, Kuala Lumpur, Mississauga, Montreal, New York City, Great Neck, NY, Toronto, and Washington DC. London opened in 1983. The 135-seater restaurant has a modern feel. Some time ago your editor ate in the NY branch, then one week later at the London branch. The menu was identical. RAL reports *'no change'*. What all BPs do is north Indian food which some describe as Indian hotel food. We think we know what that means – it's very smooth, very accurate cooking, not varying from tradition. Fine! Here is a small menu selection: Starters: Aloo Papri, Bhel, Aloo Tiiki and Vegetable Samosa, Prawn Patio over a tiny naan. Mains include Lamb or Beef Vindaloo, with chilli and Goan vinegar, Hyderabadi Lamb Chop Masala (Chef's Special), marinated with ginger, herbs, and spices, cooked in onion and tomato sauce. The most popular dish, Balouchi Raan, lamb-on-the-bone cooked Moghul-style until the meat falls off the bone. Chana Peshawari , chick peas slowly simmered with tart pomegranate seeds cooked with onions, tomatoes, and spices. and the benchmark Dal Makhani, £6.50. Set meals: Buffet Luncheon, £12.95. Set dinner £25. Service 15%. Cover charge £1 Takeaway: 10% discount. Hours: 12-2.45 (Sun. 12-3pm)/6-11.30. (Sun. 6- 11). Branches: Beverly Hills, Budapest, Houston, Kuala Lumpur, Mississauga, Montreal, New York, Toronto, Washington DC .

DURBAR NEW TO OUR TOP 100 ©

24 Hereford Road, W2 020 7727 1947

Opened when time began in 1956, by Shaimur Rahman Syed. Seats 60 diners – wicker chairs, arches, plants, Indian art, brass coffee-pots. Serves Northern Indian curries with a handful of specials which include: Chicken Xacuti, very hot with dry chilli and coconut and Chicken Silla, shredded chicken tikka. Good-value are the Thali set-meals from £8.95. Chef Shamin Syed won the International Chef of the Year Contest in Feb. 2000. He says of his winning dish – Oriental Chicken *'it's been on the menu for over 18 years'.* What more can we say about one of London's most stable and experienced venues? Well there is a bit more. RCF says *'it's one of our regular haunts. Whenever we go it is without fail packed full of Indians and Arabs. That says quality.'.* Hours: 12-2.30/6-12. Branch: Greenford Tandoori, Ruislip Road East, Greenford, Middlesex

GANGES 

101 Praed Street, W2 020 7723 4096

It's just a curry house, but it's very popular and it's been with us since our first *Guide.* Hours: 12-2.30/5.30-11.

GINGER

NEW ENTRANT 2004 AWARD FOR BEST BANGLADESHI CUISINE TOP100

115 Westbourne Grove, W2 020 7908 1990

Bangladesh's top chef, Albert Gomes was Exec at Dhaka's five-star Sonargoan Hotel when we met him there in 1996, and were stunned by his cooking. He was frankly surprised at our enthusiasm, under the impression that the UK's 7,000+ Bangladeshi-owned restaurants would offer their own food. We urged him to get a posting in London, and put Bangladeshi cooking on the UK map. And he did. Firstly with a short festival at the Red Fort, then hooray, in a permanent positition at the new Ginger, in 2001, and he brought his chef son. His style is upmarket home-cooking, and at Ginger he was given an upmarket new venue (modern wood floor, cyan chairs and white walls). I'd have preferred a more upmarket location, but it's there, and we should rejoice. Bangla cooking (*see page* 50) majors on fish, the bonier the better, shrimps, and a wealth of fresh vegetables, many only recently seen in the UK. Banglas love sweet, bitter, sour and hot. Curries are generally thinner than we get at the curryhouse, and beef, chicken, mutton are eaten on the bone. That said, the Brits are not yet ready for bones or bitter or very sweet desserts, and Gomes uses fish like Bekti, a favourite Bengali fish, which is relatively bone-free, with firm, white flesh. Even so the menu produces unfamiliar dishes, starters such as Bekti Macher Kebab, tandoor-baked. Gomes develops this further with Stuffed Squid, yoghurt-marinated squid stuffed with the same tandoori Bekti, both £4.50. Singara is the Bangla Samosa, using spiced vegetables stuffed into short-pastry, and made into a pyramid shape. Pyazi, the Bangla bhaji, their favourite street snack, both £2.95. Katti Kebab Calcutta's favourite snack, shredded pieces of spicy roasted leg of lamb served in a whole wheat wrap, £3.95. Mains do include CTM and it's done well (and yes it IS available in Sylhet's Polash hotel, no 100 on the menu!. But, please, try something new. Kashi Bhuna is a boneless goat curry, spiced hot, Kacchi Biryani, delicately flavoured, aromatic Moghul lamb biryani with dried plums and flaked almonds, Papaya Gost, aromatically spiced lamb cooked with green papaya, all £7.95. Dab Chingri is made by mother-in-laws when the son-in-law visits, using king prawns, cooked with fresh coconut milk, cardamom and a bit of saffron then served in a tender green coconut, £11.95. Surmai Macher Biryani, unique to Bengalis – fish biryani, £8.95. Raj Ash Kalia, a Bengali stir-fry of duck, capsicum and onions, lightly spiced. Moni Puri Prawns, a classic dish from the moni puri tribes people of Bangladesh, which consists of juicy king prawns cooked with ginger and light spices in a mellow sauce, £13.50. Bangladeshi vegetables appear on the menu when in season. Look out for chichinga, potol, kakrol, karela, doodi, mooli, lau, and more appearing in expertly cooked classics such as Pumpkin Bhaji, fried red pumpkin in a mild sweet and spicy taste, Green Banana Curry, fried plantain in a thick sauce, Baingan Borta, puréed smoked aubergine with ginger and garlic, Potoler Dolma, a Hindu dish from West Bengal, small gourd-like vegetables stuffed with paneer and golden sultana, Lau Dal, moong lentils and white pumpkin. No Bangladeshi meal is complete without their beloved bitter tastes. Shukto combines karela (bitter gourd) with aubergine, potato, green papaya, carrot, sweet potato, green banana and mooli cooked with a little bit of milk. All around a fiver each, and you can do no better than choose an all-veg meal at Ginger. Desserts are equally classical: Mishti Doi, a sweetened set yoghurt resembling shrikand, and Payesh, a jaggery-flavoured rice pudding. This is the break-through the UK has been waiting for. Our 7,000 Bangladeshi restaurateurs must take note. We the critics and gourmets have been saying it to you long enough; it's time to stop being complaicent by coining it by doling out curryhouse pastiche. You may be right; middle England isn't ready for you to throw out the lucrative CTM/Korma/Vindaloo baby with the bath water. but if you want your industry to be taken seriously, it's time to see why Ginger much deserves our **BEST BANGLADESHI AWARD.** Takeaway 20% Discount. Hours: 5.-11, Monday to Friday. 12 to 11, Saturday and Sunday.

INDIAN CONNOISSEURS ©

Norfolk Place, W2 020 7402 3299

Bright, cosy 46-seater which Chef Kabir Miah adds authenticity to the formula with interesting appetisers such as Bombay Roll, ground steak coated in potato paste and deep-fried, and Ayre Cutlet, Bangladeshi fish lightly spiced and pan-fried with onion. Main-course dishes include Hass Baas (spicy duck cooked with bamboo shoots) £8.50, Potato Tilli (lamb kidney cooked with potato) £6, Khashi Gazar, goat's meat cooked with baby carrots £7.50, Parrot Fish, in a thick spicy sauce, £7.75, Shorisha Ayre, £5.95, is spiced with mustard paste, or Venison, pheasant, grouse and quail Bhoona. The Meat Thali £10 was excellent value, good quality, nicely presented and very filling. Set lunch: £6.95 three courses, set dinner from £8.50. Delivery: 5-miles. Hours: 12-2.30/ 6-12.

KHANS ANP TOP 100

13 Westbourne Grove, W2 020 7727 5420

Khans was opened in 1977 by Mrs QN and Salman Khan. It seats an enormous 280 diners in two rooms (180 seats upstairs, plus 100 in the basement). The main room's high, cloud-painted ceiling is supported by a forest of gilt palm trees. There is a huge Hindi-arched mahogany bar and countless tables with pink cloths and black bentwood chairs. Here's the usual caveat: it's a love it or hate it place. They claim it is not unusual for them to do 1,000 covers a day. And therein lies the problem. This sheer volume results in a New York-style 'have-a-nice-day/take-it-or-leave-it/don't mess with me' service attitude. You'll either love that for a kind of perverse entertainment value, or you'll hate it. As first impressions count, we would not recommend it for a curry first-timer, nor to demure foreign tourist groups. Even Americans are shocked. But, for seasoned curryholics, it is an institution and decidedly not to be missed. Indeed, Khans has built up a very large customer base of frequent (some-three-times-a-week, apparently) regulars from far and wide, who certainly love Khans, and especially its Punjabi/north Indian food. It's all robust and expertly cooked. Specials such as Kastori Chicken £3.70, with fenugreek. Fish Curry £4.70, slices of fish cooked in a medium spiced sauce, on the bone. Chana Masaladar £2.60, chickpeas spiced in garlic, ginger, chilli paste, lime juice and onions. Khan's has settled down to its alcohol-free regime, and we continue to get plenty of reports from the old-hands, (who now tank up in the pub, then snatch a quick Khan's before returning to the tank), to bemused newcomers, who find it all a bit strange. What they have in common (well nearly all, not everyone reads the caveat), is praise for the food, and a kind of delight in the entertainment which is every day Khan's. It stays in our **TOP 100.** No alcohol Service: 10%. Set lunch: £5.99. Hours: 12-3/6-1030, Monday to Thursday. 12-12, Friday to Sunday.

MANDALAY NEW TO OUR TOP 100

444 Edgware Road, W2 020 7258 3696

This restaurant has the distinction of being the UK's only Burmese restaurant. Located in the unfashionable end of the road, it's run by the Ali brothers, Dwight (front) and Gary (cooking) Burmese-born and Norwegian-educated. The waiters will give good menu guidance. *'Small, very unpretentious looking place, seats 30. We started with Shrimp and*

©	Curry Club Discount	U	Unlicensed
V	Vegetarian	ANP	Alcohol not permitted
e-a-m-a-y-l	Eat as much as you like	BYO	Bring your own alcohol

Vegetable Spring Rolls £1.90 and Egg and Potato Samosas £1.90 served on a single plate in anticipation (correctly) of them being shared, accompanied by bowls of chilli, tamarind and soy – delicious. Lamb with Ginger £5.50, extremely tender lamb, in a thick, tasty sauce with right amount of ginger. Chicken Curry with Tomatoes – spicy tomato based thin curry sauce akin to Thai curries. Noodles Coconut and Chicken £5.90, a heap of soft and crispy noodles with plenty of chicken intermixed, all in coconut juices. Vegetable Rice, Chinese style with texture. All dishes were excellent, each tasting very distinct, fresh, lively, and agreeably flavoursome. Wonderful food, value tremendous. Highly recommended.' MW. Specials: A-Kyam, Fritters from £2.20, Bean Sprout; Calabash; Leafy Green; Shrimp and Bean Sprout; Shrimp and Vegetable. A-Thoat: Salads from £2.50, Vegetable Samosa Salad, Raw Papaya and Cucumber, Chicken and Cabbage, Shrimp and Lettuce. Hin-Cho: Soups all £2.50, Red Lentil; Bittle Gourd; Chicken, Shrimp and Lime. Main Courses: Spicy Lamb Curry £5.50, Pickle style Lamb – all £5.50. Chicken with Lemongrass, Chicken in Tamarind and Chilli Chicken all £5.10. Noodle Dishes: Mokhingar £5.50, rice noodles in fish soup, Noodles Coconut and King Prawns £6.90, Spice Rice and Lamb or Chicken £6.90. Licensed. Hours: 12-2.30/6-10.30, Monday to Saturday. Closed bank holidays. Welcome to our **TOP 100.**

NOOR JAHAN 2 — NEW ENTRANT

26 Sussex Place, W2 — 020 7402 2332

Opened in 2002. MD Aziz Ahmed serves the formula in 90 seats on two floors in trendy Lancaster Gate. A three course meal with wine is approximately £30 per person. Hours: 12-2.30/6-11.30.

SITARA — NEW ENTRANT

228, Edgware Road, W2 — 020 7723 1101

At Sitara, meaning 'star', chefs, Hitender Trikha and Rajesh Sharma have taken a modern interpretation on classic pan-Indian cooking and devised a menu that features dishes such as tandoori-style lobster flavoured with fenugreek, Roghan Josh, Bhel and Kadhai Murgh, and coupled it with innovative ideas like Indian-style dim sum. Run by manager, Dal Lall, the restaurant has a 6am entertainment license offering live Indian and Arabic entertainment, on its small dance floor in this elegant contemporary restaurant. Average Price £50. Mon -Fri 5.30-late, weekdays. 6-late. Closed Sundays.

London W4

Chiswick

WOODLANDS — TOP 100 V ©

12 High Road, W4 — 020 7994 9333

After many years with three branches Mr Sood has surprised Chiswick by opening this latest branch of the well-liked, small chain of southern Indian vegetarian restaurants. NP adores the Jaggary Dosa £3.75, for his pud. See SW1 branch for details.

London W5

Ealing

MONTY'S NEPALESE CUISINE

There are enough Monty's in Ealing to mount a navigation exercise in confusion. We like to clear such things up in this *Guide*. But this one is complex. The originators, three Nepalese chefs Hari Thapa, Karki and Mahanta Shrestha, set up originally in the incredibly popular Ealing Broadway venue (now closed) in 1980. They relocated to South Ealing. Since then, the members of the original group split, but they all still use the original name, logos, spin and menu. So because we have as many raving reports about any of the four venues, what we say is that all the Monty's do all the formula curries. And they all have a Nepalese specials list. *'Monty's provides excellent value for money and are a haven of quality cuisine, exquisite Nepalese spicing and caring service.'* AIE. Take your pick of which Monty's you prefer, and frankly any one is as good as any other. Here they are:

MONTY'S NEPALESE CUISINE

4 Broadway Centre, High St, W5 — 020 8579 4646

Karki converted an Italian restaurant next to the

Post Office and Club Boulevard, and refurbished it as a spacious, modern Monty's in 2000. It's a light and airy restaurant with wicker furniture, layers of fresh linen and attentive, smiley waiters. *'We are named after Sir Montgomery'*, he says, but doesn't expand on this elusive explanation. Hours: 12-3/6-12. Branch: Monty's, W13.

MONTY'S NEPALESE CUISINE

1 The Mall, Broadway, W5 020 8567 5802

Mahanta Shrestha took on this 68-seater venue, *'Monty's came from my name, Mahanta'*, he says. Details, see above. Hours: 12-3/6-12. Branch, Monty's, 53 Fife Road, Kingston. Run by Kishore Shrestha.

MONTY'S NEPALESE CUISINE

224 South Ealing Road, W5 020 8-560 2619

The reincarnation of the first Ealing Monty's opened here years ago. Still going strong with Hari Thapa in charge. Hours: 12-3/6-12am. Details, see above.

ZAYKA INDIAN CUISINE

8 South Ealing Road, W5 020 8569 7278

I'd love to say that Ealing has the best Indian restaurants in the area. It was where I was born, and it had curryhouses in the 1960s. Sadly, they come and they go. We rate them, you hate them. But the one which you all prasie is Zayka I Admittedly, the decor is basic despite the redec *'but the food (and the prices) excellent as is the service.'* AR Zayka opened in 1990 and has established itself as one of west London's favourites, serving all the popular tandooris, starters, curries and accessories including fish specialities and an extensive vegetarian menu. Sunday e-a-m-a-y-l. Takeaway. Free local delivery on orders over £5. Hours: 12-2.30 (Sun to 3)/6-11.30 (Fri & Sat to 12am).

London W6

Hammersmith

AKASH

177 King Street, W6 020 8748 4567

It's a popular long-standing venue on 'curry alley'. Specials include: Fish Peri Peri £6.95, tempered fish cooked with a blend of vinegar, chillies and spices. Fish Biran £6.95, grilled fried fish, served on a bed of fried onion and fried green chillies, and fresh herbs – a traditional Bengali dish. Chicken Hariyali £6.25, chicken with fresh spinach, mint and coriander. Delivery: 3 miles, £10 minimum. Hours: 12-2.30/6-11.

LIGHT OF NEPAL

268 King Street, W6 020 8748 3586

'*When did this one open? I remember my parents taking me there when I was what? four? five?*' [1979, Ed] '*and now I take my kids. Great.*' CP. This popular, long-standing restaurant does the 'Nepalese' curryhouse formula, which is mostly the old curryhouse favourite. JL still reminds us '*My favourite is still the Butter Chicken. It's chunks of chicken, resembling tikka, red and tender, but with a garlicy taste. With it you need their coriander dip – a pureé of mint, coriander, onion, pepper, chilli and lime juice.. After that I don't need anything else, well a roti goes well, and Cobra.*' JL. We like the Sak-su-ka, minced lamb with egg, tomato and Nepalese spices. Hours: 12-2.30/6-11.

SAGAR NEW ENTRANT TOP 100 V

157 King Street, W6 020 8741 8563

King Street is curry alley. You are spoilt for choice, and this Guide names the ones you prefer. But most are formulaic. So it is a pleasure to see a south Indian opening up here. It cooks Udipi food. Udipi is a small coastal town, a few miles north of Mangalore in the south-western state of Karnataka, celebrated for Bramin temples and cuisine. Masala Dosa originated here. By the sixth century AD, they were being made as temple feedings for thousands of worshippers. Udipi dosas are made from a thin batter cooked very thin and crisp in Karnataka and thick and small in Tamil Nadu. Also on the menu are Rasam, Sambar, Uppuma, Uthappam (*see p* 50). Curries include Kootu This is a typical Madrassi dish as found in the local homes, where it is slow-cooked in a mud pot over wood fire. It's a hot and sour curry, containing gourd, chilli, tamarind, sesame and coconut. Traditionally it's served with Kazhani meaning 'rice-washed water'. Kootu is traditionally served with that rice. At Sagar, you can order Bakabhat, a yoghurt-based rice, or Lemon rice, with cashews and curry leaves. The menu is a glossary in itself. And the staff are ever-helpful. We are delighted to place the Sagar straight into our **TOP 100.** Hours: 12-2.45/5.30-1045. Monday to Wednesday. 12-1045. Thursday to Sunday.

TANDOORI NIGHTS TOP 100 

319 King Street, W6 020 8741 4328

Mr Modi Udin is as friendly an owner as they come, as are AB Choudhury, and his staff made the more confident with the food from chef

Mabul Miah's food. Fully licensed and air-conditioned. *'Extremely well laid out and furnished restaurant on the busy King Street. Seating for 100 with several discreet areas. Very attentive, efficient and knowledgeable staff. Succulent pieces of Tandoori Chicken with those small crispy cinders that you get on the best cooked meat. Equally enjoyable and freshly cooked Seek Kebab with just the right balance of heat and spice. Cool and fresh Cucumber Raitha with a subtle sour bite. Exceptional Rogan Josh with tender chunks of lamb in an exquisite and quite the best sauce I have had to date. Mould of aromatic, al dente Pullao and a soft, fluffy Nan. Very enjoyable.'* RW. Specialities: Bataire Masala £8.95, two quails barbecued and cooked in sauce. Sunday Buffet: £8.95, familys welcome, concessions for children. *'Deservedly* **TOP 100.'** SO. Hours: 12-3/6-12.

London W8

Kensington High Street, Notting Hill

MALABAR — TOP 100

27 Uxbridge Street, W8 — 020 7727 8800

Last time we said: 'The simple decor and the eclectic menu haven't changed at Jo, Sophie and Tony Chalmers' and Anil Bis's three-floor 56-seat Malabar since it opened in 1983.' Woops! BH picked us up on such an assertive statement. *'Don't say nothing ever changes at the Malabar. Couldn't find Long Chicken on the neatly designed menu, and prices have moderately increased (Chilli Bhutta £3.75, Murgh Makhni £7, Sunday Buffet £7.50). Liked the food as much as room and service, even if sweetcorn starter came as side dish with main courses. Antje declared her interestingly smoky tasting Murgh Makhni one of the best. My Gosht Masala – plenty of fresh mint, delicious. Five Lentil Dhall – less convincing, more spices needed. All dishes very mild, surprisingly including the Chilli Bhutta (perhaps they don't want to scare the tourists). Free 20 page recipe booklet with photos is a good idea. A likeable restaurant with food quite different in spicing and presentation. I wish this were in my hom,e town, Berlin.'* BH. Remains secure in our **TOP 100.** Hours: 12-3/6-11.30. Closed one week in Aug.

UTSAV — NEW ENTRANT

17 Kensington High Street, W8 — 020 7368 0022

Entrepreneur owner of Malabar Junction, WC2, Ashok Modi launched Utsav, meaning 'festival' in 2003. It has 150 seats on two floors, almost opposite the Royal Garden Hotel. Architects Astore Harrison have designed contemporary decor, outside (striking glass, and blues, and a cute use of the first floor bay window. Inside an attractive wooden bar, white walls, creative lighting, theming blues and blondes. The food by chef Gowtham Karingi, ex Zaika sous chef (*see next entry*) is pan-Asian, a bit from here and a bit from there. OK if the chefs understand regional spicing immaculately, and that they can get difficult ingredients. We felt perhaps the Goan Prawn Balchao lacked that sourness only achieved from toddy vinegar, while Kashmiri chilli would have helped the Roghanjosh. And there were too many squiggly dots and squirls (a Ziaka trick, passée in our opinion). That said, the Tirangi chicken tikka, marinated in saffron, cheese and coriander, was masterly. The Chicken Varutha in tamarind, red chilli, shallots, curry leaves & tomato sauce had spot on south Indian tastes, as did the fine Dosa and chutneys. The Paneer was fresh and juicy. Service charge 12.5%. Hours Lunch: 12-3 daily, 6-11.30. Dinner Monday to Saturday: Sunday: -10.30 Bar: 11am-11.30. Happy hour daily 4-7 p.m

ZAIKA — TOP 100

1 Kensington High Street, W8 — 020 7795 6533

Zaika (and Tamarind) were the first Indian restaurants to get the coveted Michelin star and both still retain it after three years, despite Tamarind having a chef change and Zaika moving house. So why did Michelin give Zaika the star treatment. On arrival in London in the early nineties, Oberoi-trained Vineet Bhatia cheffed around in the inner suburbs, mostly at the aptly named Star. Vineet is good at self-spinning, he's good at cooking too. He impressed Claudio Pulze and Raj Sharma enough to offer him a partnership at Zaika which opened in 1999. We prefer the feel of this branch; despite a slight decor mismatch; the chair backs maybe? It was yet another former bank, which helps image. And it's image which gets the star, not classical Indian cooking, because although Vineet can do it admirably, he also likes to innovate. As Vineet says *'Zaika literally translates as sophisticated flavours. I aim to do justice to the name by providing a wide diversity of enticing flavours through some traditional classics and a few tantalising dishes with a slight twist'.* [Told you he likes spin]. The twists include non-Indian ingredients such as Thai lime leaves, smoked salmon, dill, cocoa, white chocolate, spring onions, shitake mushroom, goat cheese, broccoli, couscous, tuna, sago, asparagus, noodles, baby corn, and mangetout. Menu spin matches the inventions: for example, *'Spice-infused'* means tandoori-marinated, *'Jus'* means curry sauce, and '*Risotto*' means biriani. Presentation is – well it's Michelin – a kind of plated, piled-up nouveau 'enhanced' with squiggles of varying colours. We've been to both Zaika's. Our visits have found many good things, but many small flaws, not least the spelling and grammatical mistakes on the menu. Several of our most trusted reporters have also been. *'After an all-day convention at the Albert Hall, we went for a shower and drink at the Royal Lancaster where we were staying. Then over the road to Zaika for a romantic night out. We decided on the Jugalbandi Tasting menu. Five courses with wine. Course 1: Minced duck rolls, tandoori smoked-salmon chunks and coconut-kokum (sour plum) scallops. Quite divine. Course 2: Indian risotto (khichdi) with red onion and coriander (it was OK) topped with black chicken. The chicken is based on a Coorg dish, but missed the spicing and appearance quite widely. Course 3: Billed as 'Pan-fried sea bass, upma-indian cous cous ,raw mango and turmeric sauce served with carom seed nan'. Quite a flavourful innovative dish. Vineet's Upma is a variation on the south Indian Semolina Savoury Pancake. Quite an unconventional clash of flavours, fish and mango sauce. Carom (ajwain) is an acquired taste and one of our party thought the nan tasted of diesel fuel. Course 4: Billed as 'a classic Kashmiri dish cooked with lambshank in a rich onion & tomato sauce. The shank-meat was tender, though the sauce a bit uninspired. Tomato should not appear in this dish if it purports to be classical, though it does so at the curry house – it's a cheaty way of obtaining the red (rogan) colour. We confess we did enjoy it though. Served with a fluffy, golden Saffron Rice. Course 5: Malai Kulfi: egg-free Indian ice cream, Malai meaning 'cream'. No room we thought, but we loved it. You must order min two, so the prices for this are subject to £33.50, – £45 inc. wine. £55 wines matched to accompany each course. Conclusion: very interesting, and we'd go back.'* RCF. Dishes which we think hit the mark perfectly include the starter Chakaur Partridge Tikka, Tandoori – partridge breast, with partidge shammi kebab and beetroot chutney £8.75. Hunting Chakaur (or Shikar) was (is) a major sport with Indian high-borns. Quite delightful, all the combinations. Gilafi Dum Biryani (see page 50), diced lamb cooked with aromatic basmati rice, baked under a flaky crust, £15.50. Perfect, just as you'd find in Lucknow. And there's that Chocolate Samosa, Chocomaos. Marbled white and plain chocolate with chenna (paneer) and roasted almonds, enclosed in crispy envelopes. Served with malai kulfi. £4.75. A great invention. So there it is. Invention/fusion may have its place, but we feel it is unlikely to become established cuisine, since its inventors restlessly want to move on. But great cuisine isn't about what is and is not fashionable. It's about centuries of honing to perfection. And if you want classical Indian done better, with truly sophisticated presentation, matched decor and minimal spin, try the non-starred Chutney Mary. But if you and Michelin enjoy what we've described, then Zaika is for you. Service 12½%. Hours: Lunch: 12-2.30., Sunday to Friday. Dinner: 6.30-10.45, Monday to Saturday, Sunday, 10.

London W12

Shepherds Bush, White City

NEPALESE TANDOORI 

121 Uxbridge Road, W12 020 8740 7551

Prabin Pradhan's cosy 38-seater's specials include: Chicken Nepal, boneless chicken with fresh fruits and cream £5, Nepalese Murgh Masala, chicken off the bone with sauce and boiled egg £6, Vegetable Nepal, seasonal vegetables with fresh fruits and cream £3.75. Stocks Iceberg Nepalese beer Delivery: £12 min, 3-mile rad. Hours: 12-2.30/6-12.

London W13

West Ealing

LAGUNA 

1-3 Culmington Pde, 127-129 Uxbridge Rd, W13 020 8579 9992

Established in 1984 by Sunil Lamba, and it's been in this *Guide* since then, serving competent north Indian formula food in his 120-seater restaurant.. It's built up a large local following, and in its time it's seen so many new Indian restaurants come and go in Ealing, and even now it stands out above the 25 or so competitors, a chupatti-throw away. Huge frontage, decorated with individually planted conifers in square wooden tubs. Stylishly decorated in pastel shades, with arches and ceiling fans. Laguna Special Butter Chicken £5.75 is the most popular dish. Service 10%. Sun. 12-12. Branch: Laguna Banquet Hall, North Acton Road, NW10.

MONTY'S TANDOORI

54 Northfields Avenue, W13 020 8566 5364

'My curryholic daughter moved to Ealing last year and sussed Monty's out pretty quickly and invited me their on my previous visit. Lovely decor, swift service, fresh salad and yoghurt dip. Popadoms and pickles were served while we ordered and this immediately relaxed us for a pleasant evening. Spicing and quality subtle and superb. We were stuffed, enough left for a meal for two in the freezer. Why black ceilings in the toilet?' AIE. *'Highly recommended. The bill for three people with drinks was £52.* SO. Hours: 12-3 and 6-12. Branch: Monty's, Broadway Centre, W5. (and more details).

SIGIRI SRI LANKAN

TOP 100 AND PREVIOUS AWARD WINNER

161 Northfields Avenue, W13 020 8579 8000

Sigiri is a landmark in Sri Lanka, which must not be missed. If you do nothing else visit Sigiri. It is a huge mountain with a flat top (rather like Table Top mountain in Cape Town, South Africa but much more dramatic and there is no 'ski lift' to take you to the top). As you approach Sigiri you realise just how big it is and then the guide informs you that 'we' are going to climb it! It is surrounded by beautifully and symmetrically designed gardens with water pools. On top of the mountain are the ruined remains of a fabulous royal palace. Eating here, in the unlikely setting of Northfields on a corner site with its smoked-glass windows inset in red brick, reminded us of that trip as the restaurant is decorated with pictures and wall hangings and serves delightful, authentic Sri Lankan food. We ate light Popadams, Coconut Chutney, Devilled Pork – ask for spicy, Kothu Roti chopped chupatti with onions and spicy meat – all our favourites and enjoyed them all. Don't forget other dishes such as Hoppers (Apa), Dosa and Uppaamas and that glorious pudding Wattalappam – a very sweet, jaggery-based, dark egg custard. Safe in our **TOP 100**. Hours: 6.30-11; closed Mon.

©	Curry Club Discount	**U**	Unlicensed
V	Vegetarian	**ANP**	Alcohol not permitted
e-a-m-a-y-l	Eat as much as you like	**BYO**	Bring your own alcohol

London W14

Olympia, West Kensington

AL'INDIENNE

197 North End Road, W14 020 7610 2020

It's maybe not quite the best end of North End Road, but it does a good job. The frontage isn't that interesting, but inside it's a forest of palms, and foliage, wooden floor, colonial chairs, Indian artifacts and crisp, white linen. Owner MJArshad and his personable staff make it a welcoming occasion. Chef Raja cooks all the favourite curries, but his specials are worth noting. For example, try his Kunkry Bhindi starter, okra fried with poppy seeds and basil £3.15, or the mains: Guinea Fowl Tendary, smoked breast flavoured with black cardamom, and cinnamom, served with dal ajd lemon rice £11.95. Lobster ke Mezay, with poppy and dill, £12.95. Nan A Magajia £2.50 – stuffed with soft curd cheese, onion and chillies. *'Good welcome and cuisine excellent. Service with smiles and food in abundance.'* JL. Delivery. Hours: 5.30-12, daily. Sunday buffet: 5-11.30.

London WC

Area: West End .
Postcodes wc1, wc
Population: 165,000

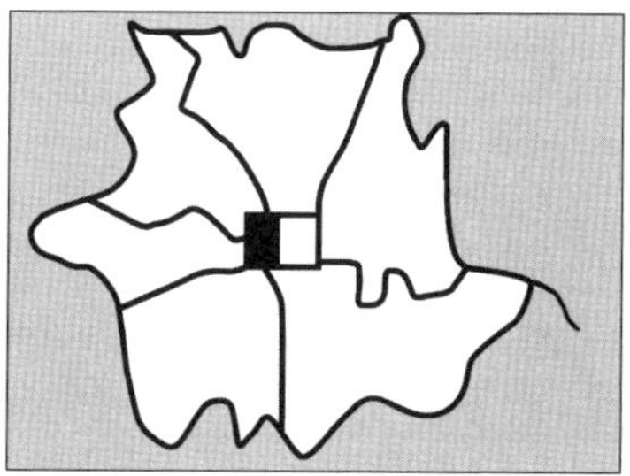

London WC1

Holborn

DEPA NEW ENTRANT

4 Leigh Street, WC1 020 7387 0613

'A great deal of attention has been paid to the decor, though the toilet could do with a lick of paint! Excellent, swift service, fresh Popadoms and Pickles, the Meat Samosa £2.10 comprised of lean, spiced, minced lamb encapsulated in rice flour pastry. Followed by a delicious Chicken Tikka Bhuna, fragrant Pullao and light Chupatti 70p. Tasty Mango Kulfi finished off the meal nicely. Mr Miah, the chef delivers classical dishes with great confidence. Prices average.' AIE. ... and Tony, just couldn't keep away... *'Consistently high quality of cuisine, attentive service and value for money but most of all the best Meat Samosas £2.10, I have had in the UK, light, crisp and just so absolutely delicious, they are addictive.'* AIE. Takeaway: 10% discount. Delivery: £10 minimum. Hours: 6-12.

HASON RAJA NEW ENTRANT

Southampton Row, WC 020 7242 3377

Rafu Miah has named his new 150-seater restaurant after a famous poet, and it' decorated in greens. There is a private room for around 20 plus another area in the basement for overflow or special functions. At lunchtime there is a 12 dish buffet for just £9.95

MALABAR JUNCTION TOP 100

107 Great Russell Street, WC1 020 7580 5230

Light, bright and airy restaurant with Victorian-styled glass sky-light giving a good summery feel. Bamboo chairs, palm trees in polished brass pots, original paintings, a marble fountain and smiling Keralan waiters complete the scene. The menu specialises in Keralan cuisine, with dishes from the cities of Cochin, Malabar and Travancore. Hot is the norm in Kerala but they cool it for *'western tastes'*! If you want it hot, tell them, the kitchen are happy to accommodate. Contrary to popular belief, meat, chicken and fish dishes are commonplace in south India, and here they do everything well. Pick from such starters as Lamb

Cutlets, £5, patties of spicy minced lamb, bread crumbed and fried, served with tomato sauce and salad, King Prawn Fry £8.50 (with ginger, garlic, spices and sliced coconut), Malabar Chicken £8.50 (with coconut, curry leaves, garlic and mustard), Spinach Vadai £3 (fried crunchy doughnut of channa dal, green chillies, onion, ginger, curry leaves and fresh spinach served with chutneys). And if you have any room left Banana Leaf Cake £4, rice with sweet filling of coconut, banana and jaggery wrapped in banana leaf and steamed – divine. The bar and further dining facilities are downstairs. *'Very courteous and hospitable. Clean, good vegetarian and non vegetarian food, prepaid in separate kitchens by different chef's. Quantities of food more than enough. A pleasant experience.'* NR. Hours: bar – 11-11, except Sun: 12-10.30; Restaurant: 12-3/6-11.30.

ORIGINAL LAHORE KEBAB HOUSE

at the Holiday Inn, 1 Kings Cross Road, WC1
020 7833 9787

Boldly going where few hotels go this 405-room Kings Cross Holiday Inn opened a 160-seater 'Indian' at this venue in 1998. Goan chefs came and Goan chefs kept on 'goan'. But the customers kept on coming. Now, still boldly going the restaurant has just (as we go to print) been taken on by Mohammed Siddique, so it's really gutsy carnivorous fare, and let's hope it's successful here (there is another restaurant in the hotel – continental! – for the limpets. *See Lahore Kebab House* E1 for details. Suffice to say Indian-born, Dean Thapar's expansion plans include sites in Croydon, Ealing, Southall, USA and the Middle East. Lunch and dinner and reports please.

London WC2

Aldwych, Covent Garden

BHATTI 

37 Great Queen Street, WC2 020 7405 5222

Taken over in 1990 by N. Ruparel. The restaurant seats 95 in two rooms and serves formula northern Indian food. It is situated in a 17th century listed building. *'Great for the theatres, and really pleasant experience here. So we go back regularly'.* HEG. Delivery: £25 minimum, 4-mile radius. Hours: 12-2.45 (2 on Sun.) / 5.30-11.45 (10.30 Sun.).

INDIA CLUB — TOP 100

143 The Strand, WC2 020 7836 0650

This time we'll leave it to you to explain. *'It took a long time to decide to give the India Club another go after finding a chicken bone in one of our vegetarian dishes.. But something this good deserves a second chance. Delighted to say that it was really very good. Immediately recognised and warmly greeted by the waiter. Vegetarian meal £10 per head is excellent value, including Popadoms, Pickles, Dosa, Chilli and Vegetable Bhajia's, four curries, Rice and Nan. Superb standard – free from bones!'* AG. *'Previously we had visited during the week, so was quieter on Saturday lunch. Warm welcome. Soon settled with an excellent bottle of chilled white wine which we had managed to extricate from 'the lady down stairs!'* [Doris: Ed] *'General Bilimoria £6 with an interesting story on the label. We were offered and accepted the set meal £11 a head, pointing out that one of our number was vegetarian. This included Popadoms – excellent with chutneys and pickles. Chilli Bhajias, Onion Bhajias, Masala Dosa and Tandoori Chicken. After a pause Lamb and Chicken Curry, Dall, Aubergine, Mixed Vegetable Potato and Chickpea, rice – plenty! Really too much for even us... but all hot, fresh and tasty. Only one waiter, even when four other tables were occupied, but he was very cheery with repeated assurances that he would bring anything else we required! Not sure about the repainted walls, glad about the retained pictures and ancient stair carpet!'* GM. *'What can you say about The India Club. The same unsmiling welcome greets you – the head waiter being the same misery who served us on our last visit. Neither the ladies nor the gents had lights, there was still no Lassi (there never is!), the chutney and onion salad were both served piled up in saucers, there was no attempt at presentation but the food was sublime and what value for money with the quantities just right.'* G&MP. And what's left to say about Britain's, nay the world's best-loved venue?? I'm not even going to explain how to get the drinks nor tell you why it remains so high in our **TOP 100.** Find out for yourself. Hours: 12-2.30/6-11; closed Sun.

MELA TOP 100

152 Shaftesbury Avenue N, WC2 020 7836 8635

When ex-Soho Spice chef Kuldeep Singh, with Sanjay Singh Sighat and Surinder Kumar Mehra (all Taj-trained chefs) opened Mela (meaning 'festival') in 2000, they pioneered an original idea to capture a vast potential lunch trade, always illusive at the Indian restaurant. Under the spin of 'dhaba' (stall) serving 'street food' and named 'Paratha Pavilion', it's the Indian equivalent of a sandwich bar. Instead of sliced loaf, choose naan, roomali, paratha, roti, puri and bhatura, appam, uttapams (served with coconut chutney), or dosa with a topping (filling) choice of as many curries as you can imagine, dozens of them. There are, it seems, over 500 combination options. Prices range from £1.95 for a simple choice to £4.50 for a Gourmet Snack Lunch. It was an instant success. The restaurant is open all day (useful to know), but it changes atmosphere in the evening. It's somehow more relaxed allowing time to inspect the decor, rather than choke on a chupatti. Clean lines of white washed walls, large seemless mirrors and a few embroidered cushion covers, from Orissa. Square terracotta floor tiles, plastic wood-effect tables (sounds horrid but not), simple wooden chairs upholstered in spicy coloured fabric. The menu describes itself as 'Indian Cuisine – Country Style', which we interpret as Indian home-cooking. Kuldeep says "*ingredients here in England are much better than back home. This is a chef's paradise.*" And he proves it with dishes such as Bater Khada Masala, marinated quails roasted in a spicy mango masala, £4.95 and Malabari Seafood Stew, mixed seafood with turnip, cauliflower, coconut milk and coriander, £11.95. *'I decided to start with Gosht Utthapams – fluffy rice pancakes topped with diced, chargrilled lamb, onion, pepper, freshly grated coconut and served with minty coconut chutney,'* £4.40. *A monogrammed square plate arrived with the promised two pancakes and a small salad of carrot, beetroot, cucumber and green leaves tossed in a lightly spiced dressing – delicious. .Pat decided on a Raj Kachauri, mini puries stuffed with seasoned potato, chick peas, onion and topped with mint and tamarind chutneys,* £3.50. *What arrived was one large stuffed puri, in a bowl, which looked as impressive as it tasted. Mains were Khatta Khargosh, curried rabbit,* £12.95 *and Kori Gassi, chicken on the bone in a thin, spicy curry flavoured with chilli, spices, coconut tamarind,* £8.50. *We accompanied our dishes with Plain Rice* £1.95, *Roomali Roti* £2.25 *– better than the offering at Benares – and Mirch Baingan Ka Salan, baby aubergines in peanut-flavoured yoghurt gravy,* £5.50, *which never arrived and I decided not to remind them. Mela is a lovely restaurant, with cheerful waiters, serving lovely Indian food.'* DBAC. This is echoed by HC: *'Charming and authoratitive person in charge. Whole place was running well. Food, again outstandingly good, definitely a very good restaurant – amazing menu..* HC. However, there are service points that need to be corrected. Firstly, forgetting a dish, next it is very rude to clear one diner's plate, when the other diner is still eating and thirdly, sticky menus and sticky tables may give the impression of a sticky kitchen – not good! Despite that, it remains high in our **TOP 100.** Hours: 12-11.30, daily. Sunday to 10.30.

PUNJAB TOP 100

80 Neal Street, WC2 020 7836 9787

The Punjab opened in 1947 in Aldgate and moved to its present site in 1951, making it the oldest UK Punjabi restaurant. For its entire life it has been in the capable hands of just three men, the late founder, son, and now grandson Sital Singh Maan. The Punjab was one of the original pioneers of the curry formula. Only here it is done as it has always been done, and as it should be. The result is unlike the newer Bangladeshi clones, and is probably what old farts think they remember when they say *'curry isn't like it used to be'.* CT is a bit suspicious if the redec; *'the wooden tree is quite striking. Seems not to have weakened the food.'* CT. The food is meat-orientated, spicy, savoury and very tasty. Specialities: Anari Gosht £7.50, pomegranate and lamb, Benaam Macchi Tarkari £7.50, nameless fish curry, Acharri Murgha £7.80, pickled chicken. Also try the Vegetable Koofta £4.70, diced pumpkin with spices and herbs made into balls. *'A year ago we had an outrageously mediocre meal. Decided to give it another go. This time Chicken Methia – beautifully flavoured and chicken was real quality. Linda had Chicken Tikka flambéed with brandy at the table – spectacular.'* MG. Regulars have their own club, the 'Punjabbers'. Remains high in our **TOP 100.** Service 10%. Lunch and dinner, daily.

SARTAJ BALTI HOUSE NEW ENTRANT

26 Earlham Street, 7 Dials, WC2 020 7831 1413

'Well established in very busy street. We caught them unaware at 6.10pm. Small, old fashioned, very long menu, unusual items, squid and scallops. Seafood Meal Thai £10.50 – very good dish of squid, scallops, prawns and white fish. Attentive service and generally very good, young waiter a bit hazy on ingredients – full marks the fish was tilapia. Curries served in large shallow karahis, presentation, quantities and overall quality were very good. More than satisfied, definitely go back.' HC. Hours: 12-3/5.30 to late.

SITAR BALTI

149 The Strand, WC2 020 7836 3730

'Can confirm that food is as good as ever and the one grumble on several earlier visits, the mean size of portions, seems to have been rectified, long may it continue. Service always friendly and generally good.' HC. *'Now opens at 5.30 so we can get to the theatre by 7.30pm without a rush. Prices are a little higher than average, but food warrants every penny. Fried King Prawn for starter – prawns coated in crunchy vermicelli, very good, served with spicy dip. Special Starter turned out to be a giant king prawn, opened out and served tail up, very eye-catching, with most wonderful mustard sauce – outstandingly good, will have main course version next visit. Brinjal Bhajee – large chunks, very good. Gulab Jamun – wonderful to have it offered and they were superb. All waiters were smiley and helpful – a most enjoyable dinner.'* D&HC.

TANDOORI NIGHTS REENTRY ©

35 Great Queen Street, WC2 020 7831 2558

Owner Mrs Yasmeen Rashid opened her first Tandoori Nights in Cockfosters, Herts, in 1988, and her second in NW1 months later. In 1993 she opened this branch with Manager Salil, and chef Waris Miah. Anyway, the delectable Yasmeen bumped into your editor at an Asian industry do recently. *'Why have you delisted me', she squealed and peeled?* To avoid funny looks at functions, she's back. Also to avoid futere squalings, Yasmeem is also running a curry ready meal company called *Organic India*, which can be contacted on 020 8805 2223. Service (at the restaurant) 12½%. Lunch and dinner, daily.

ENGLAND

The method in this Guide is to record our entries in alphabetical order: first the county then, within that, the town, then the restaurant. With the demise of Avon, we now start with Bedfordshire, the first town we record is Arlesey, and its first restaurant is Raj Villa, and so on. Our last English county is Yorkshire West, and Wakefield is the last recorded town.

BEDFORDSHIRE

Area:
Central England.
Population: 557,000
Adjacent Counties:
Bucks, Cambs,
Herts and
Northants.

Arlesey

RAJ VILLA ©

27 High Street, Arlesey 01462 835145

Akthar Ali has owned and managed this 70-seater since 1996. Branches: Raj Gat, Bedford Street, Ampthill, and Raj Moni, Upper Street, London, N1.

Bedford

CHOUDHURY'S OPEN KITCHEN
NEW ENTRANT

2 The Broadway, Bedford 01234 356162

'Choudhury's is the best and largest restaurant in Beds. It's been beautifully refurbished, bringing it bang up to date. It has a new menu with some tasty new and exciting dishes including fish. You can watch your meals being prepared in uncompromisingly modern surroundings: hence the new name "Choudhury's Open Kitchen". We have travelled quite extensively in India and Sri Lanka and all the Indian restaurants in the south of England and we have come to the conclusion that Choudhury's is best.' PE.

GULSHAN 

69 Tavistock Street, Bedford 01234 355544

Chef Shanu Miah cooks Pakistani and North Indian at S and Mrs BK Nijjer. *'Try Lamb Sharab (lamb tikka cooked in cream and almond liqueur) served with Pullao Rice.'* BB Delivery £10 min. Hours: 12-2pm/6-1am.

Luton

ALANKAR

276 Dunstable Road, Luton 01582 455189

'Took advice from the Guide and was very impressed. Looked, from outside rather peculiar for a curry house. However, the food was of excellent standard. Reminded me of Madhu's, Southall.' Not quite as good (is there better?) ..but the menu was vast. Had Kebabs and Lamb Chops, all came sizzling. Fish Masala very enjoyable. I must also say the spicy Poppadoms were the best I've had, full of flavour. Well worth a mention, would go again without a doubt. Nearly forgot, they served a beautiful dish called Begun Bortha, which is mashed aubergine. It was wonderful, trust me'. LH.

DILDAR NEW ENTRANT

1 Sundon Pde, Park Road 01582 505198

'Good formula curry house, done well. Very good Chicken Tikka.' MRW

JAY RAJ NEW ENTRANT

636 Hitchin Road, Luton

'Well done formula curry house. Very good and filling set lunch.' MRW

MEAH TANDOORI 

102 Park Street, Luton 01582 454504

'Stuffed Peppers – roasted and stuffed with minced lamb, herbs and topped with cheese. Salmon Kebabs – beautifully spiced with spring onions and potato, served with tangy sauce. Delightful.' DS. *'Very impressed with the personal service and the splendid chicken shashlick.'* AW. *'A good restaurant'.* TK.

©	Curry Club Discount	U	Unlicensed
V	Vegetarian	ANP	Alcohol not permitted
e-a-m-a-y-l	Eat as much as you like	BYO	Bring your own alcohol

BERKSHIRE

Area: Home Counties (west of London)
Adjacent Counties: Hants, Surrey, Middx, Oxon, Wilts

Cookham

MALIK'S TOP 100

Royal Exchange, High St, Cookham
01628 520085

Set in a former country pub, complete with clinging ivy, and olde beams, this restaurant takes its name from Malik Ahmed, who, with partner Mujibur Rahman, runs front of house. A huge effort is being made with the cooking. As well as popular Bangladeshi formula stuff, there are some interesting specials: Cox's Bazar Samuk – Mussels in coconut, Haash Poora – Duck breast and Annans Haash – Duck in coconut milk, Jhanglee Horrin – Venison and Mixed Seafood Bhuna with scallops, cuttlefish, squid and tiger fish. Also you'll find veal, and Bengali fish dishes. Alfresco dining in the former pub's garden. Malik's remain in our **TOP 100.**

Crowthorne

VILLAGE TANDOORI 

204 Dukes Ride, Crowthorne 01344 780118

Bangla Night every Tuesday. Good formula house.

Hungerford

MOONLIGHT NEW ENTRANT

43 High St, Hungerford 01488 685252

'We are always made welcome, especially by the head waiter - Ali and the boss, who does the cooking if he is there, he has two other branches. It is clean, though the loos are beginning to show their age. Background music is not intrusive. Good ample food, have visited at least twenty times.' Mr & Mr SH.

Maidenhead

NABHA TAKEAWAY U 

39 King Street, Maidenhead 01628 770193

A Balti takeaway, opened in 1990, Zahire Khan taking over ownership in 1997. Parking for 4 cars in front. Specials include: Nabha Special Biryani. Unlicensed. Hours: 5.30pm-12am (Sat. & Sun. to 1am).

Reading

THE GURKHA INN ©

64 George Street, Caversham 0118 948 3974

42-seater, formerly La Spice Café. A&AL comment: *'Produces exquisite food of outstanding quality but has recently been affected by local council parking restrictions. We would urge you most strongly to encourage your members to rally their support – they'll not be disappointed.'* Car park nearby. Delivery: £12 min 3-mile radius. Hours: 12.30-2.30/6-11.30.

INDIA PALACE 

83-85 Wokingham Road, Earley, Reading
0118 962 2711

The Palace is jointly owned by Mrs LC Payne and chef Bhadracen, and managed by A Ahad. *'Impressed by the cleanliness, crisp linen, light ambience of lighting and decor and background music. Chicken Chatwas delicious. Palace Spring Chicken, Haandi Saag Chicken, Pullao Rice, Tarka Dal and Bombay Aloo with Kulcha Nan, all really excellent.'* RT.

RICE N SPICE NEW ENTRANT

352 Oxford Road Reading

Pankaj Mehra formerly Executive Sous Chef of The Oberoi New Delhi has opened in Reading. This means you get gourmet food of a very high quality here.

SPICE OVEN NEW ENTRANT

2 Church Street, Caversham, Reading
0118 948 1000

'Overall - this restaurant is very special. One of the best. The food tends to be on the spicy side and not for the faint hearted. The restaurant is large, luxurious with wood carved fittings. The Taj-trained Indian chef produces authentic regional food. The prices reasonable - Sunday Buffet £7.95 - good value. On the main

menu - Haandi Gosht £7.25, Chicken Tikka Jalfrezi £6.95. A great addition to the Reading curry scene.' ¼ . Tasty Indian delights include: Murg Malai Tikka £3.75, chicken breast marinated with fresh herbs and cheese, cooked in the tandoor. Seek Kebab Khaas £3.20, minced lamb cooked on skewers and wrapped in fresh aromatic vegetables. Masala Dosai £4.50, rice pancake with potato masala stuffing served with sambhar and chutneys. Salmon Amritsari £7.50, salmon marinated in crushed garlic and Punjabi spices. Kadhi Pakoda £3.50, fenugreek, curry leaves and yoghurt curry with pakoda.

STANDARD NEPALESE 

141 Caversham Road, Reading 0118 959 0093

Established in 1980. Seats 140. 8 parking places at front. Pond and fountain as centrepiece. Nepalese specials include Katmandu Aloo. *'Three of us descended on this very spacious restaurant at 6pm on a Wednesday evening; by 8pm it was packed and queuing! Delicious spicy hot carrot chutney. Chicken tikka cooked in a specially prepared mild tomato sauce was out of this world. Chicken shashlick was brilliant. Absolutely nothing standard about this restaurant at all.'* MB. Takeaway: 10% discount. Free delivery, 10-mile radius. Hours: 12-2.30/6-11.

WATERFALL NEW ENTRANT

4 Silverdale Road, Maiden Earley, Reading 0118 926 8282

'Tastefully decorated in light sienna and pastel colours. Abundance of greenery, artificial but very clean. Tables double covered in clean white stiffly starched linen tablecloths and beautifully folded matching linen napkins. Smartly dressed waiters, quickly greeted and warmly welcomed. Moderately busy on a Friday night at 8pm, rapidly filled up, collection of people waiting for space. A Bengali menu a delight to read. Service slow, but were so many people!' RT. Some of those specials include: King Prawn Moni Puree £4.50, cooked with spices and served on a pineapple slice and fried bread. King Prawn Maknie £9.50, fresh cream and cashew nut sauce. Gosht Gata Mossala £5.85, leg of spring lamb, sliced onion, ginger, garlic and unground garam masala, thick sauce. Hours: 12 -2.30 and 5.30-11, Sunday to 10.30.

Slough

ANAM TANDOORI & BALTI HOUSE 

1a Baylis Parade, Oatland Drive, Slough 01753 572967

A typical competent curry house owned by Javeed Ali, open evenings only. *'Baltis are a speciality here and very tasty too.'* RE.

BARN TANDOORI

Salt Hill Park, Bath Road, Slough 01753 523183

We know of restaurants in old schools, fire stations, churches, garages, Portakabins, and even an ex-ambulance but the Barn takes the poppadam! It's in a rather grand, ex-cricket pavilion in the middle of nowhere – well, a park, actually, and next to the tennis courts. Taken over in 1996 by Messrs Mehbub, Rahman, Alam and Kandakar. Serves formula curries. *'I have revisited this excellent Indian restaurant in the park twice with large business parties at very short notice. The staff copes admirably, delivering many different orders at the same time, maintaining high-quality cuisine with superb service.'* TE. *'Masalla dosa was a great mixture of vegetables in a pancake. Chicken dhansak was tasty with an excellent balance of spices and chillies with the lentils. Worth a return visit.'* RH.

SKYWAYS HOTEL AND BRASSERIE

19 London Road, Slough 01753 522286

And if a curry barn isn't enough excitement, how about a curry B&B in the same town? Skyways is a family-run hotel offering an excellent *'home from home'* service with lovely warm rooms, satellite television, and full English breakfast. All at half the price of the larger hotels around Slough. Nothing unusual in that, you say, but what about the restaurant? Says TE: *'It has retained the same Nepalese chefs and waiters whose excellent cuisine and efficient service put Skyways 'on the map'. New manager is Ram Panwar, from the Cookham Tandoori, who has a long track record of success in cooking and managing tandoori cuisine. Revamped menu offers a wider variety of dishes and 'special dinners'.* TE. *'I stayed here and enjoyed an excellent meal at a reasonable cost. Chicken Patia was excellent, generous naan breads and free pickles and poppadoms. I would recommend this hotel and restaurant to curryholic business travellers and regular diners.'* RA.

TAJ TANDOORI 

7 Upton Lea Pde, Wrexham Road, Slough
01753 521674

Established in 1993. Seats 48. Room for 20 cars at front of restaurant. Changes in decor planned. Specials include: Jalfrezi, Chicken Tikka Masala, Lamb Pasanda, Chicken and Lamb Jalfrezi. Free delivery, 3-mile radius. Hours: 5.30-12am.

Sunningdale

TIGER'S PAD NEW TO OUR TOP 100

3 Station Pde, London Road, Sunningdale
01344 621215

We had a wonderful meal at Richard Green's Tiger's Pad in an almost empty restaurant. They have Indian chefs, and it is great to find the real delicious thing, rather than another formula curry house. AF said last time: *'Expensive, minimalist, open-plan decor. Oak tables. Perfect poppadams. Onion Bhajis like tennis balls, really good. Scallops Chilli Fry and Seekh Kebab, both very good. Lamb Vindaloo £6.95, excellent tender,'* and this time he says *'Gets better and better. They continually refine and change their menu. Sikadari Badi Lamb is out of this world. I'm convinced it is the "find of the decade"'.* AF. Sunday Buffet £9.95 from 12-5pm.

Thatcham

KAILASA NEW ENTRANT

35 High Street, Thatcham 01635 862228

'There are some restaurants which give you a good feeling as soon as you walk in - the Kailasa is one. Inviting eatery with white wood tables, royal blue napkins and fan shaped wall hangings - flock wallpaper enthusiasts would probably have a fit! Chefs Specials include: Boal Kofta, Sabji Bangla, Shatcora Gost, Sylheti Akni, Chingri Anana. Tandoori Chicken - seriously tender and seriously large. Excellent King Prawn Puree - juicy, tender, well spiced beasties. Chingri Ananas - chicken with pineapple, served in half a shell, with loads of fresh coriander - delicious. Sylheti Akni - kind of mixed meat biryani with a proper vegetable curry. A special mention to Sag Bhajee, obviously made from fresh spinach - a really nice change. Nan and Poppadoms were, respectively, light, moist and warm, non-greasy. All in all a very pleasant lunch.' S&ZM.

Theale

CAFE BLUE COBRA TOP 100

20 High Street, Theale 0118 930 4040

A place with a real difference owned by the enterprising Abssar Waess. The first-timer is struck by the coolness and fresh cleanliness of the decor. The bar area, with its marble and cane furnishings, seats 30. It leads on to the main dining area, whose 60 ormolu seats are designed to evoke airy oriental verandas. The light walls are a regularly changing 'gallery', home to the works of local professional artists. There is a wide range of Bangladeshi and Bengali dishes, some of which will be familiar to the curry aficionado. Delights include Tikka, Methi Saag Gosht and Birianis. But there are many other dishes. There is duckling, crab, venison, veal, pomfret, ayre, surma river fish and much more. The menu also includes Thai food. eg some classics, such as, for starters, steamed mussels, Chicken Sateh or a mixed platter. Mains: Thai Green Chicken Curry to Ped Pad Prik – Hot Duck with Pad Thai noodles. Expect to spend around £35 per head for a three-courser with drink and coffee. Waess reports that many diners happily mix and match the two cuisines. In the last guide we said that the restaurant was open all day and run as a cafe restaurant but ... *'Tried to late lunch here twice, once at 2.45pm and another at 3.15pm – both times the restaurant was positively shut. Never one to be dissuaded, I went back one evening – it was open. The meal was very good. I tried 'mix and match' option of Bangladeshi and Thai food and it worked very well – Chicken Satay to start, Methi Saag Gosht for main course and a Thai sweet for afters.'* MRW. Remains in our **TOP 100**. Lunch and dinner, daily.

Twyford

THE MITA'S 

37 London Road, Twyford
0118 934 4599

Established in 1993. Seats 32. 10 parking spaces. Specials include: Hundee dishes and Bengal fish special. Delivery: £15 minimum, 5-mile radius. Hours: 12-2.30/5.30-11.30.

HAWELI NEW ENTRANT

15 Church Street, Twyford 0118 932 0939

This is a very popular curryhouse. We have had a number of satisfied reports telling of a high level of care from reception to departure, with *'excellent food'* ANON in between. This is as it should be, and it gets the Hawelli onto the *Guide.* Owner-manager Raju Sattar tells us that Balti Chicken Saly - £6.95, mild sauce with fried potato straws on top is a major favourite with his customers. Takeaway: 10% discount. Delivery: 3 miles, £15 minimum. Credit cards accepted. Hours: 12-2/6-1.

Windsor

SPICE ROUTE

NEW ENTRANT NEW TO OUR TOP 100

18a Boots Passage, Thames Street, Windsor 01753 860720

Mridula Baljekar has written many Indian cookbooks, then she confided in us that she wanted to run a restaurant. We were surprised. She's never done it. We know she can cook, but churning it out relentlessly day in day out is another thing. Furthermore the really hard work lies elsewhere other than the kitchen. So heeding our advice, she opened here in 2001, and after a while ran short of finance, and joined forces with some Asian restaurateurs. Running a joint venture didn't work out, so she took back the reins. The site is not hard to find, but parking is. Once inside, bar on the left, and a long narrow room opening out at the end. You'll observe the glass-fronted kitchen and maybe the aptly named chef Tika Ram (formerly chef to the Oberoi family who own the Indian Hotel chain) hard at work in it. The initial traces of amateurism have disappeared, and the brigade have settled down to solid confident work. The menu is a combination of Mridula's own recipes and the chefs, and it is gourmet home-cooking. '*While we watched items being cooked, we had wonderful Egg Koftas with Date and Tamarind Chutney as well as freshly baked Naan. The Koftas were made with chopped hard boiled eggs, mixed with soft white breadcrumbs, beaten egg, lightly sautéed onion,*

ginger, green chillies and fresh coriander leaves. When we sat down to have our 'two-course express lunch' we were served more than six courses! In addition to the basic Naan that was demonstrated, we were given garlic and Coriander Naan - finely chopped garlic and fresh coriander leaves pressed onto the surface of a plain Naan then grilled in the tandoor. Besides the salmon and chicken, we had Tandoori Potatoes: parboiled and then hollowed out, deep-fried and mixed with salt, chilli, sun-dried mango powder and garam masala. They are then mixed with chopped cashew nuts and fried onions, skewered, brushed with oil and grilled in the tandoor. We also had creamy chicken tikka - chicken breasts marinated with a marinade similar to the salmon and grilled in the tandoor. Then we were served a non-tandoor dish - Kashmiri Lamb Curry (Rogan Josh), tender pieces of lamb slow cooked with the captivating flavours of special blend of spices that brought back a flood of memories of north India for me. DTH. Welcome to our **TOP 100.** Lunch 12-2. Dinner 6-11 daily, except closed Sunday.

Wokingham

ROYAL INDIAN TANDOORI ©

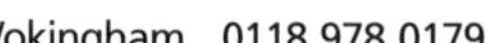

72 Peach Street, Wokingham 0118 978 0179

A 70-seater established in 1978 by T Ali, serving excellent Bangladeshi and Kashmiri-styled curries by chef M Miah. Banquets on Sundays. *'Very good food and good value, we were all very satisfied. Chicken Chilli Tandoori Masala was a superb dish, rich in colour, texture and flavour. Service friendly and attentive, some a bit slapdash.'* HC. Takeaway menu 15% discount. Hours: 12-3/6-12am.

SULTAN BALTI PALACE

7 Market Place, Wokingham 0118 977 4397

In the middle of the old town, upstairs, low ceilings, black beams, white washed walls, several small dining rooms make for an intimate and upmarket dining experience. Downstairs is modern, cafe -style, with its own menu, for light snacks while out shopping or between office meetings. We dined one night with Abdul and his wife Helena and enjoyed a very pleasant evening. Helena was in the process of updating waiter uniforms, throwing out the traditional white shirt and black tie for a blue shirt with yellow patterned tie, much more in keeping with the elegance of the venue. Good Pakistani cooking.

BRISTOL

Area: West Country
Population: 400,000
Adjacent Counties:
Glos, Soms

Bristol Centre

Consists of BS1, BS2

RAJDOOT 

83 Park Street, Bristol BS1 0117 926 8033

Established in 1970 by Indian architect Des Sarda and managed by Sukhi Sharma. The attractive decorations are very Indian with beaten copper tables in the bar area and bronze statues. *'Have had a meal at the Bristol Rajdoot twice. The food was different to the Birmingham branch. The menu looked about the same, but the food was distinctly spicier and hotter. Both meals were very good. On both visits, crowded, loads of Americans, from Wyoming on the next table, getting their first dose of curry. They had some interesting comments, expected the food to be mushy, with red hot gravy (I can remember early Vespa versions just like that!). They were pleasantly surprised at the subtlety and wondered why there were not more such places in America. A business opportunity of world dominating proportions if ever I heard one! Even though crowded, quick service.'* MRW. Perhaps it is all best summed up by DL: *'Consistently unpredictable! Sometimes wonderful, sometimes terrible, but always expensive.'* DL. Hours: 12-2.30pm (closed Sun. lunch)/6.30-11.30pm.

Bristol North East

BS5 Easton, BS16 Redfield
(for adjacent Staple Hill see Glos)

SPICE OF NEPAL TAKEAWAY 

245 Lodge Causeway, Fishponds, Bristol BS16 0117 965 0664

A Nepalese takeaway opened in 1997 by Pradeep

2004 COBRA GOOD CURRY GUIDE COUNTY Index, see page 7. Town Index, see page 359. A to Z of the Menu, page 52. Contributors Key, page 356.

Karki, head chef. Dilip Karki manages front of house. Momo, dumplings filled with mince, steamed, served with Nepalese Tomato Pickle. Kastamandapa, a mild dish, flavoured with ground nuts, cream, with a hint of garlic, good. Del £10 min 3-mile radius. 6-11.30pm; closed on Sun.

Bristol North West

Consists of BS6 to BS11

BS7 *Bishopston, Horfield*

GHURKAS TANDOORI ©

403 Gloucester Road, Horfield, Bristol BS7
0117 942 2898

A popular local with some Nepalese dishes. Seats 46. Delivery. Hours: 12-2p/6-12.30am.

PUSHPANJLI V

217a Gloucester Road, Bishopston, Bristol BS7
0117 924 0493

A vegetarian e-a-m-a-y-l establishment, whoch must be cherished.*A wonderfully informal yet smart Gujarati vegetarian restaurant fitted with formica tables and plastic chairs, with food displayed under a glass counter. All food is home-cooked. Huge variety of starters, Dal Bhajia, Samosa, Kachori, Bateta Wada, Mogo Chips, all superb. Large assorted pickle tray offering wide choice and lovely Papads. Masala Dhosas enormous with Sambar and coconut chutney. I visit this restaurant several times a month and it's truly brilliant.'* DR. *'My no. 1. Can't fault the food, sweets very indulgent.'* JM.

BS9 *Westbury-on-Trym*

BRITISH RAJ

1-3 Passage Road, Westbury-on-Trym,
Bristol BS9 0117 950 0493

Some of our scribes say this classical, upmarket restaurant, open since 1973, is one of the most highly respected in the south-west. *'A large restaurant, menu is wide ranging with few surprises but the arrangement into mild and hot sections is useful and sensible. The Lamb Dhansak I had was good and spicy with tons of life and not just 'hot'. It has stacks of character. This is a characteristic of their cooksing– the dishes have a nice, rich and very spicy quality; full and rich, not just fierce. My wife's Chicken Dopaiza had the same warm and rich quality. The Shahi dishes with fried sultanas were really palatable. The prices are extremely reasonable throughout. Service was pretty rapid and extremely accommodating. Parking not easy as the premises are bang in the middle of town. But an important plus is easy disabled access.'* RG. 12-2pm/6-11.30pm.

BUCKINGHAMSHIRE

Area: Home Counties (west of London)
Population: 693,000.
Adjacent Counties: Beds, Herts, Middx, Northants, Oxon

Aylesbury

THE CHADNIS 

43-45 High Street, Waddesdon, Aylesbury
01296 651255

Established in 1999. Seats 70. Fully licensed and air-conditioned. *'Mr Shah and the waiters provide first-class service in relaxing atmosphere.'* RB. *Price check: Poppadam 50p, CTM £6.90, Pullao Rice £1.80, Peshwari Nan £1.80, Lager £2.40. 'I booked in advance and was warmly greeted by a waiter who offered me a drink, nibbles and a paper, whilst I awaited my friend...'* [wow - that's service!] *'... once seated, Poppadoms were served promptly with choice of chutney and pickles. Plenty of time given to peruse the delicious menu. Excellent assorted starters. I would visit again, but despite advertising they took Amex, their machine could not take it!!.'* DL. David also tells us that parking is hell - so perhaps the tube and a taxi is best. Specialities: Kakra Karahi £7.60, crab with capsicum, tomatoes, onions in medium spiced sauce. Boal Satkora £7.40' Bengali Fish with Bengali lemon. £2.40 pint lager, £7.10 bottle house wine. Sunday Buffet: £6.95 adult, £3.95 children from noon to 3. Takeaway: 10% discount on orders over £10. Hours: 12-2.30 and 6 -11. Branch: Chinnor Indian Cuisine, 59, Lower Road, Chinnor, Oxfordshire.

HOUSE OF SPICE NEW ENTRANT

19 Fort End, Haddenham, Aylesbury
01844 299100

'Wonder of wonders! An upmarket restaurant in my village and within crawling distance - my wife is worried that I will be wearing out the knees in my trousers doing so! In the village centre on an 's' bend, has own car park at rear, used to be pub. Tastefully redecorated, beamed ceilings, lots of greenery, open tables, booth type seating, very comfortable and good ambience. Immaculate service. Sat down at around 7.30pm having had a snort (or was it two) at the bar. Place rapidly filled up from 8pm and seething when we left. Couldn't fault quality of meal, portions right. Calamari Chilli Fry £2.95 for me and Bharwan Baigan - gram flour coated aubergine roundels, cheese filled and herbs, crispy fried for Barbara, both different and delicious. Followed by Chicken Jalfrezi £7.50, Jangli Gosht £7.50, lamb and red chillies, Aloo Palak £2.50, Niramish £2.50, vegetable, onion, garlic, Rice and Bread, plus bottle of St Emilion. All food beautifully cooked, nicely presented and altogether terrific. We intend to go through the menu. With wine and two Campari with Orange £60.00.' MS. Hours: 12-2.30 and 6 -11.30. Reports please.

TAJ MAHAL ©

73 Buckingham St, Aylesbury 01296 399617

Opened in 1993 by Abdul Khaliq. Formula curries served competently in this 50-seater curry house, CTM, Jalfrezi and Korma being the most popular dishes ordered. Delivery: £10 minimum, 3-mile radius. Hours: 12-2.30/5.30-12am.

Buckingham

DIPALEE ©

18 Castle Street, Buckingham 01280 813151

90-seater curry house under the watchful ownership of Salique Ahmed. Head Chef Ashik. *'Visited with friends. Offered Poppadoms and drinks on being seated – excellent. Babori Mix – good value and tasty. Prawn Puree £3.50 – excellent. Onion Bhajis £1.90 – superb. Main courses took an age to be served. Hari Mirchi Bhoona Chicken £6.50 – excellent, Lamb Madras £4.95 – very disappointing. £98 for four (inc service).'* DL. *'Excellent food, surly waiter.'* SO. Hours: 12-2.30/6-11.30.

High Wycombe

CURRY CENTRE 

83 Easton Street, High Wycombe 01494 535529

Whenever the owners are personally looking after front of house (A Musowir) and kitchen (MA Mali) respectively, you can be sure of getting their best. *'Both visits have been excellent. Arrived at 7.30pm on a busy Saturday evening, after a theatre visit. We had four children with us, aged between 8 and 12, one had never had curry before. Food excellent quality, head waiter made special effort, patient and managed to fit us in as the restaurant filled around us. Samosa, Chicken Tikka, Prawn Puri, Lamb Korai Puri - interesting twist on two old favourites although a little salty. House Specials and children tested favourites in the form of CTM (sorry but they have to start somewhere!), Chicken Korma and Biriani - made with mild sauce for the main courses. Pleasant surroundings, emphatic waiters and excellent food all washed down with ice-cold bottled Cobra – what more could you want! Recommended.'* SO.

Milton Keynes

(Includes Bletchley, Stony Stratford, Woburn Sands and Wolverton)

CHILLI GARDEN 

Unit 1, Agora Centre (1st Floor), Church Street, Wolverton, MK 01908 222228

Used to be the Night of India (1988), reopened as the 80-seater Chilli Garden in June 1998. *'Grand launch with the Mayor of MK. Raita and naan both excellent.'* BG. Takeaway: 20% discount. Hours: 5.30-12am.

GOLDEN CURRY 

4 Duncombe Street, Bletchley, MK
01908 377857

MK's oldest, established in 1971, taken over by Ismail Ali in 1980. Serves formula curries. Seats 58. Takeaway: 10% discount. Delivery: £10 minimum. Hours: 12-1.30pm/5.30-11.30pm.

JAIPUR

BEST OUTSIDE LONDON TOP 100 

599 Grafton Gate East, Central Milton Keynes
01908 669796

Abdul Ahad had a dream to construct a new fantastic new restaurant, in white marble – a Taj Mahal complete with dome. We all have dreams. Few of us realise them. He spent years planning and once he decided to proceed he took a financial risk the like of which is no dream ... nightmare rather. Even his banks were dubious. But Ahad started to build. MK's residents thought he was building a mosque, which Ahad thought hilarious, as he is firmly a restaurateur. We believe the resulting free-standing restaurant is unique in the world. *See the picture on page* 28. The inside is just as plush and it cost Ahad a cool £4m. '*You can spot the Jaipur from some distance away, it really does stand out. Through double glass doors is a large circular reception. Photographs and awards adorn the walls, a sweeping staircase or a lift takes you upstairs to the as yet unbuilt banqueting rooms, and a young man takes coats, umbrellas etc. There is a sign on the restaurant door, which politely requests smart dress, no trainers or jeans. (Hooray for that). We hadn't booked, but knew there wouldn't be a problem as the restaurant is substantial. A grand, well-stocked bar dominates the room, which would be glorious if you could perch yourself on bar stools, but you can't. The bar is for drinks service only, which is a shame and in my opinion, should be moved as it occupies too much valuable table space. So, if you have arrived early or are waiting for a table, you are asked to sit in a densely populated area of colourful 'bucket' chairs on the side of the main eating arena, behind very beautiful and high, turquoise glass screens.. These prevent you viewing the dining area, and leaving you with the uncomfortable feeling that you are unwelcomingly cut off from the activities. The dining area has been divided into three spaces. The main area is encircled by more turquoise screens, which in turn encircle a lavish, four-faced, three-tiered waterfall, made from beaten copper cubes. Sparkly glass coins, in different hues of blue share the tiers with fresh orchids. Quite lovely but again dominating. The walls of the other two dining spaces have huge, tasteful, hand-painted murals of Maharajas in howdahs on elephants. Busy waiters push food-laden trolleys to and from the kitchen. (I wish they wouldn't do that – it's too much like a curryhouse – much more stylish to use a tray as they do in the grand hotels). We were welcomingly seated at a round table for four next to the waterfall. We were brought plain poppadoms with a chutney tray, which we devoured while perusing the menu. Pat chose a lovely bottle of Malbec. Bottled water was poured into wine glasses – very stylish, as was the bucket of ice with slices of lemon, left for us to help ourselves. We started with Aloo Matar ki Tikki, two potato and pea cakes, one on top of the other, drizzled with a little yoghurt and imli with a small portion of chick pea curry on the side, and Dahi Papdi Chaat, a unsparing portion of crisp flour-discs and cubes of potato and chick pea curry, all piled up in the middle of the plate with far too much imli and not enough yoghurt. Mains: Dum Ki Nalli, 'lamb shanks with bone.' Absolutely massive portion, two good shanks, smothered in a rich spicy sauce. The meat was extremely succulent, needing no encouragement in separating from its partner. Lobster Garlic Bhuna, 'grilled lobster tail with garlic-flavoured onion-tomato masala, served with rice.' A huge plate arrived, complete with lobster shell and three lobster tails – dishes used quality ingredients and were more than competently cooked, however, nothing sparkled. Put simply, we could detect curryhouse formula and chefs should do better. Just because MK isn't London, does not excuse shortcuts. We have a Malaysian friend who has a saying: 'There is no love in this food,' which perfectly sums up our experience.* DBAC. Of course we are being hypercritical. But that's what we should be. To be fair we've had loads of reports about the new Jaipur and there isn't a bad one amongst them. Ahad has a huge following of sophisticated diners, who love it. '*Had lunch in this upmarket establishment. All the reports praising the Jaipur are not surprising. Decor is very modern, very comfortable; service immaculate and with a smile – totally professional in fact, food was superb we had a mixed hor's d'oeuvre: chicken, lamb, kebabs, salad etc. Wife had Hyderabadi Gosht Biryani served in round pot, lots of nuts and lovely vegetable sauce. I went for Aachari Gosht, Jeera Pullao - cumin flavoured with saffron, Bhindi Do Pyaza Vegetable, cooling cucumber Raitha and Aloo Paratha. With a couple of Gins and a bottle of the own label house red (£10.50) and a nice soft Burgundy, plus coffees - bill was £70. Bit steep for a lunch'* [come on Maurice - you didn't go without!] *'but what the hell it's only money!'* [quite right - just have to earn some more]. *'Delightful building, superb food – an experience!'* MS. *'Can honestly say that the service was excellent, the food was excellent and the decoration beautiful. We had 10% discount and the manager sent over complimentary Brandys, when we said that we had waited nearly seven years in order to visit his restaurant. The waitresses has sari's on that were extremely attractive, and added colour to the beautiful decor of the restaurant.'* DV-W. *'Deservedly TOP 100, always excellent.'* SO. We agree but we want to go better. This restaurant is one of the most caring we know. It reeks of excellence. This *Guide* would dearly love to give Ahad our 'Best UK Restaurant Award' but some elements don't quite reach those heady heights. And we will when the food equals the service and moves up from four to five stars. Then the Jaipur will be the best in the UK. Meanwhile, we maintain its remarkable Award as the **BEST RESTAURANT OUTSIDE LONDON**, and that means it's in the Top 10. We commend everyone to visit it. 10% takeaway discount. Lunch daily 12-11.30. Snacks 2-5 except Sunday which does an £11 buffet, 12-4. *See page* 28.

JALORI ©

23 High Street, Woburn Sands, MK 01908 281239

Established in 1994 by Hai, Ahad's brother *(see Jaipur, above)* and managed by Abdul Kadi the 70-seater Jalori is bigger than it looks, and has a loyal following that includes Johnny Dankworth and Cleo Lane. Chef Abdul Hanaan prepares food that is *'First class.'* BG. Most popular dish is Chicken Cashew Pasanda. Interesting menu addition for you to try – Cheese and Onion Naan £2.50. Hours: 12-2pm/6-11.30pm.

MOGHUL PALACE 

7 St Paul's Court, High St, Stony Stratford, MK 01908 566577

'It's an old monastery school where monks once beat knowledge into the sons of local gentry.' LT. Now the local curryholic gentry beat a path through its Gothic arch, complete with wrought-iron gate, beyond which stands the imposing clerestoric building. Owners Monowar Hussain and Anfor Ali greet you and, given a chance, will tell you how much they spent in 1994 converting this Victorian former cigar-factory-cum-orphanage-cum-school into their 100-seater Palace. And impressed you will be, with the spacious reception area with its armchairs and comfortable sofas where you wait to be seated, and the scale, height, tiled floor, stonework and wood panels of the dining room. Be nice to the gargoyles, they're there to ward off bad vibes! And wonder what the monks would think of the menu offering all the familiar curry items.. *'Wow! what a place this is! Apparently an ancient school originally run by monks – no nasty habits left behind I'm glad to say!'* Ho Ho Ho!! *'Original wood panelling still in place, very high domed ceiling over half of restaurant – with mock stars in the deep blue sky and a mural copying Michael Angelo's Sistine chapel ceiling at the non-smoking end, which is raised up two or three steps. Taken here for lunch – food superb. King Prawn on Puri £4.75 – delicious, but no salad which I thought a bit mean, however, contents of the thin pancake included lots of coriander, sauce and prawns of course. Regretted choosing Chicken Tikka Bhuna £7.45 – when I say my companions Chicken Shashlik £7.25, which he said was the best ever, anywhere. Service good and friendly – I'll go again.'* MS. *'we perused the menu in the lounge, where the conversation ranged from church to curry.'* DL. Menu extracts: Stuffed pepper £3.75, stuffed with spiced chicken, vegetable or minced lamb. Macheyr Jhul £8.95, medium spiced pomfret, onion, tomato, pepper and coriander. Masala Kulcha £2.25, leavened bread with mildly spiced minced vegetables. Takeaway: 10% discount. Hours: 12-2.30/6-11.30.

Newport Pagnell

MYSORE TOP 100 

101 High Street, Newport Pagnell, Milton Keynes 01908 216426

Another high-standard goodie from the Ahad stable, this one operated by brother M Abdul Odud. *'The dining room, cleverly housed within two cottages, seats 98, yet provides a number of secluded areas, which 'give a good feeling of privacy'* HG. *'We were unsure of arrangements and numbers for a special charity dinner, so Mr Odud gave us a selection from the menu at a fixed price. Lamb Dhansak with Sag, Mixed Raitha, Pullao Rice and Paratha, all very good. The complete meal and decor (small corners and niches, then a large area with skylight, a bit colonial and glorious at full moon) to be recommended.'* BG. *'Colleague prefers the Mysore to Jaipur. He had Chingri Puri – KP's served in a thick sauce on thin deep-fried bread. I had, Jhinga Puri – KP's in a sweet and sour sauce, served on a puffed bread. Both went down a treat. Followed by Chicken Zallander, Chicken Delight, Vegetable Pullao, Bhindi and Naan. I have to admit that it was better than the Jaipur, which*

is not exactly a slouch in the curry stakes. I guess when you are choosing between very good restaurants, personal taste has to come into it and I like the cosy feel of the Mysore. I have been to the Jaipur and had just about the best meal I have bad, but it is a bit formal. I like places that are more laid back and the Mysore is that – perhaps to the extent that the service was slow. There were under 10 diners in total but you would think from the time taken to serve us that it was full. MW. 10% discount for takeaways. Hours: 12-2.30/6-11.30pm.

Wendover

RAJ

23 Aylesbury Road, Wendover 01296 622567

A 300-year-old listed building in a beautiful old street, in a picture-postcard town. Exposed beams, with walled partitions, dividing the 60 seats into almost separate rooms, creating agreeable ambience and comfort. *'Busy Friday evening but still service very good with a bit of joyful banter with the staff. Chicken Zafrani , good, Chicken Pathia , very tasty. One of our party changed order to Chicken Tikka once seeing one arrive on next table ; never seen one like it and wonderful flavour! Light and fluffy Nan breads. Very enjoyable experience in a 'not too cramped' atmosphere.'* JH.

Stokenchurch

MOWCHAK PUB AND RESTAURANT NEW ENTRANT

Wycombe Road, Stokenchurch 01494 485005

It's a good one so we hear from several connoiseurs. Good because it's a full operational pub serving English real ales, (and everything else a tradtional pub serves) and the restaurant does good quality formula curries. 'It's a dream for a CAMRA lover and Curryholic, and we find it worth travelling a long distance at least weekly, just for this delightful combination'. RL.

Winslow

MAHABHARAT ©

25 Market Square, Winslow 01296 713611

First opened in 1979, taken over by Nurul Islam in 1990, the ground-floor restaurant seats 44 diners, plus private room for 26. Takeaway: 15% discount. Hours: 6-11.30 (Sat. to 12am).

CAMBRIDGESHIRE

Area: East.
Population: 729,000
Adjacent Counties: Beds, Essex, Herts, Rutland, Lincs, Norfolk, Northants, Suffolk

Cambridge

CAFE NAZ

47 Castle Street, Cambridge 01223 363666

A branch of the well-known, well-liked Café Naz of Brick Lane. e1. The cooking is well above average, and it is master-minded by Steven Gomes, Exec Chef, whose main base is Café Naz Cardiff. See both branches for more information. Also at Chelsmford, Essex, Horsham Sussex.

GOLDEN CURRY ©

111 Mill Road, Cambridge 01223 329432

Shaista Miah's pleasant, air-conditioned, large 98-seater, is divided into booths. Chef Abdul Tahid creates: *'Wonderful tastes. Everything piping hot including the plate'* JB. *'Top of the league. A first class meal.'* RA. Minimum charge £10. Hours: 12-2.30/6-12.

INDIA HOUSE

31 Newnham Rd, Cambridge 01223 461661

'Situated in the very idyllic surroundings of Cambridge's university area. 'Location is lovely, looking across the river Cam to a green and an attractively-lit pub. Decor is almost all white, very light and summery. A very good restaurant if you are not in a hurry.' HC. *'This restaurant a mock Tudor styled building, whitewashed with black beams, is on the river opposite a very good looking pub.'* Menu extracts: Bamboo Shoot Bhaji £2.75. Garlic Chicken Masala £7.95. Bengal Chicken £6.95, with green beans in a spicy sauce. Takeaway: 10% discount. Hours: 12-2.30/6-12.

KISMET INDIAN TAKEAWAY

71 Catherine Street, Cambridge 01223 410225

Takeaway only. *'Visited dozens of times over the last decade. A Bangladeshi takeaway located in a corner house in the backstreets of studenty Cambridge. Softly spoken Mr Alos Islam is the face behind the counter. Many regulars will testify to the unwavering fabulous quality - the best curry in Cambridge. Excellent range of specials - from £7.95 - all come with huge portions of special fried rice - a meal in itself. Sylhet and Bengal Chicken both extremely rich, tasty and filling. Alos recommended - Persian Chicken Biryani. All Kebabs, Nans and Sag Bhaji the Best! Top quality, large portions, great value - deserving a TOP 100 placing even if only a takeaway. The Empress of India - one of the best pubs - lies only a few doors down. Students have never had it so good.'* CD.

KOHINOOR 

74 Mill Road, Cambridge 01223 323639

The UK's sixth-ever curryhouse and Cambridge's oldest (1937) and some say best, serving all your favourite curries and accompaniments. Some prefer it to all others. One don, who prefers to remain anon continues to tell us he's been going there for decades.

TAJ TANDOORI 

64 Cherry Hinton Road, Cambridge 01223 248063

Taken over by SA Haque in 1992. Restaurant seats 72. *'Food is very good. Puri with a large helping of Prawn Bhuna on top set the scene. Excellent Chicken Tikka Jalfrezi.'* RW. Hours: 12-2pm/6pm-12am.

Ely

SURMA TANDOORI 

78 Broad Street, Ely 01353 662281

Established 1979 by MA Ossi and SA Choudhury. Seats 64 in two dining rooms. *'This is the best curryhouse for miles. We regularly eat here once or twice a week.'* GS. *'We have always had good meals here – the quantities and quality are always good.'* JS. Hours: 12 2/6-12am.

Peterborough

BALTI HOUSE BYO

High Street, Peterborough 01733 56056

'If we had had Mixed Kebab each we would never eat all the main courses. I had Chicken Patia, my husband had Balti Chicken Jalfrezi and my cousin had Balti Chicken. Absolutely delicious. We asked for coffees, they were brought promptly, and the young lad did not leave the table until we had tasted it and said it was all right. Very friendly, clean and good service. They also do a Pizza takeaway. Ally will make any sauce to go with the Chicken Papcila, his jalfrezi is my husbands favourite, when I take my mother and Aunt there who are not curryholics he makes an omelet for my Mum who is 83, and Scampi for my Aunt to suit them. Our favourite place for work 'dos', birthdays, any excuse really.' DV-W.

BOMBAY BRASSERIE 

52 Broadway, Peterborough 01733 565606

Rony Choudhury (manager) and Mahbub Khan (chef). Attractive red-brick 70-seater interior with a brass-work bar, serving generous curries. Branch: Planet Poppadam, Park Road, Peterborough.

EASTERN GARDEN NEW ENTRANT

4 Marville Court, Thackers Way, Market Deeping, Peterborough 01778 344844

Established *'I have been a regular for over two years, and is a frequent topic of conversation in the village. Recommended.'* LM. Interesting dishes include: Kebab Sandwich £2.99, Kebab Puri £2.50, Chicken Tikka Roll £3.99. Special Fried Chicken £7.25, breast in batter, served with Saffron Rice, Salad and a Vegetable Curry – good value. Hours: 5 to 11.

INDIA GATE 

9 Fitzwilliam Street, Peterborough 01733 34616

Taken over in 1996 by Mohammed Farooq, this elegant 44-seater is full of Eastern trinkets and atmosphere. The menu consists of a full house of curry favourites, competently cooked by Chef Kamal Uddin. Air-conditioned. Sunday lunch buffet £7. Delivery: £13.50 min. Hours: 12-2/6-12AM (1am on Sat.).

KASHMIR BALTI HOUSE U

298 Lincoln Road, Peterborough 01733 894025

'It is well out of town in a slightly run down area, but the food is simply superb. Service is friendly and efficient, and special offers such as free starters are promoted frequently.' IB. *'Magnificent basic cafe-style restaurant, scrubbed clean interior, decorated with marble effect paint work and airbrushed murals. Formica table tops for 35ish diners. Enthusiastic staff. Robust and pungent food in classic Pakistani style. Perfect starters, two thin and juicy Shammi Kebabs £2.85, served on sizzling onions with fresh salad and tray of sauces – scrumptious! Excellent Lamb and Mushroom Balti £5.25, generous chunks of tender, gristle free lamb in thick sauce, heavy mushrooms, perfectly balanced. Served with pair of hot fresh Chapattis, straight off the tava - spot on. Great Tarka Dhal £1.70, thick with lentil and garlic. Salty Lassi – a litre jug of it, perfectly complimented the meal. Top 100 contender.'* RW.

TAJ MAHAL 

37 Lincoln Road, Peterborough 01733 348840

Taken over in 1995 by Haq Nawaz Seats 100. Serving Pakistani and Kashmiri-style curries. Fully licensed. *'Attractive, roomy 100-seater restaurant, profusion of red decoration, open-plan layout. Friendly, chatty staff, efficient. Set Thali £15, served on large steel tray akin to American prison films, large tandoori chicken leg – tasty, Tandoori KP – excellent, soft and juicy portion of Lamb Tikka Masala, Aubergine and Lentil Curry - both passable and little greasy. Good bread. Ice cream fresh from the tub! Average meal.'* RW. Hours: 5-1.

St Neots

JONONI NEW ENTRANT

12 High Street, St Neots 01480 219626

Mr Kadir, proprietor, sponsored St Neots Carnival 2002 and as part of that sponsorship provided the Carnival Queens Tea. Hon Secretary Michael Cullis said that everyone enjoyed it and wanted the same next year! *'Celebrated my daughters University Graduation, could not have chosen a more perfect place. Excellent food, extremely friendly, warm and welcoming staff, impeccable service.'* CG. Sunday buffet lunch: £7.95 adult, child under 10 – half price. Gourmet Night: £9.95, starter, main course, side dish, rice and coffee.

©	Curry Club Discount	U	Unlicensed
V	Vegetarian	ANP	Alcohol not permitted
e-a-m-a-y-l	Eat as much as you like	BYO	Bring your own alcohol

Menu extracts: Stuffed Pepper £2.95, green pepper stuffed with spicy vegetables. Coriander Masala £6.50, chicken breast strips, coriander paste. Sylhet Rice £2.50, fried with onion and butter. Takeaway: 10% discount, minimum £15. Hours: 12-2.30 / 6-11.

CHESHIRE

Area: North West
Population: 992,000
Adjacent Counties:
Clwyd, Derbs, Greater Man, Mers, Shrops, Staffs

Cheadle

KISMET TAKEAWAY NEW ENTRANT

132 Outwood Road, Heald Green, Cheadle
0161 437 6643

'Good honest takeaway. My local for ten years. Very consistent food particularly their Vindaloo. Have tried most things on their menu. Still the best Tarka Dal side dish of all takeaways I have ever had Typical inconspicuous decor, friendly staff and good service. I'll keep going there.' KN.

Chester

CHUTNEYBLU NEW ENTRANT TOP 100

17 Lower Bridge Street, Chester 01244 400088

'Oh what a find - absolute heaven. Specialises in Ocean cuisine. Bright restaurant, pale yellow walls, modern images of Indian dress, wooden chairs, white linen. Menu twists: Monkfish Bhuna, Tuna Dhansak, Red Mullet Sagwala, Marlin Tikka along with Java Oysters, Zanzibar Red Snapper, Shells from the Seychelles. Nearly died when I saw the prices of the a la carte — only wanted a quick lunch. Owner Younes Bakkali saw my reaction, devised set menu, starter, main meal and tea/coffee at £9.95. I nearly snatched his hand off. Decided on Onion Bhajia £3.95, three large golf balls, crisp, lightly spiced, superb, Chicken Dopiaza (inc vegetable rice) — chicken lovely and tender, sauce absolutely fantastic, white and red onions, rice lightly flavoured, excellent and two Poppadoms - crisp with chutney - fresh, on the house.' DB. [But you returned Dave, even with those HUMUNGUS prices] *'Lone diner on wet Thursday lunchtime. Chose favourite,*

CT Biryani with medium sauce – arrived plated, bowl of medium sauce. Rice was delicately flavoured but well cooked. Curryholics must support.' DB.

GATE OF INDIA

5 City Road, Chester 01244 327131

Chester's second oldest (1961), and in Moinuddin Ahmed's hands since 1992. Two floors seating 64. Chef Sundar Ali serves formula curries. Hours: 6-2.30am (Sun. to 1am). Useful for Chester night owls and curry-insomniacs.

SHERE KHAN

33 Pepper Row, Chester 01244 342349

Seats 145 in a split-level, modern, open restaurant. *'7.30pm on a Saturday night. Tried to book table, phoned six days earlier, told not taking booking, unusual! First impressions good, new restaurant, very well lit and loads of polished wood and glass. Bloody hell it was VERY busy, surprise, surprise, doorman said 'have you booked?' He had list of names – this devious place runs an unofficial list for the well-heeled... not a good start. Bar area so busy, some of those waiting were standing right next to those eating – appalling. Soon shown to table. Waiters – so quick – hyperactive? – just well practiced. Keema Samosa, fresh crisp pastry, lightly spiced. Chicken Shashlick and Shere Khan Special Tandoori – the business, succulent tikka, very tender kebab, meaty lamb chop. Chicken Dopiaza – mild, nice. Lamb Mughlai – good lamb, tender. KP Makhani - superbly buttery, succulent prawns. Chicken Jalfrezi - nice, hot, slivers of green chillies to water the eyes! No hot towel, orange segments. Scraps of food left on table wiped straight onto the floor, openly by waiter, obviously a matter of course! Overall – food was amazingly brilliant, but hated the unofficial booking list, over-crowding at the bar and oppressive 'din' from eaters, similar to a packed pub. A restaurant for the 'wannabes', well suited to the affluent life-style of Chester.'* MPW. *'Not the place for an intimate meal, but for gregarious younger customer who like noise, bright lights, bustling liveliness and clinical cleanliness without much caring about comfort, elegance of surroundings or authenticity of the food providing they can drink expensive designer lager from bottles. Not for me!'* MW.

Ellesmere Port, Wirral

The Wirral is neither a town nor a county and until 1965 was part of Cheshire. Since then the northern part (a small, digit-like, curry-rich peninsula between the rivers Mersey and Dee) has been part of Merseyside. Ellesmere Port remains in south Wirral but is in Cheshire.

THE TAJ OF AGRA FORT

PREVIOUS AWARD WINNER TOP 100

1 Cambridge Rd, Ellesmere Port 0151 355 1516

Spacious, clean and welcoming restaurant owned by Shams Uddin Ahmed. *'A couple of nice touches set it apart – the waiters, in their Agra Fort jackets, ask you how long you want between starters and main courses and give you the time requested, and slices of orange were delivered with the hot towels after the main course, whether desserts were ordered or not. Pepper stuffed with small pieces of tandoori chicken and lamb, as mentioned in the guide, was excellent. Paratha was one of the best I've had. A very good evening and I look forward to visiting again.'* OC. *'Heartily recommended.'* RW. *'We totally recommend this restaurant to you.'* MB and friends. *'Decor and service top drawer. Poppadoms – warm and crisp, lime pickle needed replenishment, garlic and ginger chutney (a new one to me) was excellent. Tikka melt in the mouth, Bhajia size of tennis ball. CTM – too red, Jalfrezi – drier than normal, both excellent. Naan warm and moist. Top rate.'* DB. Sunday Buffet. Monthly gourmet evenings. Scores 8/10 by DB. Stays high in our **TOP 100.** Hours: 12-2/6-11.30 (12.30am on Sat.). Sunday buffet 1-11.30pm.

Northwich

BENGAL DYNASTY NEW ENTRANT

Rear of Black Greyhound, Hall Lane Wincham, Northwich 01606 351597

Opened in early 2004. *As the saying goes, 'never judge a book by its cover.' This statement could have been written for the Bengal Dynasty. Situated in the car park of a pub, it is not the greatest looking of establishments being very angular, a flat roofed building, decidedly utility.; like a scout hut! However, inside is an absolute dream. White walls, blonde floor boards, original hanging art and regimented, suspended lights, dangle over each table. Running down both sides of the restaurant, are comfortably upholstered, semi-circular booths, encasing round tables, very stylish and enough space for six. Square tables, two lines of them, run parallel to the booths, giving great flexibility for dining. We were invited for the opening night party and the place soon filled up (it seats an amazing 150). We sampled varies dishes from Onion Bhajia's to Paneer to Fish to Rice, and we are pleased to report that the cooking is not curry house fare. Impressed.'* DBAC

CURRY COTTAGE ©

18 Chester Road, Northwich 01606 783824

Established in 1999. Originally called Castle Hill. Seats 60. 30 car parking spaces to rear. Takeaway: 15% discount. Hours: 5-12am.

Sandbach

THE TASTE OF THE RAJ ©

11 High Street, Sandbach 01270 753752

Opposite the old cobbled square which contains the Sandbach Cross, Anam Islam's small 38-seater *'gets very busy when the pubs close. Very neat and tidy. Panner Pakora and Fish Pakora, tasty. Chicken Lajawab with green chillies, good and spicy. Superb Brinjal.'* RK. *'High class establishment with prices to match. Folded Poppadoms and freshly made Raitha make it a bit special, staff could be more cheerful. Chilli Chicken – nicely spicy, uncomplicated flavour. Chicken Bhuna flavoursome, lots of large pieces of chicken breast.'* DM. Service charge 10%. Sunday buffet £8.95. Lunch and dinner, daily, except Sat. 3-12.30am.

Upton

Adjoined to north Chester, but is part of the Wirral; see Ellesmere Port, above.

UPTON HALAL BALTI HOUSE BYO ©

167 Ford Road, Upton , Wirral 0151 604 0166

Shofiul Miah's venture opened in 1996 and is not licensed, so BYO is a big attraction. And it's relatively cheap. Open daily except Tues, 5-11.30. Branch: Manzil, 73 Grange Road East, Birkenhead.

CORNWALL

Area: West Country
Population: 478,000
Adjacent County: Devon

Bodmin

VIRAJ INDIAN CUISINE

50 High Bore Street, Bodmin 01208 73480

'Beyond a comfortable reception area, seats 60, fairly spacious, jaded surroundings. Flowers on tables were dead - reminded me of India. Standard menu with array of spelling mistakes - again reminded me of India. Food surprisingly good. Three round, crisp, nicely spiced Onion Bhajis £1.90 came with Raitha and salad. Chicken Chat £2.50 (without puri) was very good, small pieces of chicken in a hot and tangy sauce. Extremely well marinated Tandoori Chicken £5.10, flavour ingrained, very tasty and plenty of it. Chicken Dhansak £4.90 also of good standard, lots of chicken, thick sauce, underlying hotness. Mixed Vegetable Bhajia £2.40, little greasy, nice peppery flavour. Lumpy Pullao Rice. Prices average, portions ample, service good.' MW. Hours: 12-2/5.30-11.30.

Callington

PREETI RAJ NEW ENTRANT

5 New Road, Callington 01579 383818'

Newly opened with simple, comfortable decor. *'Very good food of a high standard. Meal took a while to arrive but worth the wait.'* anon. Hours: 12-2.30/5.30 - 11.30.

Looe

MOONLIGHT

Main Street, Looe 01503 265372

'Decor smart and tasteful. Seating can either be in cosy booths or at tables in a larger room at the rear of the restaurant. There is a bar at the front, takeaway orders are dealt with here. The restaurant was never quiet! If you didn't book you were very unlikely to get a table. Reason was soon apparent - quality of food superb. Chicken Biryani, very nicely cooked, spicy and slightly

piquant, loads of good lean chicken and a very nice vegetable curry to accompany. Chicken Ceylon with Keema Nan - both VERY nice. Nicely cooked meat, crunchy vegetables and well balanced spicing. Only quibble - staff attitude - very blunt, almost aloof. No smiles, no polite comments, no chatter. A course in customer relations is highly recommended!' RT.

Newquay

INDIAN SUMMER — NEW ENTRANT

20 East Street, Newquay — 01637 872964

'Newquay's newest, opened summer 2002. Modern, light and airy, wood flooring, inset ceiling lights, plain walls, wood-effect formica table tops with red and blue chairs. Started with Onion Bhajia £1.95, three of the round variety, pleasingly light in composition, nicely crisp and Boal Biran £3.50, three spicy fillets of Bangladeshi fish, shallow fried, covered with julienne of fresh onion and capsicum - pleasant, mildly sweet flavour, lightly spiced. For main courses, my wife had Tandoori Chicken £4.75, although OK, was not the most succulent. Chicken Tikka Moricha £6.50, fried with chillies, onion, pepper, tomatoes, sour spicy sauce - served on a sizzler without any sauce. Dry Vegetables £2.10, small, diced bits of veg, little oily - however, fresh tasting and reasonably spiced. Service unprofessional. Waiters all bored and disinterested . Average prices, plentiful portions.' MW.

Penzance

GANGES BALTI

18 Chapel Street, Penzance — 01736 333002

'A large restaurant. Superb quality Chicken Kahlin, huge chunks of chicken, the largest I've ever seen. Many different flavours in the meal, top quality stuff.' GGP. *'Chicken Karahi £6.25, cooked with black pepper, attractive sour taste. Egg Bhuna £2.95. Quality very good but slightly greasy. Very prompt, efficient service. Restaurant too dark to see my meal.'* MP.

St Austell

TAJ MAHAL

57 Victoria Rd, Mount Charles, St Austell
01726 73716

'Spacious for two, raffia-screened alcoves may be a bit cramped for four. I've always liked it here. Menu covers all the usuals, and I've never had a bad meal in many years of visiting. Flavoursome, well cooked, nicely spiced dishes. Prices very reasonable, main dish portions enormous.' MW. Menu extracts: Jabra Masala £6.75, lamb, chicken, prawn, vegetable and egg cooked with cream. Bhuna Egg £2.75, medium sauce. Aloo Kofta £3.80, deep-fried potato balls in thick sauce. *'Had to write an article about Cornwall's Eden project Arrived too hungry not to eat all four Poppadoms – a bad mistake, considering main course were correctly described as 'enormous' in the Guide. Should also have left out the unspectacular Samosas. Very good bread. Chicken Dhansak came close to the limit of my heat resistance, excellent. Had a good meal.'* BH.. Hours: 12-2/5.30 -11.30.

St Ives

RAJPOOT

6 Gabriel Street, St Ives — 01736 795301

'The quality of the food was high and the meal very tasty. Down point was the prices –high for an average Indian restaurant.' R&NT.

RUBY MURRIES TAKEAWAY

4b Chapel Street, St Ives — 01736 796002

Takeaway only. *'Punjabi proprietors, moved from Leicester and offers Punjabi cuisine. Virtually impossible to park outside. Have arrangement with pub up the road you can eat your takeaway with a pint – an admirable arrangement.'* MW. Delivery: £1.50 charge, 4 miles. Menu extracts: Beef Methi (fenugreek leaves) £4.50. Mushroom and Green Pea Bhajee £5.50. Special Rice £2.95, chicken or prawn fried with peas and whole cummin seed. Onion and Tomato Salad 50p. Curry-on-the-Go £4.95, Chicken Korma or Jeera, served with plain Basmati Rice, in polystyrene carton with lid and spoon.

GANGES — REENTRANT

St Clement Street, Truro — 01872 24253

'Mohammed Udin's Ganges (situated opposite the main car park in Clement Street) is the longest established, 1987, and is by far the biggest Truro restaurant, seating well over 100 people.' rw. *Pleasant enough decor, fish tanks, mirrors with Indian scenes, red table cloths and dimly lit. Onion Bhajis £2.95, four round, pleasingly light, crispy served with extremely tasty red onion relish. Chicken Chat £3.25, sweet and spicy, very good indeed, covered by plentiful fresh cucumber. Tandoori Chicken £6.50, two generous and succulent pieces, very tasty with plenty of sprinkled fresh coriander. Chicken Patia £5.50, equally good, nicely hot in*

rich dark sauce, appropriate sweet and sour background. Mixed Vegetable Bhaji of good standard, excellent full bodied spicy flavour. Good sized portions, average prices.' MW. Takeaway: 25% discount, min £10. Hours: 12-2.15 and 6-11.15, Friday and Saturday 11.45.

GULSHAN NEW ENTRANT

Fore Street, Probus, Truro 01872 882692

'Run by Alom Ali (from Chittagong) and his English wife Sue, ably assisted by son in kitchen and daughter in restaurant. A pleasant, airy restaurant, plain white walls. Non-smoking restaurant. My wife started with Onion Bhajia £2.90, her benchmark. Three, large flat bhajis, tasty, well cooked, nicely crisp outside. Chicken Tuk Tuk £2.95, chicken tikka in batter and deep-fried - excellent, dry coating, not greasy. Excellent, pleasantly flavoursome Garlic Chilli Chicken - fairly hot, a number of green chillies to give it a zing. Chicken Arief — barbecued, superb ginger flavour, imparted into medium sauce. Peshwari Nan £2.30, fresh, light, contained fruit. Marginally, above average prices, portions extremely generous. Good quality succulent, pieces of chicken. Service efficient and friendly. A nice little gem in the Cornish countryside.' MW. Alom and Sue also provide frozen curries to locals pubs, campsites etc. Takeaway: 10% discount. Hours: 5.30-11. Monday closed, except Bank Holidays.

RAJ CUISINE

Fore St, Grampound, Truro

'An absolute gem in another curry desert. So few in the area, which are abysmal. Deserves a place in your guide, can compete with anything. Unusual dishes, personal service and very cosy. Great on a winter break.' We travel from Falmouth to eat there. D&DP.

SHANAZ

1 Edward Street, Truro 01782 262700'

The Shanaz is owned by Jammal (chef) and Kamal (front) Uddin, cousins of Mohammed from the Ganges. *'Shanaz is now situated in smart new premises at 1 Edward Street where it has been for nearly two years. It moved from very much smaller and cramped premises up an alleyway off River Street. The new accommodation is very modern — blue and green chairs, pale wood floors, high quality cutlery and linen and big enough (seats 60) to offer smoking and non smoking sections. However, it is the same ownership and chef as the previous restaurant (which is where I ate) and according to the manager "it's all the same apart from the chairs"!* MW. *'Our Truro favourite. The food is essentially Bangladeshi formula, but extremely well done and well presented. I recommend their Chicken Paneer, and Chicken Jalfrezi, the chillies being just the right heat, and their naan is the best I've tasted.'* GP.

Wadebridge

BASH BAAGAN

1a Molesworth Street, Wadebridge 01208 812500

"Occupies prime position by the old bridge over the River Camel. Owned by the same people who own the Sagor in Launceston. Food overall was fairly average. Service efficient, portions adequate. A word of caution to future first time visitors: the toilets are situated downstairs, and the stairs start directly after the door marked "Toilets". Therefore, unless you are looking where you are going, it would be easy to open the door and fall Achar over Tikka to the bottom!" MW. [Maybe that's why its called Bash Baagan!]

WADEBRIDGE INDIAN TAKEAWAY NEW ENTRANT

1 Trevanson Street, Wadebridge 01208 813339

'Opened in August 2002. Very small kiosk with a couple of chairs in front. Chicken Dhansak £3.95, hot and spicy with robust flavour, only criticism very oily. Mixed Vegetable Bhajee £1.95, good mix, well spiced. Tarka Dal £1.95, first class, good strong, full garlicky flavour. Very good Vegetable Rice £1.70. Impressed with my takeaway.' MW. Hours: 5-12. Credit cards not accepted.

CUMBRIA

Area: Lake District
Population: 493,000
Adjacent Counties: Borders, D&G, Durham, Lancs, Yorks

Barrow-in-Furness

GOLDEN VILLAGE ©

36 Dalton Road, Barrow- 01229 430133

Owned and managed by Janet Chesherwith, head

chef Aba Fateh Choudhury. The restaurant in two rooms seats 58. Delivery: £10 minimum, Barrow area. Hours: 6pm-12am; closed Mon.

MITHALI ©10%

252 Dalton Road, Barrow- 01229 432166

You give Evan Ahmed's 42-seater thumbs up for Chef Abida Choudhury. *'Excellent Thali dishes. Good selection of Biriani dishes – eight different. Curry Club members 10% discount and free bottle wine with the Kurzi Lamb (for four).'* AY. Delivery: £6.50 minimum, 10-mile radius. Hours: 12-2/5-12am (12.30am Fri. & Sat.).

Bowness-on-Windermere

EMPEROR OF INDIA

The Arcade, Crag Brow, Bowness 01539 4 43991

Some interesting dishes include Banana Raitha £1.10 and Palak Nan £2.10. *'We ordered a prawn puree to start. Fresh – an even balance of spices so as not to spoil the taste of the prawns. The main course was equally well prepared and presented. Overall an excellent meal. £36 for 2 including a reasonably priced St Emilion.'* DH. Hours: 12-2pm/5.30-10.45pm (11.30pm on Fri. & Sat.).

Carlisle

DHAKA TANDOORI ©

London Rd, Carleton, Carlisle 01228 523855

Approaching junction 42 of the M6, on the edge of town, you'll find A Harid's 100-seater smart, up-market restaurant, with its marble-effect and chandeliers. Established in 1995, the 100-seater has car parking for 100 at rear and a new large front conservatory. *'Great stop-off if returning to England via M6. Lovely country setting just off motorway with pleasant conservatory tables overlooking main road. Comfortable seating and pleasant decor. Good, friendly service. Large portions of lovely food – Chicken Pasari – very unusual and reasonably priced. Much better than motorway services!'* IB. [Say no more, Ian.] *'Consistently good. Try Chef M Ali's Kebab Kyberi, diced chicken in mild spices with fresh tomatoes, onions, served sizzling in iron karahi.'* AY. Delivery: £12 min. Hours: 12-2/6-12am. Takeaway discount: £2 off every £12. Hours: 12-2pm/6pm-12am. Sun. 12pm-12am.

Cockermouth

TASTE OF INDIA ©

4-5 Hereford Ct, Main St, Cockermouth 01900 822880

F Rahman's 60-seater is divided into two rooms with a 44-seat private room. It's *'nicely decorated, and Chef NI Khan offers good choices. Judging by the number of takeaways being collected the place is very popular with the locals. All curries excellent, if slightly milder than usual. Excellent flavours/use of spices.'* AY. Hours: 12-2.30pm/ 5.30pm-12am. Branches: Red Fort, Keswick, and Emperor of India, Bowness.

Egremont

BALTI HAVEN

8 Main Street, Egremont 01946 823186

'A most welcoming establishment. The chef Mr Mohammed Asadul Haque definitely knows his spices. I am particularly impressed by his vegetable Pullao Rice, a definite hint of the aromatics.' KD.

Kendal

FLAVOURS OF INDIA

20 Blackhall Road, Kendal 01539 722711

Yaor Miah's 95-seater *'used to be a carpet warehouse. A huge water fountain in the centre of the restaurant refreshes the senses. Choice of dishes is bewildering. Every dish is good but many are outstanding, particularly Shahi Korma. Excellent Methi dishes. Thithir Frezi, quail marinated in herbs and spices and finished off in the clay oven, then cooked with minced meat, egg, tomatoes, onions, and capsicum, served in a hot sizzler.'* AY.

Keswick

RED FORT NEW ENTRANT

Main Street, Keswick 017687 74328

'Very wet and bedraggled we tumbled through the door to find quite a large, well laid out restaurant. Now that Indian restaurants don't go for the red flock wall paper, we now know where the surplus find an outlet - it goes into the uniform waistcoats of the waiters. The welcome was a bit indifferent as was the service all night, although the dishes were served promptly. Our party of four chose to share two tandoori Special Kebabs as a starter - no

complaints here as there was enough to go around, although when we have done this in other restaurants the staff did bring another plate for the partner. The chicken, lamb, sheek kebab were excellently cooked. All our party enjoyed the main courses — Jalfrezi very hot with many added green chillies...' sounds like one for Pat! *'...Kofta Aloo and my Zeera Chicken Special — plenty of sauce and potatoes, but a bit skimpy on chicken. Excellent Mushroom Pullao.'* T&MH.

TASTE OF INDIA NEW ENTRANT

Main Street Cockermouth 01900 822880

'This restaurant is the sister of the Red Fort, above. We all had starters which we enthused about. I tried tandoori Khazana Kebab - small pieces of tandoori chicken, lamb in some kind of curry sauce wrapped up in a tortilla like puri - excellent. My wife and her sister shared a Tandoori Special Kebab as we did at the Red Fort - this was served exactly the same but had two Sheek Kebabs on it but no Lamb Tikka - deduct one point! But two minutes later, the lamb tikka appeared - add three points!...' Ah, you spoke to soon Tony. *'... My Chicken Chilli Masala the hottest. All the dishes looked different.'* T&MH.

Penrith

CAGNEYS TANDOORI ©

17 King Street, Penrith 01768 867503

Established in 1987 by Messrs Imdabul (chef) and Fazul Haque (call me Hawk!). OK! Hawk manages the restaurant, well patronised by locals. *'Table immaculate, seating comfortable and staff courteous throughout. Lamb Masala came up trumps, encompassing a depth and range of flavours. Aloo Sag was mild and fragrant'* MR. *'Unusual decor, gold leaf wallpaper. Best Pathia.'* AY. Takeaway 10% off. Hours: 12-2.30pm/6pm-12am.

CHUINI'S ©

19 King Street, Penrith 01768 866760

Established in 1998. Seats 70. Specials include: Exotic Balti. Price check: Poppadam 40p, CTM £5.95, Pullao Rice £1.50, Peshwari Nan £1.50, Lager £2.50 pint. Takeaway: 10% discount. Delivery: £1.50 charge. Hours: 5pm-12am.

RAJINDA PRADESH NEW ENTRANT

Oasis Lakeland Village, Penrith 01768

'Only open to holiday-makers at Centre Park. Highly recommended. Nicely decorated, light and airy, lovely atmosphere for relaxed meal. Superb food - a couple of Poppadoms with chutney, excellent value at 65p. Chicken Rogan Josh - a little disappointing, quite bland. Badshani Chicken - sliced chicken in tikka masala sauce with caramelised onions, fresh chillies, mint - good and spicy, excellent; Chicken Chilli Balti - good heat; Pullao Rice - good with Chapattis that could have been cooked longer. I had a Chicken Dhansak a week later, good but it lacked something. Again would recommend any members visiting Oasis should try it'. DB. Dave scores 8/10 which is high for him. Staff levels fluctuate, so ring to check the opening times and book if you want a table.

TASTE OF BENGAL NEW ENTRANT

60- Strickland Gate, Penrith 01768 891700

'Unpretentious from the outside — in the middle of an old block of cottages. I was a bit dubious because we have eaten in Penrith's other Indian Restaurant — Cagneys — where we had an excellent meal. However, it was pleasant enough once inside, if not memorable. Business was fairly quiet for a Sunday evening, about 7.30pm. Service was quick if a little brusque - unfriendly is too strong a word. Fresh and crisp Poppadoms with pickles - but no lime. Really enjoyed all the Mixed Kebabs £3.50, my companions enthused over their Sheek Kebab £2.50, Lamb Tikka and Chicken Chat £2.50. First class Lamb Jalfrez. Recommended.' T&MH. Hours: 5.30 -11.30.

Whitehaven

AKASH ©

3 Tangier Street, Whitehaven 01946 691171

Owners Abdul Karim and MK Rayman are popular hosts. Couple that with Nurul Hoque's cooking, and it attracts a loyal following. *'The food has much improved and the menu is more varied. This is now a curry house I would visit without worry. The staff are friendly and helpful but a bit on the shy side. Worthy of inclusion in the guide.'* AND *'Again, service was excellent, staff very friendly and helpful, food very tasty with good quantities. Only criticism of the Akash is that to use the toilet one has to climb some very old and narrow carpeted stairs that are pretty steep.'* RE. Takeaway 20% discount. Delivery. Hours: 12-2.30/6-12.

ALI TAJ

34 Tangier Street, Whitehaven 01946 693085

'Has recently been extended and is now a much roomier

establishment. Still proving to be the most popular curry house in Whitehaven and is full most nights. There have been many changes of staff here but this does not seem to have affected Ali's too much (the present staff are just as daft on football as the last lot). Recent takeaways have included all the usual favourites and now the menu has increased to include more house specialities: Gata Bhuna, Chicken Cheese Kufta, Chooza Shashlick, Chooza Shabzi, Mutton Shashlick. Service is fast and efficient, food very good, and draft lager the best in town.' RE. *And again: 'Two takeaways were first class with plenty of food crammed into the cartons. Good, quick, friendly service. Interesting to note that the Ali Taj never tries to compete with other establishments on price or cheap gimmicks. They rely on their reputation alone and it certainly works for them.'* RE.

DERBYSHIRE

Area: North Midlands
Population: 975,000
Adjacent Counties: Cheshire, Leics, Greater Manch, Notts, Staffs, S Yorks

Alfreton

NEW BENGAL ©

3 King Street, Alfreton 01773 831620

Established in 1986, taken over by New Bengal Ltd in 1997, managed by F Ahmed. A cosy restaurant seating just 34 diners, decorated in cream with blue furnishings. Vegetable Thali £8.95 – Poppadam, three vegetable curries, Stuffed Nan and Plain Rice. Delivery: 5-mile radius, £12 minimum. Hours: 6pm-12am (1am Sat.).

SANAM

50 King Street, Alfreton 01773 830690

'Well presented menu, good, self-confident, outgoing staff. Twelve dining – starters on the table within 10 minutes. Really excellent Chicken and Lamb Tikka/Jeera Lamb was well spiced with good flavour.' KM. *''Obviously slipped through the net and should be in the Guide. Can thoroughly recommend it, once you get passed the rather shabby exterior. Wide, varied menu; beautifully cooked food; Pleasant staff.'* HEW.

Burton-on-Trent

SPICE OF ASIA NEW ENTRANT

99 Station Street, Burton 01283 517799

Menu Extracts: Fish Chat, mashed spiced fish; Alu Tikka, grilled spiced hot potatoes; Butter Chicken; Papaya Bhaji; Onion and Chilli Nan; Garlic and Tomato Nan. *'Food of high quality and served by very obliging staff, clean table layout, quality cloths changed between courses, nice flower decorations, comfortable seating with sufficient space between tables, pleasant background music. You can bring your own drinks, with no corkage, hygienic toilets.'* BM. Takeaway: 15% discount. Delivery: 5 miles, £10 minimum. Hours: 5.30-12, Fri/Sat to 12.30.

Buxton

INDIAN PALACE NEW ENTRANT

5 Cavendish Circus, Buxton 01298 77260

'Friendly and efficient staff. Standard menu offerings. Standard Poppadoms with generous pickle tray. Lovely Mulligatawny Soup £1.50, generous portion in a large flat bowl with lemon and just the right blend of spices in a thick, rich stock. Lamb Karahi £4.10, chunks of pepper and onion, nice tender lamb, pleasant medium sauce. Well cooked aromatic rice.' RW. Hours: 5-1130, except Sunday 4.30-11.30, Friday & Saturday to 12.

TAJ MAHAL

35 High Street, Buxton 01298 78388

Established in 1997, Mr Koyes Ahmed's Taj Mahal continues to be a popular local venue. *'Cosy and clean in centre of historic peak town in centre of National Park. As Buxton is the highest town in England, the Taj Mahal must be a contender for the highest curry house in the country!'* [well, you learn a new thing every day! not only does the *Guide* inform you about the best place to go for a curry but geographical news too.] *'Seats some 46 diners in two rooms. Standard menu with smattering of specials - chef reputedly from the Curry Canyon of Rusholme. Knowledgeable and efficient staff who annoyingly were pushing drink sales with a vengeance throughout the meal. Reshmi Kebab £2.40, succulent with well cooked omelette, limp salad and no yoghurt sauce'* [I can't enjoy starters without yoghurt sauce]. *'Nicely sizzling Lamb Karahi £4.80, very good cuts of tender meat, rather swimming in excess ghee. Average Nan with little garlic, but fluffy and only slightly*

doughy. Very good Tarka Dal – perfect balance of garlic and lentils. Real tablecloths and hot towels.' RW. Menu extracts: Nawabi Steak £7.50. Pullao Rice with egg, mushroom, vegetable, onion and keema – good value at £1.90. Watch out for the Pickle Tray at a steep 80p each. Hours: 5-11.30.

Castle Donnington

VILLAGE TANDOORI ©

43-45 Borough Street, Castle Donnington 01332 814455

Taken over in 1997 by Mohammed Abdul Basit. Seats 55 in two simply decorated dining rooms. Pakistani curries on the menu. Specials include: Balti Special Cocktail. Hours: 6-12.

Chesterfield

GULAB  10%

207 Chatsworth Road, Brampton, Chesterfield 01246 204612

R Miah and A Rahman's Gulab seats 40 and serves formula curries.*'Called on spec with my son after a football match at Halifax. 10% Curry Club discount agreed although I did not book previously. Fairly good all round standard curry house and inexpensive. Chicken Jalfrezi ultra hot – Thali strength. Very clean. Service good though busy (7.30 Sat night). Deserves inclusion in guide.'* BP D. Minimum charge £6. Hours: 6-11.45 (12.45am on Fri. & Sat.).

INDIAN BLUES NEW ENTRANT

7 Corporation Street, Chesterfield 01246 557505

'Friday night at 10.30pm – it wasn't too busy and could accommodate three people easily (apparently if you get there any later they won't let you in!) Started with Aloo Chop and Mixed Kebab £2.40, chicken wing, Onion Bhajia and Seek Kebab.' EG. Menu extracts: Kashmiri Lamb Bhuna £4.10, lamb with grilled onions. Mango Delight £4.10, chicken with cream, almonds and mango. Coconut Rice £1.20. Hours: 6-12, Friday and Saturday to 1.

Derby

ABID TANDOORI BYO ©

7 Curzon Street, Derby 01332 293712

Mohammed Ilyas' 90-seater serves Pakistani and Kashmiri curries. *'This particular evening the food was delicious. It always is, but tonight the dishes were really on form. The dishes are always very generous and the service is always quick and the waiters are helpful. It's comfortable but by no means up-class, just right 'but you can BYO, £2.50 a cork.'* NH, Delivery: £15 minimum, 6-mile radius. Hours: 5.30pm-3am. Branches: Abid, Dale Road, Matlock. Abid Balti, Causley Rd, Alfreton.

SHABUZ BAGAN

80 Osmaston Road, Derby 01332 296887

Established in 1997. Seats 100. Parking for 20 cars to rear, with CCTV. Specials include: Bangladeshi fish dishes cooked in traditional style. *'Seems to be the most popular in Derby. Very friendly service, comfort and decor good. Generous portions and excellent quality - full of flavour. Sag Panir on of the best ever. Sunday evening buffet very good value at £7.50.'* GAM. Delivery: 5 miles, £10 minimum. Hours: 6-1am.

Glossop

BALTI PALACE — NEW ENTRANT

9 Victoria Street, Glossop 01457 852584

Air conditioned. *'Very small single room just off market place. Simply furnished in open plan fashion, light woods, blue wallpaper with a disturbingly out of focus pattern, which should be disconcerting for the after pub crowd. Efficient staff dealing with a large party occupying the majority of the 32 seats and obviously less than sober. I opted for a takeaway. Food prepared remarkably quickly. Mixed Kebab Starter £2.50, disappointing, rather tough and microwaved with fresh salad and Mint Raitha too piquant for my taste. Mashur Lamb Tikka Balti (inc Nan) £5.50, outstandingly good. Varied combination of tastes, nicely caramelised onion to hot chilli, rich, tasty sauce, packed with succulent, tender lamb. Good Nan, moist, fluffy and not at all stodgy, nice hint of ghee. Enjoyable. I will definitely be trying a sit down meal in the near future.'* RW. The Meal Deals are exceptional value for money, prices from £7.95 for a complete meal and the Amritsari Chicken £1.95 sound intriguing described as wings of fire! Delivery: £10 minimum, 3 miles. Takeaway: 10% discount, minimum £15. 15% discount, £20 minimum. Hours: 5-12, Fri/Sat-1.

NASEEB — NEW ENTRANT

114 High Street West, Glossop......01457 854279

'Thirty-eight seats in single room, nicely decorated with green theme! Entry is via a poorly designed outer and vestibule door, with insufficient gap to negotiate edifice. Smart staff dealt with needs of surprisingly busy Monday evening in unfussed manner. Prawn Puri £1.95, well presented, served with small fresh salad, thin sauce, pleasantly hot, splendid puri. Lamb Tikka Balti £6.95, served in obligatory Balti pan, clump of fresh coriander the size of a small Spinney, sauce identical to that of starter, addition of fried onion. A glance around showed examples of this ubiquitous ingredient! That said it was enjoyable and complimented the plentiful chunks of tangy and tender lamb tikka. Nan – soft, crispy, glazed with ghee.' RW. Takeaway: 20% discount. Hours: 5-1130, Fri/Sat-12.Sunday 4-11.

Ilkeston

SHAH JAHAN ©

1 Awsworth Road, Ilkeston 0115 932 3036

Opened 1987, taken over in 1994 by Abdul Aziz who is also the head chef, cooking curries and Baltis at his red-decorated 56-seater. Own car park. Takeaway: 10% discount. Hours: 6-12.30.

Littleover

JEE JA JEE'S — NEW ENTRANT

5 Hollybrook Way, Heatherton, Littleover 01332 523700

'Pleasant staff, lovely atmosphere, nice food.' Anon. *'Location is perhaps a little unusual, built on a new housing estate. Decor bright and modern. Extensive menu, portions are very large.'* ND. Menu extracts: Paneer Shashlik £2.95. Lamb and Tomato Kofta £3.50. Butter Chicken £7.95 inc rice. Egg and Potato Pot £6.95 inc rice. Onion and Chilli Nan or Garlic and Tomato Nan £1.70. Delivery Service. Hours: 6-12, Fri/Sat to 12.30.

Matlock Bath

ABID TANDOORI 

129 Dale Road, Matlock Bath 01629 57400

Mohammed Bashir's 70-seater is in this delightful Peak District spa town, nestling on the River Derwent, with its many pleasant walks and even a cable car to take you to the top of the cliffs. Just the thing to work up an appetite for Chef Maroof's Pakistani and Kashmiri cooking. *'The Lamb Bhuna was huge and excellent. The rice was a little al dente and the Sag Aloo was a disappointment. Massive menu.'* AGR. Delivery: £20 minimum, 5-mile radius. Hours: 6pm-12am (1am on Fri. & Sat.). Branches: Abid, Curzon Street, Derby. Abid Balti, Causley Lane, Alfreton.

Ripley

SHEEZAN II 

11 Church Street, Ripley 01773 747472

Opened in 1983, by N Hussain (head chef) and M Sharif (manager). Pakistani and North Indian-styled curries. Air-conditioned, 42-seater restaurant. Hours: 6pm-12am (1am weekends).

©	Curry Club Discount	U	Unlicensed
V	Vegetarian	ANP	Alcohol not permitted
e-a-m-a-y-l	Eat as much as you like	BYO	Bring your own alcohol

DEVON

Area: West Country
Population: 1,077,000
Adjacent Counties:
Cornwall,
Dorset, Somerset

Bovey Tracey

SPICE BAAZAAR NEW ENTRANT

38 Fore Street, Bovey Tracey 01626 835125

'A good waterhole in the Devon desert. I guess it's pretty well bog-standard, but round here it's gold dust' TR. Hours: 6-11.30.

Chumleigh

CHULMLEIGH TANDOORI NEW ENTRANT

Cooper House, Fore Street, Chulmleigh 01769 580797

'In the heart of a sleepy village in north Devon, a small - about 15-18 covers, with the best Poppadoms - brilliantly crispy and Nan breads - sensational taste with crunchy crust and moist interior, that I have ever had. Clearly a family business, mum and young daughter in evidence during the evening, providing a charming and not intrusive presence. Sometimes difficult to get a table on the off-chance, especially at the weekend.' CL.

Exeter

GANDHI

7 New North Road, Exeter 01392 272119

'Remains reliable. Good-sized tables, pleasant atmosphere and friendly staff. Lamb Tikka Karahi a firm favourite. Chicken Patia in a dark, hot, sweet and sour sauce.' PJ. *'A real find, best food by far we've had in local Indians. Staff efficient and attentive, the Birianis especially tasty. Keep it in the guide!'* CS.

GANGES

156 Fore Street, Exeter 01392 272630

'A well-appointed, caring restaurant seating 57 in a split-level arrangement. Located in the very popular and busy central area of the city, and hence it closes fairly early. Plenty of helpful staff. Great starter – two spicy fried Potato Cakes served with really tangy (chat masala?) channa sauce. Very nice salad – mangetout, sweetcorn, cherry tomato and coriander. Real tables clothes and napkins throughout and hot towels. Hot plates as standard. Superb Thali – a cold and tangy Rathia; aromatic al-dente Pullao Rice; richly flavoured Aloo Dum with potato patty right at the bottom, which had to be dug out; pleasantly hot Prawn Jalfrezi, in which the prawns had a discernable taste for once; Chicken Korma in the richest cream sauce possible and a wonderful lamb Achari Cham Cham, robustly spiced with loads of ginger and coriander. Also included. Keema Nan, light, tasty and stuffed with juicy, spicy mince - almost a meal in itself.' RW. Hours: 17.30-23.15.

TAJ MAHAL

50 Queen Street, Exeter 01392 258129

'First visit here but others in party (five) had been several times before and recommended it. Quite small inside with glass pink paint on walls and false 'copper' ceiling. Fairly standard menu with no new starters. From main courses I had Vindaloo and sampled the others' Madras, Bhuna, CTM and Roghan Josh. Most impressed at tastes and textures. Quantity just right, very good garlic Nan.' KN.

Ilfracombe

BOMBAY PALACE ©

36 Green Close Road, Ilfracombe 01271 862010

Established in 1998. Seats 60. Competent formula curry house with no surprises. Specials include: Bombay Special Mosalla and Hydrabadi. Takeaway: 10% discount. Free delivery in local area, £10 minimum order. Hours: 5.30-11pm.

RAJAH NEW TO OUR TOP 100 ©

5 Portland Street, Ilfracombe 01271 863499

Opened in 1985, Ralph Wild is the owner-chef here, assisted by his son James and his wife Janet. Good street parking. The menu is short but comprehensive. A small restaurant, seating 28, decorated in red, with Indian ornaments. *'Stumbled upon the Rajah while on holiday. Dishes very well presented, balanced. Attentive service, a strong sense of traditional family business.'* LM. *'18 years in business. Had to put pen to paper and sing the praises. Started off as regular takeaway customers. Now we eat in the restaurant twice a week. By far the best we have tasted – consistently good.'* MR & MRS D. *'WOW!! I won't forget this place for a longtime. I had a chicken Vindaloo which I can normally take with only a passing comment. My wife said it was the slowest she can ever remember me eating a meal. Sweat was pouring out of every pore. It made the Madras Potato and Pea side dishes we had with it – which was billed as fairly hot – pale into blandness. However, I persevered and enjoyed it. Fairly busy on a Tuesday night, surprised me. Everything was good or very good, rather than excellent. Poppadoms and breads on the small side, but didn't leave hungry.'* T&MH. It's time to put the Wilds into our **TOP 100.** Delivery: £13.50 min. Hours: 6-10.30pm; open bank holidays.

Newton Abbot

PASSAGE TO INDIA

137 Queen Street, Newton Abbot 01626 688443'

Often fairly crowded. Despite this the service was good and food excellent. *'A nightcap and a carnation for the ladies on the house, rounds the evening off nicely. Reasonably priced.'* JM. 25% discount for collected takeaways. *'Have yet to discover a restaurant that consistently offers food of a very high standard.'* SEJ. Hours: 12-2/5.30-11.30, (12am on Fri. & Sat., 11 on Sun.

Plymouth

JAIPUR PALACE 

146 Vauxhall Street, The Barbican, Plymouth 01752 668711

Established in 1994 by Syed Abdul Wahid. The two-roomed restaurant seats 70. Chef Rumel Ahmad's cooking is *'recommended to anyone who enjoys quality food in a comfortable atmosphere. My wife says that no one cooks a lamb pasanda like the Jaipur.'* LC. *'I can think of no better restaurant to put in your guide for the best curry I have had the pleasure to taste.'* JK. Delivery: free 10-mile radius. Hours: 12-2pm/5.30pm-12am.

KURBANI RETURNS TO TOP 100

1 Tavistock Place, Sherwell Arcade, Plymouth 01752 26677

Mr Tarafder specialises in 'home-style' Indian cooking, and we point out that since this is not the formula norm, it doesn't suit everyone. But it does suit others. *'Staff are always friendly and the service is first class. Certainly one of the best that I visit.'* PB. *'Not only is the food of high standard and very tasty and well presented, but it is also very reasonably priced. You can call me a very satisfied customer.'* JT. *'I wish to show my appreciation for the superb range of foods provided by the Kurbani. The food is excellent and is only matched by the quality of the service provided by the friendly staff.'* RT. *'Warm friendly family run establishment. Excellent service and superb food with amazing flavours. Impressed.'* NON. *'On each occasion (three), I found the food to be extremely good. My wife and I have friends who are Sikhs and Hindu and we regularly eat at each others houses. The food at the Kurbani is not exactly like Asian home cooking, it's pretty damned close. Have always found the Tarafders to be very friendly and attentive hosts.'* MRW. You all want it restored to our **TOP 100.**

JAIPUR PALACE

144 Vauxhall Street, Bretonside, The Barbican Plymouth 01752 668711

Proprietor, SA Wahid. Menu extract: Jaipur Biryani £12.95, cooked with King prawns and chicken. Seats 70 diners. *'Have dined on a number of occasions, have always been entirely satisfied with both food and service. Wahid very friendly, not rushed, we take our time, atmosphere is pleasant and relaxing.'* SJ. Hours: 12-2, Sunday only and 5.30 -12, daily.

DORSET

Area: South West
Population: 698,000
Adjacent Counties:
Devon, Hants,
Soms, Wilts

Bournemouth

BOURNEMOUTH TANDOORI 

8 Holdenhurst Road, Lansdowne, Bournemouth 01202 29620

Shuab Ahmed's 50-seat restaurant, is *'tastefully decorated in apricot and green. Poppadam and pickles arrived without asking within minutes. Started with a Madouri Kebab, new to me, diced lamb, tomato, cucumber, etc, succulent and tasty, with mint sauce in a jug to pour on, how sensible! Followed by one of my favourites, Chicken Jalfrezi and rice, bread and Mushroom Bhaji. I rate this ten out of ten. Service pleasant and swift. One of the best in Bournemouth.'* MS. Specials include:

Delight, cooked with Grand Marnier, fresh cream, almonds. Hours: 12-2.30pm/6pm-12am.

THE EYE OF THE TIGER 

207 Old Christchurch Road, Bournemouth
01202 780900

Opened in 1992 by James Dudley and Ramjan Ali. Managed by Anum Miah with Showkat Ali in the kitchen. Seats 80. 'We were a bit concerned that it was empty at 7pm on a Saturday night, but we dived in to find a pleasant restaurant with helpful waiters. It was the best curry we'd had for many a long month. I was amused to see a machine in the men's toilet selling curry-flavoured condoms! The meal (without this particular item) cost us £25 including four drinks, and by the time we left, it was packed.' CS. JS says her 'mind boggles. Imagine a Phal-flavoured version!' Really, Jane, behave yourself – this is a respectable publication! Hours: 12-2pm/6pm-12am.

Christchurch

STARLIGHT 

54 Bargates, Christchurch 01202 484111

Ian Clasper's and Abdul Hai's eye-catching, popular Starlight is decorated with hand-painted murals. Hours: 12-2pm/6pm-12am.

Poole

THE GATE OF INDIA 

54-56 Commercial Road, Lower Parkstone, Poole 01202 717061

Messrs Choudhurys' Gate, established in 1993, seats 80 in two rooms and regularly attracts praise: *'Welcoming staff, impressive service. very comfortable and cosy yet spacious. Business is brisk and even midweek you may well have to book. Busy on weekday evenings and packed to the ceiling on Saturdays. When I talk to the customers, I am impressed by the numbers who regularly come here from quite a way – Christchurch, Wareham, Wimborne, etc because it's worth the trip. Hearing us plan my birthday dinner, they offered to do us a special and prepared a Kurzi Lamb for the event – it was out of this world. Marinated for at least 24 hours, it absorbed all the mysteries of the Sub Continent. Superb. This excellent restaurant continues to deserve the highest commendations. It does a very good trade. The Gate of India thrives from tourists. I have noticed all sorts of languages and accents. The very posh Poole Yacht Club is not far away and their membership is noticeable here. Poole Hospital doctors and medical staff frequently make up parties and 'The Gate' do a fair number of charity events. Spacious (free in the evening) parking accommodation at the rear. We have been regulars throughout the year and each visit is a delight. Consistently high standard menu. Long may they prosper.'* RG. Takeaway: 10% discount. Hours: 12-2.30/6-12.

MOONLIGHT 

9 Moor Road, Broadstone, Poole 01202 605234

A Malik's restaurant seats 80, with a 30-seat function room. *'Strongly recommend a visit. Excellent food, including very interesting specials.'* JL. Mr Malik tells us of a group of customers who visit five times a week. We're still waiting to hear who they are! Declare yourselves and write in! Hours: 12-2/6-12am.

RAJASTHAN

127 Pennhill Avenue, Poole 01202 718966

Run by Kamal Mohammed (who is also in charge of the kitchen), the restaurant offers cuisine from Mohammed's native Rajasthan as well as standard high-street favourites. The venue is tasteful and very spacious, napkins are of top quality, damask. There is a well-stocked bar. We get a flow of reports telling us how good the food is. *'Rajasthani Lava Murg – a dry curry, stir-fried marinated chicken garnished with cheese was exotic, fragrant and delicious. My nephew had a splendid rich Lamb Madras Curry and my Chicken Biryani was out of this world – not the usual faked-up dish with cooked rice and a few bits of chicken, but the genuine slow-cooked classic regal dish of India. All the vegetables, including the Bindhi ,are fresh. The waiters are charming, helpful, amiable and obliging without being obsequious. Value for money. Extremely impressive. The Rajasthan is where good curries go when they die.'* RG. and many like him, have been saying superlatives Then suddenly this from RG, one of their most loyal customers. *'Rajasthan is about 4 miles away, almost in Bournemouth. Really nice, upmarket establishment. Very busy Saturday night. Meals were good, prices definitely on the expensive side. No lime pickle (my favourite) on the tray, but the next table had some! Service excellent.'* ANON. *' This formerly highly recommended curry restaurant has declined in my opinion. Portions were a bit ungenerous last time we visited. The staff seem to have grown every more supercilious. The final straw was the fact they they turned down a booking from me on a Saturday because I said that I was in a wheelchair. They said they did not accept disabled bookings at weekends. This is a policy which must be opposed. If exercised against black people or females etc there would be an outcry.'* RG. I hope you complained to the management, Roger. I presume that this happened because it was Saturday. Nevertheless, there is no excuse for it, and the incident nearly lost Rajasthan its listing. For now it loses its top **100 RATING.** Reports please for it to go out or up. Mini charge: £12. Hours: 12-2.30/6-11.30, Fri/Sat-12.

TAJ MAHAL 2 

38 High Street, Poole 01202 677315

Established in 1975. Recently taken over by A Rahman in 1999. Originally called the Prince of India. Seats 52. Ample parking opposite NCP. Specials include: Asri Gost, Badami, Makani, Gost Kalyani, Morisa. Takeaway: 10% discount. Hours: 12-2.30pm/6pm-12am.

TANDOORI NIGHTS 

50 High Street, Poole 01202 679712

Established in 1995 by AH Choudhury. Seats 100 in two rooms. House specials: Madras Sall Samba £2.25 – vegetables with lentils in Madras curry sauce. Persian Chicken Biriani £6.00 – enveloped with omelette. Takeaway: 10% discount. . Hours: 12-2.30pm/6pm-12am.

Sherbourne

RAJPOOT 

The House of the Steps, Half Moon St, Sherborne 01935 812455

Owned by Mizanur Rahman, managed by Fajul Hoque with Abdul Kussus in the kitchen, the spacious restaurant has lots of traditional tapestry and upholstery, seats for 58 in two rooms. Bangladeshi specials include Rui, Pomfret and Ayre fish, and Shatkora, a tangy Bengali citrus fruit is used, when available, in chicken, meat or prawn. *'My girlfriend and I met halfway (100 miles each) and Sherborne is the halfway point. Food was worth a 100 miles. Staff not that friendly to begin with, but gradually warmed up! Service was good and pretty fast. Bombay Spuds, £2.50 were divine. Shahi Chicken Badami £6.50 is pretty special. Vegetable Biriani £6 had raisins and okra in it.'* DB. *'As frequent customers, I would like to recommend them as a quality Indian restaurant with obliging friendly staff, great food and warm atmosphere.'* E&MP. Minimum charge: £8. Hours: 12-2.30 and 6-11.30, Friday & Saturday to 12.

Swanage

GOLDEN BENGAL NEW ENTRANT

343- High Street, Swanage 01929 427012

Formerly Taste of India. Licensed. *'Crowded on this Saturday night with a good takeaway trade. Well produced and attractive menu. 'Today's Specials' section permanently printed as part of the menu – curious! Crispy Poppadoms 50p, accompanied by four pickles 50p each, included a wickedly hot chilli pickle. Flat Onion Bhajia £2.60, disappointing, greasy, soft, although flavoursome. Much better Chicken Tikka Chat £3.95, thinly sliced chicken tikka in tangy sauce. Very pleasant Patia £5.95, nicely hot but sweeter than most. CTM £6.95, usual orange colour, creamy, heavy coconut flavour, pleasantly average. Rich Chicken Badami £7.95, creamy nut sauce with whole cashews. I had a few tastes (for research purposes of course!). Lamb Biriani £9.25, declared excellent. Portions sufficient, prices average, service could have been better.'* MW. Hours: 12-2 and 5.30 -11.30.

Wareham

RAJPOOT

39 North Street, Wareham 01929 554603

'A good-standard high street fully licensed curry house serving formula curries. Efficient service, portions good, prices average.' MW. *'Very impressed with the quality of the food and level of service.'* SEJ. Hours: 12-2.30pm/6-11.30pm.'.

Weymouth

BALTI HOUSE

24 Commercial Road, Weymouth 01305 783515

100-seater opened in 1994, owned and managed by Shalim Abdul. Chef Abdul Shahid cooks Bangladeshi-style curries a. *'Over several years, we have been impressed by consistently high standard of service and cuisine.'* M&JH. *'Lively spicy food, perfectly cooked, sensitive service.'* J&JS. *'The mangoes were great.'* R&CP. Takeaway: 10% discount. Delivery: 3-mile radius. Hours: 12-2/5.30-11.30.

COUNTY DURHAM

Area: North East
Population: 610,000
Adjacent Counties:
Cumbria,
Northumberland,
Tyne & Wear,
N Yorkshire

Bishop Auckland

THE KING'S BALTI ©

187 Newgate St, Bishop Auckland 01388 604222

Owned by Mohammed Boshir Ali Hussan. Baltis and standard curries on the menu. Chutneys and Pickles 50p a portion but if you buy a jar from an assortment they are £2 a jar – brilliant idea! Hours: 5-12am. (11.30pm on Sun.).

Chester-Le-Street

GOLDEN GATE TANDOORI

11 South Burns Rd, Chester-Le-Street 0191 388 2906

Established in 1993. Seats 45. Ample parking to front. House specials: Kaleeya Beef or Chicken £6.50 – hot cooked with roast potatoes, marinated in yoghurt. Sylhet Beef or Chicken £7.00 – strongly spiced, dry with eggs and tomatoes. Takeaway: approximately 10% discount. Delivery: £10 min, 6-mile radius. Hours: 12-2/6-12am.

Darlington

SHAPLA 

192 Northgate, Darlington 01325 468920

Established in 1980, SA Khan's green and beige 80-seat restaurant has two large trees and engraved glass divisions, with a private room seating 60. *'Brilliant.'* PJ. *'Excellent.'* DMC. Hours: 12-2 / 6-12am; closed Fri. lunch.

Durham

COPPER DOME NEW ENTRANT

Nevilles Cross, Darlington Road 0191 375 7707

'Like stepping into a South Indian temple. The smell of sandlewood, chime of designer cutlery, the motes of light refracted through laded window panes and excellent Indo-Global Cuisine made by the hands of chefs flow over from seven star hotels in India...' or so the press release says!

Stanley

MONJU TANDOORI ©

33 Park Road, South Moor, Stanley 01207 283259

Established in 1987 by Ala Miah, who is also the manager. Cooking by Moyz Uddin. A small 30-seat two-room restaurant. Delivery: £10 minimum, 8-mile radius. Hours: 12-2p / 6-12am.

Stockton-on-Tees

THE ROYAL BENGAL 

Prince Regent Street, Stockton 01642 674331

'Formula curryhouse, marginally better than the rest.' PT.

ESSEX

Area: Home Counties,
(east of London)
Population:
1,605,000
Adjacent Counties:
Cambs, Herts, Kent,
London, Suffolk

Part of Essex was absorbed by Greater London in 1965. We note affected towns/suburbs.

Basildon

LIPU TAKEAWAY NEW ENTRANT

201 Timberlog Lane, Barstable W Basildon
01268 550775

Imaginative menu: Reshmi Kebab £2.75, covered in

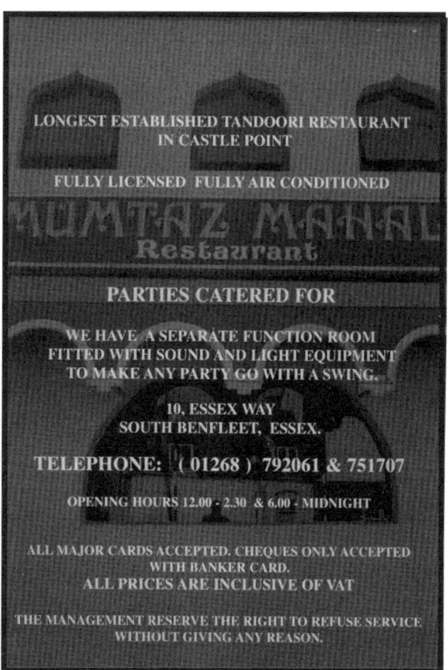

omelette. Tandoori Lobster Masala £10.95. Chef's Special £5.95, Chicken Tikka, mixed vegetables and cheese cooked in medium sauce. Tomato Bhajee £1.95. Special Nan £2.95, bread stuffed with chicken tikka, mince meat and cheese. Delivery: 4 miles, £8.95 minimum.Hours: 5-11, Friday and Saturday to 12.

Benfleet

(includes Thundersley)

MUMTAZ MAHAL 

10 Essex Way, Benfleet 01268 751707

Opened in 1977, Abdur Rahid's Mumtaz is well respected and well liked. Large car park adjacent, and inside 90 seats are split over two floors and has a cosy atmosphere. It's all standard stuff, with every variation you can imagine on chicken, lamb, prawns and vegetables, and it's all done *'sumptuously'* IDB

Braintree

CURRY PALACE 

28 Fairfield Road, Braintree 01376 320083

Established in 1975 by MA Noor. His restaurant seats 52 diners; warm, modern interior with framed canvas art imported from Bangladesh. House specials: Balti Chicken Tikka and Chicken Dhansak. Takeaway: 10% discount. Hours: 5.30-11pm; closed Mon.

Buckhurst Hill

CORIANDER NEW ENTRANT

40 Victoria Rd, Station Approach,
Buckhurst Hill 020 8504 2671

Opposite Buckhurst Hill Station. *'Well-spaced tables. My husband and I ate Badami Batar, £3.25, whole quails rubbed with lemon juice, marinated in almond paste, tandoored and Tikka Jhal Puri £2.95, small diced chicken tikka, fairly hot sauce, served on puri, Handi Lazeez £6.95, boneless chicken, aromatic, chillies, coriander, cardamom, Satkora lamb £6.50, Bengali lemon. Quality FANTASTIC and the quantities are substantial. Service very attentive, polite and helpful.'* MF.

Burnham

POLASH 

169 Station Road, Burnham 01621 782233

'Visited on a number of occasions, highly impressed by ambience, decor, service and above all, cuisine. Comfortable sized restaurant, high ceiling, tastefully picked out in soft green. Indian arches, smoky subdued pinks. Intimate lighting. Crispy Poppadoms, tasty pickle tray. Impressively generous servings of Onion Bhajia and Chicken Tikka, with fresh salad. Chicken Tikka Masala tender chicken, rich dark sauce – superb accompanied by a warm Nan wrapped in its own cloth. King Prawn Dhansak – delicious, flavoursome sauce, topped with pineapple, creamy, spicy, good helping of prawns.Deserves to be included in Guide' ASL. *'Decided to try a very hot lamb curry, I opted for Vindaloo strength. Cubed of lamb tender and tasty whilst the sauce (appreciably hot!) was full of flavour, thick and rich. Service discrete, polite, timeless and under expert management. Never made to feel rushed.'* DSL. *'We've eaten here for years - started at the old premises! Food has not changed in quality. Try the new 'special's board.' Staff and friendly and helpful.'* MC. *'Have dined*

at the Polash for ten years and have always found the food and service to be on an excellent standard. Variety of 'platter's provide good value for money.' CP & ACR. Buffet Night: Tuesday and Sundays £7.95. Delivery: 5 miles.

Chelmsford
(includes Great Baddow and Writtle)

BENGAL BLUES SHAFIQUE

30 The Green Writtle, Chelmsford
01245 422228

Mr MA Shafique's Bengal Blues Seats 180 and is decorated in the modern style. Three separate areas: lounge/bar for drinks and snacks, informal dining for Indian sandwiches – Chicken Tikka, Spicy Prawn etc – and formal dining for the house specials. It's a mile or three out of town and is in *'beautiful surroundings.'* JT. *'Elegant, well decorated, large restaurant. Sunday buffet: good selection of food with fair pricing.'* PEH. House specials: Salmon Dhaka £4.95 – fresh salmon rolled in spices, cooked in the tandoor. Tandoori Paneer Ka Sula £3.25 – home-made cheese, flavoured with mint and served with pickles. Jessore £10.95 – barbecued pepper lamb chops. Reports please.

TAJ MAHAL

6 Baddow Road, Chelmsford 01245 259618

Formula 60-seat curryhouse which it seems does a good lunch trade at £5.95. *'It was belting down with cold rain, so I went to the Taj for a warming curry. I had something from the Business Lunch menu - Meat Samosas (very nice mint sauce) followed by Chicken Kashmir - done well. Not spectacular, but what I wanted and should be a TOP 1000.'* MW. And if it's in this *Guide* it is in the top thousand Mick. Hours: 12-2.30 / 5.30-12. Sunday 1 -12.

SAGARMATHA GURKHA

2 St Botolphs Circus, Colchester 01206 579438

Established in 1999. Formerly called Oriental House. Seats 42. There are of course many if not all your old favourites on the menu, and done well too, as they are so often by Nepalese chefs. Specialities include: traditional Nepalese 'village' meal (£9.95), the most unusual dish being Shanjali Kukhura (chicken marinated in ginger, green chilli, herbs and spinach). Two large car parks with CCTV in front and rear. Takeaway: 10% discount. Delivery: £15, 5-mile radius. Hours: 12-2pm/5.30-11.30pm

Epping

RAJ

75 High Street, Epping 01992 572193

Mumin Ali tells us his 40-seater is *'beautifully decorated with artificial plants with coziness and elegance'*. Chef Abdul Ali cooks formula curries. *'Good quality food.'* SR. Delivery: £10 min, 5-mile radius. Hours: 12-2.30/6-12am.

Gants Hill (Greater London)

KANCHANS NEW ENTRANT NEW TO OUR TOP 100

53 Perth Road, Gants Hill 020 8518 9282

'Location, location, location', they say. And it is almost on the roundabout, near the tube, with a huge plate glass window with large ornately carved wooden double door with brass studs. Unmissable. But is Gant's Hill in suburban Essex the right location. Only time will tell. Because this restaurant is a real cut above anything for miles around. Inside it's a beautifully decorated restaurant, with creamy walls, crystal mirrors, Indian artifacts, lavish upholstery and place settings. Upstairs is a huge banqueting suit which is ideal for large family-and-friend parties. And does well for smaller Asian weddings. The owners have run a standard curryhouse down the road for years, but they decided to do the job properly. The chefs all imported from India, cook authentic Punjabi Indian curries and accompaniments - everything wonderful from the spicy Lamb Knuckle to the Black Urid Dal. Definitely worthy of our top 100. Gants Hill is very lucky indeed. Parking at rear. Cover charge £1.50. Hours: 12-3/6-11.30.

Heybridge

HEYBRIDGE TANDOORI 

5 Bentalls Centre, Heybridge 01621 858566

Abdul Rofik, Abdul Hannan and Nazrul Islam's 70-seater, decorated in bright colours with blue tablecloths, pink napkins, has a non-smoking room. The centre has ample 24hr security-guarded car parking facilities. *'Excellent. Everything well presented, fish specials were superb, attentive service. Four non-regular curry eaters have become converted.'* SJ. Fish specials include Chandpuri Hilsha, Boal, Ayre and large Chingri (prawns). Delivery: £10 minimum, 3-mile radius. Hours: 12-2.30/6-11.30 (Sat. to 12am.).

Hockley

KERALAM NEW ENTRANT

200 Main Road, Hawkwell, Hockley 01702 207188

Fully licensed. *'The only South Indian in the area. As good as those in Tooting and Kerala itself, which I know well. Dosas could not be bettered. Interesting vegetables like beetroot. Staff friendly, prices reasonable, well worth a detour.'* JAR. Menu extracts: Bhelpoori £2.50, poori, puffed rice crispies, potato, green chilli, sweet and sour sauces. Squid Fried £3.25, marinated squid served with salad Trivandrum style. Cashew Nut Pakoda £2.65, batter fried cashew nuts served with Date Chutney. Masala Dosa £3.95, rice and lentil pancake filled with potato and onion masala, served with Sambar and Coconut Chutney. Malabar Meen Moli £5.10, kingfish cooked with tomatoes, tamarind, onion, garlic, ginger and garnished with coconut milk and curry leaves. Kerala Erachi Olarthiathu £4.95, boneless pieces of lamb fried with fresh sliced coconut and herbs. In fact, all Pat's favourites! Delivery: £15 minimum, 3 mile radius. Hours: 5.30-11.30.

Ilford (Greater London)
(inc Gants Hill, Goodmayes and Seven Kings)

CURRY SPECIAL TOP 100 ©

2 Greengate Pde, Horns Rd, Newbury Pk, Ilford 020 8518 3005

Family-run by GL and Paul Luther, Punjabi Kenyan Asians. They are related to the Southall Anands (*see* Brilliant and Madhu's, Southall, Middlesex), resulting in a different menu from that at the formula curry house. This is the real taste of the Punjab – savoury, powerful, delicious and satisfying, and as near to Punjabi home-food as you'll get in Britain. The family signature dishes are Karai Mexican Mixed Vegetables, and the renowned Butter Chicken, Jeera Chicken and Chilli Chicken. A full portion for four is £12-13. Half-portion £6.50-7. These are starters, and are huge. And the fun is to go in large parties and share each of these. That's the way the local Asians enjoy it, leaving lots of room and lots of choice for the main course. Clues to the Luthers' Kenyan background is also in the menu. Mogo Chips are fried cassava, £3 and Tilipa Masala is an African fish curry, starter £3, main £6.50.Try the Kenyan Tusker lager. *'Food brilliant, authentic and interesting. Service quite slow but well worth the wait. Definitely not run of the mill. Worth the TOP 100 status.'* SJ. Remains in our **TOP 100**. Hours: 12-2.30, Tues.-Fri./6-12 daily; closed Mon.

HAWA BENGAL 

530 High Rd, Seven Kings, Ilford 020 8599 9778

Mr Bashir Ullah is the owner-chef here, while Mr Hudda Kabir runs front of house. *'We visit regularly and find the staff very helpful, pleasant and knowledgeable and have sampled many of their dishes. We have also been guinea-pigs on occasions and had the opportunity to try new and tasty dishes not yet on the menu. Our favourites are Sag Chicken, CTM, Balti Chicken, Chicken and Mushroom Biriani and especially the Dilkush Special.'* AN. Hours: evenings only.

JALALABAD TOP 100

247 Ilford Lane, Ilford 020 8478 1285

55-seater established in 1977 by Nazrul Islam (head chef) and Badrul Islam (manager). It serves 'good-as-they-get' formula curries. Still no new comments about this **TOP 100**, I don't know why, so reports please. Here's a précis from last time, plus up-to-date info from the restaurant: *'Have yet to find anywhere remotely up to the Jalalabad's standard.'* IB. *'Outstanding dishes of the highest quality – gorgeous.'* MF. *'Starters plentiful and delicious. Waiters very attentive without being overloading. Our main course curries were all top-class. CTM the best I've tasted. When the Peshwari Nan arrived it was the best I've had. I asked the waiter if the bread had been cooked in a tandoor, at which I was invited into the kitchen to see the tandoor. Immaculate with everything laid out ready.'* TL. *'very good'* G & MP. Stays safely in our **TOP 100**. Delivery: £15 minimum, 3-mile radius. Hours: 12-2.30/6-12 (1am on Fri. & Sat.).

MOBEEN ANP

80 Ilford Lane, Ilford 020 8553 9733

The owners of this chain of Pakistani caffs are strict Muslims, so BYO is not permitted and it's unlicensed. Go for darned good, inexpensive, value-for-money, Punjabi, Kebabs, tandoori items and curries of all sorts, selected from the counter, with specials varying from day to day. No credit cards. No smoking. Can be heaving with local Asians, who know you won't find better food, and which adds to a fab atmosphere. Being Punjabi, it's a bit short of vegetarian fodder, but for those, see next entry. Hours: 11am-10pm. Branches: Mobeen, 229 High Street North, London E6; Mobeen, 222 Green Street, London E7; Mobeen, 725, High Road, Leyton, London E10.

SURUCHI NEW ENTRANT 

506 High Road, Ilford 020 8598 2020

Cuisine is a strange combination of: South Indian and Chinese. Specialists in vegetarian dishes, Indian style, including such favourites as: Bhel Puri £2.95, Masala Dosas £3.25, Onion Uttappa £3.25, Vada (2) with chutney and Sambar £2.50. If you prefer a little Chinese delicacy, try the Mogo

Chilli Fry £3.50, Spicy Szechuan Noodles £3.50, Spinach and Bean Sprouts with dry chillies £3.50. All sounds great to me!! Service charge: 10%. Takeaway: 10% discount. Lunch Special: three courses £4.99 – good value. Hours: 12 -3/6- 12.

Leigh-on-Sea

MUGHAL DYNASTY ©

1585 London Road, Leigh-on-Sea 01702 470373

Nazram Uddin's pretty, upmarket 68-seater, serves tandooris, starters, curries and all the favourites and is a popular local.

PIPASHA ©

284 Eastwood Rd N, Leigh-on-Sea 01702 476411

Opened 1995. Taken over in 2000 by Badrul Uddin. Seats 90. Private forecourt parking in front for 10. Takeaway: 10% discount. Delivery: £12, 3-mile radius. Hours: 12-2 /6-11.30.

TAJ MAHAL ©

77 Leigh Road, Leigh-on-Sea 01702 711006

Established in 1973 and owned by Shams and Noor Uddin, manager and chef respectively. Seats 70; it's hugely popular. Recently refurbished. *'Wide menu, generous portions, service attentive and prompt. We have never had to complain in seven years.'* AGH. Specials include: Rason Mirchi, Chingri Ballichow, Chanda Fry, Lamb in Plum Sauce, Sweet and Sour King Prawns, Pomfret-Fried. *'Continues to enjoy my enthusiastic, regular patronage. Has maintained an admirable reputation for consistency of quality. Excellent reasonably priced food, produced in visibly hygienic conditions. Friendly, efficient service to both old and new customers. I personally still find the Chicken Vindaloo my favourite.'* GSH. Hours: 12-2.30/6-12.

Maldon

THE RAJ

Mill Road, Maldon 01621 858510

'excellent' G & MP

Ongar

VOJAN

Epping Road, Ongar 01277 362293

Proprietor Jamal Uddin's restaurant is worthy of notice. It has a separate bar area with comfy chairs. *'Bright and welcoming decor. Very clean and attentive waiters. Live music on Wednesday evenings. Adequate quantities of food, overall a good restaurant - recommended.'* DC. Menu extracts: Goan Crab and Mussel Puri £4.50, freshly cooked with garlic and medium spices, served on deep-fried bread. Sulimoni Kebabs £4.75, kebabs served with sliced herbal cheese. Lobster Delight £21.95, one big lobster, sweet and sour spicy gravy of red chilli, onions, tomatoes and garlic. Chilli Aubergine Bhajee £8.95, cooked in yoghurt, flavoured with peanuts and fresh coconut. Sunday Buffet: served from 1-10, £9.95 adult and £4.95 child. Hours: 12-2.30 /5.30-11, Friday and Saturday to 11.30. Sunday 1-10.

Rayleigh

RAYLEIGH SPICY TAKEAWAY 

159 High Street, Rayleigh 01268 770768

Established in 1996 by Shelim Uddin and chef Moynur Miah as the Curry Palace and renamed Rayleigh Spicy. Seats 40. Specials include: Bhuna Bahar (drumstick stuffed with spicy mince in Keema sauce) £10.95, Tangar Salon (Bangladeshi fish cooked in tangy sauce) and Mancherian, mango and peach pulp, herbs, sweet and mild £6.10. Takeaway: 10% discount. Delivery: £10 minimum, 4-mile radius. Hours: 5.30-11.30pm (Sat. to 12am, Sun to 11pm).

Romford (Greater London)

ASIA SPICE 

62 Victoria Road, Romford 01708 762623

Originally opened in 1970 as India Garden and under the present management (Yeabor Ali) since 1975. A medium-sized restaurant seating 54 diners. Branch: Rupali, South Woodham Ferrers, Essex.

©	Curry Club Discount	U	Unlicensed
V	Vegetarian	ANP	Alcohol not permitted
e-a-m-a-y-l	Eat as much as you like	BYO	Bring your own alcohol

Shoeburyness

POLASH ©

84 West Road, Shoeburyness 01702 293989

The Polash and its slightly younger branch have been in our *Guide* since we began, which makes them old friends to these pages. Manager SA Motin tells us his decor is 'wonderful, air conditioned, with water fountain'. But there's a third Polash in the same ownership. Not in Essex, nor even Britain. It's in Sylhet, Bangladesh, the town where so many of our curry-house workers come from. Polash is the best hotel in town, and their restaurant, the Shapnil, has an item on its 200-dish menu that amazed us when we visited. Item 95 is no less than CTM! It is the only place in the whole of Bangladesh where it is to be found. And, says owner Sheik Faruque Ahmed, 'it sells really well!!!' His UK partner, M Khalique, agrees. *'The food was beautifully prepared, tasty and the right strength. Service excellent. Atmosphere relaxed and friendly. Despite the fact that the proprietor informed us that they did not give CC discount on a Saturday, they accepted the coupon and gave us a discount of 10%.'* BP-D. Minimum charge £10. Hours: 12-2.30 /6-12; Sun. 12am-12pm. Branch: Polash, Burnham on Crouch.

South Woodham Ferrers

NAWAB TANDOORI

1 Chipping Row, Reeves Way, South Woodham Ferrers 01245 321006

'We LOVE the Nawab. Manager Ahad is brilliant, you mention an anniversary, birthday, special occasion and a cake always appears. The food is always good and if you have tried another dish elsewhere which is unlisted, just mention it to Ahad and it will appear.' JS.

Tilbury

MINAR BALTI HOUSE TAKEAWAY 

166 Dock Road, Tilbury 01375 855181

Takeaway only. Price check: Poppadam 35p, CTM £5.50, Pullao Rice £1.40. Hours: 5-11.30pm.

Waltham Abbey

SHUHAG ©

16 Highbridge Street, Waltham Abbey 01992 711436

21 years is how long MH Rashid has been going at his Shuhag. Everything from Roagan Goast (*sic*) to Butter Chicken is on the menu and, as you'd expect, it's all done with an experienced hand. Four-course lunch £6.95, kids half-price.

Westcliff-on-Sea

SHAGOOR

Hamlet Court Road, Westcliff-on-Sea 01702 347461

'Very large and beautifully decorated. Appearance of restaurant and staff very clean and tidy. Noorandi kebab - very pleasant, chicken and vegetable patties. Garlic Chilli Chicken - good. Tandoori King Prawn Masala - excellent, not over cooked.' AS.

GLOUCESTERSHIRE

Area: South West
Population: 566,000
Adjacent Counties:
Bristol, Gwent,
Somerset, Wilts

With the demise of Avon as a county in 1997, Gloucestershire has regained territory which was taken from it when Avon was formed in 1965.

Cheltenham

CURRY CORNER ©

131 Fairview Road, Cheltenham 01242 528449

Established in 1977. Seats 40 in two rooms. Tudor style interior. Specials include: Shagar Anna, Sweet Sylheti Surprise and Mughal Shahi. Takeaway: 10% discount. Hours: 5.30-11.30.

INDIAN BRASSERIE 

146 Bath Road, Cheltenham 01242 231350

A pretty 56-seater in pastel shades with cane furniture, managed by A Rakib. CS still thinks it's the best in town. *'Waiters always very cheerful and friendly; there's a nice atmosphere.'* Branch: Dilraj Tandoori, Dursley.

KASHMIR RESTAURANT 

1 Albion Street, Cheltenham 01242 524288

Established in 1960, name change (from Raj Vooj) in 1990. Seats 42. Takeaway: 10% discount. Delivery: £15 minimum. Hours: 12-2pm/6pm-12am (Sat. to 12.30am).

Cirencester

RAJDOOT 

35 Castle Street, Cirencester 01285 652651

Good reports at Fozlur and Ataur Rahman's place.

Dursley

DILRAJ NEW ENTRANT

37 Long Lane, Dursley 01453 543472

Standard menu. *'Delicious, ample portions, very relaxed and friendly. Excellent'* IB.

Gloucester

7 SPICES NEW ENTRANT

121 Bristol Road, Quedgeley, Gloucester

Takeaway with delivery service of Indian, Chinese and Fish'n'chips – all from the same establishment. *'If the family all fancy something different, they pass the phone around to different people to take your relevant orders. They then deliver it all together and everyone is happy. Indian food is of standard quality, usually consistent. Certainly Ok after a few beers.'* CS. [After a few beers!! - Colin, we are trying to lift the profile of this industry.]

BABURCHI NEW ENTRANT

42 Bristol Road, Gloucester 01452 300615

Formerly The Paradise. *'The menu is certainly very similar to what it was previously and it's still my favourite in Gloucester.'* CS. *'Better than ever (following a fire). Wide range of meals, service is good and prices reasonable eg: Onion Bhajia £2.40, CTM £5.95. I enjoy vegetarian meals on occasions and the menu has a Special Vegetarian Dishes section. Particularly like the Vegetable Jeera £4.95. Well worth a visit.'* DT.

HILLTOP

19 Worcester Street, Gloucester 01452 308377

'Sunday lunch, we were the only diners and felt a bit sorry disturbing the peace. Once they switched the music on and got the menu and a bottle of Cobra in our hands we were ready to go. Masala Dosa followed by Chicken Tikka Bhuna, Chicken Korma with Lemon Rice and Nan. Everything was very well presented, chopped fresh coriander and fried onion on top of the main dishes. Unfortunately, they still don't use plate warmers and we didn't get get the usual side plate of raw vegetables, which makes a nice nibble between courses. £32 for two. All in all a nice Sunday lunch which made us want to go home and put our feet up.' CS. [The sign of a good meal.] Special lunchtime meal £4.95. *'Always enjoy their Nepalese dishes. Service is good, friendly and attentive. My only complaint is that it is so popular, on occasions difficult to get a table.'* DT. *'Had a takeaway - wasn't recommended. It didn't travel well - very authentic Masala Dosa but should have expected it soggy after a 15 minutes car journey. Curries very watery, almost low calorie version(!) Won't bother with takeaway again, but happily eat in.'* CS. *'Good '* G & MP.

SHAHI BALTI NEW ENTRANT

72 Westgate Street, Gloucester 01452 385386

Formerly Indian Dynasty. *'Very good service and everyone friendly. Tasty, plentiful food and very good value for money eg: Onion Bhajia £2.10, Chicken Chat £2.40, very popular. CTM £5.95. My favourite vegetarian Spinach and Vegetable Balti £4.50 and Pullao Rice £1.60.'* DT.

Newent

NEWENT TAKEAWAY NEW ENTRANT

34 Broad Street, Newent 01531 822748

A New Entry, the Newent of Newent (Good gag? No? ... well we all get bored, don't we?) *'Murgh Jalable £5.95, Jeera Gosht £5.95, Chicken Tikka Paneer £5.95, all three very good, the Murgh sweet and hot, Jeera smokey and meaty, the Tikka a strange but successful use of cheese in an Indian sauce. We'd have loved to try more! One of the best*

©	Curry Club Discount	U	Unlicensed
V	Vegetarian	ANP	Alcohol not permitted
e-a-m-a-y-l	Eat as much as you like	BYO	Bring your own alcohol

takeaways we've had. Decent sized portions, rice average, but flavours were the great attraction.' RB. Hours: 5-late.

Stroud

JEWEL IN THE CROWN

Gloucester Street, Strood

'Good' G & MP

Thornbury

MOGHULS BRASSERIE

8 High Street, Thornbury 01454 416187

'Converted Inn, wood panelling, low beams. Waiters very smart, food formula curry house. Tasty Sheek Kebab £2.95, Ayr-Biran £3.50 – colleague had to contend with bones [well, fish often do have bones!], removed the relish tray. King Prawn Dhansak, nicely sauced, prawns overcooked. Service OK.' MS. Hours: 12-2/6-11.30.

MUMTAZ INDIAN 

7 St Mary's Centre, Thornbury 01454 411764

The Mumtaz is on two levels. The downstairs seating area and small bar are for takeaway customers and perusal of the menu. The restaurant is upstairs. *'Menu not too extensive, but food extremely good and large portions. Clean European-style decor and music! Very helpful staff and friendly. Would go back.'* WW. KB was less enthusiastic about the decor and other reports talk of standard curries of generous proportions. AE-J found the Phal too hot on one occasion and too mild on another, although his fiancée *'loves the Kormas'. 'good'* G & MP. Evenings only.

Wotton-under-Edge

INDIAN PALACE

13 Church Street, Wotton 01453 843628

'We had a special price offer for a medium-sized party. £13.95 each. Food delicious, service good and informative and we were well looked after – an excellent night!' SC. *'Good menu and service, but food a tad disappointing'.* IB.

HAMPSHIRE

Area: South
Population: 1,644,000
Adjacent Counties:
Berks, Dorset, Surrey, Sussex, Wilts

Aldershot

JOHNNIE GURKHA'S 

186 Victoria Road, Aldershot 01252 328773

'Glad to see the restaurant is still as seedy as ever, although it's not quite so easy to accept since the prices are now as much as anywhere else. Mint sauce is excellent. Famous Dil Kusa Nan – an enormous bread topped with cherries and coconut.' PD. *'Food is very plentiful, beautifully cooked and spiced and nothing was left!'* JW.

TASTE OF INDIA NEW ENTRANT

319 Vale Road, Ash Vale, Aldershot 01252 334084

'Light and airy, considering its size. Painted murals on walls. Welcome friendly. Full and varied menu, always enough food, don't be tempted to have a snack at home before going here! Prawn Puri is recommended as a starter, light and crisp and the Sag and Chana Bhaji is very tasty.' JGR. JGR. Sunday Buffet: £5.95 adult, £3.50 children, 12-2.30.

Alresford

SHAPLA

60 West Street, Alresford 01962 732134

'A group of retired officers of The Royal Hampshire Regiment, who are addicted to curries, meet once a year as members of The Vindaloo Club (15 of us). A fortnight previously I'd visited and explained to manager, Mr Moon, what I wanted. Much pleasure in letting you know – my instructions were carried out to the letter. Poppadoms the largest I have ever seen, extremely tasty Lamb Vindaloo and Garlic Chilli Chicken.' JK.

Alton

ALTON TANDOORI 

7 Normandy Street, Alton 01420 82154

48-seater, owned and managed by M Shahid. *'Usual menu with a few unusuals. Linda's special comprising Tikka Chicken with spinach and chickpeas was underspiced and bland. Meat Vindaloo was hot and rather good. Nice dry poppadoms, flavoursome rice. Excellent service.'* MG. *'Greeted by the manager like long lost friends. Service was very good. There were 14 of us, and we were treated well. Food was excellent. Madras Chicken, Meat Rogan, Chicken Morrissa (beautifully spiced and hot, succulent chicken). Rice, Bhajis, Naans, all superb. We were very impressed.'* JW. Hours: 6-11.15pm.

Andover

MUGHAL 

33 Andover Road, Ludgershall, Andover 01264 790463

Owned by Towidar Rahman, managed by S Miah. *'Tucked away at the end of a modest row of suburban shops is a trip down memory lane. The food is remarkably reminiscent of the kind of curries we used to eat as students in the late 1950s. Old favourites recycled with modern subtlety, style and art. Zappy specialities such as Murgh Massala, Garlic Chicken, Achar Gosht, Jhingi Kodu. Well worth looking out for.'* RG.

Ashurst

EURO ASIA INDIAN CUISINE 

179 Lyndhurst Road, Ashurst 023 8029 2885

Azad Miah runs the front while Mr Rahman cooks the food, which we continue to hear is fine. Hours: 6pm-12am. Branches: Prince of Bengal, Hythe, Dynasty, Brockenhurst, Lal Quilla, Lymington, all Hampshire.

Basingstoke

BENGAL BRASSERIE 

4 Winchester Street, Basingstoke 01256 473795

This 'old hand' originally opened in 1978 and has been under Shelim Ahmed's careful ownership since 1985. *'Very, very good restaurant. Didn't have time for starters - working at the Anvil Theatre - shame. Nepalese specials styled up on A4 paper. All main courses very, very good. Nepalese Chicken cooked with lots of thin strips of fresh ginger and tomatoes, really tasty, well balanced sauce. Special Rice small vegetables and egg, really great! All dishes more than competently cooked.'* CT. *'Outstandingly good meal. Every dish was well above average, even the poor Brinjal Bhajee last time was good and portions generous. First class chicken dishes. Onion Bhaji – superb. Small grumble re: service – friendly, well-intentioned, delivery slow and no excuse for not being instructed on how to present, open and serve wine correctly.'* HC. *'We tried again because the food is so good. This time the service was much better, although far from brilliant and the disastrous waiter was notably absent. Determined to have the dish I ordered last time but did not get– did not come as menu described but never-the-less wonderful. All dishes so good. Expertise of kitchen staff no doubt keeps diners returning.'* HC. But on a later occasion HC tells of slow service by precious waiters who caused diners to leave their meal rather than risk missing curtain up for a local concert. Hours: 12-2.30/6-12.

KASHMIR

4 Church Street, Basingstoke 01256 842112

Now whose favourite Basingstoke restaurant is this? *'We're regulars here when we're in Basingstoke for concerts at the Anvil, partly because it is the nearest and luckily the best. Food always good but on the most recent visit it really hit an all time high, every dish was exceptionally good. It is a joy to find a restaurant that is not let down by its service.'* HC. *'Waited for over an hour for the food (usual marvellous quality) to arrive. Busy with takeaways. Not impressed.'* HC. *'Redeemed itself on Friday, table was laid in favourite corner, even having two bottles of our usual wine. By design or accident the hopeless waiter was kept occupied behind the bar. All impressed with food, general ambience, everything about the restaurant . Can understand why we keep returning.'* HC . [Have you spoken too soon, Hilary?] *'Reported previously that very disillusioned, but virtually forced to go back, as torrential rain and it was the nearest. Food as good as ever, if not better - Fish Tava - with tomato, garlic and lots of pepper, very good, but service hadn't changed - not a glimmer of recognition, not a word was said not related to order - quite extraordinary. Very great shame as kitchen obviously very competent, deserve better serving staff. £38 for two - good value.'* HC Delivery Service.. Delivery. Hours: 12-2.30 (closed Sun lunch .)/6pm-12am, daily.

POPPADOM EXPRESS

Unit 5, Festival Place, Basingstoke 01256 321222

Full-width, open-plan kitchen in clean-lined, well-designed modern setting, with ample seating inside and *al fresco* in the covered food court. Poppadom Express is clearly planned to roll out nationwide. There are already two branches with another due soon. Established in 2001 by Kal Dhaliwal, a determined restaurateur. After time in Scottish restaurants he started Simla Pinks, which ran out of money and was bought by the Oriental Group. Dhaliwa is also a master of spin. This is what he says: *'Kal Dhaliwal – Man of inspiration. Most restaurants have the Tandoor as the only authentic piece of kitchen equipment. We have bought across seven different cooking utensils used in India for thousands of years, such as the Sigrhi (open fire grill), Tawa (griddle), Mahi Tawa (walled griddle), Kadhai (wok), Lagan (steam pot) and Shilajit Stone (special stones from Hyderadbad, with aphrodisiac properties).The Poppadom Express experience will be a first for many.'* Apart from some fusion dishes, we don't agree, at least not for readers of this *Guide*. And as for the *'special cooking gear'* – a wok? However all this does impress young spender.s Here are some menu examples: Starters Deep Fried Stuffed Hot Green Chillies, £3.25, Dahi Bhalla Papri Chaat, £3.50, Fusion Boti-Kebab Naan-wich, Charcoal grilled lamb picattas with mint spread and sandwiched with an apple and mint chutney, £3.95. Main Course: Most standard curryhouse items eg: Karahi Chicken, £6.75. Side Dish: Baingan Bhartha, Side Dish, £3.50. Dessert: Gulab Jamun A classic dessert from North India, deep-fried, reduced milk balls soaked in sugar syrup, served warm, £2.95. Hours: 11-3 / 6-11, daily. Branches: Popadom Express, Basingstoke, Hants, Manchester and PickleJohns, Swindon, Wilts.

Farnborough

GURKHA PALACE

78 Farnborough Road, Farnborough 01252 511550

The home of the Gurkhas, Church Crookham, is no longer. And huge numbers of Britain's favourite warriors are being disbanded. Throwing the baby out with the bath water, we think. One legacy, fortunately for curry-lovers, is the relatively high number of Nepalese restaurants in this area of Hampshire . This is one where the food is authentic, the staff are Nepalese, and they serve a good range of formula curries to. See branch for menu details. Branch: Gurkha Palace, Liphook, Hants. Hours: 12-2.30/6-11.

POPPADOMS 

33 Medway Drive, Cove, Farnborough 01252 376869

Owner Sean Usher claims to be the UK's only English owner [you're not, Sean – read this *Guide!*]. The 36-seater is painted cream and earthy red, the woodwork indigo blue, the furniture is simple wood giving an airy feeling. Swathes of cream, red and blue hang from the ceiling. Nepalese Bikash Devkota is manager. Sanjiv Singh's specials include: Chicken Monsourri – slices of chicken tikka in Madras sauce with green chillies and soy. Delivery: £8 min. Hours: 6-10.30.

Fleet

GULSHAN INDIAN

264 Fleet Road, Fleet 01252 615910

'Greeted in a most friendly way. The restaurant appeared to be divided into two halves, one for couples and well-behaved diners, one for noisy oiks – what a good idea.' [and which are you?]. CP. *'Standard is consistently high. It has to be one of the best restaurants in Hampshire and Surrey. We use as our local takeaway and their food is of a consistently high standard and good value for money. If you spend £15 you receive a free Onion Bhajia and if you spend over £20 you receive a mystery dish which is a very tasty little chicken number! They are always pleased to see you. Sixteen of us went for a curry at 10pm. Superb food. Excellent service.'* JW.

THE GURKHA SQUARE TOP 100 ©

327 Fleet Road, Fleet 01252 810286

Of the several Nepalese restaurants in the area, reports received place this one at the top. And it is actually patronised by Nepalese. This 67-seater, owned by AB Gurung, managed by Om Gurung, is as good as you'll find. *'Rather twee and overrated.'* MG. *'Delighted to see the Gurkha Square in the* **TOP 100**. *My wife* *and I can certainly back this up. Perhaps slightly on the pricey side, but superb value for money. We particularly like the Mis-Mas, and the rice and naan are quite excellent.'* DT. *'Comfortable, polite service, excellent food.'* GR. Delivery: 3-mile radius. Hours: 12-2.30/6-11.30

Four Marks

SAFFRON

8 Oak Green Parade, Wincvhester Road, Four Marks, Alton 01420 561872

From mild aromatic Kurmas and Mossallas to spicy Madras, Baltis and House specialities, it's all here at the Saffron. 10% discount on takeaways, Minimum order £10. Hours: 12-2,30/5.30-11.30. Friday / Saturday -12.

Hamble

CINNAMON BAY NEW ENTRANT ©

4 High Street, Hamble 023 8045 2285

Formerly Last Viceroy. *'Clean, modern decor, beautiful table linen, very different menu. Great place.'* BF. Specialities include: Batak Biran Jalfrezi £11.50, boneless duck with fresh green chillies. Ayre Mass Jalfrezi £8.95, fillet of Ayre in hot spicy sauce. Mahaan Shabji Kashmir £5.95, vegetables soaked in butter, cooked in creamy sauce with tropical fruits. Khasi Amchor £8.95, charcoal roasted lamb tikka, sweet, creamy yoghurt sauce, with mango slices. Expensive Chutney Tray at £1.50 – you could buy a whole jar for that! Takeaway: 20% discount. Hours: 5.30 -12.

Hindhead

MOWJAR NEW ENTRANT

5 London Road, Hindhead 01428 606066

Newly opened on the top of the Hog's Back Hill is this branch of Liss Madhuban. See later. It does a standard range of hot takeaway items, but like the Madhuban it does it well and with care. Two features of note: it does a meal-for-one cold takeaway. Designed for speed, it's been packed already. Simply take it and when you get home heat it in the microwave. For a tenner you get Poppadom, Tandoori Mint Raita, Onion Salad, Onion Bhaji, Meat Samosa, Chicken Tikka

©	Curry Club Discount	U	Unlicensed
V	Vegetarian	ANP	Alcohol not permitted
e-a-m-a-y-l	Eat as much as you like	BYO	Bring your own alcohol

Masala, Chicken Jalfrezi, Bombay Potato, Pullao Rice and a Naan. Great value. Then there's the e-a-m-a-y-l buffet when you dine in. At least six different dishes, including starters, plus rice & bread. Menu changes nightly. Fabulous value £11.95, Kids (under 14) £4.95. Bring Your Own (wine & beer only). Hours 5.30-1, Wednesdays to Monday. Closed Tuesday. *See page* 23.

Hook

HOOK TANDOORI 

1 Fairholme Pde, Station Road, Hook
01256 764979

Syed Ahmed's 67-seater is: *'Highest quality, full of flavours. Particularly the King Prawn, Chicken Vindaloo really good. Staff well presented and friendly.'* MJBK. Hours: 12-2.30/6-11.30. Branch: Mogul, 13 London Road, Bagshot.

Horndean

INDIAN COTTAGE 

4 The Square, Horndean 023 9259 1408

Established in 1978. Taken over by Anwar Miah in 1996. Seats 48. *'Have tried this restaurant a couple of times before and have never been disappointed. Excellent parking, tasteful decor, keen staff. Garlic Chilli Chicken was excellent and not overladen with chillies. Chicken Dorai was served sizzling with large cubes of breast chicken. Peshwari Naan very nice. Well worth a visit. Will go back again.'* DL. Hours: 12-2.30/6-12.

Liss

MADHUBAN TOP 100

94 Station Road, Liss 01730 893363

Owned and managed by Lodue Miah, with help from his brothers Bedar, Didar and Dodo and some experienced waiters, all in smart blue shirts and yellow ties. 'Uncle' Ahad runs the kitchen. It has 96 seats and plans for a conservatory extension. Then it will take 120 diners, and it will fill many of those seats 365/7. The Madhuban is located in a small, typical southern village, which just a few years ago would have been an unlikely setting for an Indian restaurant. Now the village has two. There are no big name eateries there. In the 'Location, Location, Location' stakes, no one with sense would invest in an 'Indian' here. We are often asked what makes a curryhouse good. And this is as good a place to explain as any in this *Guide*. It's a venue, be it a pub, shop, sports club, or a restaurant, where one wants to return. It becomes one's local. Many of our correspondents tell us about their locals with some affection. Many are listed in this *Guide*. But Liss has just 2000 population, not enough to fill 120 seats daily. Ergo, most customers come from further afield, some making as much as 150-mile round trips. What makes them come this distance? The answer is care. If the owner cares, it shows. It begins with a prompt hello at the door. Names are remembered, and favourite drinks and dishes. In between everything is done well: phone manner, the reservation system, the service, the cooking and the ambience. Service is attentive and it ends with a courteous goodbye on departure. *'This restaurant is not our local in the sense that it is the nearest Indian restaurant to our home, it isn't, but we make the extra effort to travel to the Madhuban to eat because it is so good. But I have to say that I do think that Uncle Ahad cooks a tastier Chicken Dhansak than Lodue – though Pat says Lodue cooks him a tastier Chinga Sag. It's what this guide is all about – personal opinions.'* DBAC. Blue is the house colour, used on the exterior, the chairs, the decor, and even the menu. Like everything else, this eight-page document epitomises the Madhuban's attention to detail. It is illustrated in full colour and fully describes all the dishes. There are 22 starters, 7 items from the tandoor, plus 5 nans. There is an ample choice of old favourites, and they are all done well. *'Given the extensive menu, it took some time to make any choices. I ordered Keema Khumb for a starter (excellent and flavoursome) and Dhaba Gosht with Pullao Rice as a main course (superb). Service was friendly and attentive. A most pleasurable lunch – Madhuban deserves its laurels.'* RH. *'Very stylish, great ambience. Six of us went for my daughter's 19th birthday. Food was very good as always. My Methi Gosht was very well spiced and my daughter's King Prawn Masallah superb. Pretty good value, but portions not over-generous.'* MG. Being busy and popular (not to mention acclaiming such a place in this *Guide*) can lead to problems, as this quote from HC tells *'Eye-catching decor, spectacular food. A shame that it was all spoiled by the unreasonably long wait. We arrived 7.30pm and the food arrived at 8.48pm. True, a busy restaurant is lively and fun but serving delays can be quite annoying.'* HC [It was a Saturday night, which as we always say, we avoid like a plague if at all possible. One Saturday in June they served 250 seated diners, and 120 takeaways. They had to cook new items and kept going until the wee hours giving free drinks until every one was satisfied. AND they turned away another 50 diners, as they do every Saturday.] But JL: *'first discovered this restaurant shortly after it opened. Since that time it has gone from strength to strength, and is now on my list of top restaurants to visit when I am away on business. Thoroughly recommended. I live too far away to visit regularly, but their chilled curry sauces (Balti, Tikka Masala Korma, Madras and Bhoona) are now available nationwide* . JL. *'The food, decor, service and general ambience were still as good as ever. Good starter – Onion Bhajia, one of the best I've had. Excellent Chicken Jalfrezi, hotted up to Vindaloo strength, Pullao Rice, Mushroom Bhajia and Nan couldn't be faulted. Plus a pint of Dortmunder Union lager – very nice. Followed by Almond Kulfi – inverted it into a special glass so did not look too rude!! – not that I mind!'* BP-D *'We used to live in the area and fell in love with the place. Never changed the high standard that it sets. The proprietors treat you like long lost friends, remembering you even if you haven't been for a while. Quality of food matches quality if service. Never been disappointed. Belated Valentine's meal. After greetings, we were shown to our table, drinks and Poppadoms– good, warm and crispy, promptly arrived. Chicken Tikka – moist, delicately spiced and Meat Samosa, both very good. I love the Jalfrezi– fresh green chillies, my wife Dhansak – good. The Stuffed Wild Mushrooms are excellent. Saag Paneer – prepared with paneer cheese and fresh spinach. Nan – warm and well cooked. Preparation and presentation is done with care. Highly rated as a TOP 100 – long may it remain.'* J&JM. One more thing: Prices here are among the cheapest in the area. This helps its appeal, but there is much more to it than that. We are pleased to keep this restaurant high in our **TOP 100.** Hours: 12-2.30pm/5.30-11.30pm. *See page 23*

Lymington

FOREST TAKEAWAY NEW ENTRANT

24 Milford Road, Pennington, Lymington
01590 688 446

'Heard good reports from locals. Can see your meal being cooked, no microwave. Lamb Dopiaza (the only curry my wife will tolerate!) Chicken Vindaloo (for me!) excellent, bordering on Phal strength. Pulao Rice, Nan Bread and free Pops. Food was excellent and plenty of it. Impressed with the cleanliness of the kitchen.' BP-D.

Portsmouth

NEW TAJ MAHAL 

54 Kingston Road, Buckland, Portsmouth
023 9266 1021

Nothing 'new' about this 1965 curry house. It's an old hand, now owned by Lilu Miah and Abdul Matin – it's a safe bet on curry alley!

STAR OF ASIA 

6 Market Way, City Centre, Portsmouth
023 9283 7906

Great little 40-seater restaurant, established in 1992 by Abdul Mothen, who also manages. Chef Gian Uddin cooks the curries. *'Far enough away from the circuit drinking area. Standard range of dishes. Hot and crispy Poppadoms. Excellent Rashmi with large portion of succulent kebab, topped with fluffy and tender omelette. Tandoori Chicken beautifully tender. Lovely Meat Bhuna and tangy Chicken Dhansak. Late generally means 1am, I left at 2.30am and people still arriving.'* RW. Hours: 12pm-2.15am (Fri. closed)/6pm to late; Sat. & Sun. 12pm to late.

Ringwood

CURRY GARDEN 

10 High Street, Ringwood 01425 475075

Between them, Feroze Khan and chef Runu Miah continue to satisfy the needs of their diners.

Southampton

KUTIS BRASSERIE

37 Oxford Street, Southampton 023 8033 3473

Exotically decorated with marble effect walls, large plants, chandelier and tented ceiling. Kurgee Lamb – a whole leg of lamb marinated in spices and slowly roasted or Kurgee Ayre – whole Bangladeshi dish marinated and roasted – 24 hours notice required for both of these dishes. Duck and venison features highly on the menu. *'Usually very good.'* SO. *'Have visited twice– once for the lunch time buffet and once in the company of Asian colleagues in the evening. Both times, I thought, deserved its place in the TOP 100, particularly for the venison dishes.'* MRW. Shall we restore it to that status? Reports please.

NATAJ BALTI

3 Winchester Street, Southampton 023 8036 6344

'I am vegetarian and the Vegetarian Baltis are very good. Also, according to friends that eat meat, the other Balti dishes are excellent too. The building was once a night club and the owners have kept the dance floor and they play live Indian music on Fridays and Saturdays.' MD. Hours: 12-2/6-11.30.

POPADOM EXPRESS NEW ENTRANT

48 Oxford Street Southampton 023 8063 2444

Details on Basingstoke branch. *'Couldn't get in to Kuti's for 2½ hours just before Christmas, so went to Poppadom Express. WOW, it was all happening, with a lively bar, disco being set up, restaurant in the middle distance and kitchen going hammer and tongs at the far end! Found a table, couldn't hear waiter (plenty of efficient) so just said "I'll have what they're having" pointing to table next to us. This was their Christmas Dinner, with Poppadoms etc, starters, amuse–bouches of Kebabs and grilled spicy cheeses, three main course Curries and Naan, and if you still had room, kuli with mango sauce– all for £16.99. It was a bit of a struggled getting back up to the station for the train, I can tell you.'* JGR. *'The menu had a dessert selection, several fruit based dishes. I had gulab jamun, arrived sliced on eye catching square white plate, with brandy snap basket, halved strawberries and cream – disappointing, not a happy combination. We enjoyed our meal, but prefer a more traditional style. Restaurant almost full, so obviously pleasing many.'* HC. *'A friend (originally from Gujarat) said he had had the best curry in the UK here. My first visit, really good formula. We ate in, but they do takeaway.'* H&HM. Hours: 11-3/6-11, daily. Branches: Popadom Express, Basingstoke, Hants, Manchester and PickleJohns, Swindon, Wilts.

P.O.S.H. NEW ENTRANT

1 Queensway, Southampton 023 8022 6377

Port Outer Starboard Home, it means, and it's apt in this city. When entering, you have a slight feeling of entering a night club, however, the restaurant is upstairs, not down. Large and generous reception area, with hygienic 'his' and 'her' toilets. Double doors take you through to a good sized lounge, arranged with expensive and comfortable sofas and chairs, grouped around coffee tables. More double doors open to an immense dining room (300 seats), complete with grand piano, band stand and dance floor with flashing lights. Self-serve area (which is a permanent feature, not the usual linen-dressed tables with chafing dishes) and a enormous bar, which impressively runs from one end of the room to the other. The restaurant, though large, doesn't feel like a warehouse, but more like a pleasant banqueting room, and with its distinctly nautical decor theme, redolent of the grand liners' dining rooms. We were meeting friends and sat in the lounge for a while, sipping spritzers. The owner told us he wasn't interested in serving the 'rif-raf' of Southampton, and that the many new trendy flats, which surrounded his establishment, were full of people who had no money. His chefs all came especially from India and had developed new, special dishes. While the place is very striking, the food is not. Firmly curry house stuff of reasonable quality. Lunch and dinner, daily.

SPICE OF INDIA

42 Commercial Rd, Southampton 023 8022 0201

'Location is unlikely, in a really awful concrete courtyard of an equally awful concrete block of flats, typical 1960's ugliness. Extensive menu, our dishes exceptionally competent. Poppadoms served cold but very crisp and light. Batak Karai, excellent, Karahi Ayre, successful. Best ever Nan, large, light and fluffy. Generous portions, service good, most impressed.' HC. *'Very good, but what an awful location as mentioned.'* JGR. Hours: 12-2.30/6-12.30 (Fri. & Sat. to 1am).

Southsea

GOLDEN CURRY TOP 100 ©

16 Albert Road, Southsea 023 9282 0262

Some years ago, I was interviewed here,by the then local TV station Meridian, and I sampled many dishes from the korma to the phal. As a definition of the formula, they were spot on. Colours, aromas, tastes, textures, service and price – all done right by experienced 'old hands'. In fact the 52-seater has been owned by Salim Hussein (manager) and Razak Ali (head chef) since 1979, and has a justifiably loyal following. Menu extracts: Chicken Tikka Chilli Masala £7.05. Special Mixed Fried Rice £2.75, with prawns and

cabbage, garnished with omelette. Vegetable Thali £7.30, Vegetable Bhajee, Brinjal Bhajee, Cauliflower Bhajee, Tarka Dal, Mushroom Bhajee, Nan and Pullao Rice – great value! *'An excellent restaurant which my husband and I go to for a "curry fix". Salim is a wonderful host, greeting his clients with courtesy and friendliness, the waiters follow his lead. Ali runs a wonderfully efficient and clean kitchen.'* C&CH. *'Excellent food and service. Our regular curry restaurant.'* DKM. *'Staff always friendly and attentive. Extremely clean and cosy restaurant. Meals range from very good to superb!!. Good sized portions which are very filling.'* GB. *'An excellent restaurant. Received a nice welcome. Table, decor– clean and tidy. Meal was as I ordered it– HOT! I have been all over the country but it would be hard to beat this curry house.'* EC. The takeaway menu gives prices for eating in and taking out – what a good idea. Delivery Service. Hours: 12-2 /5.30-12.30am; Sun. 12-12am.

Stubbington

STUBBINGTON TANDOORI 

35a The Green Stubbington, Nr Fareham
01329 664615

Mr Rahman's 40-seater. Specials include: Balti £5.95, Murag Makhan £5.95, chicken cooked with butter and fresh cream.Takeaway: small discount. Delivery: £12 min, 4-mile radius. Hours: 5.30-12.

Waterlooville

INDIAN COTTAGE ©

51 London Road, Cowplain, Waterlooville
01705 269351

D&BR and L&AC have been coming as a foursome for many years to Sheik Shab Uddin's tiny 30-seater (exposed oak beams, blue walls and tablecloths, red velvet chairs) because chef AH Khan's *'food is excellent and the staff always attentive'*. Hours: 12-2.30/5.30-12. Branches: Indian Cottage, Port Solent, Gunwharf Quays and Horndean.

SHALIMAR 

9 Hambledon Pde Hambledon Rd,
Waterlooville 023 9225 1565

56-seater, with smoking and non-smoking

sections, managed by Mujib. *'Shalimar's greatest asset is that it does the simple things well. The Lamb Jalfrezi is a little hotter and more adventurous than usual, and the Chicken Shaslit is another highlight. A quiet, friendly establishment with young staff who are both polite and efficient.'* GS. Hours: 12-2.30/5.30-11.30.

Winchester

THE FLOWERPOTS INN
NEW ENTRANT

Cheriton, Winchester 01962 771318

'Wednesday nights are Curry Nights with Punjabi cuisine prepared by a local family who originated from The Punjab. A Popadom starter, choice of two main courses rice and Naan Bread is just under £9. The pub doesn't do Cobra as they brew their own inimitable ales which hansomely complement the meal.' JGR. Hours: (for curry night) Wednesdays, 7-9.30.

BALAKA

75 Stoney Lane, Weeke, Winchester
01962 855118

Ali Forid Miah's Balaka is modern and clean-lined inside. It is in all respects an good formula curry house, where you will be able to find all your favourite dishs. Cooking is, we hear, well up to scratch,a dn the venue has many regulars. Hours: Lunch and dinner, daily.

HEREFORDSHIRE

Area: Welsh Border
Population: 215,000
Adjacent Counties:
Gwent, Powys,
Shrops, Staffs,
Worcs

Bromyard

TASTE OF INDIA NEW ENTRANT

22 High Street, Bromyard 01885 488668

Fully licensed and air conditioned. *'Had a good sit down meal in here. Waiters very friendly although three other tables taken at about 8.30pm on a Friday night. Goa Murgh £5.95 – not particularly hot, although colleagues at work call me 'Asbestos Gob'. Decor– typically small town curry house.'* ANON. Hours: 12-2.30/5.30-11.30, closed Tuesday.

Hereford

KAMAL NEW ENTRANT

82 Widemarsh Street, Hereford 01432 278005

A narrow-fronted and impressively named enterprise that fronts a surprisingly long and capacious curry house. Helpful and friendly staff. Menu contains usual suspects, plus specials. Real cloths and hand towels. Jangra Purr – unusual, almost spring roll, delightful chat style curry with salad and sweet sauce, enjoyable. Lamb Tikka Biriani – very good, well cooked, a shade greasy, boiled egg rather than usual omelette topping. Lamb absolutely top quality, mouth watering. Recommended.' RW. Sunday Lunch Special: three courses, £7.50. Delivery: city radius, £13 minimum. Menu Extracts: Chicken Pakora £2.75, Stuffed Mushroom £2.40, Garlic Chicken Jalfrezi £6.95, Tarka Dal £2.30; Garlic Nan £1.70. Hours: 12-2/5.30-12.

KHAN'S NEW ENTRANT

Plough Inn, Canon Pyon, Hereford 01432 830577

'Curry restaurant in a pub! Excellent food at very reasonable prices– best in hereford. Portions good, Nan too big for one person' [I don't expect they get many complaints about that!]. *'Jalfrezi – excellent fresh chillies. Specialities: Lamb Paprika £6.50. Well worth finding.'* PJM. No credit cards. Price Check: Popadom 25p, CTM 34.95, Pullao Rice £1.25. Hours: 5.30-12.

Leominster

JALALABAD

33 Etnam Street, Leominster 01568 615656

Well promoted by the ebullient owner-manager Kamal Uddin (though, curiously again, not to us). Owner-chef Abdul Mukith's food menu attracts regular praise from Leominster locals, though G & M P found the Shahagh *'excellent'*. IB on the other hand, found the service *'appaling and miserable by all three waiters, but the food reasonable.'* IB.

TASTE OF RAJ NEW ENTRANT

67 St Ownens Street, Hereford 01432 351075

'Plainly decorated, attractive establishment, bustling corner of city. Policed by efficient, almost surly staff. Good menu to tempt the palate. Reshmi Kebab £3.40, slightly dry, nicely hot, excellent texture, crisp salad, lurid green yoghurt sauce. Lamb Tikka Biriani £7.40, mouthwatering, well cooked, greaseless rice, packed with vegetables, accompanying vegetable curry better than 'bog standard' house curry sauce. Very good Garlic Nan £1.95, light and fluffy, plenty of finely chopped garlic. Tarka Dal £2.45, unusual, pieces of tomato and cucumber, thick, subtle flavours. Very enjoyable overall, definitely recommended.' RW. Takeaway: 10% discount. Delivery: £12 min. Hours: 6-11.

Ross-on-Wye

OBILASH

19a Gloucester Road, Ross-on-Wye 01989 567860

First opened 1980. Seats 40. Some unusual Bangladeshi authentic dishes on the menu include Shathkora Curry and Ada Lembu Curry. Specials include: Anderi Raat (half chicken marinated in

©	Curry Club Discount	U	Unlicensed
V	Vegetarian	ANP	Alcohol not permitted
e-a-m-a-y-l	Eat as much as you like	BYO	Bring your own alcohol

Obilash special spices, served with rice). Takeaway: 10% discount. Delivery: £18, anywhere in Ross. Hours: 6-11.30pm (1am on Sat.).

HERTFORDSHIRE

Area: Home Counties, (north of London)
Population: 1,028,000
Adjacent Counties: Beds, Bucks, Cambs, Essex, London

Part of Herts was absorbed by Greater London in 1965. We note affected towns/suburbs.

Abbots Langley

VICEROY OF INDIA TOP 100 

20 High Street, Abbots Langley 01923 262163

Established in 1989 by Ronney Rahman. *'Food delicious, always fresh and elegantly presented. Waiters friendly and attentive.'* D&PM. *'Menu was full and standard with the unique addition of a number of hash (duck) dishes. Makhoni Hash – wonderfully flavourful, distinctive but mild spices in a cream and tomato sauce.'* RH. House specials: Makhoni Hash (mild) tandoori grilled duck, tossed in butter, cultured yoghurt, fresh cream and mild spices and Karahi Jhinga (hot), jumbo prawns cooked with a medium dry gravy, herbs, tomatoes, onions and green pepper, served from a iron karahi. Hours: 12-2.30/6-11. *See previous page.*

Baldock

BALDOCK INDIAN CUISINE NEW ENTRANT

8 Bell Row High Street, Baldock 01462 491226

'I have been moved to write after another very good meal. Spotless, minimalist decor, toilets very clean. Fresh Pops, varied Pickles. Balti Keema – tender and tasty, Shashlik – loads of chicken, Vegetable Dhansak – large portion, pleasantly hot, Madras standard, Tarka Dhal – the business, good Chapati. Excellent service, ordering is prompt and polite. Often served with complimentary liquor before settling up. Good value for money.' JMF. Hours: 12-2.30/6-11.30.

Barnet (Greater London)

(inc East Barnet and New Barnet)

KING TANDOORI 

92 East Barnet Road, New Barnet 020 8441 9272

MD Salim opened his 46-seater in 1995 and we hear well of it, especially of the Happy Hour Half Price Meal. *'It makes me happy at that price.'* NL. Evenings only, except Sun. e-a-m-y-l buffet £6.95, lunch and dinner.

SHAPLA TANDOORI 

37 High Street, Barnet 020 8449 0046

Established in 1981. SI Ahmed's smart restaurant seats 50 and is popular. *'My local, always very reliable. Standard menu. Excellent Dhansak, generous Shashlik and very good side dishes. A clean, cosy restaurant.'* CT. Delivery: £1.50, 4-mile radius. Hours: 12-2.30pm/6pm-12am.

Berkhamsted

AKASH 

307 High Street, Berkhamsted 01442 862287

'We particularly like owner Foysol Ahmed's service – greeted at the door, coats taken, napkins placed in your lap, staff are attentive without hovering.' LB. Hours: 12-2.30pm/6pm-12am.

CURRY GARDEN 

29 High Street, Berkhamsted 01442 877867

'An old converted pub, lovely low beams and cosy booths. Very impressed. Will most definitely be back.' SW.

Bishops Stortford

SHADONA NEW ENTRANT

High Street, Bishops Stortford 01279 508149

'In centre of BS. Looks fabulous, rather crisp, almost Scandinavian. Excellent cuisine and sharp service. Enjoyed Cobra with fresh Poppadoms and Pickles. Shared different starters of Meat Samosas – lean and crisp, Bhajis – great, Sheek Kebab – beautifully cooked. Mains curries – Bhuna, Tikka, Korma

were all served with Pullao Rice. Sag Aloo, Nan and Chapatti . Quantity and quality outstanding, we were all stuffed! Prices above average. Fabulous experience.' AE. Hours: 12-2.30/6-11.

Cheshunt

RAJ VOGUE ©

48 High Street, Cheshunt 01992 641297

Established in 1991 by Khalek Quazi, who also manages the 82-seater restaurant. Room for 50 cars at the back. GR likes the Nawab Nargis, cooked with spicy minced chicken and fresh mint. Takeaway: 10% discount. Delivery: £15, 3 miles. Hours: 12-2.30/6-11.30; Sat. 12-2.30 (Sun. 1-2pm)/6pm-12am (Sun. to 11pm). Sunday lunch buffet £6.95.

Hatfield

PRINCE OF INDIA ©

10 Market Place, Hatfield 01707 265977

Established in 1993, managed by SF Ali. The restaurant seats 48 diners, and is a romantic and pleasant atmosphere. Delivery: £8.95 minimum. Hours: 5.30-11.30.

TASTE OF INDIA 

33 Salisbury Square, Old Hatfield 01707 276666

Owned by Mrs A Khatun and managed by Golam Yahna, the Taste has become a popular local haunt. Specials include: Duck Korai, and Balti Tropical. Mondays, four-course banquet.

Hemel Hempstead

GURU TANDOORI 

5 Bridge Street, Hemel Hempstead 01442 254725

Owner SM Rahman. Chef S Uddin. 36 seats. MBS says he has eaten here twice a week for twenty years, and that he always recommends it to his friends, who in turn have become satisfied customers. *'The only Indian in Hemel in bad need of a refurb– including the toilet! Food, however was great and good portions, Chicken Tikka Garlic Balti £7.50 – fantastic. Prawn Vindaloo £4.95 – wow! Tandoori Mixed Grill– how much meat! Cramped– next table almost joining!'* JH. Justin's next visit: *'Good service, good food. Chicken and Lamb Bormani £6.30 served piping hot on a skillet was fantastic. Chicken Tikka Garlic [you had that dish last time] also well worth a return visit! £57 for four.'* JH. Delivery: £15 minimum, 5-mile radius. Hours: 12-2.30pm/6pm-12am. Branch: Guru, 630, Uxbridge Road, Hayes, Middx.

MOGUL NEW ENTRANT

91 High Street, Old Town, Hemel Hempstead 01442 255146

'I feel this is the best in Hemel– beautifully decorated and always good food and service. 'Took two work colleagues and two customers – all agreed the best meal! Chicken Roushini, Chicken Rezala and Mogul Special Masala– all fantastic. Side dishes and breads– all very good.'Takeaway for two.' [and JH returns]: *'Phoned and collected within half an hour, all hot plus free Poppadoms!'* [and JH keeps returning]: *'Busy Saturday night, party of nine. Table booked for 9.30pm, sat down at 10pm. Main courses at 10.45pm, no starters. Food as good as ever– well loaded chicken and mushroom Rizato, thoroughly enjoyed by two. Only let down was Tandoori King Prawn looked great but lacking in flavour. Bill at 12.20am. An enjoyable night but too long!* [and JH keeps returning]: *'Busy Thursday night. Deep fried aubergines on the house to start absolutely gorgeous. Roushini seemed a but rich. Mushroom Rizoti and Chicken Gastoba– as good as ever.!'* JH. Takeaway: 10% discount. Hours: 12-2.30 and 5.30-11.30, Friday and Saturday to 12.

ROYAL TAKEAWAY NEW ENTRANT

6 The Queens Square, Adeyfield, Hemel Hempstead 01442 247171

'Their regular customers since it opened, three years ago. Very nice Korma and Tikka Masala– the best takeaway in Hemel.' MR & MRS D. *'we order meals from here three to four times a week, as do our friends.'* R.D. Delivery: £12 minimum.

THAAL NEW ENTRANT

38 Lawn Lane, Hemel Hempstead 01442 252080

'Chicken Vindaloo – nice sauce but chicken not very big. Mushroom Fried Rice is always wonderful and a meal in itself. £6 for one.' JH. *'Hector and Raj are very nice people, been a great help to me supplying Naga chillies to aid my home-cooked curries. Food always cooked to high standard, generous portions and extras often thrown in.'* MC. [Naga is the hottest chilli on earth. Beam me up Scottie. Certainly gets it into

©	Curry Club Discount	U	Unlicensed
V	Vegetarian	ANP	Alcohol not permitted
e-a-m-a-y-l	Eat as much as you like	BYO	Bring your own alcohol

the *Guide.* Ed.] Menu extracts: Chicken or Lamb Naga £6.95. Chicken or Lamb Shatkora £6.50, with citrus fruit. Takeaway: 10% discount, minimum £12. Delivery: £12 minimum. Hours: 5.30-11.00, Friday and Saturday to 11.30.

Hitchin

INDIA BRASSERIE ©

36 Bancroft Road, Hitchin 01462 433001

M Chowdhury's restaurant seats 32. Specials: Chicken Makhani Tikka, Rezala Chicken and Fish Bhuna5. *'The best in Hitchin.'* SW. Hours: Tues.-Thurs. 12-2.30/5.30-12; Sun. 1-11pm, buffet £7.95.

Letchworth

CURRY GARDEN 

71 Station Road, Letchworth 01462 682820

Afiz Ullah is the head chef and owner of this 72-seater, which has a *'huge friendly menu.'* MT. Hours: 12-2.30pm/6pm-12am; Sun. 12pm-12am, buffet 12-5.30pm. Branches (all named Curry Garden) at: Berkhamsted; Rickmansworth; Dunstable, Beds; Hornchurch, Essex.

SAGAR 

48 The Broadway, Letchworth 01462 684952

Motiur Rahman's *'Trout Masala is one of the best.'* LV. Service 10%. Lunch buffet, weekdays £5.50, Sun. £5.95. Branches: Aashiana, Broadway, Beds; Ahkbar Takeaway, Abbot's Walk, Biggleswade, Beds.

PAVILLION

38 High Street, Markyate, St Albans
01582 841436

Air conditioned. *'Located just off the A5, close to junction 9 of the M1, an excellent stop off point on a long journey. Arriving at 10pm we were greeted with warmth and offered drinks, Poppadoms etc. Quality of food excellent, although could not tell any difference in temperature between Madras and Vindaloo. Overall good meal washed down with draught Kingfisher.'* DL. Hours: 12-11, Friday and Saturday to 11.30.

Royston

BRITISH RAJ

55 High Street, Royston 01763 241471

Established in 1976 by Nazir Uddin Choudhury, and it has been in this Guide since we began. It is certainly an old hand and Mr Choudhury has a wicked sense of humour. It is really worth a trip just to get his 'mini-menu', which is a 20 page booklet packed with jokes, cartoons, facts, and goodness knows what.The restaurant is decorated with embossed ivory wallpaper and pictures of the Raj. Seats 44 in an L-shaped dining room. House Special: Bengali cod fish curry with tomatoes, chillies in a sauce £6.55. After your meal you can finish the night off by ordering the fifth course – Hukkah (Hubble Bubble). Takeaway: 10% discount. Hours: 12-2/6-12am.

Sawbridgeworth

STAR OF INDIA 

51 London Road, Sawbridgeworth 01279 726512

Established in 1981 by Dilwar and Jamal Ahmed. Seats 70 in two rooms. Free car park opposite. Specials include: Kurzi Lamb and Kurzi Chicken. Takeaway: 10% discount. Delivery: £12 minimum, 5-mile radius.Hours: 12-2/5.30-11.30.

TANDOORI NIGHT

Knight Street, Sawbridgeworth 01279 722341

'We had our wedding reception in this great restaurant. Food and service excellent.' JP. *'Chicken Tikka, excellent huge pieces, very tasty. Onion Bhajis size of tennis balls.'* [must be the thing round here – Ed]. *'Very hot and tasty Madras, plenty of Vegetable Biriani. Friendly staff.'* JP. Hours: 12-2.30/6-11.30 (12am on Fri. & Sat.).

St Albans

MUMTAJ TOP 100

115 London Road, St Albans 01727 858399

Originally opened as a restaurant way back in 1962. Present owner, Muklasur Rahman Mojumder took over in 1983 and has established himself as a highly regarded source of Indian cuisine. Seats 44 diners in two rooms partitioned by an archway. The owner's son Chad Rahman now runs the kitchen. He loves to try out new ideas, and has been experimenting for a new menu. He worked some time in curry houses in Houston Texas. More recently he entered the Curry Chef of the Year competition, run by the Chartered Institute of Environmental Health. (CIEH). I wouldn't enter a cooking contest myself. What if you loose? Chad entered and won in 2002, and bless me he did it again in 2003, and again he won. St Albans MP Kerry Pollard loves the place but agreed with me that Chad is 'a

©	Curry Club Discount	U	Unlicensed
V	Vegetarian	ANP	Alcohol not permitted
e-a-m-a-y-l	Eat as much as you like	BYO	Bring your own alcohol

brave man, and a brilliant chef'. Chad is not without plagiarism problems. *'I create original dishes',* he tells me *'and within a trice, other restaurants copy me – dishes of the same name (names I've dreamed up) soon show up on their menus, and I know they can't cook them like I do'.* One such restaurant was Vindaloo, opposite the Mumtaz and because of it delisted from the Guide. *'I am lucky enough to travel widely on business, and never travel without your Guide. I aim to visit every TOP 100. I agree with all but one of those visited. Having visited many, many U.K. curryhouses in the U.K, as well as in Brussels (ugh), Amsterdam (great), Stockholm (ugh), Riyadh (ummm), and the USA (hmmm), I am always pleased to get home to St Albans, and eat at my local, the Mumtaj.'* PFM. *'Smart, elegant restaurant just outside historic St Albans. Fairly small, intimate, air of refinement. Attentive and friendly service. Excellent Prawn Puri £3.65, really aromatic sauce, plenty of prawns, slightly crisp, oil–free puri. Lamb Nashilee £7.95, very good combination, robust spices, plenty of ginger, texture added by peppers and chillies, good cuts of gristle-free lamb, very enjoyable. Peshwari Nan £1.90, moist, well cooked, too much filling, sweet and delicious. Enjoyable, just a* **TOP 100** *restaurant.'* RW. Delivery: 2 miles, £15 minimum. Hours: 12-3/6 -12.

Stevenage

GATE OF INDIA 

20 The Glebe, Chells Way, Stevenage
01438 3176195

Abdul Salam has dropped the word 'New' from his restaurant's name, but our scribes tell us not to worry, everything else is as before. Its 57 seats are divided between 4 rooms. Chef Arosh Ali cooks all the favourites. Delivery: £10 min, 4-mile radius. Hours: 12-2.30pm/6pm-12am.

TAJ MAHAL NEW ENTRANT

70 High Street, Stevenage 01438 313290

Full of customers ate 8pm on a Wednesday night! Moderate prices, good range of dishes, very stylish decor. Kingfisher but no Cobra. Recommended.' AE.

Tring

JUBRAJ 

53a High Street, Tring 01442 825368

Special dinners for two at Monnan Miah's 90-seater, adjacent to the town car park. Hours: 12-2.30/6-11.45.

Ware

NEELAKASH

1-3 Amwell End, Ware 01920 487038

'Busy but service was still attentive. Slightly larger than usual menu – fish curry is quite rare to find as is a restaurant that actually has rasmali.' SJ.

Welwyn Garden City

PAVILLION

49 Wigmore Street, Welwyn 01707 333014

'Certainly worthy of your attention.' GF.

KENT

Area: South East
Population: 1,572,000
Adjacent Counties: Essex, London, Surrey, Sussex

Part of Kent was absorbed by Greater London in 1965. We note affected towns/suburbs..

Ashford

ZARIN 

31 Bank Street, Ashford 01233 620511

Bajloor Rashid came to the UK in 1978 and began his career as a restaurateur. He is currently a director of the Bangladesh-British Chamber of Commerce and plays an active role in supporting the Bangladeshi community in Britain. His Curry Garden has been refurbished, and renamed Zarin. It's decidedly modern, with pale wooden floors, and chrome and different levels. At the back is a water feature. Plasma screens and lively music play constantly, and Elvis night are held monthly. Menu Extracts: Chicken Chat Puri £3.95, Maccher Torkary £7.95, seasonal freshwater Bangladeshi fish, Ginger Muragh £7.25, Palok Gajor Cashew Nut £5.25, with spinach, Peas Pullao Rice £2.25. Takeaway, 20% discount. Hours: 12-2.30/6-11.30 Fri. & Sat. to 12am. Sunday 12-11.

Barnehurst (Greater London)

JHAS TANDOORI ©

158c Mayplace Road, East Barnehurst 01322 555036

Est.1989 by Kuldip Jhas, who is also head chef; Robinder Jhas is the manager – a family business. Seats 50. Recently refurbished. Punjabi style Chicken and Lamb Balti is a house special and most popular with customers. 10% discount on takeaways. Hours: 6-11.30 (Fri. & Sat. to 12am); Sun. closed.

Bexley (Greater London)

CURRY HUT TAKEAWAY 

166 Mayplace Road East, Bexleyheath 01322 550077

Established 1995 by Muhammed Jahangir Alam. He tells us it's very modern, with an open kitchen. Set dinner £12.95 vegetarian, £14.95 non-vegetarian. Delivery: £10 minimum, 3-mile radius. Hours: 5-11.30.

SAGGOR 

145 Blendon Road, Bexley 020 8303 7549

Ali Uddin's *'pleasant restaurant, had a nice ambience, appetising smell as we entered – always a good start. Good menu featuring all the usuals plus a few less common names, particularly one or two interesting looking fish dishes. One of the most tasty Chicken Chats I've had for some time. Prawn Puri also unanimously approved. Subze Tandoori – a mixture of vegetables either whole or large slices, was very different. Certainly worth going to again.'* MW. Hours: 12-2.30/6-11.30.

Biggin Hill

RAJ 

187 Main Road, Biggin Hill 01959 572459

70-seater, managed by AM Crorie, decorated in an 'olde worlde' style. Delivery: £10 minimum, 3-mile radius. Hours: 12-2.30 (3.30 on Sun.)/6-11.30 (12am on Sat.). *See page* 23.

Bromley (Greater London)

CAFÉ EAST

123 Masons Hill, Bromley 020 8460 5452

Part of the Tamasha Group, owned by Shekor Tarat and Anil Deb, seats 76 diners. Brightly coloured menus, turquoise with orange for the food and fushia with orange for the wine list. Somebody has rather a *'Carry On'* sense of humour with starters like Tossing the Kyber, (Scottish salmon marinated with ginger and garlic, flavoured with caraway and char-grilled on the tandoor), Hey Griddle, Griddle, (chicken cooked on the tava with green peppers, onions, tomatoes and fresh herbs), Goan, Goan, Gone! £10.95 (in a trice, these Goan prawns with a Portuguese influence – hot and spicy!), It's all Fenugreek to Me, (nuggets of soya delicately spiced with garam masala and cooked with fresh fenugreek), Kebab's your Uncle! £6.95 (potato, cauliflower and paneer chunks skewered with green peppers, onion and tomatoes, then popped in the tandoor to char grill, and, probably the worst joke of the lot, Grandma, we love you! ,(she may be plain, nutty or even highly scented, but we know you all love your nan). I can hear the groans [gro-naans?] already! It's perhaps not the longest menu in the world, but there are some great dishes for everyone. Sunday brunch: three courses, £10 per person, live jazz band, 12-3pm. Hours: 1-2.30/6-11.00. Branch: Tamasha, Bromley.

HOMESDALE TANDOORI 

28 Homesdale Road, Bromley 020 8290 0671

Established in 1986. Seats 60. Undergoing redecoration. House specials: Haryali Chicken Masala £7, baked chicken in a marinade of spinach, mint and coriander puree, served in a creamy sauce. Takeaway: 10% discount. Delivery: £10 minimum, 3-mile radius. Hours: 12-2/6-12am.

SURUCHI 

466 Bromley Road, Downham, Bromley 020 8698 8626

Modern, simply decorated, 60-seater. North Indian curries. Recommended: Kaliya Galda, tiger prawns prepared with fresh coconut, ground mustard and ghee. Sunday buffet £6.50, kids £4.25, babies free. Owner Mr Dey promises CC members a free drink as their discount. Service 10%. Delivery: £12 min, 2-mile radius. Hours: 12-2.30/6-12.

TAMASHA TOP 100 

131 Widmore Road, Bromley 020 8460 3240

Established in 1993. Owner is Shekor Tarat and manager Pramod Dey. Attached to a small hotel, so if you need a decent curry followed by a bed for the night, now you know. Tamasha means *'something worth seeing'*. And it is! There is ample car parking, and you enter past a smartly saluting geezer, via an awning flanked by tub plants. Inside, there's a well-stocked bar. The dining room, in two parts, seats 120 in seven rooms, and is superbly decorated like a British Raj Club, with polo sticks and hats, black and white photos of polo teams, Maharajas and sumptuous banquets. Cane furniture with palms in copper planters. Head chef Rajinder Kumar cooks food from north and south India, Goa and Kashmir. Curry house formula, it certainly is not. Favourite starters include Bhajis (Pakoras), Kebabs and Tikka, and main courses Jalfrezi and Chicken Tikka Masala. Good they are, too. But a little exploring can yield some treasures: Chicken Nilgiri Tikka, boneless chicken marinated in spices, fresh coriander and mint, cooked in the tandoor. Goan Fish Curry, fish cooked in coconut and red chillies and garnished with fresh coriander leaves. Dum Pukht Gosht, marinated sliced baby lamb in a variety of spices and then steam-cooked in sealed earthenware, and Chicken Mirchi Wala, boneless chicken cooked in strongly spiced red chilli curry with potatoes, is popular, and Abrakebabra! so is the table magician who entertains the kids during Sunday lunch buffet. *'Crowded right through the evening and booking in advance whatever the night is to be recommended. Real orchids on the tables and everything about it shouts quality. Many unusual and imaginative dishes. Chicken Nilgiri Tikka was an intriguing shade of green, caused by being marinated in mint and coriander, flavours came through as I ate. Fish Punjabi crisp and spicy, Aloo Tikki very tasty. Raan Jaipuri and Rara Gosht equally tender and delicious. The only thing that did not suit our taste was the Peshwari Naan which was very sweet and overloaded with ground almond, but no fruit. Portions ample, service efficient and polite (but not particularly friendly, except for welcoming doorman). Prices above average, but not excessive for quality of restaurant and location. Well deserves its* **TOP 100** *status.'* MW. Menu Extracts: Malai Tikka £4.75, chicken marinated in cream cheese, cooked in tandoor, Aloo Tikki £3.95, minced potato burger, filled with lentils, served with mint and imli chutney, Aloo Pappri Chatt £4.25, chick peas, potatoes, coriander leaves, mint, yoghurt, imli sauce, crispy puri bread, Murgh Nawabi £10.50, chicken marinated in white wine, rich sauce of onion, tomato and saffron (sounds delicious!), Goan Chicken Xacuti £8.50, with coconut, Jhinga Tariwala £10.95, King prawns, spicy, tangy, red chillies, turmeric, bay leaves, Banarsi Dum Aloo £6.50, new potatoes stuffed with mint, cheese, tangy dry gravy. Service charge 12.5%. 20 car parking spaces. Live jazz and blues on Sun., Mon. and Tues. evenings. Sunday lunch buffet with in-house magician for children. Takeaway: 10% discount. Hours: 12-2.30/6-11pm. *See page* 23.

ZANZIBAR 

239 High Street, Bromley 020 8460 7130

Ebullient owner Ken Modi opened his Carioca in 1971 but changed its name because 'I got fed up with Karaoke requests'. The main room seats 50, its walls and ceiling decorated with coconut matting, giving the feeling of being in a fisherman's hut '– a very glamorous one' according to Mr Modi. The party room, which includes a mock Pullman railway carriage, seats 70. The menu contains the regular favourite tandooris, baltis, curries and accompaniments. *'After a morning shopping on a Saturday, we headed to the Zanzibar for a lunchtime buffet. The food is on view from the outside, as it is displayed on a warming table in the window. This sounds awful but it's actually well done, the dishes, polished and spanking clean, the food, fresh. We were politely served our starters first: a fresh, crisp salad with flat Onion Bhajis and half a Nan with chutneys, raita and a Coconut Chutney which was incredible, with a slight hint of heat from its mustard seed. The service became very friendly and helpful when we were given huge warm bowls for the self-serve buffet. The dishes were explained to us: Chicken Tikka Masala (smoky flavour – great), Bhoona Gosht, Mild Chicken Curry, Meat Madras, Bombay Aloo (excellent – new potatoes), Cauliflower Bhajee, Dal Makhani, Brinjal Bhajee, Plain and Pullau Rice and Nan bread. After two visits to this array of food, I was stuffed and delighted. Good food from a clean, well-decorated restaurant.'* MPW. Hours: 12-2 (Sun. 12.30-3.30)/6 (Sun. 6.30)-10.30.

Canterbury

TASTY SPICE

9 Longport Road, Canterbury 01227 463326

'Smart waiters provide efficient service to a mature and refined clientele . Prtions are plentiful, prices very reasonable for a better than average restaurant). Deserves its entry in the guide.' MW.

Chatham

LADY CHUTNEYS

74 High Street, Chatham 01634 400450

'Food reasonably priced and good sized helpings. Beer rather pricey – £7 for two bottles Cobra. Very clean throughout. Nan Bread £1.50 – nearly 24" long – Sparkbrook, Birmingham size!! Very pleased with ambience and quality and I consider the quality worthy of entry in the Guide.' BP-D. *'Punjabi restaurant. Plain, cream walls, large prints, mirrors, inset lights, all provide clean appearance. Extensive selection of continental dishes for the unbelievers. Onion Bhajia – two flat, small salad, good, thick Mint Raitha, extremely tasty, hot spicy flavour, bit stodgy, glutinous inside. Chicken Chat – nice, succulent, very tasty sauce, fresh coriander, just right. Mains – Chicken Masaleder – mild, very rich sweet and sour sauce, bordering Chinese. Mathmandu Masala - thick lentil base, plenty of capsicum, chicken, very tasty. Good rice and bread – twice the size of most places – be warned! Pleasant and efficient service. Average prices, portions plentiful.'* MW. Menu Extracts: Cheese Pakora £2.75, Channa Poori £2.90, chickpeas on bread, Chicken Mirchi Masala £6.50, barbecued chicken, green chilli, spring onions, Lamb Dilrazia £6.95, barbecued lamb, garlic butter, pineapple, apricot, onion, lime, mild sauce, Sambuca kick!, Peas Rice £2.25, Chilli and Coriander Nan £2.25. Takeaway: 10% discount. Delivery: £15 minimum, 5 miles Credit cards accepted. Sunday night Buffet: £8.95 adult, £4.95 child. Hours: 12-2.30/6-1. Sunday 5.30-10.30.

THE ROYAL

50 New Road, Chatham 01634 827799

Formerly Monuments of Bangladesh. *'Situated in a former pub, seats forty, fairly comfortable. Surprisingly crowded on Thursday night. Interesting menu – expensive Poppadoms 75p plus 75p for a small portion of pickle. Excellent starters, my wife's favourite Onion Bhajia – four bhajis, very crisp, tasty, a better version. Chicken Tikka Chat – extremely tangy. Tandoori Mix – tasted good. Mains – Chicken Bhuna – medium strength, good well rounded flavour, very moist, fresh coriander leaves. Chicken Tikka Chilli Masala – rather rich red colour, very spicy, plenty of green chillies, pleasingly hot for my tastes, although too much for my wife (all the more for me!) Buttery Chana Masala, melting in the mouth.'* MW. Delivery: £10 minimum, 4 miles. Takeaway: 10% discount, £20 minimum. Hours: 12-2/6-2 Friday closed lunchtime.

Chislehurst (Greater London)

JAIPUR 

53 Chislehurst Road, Chislehurst 020 8467 9390

Owner Abdul Mushahid and manager Abdul Hannan have put together *'an exciting, different menu.'* PP. Starters include Lacy Cutless, an Anglo-Indian Keema-stuffed potato rissole, and Fish Roe, breadcrumbed and deep-fried. Main courses include a wealth of interesting items, such as Green Goan Chicken Curry and a Sylheti red version. There is a creditable selection of Bangladeshi dishes. Ayre and Roop, Bengali fish, and the Baingan Torkari – aubergine with tamarind cooked Sylheti-style in black terracotta. Minimum charge £10. Hours: 12-2/6-11.30.

Crayford (Greater London)

CRAYFORD TANDOORI NEW ENTRANT

4 Empire, Waterside, Crayford 01322 524539

'Boss called Vicram. Cosy establishment with about 50 seats.

©	Curry Club Discount	U	Unlicensed
V	Vegetarian	ANP	Alcohol not permitted
e-a-m-a-y-l	Eat as much as you like	BYO	Bring your own alcohol

Poppadoms always fresh and crispy. Chicken Chat is unsurpassed oozing flavour!! Chicken Tikka Korai Madras, hot, just excellent. Quality of curries is very high with juicy tender chicken. All staff friendly, prices fair though price of Cobra has gone up!' MS.

GHANDI SPICE ©

108 London Road, Crayford 01322 559191

A standard curry house, established in 1997. Seats 40. Parking at front. Sunday buffet. Takeaway: 10% discount. Delivery: £10 minimum. Hours: 12-2.30/5.30-11.30; Sun. 12-11.30.

Dartford

GREEN TANDOORI ©

Green Street, Green Road, Darenth, Dartford 01474 708885

Opened in 1996. A pretty boring curry house from the outside, but don't be put off – inside it's really quite nice. Air conditioned, hanging plants, green (what else!) tablecloths. Seats 45. Six car parking spaces at front, 20 at rear. Specials include: Kebab Raj Bahar, Chicken Shagorana, half tandoori chicken with keema, garlic, tomato, green pepper, onion, egg, almond, cream and butter served with Fried Rice. Chingri Raj Bahar, king prawns with garlic, onion, green pepper, tomato and coriander, slightly hot. Takeaway: 10% discount. Delivery: 4½ mile radius. Hours: 5-12; Sun. 12-12am.

SHER E BANGLA NEW ENTRANT

33 Station Road Longfield Dartford 01474 704627

'Takeaway opened for 4 years and linked to a restaurant in Crayford of same name. Chicken Jalfrezi pleasingly hot and flavoursome in a thick sauce with the chillies cooked in to give some zest. Sylheti Bhajee a nice vegetable mixture well cooked and tastily spiced. An enjoyable and good quality formula curry takeaway.' MW. Menu extracts: Tandoori Trout Masala £7.95, Sylheti Bhajee £2.20.Hours: 5.30-11, Friday and Saturday to 11.30.

Downham

SHANTI INDIAN CUISINE 

419 Bromley Road, Downham, Bromley 020 8461 4819

Established in 1988. Taken over by Anwarul Azim and Rukhsana Faoir in 1998. Air conditioned. Seats 48. Specials include: Chicken Achari, cooked in a thick sauce with hot pickles. Sunday buffet: 12.30-3.30, adults £7.50, children under ten £4.50. Takeaway: 10% discount. Delivery: free, 10% discount, 4-mile radius. Hours: 12-2.30/6-11.30 (Sat. to 12am).

Dunton Green

TAJ

110 London Road, Dunton Green 01732 462277

'Probably my favourite of all time. I have tried nearly every dish. Never disappointed. King Prawn Patia the best. Ample portions. Guideworthy.' KT. *'Owner tells me that he has been in the business for thirty years. Doing something right? Comfortable surroundings. Nothing outstanding, food overall a good standard formula. Chicken Dhansak, fairly spicy, thick lentil sauce. CTM – creamy, sweetish, a good example, can't comment critically, not a favourite of mine. Excellent Dry Vegetable Curry – lightly cooked, well spiced. Tarka Dal – fairly thick, porridge like consistency, nice garlic under taste. Prices and portions average. Efficient service.'* MW. Menu Extracts: Lamb Tikka £3.30, Hasina Kebab £6.75, Butter Chicken £6.55, Saag (spinach) Cream £2.90, Moti Pullao Rice £2.90 – minced meat and boiled egg, Roti £1.65. Minimum charge: £10. Hours: 12-2.30/6-11.

East Peckham

SPICE COTTAGE NEW ENTRANT

2 Bullen Lane, Addlestead Road, East Peckham 01622 871282

'The building is a converted public house, once the Addlestead Tavern. – a sign of the times? The entrance and exit doors still carrying the etched indications of saloon and public bars. Pale pastel walls, adorned with mirrors and pictures of eastern scenes. Plenty of smart staff, helpful and attentive. NO background music – great blessing. Smoking and non–smoking sections. Very

good quality menu, large starters. Poppadoms come with five pickles. Rezala, well cooked, quite hot, chillies. Achari, redolent of lime pickle. Meat Biriani, best ever. Dupiaza, mild, flavourful, satisfying richness. Our daughters' Vegetable Balti– excellent, underlying richness. A delight.' JDL. *'Very busy Saturday night, but plenty of helpful, efficient staff on duty. Bright and welcoming. Food very good.'* DB. *'For those who like things hotter, as I do, the Lamb Tikka Dhansak, excellent, good tender chunks of well cooked lamb in thick, dark, full flavoured spicy sauce. Bombay Potato – good example. Found the Tarka Dal, thick and creamy, rather like custard, but had right garlic and spice flavours. Portions quite sufficient. Service efficient. A good meal in pleasant restaurant.'* MW. Menu extracts: Vegetable Kasuri £2.50, mixed vegetable covered in crunchy crum. Chicken Roll £2.95, chicken cooked with tropical vegetables, covered with thin bread. Staff Curry Dishes from £4.75, Keema Methi, Sag Gosht, Sag Prawn. Courgette Bhajee £2.95. Saffron Navrattan Rice £3.50. Cheese Nan £1.95. Sag Nan £1.95. Sunday Buffet: £7.50 adult, £4.95 children. Takeaway: 10% discount, £10 minimum. Hours: 12-2/6-11.

Farnborough

VILLAGE CUISINE 

145 High Street, Farnborough, Nr Orpington 01689 860077

Modern decor and wooden floors at the Village. Established in 1991, it seats 40 and is not your run of the mill curry house – check out some of these fantastic dishes on the Summer Set Menu. Samosa – choose from meat, vegetable, coconut or fish. Creamed Mussels – served in their half shells, lightly spiced with saffron cream sauce. Murg Khasthri Kebab – chicken marinated overnight in yoghurt and herbs, skewered and cooked in tandoor. Hariali Lamb – boneless meat marinated in freshly ground coriander, spinach, mint and green chillies. Cucumber Rice, Spinach Nan, Mint Paratha and this list goes on! If you are not tempted by this extraordinary menu then there are of course the usual curry house curries. Proprietor Mr Fahim Maksud has promised to give a discount of 10% to Curry Club members, please ring him for booking confirmation. Takeaway: 10% discount. Delivery: £10 minimum, 4-mile radius. Hours: 12-2.30 / 5.30-10.30; Sun. buffet 12-6.30pm.

Faversham

INDIAN ROYAL — NEW ENTRANT

16 East Street, Faversham 01795 536033

'Faversham's first Indian restaurant, opening in 1991 in an older Tudor style building. Probably seats forty comfortably in pleasant wood beamed restaurant – nice ambience. Standard menu, plus interesting additions such as Malai Kasa, cooked with coconut, almonds and chilli, Makhoni, cooked with mangoes, Manchurian, sweet and sour. However, I was told it was less hot than Pathia, I had visions of Chinese sweet and sour dishes so stuck to Chicken Tikka Pathia. This was very good – a nice thick hot and tangy sauce. Cauliflower Bhajee, a bit salty, but Vegetable Sambar, with lentils was excellent, delicious. Efficient and friendly service. Sufficient portions with average prices.' MW. Tuesday Night Special – £9.50 for starter, main, side and sundries– booking advisable. Sunday Buffet – £6.95 adult £3.50 children from midday to 5. Hours: 12-2.30/5-11.30.

Folkestone

INDIA — TOP 100 

1 The Old High Street, Folkestone 01303 259155

Mr Ali Ashraf chose Folkestone to establish his 42 seat India in 1985. Being a French-trained Indian chef and speaking French too, perhaps he felt being close to France would be *au fait*. In some cases he combines French methods (cream, wine and brandy) with Indian spices to provide an original interpretation of his Indian dishes. Since being a little critical last time (and we are just the messenger) we've been inundated with letters praising the India, strangely though, some typed by the same type-writer arrived in same-type envelopes. But we like the ebullient Ashraf, and it's great to hear from new reporters (but let's also hear from our old hands next time, please). So here are some examples: *'For many years now, my family and I have been making the India our first 'obligatory' stop after crossing the Channel from our home in Belgium. We enjoy outstandingly fine cooking accompanied by impeccably discreet, relaxed service from Sheuli. Helpings are generous. Repays any effort required in order to go there.'* BH. *'Ali Ashraf and his charming wife unfailingly serve us excellent food and wine, at reasonable prices coupled with warm hospitality.'* C&AN. *'As a regular customer, over ten years, I am delighted to take business visitors from around the world to this restaurant, the proprietor and his wife always make these occasions a gastronomic and social success.'* MF. *'Your write-up of this restaurant, written some time back, seems as appropriate today as it did then. Have patronised this excellent restaurant for at least fifteen years, quality is high, certainly far superior to any other. Outstanding starters – Sita's Dosha £3.25, pancake stuffed with prawns, mushroom, crab, coriander and minced meat, Crab Kochin £4.50, crab with ginger, coriander and white wine, Prawn Puree and Ghungni £3.25 – split peas and potatoes with fresh coriander, cumin and tamarind. I particularly like the main courses – Khobani £5.75, medium spiced with cinnamon, cardamom and apricot, Pahari Chicken £5.50, fairly hot with cardamom, ginger, fresh coriander and tamarind, Lamb Mysore £5.95, fairly hot and Beef Hyderbadi £5.25, with cumin, coriander and mustard seeds. My wife says the best is yet to come with the home made desserts – Firni, Almond Pudding and home-made Kulfi.'* RFB. *'Small, simple, spotlessly clean. Never fails to produce the most elegantly flavoured authentic recipes. Gets our vote every time.'* F&PD. Hours: 12-2 / 6-10.30.

Gillingham

SPICE COURT NEW ENTRANT

56 Balmoral Road, Gillingham 01634 570555

The 2001 *Guide* had the Tiffin in Gillingham (see Tiffin E1) as a 'New Entrant', taking over from the short-lived Mango Tree. However, Tiffin closed at the end of 2000 re-opening a year later as Spice Court and *'run by a guy who used to work for Cobra lager and is married to sister of Mr Choudhury who owns the Bengal chain. Sizable and comfortable bar with reception area. Dining area, modern, roomy, bright, fresh, brightly coloured plain walls. Crisp white table linen, glasses and cutlery, smart waiters. Mangalorean Crab – a little sand castle of minced crab and rice, lightly spiced. Crispy fried to perfection Onion Bhajia, very tasty, not greasy. Chicken Dhansak – tongue tinglingly hot, good underlying flavour. Lamb Pathia – slightly sweetish, very flavoursome sauce. Absolutely delicious Tarka Dal, lovely underlying flavour of garlic. Prices very reasonable, portions perfectly adequate. All in all a first class restaurant, a gem.'* MW. Sunday Buffet: £6.45, £3.50 child. Delivery: £15 min, 3 miles. Takeaway: 10% discount. Credit cards accepted. Hours: 12-2.30, Sunday to 4/6-11.30, Sun-11.

Gravesend

(inc: Meopham)

BADSHAW NEW ENTRANT U BYO

65 Wrotham Road, Gravesend 01474 534910

Formerly the Ajay. Refurbished in summer 2002. *'Fairly plain with tiled floors, plain walls with large Indian pictures, quite roomy. Onion Bhajia £1.50, two flat type, crisp outside, plenty of onion, light and moist inside. Served plainly without any salad, although a bowl of Raitha was provided. Chicken Chat £2, pleasantly spicy and tasty. Chicken Tikka Dhansak £4.50, excellent, thick lentil based sauce with lots of taste, hot enough to set the tongue tingling. Chicken Patia £3.50, distinctively different, thick, slightly darker sauce, hotter than the Dhansak, underlying sweet and sour flavour. Sizzling Mixed Vegetables £2.90, good variety, lightly cooked and spiced. Rice – Ok, as was Chapati 75p. Bhatura 75p, pleasant and different. Adequate portions, extremely reasonable prices. Very friendly waiters.'* MW. Takeaway: Free Chicken Tikka starter, £10 min. Free bottle of Bacardi breezer, £15 min. Free bottle of wine, £25 min. Delivery: £10 minimum. Hours: 5.30-1130.

CAFE TAJ NEW ENTRANT

170 Parrock Street Gravesend 01474 365700

Popular with quite a few, it seems. Menu extracts: Sizzler Jullett £7.90, chicken or lamb with brandy and Tandoori spices. Rupchanda Boal £6.50, freshwater fish marinated in garlic, fenugreek and tomatoes. Sarisha Murgh £5.50, chicken kebab, ground mustard, green herbs, medium sauce. Egg Pullao £2.20.Takeaway: 10% discount. Delivery: £15 minimum, from 6-11. Hours: 5.30 -11, Friday and Saturday to 11.30.

GANDHI BALTI HOUSE ©10%

66 West Street, Gravesend 01474 536066

Owned by Abdul Basith Khan, serves Bangladeshi-style curries. Restaurant decorated in light pinks and light green, seats 60. *'Standards as good as ever. Chot Pote (spiced chickpea and egg mixture) tasty, Chicken Pathia always good, Vegetable Pullao had plenty of vegetables and nuts, a was an excellent value alternative to plain pilao rice. Service friendly and efficient and 10% Curry Club members' discount given without hesitation. Price average, portions ample. Usually fully booked in advance Friday and Saturday nights!'* MW. Sunday lunch buffet £7, children £6. Hours: 12-2.30/5.30-11 (11.30 on Sat.).

MEOPHAM TANDOORI ©10%

2 The Parade, Wrotham Road, Meopham, Gravesend 01474 812840

Jahir Ali's 60-seater is *'Comfortable, small fountain, glass partitions, pleasant atmosphere. Comprehensive menu, usual dishes.'* MW. Sunday Buffet £6.95. Mr Ali give a generous 10% for Curry Club members. Menu extracts: Bombay Spice Chicken £6.95, with fresh green chillies and carrot – fairly hot. Meopham Tandoori Special £7.95, with Tia Maria, fresh cream, mild spices. Chicken Juleat Special £7.95, chicken and lamb chops, brandy. Sunday Buffet: £6.95 adult, £4.95 children, 12-2.30. Hours: 12-2.30/5.30-11.30. Branch: India Palace Balti House, Station Approach, Meopham, Kent.

PUNJAB KARAHI U

4-5 Milton Road, Gravesend 01474 322222

As its name suggests, this is not a standard high street curry house, but cooks good, well spiced Punjabi food while you wait. It's what you find in Southall and Tooting. and other Indian areas. *'Spotless surroundings, no license. Full on a Friday night, and we were the only non-Asians. Limited but sufficient selection. Good, well spiced Punjabi food cooked while you wait. Aloo Tikki and Kebab Roll starters were excellent, and main dishes were first class, gutsy and well spiced. Service interestingly amateur. All in all, a good, inexpensive meal.'* And a second visit *'Plain tables now covered in tablecloths, napkins etc, and new more efficient waiters. But I am happy to report that the menu, prices and food remain the same, and the clientele was still all Asian. Food again delicious – all freshly made and extremely tasty. Reasonable prices.'* MW. Delivery: £8 minimum. Hours: 5.30-2; Sat. & Sun. 12-12am.

Halstead

BENGAL MANGROVE

London Road, Halstead 01959 534688

Owned by the Choudhury family and seats 180 in spacious, modern surroundings, formerly a Spanish restaurant. Cooking by Chef Ram Das, ex Bombay Brasserie and the Three Monkeys, SE23 Menu extracts: Goan Chingri Palok, marinated king prawn wrapped in fresh spinach and deep-fried. Chicken '65, cooked Hyderabadi style with green chillies and curry leaves. Chicken Peshwari, marinated in mango pulp, cream, almond and sultanas. Dum Pukht Gosht, subtly flavoured lamb cooked with saffron and brown onions. Golda Chingri Pardanashin, Goan-style, coconut flavoured giant prawns served in coconut shell. Roshoni Khaju Gobi, cauliflower, garlic and cashew nut. *'Food was superb! Very lucky to have this restaurant.'* KT. *'Food all very enjoyable although the vegetables – Dal Palak, Sabzi Curry and Sabzi Haryali all very mildly spiced and could have done with more zip. Nevertheless, all dishes good, subtle spicing and flavours but oily. Service generally good, although frenetic at meeting and greeting stage. Portions quite adequate, prices slightly above average, however, extremely irritating practice of leaving credit card open after 10% gratuity has been added.'* MW. And Malcolm isn't alone with this complaint. Last Guide we said *'We'll put the Mangrove straight into to our TOP 100 category, despite this practice, though we'd like to hear from you that it has stopped.'* It hasn't stopped. This odious practice borders on the dishonest and shows a complete disregard for customers. So as we promised this, and any other restaurant you tell us which operates this scam, will be downgraded and/or delisted. And there is another reason. One of the *Guide* researchers (Claire) phoned to check details with the manager. The response was very rude. *'I don't want to speak to you'* he said, and put the phone down. Usually the *Guide* gets a great response from restaurateurs and staff. Claire was deeply upset, and we simply do not tolerate rude behaviour. Reports, reports, reports, please.

Hayes

CINNAMON LOUNGE
NEW ENTRANT

18 Station Approach, Hayes 020 8462 8594

Trendy name, trendy place. *'Clean, bright, airy, plenty of space between tables. Arrived at 7.30pm, only 2nd table occupied, worried me, however by 9.30pm, very busy and quite rightly. Well presented, nicely spiced, generous portions. Polite and attentive service. Aloo Bora and Rampuri Sheek kebab, both excellent. I do appreciate a cool, crisp salad, rather than a limp one. Xacuti Chicken – great taste of coconut. Posh toilets.'* MPW. Menu Extracts: Hyderabadi Lamb Chop £3.25 – marinated in ginger, charcoal roasted, Akbari Murg £3.25 – diced chicken, green chillies and curry leaves, Dhaniya Fish £7.95 – fish of the day in light coriander curry sauce, Chana Masala £2.95 – chick peas cooked with lemon and tamarind sauce. Tandoori Roti £1.50.

TASTE OF BENGAL TAKEAWAY
NEW ENTRANT

96 Sea Street, Herne Bay 01227 374763

Takeaway: only. *'Nice, clean appearance, which is enhanced by a small smart, sparkling van for home deliveries, parked outside with the name of the restaurant emblazoned on it. All dishes were of a good standard formula. Pathia £5.40 (inc Pullao Rice) – hot with a nice lentilly sauce. Mixed Vegetables Bhaji £2.00 – good selection, well cooked, tastily spiced. Excellent Tarka Dhal £2.30. Portions very good, prices about average and service at reception very friendly. A good decision.'* MW. Great value set meals, from £8.50. Delivery: £12 minimum. Hours: 12-2/5.30-11.30, Friday and Saturday to 12.

Hythe

KAI'S NEW ENTRANT

1 Red Lion Square, Hythe 01303 237080

Outshines in terms of food quality, service and atmosphere. Owned by a Bengali, with the cooking done by his mother in the kitchen – home-cooking. *'Without a doubt deserves to be put on the map.'* PB. Agreed. The curryhouse trade whinge about labour shortage but don't let their women work. And guess who cooks all the gorgeous Bengali (Bangladeshi) food at home? Starter Specials include: Indonesian Fish Cake £3.20, Grilled Meat with Stuffed Cheese £3.20. Main Courses include: Thai Beef and Coconut Curry £6.30, Bengal Minced Lamb and Potato Curry £5.00, Tamarind Beef and Pepper £6.10, Malaysian Egg Curry £4.30, Coriander and Tomato Scallop £6.10. Hours: 6-11, daily. Friday and Saturday no takeaways after 8.

Maidstone

CURRY INN NEW ENTRANT

98 King Street, Maidstone 01622 756094

'Small, unpretentious in quieter end of town. Tables set closely together. Starter portions absolutely enormous! – four round Onion Bhajias, tightly packed onion, not stodgy, tastily spiced. Feeling quite full, we went for the mains. Tandoori Chicken – two pieces, very good, darkly coloured with marinade, char grilled and Chicken Pathia – included full portion of rice, strong, gutsy spicing, set the mouth a tingle. Reasonable prices. Waiter anything but professional, took order without a flicker of a smile or friendly word.' MW. Menu Extracts: Jeera Chicken Masala £5.95, Lamb Mirch Masala £5.95 – tikka with green chilli, Mushroom Rice £2.20, Egg Paratha £1.80. Credit cards accepted. Licensed. Hours: 12-2.15/5.45-12.

HILLTOWN NEW ENTRANT

102, Union Street, Maidstone 01622 753575

Formerly Monsoon. *'Narrow premises, with small bar and reception area. Chicken Chat – tikka in sauce, not tangy but tasty. Onion Bhajia – nicely crisped on the outside, bland inside, fresh salad and Mint Raitha. Green Chicken Curry – pleasant enough, cooked with spinach, fairly mild, no green chillies, certain it was Chicken Sagwalla, my friend and I said nothing. Chicken Dhansak – an old favourite, large chunks of chicken in a very tasty and pleasing hot sauce. Tarka Dhal and Niramish – up to standard. Efficient and friendly service, adequate portions, average prices.'* MW. Menu Extracts: Hawali Chicken £2.50 – green paste of spinach, Aromatic Duck Tikka £7.95, Lamb Nehari £6.95 – fillet of lamb, spring onion, paprika, garlic, Shobji Bhuna Masala £6.25 – vegetables, cream, almonds.

TANDOOR MAHAL NEW ENTRANT

Medway Street, Maidstone 01622 762459

'Interesting restaurant, two staircases go up to mezzanine dining area. Comfortable place, pastel green, potted palms. Friendly efficient service. Excellent meal.' MW. Menu Extracts: Seek, Nargis or Reshmi Kebabs £2.50, Chicken Razala £7.50 – Tandoori chicken, mince meat, medium sauce, Egg Paratha £1.80. Takeaway: 10% discount on cash orders over £10. Hours: 12-2.30/6-11.30.

Marden

MARDEN TANDOORI NEW ENTRANT

Rutland House, Albion Road, Marden 01622 832184

Established twenty years. Has a good local reputation. *'Pleasant, comfortable, nicely decorated. Chicken – tasty, plentiful, good salad. Chicken Tikka Dhansak – good, thick lentil sauce, well spiced, several pieces of lemon for sharpness, not particularly hot. Chicken patia – flavoursome, good thick sauce. Extremely tasty Bombay Aloo, lots of spice and onion. Excellent Tarka Dal, strong onion and garlic flavour. Efficient and friendly service, ample portions.'* MW. Menu Extracts: Rezala £8.50 – Tandoori chicken, mince meat, medium sauce, Trout Bhuna £4.50, all vegetable curries, good value at £2 a dish. Hours: 12 -2.30/6-11.

Northfleet

PREETI RAJ TAKEAWAY NEW ENTRANT

141 Waterdales, Northfleet 01474 353022

'Another good formula curry. Chicken Chat £2.50, tasty if a little salty. Dhansak £4.10, well spiced and hot, various vegetable curries all nicely spiced but Bombay Potato £1.80 and Aloo Gobi £1.80 had the same taste. Special Rice cooked with diced vegetables. Value particularly outstanding.' MW. Delivery: £10 minimum. Sunday Set Menu: two courses (inc accompaniments), £8.90. Hours: 5.30-11, closed Monday.

Minster

SHERAZ

10 High Street, Minster 01795 876987

'Interior looks like a Kebab House. Punjabi cooking. Friendly service. Food surprisingly good. Nappali Chicken – good, hot, chillies. Dhal Samba – tasty. OK, but oily Cauliflower Bhajee. Prices average, portions good.' MW. Delivery: £12 minimum, 3 miles. Credit cards accepted. Menu Extracts: Kofta Masala £6.95 – meatballs, cooked with yoghurt, spicy sauce and egg, Bindi Ghost £6.95 – orka, lamb, rich spicy sauce, onions, Peas Potato £2.40, Butter Chapatti or Onion Nan £1.90. Hours: 11-11.30, Friday and Saturday to 12.

Orpington (Greater London)

CURRY HOUSE 

24 Station Square, Petts Wood, Orpington 01689 820671

Basth (Baz) Wahab runs 42-seater. *'Food good but atmosphere non-existent. Eventually won the waiters round and managed a laugh and a little conversation. Flavoursome fish tikka. Main dishes were well up to expectation.'* C&GM. Hours: 12-3pm (not on Fri.) and 6pm-12am; closed Mon.

RAJ OF INDIA 

4 Crescent Way, Green Street Green, Orpington 01689 852170

Established 1987. Owner-manager Muzibur Rahman. Seats 72. Chef recommends: Akbori Lamb, cooked with sultanas and almonds in a yoghurt sauce. Takeaway: small discount. Hours: 12-2.30/6-12am. Branches: Raj of India Sheerness, Swanley and Sittingbourne; Raj Bari Sevenoaks; Maharajah Bexley; Juboraj Brentwood, Essex.

BARABA NEW ENTRANT

215 Petts Wood Rd Petts Wood Orpington

Close to the Station. Airy air-conditioned, well spaced tables, light and modern decor Well-dressed and helpful friendly staff. *'Meal for Two. 1 meat Madras, 1 Chicken Xacuti, 2 Pilau. 1 Bhindi (fresh), 1 chapatti, 2 papads, 2 small Kingfisher. Enough left over for a doggie bag for a snack lunch). By far and the best meal out or takeaway we have had for a long time. Total cost £27 inc tip. Menu has a good range of specialities which are worth trying plus the usual curries but this is a cut-above average for the local establishments. A wee bit more expensive but well worth it. Takeaway now but no delivery at the moment. A must for anybody'* NC.

Ramsgate

RAMSGATE TANDOORI 

17 Harbour Street, Ramsgate 01843 589134

70-seater, owned by Rezaur Rahman, managed by Mrs Rahman. Bangladeshi and Pakistani curries cooked by head chef Joyanti Mendas. Sunday buffet. Delivery: £10 minimum. Hours: 12-2.30/6-12.

©	Curry Club Discount	**U**	Unlicensed
V	Vegetarian	**ANP**	Alcohol not permitted
e-a-m-a-y-l	Eat as much as you like	**BYO**	Bring your own alcohol

Rochester

CUMIN CLUB NEW ENTRANT

188 High Street, Rochester 01634 400880

'Very modern style, plain cream walls, occasion square bright fabric, pale wooden floors, white linen. Light, airy, spacious, rather cold. Aloo Tikki – two flat, fairly thin patties of spiced mashed potato, small portion of imli and another sweet and sour channa sauce. Extremely tasty, subtly spiced, unusual flavour. Onion Bhajia – very large onion rings, batter coated and deep-fried. Attractive but disappointing, no spiciness. Dhuba Murgh – large pieces of well marinated, succulent, moist chicken tikka in creamy, smooth, mild sauce – pleasant. Chicken Patia – very tangy, fairly hot sauce, plenty of onion, good flavour. Benguni Aloo – potatoes and aubergine, excellent. Peshwari Nan – lovely, fresh, but lacked content, I wasn't expecting whole coconuts, but hoped for something more substantial than a sweet paste. Prices above average, portions adequate, efficient and friendly service.' MW. Business Lunch: Poppadoms with condiments, choice of starter and main course, served with Pullao Rice and Nan – all for £6.95, exceptional value I think! Menu Extracts: Salmon Pakora £5.50. Shahi Malai Tikka £3.50 – chicken marinated in cummin, cream, cheddar and coriander leaves. Maynamothi £12.95 – king prawns, white wine, almonds, honey, sag and vegetables. Takeaway: 20% discount. Hours: 12-2, Friday lunch closed and 6-11.30.

A TASTE OF TWO CITIES NEW ENTRANT

106 High Street, Rochester 01634 841327

Smallish 52-seater. *'Fairly standard selection on menu. Onion Bhajia £1.80, four round small type, good, well spiced, not stodgy, accompanied by small garnish of strips of mustard sauce, marinated onion, peppers – pleasant and tasty. Chicken Chat £2.60, Ok, hot and spicy, too salty. Chicken Dhansak £6.50, hot and spicy, lacked sweetness and lentil flavour, rice was included. Shahi Chicken Tikka £6.90, with onions, tomatoes, peppers skewered and barbecued– dark coloured, fairly dry curry, strong smoky flavour, slightly burnt caramelised onion, very pleasant. Dry Mixed Vegetables £2.20, very tasty, nicely cooked, heavy on carrots. Service was reasonable and polite without being friendly. Portions and prices average.'* MW. Takeaway: 10% discount. Hours: 12-2.30/6 - 11.30.

BENGAL BRASSERIE 

356 High Street, Rochester 01634 841930

Opened in 1993. Seats 46. Ashahin Ali (manager), Abdul Roob (chef) and Ashamim Ali (chef). *'Indian music was too loud. Good, comprehensive menu. Slightly disappointed with the spicing and flavourings of all dishes.* MW. *'My favourite Indian restaurant.'* BP-D. Takeaway: 10% discount. Menu extracts: Honey Murghi £5.95, tender chicken, honey, sultanas, creamy sauce. Anda Bhuna £4.90, omelette shredded and served in a heavily spiced thick sauce. King Prawn Puri £4.70, tomotoes, onions, fresh coriander herbs and spices, served on a small pancake. Delivery: 6 miles, £12 minimum Hours: 12-2.30/5.30-12am.

BOLAKA NEW ENTRANT

17 Parkside Pde, Cliffewood, Rochester. 01634 222231

'Small, 28 seats, dining area. Pleasant modern exterior. Standard menu with a few Nepalese dishes (the Chef's Nepalese). Mixed Starter – Onion Bhajia, Sheek Kebab, Chicken and Lamb Tikka – each quite small, but what can you expect for £3 – provides a taste which is sufficient for an appetiser. Obliged for try Nepalese dishes – tempted by Capsila Chicken (menu warned of aphrodisiac properties)' [only tempted Malcolm?] *'plumped for Chicken Gurkha– extremely tasty, slices of Tandoori Chicken in very dark, thick medium hot and spicy sauce. My wife had Nepal Chicken – Tandoori Chicken off the bone in rich, thick, smoky flavoured and again very dark sauce – delicious Mixed Vegetable Bhajia nicely cooked selection of vegetables. Prices average, portions a little smaller but adequate. Extremely chatty and friendly waiter.'* MW. Sunday Buffet: £7.50 adults, £3.75 kids under 12. Hours: 12-2/5 -11. Sunday 12-10.30.

SINGAPORA 

51 High Street, Rochester 01634 842178

Dr and Mrs Shome's 150-seater spreads over three floors, with tables in odd alcoves. Specialising in Malaysian, Chinese, Indonesian, Thai and Japanese cuisine. *'Cosy, but deceptively larger with upper floors and basement. Aromatic Duck, shredded with sliced spring onions, cucumber and plum sauce rolled in pancakes. Udang Roti, King prawns on sesame toast – substantial flavour. Ayam Penang, Malaysian dish, crispy chicken with ginger and onions, tasty. Ayam Iblis, sliced chicken, chilli and ginger, very tasty. Washed down with red house wine £8.95, smooth and excellent value. Portions a little on the small side. Efficient and friendly service. Pleasant alternative.'* MW. Delivery. Hours: 12-3pm/6-11pm (Fri. & Sat. to 11.30); Sun. 12-10.30. Branch: 73, Brewer Street, Maidstone.

Sevenoaks

ASIA CUISINE

107 London Road, Sevenoaks 01732 453153

'My local. Does a brilliant CTM with rice and always friendly service.' KT. *'Nice place, very cosy, love the Indian music. Portions more than ample and prices just right.'* RL.

SPICE CLUB NEW ENTRANT

57 High Street, Sevenoaks. 01732 456688

'First class Indian restaurant. Staff smartly dressed in black, very helpful. Food is outstanding. Connoisseur starter section along with traditional Fish Pakora £3.25 very light. Lamb Boti Kebab £3.25 very succulent. Boal Malchi £10.95, very good (Gourmet). South Indian Garlic Chilli Chicken £6.95, very popular. Sevenoaks best!' KT. Hours: 12-2.30 / 6- 11.30.

TANDOORI NIGHTS NEW ENTRANT

47 High Street, Seal, Sevenoaks 01732 763055

Light green decor, padded cane chairs, pleasant ambience. *'Onion Bhajia £2.10 (4 pieces) – crisp, tasty. Chicken Chat £3.10 – as it should be, small pieces of chicken, very tangy sauce. Duck Reshmi £3.60 – pieces of duck cooked in egg, quite tasty, a little cool. A flavoursome, piquant tamarind sauce served with starters and left on table throughout meal. Murgh jal Ferizi (sic) £6.80 – excellent with chillies properly cooked in the sauce, good underlying flavour. Meat Dhansak £7.40 (inc PR) – quite hot, but softer and sweeter flavour in nice lentil based sauce. First class Kulcha – stuffed with paneer and vegetables, extremely light and tasty.'* MW. Menu extracts: Narkel Rami £2.70, beans & coconut. Lamb Rajitha £6.80, tender lamb with tomato and fried raisins.

Sidcup (Greater London)

BLACKFEN BALTI 

33 Wellington Parade, Blackfen Road, Sidcup 020 8303 0013

A friendly, pleasant, competent 48-seat curry house, owned by Muzammil Ali since 1983.

OVAL BRASSERIE 

49 The Oval, Sidcup 020 8308 0274

Ansar Miah has owned and managed the aptly-named Oval since 1988 (head chef Mohibur Rahman). Monday and Tuesday £7.95, starter, main course, side dish, rice or Nan – excellent value. Delivery: £10 minimum, 3-mile radius, free Poppadam. Hours: 12-2.30/6-11.30. All-day Sunday 12-11.30, buffet £6.95, £4 for kids.

Snodland

AGRA

16 Holborough Road, Snodland 01634 243320

'Recommended by friends, and we were not disappointed. Excellent King Prawn Bhuna on puree followed by Garlic Chicken which was as good as it gets! Service first class. Will go back.' KT. *'Pathia always my favourite, hot, spicy, rich dark sauce - delicious. Portions prices still about average. Good formula curry.'* MW. Menu Extracts: Chicken or Lamb Tikka Peaza £5.85 – onion flavoured thick sauce, Courgette Bhajee £2.15, Egg Paratha £1.75. Credit cards accepted. Hours: 12-2 .30/6 - 11.

DHAKA TAKEAWAY NEW ENTRANT

Snodland Railway Station 01634 245762

Takeaway: only. Situated at the Paper Mill End. *'Well produced menu for a small takeaway, good value set meals, well patronised. Chicken Patia £5.10 (inc Pullao Rice) was excellent, being hot with a very distinct sweet and sour contrast, well balanced. Shobze Bhaji £2.10, first class, good mix of vegetables, whole chillies, nicely spiced. Fairly ordinary Tarka Dal £1.95 – thick. Portions very good, prices reasonable and two complimentary Poppadoms. One to remember.'* MW. Hours: 5-1.

Staplehurst

MALONCHO NEW ENTRANT

17 The Parade, Staplehurst 01580 892769

Fully licensed and air conditioned. *'First impressions were good – it looks smart and fairly modern, comfortable takeaway waiting area, with busy regular trade. Restaurant seats 50, nicely decorated with hanging letters, wooden pictures, comfortable seating arrangements with reservation system that actually works! Standard menu with three Bengal Fish dishes. Vegetable Bhoona £3.50, completely tasteless, absolutely no hint of spicing. Dry Mixed Vegetables – similarly lacking in flavour. Chicken Patia £3.95, fairly tasty, but not hot. Prices were reasonable, portion very small. Service pleasant, but slow.'* MW. Hours: 6-11. Sunday 7-10.30.

Strood

SHOZNA INDIAN CUISINE 

28 High Street, Strood 01634 710701

Established in 1978. Taken over by J Ahmed in 1996. Seats 38. Parking at rear for 50 cars. Chef Jamal Uddin Ahmed was the 2003 runner-up winner of the Curry Chef of the Year contest run by the CIEH, (Health officer's institute) and the food is good. *'Does not look much from the outside, inside pleasantly cosy. Relatively small, seating 48. Custom made furniture, all good quality. Started with my benchmark – Onion Bhajia. Four, small, round, plenty of onion, crisp outside, moist inside, excellent. Bhari Kebab – small pieces of kebab, spicy, rich sauce, extremely tasty, first class. Long debate over mains, chose Badami Chicken – delicious full bodied sauce, chopped cashew nuts, slightly herby. Dhansak – included Pullao Rice, well spiced lentil sauce. Smart, clean toilets. Portions just right, prices average. The car park is behind the restaurant, up a small alleyway, easy to miss. An excellent little restaurant, packed on a Thursday night.'* MW. Menu Extracts: Monchorian Chicken £5.70 – chicken fillet, mango, cream. Naga Lamb £5.70 – garnished with Naga chillies. Naga chillies are incendiary – so be warned! Takeaway: 10-15% discount. Hours: 12-1.30/5.30-12am.

Swanley

RAJ OF INDIA 

23-25 High Street, Swanley 01322 613651

'Popped into the Raj of India, on mentioning The Curry Club and the possibility of a discount (I always ask - even if it not shown in the Guide), the proprietor for some ungodly reason took to me and said I could have a free drink. Started with two Poppadoms, pickles and surprise, surprise they actually asked me if I would like pickles with my main course! wonders will never cease!! Very good and hot Chicken Vindaloo, Pullao Rice and Nan Bread - excellent meal, just right.' BP-D. Menu extracts: Noorani Kebab £2.90, minced chicken, coriander, onion and green chilli. Aliza Chicken £3.50, deep-fried chicken pieces in chick pea flour.

Other members take note of Bill's persistence in getting his discount. Branch: Raj Bari, Sevenoaks, Kent and Alishan, Tonbridge, Kent.

GINGER GARDEN NEW ENTRANT

49 Grosvenor Rd, Tunbridge Wells 01892 616742

'As we suggested, they put pictures up on the walls to make it more cosy.' RL. *'Perhaps one of the best of a dozen or so indifferent restaurants in this town of 75,000 souls. Everything about this place was spotless and tastefully decorated. A smallish restaurant (48 covers) and seemingly ardent Curry Club fans. I got 10% discount from whole bill* '[Well done, Bill] *'and without previously having booked. Food well cooked and plenty of it, good quality. My son, Nigel and I ate four Poppadoms, two Onion Bhajis £1.85, Chicken Tikka Jalfrezi £6.50, two Pullao Rice and a Naan, Mushroom Bhajee £2.50, Lamb Dhansak £5.10 with two pints of Draught King Fisher – The whole Bill inc discount £28.80.* BP-D. Hours: 12-2.30 / 6-11.30.

MUNA'S RESTAURANT & BAR 

70 High Street, Tunbridge Wells 01892 537113

Established in 1996. Seats 38. Modern design, black and chrome. Punjabi curries – à la carte and buffet is available every evening. À la Carte – Deluxe Grill £11.95 – assortment of lamb and chicken tikka, kebab and prawns, served with potato salad and rice. Naan Toppers – warm nans topped with: Chicken Tikka Masala £7.50, Tandoori Prawn Masala £8.50, Lamb Boti £7.50. Buffet £13.95 – e-a-m-a-y-l from Poppadams with Chutney and Raitha, Vegetable Pakoras, Spicy Savoy Cabbage Stir-fry, Aubergine Masala, Fried Okra and Onion in Chickpea Batter, Indian Salad in lemon and mint Dressing, Hot Stuffed Red Pickled Chillies and that's just for starters! Buffet main courses include: Lamb Rhogan Ghost, Chicken Bhoona, Vegetable Balti, Saag Aloo, Tarka Dal with Rice and Bread, tremendous value. Hours: 12-2 / 6-11; Sun. closed.

Welling GL

TAGORE TOP 100 ©

3 High Street, Welling 020 8304 0433

Nur Monie's 40-seater is decorated with swathes of silk on the ceiling and pleated saris on the walls. Bombay-trained chef Rajendra Balmiki cooks Northern Indian curries and specials from Pakhtoomn, assisted by head waiter Tapesh Majumber. This refers to the Pathan tribal people of Afghanistan and the rugged Pakistani passes, whose name for themselves is Phuktana or Pukhtun. Afghan food is pretty basic (see page 37), especially at tribal level, involving kebab-skewer cooking and slow-cooking in pots. This is translated at The Tagore into a select menu. Kebab Ke Karishma, a selection of kebabs £16 for two, is popular). Main dishes are divided between six chicken dishes, five meat, six from the tandoor and three fish dishes. At £6, Patrani Mahi, pomfret coated in herbal chutney, leaf-wrapped and baked, is a rarity to be treasured. Murgh Chennai, £5, is none other than Chicken Madras, and Koh-e-Avadh, £5.50, is lamb knuckles simmered in the dum method. Raan E Buzkazi, leg of lamb from the NW Frontier £19.50. The fact that it's not formula leads to adverse comment: ' DW. Others like it: *'On all occasions I have found their food to be a world apart from the traditional curry houses with the dishes being expertly cooked. Excellent value for money, service and explanation of the dishes is of a very high quality.'* PG. Takeaway 20%discount. Hours: 8-11pm. Branch: Kasturi, London EC1.

West Kingsdown

RAJDANI NEW ENTRANT

17, London Rd, West Kingsdown 01474 853501

Proprietor Suna Meah. Visited for dinner. Ate plain pops with chutney tray. Onion Bhajia, Chicken Aliza (chicken pakora), Tandoori Prawn, Chicken Chat in puri with plenty of crispy salad main course, huge tandoori king prawns in a cashew nut korma sauce, chicken with cashew nut sauce – delicious chicken tava – spicy but not hot. Plain Nan – light, fluffy – all breads that came out of the kitchen were really good. Red rose on leaving; good sized car parking; two ponds; a little decking-style bridge to cross over the ponds. Separate area for takeaway. We were introduced to a couple who dine here six days every week, and on the seventh, they visit other Indian restaurants. There's loyalty. *See overleaf.*

©	Curry Club Discount	U	Unlicensed
V	Vegetarian	ANP	Alcohol not permitted
e-a-m-a-y-l	Eat as much as you like	BYO	Bring your own alcohol

West Wickham

BLUE GINGER

101 High Street, West Wickham 020 8777 4080

'Attractive, not as minimalist and basic as some new wave establishments. Staff, welcoming, knew what they were doing. Pops with good chutney in an unusual container. Aloo Bora, particularly good and flavoursome. Spicy Bindi, hot and crispy. We'll be back.' G&CM. Takeaway: 10% discount. Banquet Night: Wednesday £9.95. Sunday lunch buffet £7.95.

Westerham

RHONDAN AT PITTS COTTAGE

TOP 100

High Street (Limpsfield Road), Westerham
01959 562125

Established in 1995. Taken over by Sujit Dey in 1997. Own car park opposite, for 80 cars. 200 seats in four separate rooms in a 700-year-old listed cottage, once the home of William Pitt. Upstairs toilets. *'If you do nothing else this year visit here'.* CRC. *'Very pretty and does consistently good curries.'* KT. *'An interesting menu – a few of the familiar dishes, but plenty of more unusual ones. Tandoori Trout has nicely moist flesh although most of the flavour was in the crisp skin. Delicious Aloo Tikki, Mixed Vegetable Bhaji nicely flavoured. Generous portions. As one might expect, prices slightly higher than average. Service excellent. well above average.'* MW. Twelfth-century cottage famed for its old-world charm and tranquillity. Specials include: Prawn Massala Puree, Tandoori Trout, Mutton Cutlet, Papaya Ghosht, Rajenya (King prawns with onion and potato). *'First impression is fabulous. Pitts Cottage is an old historic building, which is a pleasure to enter and is warm and inviting. First class service. Excellent food.'* JH. *'Welcoming staff. Enjoyed their Special Punjabi Menu. Quality and quantity of food excellent, attractively presented. One has the feeling that client satisfaction is important– more than just making money!'* M&DS. *'Excellent– excellent– excellent.'* SR. *'Coming from Bangladesh, one may imagine I would be tired of the spicy Indian type food– however Pitt's Cottage is one place I truly enjoy spending time and money at.'* MR B. . *'Perfect settings and atmosphere. Fantastic food with flavours to remember. Exceptional!'* MR & MRS D. *'Having spent several months in India, find it the most authentic restaurant around. Punjabi Menu a triumph! Methi Paratha– exquisite. New staff from Calcutta add an extra dimension.'* PDM. . *'Worth going out of your way for.'* pga.. *'Fabulous first impression, pleasure to enter, warm and inviting. First class service. Varied main menu. Definitely worth a visit!'* IH. Takeaway: 10% discount. Hours: 12-2.30/6-11.30.

TULSI

20 London Road, Westerham 01959 563397

Tulsi (biological name *Ocimum sanctum*), is the sacred basil plant of India, where it is grown as a symbol of good luck and good health. Owned by AK Deb, it has a small waiting area with tables and chairs, and an extended, slightly elevated, well-decorated eating area, with a polished wooden floor. Walls covered by framed posters of Bollywood film stars. Ambience is good with very friendly staff, well-dressed in national costume. Chef Anil K Hazra cooks wonderfully innovative Indian cuisine – just how we like it and many others agree... *'Have been coming for seven years and every occasion the food has been excellent. Perfect in every way.'* MR&MRS W. *'Exceptional.'* MO. *'Delicious, consistently excellent. The best we know.'* LBP. In fact we have numerous reports, so why have we delisted Tulsi from our **TOP 100.** Read on. *'Under same ownership of the very excellent Tamasha, Bromley, is sufficient recommendation. Were greeted by the diminutive manager and ushered past small bar and comfortable waiting area to table. Polished wooden floors, slowly revolving ceiling fans, brass Indian figures in the corners and plain emulsion walls covered with pictures of Indian film stars and scenes gave an air of elegance. Two attentive waiters unrolled napkins, made sure we were comfortable. Appealing menu. Chicken Tikka Nilgiri £3.95, four succulent, very tasty pieces, marinated in green coriander base. Aloo Channa and Palek Kebab £3.50, two potato, chick pea, spinach pattie, deep-fried, served with sauce, crisp salad. Both excellent. Chicken Manchoori £7.50, plenty of chicken, good flavoured sauce, lovely little green chillies – excellent. Raan Jai Puri £8.50, sliced roast beef, sauce poured over – disappointing. Tarka Mila Juli – first class, large pieces of vegetables, lightly cooked, very tangy sauce. Browned tarka on Pullao Rice gave very attractive appearance. Glistening ghee brushed Peshwari Nan £2.25, lightly cooked, no raisins. Prices above average, portions quite sufficient. Service excellent, 10% added to bill, left blank open on credit card. This greediness irritates me.'* MW. Because of this open credit card slip business, as with Bengal Mangrove, Halstead, Kent, we have delisted Tulsi from our **TOP 100**. Hours: 12-2.30 (closed Sun. lunch)/6-11.30. Branch: Tamasha, Bromley.

LANCASHIRE

Area: North West
Population: 1,434,000
Adjacent Counties: Cumbs, Greater Man, Mers, N Yorks, W Yorks

Adlington

SHAPLA TAKEAWAY ©

178 Chorley Road, Adlington 01257 474630

Est. 1992 by Shiraz Ali (manager) and MD Rahmin Ullaj (chef). *'Addiction from an early age, satisfied on my doorstep.'* AL. *'A wide range of excellent food.'* AH. Hours: Sun.-Thurs. 4-12.

SHARJU TOP 100

Church Street, Adlington 01257 481894

Managed by BB Choudhury, this is an old favourite of our *Guide*, and of its loyal following. *'Congregation'* may be a more appropriate word because this was surely the first restaurant to occupy a former church. And, yes, they've heard all the gags: from Vestry Vindaloo, RC Roghan, Baptistry Biriani, C of E Tikka to *'will they be serving papadoms with communion wine?'* Now owned by Mithu Dhar, the opportunity was taken in 1984 to convert this building to its now ideal use. In fact, it is not a large room, in clerical terms, but it has made for a large number of seats in restaurant terms. Reached by an imposing staircase, the plum seats are on the balcony, which extends around the remaining three sides of the room. From here one has a view of downstairs diners. DB says: *'It has bags of atmosphere, with its oak beams and strategically placed Indian artefacts. Back to dining on my own again. Lovely restaurant, converted from old church. Friendly and attentive service. Chicken Tikka Biryani – nicely presented ring of rice, wonderful aromas. Chicken subtly spiced, cut into small pieces, relatively good portion, thin Madras sauce. Not cheap, but treat yourself...' quality is never cheap! ...reports will slow down a bit now. I have been back at work and eating two curries a week has caused the weight to jump one and a half stone!' db. You were back five weeks later. 'Back to lunch time dining even though I promised her who doesn't eat curry that I'd lose weight. What she doesn't know can't hurt me...' David, I think the bathroom scales might give you away! '...nice and fresh Popadoms with excellent chutneys. Chicken Tikka – good portion, served on sizzler, naturally coloured, no lurid red, very subtle flavour. Pullao Rice – flavoured with aniseed, a new trend? They prepare dishes with superb individual flavours which require a retraining of the taste buds.'* DB. Chef Faruk Ali's signature dishes, Chicken Shagorika and Lashuni Chicken Flambé, both with rice. The former is tikka pieces twice-cooked in a very spicy sauce with peas, the latter consists of a tandooried long fillet of chicken breast, which is flambéed in brandy, in a creamy garlicky sauce at your table. e-a-m-a-y-l Sunday lunch, 12-4.30, £10, kids (under 10) £5. Thursday evenings for the Candlelight Dinner. Hours: 12-2/6-11. Fri/Sat 5.30-12. Branch: Shanti, 466 Bromley Rd, Bromley, Kent. Remains in our **TOP 100.**

Blackburn

SHAJAN 

Longsight Road, Clayton-le-Dale, Mellor, Blackburn 01254 813640

Mohammad Ali Shaju's 144-seater is easily found on the A59. Its resemblance to a residential bungalow ceases on entry. It is stylishly decorated with cream walls, ceiling and table linen, blue carpet, and 144 wicker chairs, in two dining rooms. Wooden fretwork screens give tables privacy. *'Modern, out of town restaurant, conservatory. Arrived at 6.45pm, as the large car park was filling up. A few moments wait before being ushered into conservatory, restaurant already full. Couldn't fault any of the dishes. Despite being busy, service was good, but indifferent. Not pressurised to leave, however it was all hands to the pump to get the table changed for the next sitting. We will return with our caravan, there is a site next door.'* T&MH. Takeaway: 20% discount. Hours: 12-2 / 5.30-11.30. (12am on Fri. & Sat.). Sunday 1-11.

Blackpool

BOMBAY 

227 Dickson Road, Blackpool 01253 296144

Askor Ali's dusky pink restaurant seats 30. *'The Chilli Masala is just fabulous'* RT. For delivery, you pay for the taxi!!! Hours: 12-2/6-12. (Fri. & Sat. to 1am).

Burnley

SHALAMAR 

56 Church Street, Burnley 01282 434403

'Service good – not pushy. Food presented well, portions ample, but not generous. Karahi Lamb and Chicken Bhuna – excellent with delicious side dishes of Tarka Dhal & Aloo Palak. Definitely revisit.' AC.

Chorley

BLUE ELEPHANT NEW ENTRANT

Dauwbeers Lane, Chorley 01257 451155

Under same ownership as Veena, Chorley. *'Was shabby, run-down country pub, now fabulous, attractive, Indian restaurant, with night club. Led to a table set with fresh linen and even fresher Popadoms with delicious Pickles. All food of superb quality and portions family sized, excellent value for money. Pullao Rice, fragrant, delicious Sag Aloo, the Garlic and Peshwari Nans were succulent.'* AE. Takeaway: 10% discount. Hours: 12-2/5.30-11, Saturday and Sunday 1-1.

Clitheroe

DIL RAJ 

7-9 Parsons Lane, Clitheroe 01200 427224

Seats 48, owned by Mr Raj. Set dinner £14 each, four people share. Papadams, Tandoori Chicken, Lamb and Chicken Tikka, Sheek Kebab starters, Beef Roghan Josh, Karahi Gosht, Mogulai Chicken, CTM, Vegetable Pullao, Raita, pickles and chutney, followed by desserts and coffee. 10% off takeaways. Hours: 5-12.30. Sun. 12-12.

Fleetwood

AL MINAR 

26 Larkholme Parade, Fleetwood 01253 777787

Opened 1996. Three rooms with parking for 30 to 40 cars out front. Banquets on Wednesday nights. Delivery: £7 minimum, 4-mile radius. Hours: 5-12.

Haslingden

SUNAR GAW 

16 Regent Street, Haslingden 01204 364915

Owner-manager NA Malik and owner-chef A Quddus share ownership and roles at this popular 1987, evenings-only restaurant. RK says: *'The Kyber Murghi Maladari – chicken cooked with ginger, green chilli, onion, garlic and coriander – was out of this world.'*

Lancaster

ASHIANA NEW ENTRANT

Fleetwood Rd, Greenhalgh, Nr Kirkham 01253 836187

'Celebrated my 40th birthday here, some time ago. An excellent and memorable experience. Their blue lit gables stood out like a guiding beacon in torrential rain. Warm reception, cold lager, tastefully decorated with red leather seats, pink and cream decor, Indian pictures and brassware. Popadoms and Pickles were followed by lean and crisp Meat Samosas, large and crisp Onion

Bhajia and salad. Lamb Bhuna and Chicken Tikka Dopiaza both nicely spiced served with Pullao Rice, Sag Aloo, Nan and a platter of chips (why not!)...' [why?] *'...Excellent value for money.'* AE. I notice Bombay Duck on the menu. Hours: 12-2/6-12, Sunday 12-12.

BOMBAY ©

16 Jubilee House, China Street, Lancaster 01524 844550

Askor Ali's his 70-seater serves chef Babul Ahmed's curries.Takeaway 20% discount. Hours: 12-/6-12.

Lytham St Annes

MOGHUL ©

12 Orchard Road, St Annes 01253 712114

M Liaquat Ali owns and presides over a very sunny, friendly 60-seat restaurant, which is a good standard curry house. We hear well of the Keema Patila, a tasty mince curry, which one couple enjoy for takeaway and they also like the special box provided. *'Lamb Rogan Josh was delicious. I enjoyed every last bite.'* MB.

Rawtenstall

SAMRAT 

13 Bacup Road, Rawtenstall 01706 216183

Alkas Ali is owner-chef here, and he's proud of his cooking – so proud, in fact, that you can ring him on his mobile on 0973 328426 and he'll explain about his dishes. A unique service, we believe. *'Most fabulous night out we have had and food absolutely gorgeous. Reasonably priced.'* SH. Hours: 5-12.

ASHOKA

255 Bacup Road, Rawtenstall 01706 231665

'An amazing find in that slightly run down area. Smart and elegant, air-conditioned, beautifully decorated with taste and style. Exceptionally welcoming and gracious staff, a comfortable atmosphere. Good, well spiced food, served in ample quantities. Plus factor the waiters don't stand over you, filling up glasses after every sip. We were left in peace to sample Liver Bhajia, Lamb Chops, Specials of Fish and Aubergine, rice and Aloo Methi. We'll definitely return on our next trip north.' G&CM. Takeaway: 20% discount. Hours: Monday to Thursday 5-11.30, Friday 3.30-12. Saturday 12-12, Sunday 3- 11.30.

LEICESTERSHIRE

Area: East Midlands
Population: 945,000
Adjacent Counties: Derbs, Lincs, Northants, Notts, Rutland, Staffs, Warks

Broughton Astley

BENGAL PALACE 

1 Green Road, Broughton Astley 01455 282280

Mohibur Rahman's venue seats 48, with spaces for 15 cars opposite. Old cottage-style restaurant. Specials include: Chicken Jaflong (marinated chicken on the bone, with minced meat garnish with various green herbs). Hours: 6-12; Sat. 6-1AM.

Leicester

Leicester is home to a good number of Gujaratis from India. In addition, many of its Asian community settled there in the 1970s when they became exiled from Africa, specifically Kenya and Uganda, where they had lived for generations, having been taken there as clerks and semi-skilled plantation labour by the British. Most contemporary Leicester Asians have little concept of the Indian subcontinent, few having ever visited it, but you would not know this from the quality of the food, particularly in the cheap and cheerful cafés, snack bars and sweet shops all over town. The first curry house, the Taj Mahal, opened in 1961 and is still there! I dined there that year, and when I asked for chilli pickle the anxious owner appeared and spent half an hour counselling me against eating hot food! (To no avail, I might add!) Now there are over 80 'Indian' restaurants on our database which, in a city of around 300,000 population, is a ratio of one 'Indian' restaurant per 3,750 people, making Leicester our second most densely curry-housed city in the UK (see Bradford, West Yorkshire). However, over a two week visit period, we found Leicester's restaurants, Indian and otherwise, to be virtually empty on weekday evenings. The City simply closes at around 6pm. What a terrible waste. We were also surprised to find that Leicester council do not allow pavement trading, so vital to the charisma of London's Asian communities. They say vegetables on the street is a health hazard!

©	Curry Club Discount	U	Unlicensed
V	Vegetarian	ANP	Alcohol not permitted
e-a-m-a-y-l	Eat as much as you like	BYO	Bring your own alcohol

Get real Leicester, and get using your restaurants, before they close on you. Oh and yes, if you choose to have a go at me about this, your comments will be published here next time.

AKASH — NEW ENTRANT

159 London Road, Leicester 0116 255 9030

'Very popular with student population. Nicely decorated with pleasant atmosphere. Highly efficient waiters, the place is perpetually busy. Real tablecloths. Bhuna Prawn Puri £2.95, good, plenty of well textured, delicately flavoured prawns, served in a deliciously tangy, slightly crunchy sauce, served with grease free bread. Lamb Biriani £4.95, good cuts of meat, fat and gristle free. Tarka Dal £1.90, pleasant but a little oily. Friday and Saturday nights are to be avoided if you are a shrinking violet!' RW. Business Lunch: £3.75 Licensed. Credit cards accepted. Delivery: £10 minimum, 6 miles. Takeaway: 15% discount. Minimum charge: £7. Hours: 12-2 and 4.30-11.

BOBBY'S GUJARATI VEGETARIAN — V

154 Belgrave Road, Leicester 0116 266 2448

Atul Lakhani (aka Bobby) owns a restaurant with two advantages – a license and very reasonably priced food, so it's ever-popular with a cafeteria-type atmosphere. Mostly Gujarati food, which is light and slightly sweet. You pay (credit cards at last taken) at the till. Hours: 11-10.30.

CURRY FEVER — AWARD WINNER 

139 Belgrave Road, Leicester 0116 266 2941

Established in 1978 by Anil Anand (head chef) and Sunil Anand (manager). They are related to the Brilliant and Madhu's Brilliant of Southall and Curry Craze of Wembley (*see* entries in Middlesex). The food is Punjabi, cooked just as they eat them at home. House specialities, which show the owners' Kenyan background, include: Jeera Chicken, Butter Chicken and Pili-Pili Chicken. A yellow sign board stands out on the pavement, among other restaurants, sari shops and a lot of large, expensive-looking jewellers. The restaurant is painted in a pale, pretty pink, the bar is towards the back, tables with comfortable chairs are politely spaced, green carpet and chandeliers finish off the scene. Light, crisp and warm plain Popadoms were served with a tray of puréed mango chutney and finely chopped mint and onion chutney – very good and a nice change from the normal selection. Our waiter served us with a large bowl of their Special Salad, a combination of cubed tomato, cucumber and onion with sprinklings of chopped coriander leaves, stubs of green chilli and hot chilli powder. We ordered for starters a portion of their famous Jeera Chicken (half). An absolute must when eating Punjabi cuisine. This is served on the bone, giving so much more flavour, but it can be rather a messy business if using your hands, though Pat and I don't care about that, so hands it was. Anil had added plenty of black pepper to the butter and jeera, making it quite delicious. Sunil recommended we follow with their Piri Piri Chicken – it was not as hot as we were expecting, but spicy never the less and Methi Lamb, cubes of succulent and tender lamb wrapped in a pungent herby spinach sauce. To accompany our main courses we ordered Maharani Dhal, aromatic, creamy, black urid dhal, Pullao Rice, not brightly coloured but natural with whole spices and peas, Nan Bread, buttery and light, sliced in half and (Anil's surprise) a fabulous Kulchay £1.40, a puri made of nan bread dough, absolutely delicious, crisp, light and not at all greasy which is surprising since it had been deep-fried. Everybody must try one – I insist! We drank a bottle of house red, which was very acceptable. While we were eating, Sunil chatted to us about business and Anil joined in when he wasn't in the kitchen conjuring up his next master-piece. A very satisfying evening to end a busy day. 10% discount on takeaways. Delivery: £50 minimum. Hours: 12-2.30 (Sun. lunch closed)/6-11.30 (midnight on Fri. & Sat.); Mon. closed all day except bank holidays. Last time we gave it our **BEST IN THE MIDLANDS** Award. Though this time the award has moved eleswhere, it is an award which lasts for ever. Curry Fever remains outstanding, and we commend you to try it.

FRIENDS TANDOORI — TOP 100 ©

41 Belgrave Road, Leicester 0116 266 8809

The restaurant is on a corner site, smokey glass windows and huge crystal chandelier. Its

©	Curry Club Discount	U	Unlicensed
V	Vegetarian	ANP	Alcohol not permitted
e-a-m-a-y-l	Eat as much as you like	BYO	Bring your own alcohol

cleanliness is quite superior – there is not a spot of dust or dirt anywhere (and that includes the toilets). We started with crispy, light Papadams served with two chutneys – both green, herby, minty, yoghurty – lovely, we kept these on the table. Onion Bhajia and Vegetable Samosa – not the usual triangle-shaped version, but shaped rather like a pyramid, reminiscent of the samosas that I am served in India and Bangladesh. Both were served in threes with a fresh mixed salad including lemon wedges – very tasty, we ate the lot! Main courses: Tandoori Mixed Grill – served on a sizzling dish, large prawn, chicken leg, lamb and chicken tikka and a Sheek kebab, what a portion! Chicken Tikka £6.75 – generous chicken, not the overly red marinade which is so prevalent in the south of England, succulent and I ate most of it. Stays in our **TOP 100.**

KABALOU'S

23-25 Loughborough Road, Leicester
0116 268 2626

Kabalou's is an hotel and Indian restaurant residing in a very imposing building, painted in buttermilk yellow. There is parking by the side of the restaurant in a private courtyard. Creating Kabalou's took an alleged £1.8 million. The interior of the restaurant is absolutely amazing, an incredible amount of money has been spent and the overall effect is spectacular. A mirror ball, in the centre of the restaurant, sprays sparkling light over the diners – sounds irritating? It wasn't. The head waiter, Joe (who thinks quite a lot of himself), is quite a performer; he specialises in silver service which is quite showy, when done correctly. We nibbled on crisp light Papadams, with cachumber, mint yoghurt – very good, mango chutney puree and a mixed pickle, not your average pickle, authentic and hand-made. We followed this by Chicken Tikka, not the usual bright orange/red colour, more natural and tasty, Jeera Chicken, good pieces of chicken in a light spicy sauce both accompanied by fresh salad and served sizzling from the trolley. Jeera Chicken is actually a Punjabi dish (*see* Curry Fever, Leicester). For our main courses we chose King Prawn Chilli Chilli, large prawns and plenty of sliced green chillies, and Chicken Butter Masala, this dish is very similar to CTM but much nicer with Brinjal Bhaji, not particularly smoky which I like, bulked by onions and tomatoes which I don't. Pullao Rice, basmati, good aroma and Nan Bread, brought to the table sliced in half, very light, butter ghee taste. A very enjoyable meal in extraordinary surroundings and not as expensive as you might expect at £40.45 inc. the wine. We asked to see the hotel rooms and can report that they are very nicely appointed and clean. Before we left we sat in the bar with the manager, Harshad and his wife, Indira and chatted, over an Armenac. A lovely evening and great establishment for a celebration.

MONSOON ©

194 Evington Road, Leicester 0116 273 9444

Established in 1995 by Mokhtar Hussain and Monrul Huda. A pretty, formula curry house, seating 40. Blue hand-printed curtains with white elephants hang at the large plate-glass windows, comfortable rounded wooden chairs, square and round tables (I prefer round tables). Some unusual items. Halim (*sic.*) soup is a meat- and lentil-based spicy broth, Haash Masala is half a duck on the bone, marinated and deep-fried, and Roup Chanda Bhaza is Bangladeshi fish, marinated and pan-fried. With 24 hours' notice and a deposit, you can have Shagorana (£35), a feast for two, with, amongst other things, mussels, crab, lobster and Bangladeshi vegetables. Takeaway: 10% discount. Delivery: £10 minimum, 4-mile radius. Hours: 12-2/6-11.30; closed Mon.

NAMASTE 

65 Hinckley Road, Leicester 0116 254 1778

Proprietors Dwssendra Kumar Dey (manager) and Rakhal Paul (chef) opened in April 1994, serving formula curries in a restaurant seating 52 diners. Balti Mixed is the most popular dish ordered. Minimum charge £9.50. Sunday buffet lunch £5.95. Tuesday and Wednesday £8 e-a-m-a-y-l dinner. Hours: 12-2/5.30-11.

SAYONARA THALI V

49 Belgrave Road, Leicester 0116 266 5888

Pure vegetarian Gujarati restaurant owned by S and V Pandya. *'We visited on Tuesday for an early dinner, two other tables occupied, but the venue soon filled completely, with mainly-Asian clientèle of all ages. The 63-seat restaurant is quite small, clean and smart. The main attractions were the license and the Gujarati food. Our waiter welcomed us and showed us to a table. He didn't smile but wasn't grumpy, I think shy and perhaps a little fed-up (he waitered to an almost full restaurant single-handed). We ordered plain Papadams, crispy and light with chutneys. Bhel Puri, good portion (too sweet for me, though this is a typical Gujarati trait) – a combination of mamra (puffed rice), potato, onion and tamarind with a dollop of green herby chutney on top. Dahi Puri, crispy puri topped with potato, onion, tamarind and plain yoghurt – not so sweet, good portion. We followed these with Masala Dosa £3.95 – large, light, crispy dosa, filled with mashed potato and onion, flavoured with seeds. No turmeric or curry leaves normally associated with the South Indian Dosa. These were served with Sambar again a Gujarati version, no drumsticks (which I adore) but had a good flavour and contained a sprinkling of desiccated coconut, could have been a little thicker. Coconut Chutney, a thick sauce of coconut and yoghurt, lightly spiced. We drank glasses of Perrier water from very large brightly coloured plastic sundae glasses (bizarre) with a bottle of red wine. Amazing value at £25.55.'* DBAC. Brigette at local Pukka Pies thinks this restaurant is great, she orders the Thali, because *'you never know what you're going to get!'* (and the portions are huge). Hours: 12-9.30pm (Sat. to 10pm).

SHARMILEE VEGETARIAN V © 10%

71-73 Belgrave Road, Leicester 0116 261 0503

Opened way back in 1973 by Gosai brothers (manager, LK Goswami), this is a two-part venue. The sweet mart serves a rich assortments of Indian sweets, and such delightful items as Vegetable Samosas, Pakoras and Dahi Vadia, from 9.30am-9pm daily, except Mondays. The licensed restaurant is upmarket and vegetarian, decorated with marble pillars in shades of brown and dusky blue marble-effect walls, high-backed black chairs, white table linen. Tasty starters of Pani Puri, crispy puris served with spicy sauce, chickpeas and onion. Chanabateta, chickpeas and potatoes in a tamarind sauce garnished with onions. South Indian specialities: Masala Dosa, thin crispy pancake filled with potato and onion, Idli Sambhar, flat pulse balls, both served with Sambhar and coconut chutney. *'Elegantly simple surroundings, food delicately flavoured, and best recommendation of all, 50% of clientèle were Asian. Food was beautifully cooked and incredibly cheap (Navratan Kofta, Jeera Rice, Handi Birianee, Naan and drinks for just over £12). Decor was simple, bright and cheery and the service was pleasant. The clientele comprised of mainly Asian family parties which made the atmosphere very pleasant and relaxed. My wife and I wholeheartedly recommend visiting this restaurant.'* P&SM. Takeaway 10% discount. Minimum charge £4.95. Hours: 12-2.30/6-9.30, Sat. 12-9; closed Mon. except bank holidays. 10% discount to Cury Club Members.

LINCOLNSHIRE

Area: East
Population: 630,000
Adjacent Counties:
Cambs, Leics,
Norfolk, Notts,
E & S Yorks

Boston

ROSE OF BENGAL ©

67 West Street, Boston 01205 363355

Established in 1996, taken over by Mr M Jay in 1998. Seats 58. Car parking for 10 cars to the rear. Specials include: Shashk Korai. Takeaway: 10% discount. Delivery: £10 minimum, 7-mile radius. Hours: 12-2/5.30-12.

STAR OF INDIA TOP 100

110 West Street, Boston 01205 360558

Owned by Tanvir Hussain. Air conditioning and completely redecorated in 1997, seating increased from 52 to 76 diners, serving Pakistani formula curries with traditional accompaniments. *'Very pleasant decor, typical Indian restaurant style enhanced by large numbers of cotton flowers. Service attentive but not intrusive. Balti Chicken was quite delicious. Keema Nan was piping hot and filled with ample quantity of minced meat. Highly recommended.'* MS-R. *'Best-ever Tandoori Chicken starter followed by superb Dhansak.'* AG. It continues to get plentiful one-liners of satisfaction. *'We have been to Indian restaurants all over the country and we have not come across anywhere which beats it for great food, friendliness and cleanliness. We hope to be going there every Friday for the next 18 years.'* PDEP. Minimum charge: £5. Takeaway 10% discount.Hours: 12-2.30/6-12. Branches (both takeaways): Chilli Master, 2 Red Lion St, Stamford; Chilli Master, 11 Winsover Road, Spalding.

Bourne

SHALIMAR BALTI HOUSE 

8 Abbey Road, Bourne 01778 393959

Co-owners Ali Ashker, Ali Akbar (chef), Ali Arshad and Ali Amjad, told me last time that they have made a lot of new customer friends since they appeared in the Guide, and they really welcome Curry Club members for their discount, so get booking and enjoy all your favourites. Hours 5.30-12 (12.30am on Fri. & Sat.).

Grantham

BOMBAY BRASSERIE 

11 London Road, Grantham 01476 576096

Large 104-seater in the town centre. Well-spaced tables achieving intimacy in a large restaurant. Festoons of red silk and satin hang from the ceiling, blue and pink chintz curtains hang by an arch dividing the dining room. Pink and white table linen, air-conditioned. *'Acknowledged as the best in the area. Wide ranging menu. I recommend the Shahi mix, a generous dish of tandoori meats in a medium sauce with plenty of herbs. Friendly and efficient staff.'* RW. *'One of the best restaurants in the area. Offers a 10% discount to Curry Club members. Boti Kebab, Chicken Chaat, Murghi Jalfrezi, all very tasty. Waiters all polite.'* IW. Hours: 5.30-12, 1am on Sat.

Grimsby

SPICE OF LIFE 

8-12 Wellowgate, Grimsby 01472 357476

A perfectly satisfactory curryhouse, established in 1999 and seating 100. Delivery: 3-mile radius. Hours: 12-2/6 -12.

Lincoln

THE BOMBAY

6 The Strait, Lincoln 01522 523264

Lincoln's oldest curry house, says NTT. *'Onion Bhajia, Vegetable Korma, Vegetable Rice, Stuffed Paratha. All very delicious.'* NT. Serves Pullao Rice, Curry Sauce and Salad with all Tandoori main dishes. Licensed. Takeaway: 20% discount. Menu Extracts: Chicken or Lamb Bangalore (extremely hot) £5.95. Egg Biryani (with Curry Sauce) £5.45. 20% takeaways discount. Lunch and dinner, daily.

MAHARAJAH NEW ENTRANT

Newark Road, Auborn, Lincoln 01522 681160

'Aloo Paratha and Paratha very tasty. Lemon Rice refreshing.' NT. Licensed. Credit cards accepted. Takeaway: 15% discount.

MALABAR JUNCTION AT BARBICAN HOTEL NEW ENTRANT

11 St Mary's Street, Lincoln 01522 522277

Malabar is in the South of India. It is a mistake to think that the majority of people from this region are vegetarians. There are, of course, many people who do not eat meat, however, there are many who do. This style of food is quite different from 'curryhouse', but is really delicious. (*See page 51*), *'The meal was delicious, including Vegetable Korma, Lemon Rice, Mushroom Rice, Coconut Rice.'* NT. Menu Extracts: Ghee Roast Masala £6, crispy pancake roasted in purified butter, filled with potato masala, served with sambar and chutney; Spinach Vada £3.50, fried doughnut made of split black gram batter, ginger, onions, green chilli, curry leaves, cumin soaked in seasoned and tempered yoghurt; Minced Lamb Cutlets £3.50, patties coated with breadcrumbs, served with tomato sauce and salad; Cashew Nut Pakora £2.50, cashewnuts dipped in spicy batter and fried; Lamb Chilli Fry £6.50, stir-fried lamb, mustard, red chilli, curry leaves, ginger, garlic, onion, tomato, garam masala and coriander leaves; Konju Kanava Masala £7, shrimps and squids cooked in thick gravy, flavoured with kokum. *'Yum yum!'* NT.

PASSAGE TO INDIA — NEW ENTRANT

435 High Street, Lincoln — 01522 526166

'To celebrate Valentines Day, I had a takeaway. Stuffed Paratha, actually tasted more delicious than Plain Paratha, which was small and thin. Vegetable Curry, Rice and Bindi and Brinjal Bhajee on the small side, but so was the bill.' NT. *Licensed. Set menus are are all excellent value, from £10.50 for one, you get a good three course meal.'* NT. Delivery: £10 minimum, 3 miles. Takeaway: 10% discount. Hours: 6-12.30, Friday and Saturday to 1. Sunday 12-2.

Stamford

RAJ OF INDIA ©

2 All Saints Street, Stamford — 01780 753556

Rohom Ali's well established (1982) 84-seat Raj has promised a 10% discount off the bill for CC Members. *'On being asked by friends to find a good curry house near Peterborough, I opened my trusty bible to the Raj of India. Staff very pleasant. Couldn't fault it. Fifteen of us. Xal Fari very hot but very tasty, good sized portions, lovely surroundings. Another great, successful curry.'* DP. *'Given I didn't have much time, I telephoned ahead and found crisp fresh Papadams waiting at my table for one. Large portion of Pullao Rice, equally big CTM – quite spicy, required a Cloret or two before my afternoon meeting, quite simply the best Mushroom Bhajee I have had, lightly spiced, thinly sliced button mushrooms, garnished with chopped fresh coriander – excellent. Clean and inviting restaurant, well worth its entry in the guide.'* AG. Raj Suite for private parties. 10% discount on takeaway. Hours: 12-3 (except Sun)/6-12, daily.

MANCHESTER (Greater)

Area: North West
Population:2,590,000
Adjacent Counties:
Cheshire, Lancashire,
Merseyside,
Yorkshire

Greater Manchester was introduced as a county in 1965, though this was regarded as an imposition by many of its residents, who still prefer to refer to the counties that Greater Manchester gobbled up, e.g. parts of Lancashire and Cheshire. We have adhered strictly to the official current Greater Manchester territory for town locations in this Guide. The city area is shown in white (below), while the remainder of GM is shown in black

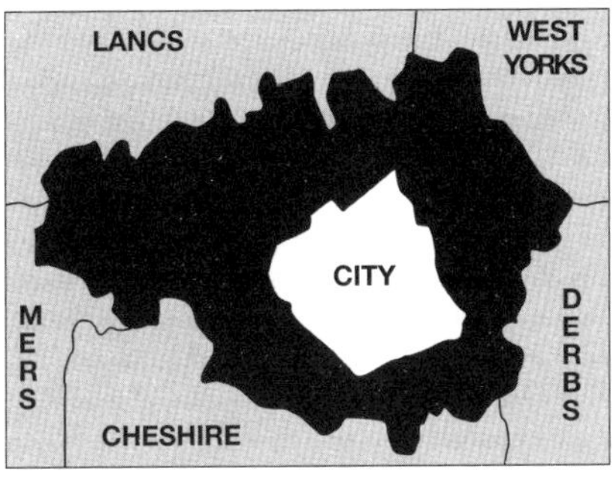

Altrincham

(inc Hale, Halebarns and Timperley)

BARINDA — NEW TO OUR TOP 100

134 Ashley Road, Hale, Nr Altrincham
0161 928 3696

First opened in 1982, taken over by Javed Akhtar in 1998. Seats 70. Standard range of Curries, Tandoori, Karahi and Balti dishes. *'If you are a stranger to an area, you are never sure what a suburb of a major conurbation is like. When I saw 'Hale' in the Guide, I thought that sounds like 'Sale' and is likely to be the same!! What I soon appreciated is, to quote a colleague, that 'Hale is the poncey end of nicey – nicey Altrincham.' Having paid this area a visit, I can see what he means. It is a very designer conscious part of the Cheshire set– loads of restaurants and Mercs and Beamers to match.'* Well Mick, thanks a million. I'll forward the disgusted-of-Hales letters to you. that's Mick Wright of Bedfordshire. MW goes on *'Anyway, I found the Barinda without any difficulty– almost opposite the station on Ashley Road. I started with tandoori Chicken which has real melt in the mouth stuff, and then had bengan Murghi– I love Brinjals in the Asian cuisine, and this was a very good chicken and aubergine dish. I would say on my experience, albeit limited, it should at least be considered for the* **TOP 100'.** MW. OK Mick let's give it a whirl. Takeaway: 10% discount. Delivery: £12 min, 3-mile radi. Hours: 5.30-12.

SHERE KHAN

9 Old Market Place, Altrincham 0161 926 8777

Sister restaurant to the famous Shere Khan in Rusholme. Owned by Rafiq Awan and managed by Saleem Bakir. Located next to the Orange Tree Pub (CAMRA award-winner) in an attractive old town, its reputation has grown – it's busy every night. *'Waiters pounce from all corners, service is excellent. Papadam, perfect with complimentary side salad and the usual pickles. Delicious Chicken Tikka curries, slightly spicier than expected. Breads and Rice very tasty.'* TE. *'Decorated to attract the wine bar set with pale yellow, green pastel colours, fake bamboo chairs. Brusque staff. Plate of Coleslaw, Chutney, Raitha and Onion of indeterminate age on every table, charged 50p regardless whether brave enough to tackle it. Small Papadams, requested fresh tray of Chutneys. Shami Kebab £1.70 – blend of spices, onion, dal and keema bound with egg, tasty if dry, limp salad. Karahi Simla Keema £5.90 – delicious, served sizzling, tamely spiced, quality mince. Garlic Nan £1.60 – very good, plenty of chunks of garlic. Service automatically added to bill.'* RW. Hours: 5-12 (1am on Fri. & Sat).

Ashton-under-Lyne

ASHTON BALTI TAKEAWAY
NEW ENTRY

49 Oldham Road, Ashton 0161 343 6323

Takeaway: only. Their motto: *'Never Hurry a Good Curry!' 'Rather shabby, relies on pub and passing trade. Very good freshly cooked Sheek Kebab - served with small portion of salad and optional extra garlicky yoghurt sauce 4p - lovely. Chef's Special - enjoyable blend of lamb, prawn and chicken with mixed vegetables, packed in microwavable plastic tubs with lids, an improvement over the foil tray and card lid, no hint of leak despite a three mile drive home over what laughably passes for metalled roads in Tameside. Fluffy Pullao Rice - al dente, perfumed.'* RW. Hours: 6-1am, Fri and Sat to 3, closed Tuesday.

INDIAN OCEAN NEW TO TOP 100 ©

83 Stamford Street East, Ashton 0161 343 3343

This is one of those remarkable establishments. It's a perfect curryhouse, the like of which we described at length in the Madhuban, Liss, Hampshire entry. It is the extraordinary level of care which we're talking about. It is a Pakistani curry house owned by Nahim Aslam. Seats 120. Large lounge with regular entertainments which attracts diners to stay and enjoy after dinner drinks with a cigar (there is a smoking menu). House specials: Chicken Chilli Masala – cooked with fresh green chillies. Chicken Chat Masala £5.25 – chicken pieces with chick peas, garnished with roasted cashew nuts. Minimum charge: £8. Buffet £8.95. Delivery: £7.95 minimum, 3-mile radius. Hours: 5pm (Sun. 4pm)-11pm (12am on Fri. & Sat.). *'We are regulars, where the welcome is always warm and friendly. First impressions are good as it is an attractive, clean and well presented restaurant. Good menu, appetising food, served pleasantly. Recommended.'* PR. *'Have had a few parties here and have really been looked after.'* JW. Menu Extracts: Chicken Gorkali £9.95, red and green peppers, whole dried red chillies, tomatoes and Nepalese chilli sauce, spicy, served with Aloo Bhajia. Shahi Machlee £12.95, chunks of salmon, fresh coriander, ginger, garlic and mustard oil, with little green chilli and capsicum, medium spicy taste, served with Kulcha Nan and side salad. Delivery: 3 miles, £10 minimum. Hours: 5-1, Saturday -12, Sunday 1-1. Welcome to our **TOP 100.**

MOSSLEY TANDOOR NEW ENTRY

181 Manchester Road, Mossley, Ashton
01457 834983

Air conditioned. Licensed. *'Small, homely 36 seater on main road with a gene pool that makes some backwaters of Arkansas appear positively cosmopolitan by comparison.'* [are you referring to 'Middle England' Ralph?] *' Single room with booths and open tables, staffed by friendly and efficient waiters. Well but plainly decorated. Good starter - Mixed Kebab £2.95, fluffy bhajia crisp exterior and delicate perfume. Freshly prepared shami, strong spicy taste, good twang of ginger. Well matched sheek kebab, hot, lean and tender. Crisp salad and piquant yoghurt sauce - marvellous. Lamb Tikka Sylhet £6.10, luscious, well balanced packed with gristle free hunks of marinated and barbecued lamb — spicy. Garlic Nan £1.75 - good, light and fluffy, lacking in garlic. When we order a Garlic Nan - we mean GARLIC Nan. Enjoyable.'* RW. Hours: 5-11.30, Fri/Sat -12.

MINA — NEW ENTRY

71 Oldham Road, Ashton 0161 339 1150

Situated opposite Ashton Baths. *'Warm and friendly restaurant. Seats for 40 diners, booths and tables, decoration of the mood lighting and flock wallpaper variety. Very affable staff, complimentary popadom with nice chilled daba of chutneys — onion salad, robust lime pickle, mild, sweet red chutney with hint of aniseed. Excellent starter of Nargis Kebab £3.10, boiled egg wrapped in a moist and pleasantly spiced mince jacket topped with a savoury sauce with a tamarind tang and cool fresh salad. Main dish - Lamb Tikka Biriani £6.50, enjoyable. Better than average place to eat.'* RW. Hours: 6-12.30, Fri/Sat/Sunday 1

MOGHUL CHEF — NEW ENTRY

149 Manchester Road, Mossley, Ashton
01457 836077

'Possibly the most 'Bog Standard' restaurant you will find. Average decor, size, menu. Everything you expect to find but nothing else. Some of the best serving staff I have encountered, remarkable efficient and aplomb. Good starter Mulligatawny Soup £1.75, thick, pleasant texture, good zing of lemon. Well executed Lamb Biriani £5.50, completely grease free, fragrant, plenty of nuts and whole spices, generous tender lamb chunks with Madras strength sauce, topped with full sized omelette and salad - very pleasant. Tarka Dal £1.70, disappointing, tasteless, thick. Good value for money.' RW. Delivery: £10 min. Hours: 5-11, Fri/Sat -12.30.

Atherton (M46)

RAJ — NEW ENTRY

39 Mealhouse Lane, Atherton 01942 875544

Formerly Savar, a **TOP 100** restaurant. *'Cosy sixty seater restaurant in the centre of post-industrial Atherton. Clean and tidy, welcoming staff. Arrived shortly after opening time to find the manager pushing a vacuum cleaner around, immediately put away and table prepared for me. House specialities - Balti dishes. Never one to turn down a good Balti, I selected one of my favourite combinations - Lamb and Mushroom £5.80, and a starter - Sheek Kebab £1.90, excellent, freshly prepared pair of kebabs of the highest order, sizzling with bed of onions, salad and mint sauce. A large 24" x 13" Nan — light texture, quite thin - all good so far. Sizzling Balti bowl arrived - uninspiring lacklustre sauce, generous quantities of quality lamb and fresh mushrooms could not make up for this sauce, a severe disappointment.'* RW. Hours: 5, Sunday 4-11.30, Fri/Sat -12.30.

Bolton

ANAZ TAKEAWAY 

138 St Helens Road, Bolton 01204 660114

Takeaway established in 1993 by Yunus Ahmed. Specials include: Moglai, Masala, Aloo Gosht, Aloo Methi, Chilli Masala and Garlic Curries. *'Spotless, service first-class and I was offered a fresh cup of coffee whilst I waited.'* MB. Delivery: £7.50 minimum, 2-mile radius. Hours: 5-12 (Sat. to 1am); Mon. closed.

HILAL TANDOORI 

296 Chorley Old Road, Bolton 01204 842315

Opened in 1975 by Surat Ali, and he's still here with Anor Liiah as manager. Chef Abdul Monaf cooks the curries. A nice touch is the free liqueur at the end of the meal. Takeaways qualify for a free can of lager and Papadam. The Bangladeshi Dishes are in demand, we hear. Shandus Baja (£4.25) is chicken or meat, roasted, then stir-fried with bamboo shoots and fresh hot chillies. Delivery: £6 min, 3-mile radius, 95p charge (!!!); £12 order, 4-mile radius, £1.95. Hours: 5-11.30; Sat. 4.30-12.

Cheadle

MILLENNIUM MASALA — NEW ENTRANT

1 Gatley Road, Cheadle 0161 428 0888

Balti cuisine and of course Tandooris and Tikkas, Karahis and Curries, Bhunas and Birianis, in fact everthing you like in an olde oak-beamed mock-Tudor building with chandeliers, fountain, waterfall and goldfish. It's popular and busy at times, so it's advisable to book. *'A well known restaurant in a popular area - overwhelming at weekends, service can be slow. Typical menu, standard fare, value for money.'* KN. Several set meals from £12.95. Sunday 5-course £7.95 to 6pm. Takeaway: free pop & chut. Delivery: min £12, cash only. Hours: 5.30-11.30.

Sunday: 12.30-11.30.

Dukinfield

BENGAL SPICE TAKEAWAY
NEW ENTRANT

55 Armadale Road, Dukinfield 0161 330 2212

'Small clean takeaway in middle of housing estate. Friendly staff. All main meals include Nan or Pullao Rice. Two large, thin Shami's £1.40 - tender, delicious, served with fresh crisp salad but NO yoghurt sauce. Chicken Chat Puri £1.50 - light puri, fluffy, topped with generous medium curry and Chat Masala, distinctive bittersweet tang, very nice. Balti Kashmiri Masala and Pullao Rice £5.10 - bore passing resemblance to Tikka Masala sauce, homogeneous, dark red, coconut, marvellous concoction of garlic, herbs and spices - excellent flavour. Moist chicken and lamb tikka, cooked to perfection, no gristle and residual ghee. Strongly perfumed rice, lacked flavour. Excellent meal - good price.' RW. No credit cards. Hours: 5-12, Friday & Saturday to 12.30.

HERB & SPICE NEW ENTRANT ©

99 Foundry Street, Dukinfield 0161 343 5961

Kutub Uddin – manager. *'A restaurant of many guises, most recently Millennium Brasserie. Smartly laid out, 120 seats across two rooms, particularly spacious. Comprehensive menu, variety of tempting specials, including Afghan, Nepalese and section devoted to fish. Standard Popadoms with better than average Daba of Mango Chutney, Paprika Onion, Mixed Vegetable Pickle with boats of Yoghurt and Chilli Sauce. Chicken and Chana Chat Puri £3.50 - enjoyable, very dry sauce, al-dente chickpeas, small piece soft chicken, could have been better, served on outstanding, very light, flaky, marvellous flavoured, puri. Lamb Tikka Biryani £8.50 - very good, well cooked aromatic rice, plenty of texture, nice chunks of lean lamb, well presented on salver with a small omelet, tomato and cucumber garnish. Accompanied by generous portion of Roshunee Vegetable Curry, dark and robust, seriously packed with garlic. After that Nosferatu would be giving me a wider berth than Buffy the Vampire Slayer for a week! A very enjoyable meal.'* RW. Menu extracts: Paneer and Sag Puri £2.45, Indian cheese and spinach cooked with herbs and spices and served on a deep-fried flaky unleavened bread. Ameri Murgh £6.95, chicken pieces cooked in mango pulp and double cream. Delivery: 3 miles, £9.95 minimum. Sunday Buffet: £7.95. Hours: 5-11, Sat to 12. Sunday 1-10.

Hazel Grove

THE MAHARAJ ©

2 Jackson Lane, Hazel Grove 0161 439 1041

Bangladeshi restaurant and takeaway. Haroon's Specials: Shaskhick Maharaja – Tikka with sauce of cream, cinnamon and chopped nuts. Hyderbadi Hake – fillets in light batter with garam masala. Hours: 5-12; Sun. 1pm-12am.

Hyde

ASOKA NEW ENTRANT

43 Claredon Place, Hyde 0161 368 7479

Formerly The Balti House. *'Full refurbished, change inside is miraculous. Utterly contemporary decorative scheme, white walls, loads of pale wood, attractive artwork and careful lighting keeps it just the right side of looking like Cologne Airport. Modernity is matched by youthful and dynamic waiting staff. Furniture is well spaced, and seats 38. Hot Popadoms and a good Daba of pickles and sauces. Non Vegetarian Thali £14.95, excellent combination of Sheek Kebab, Chicken Tikka and Tandoori Lamb Chop for starters. All very nicely spiced, gristle free, succulent. Excellent Korai Chicken, slightly fatty Lamb Balti, though sauce exquisite and pungent and a cloying Bombay Aloo. Spot on Pullao Rice, doughy Nan. Overall a good meal, recommended for a second visit.'* RW. Cute and expensive takeaway menu, full of colourful pictures and full descriptions of dishes. Hours: 5-11.30, Friday and Saturday to 12. Sunday 4- 11.

BALTI JUNCTION PUB NEW ENTRANT

2 Mottram Moor, Mottram, Longendale, Hyde 01457 763102

'Enterprising authentic restaurant located inside a traditional pub on the edge of the peak District. Run separately from the pub. Sunday Special: Popadoms with chutneys, including Onion and Yoghurt Raitha. Mixed Starters – fiery Sheek Kebab, two large juicy pieces Chicken Tikka, served with fresh crisp salad. Prawn Bhuna – aromatic, mild, well balanced, generous, tender prawns, added texture of onion, coriander, tomato and peppers. Mushroom Bhajee – really tasty. Fluffy Pullao Rice. Very enjoyable meal particularly as it serves well-kept cask beers.' RW. Delivery: 7 miles. Sunday Special: five courses, served between 1-10.30: adult £4.95, child £3.95. Hours: 5-11, Fri/Sat -11.30. Sun 1-10.30, closed Tuesday.

RAJ2.COM NEW ENTRANT

Unit 3 Pine Street, Newton, Hyde 0161 368 9500

A novelty. Order on the web – <www.raj2.com>. Deliveries will take an hour. You will find all the regular curries and accompaniments at this takeaway /delivery service, plus Pizza, Chinese Noodles and Rice, Southern Fried Chicken, Kebabs, Chips etc. Hours: 5-11, Fri/Sat/Sun -11.45.

SAFFRON BALTI HOUSE
NEW ENTRANT

100 John Kennedy Road, Mottram, Hyde 01457 762222

'Previously the dismal Shahin, Ali Raj, Mottram Tandoori and currently Saffron. Much cleaned and improved. Menu with a sense of humour! (note the Britney Special with honey). Menus includes burgers, kebabs, pizzas etc. Good starter, Fish Puri £2.70, piquant, well balanced and served on non-greasy bread. Butt-Bastic £4.10, incredibly rich, I watched the chef putting copious quantities of cream into my dish in the open kitchen. Plenty of good cuts of tasty lamb, though some gristle was evident. Average Nan, barely smeared with garlic. A deserving business in a deprived area.' RW. {and now for the bad news] *'WARNING: the area is famous for the voracity and skill of local car thieves. Park your car in view of the takeaway and lock it. Be aware of your surroundings when going back to it and lock the doors as soon as you get in. Ignore anyone lying in the road apparently injured - it's a car-jacking scam.'* RW. No credit cards. Delivery: £8 minimum, 2 miles radius. Hours: 5-12, Friday and Saturday to 12.30.

SPICY KITCHEN TAKEAWAY
NEW ENTRANT

100 Market Street, Hollingworth, Nr Hyde 01457 765655

'Friendly and bustling takeaway. Very clean waiting area. Chicken Chat Puri £3, a really great starter, well cooked bread, with generous sprinkling of Chat Masala. Lamb Tikka Biriani £4.50, a Curate's Egg, very good pieces of tasty lean lamb and really nice medium spicy sauce, poor vegetables. Worth a second look.' RW. Set Meal for two - excellent value at £11 for two courses. Pizzas also available for the curry uninitiated! Opposite The Organ Pub. Cash and cheques only. Delivery: £8 minimum, 3 miles. Hours: 4.30-12, Friday and Saturday to 12.30.

MANCHESTER CITY

(Manchester postcodes, M1 to M46
Population: 433,000)

For the purpose of this Guide, we have included M postcodes (M1

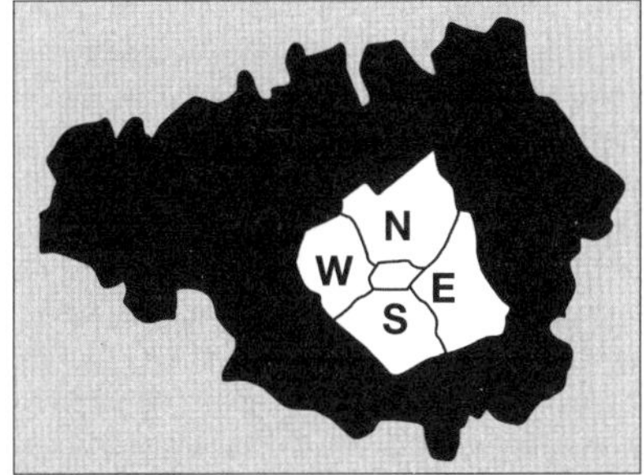

to - M46) in all our Manchester City entries. There is no geographical logic to our putting postcodes into numerical order. They are frankly a jumble. But it is the system which exists, and to help narrow things down, we have divided the city into Central, East, South, West and North, using major roads as our arbitrary boundaries.

©	Curry Club Discount	U	Unlicensed
V	Vegetarian	ANP	Alcohol not permitted
e-a-m-a-y-l	Eat as much as you like	BYO	Bring your own alcohol

Manchester Central

M1 to M4

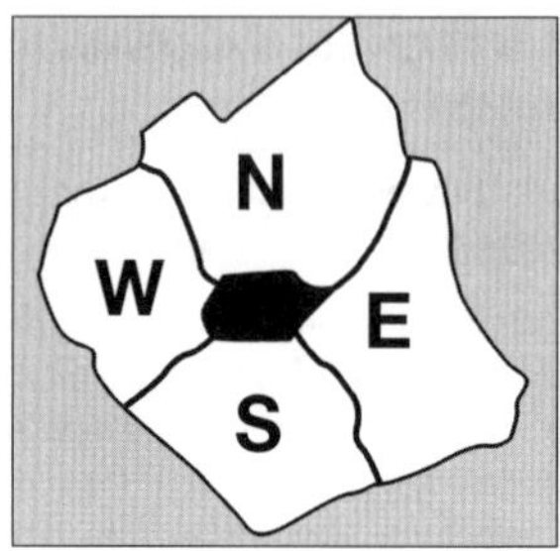

(restaurants listed in alphabetical order)

ASHOKA

105-107 Portland Street, Manchester M1
0161 228 7550

'The service can be a little slow, but the standard of food here is well worth the wait. Rashmi Kebab – god what taste, beautiful! £19.00 for one, but worth every penny.' MB. *'Lunch time and there's only one other sad git needing a fix. Reasonably well decorated, but could do with a touch up. Asked by waiter if I was having lunch, I said yes, he walked off, came back with two Popadoms and Chutneys. Raita - too salty and Onion Salad - devoid of anything but onion. Not impressed. Apparently, lunch £4.95 has no choices. Mystery Course Two - plate of salad arrived with good portion (six) of Chicken Shashlik along with half a Nan. - excellent flavour, nicely spiced, very definite smoky flavour, tired salad, good Nan. Mystery Course Three - Chicken Jalfrezi - generous helping, good nicely spiced sauce, Vegetable Curry - good selection of vegetables but bland, Pullao Rice - generous portion, good flavour, light and fluffy.'* DB. Menu extracts: Chilli Chicken £4.50, green chillies, ginger, fresh coriander, capsicum and red chilli sauce. Rashmi Kebab £3.00, minced chicken, onion, green chillies, fresh mint, coriander, cooked over charcoal. Quail Makhani £7.50, butter, tomatoes, cream sauce. Hours: 12-2.30, Sunday closed and 6-11.30.

BALTI BASEMENT — NEW ENTRANT

Hilton Street, Manchester, M1 0161 237 1893

'Lunch time and it's chocka! A down market cafe rather than a restaurant, with limited restaurant. A couple of starters, Samosas 60p each, four meat curries and something for those sad old veggies, food served over counter, bread brought to your table. By the time I got my food, found a seat, queue was to the door. Chicken Jalfrezi with Chapati was out of this world – large and moist. I can honestly say that it was the best bread I've eaten.' DB.

GAYLORD — TOP 100

Amethyst House, Spring Gardens, Manchester M2 0161 832 6037

Owned by PK Chadha and R Kapoor, since '93. When it opened in the 1960s it was Manchester's first up-market Indian restaurant, and it poineered the Tandoori oven in the city. The name is a play on the names of the original owners Gai and Lamba, who had opened one of Delhi's very first Indian restaurants called Kwality in 1948. By the 50's there were Kwalities all over India. But they were little more than caffs.

Having made a fortune producing ice cream, the pair decided to go up market with their first Gaylord which opened in Delhi in 1958. Other branches soon followed in Bombay, London, San Francisco, Kowloon, Kobe Japan, and the Bahamas. The Gaylord seats 92 diners, and serves northern Indian cuisine. *'Reasonable menu selection, but what they offer is excellent. Good service in a very relaxing atmosphere.'* AKD. *'All four of us agreed that it was a wonderful curry with such different tastes. Started with Tandoori Fish, Onion Pakoras, Vegetable Samosas and Chicken Chat – very interesting salad, quite spicy – all good quality. Hot green chutney, harissa like substance was a favourite, to be used with caution. Superb Sag Chicken, best we have tasted! Excellent Chilli Chicken Tikka, char grilled flavour. Stunning Channa Kabuli, very hot, small pieces of raw chilli. Very impressed.'* KW. Sunday lunch buffet £7.95. Service: 10%. Takeaway 10% discount. Hours: 12-2.30/6-11.30. Sun. to 11.

KAILASH ©

34 Charlotte Street, Manchester M1 0161 236 6624

As ever, at NP Bhattara's 'Nepalese' 75-seater basement restaurant established in 1989, all the curryhouse dishes are on the menu and you need to search for Nepalese specials. But they're there. For £14.50, try the Nepalese Dal Bhat. With momocha, makhan chara, masu bhutan, kalo dal, palungo aloo, bhat, dessert and coffee. *'Basement restaurant on the outskirts of China town. A well lit, spacious restaurant in need of redecoration and carpet cleaning. Not a great choice of Nepalese dishes. Executive Lunch £4.99 - Popadom and Chutney not the freshest I've tasted. Rashmi Kebab, two minced chicken sausages, well presented, with subtle spicing and strong flavour of lemon. Nan crisp around the edges, yet soft and fluffy in middle, one of the best I've tasted. Rogan Josh - small portion, five pieces of tender lamb in pleasant spicy sauce, cashew nuts thrown in. Large portion of plated, well flavoured, light steamed rice. Ubiquitous Vegetable curry.'* DB. Nepalese Menu extracts: Masu Nariwol £6.25, lamb, coconut cream and curry leaves. Aloo Tareko £3.80, thin and crispy sliced potato, cooked dry. Kalo Dal £3.80, black lentils. Sag Palungo £3.80, spinach, fresh garlic and dried red chillies. Service Charge: 10%. Hours: 12-2.30 (Sun. closed)/6.30-11.30.

SHIMLA PINKS

Dolefield, Crown Square, Manchester M3 0161 831 7099

Near the Law Courts by Deansgate at a former Italian restaurant, with a massive 7,500 sq ft and 80 covers, with a further 40 outdoors but under cover. Plenty of money went in installing the decor, furnishings and kitchens. Enough indeed to bring its founder Kaal Daliwal into receivership in 2001. (He's back – see Poppadam Express, Southampton, Hampshire.). The food has always been curryhouse formula stuff with spin. It's designed to appeal to young spenders whose attitude is matched by the servers – I mean arrogant. Maybe it's what they each deserve. But we get reports from real curry-lovers who also enjoy the place, so we keep it in the *Guide*. Hours: 12-3/6-11.

THIS AND THAT CAFE 

3 Soap Street, Manchester M4 0161 832 4971

Established in 1980. Taken over by Ismail Musa Mallu in 1992. Seats 55. Specialises in Northern Indian, Pakistani and Vegetarian meals. Different simple menu to choose from each day. Lamb and Pumpkin £2.00, Cabbage Curry £1.60, Spinach and Vegetable £1.60, Fish Curry £2.30, Lamb and Okra £2.00, Lamb Courgette £2.00, Dal £1.60. Hours: 11.30-5.30 (Sun. to 4pm); Sat. closed.

Manchester North

Consists of M7, M8, M9 M24 (Middleton), M25 & 45

(Whitefield) M25 (Prestwich), and M26 (Radcliffe)

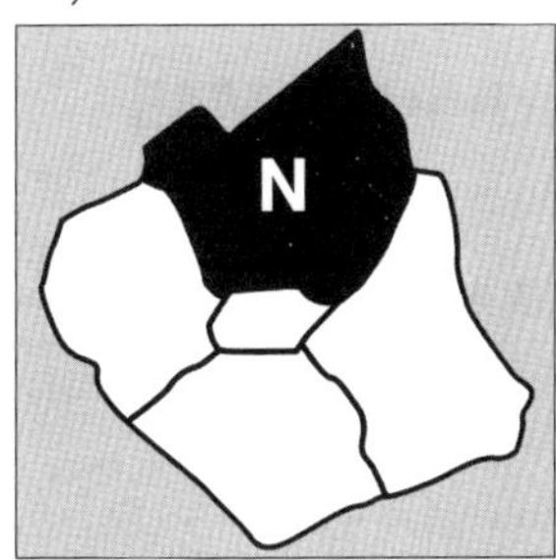

©	Curry Club Discount	U	Unlicensed
V	Vegetarian	ANP	Alcohol not permitted
e-a-m-a-y-l	Eat as much as you like	BYO	Bring your own alcohol

Manchester M25

Gorton (see also M45), Prestwich

GARDEN OF INDIA ©

411 Bury Old Road, Prestwich M25 0161 773 7784

An 88-seat restaurant, opened in 1984 by Hafizur Rahman and managed by A Quyum. *'Chicken Samber, very reminiscent of a Dhansak, hot, but not as sweet, which was a very pleasant change and one which I shall look out for again. Chicken Paneer met with total approval.'* SN&RA. *'Have visited several times and have always found it quite acceptable.'* MB. TT likes the Fish Kufta Masala – fish balls in a creamy sauce. Hafizur Rahman has plans for refurbishing his 68-seater. Curries, cooked by head chef Ataur Rahman. Thalis recommended. Service 10%. Cover charge £1.25. Takeaway 20% discount. Hours: 5-12.

Manchester M26

Radcliffe

RADCLIFFE CHARCOAL TANDOORI ©

123 Blackburn Street, Radcliffe, M26 0161 723 4870

At MLA Khan's very smart, long-standing (1966 – then the Taj Mahal) up-market 100-seater, chef SN Ali's interesting starters include: Balti Chana Masala and Puri, and Lamb Chop Tikka. *'Very comfortable restaurant but the food tends to be a little up and down. I have called in here and ordered a takeaway only to find it disappointing; on the other hand we have gone in and the food and service have been brilliant.'* MB. Takeaway 30% discount. Sunday lunch £7. Delivery: 3-mile radius. Hours: 6-12.30. (1.30am on Fri/Sat.); Sun. 12pm-12.30am. Branch: India Brasserie, 105, Stockport Road, Marple, Stockport.

Manchester M45

Whitefield (see also M25)

LA IMRANS ©

Top of Elms Centre, Whitefield, M45 0161 796 0557

'Our party called for a light meal after our bowling night. Food excellent, all knocked out by the price (£53.20 for seven!), staff all knocked out by being in the 1999 GCG. Must return soon for a full meal. From outside, we would not have ventured in without the guide.' RN. Popular Balti Night' Tuesday and Thursday, seven dishes £7.50. Sunday buffet 1-6. e-a-m-a-y-l £7.95 adult, £4.95 kids. Takeaway 30% discount. Free parking at rear. but please ask. Hours: 5 (Sun. 1)-11. (1am on Fri/Sat.).

MOGUL NEW ENTRANT

Sefton Street, Whitefield, Manchester, M45 0161 796 0403

'My newly graduated son held his first housewarming and suggested we visit as it "looked impressive." Converted Church Hall, external blue flood lighting, invested in trendy decor, very tasteful conversion, lots of wall lighting, illuminated alcoves, Indian antiques, elevated area, marble top tables, long ladder-back chairs and clean toilets. Two lovely young Indian ladies showed us to table. Have spent a lot - reflected in bill 15% meat surcharge and 10% service charge (slow but quality of cuisine excellent). Five curries - all sauces delicious, large chunks of chicken beautifully tandoor cooked.' AIE. Service: 10%.

Manchester East

Consists of M11 to M13, M18, M34, M35, M40, M43

Manchester M34

Audenshaw, Denton

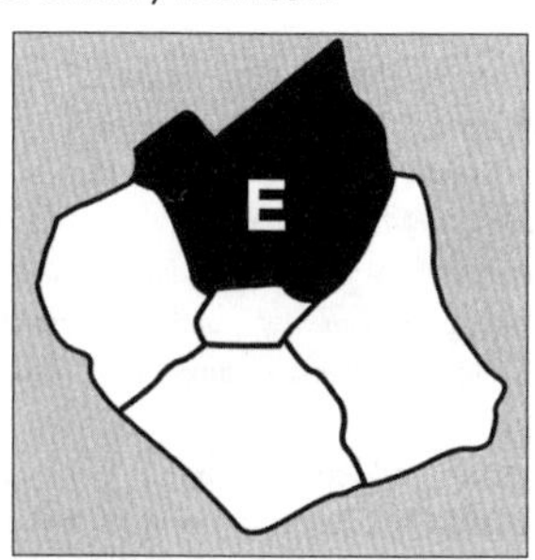

AASHIANA

17 Ashton road, Denton 0161 336 3677

'Smart, clean lines, very relaxing, seats seventy in comfort. Bright, lively young staff, very efficient as place filled up. Extensive and

varied menu, some genuinely interesting offerings. Really good Lamb Garlic Tikka, tender, fat and gristle free, oozing garlic served with crisp, fresh, shredded salad. A proper Bhuna, dry consistency, well spiced, complex, with stir-fried onion and green peppers — superb. Outstanding Nan, really light and fluffy, crispy underneath, melt in the mouth, plenty of grated garlic with aromatic brushing of ghee. Kulfi appeared to have been stored in the same facility where Walt Disney's head currently resides, as it totally deflected the attentions of my spoon for a good quarter of an hour. Taste of Tarka Dal could not be faulted, but a little too runny. Very highly recommended.' RW. Delivery: £10 min. Hours: 5-11.30, Fri/Sat 4-12, Sunday 3-10.30.

BARAKAT BALTI ©

699 Windmill Lane, Danebank, Denton, M34 0161 320 3232

Chomk Ali's Bakarat was established in 1988. *'Bright and scrupulously clean takeaway, located in a small precinct. Smart open kitchen populated by immaculate staff, exemplary waiting area with over-stuffed leather sofas, TV, Bombay Mix and current newspapers and magazines to read - I was almost sorry to go home when my curry was ready. Fish Puri £1.90 - unusual blend of lightly spiced curry with a delicate piece of cod on a very good puri. Unfortunately the curry was not well suited to the taste of the fish, I had to resort to lemon juice and chat masala to save it. Main meal - Balti Lohari Chicken £4.75 - faultless, superb sauce, generous portion, perfectly cooked chicken tikka. Garlic Nan £1.30 - measly in garlic. Cracking Tarka Dal £1.30 - not greasy, not thin, exquisitely balanced, a real treat.'* RW. Tandoori/Curry set meal for two good value at £12.99. Hours: 5- 11.30, Fri/Sat to 12.

SHIREEN TAKEAWAY NEW ENTRANT

266 Manchester Road, Audenshaw, Manchester, M34 0161 371 7397

Established 1993. As the saying goes - never judge a book by its cover - I think the same can be said about a restaurant. *'Rather seedy looking establishment hard against a busy main road with limited parking. Run down but clean interior. Enjoyable Sulaimani Kebab £3.75 - combination of chicken and lamb tikka and sheek kebab covered with melted Paneer, served with crisp salad and tangy Raitha. Very generous Chef's Special Biriani £6.40 - well packed with chicken, good quality lamb, prawn an mushroom in a highly aromatic matrix of well cooked Basmati rice, accompanied by a large portion of medium sauce with well cooked vegetables, topped with omelette, sliced cucumber and tomato. Very pleasant and filling, better than average and shop front.' RW. Specials: Komla Murghi £6 - chicken with mandarin. Chops Chom Chom £6.45 - with pickled onions and roasted panch phoran. Lamb Pardesi £6.10 - with garlic, spinach and mushroom. Very unusual for a curry house - beef is listed on the menu. Free Onion Bhajia or Popadoms with takeaways over £10.* ANON. Delivery: £10 min, 3 miles. Hours: 5-12, Friday/Saturday to 12.30.

SPICE OF INDIA TAKEAWAY
NEW ENTRANT

86 Manchester Road, Denton, Manchester, M34 0161 337 9493

'Clean and welcoming takeaway, spotless kitchen and smiling staff. Marvellous starter - Reshmi Kebab £1.90 - two generously sized tender kebabs topped with whisked scrambled egg and fresh salad and Raitha. Lamb Nowabi £5.30 (inc rice or nan) - robust, remarkably rich sauce with plenty of hot chillies and packed with potato and juicy lean lamb. Fluffy Nan - of good proportion.' RW. Delivery: 3 miles, £8 minimum. Good value set meals from £7.50. Hours: 6-1am, Fri/Sat to 1.

Manchester South

Consists of M14 (Wilmslow Road, Rusholme) M15, M16, M19 to M23, M32, M33 and M90

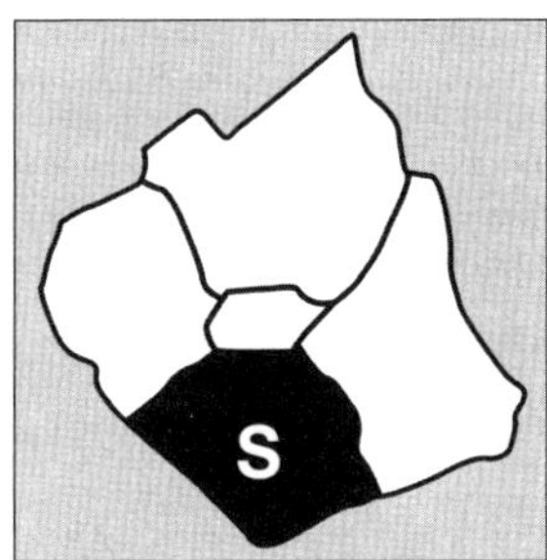

Manchester M14

Wilmslow Road, Rusholme

Wilmslow Road, extends for nearly 6 miles south from Manchester Centre. It passes through Rusholme, Manchester's main Asian area. To get there from the city centre it's best to walk – parking is normally a joke. Face south on the Oxford Road, with the BBC on your left, and go for about 800 metres, passing

©	Curry Club Discount	U	Unlicensed
V	Vegetarian	ANP	Alcohol not permitted
e-a-m-a-y-l	Eat as much as you like	BYO	Bring your own alcohol

the Uni and then the Royal Infirmary. At the Moss Lane East junction, Rusholme and Little India starts. In the last five years the expansion has been amazing and is continuing unabated. From a drab and run-down look it now sports neon lighting to rival Las Vegas. Now, in the 600 metres from Moss Lane to Claremont Road, there are no less than 42 curry eateries – Indian snack and sweet shops, cafés and restaurants. As if that's not enough, there are numerous pubs, offices, chippies, Chinese, pizza joints, kebab houses and burger bars, Asian grocers and halal butchers. Some of the cheap and cheerful all-day cafés allow BYO (but always ask – it can offend some Muslims). Some are quite expensive licensed restaurants, the largest of which seats 400! A conservative estimate on curry consumption is 50,000 curries a week here. We believe this to be the curry record for a district. Any challenges? Go a further 900 metres along Wilmslow Road, and there are some 35 more curry eateries, making this a genuine Golden Mile. Almost any are worth trying. Most open all day.. Don't try reserving, you'll be lucky if they answer the phone. Just turn up, and if one is busy go to another. Our regular and prolific correspondent – DB *– tells us that, '...my overall experiences of Rusholme have been a little disappointing both culinary and service wise, considering there are so many curry houses vying for your custom.'*
Here are some of your favourites:

Rusholme

AL NAWAZ NEW ENTRANT

74 Wilmslow Road, Manchester M14
0161 249 0044

'Working near curry heaven, Rusholme. Good, spacious, light, well decorated. Popadoms with five chutneys, very acceptable. Massive portion of Chicken Tikka Biriani with Madras sauce, good tikka, decent flavour to rice. Will return.' DB.

HANAAN

54, Wilmslow Road,Rusholme 0161 256 4786

Scores: 8/10. DB.

LAL HAWELI NEW ENTRANT

68-72 Wilmslow Road Manchester M14
0161 248 9700

'Good formula curry house. Chicken Tikka, eight pieces served on sizzler with onions and peppers. Good portion of nice, fluffy, nutty Pullao Rice.' DB.

ROYAL NAZ NEW ENTRANT

18, IFCO, Wilmslow Road, Rusholme 0161 256 1060

Scores: 6/10. then 8/10. DB.

SANAM SWEET HOUSE 

145 Wilmslow Road, Rusholme, M14 0161 224 8824

Despite AQ Akhtar's restaurant being huge (seating 160, plus a further 200-seat function room), it is so popular locally that it's often full, with queues waiting to be seated. *'The standard fare was very, very good . . . the Aloo Tikka was very tasty. A good first time visit.'* TOC. *'Quite nicely decorated, staff not overly friendly. Excellent Popadoms and chutney. Chicken Biriani, had flavour, fried onion garnish, tender chicken.'* DB. Hours: 12pm-12am. Branches: Abdul's, 121 318 Wilmslow Rd, and 298 Oxford Rd.

SHERE KHAN

52 Wilmslow Road, Rusholme, M14 0161 256 2624

This is Manchester's version of Khan's, London W2. It is popular beyond belief and does a massive *'love-it or leave-it' trade. The decision is yours. Examples of both: 'One of the busiest restaurants on the Curry Golden Mile. Clean, a/c (sometimes) and so busy that people stand around waiting for tables, wishing you to hurry up. Food quality can vary widely on different days of the week, portions not generous and it is not cheap. Uniformly surly staff, probably a result of their constant harassment by management. Look after your valuables, had two purses and a handbag stolen. No help and sympathy from the management – only the bill. £131 for nine, no service, definitely no tip.'* NSC. *'I've been there 100 times and it's great, but still they don't recognise me!'* GR. *'Filling up rapidly as we sat down, and heaving within half an hour. Kitchen and meal assembly area in clear view at rear which is encouraging. Service was pleasant with smiles, but according to the local I was with, it depends where you sit in this very large place. Lamb Tikka starter was tasty and tender with Chicken Chillies, very tasty but didn't blow my brains out. Mushroom Bhaji excellent. Enjoyed it all. Seems a safe one to me out of the amazing choice of restaurants cheek by jowl in this area.'* MS. *'Tuesday night - bustling! great atmosphere, great smells. Sheek Kebabs - no artificial colourings, lovely taste. Good portion of Chicken Tikka. Kofta Madras - my favourite, received well and hot. Bombay Aloo - Ok. Very tasty Mushroom Bhajee. Recommended.'* JH. 'Scores: 6/10' DB. Hours 12-12. Branch: Manchester M16, *see next page.*

SHEZAN

119 Wilmslow Road, Rusholme, Manchester, M14 0161 224 3116

'Chicken Tikka Biriani with Madras Curry sauce. Rice had flavour, good portion with plenty of chicken, heavy on peas. Nicely garnished with omelette, heavy on tomatoes. A good meal.' DB.

SPICY HUT U BYO 

35 Wilmslow Road, Rusholme, M14 0161 248 6200

MS Mughal's simply decorated 60-seater serves traditional Pakistani curries and side dishes. *'A must whenever we visit Manchester. Always assured of a warm welcome and a good curry. Popadoms, pickles and generous portion of Indian salad provided as soon as you sit down - used to be free, now 30p a head. We often take a bottle of wine with us which is uncorked without delay. Jugs of iced water provided without fuss, replenished automatically. Rice portions are so big, one between two is enough. Garlic Chicken £5.80 - very good, large portions. Naan always good, light, fluffy, not too doughy. Meal for two £16 - what a bargain!'* EG. Discount Scheme. Delivery: 2 miles, £10 minimum. Hours: 5-2am; Sun. 3-1am.

TABAK

199 Wilmslow Road, Rusholme, M14 0161 248 7812

Mohammad Nawab's restaurant seats a MASSIVE 350 diners, on two floors. Pakistani curries and accompaniments on the menu cooked by chefs Raj Kumar and Abrahim Ali. *'A Bit scruffy, in need of redecoration. I was the only diner at first, but joined by some others later in my adventure. Sent the Popadoms back – stale. Chutney tray – poor, Raitha good. Excellent main meal, well flavoured rice, very good succulent chicken and a curry sauce near to perfect.'* DB. Hours: 12pm-1am.

Manchester M16

SHERE KHAN EXPRESS
NEW ENTRANT

Orient Food Hall, Trafford Centre, M16 0161 749 9900

Opened on a prime corner location in the upper rotunda of the Trafford Centre. and must be one of the trendiest in the area. Seats a considerable 430. *'Innovative food franchise in the monument to avarice that is the Trafford Shopping complex. An off shoot of Shere Khan that has been a love-it-or-hate-it (I am of latter persuasion) fixture of Rusholm's curry Canyon since the 60's and trading on its forebears' name and success. Limited choice served with a world weary disinterest by haggard staff. Two Kebabs - very good, fresh not microwaved, you have to ask for complimentary salad, sauce. Lamb Karahi £6.20 - just recognisable as it's description, quality of meat beyond reproach. Passable rice. Overall, reasonable, unexpected, streets ahead of the premium priced McNasties and Unlucky Fried Kitten nearby.'* RB. *'It is MASSIVE inside! Split level, spacious, light wood and chrome theme with open kitchen. We plumped - appropriate - for the special lunch menu £6.99 - Popadoms and Pickles, Meat Samosa, Kebabs, Lamb Korma, Chicken Bhuna, Lamb Madras, Pullao Rice, Nan and chip - excellent. Highly recommended.'* AIE. *'Massive restaurant, light, airy, vibrant purples, pinks and yellows — a bit garish. Lunch buffet, not cheap at £9.99. Popadoms with chutneys, served with very fresh side salad, great value at 65p. Service wasn't quick. Portion not the biggest, rice had flavour, Chicken Tikka was a hideous pink colour, good flavour. Well spiced Madras sauce. Disappointing, no omelette garnish.'* DB. Menu extracts: Chicken Pakora £3.40. Aloo Kebab £1.50, spicy potato, green chillies. Chicken Chilli Masala £6.50.

Manchester M19

Burnage, Kingsway, Levenshulme

NAWAAB — NEW ENTRANT

1008 Stockport Road, M19 0161 224 6969

Mahboob Hussain bills this as the biggest curry house – 350-seats on the ground floor plus 600 on the first floor. *'Located in a former art-deco cinema, which became a bingo hall then a cash-and-carry, it has had a £1m make-over, including restoring the original 50 ft domed ceiling to its former grandeur. Bollywood prints and hanging silk saris add dramatic statements. For kids who get into masala mischief, an in-house creche gives parents a chance to concentrate on perky pickles instead of being caught in one. Executive chef Mahboob Hussain, jnr, over sees chefs brought in from Pakistan and has opted for an e-a-m-a-y-l buffet, £9.99 (£5.99 for children under five). Includes a salad bar, starters such as Fish Masala, Samosas and Pakoras and Pakoras. Six different meaty mains, assorted veggies and Indian add-ons plus a selection of puds from the subcontinent make for a decent night out.'* PV. Branches: Bradford etc.

THIRD EYE 

198 Mauldeth Road, Burnage, M19 0161 442 2900

Nepalese restaurant. Opened 1998. Seats 72. Cosy, traditional decor. Specials: Tangri, chicken drumstick stuffed with saffron minced lamb and nuts. Bhutan Chara, chicken with mushrooms and tomatoes. Kidney Masala, lamb kidney in spicy sauce. Takeaway: 10% disc. Del: £15 min, 3-miles. Hours: 5-12.

TONDORI ROYALE ©

682 Burnage Lane, Burnage, M19 0161 432 0930

'Bob Hoque's 110-seater is very well-established (1980) and very well spoken of by the locals. 'It was packed! It is not difficult to work out why when you taste the cuisine. Atmosphere is electric and food well worth the 40-mile trip.' MB. It has a full house of familiar dishes. Fish dishes include Boal and Ayre. NW's favourite is Zhal Golda Chingri, king prawn cooked with chilli and ginger. *'Very good. Vegetable Pasanda had excellent flavour.'* RWI. *'A pleasant surprise tucked away in the Manchester suburbs. Try the Hopi for your starter – an interesting variation on the Chinese spring roll. Sizzling baltis with quality ingredients and accompanied by fluffy naans. Worth a go!'* PW. Delivery: £15 min, 3-miles. Hours: 6-1AM; Sat/Sun. 5-2.30am.

Manchester M22

Northenden

CURRY RAJ — NEW ENTRANT

331 Palatine Road, M22 0161 945 9959

'Very compact; seats 30. Well decorated and maintained. Friendly staff. Standard menu.. Really good, crumbly, succulent Reshmi Kebab, well spiced, tangy, got the digestive juices flowing, topped with perfect small omelette, and served with a cold, crisp, salad and cool Raitha – spot on. Well cooked Lamb Tikka Biriani – equally pleasing, very pungent, full of flavour, topped off with another perfect omelette, and a sprinkling of diced tomato and cucumber. Tarka Dal, the star of the show – cooked to perfection, right balance of garlic and onion, outstanding.' RW. Takeaway: 15% discount. Hours: 6-11.30. Sunday 12-2.

Manchester M33

Ashton-upon-Mersey, Sale

SPICE CHEF 

85 Washway, Sale, M33 0161 976 4577

Established 1994. Seats 50, parking for 10-15 cars. Sunday buffet: 2-6pm, five courses £5.95, children half-price. Vegetarian Night: every Tuesday, five courses £14.95. Delivery: £10 minimum, 3-mile radius. Hours: 5-12. Sat. 5-1am.

Manchester West

Including M5, M6 (Salford) M17, M27 to M31, M41, M44.

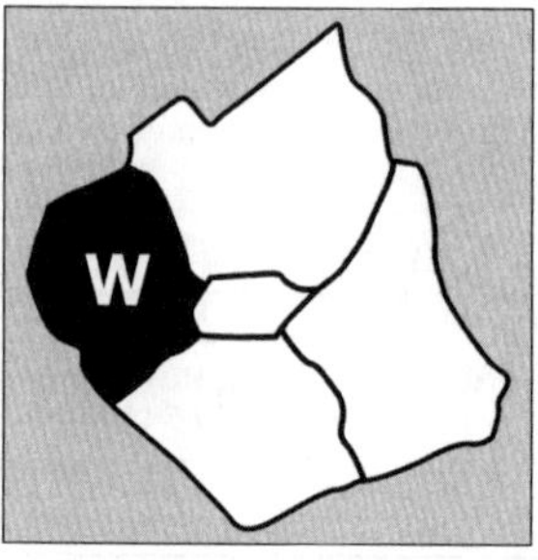

Manchester M28

Disdbury

THE ORIGINAL THIRD EYE
NEW ENTRANT

661 Wilmslow Road, Didsbury, Manchester M28
0161 446 2300

'I have visited at least 10 times over two years and it is still one of my favourites. Run by the same family who started Katmandu on Burton Road and Third Eye on Mauldeth Road - the best chef is definitely in Didsbury. Small, seats forty and decorated in Didsbury chrome and glass style. Superb menu [which we will see more of later]. Particularly recommended is the Aloo Chilli, Kidney kebab, Tarka Dal and they do a brilliant Garlic Nan with more garlic than Nan! [sounds just fantastic]. *I love their Vindaloo with little pieces of chopped ginger garnish. Portions can appear small, but you will end your meal feeling nicely full rather than stuffed full.'* [I too, prefer the former feeling over the latter one]. *'Staff polite and friendly.'* KN. Menu extracts: Fish Tikka £2.75, cod marinated in spiced yoghurt and barbecued. Kidney Kebab £2.75. Bari Masala £4.90, mince balls seasoned with herbs and cooked in a curry gravy. Bhutan Chara £4.90, chicken with mushrooms and tomatoes. Pommi Nan £2.20, stuffed with potatoes, cheese, herbs and spices. Hours: 12-2.30 (Weds to Sun) /6-12.

Manchester M30

Eccles, Irlam

PASSAGE TO INDIA ©

168 Monton Road, Monton, Eccles, M30
0161 787 7546

M Hassan Choudhury and H Uddin's serves 90 diners all the formula curries. Open 12pm-11.30pm. Branch: Gate of India, Swinton.

Elsewhere in Greater Manchester

Oldham

BENGAL BRASSERIE NEW ENTRANT

31-33 Milnrow Road, Shaw, Oldham

'Large detached restaurant with own car park. Smart and unfussy decoration, just a little frayed at the edges. Well presented and efficient staff. Excellent starter - Reshmi Kebab £1.70, moist, well spiced, omelette on top, crisp salad and yoghurt sauce. Lamb Zamdani £6.40, pleasant combination of basic sauce with a sprinkling of green chillies and almonds, topped with egg noodles. Lamb chunks were plentiful, well sized, but some fatty. Well cooked fluffy Garlic Nan, sprinklings of garlic on top, brushed with aromatic ghee.' RW. Hours: 5-11.30, Fri/Sat to 12.

BRITISH RAJ 

185 Lees Road, Oldham 0161 624 8696

Oldham's oldest (1970), taken over by Mr S Rahman in 1997, of which RK says: *'It's tasteful, right down to the Union Jacks embroidered into the chairbacks. The food is really good. The Shan Special Chicken and Bombay Chicken were both like a dream — hot and spicy and unlike the normal formula stuff. Pullao Rice exceptionally light and perfumed. The meal was finished off with hot towels and orange segments. They do special evenings with home-cooking, food as eaten by Bangladeshi families. One to return to.'* RK. RW likes it too: *'Well laid out smart interior belies the tatty facade. Very polished service. Standard range of curries with large range of house specials. Started with Tandoori Fish — whole large trout, with tail and head on, dominated dinner plate, well marinated in tasty blend of spices, brought out best in flesh and served with crisp fresh salad. Handi Exotica Masala — superbly balanced curry sauce, deliciously hot, chunks of Chicken and Lamb Tikka with prawns filled a generously sized Handi. A thoroughly enjoyable meal.'* Seats 50, car parking for 50 at rear. Delivery 10% discount. Takeaway 20% discount on collection. Sunday buffet – 10 courses. Hours: 5.30-12.30 (Fri. & Sat. to 2.30am); Sun. 4-1am.

MILLON RESTAURANT 

Westwood Business Centre, Featherstall Road, South Oldham 0161 620 6445

Abdul Momin and Ashik Ullah opened their Millon, meaning 'meeting place', in 1993 in a purpose-built, elegant building. The inside is as smart as the outside. There is a pub-ish, comfortable bar and a 96-seat dining room, with

©	Curry Club Discount	U	Unlicensed
V	Vegetarian	ANP	Alcohol not permitted
e-a-m-a-y-l	Eat as much as you like	BYO	Bring your own alcohol

alcoves and pillars and smart upholstery. Since the chef is Mr Momin, the food is of a high standard. *'Plush surroundings. Popadoms and a lovely, very tangy chutney, Amishi Chicken, very creamy and fruity and Chicken Jhali Bhuna, spicier and better. Totally approved of the Sag Paneer.'* RK. Takeaway 5% off. Hours: 5-11.30 (Sat. to 12.30am; Sun. 4-11.

Rochdale

LA TANDOOR NEW TO OUR TOP 100 ©

A7, Bamford Precinct, Rochdale 01706 642037

Mrs S Habeeb's 68-seater is decorated with a paint effect of waves in the ocean and trees on banks. Eight spice boats have been fixed to the walls with sacks of spices in them. Fishing hammocks are tied to the ceiling. *'A superb restaurant, and be warned – book a table, as it gets very busy. We had Nargis Kebab and Vegetable Chaat for starters – a dream – and we followed with a main-course choice of Chicken Tikka Biriani and Chilli Chicken Balti, with a side dish of Malayee Kufta (vegetable balls in a coconut sauce with pineapple and peaches), Pullao Rice and Chupattis. It was all excellent, followed by ice cream, face towels, a free drink and after-meal sweets. All this cost us just* £26.45. *We'd eat there every day if we were locals!'* RK. *'Now enlarged. Food still fab. Had forgotten this place until we read the Guide.'* RN. Takeaway 20% off. Hours: 12.30pm-12.30am (1am on Sat.). Family banquets: Sunday £8.50 – 12.30-6. Welcome to our **TOP 100.**

Stockport

(includes Chapel-en-Le-Firth, Heaviley Heaton Moor, Marple, Offerton, Romiley, Whaley Bridge)

KUSHOOM KOLY 

6 Shaw Road, Heaton Moor, Stockport 0161 432 9841

Meaning *'flowerbud'*, Mrs Kulsum Uddin's 80-seater with bow window and an open kitchen has been in the same family since it opened in 1971, with Fakuk front of house. The 8 rooms are decorated in pastel shades of peach and blue with carved teak screens on the walls. Sami and Kashim in the kitchens will cook Bengali fish dishes to order. *'A group of business consultants in Stockport consulted the Guide for reviews. Maturity, family ownership and positive reports prompted*

us to try on Thursday (busy) night. As taxi pulled up, impressed with garden exterior, trailing flowers. Primed with beautifully fresh Popadoms and exceptional pickles but no Cobra. Starters: Onion Bhajia – crisp, Sheek Kebab – lean, no fat, Samosa – pastry not crispy, all with salad, overall good start. Main courses: CT Bhuna – superb, Chicken Rogon Josh – very good, Beef Bhuna – the best ever! Sag Aloo – tasty, Pullao Rice – fluffy and tasty, Nan – sweet roasty taste and "proper chips" as Farouk called them! Portions generous, absence of hot-plates, delicious dishes, service attentive. Lives up to its reputation.' LL. Takeaway 15% off. Delivery. Hours: 5-1am (2.30am on Sat.). Branch: Kaya Koly Takeaway, Heaton Road, Heaton Moor, Stockport.

PRIDE OF BENGAL NEW ENTRANT

2 George Lane, Bredbury, Stockport 0161 406 6451

Fully licensed and air conditioned. *'Peculiar building sitting on its own next to a car park. The decor, colour scheme and not least the waiters in leather waistcoats make the place look like one of those nightclubs where the gentlemen dance with each other! Extensive menu with good assortment of house specials. Excellent Malagathani Soup £1.50 - thick, made from good stock, generous portion. Aromatic Pullao Rice. Good rich Karahi £5.30 sauce, served on a violently sizzling dish, which had to be left on the side to calm down! Good chunks of moist tender lamb.'* RW. Hours: 5-12.

SANJOYS INDIAN CUISINE
NEW ENTRANT

59 Petersgate, Stockport 0161 476 2077

'Owner/manager Debrash (Deb) used to own Heatons tandoori. He is keen to cultivate the office/business trade as well as local residents, so the interior and decor are top class - brassiere style, fresh white linen and sparkling cutlery. Five of us on a wet Wednesday night to be greeted by Deb and his waiter who quickly disposed of our coats and sat us at one of the immaculately laid tables. Cobra on draught was quickly dispensed followed by fresh popadoms and pickles - in such small containers that the overflow soon mucked up the fresh linen! Starters of Meat Samosas £1.95, Onion Bhajias £1.95, Lamb Chop Tikka, Mixed Kebab and a Prawn Cocktail £2.25 (who had that?) were all good, well presented and quickly demolished. Followed by Chicken Jalfrezi, Chicken Tikka Bhuna, Chicken Korma, A Sanjoys Special Balti and a scampi £4.85 and chips £1.15 for our more mature colleague. All dishes were generous, chicken exceptionally good. £86 for five with complimentary brandys, needless to say, we are all looking forward to revisiting.' TE. Sunday Lunch Special: £5.95 per person from 2 to 6 including five starters, ten main courses and two puddings. Complimentary chutney tray.

Wigan

CINNAMON NEW ENTRANT

487, Preston Road, Standish, Wigan 01257 426661

From the house of Sagar, owned by Mr Amin. 'Driving up the M6, needing a rest and some sustenance. The pastel decor, light wood floor, cream seating and fresh linen looked fabulous, immediately greeted with large smiles from smartly dressed staff. Busy on a wet Wednesday night, yet service was relaxed if swift. Ordered by test meal of Popadoms (fresh), Pickles (piquant), Meat Samosa (light filo pastry, lean spiced lamb with salad on a stylish triangular plate), Chicken Tikka Bhuna (large chunks of chicken in best sauce I've ever tasted) with warm Chapati. Considering the quality and size, washed down with a lager the bill surprisingly modest at £15. I felt invigorated after this experience and will return with my family.' ae. Takeaway: 10% discount. Hours: 12-2/6-11.30, Saturday and Sunday 1-11.30.

TASTE OF BENGAL NEW ENTRANT

11 High Street, Standish, Wigan 01257 473119

'Great service, food and prices. Prawn Puri Garlic - lovely. Two Balti Dishes - piping hot, loads of thick spinach in Chicken Sag Balti.' JH. Probably of little interest to the gourmet readers of this *Guide*, there is the novel 'Weightwatchers' Special Start with tangy grapefruit chutney, Main: quarter chicken breast tandoori, or fillet of chicken tikka shashlik, boiled rice, chapatti, pineapple & cucumber raita and salad.

©	Curry Club Discount	**U**	Unlicensed
V	Vegetarian	**ANP**	Alcohol not permitted
e-a-m-a-y-l	Eat as much as you like	**BYO**	Bring your own alcohol

MERSEYSIDE

Area: North West
Population: 1,415,000
Adjacent Counties:
Cheshire, Lancs,
Greater Man

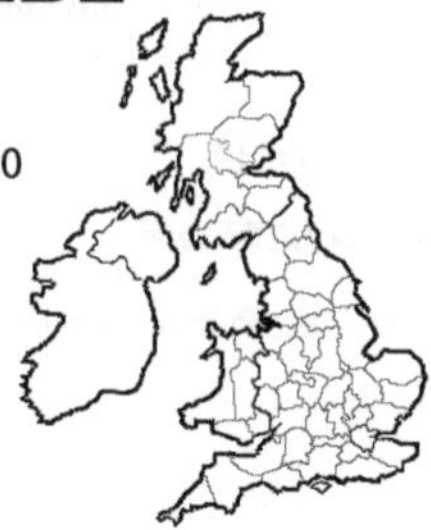

Liverpool

ASHA

79 Bold Street, Liverpool 0151 709 4734

'The oldest Indian restaurant in Liverpool, established 1964. *'Thursday lunch time, flourishing including toddlers chomping away happily on Bhajias and Samosas. Ordered the Business Lunch £3.50: Bhajia - flat, crisp outside, moist outside, excellent spicing and Samosa - small, filling more than acceptable, served with yoghurt and fresh crisp salad. Chicken Madras with Pullao Rice (offered, wait for it, CHIPS). Sauce good strength, five good sized pieces of chicken. Pullao Rice OK. Service reasonably good. Value? how can you argue with £3.50 a must for any curryholic needing a quick lunchtime fix! I think I may become a regular.'* DB. [And you have, haven't you Dave.] *'Chicken Tikka Biryani with Madras sauce was exquisite.'* DB. *'Friday lunch and restaurant wasn't busy. Lunch Special £3.95,Onion Bhajia, Samosa, Chicken Madras and Pullao Rice.'* [you get quite a lot for £3.95 don't you] *'Bhajia and Samosa very good, madras - good portion, six pieces of chicken, good spicy and tasty sauce, rice average. Superb value.'* DB. Sunday Early Bird: £7.95 from 5-7. Takeaway: 10% discount. Hours: 12- 2, closed Saturday and Sunday and 5-12, Friday and Saturday to 1

GULSHAN TOP 100 AWARD WINNER ©

544 Aigburth Road, Liverpool L19 0151 427 2273

Established in 1986. Seats 72. One look at M and S Rahman's venue tells you that it is likely to be good. Along its three-shop frontage is a white fascia, supported by twelve pillars, above each of which resides an attractive uplighter resembling an ice cream cone. Between each light is a small canopy that crowns each of the tinted, partially-curtained windows below, beyond which one can see an inviting restaurant scene. There's a smart lounge complete with leather Chesterfields, and the 76-seater restaurant, in 3 rooms, with equally impressive leather-backed chairs. The toilets are very expensively fitted out and they're spotless. The 'ladies' powder room contains hairspray, perfumes, deodourants, hand-creams, cotton-buds and its very own resident resplendent black elephant. Sorry, chaps, no can see, not even if you're Lily Savage in full drag. DR says *'you could eat your dinner in there'*– you're welcome, Denise, and we get your drift, but the Toilet Tikka has limited appeal, no matter how long the queue. The waiters wear striped waistcoats, and the tables are all well-dressed too, with crisp linen and decent cutlery. *'Even before we started to study the menu, complimentary Papadoms and chutneys were discreetly served . . . why doesn't every Indian restaurant do that?'* asks GB. This is clearly a caring restaurant. They give a nuts-warning where relevant and are great with kids. Several regulars have remarked that the prices, though a little high, have hardly varied in several years, indeed we can confirm that they are the same now as in 1998. Starter Specialities include: Dahi Begoon with Puri £2.70, finely spiced aubergine with onions and topped with plain yoghurt, served on a puri. Fish Kofta £3.70, delicately spiced minced trout kebabs. *'Definitely a* **TOP 100.** *Took the Guide's advice and had a Mustard Balti Chicken, £4.95 cooked with mustard and wine, and Green Balti Masala, £4.95 containing puréed coriander, tamarind, green chilli and green herbs. Great when places experiment, thoroughly satisfied and went to the good pub opposite, then braved Liverpool's occasional public transport.'* rdl. *'Recommended. Delighted to go.'* RC. *'Very, very good, especially, as recommended, the Chicken Zeera and Green Balti Masala.'* LH. The imaginative use of wine is rare in Indian restaurants and, done well as it is here by owner-chef M Rahman, it gives traditional dishes an unexpected and subtle lift. Takeaway: 30% discount, free popadom with Chutneys with every order. Hours: 5-11.

Newton-le-Willows

TASTE OF INDIA 

56 Market Street, Newton 01925 228458

Akhlaqul Ambia's 80-seat Taste's house specials include: Balti Exotica – meat, chicken, lamb and king prawn, medium spiced. Balti Ruhabja – tikka cooked in mincemeat, highly spiced. Balti Garlic Chicken – tikka with fresh garlic and green peppers. Takeaway: 15% discount. Sunday buffet £7.95 between 3pm and 10pm. Hours: 5-12. Branch: Haydock Tandoori, Kenton Lane, Haydock.

Southport

THE KASTURI NEW ENTRANT

40, Eastbank Street, Southport 01704 533102

'Very nice, good decor, facilities. Prawn Puri very good, not greasy, Mixed Kebab tasty. Really hot Tandoori Mixed Grill, plenty of meat, lovely flavours, served with a curry sauce and Nan. Pleasant service..' JH. Hours: 5.30-12, Fri/Sat -1.

WIRRAL

The Wirral is neither a town nor a county and, until 1965, was part of Cheshire. Since then the northern part – a small, digit-like, curry-rich peninsula between the rivers Mersey and Dee – has been part of Merseyside. Ellesmere Port (q.v.) remains in south Wirral but is in Cheshire. Our choice of Merseyside Wirral curryhouse towns are in alphabetical order:

Moreton, The Wirral

EASTERN STYLE TANDOORI ©

11 Upton Road, Moreton, Wirral 0151 677 4863

'Shahan and Miah manage and cook respectively at this standard takeaway with better prices locally., DB. Hours 5-12.

SURMA TANDOORI 

271, Hoylake Road, Moreton, Wirral 0151 677 1331

Jamshed Ullah's first-floor restaurant seats 52 diners. *'Good food, tasteful decor and friendly service. Side dish of Matter Paneer and the Chapatti were excellent.'* RK. Takeaway 20% discount. Takeaway: 20% discount. Hours: 5.30-11.30. Scores: 7/10. DB.

©	Curry Club Discount	**U**	Unlicensed
V	Vegetarian	**ANP**	Alcohol not permitted
e-a-m-a-y-l	Eat as much as you like	**BYO**	Bring your own alcohol

New Brighton, The Wirral

KHAN'S TAKEAWAY NEW ENTRANT

243 Rake Lane, New Brighton, Wirral 0151 639 7017

Formerly Lucky Balti. *'So, my beloved Lucky Balti is no more, chef and staff have up and left to pastures new. Now closes as 11pm, so my visits have been curtailed. Advertised as a Bangladeshi takeaway - the first in the area. New dishes for me to try. Nawaabi Murghi £4.95 - tandoori chicken cooked with mint and garlic. Narangi £4.80, chicken or lamb in a tandoori sauce with ginger, tomato and coriander. Asari Chicken £4.95, cooked with mixed pickle, and green chilli. However, started with my usual Chicken Tikka Biriani £6.50 with Madras sauce - good portion, well cooked, no omelette, excellent sauce, nice and spicy. Second visit ordered Chicken Sylhety £4.85 with plain rice - good portion of sauce, massive portion of rice, good amount of chicken with plenty of green chillies and a sauce to die for - hot, vibrant, bursting with flavours in the mouth. Very impressed, but I may have to change my drinking habits to make sure I get there before they close.'* DB. [Careful Dave!] Hours: 5-11.

Wallasey, The Wirral

ANAZ NEW ENTRANT

137 Saughall Massie Road, Upton, Wirral
0151 606 1040

Formerly Saughall Massie Balti and Tandoori Takeaway. Now has a sit down restaurant, menu the same. *'Popadoms fresh and crisp, but chutney portions were a little on the poor side. Mixed Kebab - Onion Bhajia, soggy but generous size; Seek and Shami Kebab, nicely spiced, fair portion served with fresh green salad and kebab sauces. Main meals consisted of Chicken Tikka Balti jalfrezi - good portion of tender chicken, plenty of green chillies. Described as hot on menu, I wasn't disappointed, but large pieces of green pepper had gone mushy. Chicken Balti Bhuna, good portion of chicken, lightly spiced sauce, ideal for Jaqui, who is a bit of a wimp when it comes to the curry art, she did enjoy it. Caz chose Chicken Balti Hasina - good portion fo chicken, lots of garlic, sliced mushrooms, best meal of the lot. Chicken Garlic, loads of chicken tikka, and I mean lots of garlic, a little overpowering, even for me. Biggest portion - but Roger polished it off. Rice light and fluffy. Chapattis - OK, a little crisp. Service was slow.'* DB. Delivery service.

TANDOORI MAHAL

24, King Street, Wallasey 0151 639 5948

'This restaurant continually produces a decent standard of food for late night revellers. Very , very drunk. Had Chicken Rezala. I'm sure it was excellent.' On the next occasion, got there about midnight after watching England beat Turkey, so a few beers had been sunk. £42 for four. No alcohol, only water' DB. *'Nothing seems to change in this long established haunt. Usual friendly services - always laugh when we ask for jug of parni (water). Not best in the world but suits occasion ie: past midnight on a Saturday. Mixed Kebab - excellent as were Onion Bhajias and Chicken Chat. Chefs Special, basically a mixed meat curry - excellent, CTM - very good, Chicken Biryani - OK, Chicken Tikka Dhansak - bland. Rice and Breads - good.'* DB

West Kirby, The Wirral

ROYAL BENGAL

150 Banks Road, Kirby 0151 625 9718

'Clean, bright and modern decor. Service good, although slow between Popadoms - crisp and warm with uninspiring chutneys and Starters - excellent Mixed Kebabs. Chicken Tikka Masala was good, thick sauce, sweet, good portion. Chicken Garlic Chilli - excellent, good portion of chicken, chillies and garlic. Rice fluffy, Nan large and superb. Small Cobra £2.30 each - a touch expensive.' DB.

MIDDLESEX

Area: All part of Greater London (west of London)
Population:1,000,000
Adjacent Counties: Berks, Bucks, Herts GL, Essex GL, London NW & W and Surrey GL

The county of Middlesex is very ancient. It once contained most of London, though this distinction became diminished when central London became autonomous during Victorian times. What was left of the county (located west and north of London) was completely 'abolished' when Greater London was formed in 1965, a move unpopular with Middlesex residents. Confusion exists because the

Post Office still use Middlesex as a postal county. Postcodes add to the confusion. Enfield, for example, is EN1, EN2, EN3 *in postal Middlesex but is in (Hertfordshire) GL county. Potters Bar* EN6 *is the same. Barnet is in postal Hertfordshire with* EN4 *and* EN5 *codes. It used to be in geographical Middlesex but is now a GL borough!*

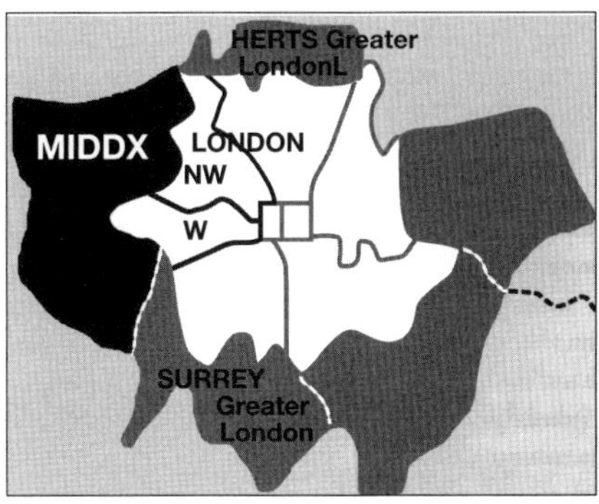

Ashford

TAMANNA'S 

15a Station Road, Ashford 01784 420720

Opened in 1998 by Azizuk Rahman. Seats 70 diners in a clean, modern restaurant with cane furnishings and wooden blinds. Specials: Bengal Fish Zafrani £10.95 – fresh water fish from Bangladesh served on a bed of baby spinach with lime and butter sauce, topped with fried shallots and spring onions, garnished with Karari Bhindi (sliced okra tossed in gram flour, fried until crispy). Sunday lunch: £6.95. Takeaway: 20% discount. Hours: 12-2/5.30-11.30..

Brentford

PAPPADUMS NEW TO OUR TOP 100

GC1 and GC2, Ferry Quays, Ferry Lane, Brentford. 020 8847 1123

Once a bustling market town, Brentford has long been associated with grimy industrialisation, and the image has only recently been shaken off following the redevelopment of the riverside area. Pappadums, the latest restaurant to open on the banks of the River Thames is sited close to luxury apartments and over looks Kew Gardens. Owner, Narinda and Satvir Sindhu pulled out all the stops at their recent restaurant opening where guests included Bollywood celebs, and Euro MP, Robert Evans. The smart, modern looking 150 seater restaurant has the bonus of a patio area in addition to a private dining area. Inspired by traditional Indian decor, the restaurant's weighty wooden doors have been shipped over from the subcontinent, but Pappadums remains a contemporary restaurant with a healthy take on many well-known dishes featured on the menu. and his restaurant menu features pan– Indian as well as occasional dishes from South East Asia. besides more substantial main courses, Pappadums also has a light lunch menu where spiced bites include Wraps, Kath Rolls and even Indianised paneer Spring Rolls. Pappadums is situated in a new development of riverside apartments – Ferry Quays. Plate glass wraps itself around contemporary dwellings. Some apartments view the river, others, open spaces. It is the only Indian restaurant within the complex and has a modernistic, double frontage, which looks out onto a large promenade area. Steps then lead you down to the Grand Union Canal and Thames. When weather permits, diners are welcome to eat outside, on wooden benches with chairs. Owners Narinder and Satvir Sidhu (who also owned a restaurant in Weybridge), Chef Gupta from Oberoi hotels, and young personable Alston Wood from Sri Lankan are the team. Park in the underground car park (or you'll get a wheel clamp). '*Our waiter delivered two crispy and light plain Popadoms with a tray of mango chutney, mixed pickle (not your average but with carrot sticks and gunda), mint raitha and cachumber (onion salad). The menu at Pappadums is varied and includes dishes from other spicy countries, such as China and Thailand. Under the heading of 'Exotic Oriental Delicacies', you will encounter Nasi Goreng £13.90, 'lamb and chicken satay served with spicy fried rice, topped with fried egg and peanut sauce,' Honey Spiced Chicken £8.80, Thai Gaeng Pak £8.80 'stir-fried vegetables, tofu, scallions, mushrooms, hot and sour sauce.' I decided to stick to the Indian section and spied Machhli Ke Pakode £4.95, 'fried cod dish strips coated with mild spiced gram flour.' A generous portion was presented with a good salad and I enjoyed it very much. Pat had Kashmiri Lamb Seekh Kebab £4.50. Again a generous portion of tender, well pounded, spicy meat with salad. The chutney tray was left on the table for us to help ourselves. The menu highlights various dishes with a chilli logo, so we homed in on those choices. Chicken Chettinad £7.25, '...tempered with curry leaves, sun-baked red chillies and peppercorns,' (three chillies). My portion contained large pieces of tender and succulent chicken, smothered in a spicy, tomato-puree sauce, topped with fried curry leaves. Pat chose another Kashmiri favourite, (the kebabs being the first), Mutton Roganjosh £6.95, '... spicy onion gravy flavoured with Rattan Jog,' (two chillies). He did enjoy the dish, however, it was not very hot. In fact, neither was the Chettinad, even though Alston, warned us that the Rogan was 'incendiary level'. I hadn't tried the next dish before, so ordered Aloo Udaigiri £4.50 (two chillies) 'potatoes braised with coriander, cumin and Bikaneri spiced chillies.' Have to tell you that again it wasn't very hot, but pleasant. Pat spotted my favourite lentil dish - Dal Makhani £6.80, 'slowly simmered black lentils.' A small, highly polished brass bucket, complete with handle, filled to the brim and decorated with a swirl of fresh cream came to the table - quite delicious. A portion of Steamed Rice £1.95 escorted everything.'* DBAC. Welcome to our **TOP 100.** Lunch and dinner, daily.

Enfield

MEHEK — NEW ENTRANT

424 Hertford Road, Enfield 020 8443 1844

Large, glass-fronted restaurant. Wooden flooring, stainless steel and wooden seats, mauve and cream walls. Plates, napkins and waiters shirts all match. *'An appealing restaurant, exceptional service and staff well dressed, polite and friendly. A wonderful evening.'* EG. *'Very modern looking - French café style. Very clean, good a/c, no smells of curry which I hate. Food 'different' and top quality in taste, sufficient quantity. Best Indian I have had in twenty years - highly recommended.'* BF. *'Great telephone manner. Deliveries arrive on time, double wrapped, with freebies! My favourite Mutter Panir, lightly spiced, really gooey. Shahi Pullau - load os cashews. Tarka Dal - wonderful.'* RMC Q. Menu extracts: Tandoori Machli Tikka £6.50, fish marinated in Bengali spices and grilled. Badami Murgh £6.95, boneless chicken with mace, cardamom and almond sauce. Gosht Pasanda Nawabi £6.95, thin fillets of lamb, cultured yoghurt, almonds, coconut, pistachio and fresh cream. Mehek Ka Pilau £11.95, tiger king prawns, sweetcorn, potatoes in rice. Hours: 12-2, not Friday /6-11, Fri/Saturday -12.

Feltham

CURRY NIGHTS — NEW ENTRANT

4 Hamilton Parade, Feltham Hill Road, Feltham 020 8751 3300

'Please, please include Curry Nights in the GCG . Both the service and food are excellent. I am thinking of moving to Leicester this year and I already miss Curry Nights.' ES. Menu extracts: Dhal Soup £2.25, Aloo Chat £3.25, Chicken Biryani £5.95, served with Vegetable Curry, Achari Lamb £5.95, hot and spicy and sour, Garlic Nan £1.75. Set Meal for Two: £19.50, Onion Bhajia, Shami Kebab, CTM, garlic Karahi Gosht, Bombay Aloo, Pullao Rice, Nan, Popadoms. Delivery: 3 miles, £15 minimum. Takeaway: 10% discount, cash only. Lunch and dinner, daily.

Greenford

SPICEWORLD

11 Ruislip Road, Greenford 020 8575 6505

'Wide variety of excellent Indian food, where the staff could not be more helpful and friendly, all at very affordable prices.' DP.

Hampton

MONAF'S

119 Station Road, Hampton 020 8979 6021

Named after its owner, Mr A Monaf, we hear good things about this restaurant, and its Sheesh Mahal sister. Monaf's is a well run, popular local. Sunday buffet. 10% takeaway discount. Delivery 3-m radius. Hours: 12-2,30/5.30-12. Branch: Sheesh Mahal.

Harrow

CONNOISSEUR CUISINE OF INDIA

NEW ENTRANT NEW TO OUR TOP 100 ©

37 High Street, Harrow-on-the-Hill 020 8423 0523

It's near the School, right up on the hill. Once you've found a parking place, admire the views overlooking London. Proprietor Sonny Walia and his team ensure you get a warm and professional welcome. Chef Ramesh Honatha trained at India's Sheraton Group. *'He's attractive and single – girls should try to book a table in the kitchen!'* DBAC. [Last time I go there with my wife, Ed.] *'Piaz Ke Pakode, gram flour coated crisp onion slices, sprinkled with chat masala, a large plate of crisply fried onion Bhajias as most know them arrived with a neat pot of coriander chutney – delicious. Pat loved his soft shelled crab, which came with a small salad of cubed tomato, onion and cucumber. Lachadar paratha was light and buttery. Aubergine, the smallest, plump baby aubergines, smothered in a spicy sauce. Chicken with pepper, lovely and spicy. Portions are generous.'* DBAC. Well worthy of joining our **TOP 100**. Hours: 12-2.30, except no lunch on Saturday and Sunday /6.30-10.30, Friday to 12, closed Monday.

PAPAYA — NEW ENTRANT

14,Village Way, Rayners Lane, Harrow
020 8866 5582

Sri Lankan and South Indian Food, which is great in this area. Reports please.

Hayes

ASHA

60 Station Road, Hayes 020 8573 4717

Established in 1977. Fully licensed and air-conditioned. *'Our regular port of call when staying at Heathrow – always an excellent beginning to a holiday...'* [here, here!] *'...Popadoms, crispy and hot with chutneys. Tikka Kebab Platter, brought hot, spicy and sizzling to table on bed of succulent onions with good salad. Good Jeera Chicken with well flavoured Methi Chicken, tender and moist. Ample portions of Pullao Rice. Wine well chilled and nicely serviced. Attractive and comfortable, tables separated by etched glass panels, lots of plants, a lively and pleasant atmosphere.'* G&CM. Takeaway: 10% discount, free bottle of Coke, £10 minimum. Delivery: 5 miles, £10 minimum. Hours: 12-2.30/6-12.

THAMOULINEE SRI LANKAN RESTAURANT

128a Uxbridge Road, Hayes 020 8561 3723

We are often asked what makes a good restaurant, and by all our own yardsticks, Thamouline shouldn't! But, as any regular visit to the subcontinent will vouch, dirt and decor are not in the frame over there. It's service and good food which matter, so welcome back Thamouline, and there are precious few Sri Lankan eateries in the UK. *'Delighted to report that the food is still very good – they can still cook. With our usual bottle of red wine (£5.95) we nibbled Papadams, still the lightest we've ever tasted, with mango chutney, mint raita and a red-tinged coconut chutney. Then our usual Mixed Special starters: Vadai, Mutton Roll, Crab Claw and Prawn Kebab, with a green-tinged coconut chutney and tomato sambol all fresh, and enjoyed, still for just £2.50. I ordered my usual Kothu Rotti, chopped chapatti prepared with mutton, egg, onions and spices. It looks unpromising, but at £4.10 it's a huge, filling portion – dry, spicy and a lovely change to wet curries. Pat's Thamoulinee Special Crab Curry, two crab shells, legs and claws, packed with meat, smothered in rich hot gravy, lived up to expectations at just £3.90. Special Fried Rice £2.80, was huge, with more coconut, tomato sambols and Achcharu (mixed pickle)'* DBAC.

Hounslow

HOUNSLOW BRASSERIE ©

47 Spring Grove Road, Hounslow 020 8570 5535

Open-plan restaurant owned and managed by Naveed Sheikh. Chef Ali cooks Pakistani. Specials: Zeera Chicken, cooked with ground cummin, fairly dry £6.25. Karahi Lobia, black-eye beans, herbs, spices, onions, capsicum and tomatoes £4.25. *'Meat Samosas, £1.50 are absolutely outstanding, the holy grail of samosas!'* TE. *'A very quiet Thursday evening, and there were no other diners until I left at 2030 hours. Samosas were fantastic, certainly the best I can recall. Chicken Tikka was very good with a smoky flavour and nice use of ginger as a garnish. Rice was fine. Three bored waiters gave okay service. Worth another visit if they stay in business.'* RH. Takeaway: 5% off. Hours: 12-3 (Fri. closed lunch)/6-12.

KARAHI MASTER LAHORE TANDOORI — BYO ©

795 London Road, Hounslow 020 8572 2205

Pakistani (Halal) 40-seater opposite Hounslow Bus Garage. Taken over by Mohammad Akmal. Specials include: Roast Lamb Leg £17.50, or, if celebrating with friends, Stuffed Whole Lamb £100 sounds great. Lunch-time specials for £5.95, please ask. BYO is allowed, 1 bottle per person. A free drink to Curry Club members from Mr

Akmal – cheers! Delivery: £15 minimum (6 free Papadams), 4-mile radius. Hours: 12-12.

NEW HEATHROW TANDOORI
NEW ENTRANT

482 Great West Rd, Hounslow 020 8572 1772

'The original Heathrow Tandoori was founded in the 60 s, but has been sold to the Rahman family, who completely refurbished and reopened in 2002. They have made the NEW an even bigger success than its predecessors. Smoked glass windows, light wood floor, new cane furniture with expensive linen and cutlery present an upmarket image, yet prices are highly competitive. Meat Samosas £1.95 - exquisitely cooked and stuffed with lean, spicy minced lamb Balti, Tikka Bhuna £5.85 and Tikka contained large slices of piquant breast meat. Superb Pullao Rice £1.65, Onion Bhajia £1.95, chips' [WHAT?] *'and Paratha £1.50. The Obligatory Cobra lager was ordered to wash this all down. Meojanur kindly offered us a drink on the house - Kuch Nai - Indian whisky that was delicious!'* TE. Menu extracts: Kufta Bhuna £5.85, meat balls in thick, medium sauce. Lamb Ginger Masala £4.35. Prawn tangy Masala £5.15, rich garlic flavour. Dal Lalmirch £2.50, lentils with fried red chilli. Takeaway: 10% discount. Delivery: £12 minimum, 4 miles. Hours: 12-2/5.30-11.30.

Ickenham

DARJEELING NEW ENTRANT

89 High Road, Ickenham 01895 679300

Darjeeling is a popular local restaurant, serving the formal curry competently and successfully. It even offers roast chicken and chips!!! What's wrong with curry, we ask, but I suppose the restaurant has all the angles covered! From what we hear, there are many regulars, and the establishment has been going for many a year. Takeaway 5% discount. Deliveries, min order £30, 2 mile radius.Hours: 12-2.30/6-11.30.

Northolt

EMPRESS OF INDIA ©

40 Church Road, Northolt 020 8845 4361

Est. 1974, Ali, Zaman and EH Khan's a/c 52-seater serves popular curries. Specials include:

Butter Chicken Massalla, CTM, Balti dishes. Sunday lunch buffet – 12-6pm £6.95. Takeaway: 10% discount. Delivery: 4 miles, £13 minimum Hours: 12-2.30/6-12; Sun. 12-12.

Northwood

ROYAL COTTAGE ©

59 Green Road, Northwood 01923 824444

Opened in 2000. Seats 85. Specials: Papadam Spring Roll – papadoms roll filled with minced chicken or prawns. Chicken Bhutuwa £7.95. Mari Chicken £7.95 – peppercorn and green chillies. Hours: 12.30-2.30/6-11.15.

SHANTI 

48 High Street, Northwood 01923 827856

Established in 1984, formerly the Viceroy, this 60-seater, taken over by Mofiz Miah in 1994. Decorated with carved wooden art hanging on white walls. Specials: Lamb Shahjanee – lamb tikka cooked with spicy kebab mince and sautéed onions served with rice or naan. Sunday buffet: 12-3pm, £7.25 adults, £4.25 children (under 10). Takeaway: 15% discount. Delivery: £10 min, 3-miles. Hours: 12-2.30/6-12. (Sunday buffet £7.25 to 3)

Osterley

MEMORIES OF INDIA

160 Thornbury Road, Osterley 020 8847 1548

'After an intensive sailing weekend in the Solent, I was gagging for a curry. Popped in to see my aunt and uncle (ex-army), they recommended Memories. Good, light, brasserie-style decor, interesting carved wood panels and screens, service swift and attentive. Superb Meat Samosas, light pastry, flash fried lean lamb. Curries all contained ample portions of meat, fragrant Pullao and breads all truly delicious.' AIE. Branches: Memories of India, 18, Gloucestershire Road, SW7. 020 7581 3734. Memories of India, Reguliersdwarsstraat Amsterdam, and Drieharingstraat 16, 3511 BJ Utrecht, Netherlands.

Ruislip

RICE N SPICE TAKEAWAY ©

73 Station Approach, South Ruislip
020 8841 5498

Kaizer Ahmed Chowdhury has agreed a drink for CC members as their discount at his (unlicensed) takeaway. Chef Cherag Ali's specials include: Chicken Tikka Mushroom Korai £4.30 and Peshwari Chicken or Lamb. Delivery: £12 minimum, 3-mile radius. Hours: 12-2/5-11.30.

RUISLIP TANDOORI 

115 High Street, Ruislip 01895 632859

This air-conditioned venue is an old friend of this *Guide*. It's a 52-seat Nepalese restaurant in black and white with flowering trees, Nepalese handicraft, pictures and a beautiful golden Buddha, which is, we're told, 'the main attraction apart from the Nepalese food'. Owner KB Raichhetri enjoys explaining about his Nepalese house specials on the menu. Takeaway: 10% off. Minimum charge: £8. Sunday buffet £7.95. Delivery: £15 min, 2-miles. Hours: 12-2.30/6-12.

Southall

From a single acorn the former Maharaja, there is an satisfying number of sweet/snack centres, cafés and restaurants to be found on South Road and the Green, but mostly on the the Broadway, the main artery through Southall. Expansion westwards continues, where its unexpected bonus is a pleasing growth of Sri Lankan suppliers. These places cater primarily for their indigenous Asian population, a generally peaceful mix of Indian and Pakistani Sikh and Punjabi carnivores, enhanced by East African Asians and most recently, Somalis. If you are none of these, do not feel inhibited from entering. Everyone is treated equally and all are welcome. Some venues are licensed and modern, aiming at the younger Asians. Others are café-style and unlincensed. At all of them you'llll find good, authentic cuisine in straightforward, functional eating-houses, at realistic prices. The food is served from early morning to late night, fast and fresh. One or two corres-pondents have bemoaned the use of the microwave to heat the food. We point out that a microwave is merely a heater, which has gained a poor reputation because it cannot heat pastry well (samosas for example). It is not to be despised, and does not demean the food it heats. Better that than unhygeinically keeping the food warm in bainmaries for hours on end. Overleaf we examine our (and our correspondents') favourite eating holes:

BALTI & TANDOORI WORLD U

185- 187 The Broadway, Southall 020 8867 9991

'There is no such thing as Balti', I was earnestly told by a wealthy Indian lawyer who lives in Southall. Readers of these pages will know I'm always being told that by Indians. When I queried this restaurant with him, he poo-pooed it, telling me *'it's not a place I'd visit'*. Strange isn't it how often people form opinions without ever trying the goods. Fortunately our inquisitive scribes try everything, and they like this one. *'World'*, is the focus word at this newish venue in the westward expansion, mentioned above. Not only does it do Balti dishes, aka Karahi by the Punjabis, and Tandoori items, it does a fascinating mix of dishes from the culinary subcontinental world: Representative dishes from Gujarat, Punjab, Kenyan Asia, and north and south India are all on offer. *'Service is very quick and informative. Waiters kindly fetched beer and soft drinks from the adjoining off-license. Customers can try their hand at cooking their own dishes. All dishes were of a high standard and were more authentic Indian-style cooking than some other restaurants we've visited. A memorable evening.'* SF. Hours: 11.30am-11.30pm.

BOMBAY

177 The Broadway, Southall 020 8560 4646

This restaurant has been around for a few years and has breathed fresh air into the 'formica cafes' of Southall – it looks very modern and trendy inside and out – all black and white paint and stained wood. There is a bar on which to prop yourself up on (if you can elbow the proprietor's friends out of the way who seem to treat the place like their local pub), a big TV for entertainment, many framed pictures of 'stars' and a party room which always seems to be full of beautifully sari-ed ladies having a roaring time with a booming disco and disappearing trays of steaming food being carried upstairs by some gormless youth. The menu is small but that's OK, with all you really need listed. The waiter noticed me gaping at the TV, turned over to Eastenders and put on the subtitles – how kind! Papadams are good with an excellent chutney tray – definitely hand-made, lovely. Curries are well above average but with one criticicsm, they are a little salty for my taste. Good value wine list. Enjoyable.

BRILLIANT TOP 100 AWARD WINNER ©

72-76 Western Road, Southall 020 8574 1928

Owned by Kewel and Davinder (Gulu) Anand since 1975, who settled in the UK, having been forced to flee from troubled Kenya. Over the years they have expanded their operation from one shop front to three.. Now, when driving down the Western Road, the Brilliant seems to light up the whole road. Redecoration and expansion, have taken place. Now seating 180, also there is a first floor party room, with its own bar and music equipment (for discos etc.) which seats 80. ¾t is still always full to bursting, being especially popular with happy, chattering Asian families, with rather more reserved whites in smaller groups. It simply proves that when something is really good, price is not the all-important criterion. It also indicates that Southall wants more luxury licensed restaurants than it currently has. The tables are large, and groups of 10 to 20 are the norm. Half of these will be kids, and Asian kids are always well-behaved at the restaurant, loving the experience as much as their parents. The restaurant has many large tables, laid out banquet-style, white linen cloths and burgundy paper napkins. Small matching chandeliers and wall-light fittings, padded velvet chairs. On busy nights you may find yourself sitting next to an unknown dinner companion, but conversation soon flows, as does the Punjabi cuisine, which is deliciously robust and spicy but not necessarily hot. Carrot and mint home-made pickles are on the table, Masala (only) Papadams, which can be either fried or roasted, will be served while you peruse the not overly large menu. You say: *'Visited many times! An exceptional restaurant! Standard of food, the way it's served, atmosphere, beyond compare. Cannot enthuse about enough! Well worth a 280-mile round trip from Weymouth! Vegetable Keema, CTM and Kofta are all wonderful. In fact, I might just drive up there now!'* RC. And we thought our 80-mile trip heroic. Can anyone beat Roger's distance record?

'Easy to find, difficult to park. Very popular with the locals. Friendly and helpful service. Enormous helpings.' R&NT. *'On our spur-of-the-moment visit, Gulu was behind the bar, holding the fort, as Kewal had the night off. He greeted us and sat us on a generous table for four. A Brilliant restaurant hallmark, is the chutneys already on the table. Both are homemade and are expected to be devoured with the popadoms and starters. Our particular favourites are the spicy but sweet, Imli and the chilli hot, minced Podina. Pat and I both agreed that Jeera Chicken was a must. Jeera, along with its sister dish 'Butter Chicken' are legendary, absolutely delicious, you will not be disappointed. And at £8 for half a chicken (plenty for two) is exceptional value. Other starter dishes that might catch your eye include: Fried Masala Egg £2, boiled eggs filled with spices and fried in batter; Fish Pakora £5, Talapia fish traditionally marinated in Keynan style coated in batter and fried. While we were chomping into legs and thighs of chicken, Gulu's chef appeared with a dish laden with tandoor items, including Lamb Chops, Chicken Tikka and Seekh Kebabs, which we happily ate. Curries here are firmly Punjabi in style, which means spicy, but not necessarily hot. Pat chose one of his all time Brilliant favourites: Palak Lamb £8, chunks of lamb cooked with spinach. It was very good indeed, tender lamb intermingled with spinach, which did not over dominate, as it sometimes can do and I, Karahi Chicken £9, chunks of chicken smothered in a spicy sauce with fresh capsicums. Our main courses were accompanied by Plain Rice and Tandoori Roti. However, because we had over indulged with Popadoms and Starters (not entirely our fault!), we failed to clear our plates, so Gulu had them packed up for us to enjoy the next day.'* DBAC. Specials are served in decorative copper beaten pots with serving spoons to match, balanced on individual heaters. The Anand signature dishes remain their most popular. Chilli Chicken, Butter Chicken, Jeera Chicken £16 whole bird or £8 half, on the bone, Methi Chicken £8, spicy fenugreek sauce; Keema Peas £8, minced lamb with garden peas; Alu Chollay £5, chickpeas in spicy sauce; Lamb Biriani £13; Kulcha £1, bread rolled and fried.*'finger lickin' good, leaves the Colonel at the starting gate'* DD. 100 parking spaces opposite in Featherstone High School. Takeaway: 10% discount. Free delivery only to regular customers. Hours: 12-3 Tues.-Fri (no lunch Sat. & Sun)/6-11.30 (12am on Fri. & Sat.); closed Monday.

GIFTO'S LAHORE KARAHI AND TANDOORI BYO

162-164 The Broadway, Southall 020 8813 8669

Asif Rahman's Gifto has for many years operated one of Southall's best-stocked Asian grocery stores (at 115-119 The Broadway). Mr Rahman also takes a stand at the BBC Good Food Show cooking and selling his food at the exhibition. He has recently added 'Gifto's' to the name of his well-established and extremely popular restaurant' a few doors down from the shop, on the other side of the road. Its huge plate-glass window with sliding doors dominates the front of the 120-seater. The open stainless-steel kitchen runs down one side, the tandoor oven being in view from the street. Watch the chefs prepare Pakistani curries and accompaniments, with a noisy tossing of karahis and thumping of nan bread-making accompanying the beat of the Bangra background (make that foreground) music. Sit at simple formica tables at the front, or at the back in more 'glamourous' ones with high-backed padded seats. It's all pure show business, and it's good business, as the crowds of young Asian prove. Kebabs are the most popular, though the food, uncompromisingly Punjabi, is all of very high quality. Specials include: Niharhi – spicy leg piece with spicy gravy £5.50, Paya – lamb trotters with thick gravy £5.50, Haleem – crushed lentils and lamb £5.50. There is also another counter with cold savoury items, Paan and sweets. Gifto's is rare in Southall for serving Bhel Puri (see A to Z of the Curry Menu) *'My favourites include: Dahi Vada, Alu Tikki and Chana Masala £1.80, Bhel Puri £1.90, Papri Chat £1.70 – Yum Yum! ie very passable and the only place to get this in Southall. Waiters have a leisurely approach to service but are happy about it.'* DBAC.. Papadam complimentary. Delivery free locally. Room upstairs holds 350 for weddings etc. Hours: 12-11.30 (Sat & Sun to 12am).

GLASSY JUNCTION

97 South Road, Southall 020 8574 1626

Drive north over Southall railway station bridge, observing the tiny (and excellent) kebab house on its brow on the left and ahead you can't miss the

©	Curry Club Discount	U	Unlicensed
V	Vegetarian	ANP	Alcohol not permitted
e-a-m-a-y-l	Eat as much as you like	BYO	Bring your own alcohol

amazing vista of Glassy Junction. It's a pub, whose exterior is clad with gigantic Hindu figures. Being a pub, it serves booze just like any other pub. Its clientèle is largely young trendy Asians, the like of which abound in Southall. Bangra and Hindi movie music blares out. Add the chattering, and the noise is more deafening than a migrating flight of starlings. As to the food, there's a splendid selection of tandoori and curry items.

KARAHI TANDOORI KABAB CENTRE ANP

161-163 The Broadway, Southall 020 8574 3571

Owner AF Choudhury and Manager Dalawar delightedly tell that their venue, known locally as TKC, was an original of the genre, founded in 1965, early days in Southall's currinary development, and that there have been numerous copiers, not least the ones dead opposite. And what is the genre? Firstly, it is and was uncompromisingly Asian in food style and service, though, all are welcome, of course. In 1965, few whites visited it, now things have changed, and they are as taken for granted as the Asian clientèle. The venue is open-all-hours, and the price is right – inexpensive, and designed to attract regular local custom several times a week at breakfast, lunch tea or dinner. Next, standard shop full-length windows ensure that when walking past, you are immediately attracted to the display cabinets containing all sorts of tempting snacks such as Pakora, Bhel Poori, Gol Goppas, Jeera Pani (cumin water), Tikki, Samosa, Indian sweets, etc. Alongside, and equally on show are the chefs, under head chef Farooq, and they soon learn to show off, much as do Tepiyakki chefs in the Japanese equivalent. Their freshly cooked Tandooris, Kebabs and breads, Punjabi Karahis and curries are cooked to order, and are quite delicious. Inside is a clean and tidy, no frills café-style restaurant, seating 66, with formica tables, and waiter-service. Head chef Farooq's menu says 'please specify your taste of chillies when ordering. His Appetisers include: Reshmi Spring Lamb Boti, tender succulent pieces of lamb marinated in double cream roasted in the tandoor £3.50. Paneer Tikka, chunks of vegetarian cheese marinated with spices and baked in tandoor £3. Main courses: Nehari, shank of lamb served in a spicy sauce £4. Zeera Chicken, made with butter and cummin seeds £5. Sarson Ka Saag, mustard and spinach leaf £3.50. House Specialities: Chargha, fully roasted and tenderly spiced, free-range chicken, a recipe from the inner Punjab £6.50. Chappal Kebab, beaten mince steaks cooked and served on a sizzler, a speciality from the North-West Frontier Province £4. Try the Kulfi Faluda, a Pakistani version of the Knickerbocker Glory £1.80. Pinad Da Buffet £6.99. All food is prepared with Halal meat. Alcohol is strictly prohibited. Hours: 10am-11pm. I wish this were the formula all over the country, rather than the exception in the various Asian communities. No wonder it gets very busy with all age groups, from the pensioners, mums and babes in the day to the young trendy ebullient fun-loving Asians at night and weekends. Hours: 9am-12am. Branch: Tandoori Express on Jalebi Junction, 93 The Broadway, Southall.

MADHU'S

BEST IN UK AWARD WINNER 

39 South Road, Southall 020 8574 1897

It is with great pleasure that we announce that our **BEST RESTAURANT AWARD** is, for the first time ever,out side central London. Not far outside, but far enough to raise eyebrows, and no doubt to raise suspicions. Owner Sanjay Anand, of whom more later has absolutely no idea that we are doing this. But he has been a great friend over the last twenty years or so. He has catered for our Awards ceremonies in Central London, and he and his delightful wife Rena have been twice to India with us on our Gourmet Tours. We have been to his home and he to ours. He is unsparingly generous, and spectacularly successful at operating his Asian wedding department in several major London hotels, including Grosvenor House Hotel which he fills with 1,500 guests at a time. We have been his guests at some of his own family occasions and at the show he puts on. We are proud to be considered 'one of the family'. Sanjay will worry that we have therefore given him this award because of this friendship. Well, we haven't. We have done it because this *Guide* always leads the way. There are numerous central London contenders, with far more prestigious addresses. But Sanjay, his Madhu's, his chefs, waiters and team, and his totally positive can-do attitude, simply cannot be bettered. So watch out Sanjay, Madhu's will be busier than ever, with people, being hyper-critical because of this Award. Let them. First, let's look at the background. Opened in 1980 by JK, KK, Sanjay and Sanjeev Anand, nephews of the great Mr Anand of the Brilliant (*see entry above*). The restaurant seats 94 on two floors, the upper floor, toilets and second bar being reached by a large spiral staircase at the front of the restaurant. You will often find Sanjay in the restaurant, welcoming diners as old friends – you will know which one he is, because of his very distinctive laugh. Our *Guide* was the first to recognise this restaurant, back in 1984, when the clientèle was mostly Asian. Today, and dozens of awards later, there are as many non-Asians as Asians enjoying the food and ambience here. In 1999, the homely venue was totally revamped at considerable expense. We said then: '*It is now absolutely amazing and would not look out of place in the West End. Walls are a creamy buttermilk, squares of gold leaf have been hand-brushed onto one wall making for a very dramatic look. All chairs have been replaced and upholstered in a heavy brocade style material, green and cream. Indian art and lighting is discreet. It has to be the poshest restaurant in Southall.*' DBAC. And then, in 2002, the place was gutted by fire. '*The police phoned at about 3am. As I drove in I could see an orange glow in the distance, which grew bigger as I came nearer I knew was mine*' said Sanjay. '*And I had under insured!*' It took Sanjay ten months to sort out finance and rebuild. The new-look is even better than the last. A water feature is located under a glass floor at the entrance. Black granite and wooden flooring are set off by plain but modern high back chairs, white table linen upon which invitingly laid smart glasses, cutlery and plates await you. The spiral staircase has been retained, but, whereas before, upstairs was just an unappealing overflow room, it's now as inviting as downstairs. Both floors seat around 50, and have well-stocked bars at the end. The new kitchens are space-age, and upstairs has a party room, noisily partying on most nights, and a small office suite, from where Sanjay holds court. Waiters wear smart black uniforms with the new red Madhu's logo, discretely displayed. You will not find more up-market surroundings at any other restaurant. Sanjay says it cost £800,000. And it looks it. House manager is new-comer, Adi, of Taj hotels fame, assisted by Ghandi who has been there since time began. To allow brother Sanjeev (Mint) to pay full attention to running the all-important function production kitchens, new Indian-Hyatt-trained chefs have been brought from Delhi. The first thing that happened was that Mint trained them to cook the Anand signature dishes, typically Punjabi with that wonderful Kenyan Asian twist. More importantly, they have brought a whole new range of dishes to the menu. Here are some menu extracts: Butter, Methi, and Jeera Chicken, all £8 for half a chicken on the bone, are an absolute must when dining here.; Nyamah Choma – spring lamb ribs seasoned and marinated and cooked in tandoor. Machuzi Kuku – spring roaster – on the bone, in a thin curry, medium-spiced, a Kenyan speciality – three-person portion £7; and Sanjay's favourite, Boozi Bafu – spring lamb chops from Kenya's Boozi, cooked authentically in a spicy medium sauce, – three person portion £16. Chicken Malai Tikka £8, tender, juicy mildly spiced boneless chicken roasted in tandoor, kept over night in a cream and cheese marinade, flavoured with garlic. Aloo Papri Chat £4, combination of papri (fried crisps), boiled potato cubes, chick peas and yoghurt in fresh mint and tangy tamarind sauce, garnished with fresh coriander. Aloo Tikki £4, pan-fried potato cakes, lightly spiced, flavoured with pomegranate seeds, topped with yoghurt, chickpeas, and a sweet and sour tamarind sauce. Makhni Chicken £8, mild chicken, cooked in rich butter cream gravy, spiced with cardamom and cinnamon. Bharwan Shimla Mirch (Keema) £7, fresh green peppers stuffed with minced lamb seasoned with cardamom and nutmeg, roasted in oven. Bharwan Shimla Mirch (Aloo) £6, fresh green peppers stuffed with potatoes and onions, seasoned with pomegranate seeds, roasted in oven. Bhuna Karela £6, bitter gourd stuffed with its rind and onion masala, flavoured with pomegranate seeds, then oven-roasted. Some of these items are as eye-opening to Southall's Asian community as to the white folks expecting the Bangladeshi curry house formula. Although we say every time, that the food is authentic, and not formula, we continue to get disappointed comments. But most are like this one: *'Definitely one of the best curries I have ever had in my life. Decor was much more modern than I expected as I am fairly used to Brilliant up the road. However, after enjoying Curry Fever in Leicester enormously this was definitely on a par. There were five of us – all brothers – who absolutely love curry and we all thoroughly enjoyed our meal. We arrived very late (around 10.35pm) and I have to say that the service we received was unsurpassable. Our host knew I was a Curry Club member and gave us all the help that we could possibly have needed. Our meal consisted of Tandoori Lamb Chops £6, Jeera Chicken £6.50, an unbelievably mouthwatering flavour, Fish Masala £6.50, quite beautiful, Chicken Makhani £6.50, full of flavour, Prawn Korai etc. This is one restaurant that will most definitely be revisited on many a future occasion. Very reasonable at £125 for five including beer and service.'* LH. *'Never had better meal. It was quite different from the usual place.'* PE. *'I ate here and can confirm its status in the Guide. Food a little pricey, but probably reflects London effect and reputation. Wonderful atmosphere as it was crowded with the local Asian community. Only 30 minutes from Heathrow, so good place to eat between flights. Parking can be difficult.'* PAW. *'Having been going here since 1980,'* [like your Ed] *'It just say it gets better, and better, and better and better.'* DM. Takeaway: 10% discount. Hours: 12.30-3 (Sat. & Sun. closed)/6-11.30; closed Tues. Some 100 plus Indian restaurants up and down the UK proudly display their 'Best in Britain' certificates, awarded by another organisation, with whom we have no axe to grind. But in that context 'Best in Britain' is a brand name, equivalent to our **TOP 100**. Our **BEST IN THE UK AWARD** is just what is says, applied to just one restaurant in each edition of this *Guide*. Previous winners are Chutney Mary, SW10 1992-5 and 1999-2000; Bombay Brasserie 1995-7; La Porte des Indes 1998-9, Quilon, SW1, 2001-3. Welcome to this elite group, Madhu's 2004-5. *See pages 33, 34 & Rear cover.*

OMI'S TOP 100

1 Beaconsfield Road, Southall 020 8571 4831

Big news from long-standing Omi's located off South Road, on a side street. It has taken over the shop unit next door and has doubled capacity to around 80 seats. Rumour has it that the van-hire double act has gone, which means my gag has to go; well just one more time, please!. 'One phone call can order you a lovely, soft, delicious Garlic Naan and a noisy diesel-fumey Transit Vaan!' Owner-chef Mykesh Kharbanda cooks north Indian and Kenyan Asian curries at Omi's. The shop front stands slightly back from the pavement, making room for parking for 6-8 vehicles. A short menu above the counter describes what is on offer, along with the Specials of the Day. The most popular dishes are Ginger Chicken and Palak Chana. Since we were taken here years ago by Indian journalist KN Malik (*'I want to show you Indian food at its best'*), we can safely say this is the Indians' Indian restaurant. We love his food and adore Mykesh's idiosyncrasies. It has the usual plastic tables and chairs, making for a clean and tidy restaurant, but it's the freshly-cooked food you go for. Licensed. Delivery: small charge. Hours: 11am-9pm (Fri. & Sat. to 9.30pm).; closed Sun. Remains in our **TOP 100.**

PALM PALACE

80 South Road, Southall 020 8574 9209

Following four incarnations in as many years up to 2001, Palm Palace has remained in one ownership and mercifully still does Sri Lankan/south Indian, a scarce resource in the UK, and unique in Southall. The place is simply decorated, licensed and all restaurant. And this seems to be working. It is now busier than we have seen before, not over full, mind you – Southall's Asians are a conservative lot – but the if-it-ain't-Punjabi-it-ain't-edible view is hopefully changing. And, as we say every time, so it should. My bench mark crab curry from an early ownership has never matched, but it's still an exciting dish, especially fired up to incendiary level for those of us who cannot do without chilli. There's nothing like picking and sucking out crab meat from legs and shell and dousing it in rich Sri Lankan gravy. Messy shirt-sprinkling stuff, yes, but a slow, pleasurable experience, which is a contender for my desert island luxury. *'Palm Palace never changes and neither does our choice, we don't even bother to look at the menu. Service can be a little slow, so do order everything at the same time and ask for it at the same time. Two plain popadoms with chutneys, Masala Dosa with Sambar and Coconut Chutney and Rasam - lovely Note, the toilets are pretty grim.'* DBAC. Licensed. Hours: 12-3/6-11.

PUNJABI KARAHI 

175 The Broadway, Southall 020 8574 1112

Chef Khurrum Choudhry's restaurant seats 150 and he warns that parking after 6.30pm is 'thin on the ground'. Pakistani and Balti dishes are his speciality, including Mixed Grill £10, Kebabs 60p, Chicken legs £2.60 and Tandoori Batera (quail), £2.90 for starters and Methi Chicken £5.40, Paya – lamb trotters in a spicy sauce £5. Hours: 11.30am-11.30pm (12am on Sat.).

ROXY – NEW ASIAN TANDOORI CENTRE TOP 100

114 The Green, Southall 020 8574 25791

There is nothing new about this venue. It began trading in 1959. Indeed it is still known as The Roxy, although its English transport caff namesake closed over four decades ago. In its place came an Asian version of the same – one of those long-standing restaurants which serve the local community morning, noon and night. Founders Mr Sagoo and Mr Thakhar strategically set up two such venues, located at either end of Southall. have finally retired and sold their 157 The Broadway venue to the next door halal butcher, who has renamed it The Kashmir. Well, I say nothing new, but they have had a smart redec. When you enter the Roxy, there may be a queue, even outside the door, but it won't take long before it's your turn. Long glass counters display tempting Indian sweets and savoury snacks (Bhajias, Kebabs, Samosas, Aloo Tikki, Dahi Vasa, etc.), curries (Murgh Masala, on the bone, Bombay Potato, Sag Paneer, Sag Gosht and more, all cold but will be reheated in the microwave on request), Channa Dal, Rice (Plain, Pullao and Biryani) and breads. *'Pick up a tray and tell the chap behind the counter what you want and whether you are eating in or taking out. Portions are generous and I have to restrain myself from over-ordering. When you have paid (cash or cheques only), take your tray to the other room and seat yourself.'* DBAC. *'The absolute curry experience, should be compulsory for all members to visit! Sample the vast range of dishes on offer, all authentic and served up in a no-nonsense style. We ate vast quantities of food, including Pakoras, Dal (black bean), Chicken and Meat Curries, Rotis and rice. Service with a smile, staff friendly. Highly recommended, must be very high in the* **TOP 100.'** DB. They also serve a wonderful chutney, sticks of carrot, slices of onion, embalmed in a tamarind and yoghurt sauce, delicious, I can't get enough of it. You can BYO (but please ask) though they do sell Cobra, which all makes for a great meal out. Fresh fruit juice and Lassi are available. Hours: 10-10.30 (11pm on Fri.-Sun.). It is high in our **TOP 100.**

SHAHANSHAH VEGETARIAN V ©

60 North Road, Southall 020 8574 1493

Gill Baljinder (manager) and Johl Sarbjit, have since 1984 specialised in cooking from north and south India at their vegetarian restaurant, which seats 30 diners. Samosas and other snacks are the most popular items ordered. Indian sweets are made on the premises, so you can be sure they are fresh. Set dinner £5. Sunday lunch £4.Branch: Shahanshah Vegetarian, 17 South Road, Southall.

TANDOORI EXPRESS ON JALEBI JUNCTION ANP ©

93 The Broadway, Southall 020 8571 6782

Owner Abdul Chaudhury, manager Mr Shauket, and head chef Rassaq's bright and colourful venue appeals to the local young and trendy population. It is often full of chattering, bright young Asians babbling on in animated Southall cockney accents. A richly painted and decorated rickshaw can be seen outside on the wide pavement which enhances the environment. Also a cook makes Jalebis, those crispy, deep-fried squiggles, immersed in syrup, right there on the pavement. You can't get fresher than that, and if you've not seen it done, here's the only place in Britain we know of that does it on view. Great Pakistani curries and fresh breads are a big pull, along with snacks such as Samosas, Pakoras, etc. There is also a vast sweet counter to pile on the pounds (weight that is, not the bill). Starters include: Club Sandwich, finest chicken and lamb BBQ fillings £3. Shami Kebab, mince meat and lentil burger 50p. Dahi Bhalla, lentil flour doughnuts soaked in yoghurt £1.50. House specials: Masaladaar Raan, whole leg of lamb roasted in the tandoor with all the natural juices and flavours sealed within, a Moghul dish from Lakhshmi Chauk, Lahore, £15. Alcohol is strictly prohibited. Hours: 9am-11pm. Branch: Karahi Tandoori Kebab Centre, 161 The Broadway, Southall.

Shepperton

SCHOOL OF SPICE NEW ENTRANT

The Old School House, High Street, Shepperton 01932 242728

'As usual, the welcome was warm and cordial without being smothering. Reasonably standard fare, without anything to scare seasoned curryholics. We had Chicken Tikka, Chicken Shashlik, Plain Rice, Garlic Nan and Bombay Potatoes – a good, tasty, filling meal that didn't leave us feeling bloated.' DD.

Teddington

BENGAL BRASSERIE 

162 Stanley Road, Teddington 020 8977 7332

Established in 1986. Managed by Ali Kausar, head chef Sufian Khan. Air conditioned, seats 44, decorated with Indian and Bangladeshi art on the walls and fresh carnations on the tables. House specials include: Chicken or Lamb Balaka, marinated, cooked with potato, egg, green chilli, red wine, spicy hot. Jeera Chicken, marinated, cooked in cummin. Bangladeshi style Rezela and Jeera Chicken. Min charge £8.50. Collected takeaway: 10% discount. Delivery: £20 min, 2-miles. Hours: 6-12.

Twickenham

PALLAVI SOUTH INDIAN

Unit 3 Cross Deep Court Heath Rd, Twickenham 020 8892 2345

Specialises in South Indian Keralan cuisine, with dishes from the cities of Cochin, Malabar and Travancore. Hot is the norm in Kerala but they cool it for 'western tastes'! So if you want to up the chilli strength, tell them and the kitchen will be more than happy to oblige. Contrary to popular belief, meat, chicken and fish dishes are the norm there. Try Lamb Cutlets: patties made of minced lamb and spices with bread crumbs and fried. Served with tomato sauce and salad. Malabar Chicken is cooked with coconut, curry leaves, garlic and mustard. Fish Mollee is a classic dish, so mild and gentle in its coconut base that even the Raj allowed it at table. And for pud Banana Leaf Cake: made of rice with a sweet filling of grated coconut, banana and jaggery wrapped in banana leaf and steam cooked. *'Visited on return from Kerala, S. India. Authentic food and very good quantity and quality. The waiters came from the region, which makes it better. Keralans are charming people with a special mannerism all their own! On leaving we were given a bag with information from Kerala Tourist Board.'* RH. Hours: 12-3/6-12.

AMIS RENAMED ANP

98 Heath Road Twickenham 020 8891 1100

'Same family who ran the now defunct Rawalpindi in

Twickenham for 40 years. Moved up the road and have re-opened as Amins. Delighted to report the food as excellent as ever. Best curry in the area. No alcohol on the premises these days – a positive for some, a negative for others no doubt.' AJ. A big fat negative for me, Andy, but who am I to judge and you all say the food warrants retaining it in the *Guide*.

Wembley

Rapidly gaining ground as the second Southall. Unlike Southall, its large Gujarati/East African population gives Wembley food a different (predominantly vegetarian) taste from Southall. As with Southall, there are many good sweet/snack shops/cafés and restaurants crammed with Indian goodies. Here are your favourites:

ASIAN KARAHI

272 Ealing Road, Wembley 020 8903 7524

Small venue (25 seats) which exudes careful service and thoughtful cooking. The usual range of Karahi style cooking is available all week, but at the weekend, they offer some really authentic stuff, not for the faint-hearted: Niharhi – marinated leg piece (shank) of lamb served with a spicy gravy, Paya – lamb trotters with thick gravy, Haleem – an almost gruel-like mash of crushed wheat and lamb and Haandi dishes all of very high quality. Spicing is done to taste.

CHETNA'S BHEL PURI TOP 100 V

420 High Road, Wembley 020 8903 5989/8900

A large, very popular vegetarian licensed restaurant with vegan dishes. *'You often have to queue here. We waited on the pavement until they called out our number, but it is well worth it. They do deluxe Masala Dosas, and a great Vegetarian Thali main course. Their Bhel Puri is gorgeous, with its crispy, crunchy textures, and its tart, hot and savoury tastes, and there is a variant called Aloo Papdi Chaat'.* JM. Alongside dishes from Gujarat and south India, they serve pizzas , reflecting the craze, not only amongst Wembley Asians, but continuing to sweep Delhi and Bombay! Hours: 12-3/6-10.30.

KARAHI KING U BYO

213 East Lane, Wembley 020 8904 2760

Fabulous food, Kenyan Asian curries. Try the Mogo Bhajia a pakora of sweet potato complete with a super imli (tamarind) chutney, or the fabulous tandoori (including the breads), curries for meat-eaters and vegetarians. Methi Murgh divine. Hours: 12pm-12am. No credit cards. No corkage, so BYO.

KARAHI RAJA U BYO

195 East Lane, Wembley 020 8904 5553

Established in 1993 by Mushtaq Ahmed. Restaurant seats 150 in two rooms. Pakistani curries are cooked by B Hussain. House specials include: Haandi Chicken – chicken on the bone cooked with herbs, tomatoes and spicy thick sauce. Paya – lamb trotters Lahori style. Vegetarian dishes: Karahi Egg, scrambled egg, tomatoes, coriander and green chillies. BYO allowed, no corkage. Hours: 12pm-12am.

MARU'S BHAJIA HOUSE V ANP

230 Ealing Road, Alperton, Wembley 020 8903 6771

Opened by Maru over 20 years ago, it provides superior family unique style of vegetarian curries and accompaniments from East Africa. Their Bhajias are the real thing, and they are even spelt correctly, rather than the formula Bhaji. Try their Potato Bhajias, besan-batter-coated, deep-fried and served with tamarind (imli) chutney as a real treat to die for. Hours: 12-9.30pm..

MARUTI BHEL PURI V

238a Ealing Road, Wembley 020 8903 6743

A vegetarian restaurant serving inexpensive melt-in-the-mouth delights, such as Dosas with Sambar and, of course, the namesake Bhel Puri. Try their Karahi Corn-on-the-Cob. *'All fantastic stuff for the lucky residents of Wembley. I wish I lived nearer.'* DC. *'After eating our fill of Papadoms, we started the proceedings with Jeera Chicken. Good value in terms of standard of cooking. When there is a concert or football match at the Stadium, a set dinner buffet is provided. Dishes were full of spices and excellent. Service was very friendly.'* AN. Hours: 12-10; closed Tues.

PALM BEACH

17 Ealing Road, Wembley 020 8900 8664

A licensed Sri Lankan and south Indian restaurant, but this doesn't mean there is no meat on the menu. Alongside the Dosas, Vadas and

Hoppers, you will find Mutton Ceylon Curry, tender lamb, steeped in a richly spiced, meaty, juicy gravy. Decorations are relaxed, with batiks and wood carvings. Hours: 12-3/6-11.30; closed Tues. Branch: Palm Beach, 18 The Avenue, Ealing, W13.

POOJA COTTAGE ©

305 Harrow Road, Wembley Triangle
020 8902 4039

Established in '85 by T Moniz, as Wembley Cottage, this 45-seater is one of the few Nepalese restaurants. Baban in the kitchen cooks up unusual delights which include Mariz (pepper) Chicken £5.95, Nepalese Chicken Bhutuwa – highly spiced £6.25. Chicken Chowla – cooked in tandoor, mixed with ginger and garlic £5.95. *'Not terribly impressed with the food.'* RM. *'Very impressed with the food. Recommended to me by so many of my colleagues.'* CT. Hours: 12-2.30/6-11.30.

SAKONI V ANP

119 Ealing Road, Alperton Wembley 020 8903 9601

Alcohol is not allowed at Sakoni, which to some (including Asians we know) is a shame, but which seems not to deter from its popularity and its expansion (see branches below). The founder branch is now enormous, with its conservatory extension serving that Asian of Asian delights, Paan (*see page* 56) It's family-run by Gujaratis Kenyans who know about the food and tradition. But they offer variety to their regular Asian customers (of whom there are many) – dishes such as Chinese vegetarian noodles and Bombay Sandwich, white sliced bread with spicy spreading, a kind of relic of the Raj, the like of which you still, amazingly find in Indian public schools and army messes. Such things make a change, but I for one prefer Sakoni's authentic Indian items (Dosai, Vadai, Uthappam et al, in a pleasant and informal atmosphere. *'Service good and quick. Generous portions. Chutneys are freshly prepared and not removed from the table every few minutes, which makes a change from most other Indian restaurants. Recommended.'* RM. Hours: 11am-11.30pm. Branches: 116 Station Rd, Edgware; 6 Dominion Parade, Station Rd, Harrow.

WEMBLEY TANDOORI 

133a Wembley Road, Wembley 020 8902 2243

First opened in 1984, taken over by Mr D Chhetry in 1999 and given a Nepalese menu. Specials include: Momo, Simi Soup, Nepalese Chicken Bhutuwa, Nepalese Vegetable, Aloo Tama. Delivery: £16 minimum, 2-mile radius. Hours: 12-2.30/6-11.30; Sat. 6-12.

WOODLANDS TOP 100 V ©

402a High Street, Wembley 020 8902 9869

See reports in the branches Hours: 12 -2.45/6-10.45. UK Branches: London SW1 and W1, W4.

NORFOLK

Area: East
Population: 793,000
Adjacent Counties:
Cambs, Suffolk

Dereham

BOMBAY NEW ENTRANT

8 Norwich Street, Dereham 01362 690708

'First class service, good food and drink, shame about the toilets! Hasky Pancakes very tasty, King Prawn Butterfly – OK. Moris Gosht - fantastic flavour. Tandoori Mixed Grill – tasty colourful hot and plenty of it. Washed down by a new experience for me, draught Cobra – lovely!' JH. Menu extracts: Hasky Pancakes £3.50, duck stir-fried. Moris Gosht £5.95, tender strips of lamb and spinach, stir-fried with red and green peppers and fresh chillies. Piaza Nan £1.50, stuffed with onion. Hours: 12-2.30/5.30-12.

Great Yarmouth

BOMBAY NITE 

25a King Street, Great Yarmouth 01493 331383

First opened in 1995. Seats 60. Raza is the owner and Louise Hughes is manager. We hear well of the Roast Chicken Masala and the Sylhet Supreme. Minimum charge £12.50. Service 10%. Takeaway: 10% discount. Delivery: £15 min. Hours: 6-12.

King's Lynn

INDIA GATE 

41 St James Street, King's Lynn 01553 776489

Taken over in August '97 by A Miah (manager) and S Ahmed (head chef). Bangladeshi curries and Balti. *'Warm and welcoming. Seats forty in open layout. Friendly and efficient. Prices a little above average. Very good Reshmi Kebab £3.10, really meaty, excellent balance of spices, topped with small omelette, served with fresh, crisp salad and tangy yoghurt sauce. Better than average Tarka Dal £2.70, rich in garlic, nice and thick. Prices a little above average.'* RW. Takeaway: 10% discount, £12.50 min, cash only. Hours: 12-2/6-12..

Norwich.

NAZMA 

15 Prince of Wales Road, Norwich 01603 616101

Glad to report that Mohabbat Ali's 1996 Nazma venture is thriving. PM says *'Recommended by locals. A delightful meal.'* PM. Minimum charge £5. Open daily for lunch and dinner. Branch: Nazma, 15 Magdalen Street, Norwich.

NORWICH TANDOORI 

98 Magdalen Street, Norwich 01603 621436

Kuti Meah is the managing owner. His 50-seater restaurant has: *'A straightforward comfortable interior. Lamb Pasanda best tried so far in the city. Chicken Tikka Pasanda, mildly creamy, cooked with butter, almonds and sultanas, exceeded expectations.'* TW. Hours: 12-3/6-12.

Thetford

SAFFRON INDIAN CUISINE 

17 St Giles Lane, Thetford 01842 762000

Established in 1999. Seats 30. Specials include: Bengal Chicken Jelfrezi £7.50 – with onions, peppers and crushed Bengali chillies, Madras hot. Achari Chicken £5.75 – in thick sauce with pickle. Delivery: £10 minimum, 5-mile radius. Takeaway: 10% discount. Hours: 6-12.

Wells Next the Sea

WELLS TANDOORI NEW ENTRANT

6 Freeman Street, Wells 01328 710280

Menu extracts: Onion Bhajee £1.95. Muglai Chicken £6.75, mild, creamy sauce, egg yolks, fairly dry. Lamb Tikka Rezala £7.25, medium hot, red wine, chopped onion, green pepper. Aloo Gobi £2.50 potato and cauliflower. Keema Nan £1.90 stuffed with spicy minced meat. *'We've been birdwatching in north Norfolk for at least 10 years and at last someone is on the same wavelength as us and opened a curry house. Placed very handily – almost next to Wells harbour. Very small, perhaps 6 or 8 tables with small waiting area next to the bar. The floor had just been varnished and our walking boots clung to the floor. The bored waiter lightened up tremendously when I engaged him in conversation, he became positively friendly, telling me that the owner came from Birmingham. The chef was obviously starting from scratch – there was a fairly lengthy wait. Roghan Chicken £4.95 and Chicken Vindaloo £4.40 both very similar – bright yellow orange but my worst fears were groundless, tasted completely different. Plenty of large chicken pieces, struggled to find the potato in mine! Ample quantities, but Pullao Rice a bit stingy. Paratha £1.75 really really excellent. Prices slightly on the high side..'* T&MH. Hours: 12-3/6-11.30.

NORTHAMPTONSHIRE

Area: Central
Population: 620,000
Adjacent Counties: Beds, Cambs, Leics, Oxon

Brackley

PRINCE CALCUTTA 

36 Market Place, Brackley 01280 703265

First opened in 1994, taken over by Azizul Islam in 1998. Seats 50. Chicken Moricha £5.95 – barbecued chicken with green chillies, fairly hot.

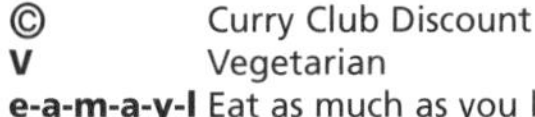

©	Curry Club Discount	U	Unlicensed
V	Vegetarian	ANP	Alcohol not permitted
e-a-m-a-y-l	Eat as much as you like	BYO	Bring your own alcohol

Lamb Bakera with Pullao Rice £7.50 – chicken tikka, minced meat in rich medium sauce. Hours: 5.30-11.30; Fri., Sat. & Sun. 12-2.30/6-11.30.

Kettering

MONSOON BAR & INDIAN ©

Ebenezer Place, Kettering 01536 417421

Established in 1998 by P Sadrani. A colourfully painted Tudor style restaurant, seating 90. Specials: Jeera Tikka Masala £5.95, marinated chicken or lamb cooked with cummin, onion, capsicum and herbs. Punjabi Masala £5.85, Chicken or lamb flavoured with green chillies, yoghurt, capsicum and fresh coriander. Takeaway: 20% discount. Delivery: 4-mile radius. Hours: 5.30-12.

THE RAJ ©

50 Rockingham Road, Kettering 01536 513606

Established in 1991. Seats 110 in two rooms. Goyas Miah has newly refurbished in modern style – wooden floor, marbled walls, chrome downlighters. *'This Bangladeshi restaurant has had such a transformation – I thought I was in Brick Lane. Not only the appearance, the food is much better, more tasty, however with fewer colourants, which has got to be better for the consumer! Very friendly staff and helpful, have good knowledge of their indigenous food! What a wonderful time.'* FAV. *'Just to let you now about wonderful restaurant. Took my drummer and my wife, he was absolutely "gobsmacked" with food and service.'* AB. Specials include: Muktaj, Sharabi, Batera, Chittol. Takeaway: 15% discount. Delivery: £7.50 min, 3-mile radius. Hours: 12-2/5.30-12am; Sun. 12-12am.

Kingsthorpe

BOMBAY PALACE 

9-11 Welford Road, Kingsthorpe 01604 713899

Abdul Ahad's restaurant first opened in 1988 and seats 40 diners. Of chef Abdul Husain's curries, CTM is the most ordered. *'Arrived without booking, offered a choice of smoking or non smoking area (excellent). Jayne, my girlfriend says this is the best Chicken Malaya in Northants! Jayne given rose as we left! (Nice touch). Well worth trying – don't be put off by the location.'* DL. *'20% off all meals including takeaway, Sunday to Thursday. Service was attentive and friendly. Popadoms fresh and crispy. The whole meal was excellent, with fresh vegetables and not a hint of unnatural spices. Cracking restaurant!'* DL. Takeaway: £3 discount on minimum £10 order. Delivery: £10 minimum,Northampton & surrounding villages of Kingsthorpe. Hours: 5.30-12.

Long Buckby

VOUJON NEW ENTRANT

1 Church Street, Long Buckby 01327 843571

Formerly India Village. Licensed and air conditioned. *'Now the only Indian in Long Buckby. Booking is essential. Tables situated nicely apart, allowing privacy of conversation. Very attentive service without pestering! Popadom and Chutneys - good, but spiced ones too salty. Panch Mishali £3.55 and Jhinga Bhuna on Puri £3.65, both excellent. Murgh Tikka Jalfrezi (£6.95 Mogul style), Duck Kabuli Bhuna £6.95, Keema Rice £2.35, Tarka Dal £2.35, Peshwari Nan £1.60 and Plain Paratha £1.60, all superb, generous portions.'* DL. Banquet Night: £8.95, Wednesday. Sunday Buffet: £6.95, child eats free with paying adult, five starters, ten main courses with side dishes and accompaniments, from 12-10.30. Delivery: £10 minimum, 7 miles. Takeaway: 15% discount. Hours: 12-2/5- 11, Sunday 12 -10.30.

Northampton

ASOKA NEW ENTRANT

151 Wellingborough Road, Northampton 01604 231194

'What a recommendation! Quality and presentation of dishes first class. Every dish tasted fantastic!' DL.

BALTI KING U BYO NEW ENTRANT

76 Earl t, Upper Mounts, Northampton 01604 637747

'Visited to celebrate England's fine victory. Arrived at 6.30pm, we were quickly shown to a table and offered popadoms and drinks - you can BYO alcohol. Sheek and Shami Kebabs 75p - excellent quality, served with mint yoghurt sauce and spicy tomato sauce. Balti Chicken Tikka Chana Dal £4.40 and House Special Balti £6.95 - Madras heat with Table Nan £1.85. Both generous and full of meat. Service prompt and attentive. Worth a visit!' DL. Hours: 12-2/5-11, Sunday 12-10.

FAR COTTON TANDOORI 

111 St Leonards Rd, Far Cotton, Northampton 01604 706282

'Far out' wrote a local scribe (IM) of the three Alis: chef Haruni, Ansar and Soub's above-average takeaway in the southern outskirts of town. Specials include: Mint Lamb, tikka meat, mint and almond. Chicken Dhakna, medium spiced, tomatoes, capsicums, fried garlic and mushrooms. Hours: 12-2/5-10.30 (Sat. to 11pm, Sun. to 10pm).

IMRAN BALTI HUT BYO

285 Wellingborough Rd, Northampton 01604 622730

Fully licensed (BYO welcomed). *'Having booked for 8pm, I knew the place was popular, we duly turned up to find a queue to people who had also booked in advance waiting for tables! Entrance area was full and chaotic. After 30 minutes we got a table, too small for our party. Food and service was exceptional, quality and large portions. Family Nan £2.50 were excellent. BUT the experience was ruined by front of house lack of organisation. Can't fault otherwise.'* DJL. *'If you can get inside the door of this extremely popular restaurant and push through the crowds of people also trying to get a seat you are guaranteed an excellent meal. Always best to book* [see above -Ed]. *At the weekend people queue out of the door! Simply decorated, pleasant waiters. A large vegetarian choice. After papadoms and chutneys, don't order starters unless you have a particularly huge appetite, though a must is the family Naan – 2 feet by 18 inches – a highlight. Can BYO for a small corkage charge.'* SS. *'Always excellent.'* SO. Hours: 5.30 (Fri. & Sat. 5) -1am.

MEMSAHIB NEW ENTRANT

357 Wellingborough Rd, 01604 630214

In a former shoe factory. Millionaire businessman Satbachan Singh Sehmi bought the site some years ago and flattened it, for a £4.5 million residential development known as Burlington Court. The front of the factory was left intact and that holds the restaurant. John Dahaliwal, leases the building and his restaurant opened in 2002. *'We decided our first visit should be on Valentines Day! Pleasantly refurbished, minimalist style. Plush high back chairs, modern art, intriguing clock that shines onto a wall, jazz music, dried flowers. Secure parking. Arrived at 7.45, managed advised us that they had bookings for 120 people and the restaurant seats 70. Offered drinks and Popadoms. Samosa Duo £3.25, two pastries, one meat, one veg, served with curries chick peas. Chicken and Fish Pakora £3.34, fillets crisp-fried batter, served with dip - arrived promptly, excellent. Tandoori Combination £11.95, Tandoori Chicken, Lamb and Chicken Tikka, Tandoori Ginga (King prawn), Tarka Da,. Tandoori Masala (Madras strength) £7.95 - Tandoori chicken with green chillies, served with Pullao Rice, Garlic and Keema Nan – all beautifully presented and of excellent quality. Accompanied by superb Mondavi Zinfandel rosé wine. Service, whilst very attentive and polite, everything was done at 100 miles an hour. We were very impressed and will return soon.'* DL. [And you did!] *'all beautifully presented, reasonable portions, excellent combination of flavours. Throughout meal, received attentive service, never once had to pour our own wine. A venue for people seeking non standard Indian cuisine.'* DL. Lunch and dinner. Branch: Memsahib, Leicester.

RAJPUT BALTI 

224a Wellingborough Rd, Northampton 01604 637336

Taken over in 1996 by Shahab Uddin. Seats 50, serves Bangladeshi formula curries, cooked by chef Shofor Ali. Set dinner £8.95. Free bottle of wine with orders over £20. Delivery: £8 minimum. Hours: 12-2.30/6-12.

STAR OF INDIA 

5 Abingdon Avenue, Northampton 01604 630664

Fully licensed and air-conditioned 50 seater, established in 1964, and taken over by Abdul Noor in 1983. Managed by Bodrul Islam. Parking opposite on race course. *'Quality of food, service etc just gets better and better. Popadoms excellent, served with fresh chutneys and pickles. Tandoori Shahjahni and Murgh Pakora, both super, served with a tasty sauce in a silver jug. Batak Mossaladar, lean meat, not fatty with a subtle sauce, gorgeous. Star Mixed Thali, incredible, too much even for me to eat!! washed down with chilled Cobra, served with Pullao Rice and Roti Khasta. Excellent – deserves an award. Booking advisable.'* DJL. *'Having dined here many times, we decided to try their 24-hr notice. Murgh Mossala, a complete meal for 4 including a bottle of Indian red wine (£25 per person, min 4). After crisp Popadoms, with the usual accompaniments, were starters, including Onion Bhajis, Samosas and Tandoori Shah Jahni. Main course, two whole chickens marinated and stuffed with spices and two whole boiled eggs! and Special Fried Rice – did not disappoint!'* DL. Tandoori dishes and Vegetarian dishes can be ordered in half-portions – what a great idea. Takeaway: 25%

discount. Delivery: £9.50 minimum, within Northampton. Hours: 12-2.15/5.30-12 (1am on Fri. & Sat.); Sun. 12-12.

Oundle

ONKAR NEW ENTRANT

26 West Street, Oundle 01832 274312

'Tasteful sixty seater in two rooms, the back being newer with mood lighting, both are permeated with dreary non-asian musak. English waiting staff. Manager helpful and polite. Good, if limited menu. Permanent waft of mouthwatering smells from the kitchen. In a hurry and on diet [yuk!] skipped preliminaries. Enjoyable Chandigar Lamb Karahi (in Pullao Rice) £7.95 - well balanced, spicy, if lurid red, onions, peppers, generous chunks of lamb. Excellent rice, perfectly cooked and fragrant. Presentation of thin, tear-drop Nan superb, plenty of garlic - £1.95.' RW. Special include: Onkar Mushroom £2.95, garlic soaked mushrooms with Punjabi spices. Onkar Royal Shahi Bhuna £6.45, garnished with onions, garlic, ginger, tomato and green chillies. Takeaway: 10% discount. Hours: 6 -11, Friday and Saturday to 11.30. Sunday Lunch Buffet 12-2.

NORTHUMBERLAND

Area: North East
Population: 310,000
Adjacent Counties: Borders, Cumbria, Durham, Tyne & Wear

Bedlington

FRONTIER KARAHI HOUSE 

46 Front Street, West Bedlington 01670 820222

Established 1997. Seats 66. New, modern decor. Specials include: Balti as well as Karahi. *'Discovered by accident on an evening trip for petrol. A considerable amount of thought and effort has gone into the decor and ambience. Presentation of food and quality were excellent. Best Tandoori King Prawns that I have ever come across. Proprietor, Nazir is a wine buff – excellent wine list.'* AMcC. *'Food always excellent, selection of wines cater for every taste. Owner very polite, helpful and always on hand if you would like a chat. Extremely helpful staff, exceeds expectations. Recommended.'* MT & JS. Hours: 5.30-1; closed Mon. Open for lunches in the month leading to Christmas.

Berwick-upon-Tweed

MAGNA TOP 100 

39 Bridge Street, Berwick-upon-Tweed 01289 302736

Free car park 100 yards from restaurant. Jahangir Khan's 80-seater family business – a pretty restaurant is a pretty restaurant with smartly dressed black-tie waiters,. It has been in our *Guide* since we started it in 1984. *'And no wonder.'* says CC member Michael Fabricant, MP. The food, which is the standard formula stuff beloved by all curryholics, is as well described on the menu as it is cooked. It's a port in a storm right there on the A1-Scottish border, with the ghosts of Lindisfarne not far behind. *'Most pleasing and memorable way to spend an evening with friends.'* GFB. Says WA" *'Being a B&B House, we are pleased to send out guests to recommended restaurants. The feedback we receive on the Magna is excellent to say the least, not only for the high standard of Indian cuisine, but also the warm, friendly welcome and very cosy surroundings. Clean, comfortable restaurant, friendly and helpful staff, superb food, generous portions. It's always been well looked after by the family.'* WA. Specials include: Murghi Mossalla, Ash de Bash and Chandee Dishes, very mild with fresh cream and mango from £7.50. Shim Dishes, cooked with green beans from £7.50.. Stays in the **TOP 100.** Takeaway: 20% discount. Hours: 12-2/5.30-12.

Corbridge

CORBRIDGE TANDOORI 

8 Market Square, Corbridge 01434 633676

SM Shahjahan's small restaurant hidden above a shop was est. in '89. Specials: Murghi Masala, succulent cubes of chicken tikka, cooked with mincemeat £6.95. Takeaway: 15% discount. Lamb Karaya, marinated diced tender lamb, barbecued over charcoal then cooked in a slow process in a pot called karaya with garlic . MH continues to dine here regularly (though he lives in Wales) *'It is as good or better than the Valley.'* [see entry] *'and I go to both. If you want excellent decor and different dishes, go to the Valley. If you want excellent "standard" dishes, come here. It has only two drawbacks: it is small and can get stuffy and hot when busy, and it does get busy, especially at weekends. I cannot recommend it highly enough.'* Hours: 12-2.30/6-11.30.

THE VALLEY TOP 100 

The Old Station House, Corbridge 01434 633434

Corbridge station building in the beautiful Tyne valley, was built in 1835 for Stephenson's railway. It is no longer used as a station although it is on the important Newcastle-to-Carlisle railway line. Trains stop at Corbridge station throughout each day, but passengers do not use the old building any more. That is until Daraz (Syed Nadir Aziz) turned it into a stylish, up-market Indian restaurant in 1991. Seats 80, car parking for 20 directly outside. A feature of which is a unique service, for parties of 10 to 80 at £20 a head, including return travel. Uniformed restaurant staff welcome you at Newcastle Central Station and escort you by train to The Valley. En route, choose four courses from the à la carte menu. The order is rung through on a mobile. Your starter is awaiting your arrival. *'It beats ordering a taxi.'* GM. Of course, individuals can make their own way here and back by scheduled train – but beware a fairly early last train. Or, there is parking for 12 cars. Why not book your takeaway by phone en-route, collect, pay and eat it, without leaving the train? As for the restaurant, there is a reception room and 80 seats in four connecting rooms (one of which opens onto the eastbound platform). Decor is lush and Indian. And the food? Chef Abdul Khalick's menu contains all the CC (currinarily correct) favourites plus some good specials. Chingri Moslai, prawns with garlic and mustard. Macher Bora, tuna fish kebab. Luari Mangsho, medium hot lamb dish, cooked with tomatoes, green pepper and fresh coriander. Rajha Chingri Sagwala, king prawns cooked with fresh spinach, coriander and green chilli. Dahi Baigon, large grilled aubergine stuffed with spicy mixed vegetables, topped with yoghurt. *'I decided to visit having read the Guide write-up and was not disappointed. Food superb, one page devoted to house specialities, none of which I had ever come across before. An absolute must.'* TOC. *'Overlooking one of England's finest town squares with panoramic views from the Moot Hall to the Abbey. Decor is quietly sophisticated with citron sponged walls and distressed terracotta and gold screens, a circular drum links the two floors giving a sense of spaciousness, all of which is set off by tables covered with persil-white damask table cloths, napkins and Wedgwood china.'* ANON. Menu Extracts: Murgh e Khazana £8.50, chicken with mild spices, honey and cream. Salmon Bahja £11.50, salmon steak, fried in herbs, garlic, ginger and onion. Remains high in our **TOP 100.** Takeaway: 20% discount. Hours: 6-10; closed Sun. Branch: Valley Junction 397, The Old Station, Archibold Terrace, Jesmond, Newcastle.

Cramlington

LAL QILA 

Dudley Lane, Cramlington 01670 734268

Established '86 by Sabu Miah. Seats 60, serves formula curries. Red brick building, with private parking for 20 cars. Framed Indian art hangs, padded yellow and blue chairs, yellow table cloth, red patterned carpet, flowery wallpaper and curtains, makes for quite an eye full. Baingan Pakora, deliciously spiced, deep-fried aubergine served with minted sauce. Samba Gosht, lamb fairly hot, spiced cooked with lentils and fresh coriander. Specials include: Ajjwan Chicken – fillet of chicken with braised ajwan, onion, peppers, served on sizzler. Restaurant owns parking area for 40. Business lunch Mon.-Fri. £3 -£6. Takeaway: 20% discount. Hours: 12-2/6-11.30.

Hexham

DIWAN-E-AM 

4-5 Country Mills, Priestpopple, Hexham 01434 606575

Established in 1983. Seats 86. 'Pleasant decor and environment, friendly and helpful staff. *'Menu extensive, but no curry house inventions such as vindaloo here. Starters include the excellent Diwan Khata Mita Soup (garlic and lentils) and Mathu Vortha (grapefruit with chilli and coriander). Main course selection includes a wide range of duck and fish dishes.*

More expensive than the 'usual' curry house, but good value given the high standard of the meals.' CF. House-style cuisine on demand for regular customers. Takeaway: 20% discount. Hours: 5.30-11pm; Sun. 6.30-10.30pm.

Morpeth

TANDOORI MAHAL 

17 Bridge Street, Morpeth 01670 512420

60-seater, owned by chef Afrus Miah whose menu gives very good descriptions of every dish. Specials include Murgh Masala, spring chicken off the bone, soaked in spiced cream, roasted and served with Basmati Rice £8.50. Sabzi Ka Khazana contains Bhindi Bhaji, Milijuli Sabz, Dal Masala, Palak Bhaji, Chawal (rice) and two chapattis. *'An absolutely first-class establishment. Prices fair, service good, decor of a very high standard, parking no problem.'* MB. Manager Surot Miah has promised to give a discount to Curry Club members at lunch times. Takeaway: 10% discount. Hours: 12-2.30/6-12.

Ponteland

PONTELAND TANDOORI

11a Main Street, Ponetland 01661 860292

Family-run since 1992. *'Friendly and fun and a stone's throw from Newcastle, and we think it's worth the trip'. Be sure you go too. Great place. great food.* , says GM. All the favourite curry dishes are on offer here. Takeaway service. Restaurant hours: 12-2/5.30-12.

NOTTINGHAMSHIRE

Area: East Midlands
Population: 1,043,000
Adjacent Counties:
Derbs, Leics,
Lincs, Yorks

Nottingham

(includes Basford, Beeston, Mapperley, Radford, Sherwood, and West Bridgford.)

4500 MILES FROM DELHI NEW ENTRANT

41 Mount Street, Nottingham 0115 947 5111

No it is the name, not an error. Danny Punia is the main partner in the Poppadom Express restaurants in Southampton and Basingstoke Hants. This restaurant is in a 4000 sq m former public house, which has been transformed internally and externally to include a ten metre high glazed atrium in which the bar is located. A halved motorised-rickshaw gives a new meaning to wall-hanging. Suspended cylindrical stainless steel lights over the bar, a bronze staircase and solid oak and recycled slate flooring on which sit 130 Italian made chairs with bronze inlay work in the dining area overlooking an open kitchen. Chef Mahaneshwar Pal, previously with Delhi's Taj Palace Hotel has developed a North Indian menu that also includes a choice of set meals priced at £16.95 per person. Popular dishes include Tikkas, and Seekhs, Aloo Tikkis and a selection of simmered curries cooked by the Dum Pukht pot method. (*see p50*). Punia hopes to open further branches, naming each after its distance from Delhi and has plans to open a 4320 Miles from Delhi in London, and 4480 Miles from Delhi in Sheffield. Hours: 12-2.30/5.30-11.

BEESTON TANDOORI 

150 High Rd, Beeston, Nottingham SW 0115 922 3330

S Choudhury's cosy 40-seater. Chef recommends Uri and Muki Specials, described as fairly dry but well-spiced. Hours: 12-2.30/6-12.

BOMBAY BICYCLE SHOP TAKEAWAY 

511 Alfreton Road, Basford, Nottingham NW
0115 978 6309

Takeaway only, interior in shades of grey, exterior red and yellow. Specials include: Chicken de Goa, fresh cream, flaked coconut, mango sauce. Sag Aloo Paneer. Garlic Chapatti. 6 parking spaces behind takeaway. Credit cards not accepted. Delivery: £8 min. Hours: 5.30-12.

CHAND TOP 100 

31 Mansfield Road, Nottingham Centre
0115 947 4103

38-seater, jointly owned by Mohammed Shanaz, front of house, and chef Mohammed Riaz. The menu contains a very good selection of vegetarian dishes. Dhava Thaum £2.20 – garlic mushrooms served on a thin bread, and Mixed Vegetable Karahi £5.15. There are plenty of meat, fish and fowl dishes, too. *'Food excellent, owner and staff always extremely friendly, very good choice of menu, comfortable and clean, very good sized portions. I highly recommend it to all my friends.'* SW. And says TA: *'Finest of fine restaurants. Onion bhajis are simply the best I have tasted anywhere in the world, truly mouth watering and the perfect introduction to the delights to follow. Chandni Murgi Tikka was sublime, a perfect balance of subtle flavours in a rich sauce. I can wholeheartedly recommend the Chand to anyone who hankers after delicious eating experiences'.* TA. *And* BH: *'We've been eating here for many years, and whether it be meat or vegetarian dishes, the food is still the best we have eaten, made better with relaxed and pleasant atmosphere and very friendly and helpful staff. Large portions, and good value for money.'* BH. Paradise Balti, chicken, lamb, prawn and vegetables, all in one medium-spiced sauce with a mesh of omelette £7.50. *'Cosy restaurant, unimposing exterior. Smartly furnished open plan layout seating for fifty. Efficient waiting staff, annoyingly change tables at frequent intervals, so you don't know who's attention to attract for service. Standard Popadoms and chutneys. Lovely Lamb Paseena £3.30, highly spiced, flavoured sauce, quality lamb, small fresh salad and cool Raitha. Delicate Bombay Kofta £7.50, full of onions, peas and peppers, plenty of garlic and coriander. Well cooked Nan, generously packed with slivers of garlic – a perfect accompaniment.*

Definitely **TOP 100**.' RW. Credit cards accepted. Takeaway: 10% discount. Delivery: £15 min, 3 miles. Hours: 5.30-12, Friday and Saturday to 1.

THE INDIAN COTTAGE ©

5-7 Bentnick Road (off Alfreton Road), Radford, Nottingham W 0115 942 4922

Pretty black beams, white frontage and inviting curtained windows at Naj Aziz's 40-seater in 2 areas (smoking and non-smoking). Very stylish restaurant, un-Indian, unfussy, light and bright, Wedgwood blue ceiling and magnolia walls. Walls are decorated with hanging carpets and back-lit fretwork, tiled floor, large palms in white pots. We hear that the food is family-style. *'Aubergine Paneer and Garlic and Mushroom Bhaji for starters, served with crisp salad. Murgh Makhani, Chicken Tikka cooked with garlic, coriander and brandy, and I can honestly say it was among the best curries I have ever eaten. Rice portions were large. Staff extremely friendly and food is outstanding.'* CY. *'I feel compelled to write to you, having recently indulged in a remarkable gastronomic experience! A little 'oasis' in the middle of Radford, our first impression of The Indian Experience was a deep feeling of India. A veritable wealth of dishes, many quite original. From the papadoms right through to the coffee, the flavours were exquisite, presentation faultless and service wonderful. Hard to single out the best part of meal, and probably unfair to do so, but Peshwari Naan, which arrived dripping in honey, was an absolute delight. I urge you to pay a visit!'* D. 10% service charge for parties of 6 or more [why???]. Takeaway 10% off. Sunday lunch £16. Hours: 6-10.30 Tues.–Sat. Closed 16-30th August, a week at Christmas.

KASHMIR BYO 

60 Maid Marian Way, Nottingham Centre 0115 947 6542

At A.D. Satti's 100-seater, BYO allowed, no corkage. [Hooray!] *'Service was very good and friendly. Food excellent. Relaxed atmosphere. Have visited for many years, always had enjoyable time.'* Anon. *'A star place! consistently efficient and friendly service, brilliant and inexpensive. No pressure to eat and leave – a huge bonus.'* CN. *'Good variety, some unusual dishes, always good.'* JH, *'Attentive, keen and efficient service. Cosy atmosphere. Good value for money.'* AW. Hours: 6-1AM (Sat. from 2pm, Sun. from 1pm).

LAGUNA 

43 Mount Street, Nottingham Centre 0115 941 1632

Taken over in '85 by manager Tony Ranjit Verma. Seats 62, serves Northern Indian curries, cooked by Bharat Desai. *'Very efficient, food well above average. Laguna Special, a sort of Tandoori Masala sauce is good, its vegetarian counterpart is potatoes in the same sauce, but is curiously called Bombay Aloo. Many vegetarian dishes and beautifully cooked.'* PT. Menu Extracts: Hot Chicken Wings £3.60, good one for the kids! Lamb Shahjehani £7.80, with fruit and herbs. Stuffed Paratha £2.60, with cauliflower, potatoes and peas. Lettuce and Tomato Salad £2. Set Menus: Mixed Grill £10.20, Tandoori Chicken, Seekh Kebab, Boti Kebab, Chicken Tikka and Nan – good value. Service 10%. Takeaway: 10% discount. Hours: 12.30-2/6.30-11.

MEHRAN 

948 Woodborough Road, Mapperley, Nottingham N 0115 955 1005

Taken over in '98 by Mr and Mrs Mohamad Akram Khan. Balti – chicken balti most popular – restaurant seats 80. *'Excellent restaurant, good service. Very original recipes such as Chicken Sommerkhand (made with strawberries, cherries, cream and pistachio nuts). Unfortunately it appears to be going through a bad patch, not helped by being situated next door to Nottingham's most established Chinese restaurants.'* DE. Despite the above sounding like a fruit salad, we do know this restaurant, and have always heard well of it. Delivery: 2-mile radius. Hours: 6-12 (2am on Fri. & Sat.).

MILAAP TANDOORI 

67 Chilwell Road, Beeston, Nottingham 0115 925 4597

Owner chef Pervaz Iqbal seats a snug 28 diners and cooks Pakistani curries. All prices include Poppadom, rice and chutney. *'A welcoming smile and friendly banter from manager Yousef (or 'Chippy' as he is better known) makes the journey seem worthwhile. The Makhani Chicken Tikka is the mouth-watering combination of boulders of fresh moist chicken served in an indescribable tandoori sauce – truly magnificent!!!!!'* PB. *'The clientele are welcomed as part of a*

family, and many people who have met over a meal have become good friends. Whatever I choose, I am never disappointed. The quality of the ingredients, and the care taken in the kitchen never vary.' CF. *'Whilst the food is excellent, the service is second to none.'* pb. *' Pervez is an excellent cook, who manages to combine just the right amount of spice with the subtle flavours of Indian cuisine.'* JB. *'We visit here frequently and can honestly say that we have never had a disappointing meal in over 10 years. The staff are always friendly and welcoming, take a pride in the food that they serve, are willing and able to give advice about food on the menu, and remember customer preferences. Food is always good and reasonably priced.'* S&BA. Minimum charge £8.50. Hours: 5.30-12 (12.30am on Sat).

MOGAL E AZAM NEW TO OUR TOP 100 ©

7-9 Goldsmith Street, Nottingham Centre
0115 952 8777

The Mogal was opened in 1977 by Mr SN Miah, and seats a huge 300 diners on ground and 1st floors, and serves very good, very popular formula curries, CTM the most popular dish ordered. *'Like the Taj Mahal inside, with arches and minarettes built into walls and hallway, marble-effect look, creamy white in colour, with large brass bric-a-brac as decor.'* SNM. *'Recommended by the student son of friends of ours. Portions enormous, well presented, good decor but pricy. Varied menu, slightly larger than most. Service excellent – they try very hard.* SJ. Specials include: Bengal ka Boul, Bangladesh fish £11.95. Hours: 12-2.30 / 5.30-1am.

SAAGAR TOP 100 

473 Mansfield Road, Sherwood, Nottingham N
0115 962 2014

Mohammed Khizer opened his Victorian-styled 98-seater on two floors in 1984. Front of house is managed by Imtiaz Ahmed, leaving Mr Khizer to do his thing in the kitchen, assisted by Amjaid Parvaiz. This time we had one 'hated it' report from one scribe (MR) but all other reports are happy. *'Everything it is cracked up to be, expensive but worth it. Vegetarian Thali for two is not just a tray but a seemingly endless train of small bowls provided as fast as you can eat.'* PT. *'The pops and picks were gorgeous. My Mixed Kebabs £4.90 were tasty. Chicken Kaallan £9.10 was very sweet, yet very sour too, with tender chicken cooked in a south Indian style, with mango, coconut and yoghurt. My girlfriend was brave enough to tackle Chilli*

Chicken Tikka Masala £9.50 incl. rice, and our Garlic and Tomato Naan £1.95 was excellent, covered in fresh tomato chunks. Everyone felt the food had been made freshly, and it was cooked to perfection. It makes a nice change to come to a decent restaurant which has the edge over others because of little things that just make a difference, like fresh flowers at every table, proper lemon-squeezers, spotless toilets, etc.' NH. Discounts for CC members at lunch times. Hours: 12-2.15/5.30-12.30am (closed Sun. lunch).

Southwell

SANAM BALTI HOUSE ©

15-17 King Street, Southwell 01636 813618

Early Victorian listed building, established in as the Taj Mahal in 1990, and taken over by Khalid Mahmood in 1994. The 50-seater boasts a splendid spiral staircase. Rooms are open plan with ornate Moghul style arches to doorways. Beautiful jade colour, lighting subdued crystal reflecting the traditional Indian art. All tables are covered in fine contrasting linen, sparkling silverware and fresh flowers. Centre of attention has to be a 26-cubic-feet fish tank, which is set within an existing chimney and can be viewed from both rooms. Chef-owner, Khalid Mahmood or *'Chef Saab'* as he is known to staff and customers, originates from Pakistan's Kashmir. *'Tastefully decorated. All food was hot, excellent Pullao Rice and Peshwari Nan.'* LW. Specials include: Makhani Tandoori Chicken, Marinated Tandoori Chicken with Makhani Sauce (green peppers, onions, tomatoes, methi, garlic sauce). Hours: 5.30-11.30.

Stapleford

MOUSHUMI ©

124 Derby Road, Stapleford 0115 939 4929/ 917 0170

Established in 1993. The Moushumi is a tastefully decorated 70 seater decked out in sea greens and stained wood. Large and expensive engraved glass panels divide the restaurant. Proprietor Sanawor Ali is a romantic soul. His Valentine's Night at £25 per couple, with free cocktails for her and champagne for him, sounds good. No reports on proposals. Specials: Dakeshwari Murgh, chicken in cream and yoghurt. Car parking for 50 at side of restaurant. Takeaway: approximately 20% discount. Delivery: £10 minimum, 3-mile radius. Hours: 12-2.30/6-11.30. Branch: Amrit Takeaway, Mapperley Top, Nottingham.

Sutton-in-Ashfield

HUTHWAITE TANDOORI ©

17 Market Street, Huthwaite, Sutton in Ashfield 01623 557716

Established in 1990. Seats 80, parking for 30 at front. Specials: Rish Rosha £6.20 – marinated trout cooked in the tandoor, served with thick sauce. Kufta Khana £5.70 – minced lamb rolled into balls, roasted and served with spicy sauce. Takeaway: 10% discount. Hours: 12-2.30/6-12.

OXFORDSHIRE

Area: Central
Population: 619,000
Adjacent Counties: Bucks, Berks, Glos, Middx, Northants, Warks, Wilts

Banbury

SHEESH MAHAL ©

43 Oxford Road, Banbury 01295 266489

M Khalid is the owner-chef at this 64-seater, managed by M Manwar, and it serves standard formula curries. *'Decided to visit on a friend's recommendation. Tandoori Fish for starters, very good. Chicken Moghlai, excellent, Naan breads were massive. Coffee pot and cream were left on our table so we could help ourselves.'* JSK. 20 private car parking spaces at rear. Takeaway: 25% discount. Hours: 6-12 (Sat. to 1am).

Bicester

BICESTER TANDOORI ©

15 Market Square, Bicester 01869 245170

The Sahana was taken over in 1994 by Mrs

Dilwara Begum. Decorated in pink with a blue marble bar, seats 40. Formula curry house.Delivery: £15.95 minimum, 3-mile radius. Hours: 5.30-11.30 (12am on Sat.).

Chinnor

CHINNOR INDIAN ©

59-61 Lower Road, Chinnor 01844 354843

Saidur Rahman has been the owner of this 60 seater since '97. *'The food is superb. A great evening. I can't fault them. Highly recommended. Decorated in green with artificial plants, to look like a garden, bamboo chairs, apricot table linen'* MS. *'Having eaten in many curry restaurants and having spent a great deal of my working life in Dhaka, Bombay and Delhi, as well as over 60 other countries in the world, I can safely say the food offered here ranks with the best I have ever tasted. Tandoori dishes are freshly made, curry dishes are subtle, chicken is succulent, lamb tender and well marinated, presentation is superb. Hospitality is warm and welcoming.'* JR *'I recommend it to all my friends.'* DGG. Parking for 30 cars. Hours: 12-2.30/6-11.30.

Chipping Norton

ANARKALL ©

6 West Street, Chipping Norton
01608 642785

'Good selection on menu, good-sized portions. Best-ever Naans, light and fluffy. Onion Bhajis out of this world. Bank Holiday weekend was busy but manager still had time to talk to us.' PA. Proprietor A Uddin. Hours 12-2.30/6-11.30.

Didcot

DIDCOT TANDOORI NEW ENTRANT

222 Broadway, Didcot 01235 812206

'Nice decor, excellent service and extensive menu. Excellent Chicken Jalfrezi and Mushroom Rice.' IB.

SUNKOSHI TANDOORI

226a Broadway, Didcot 01235 812796

Nepalese Menu Extracts: Shak Shuka £6.20 – minced lamb, fresh cream, topped with egg, mild. Prawn Chatpat £6.50 – green chillies, green peppers, onions, ginger, hot. *'Hasina Kebabs and Chicken Chats were incredible, served piping hot and full of flavour. Karai Mixed Grill, Chicken Karai wonderfully cooked and huge portions. Service excellent. Having never knowingly eaten at a Nepalese restaurant before, we were very impressed and will return again very shortly'.* DL. *'Revisited and did not disappoint. Chicken Choykola, particularly good. Excellent portions and beautifully cooked – offered doggy bag for leftovers!'* DL. Delivery: £10 minimum, 5 miles. Takeaway: 10% discount, £10 minimum. Sunday Buffet: £9 adult, £5 child under 10. Hours: 12-2.30/6-11, Fri/Sat to 11.30.

Faringdon

AZAD TANDOORI & BALTI 

14 Coxwell Street, Faringdon 01367 244977

30-seater owned by Rabia Khanom Ali, since '95. *'Nicely decorated since he took it over.'* RK. Serves Bangladeshi formula curries, Tandoori dishes are very popular. *'Standard menu, basic decor, small restaurant. Fair portion of Chicken Dhansak and Mushroom Rice – excellent.'* IB.Takeaway: 15% discount. Delivery: £10 minimum, 4-mile radius. Hours: 5-11.30. Sun. 12-11.30.

Henley-on-Thames

GAZAL 

53 Reading Road, Henley 01491 574659

Gazal means gentle Indian love songs. It has nothing to do with guzzling. (*'I hope that puts one reporter right, who told me that's why he came here in the first place – to get big portions!'* PJ.) He loves the place, though, visiting whenever he's in town. Hours: 12-2/6-11.

Oxford

AZIZ TOP 100 

228 Cowley Road, Oxford 01865 794945

Smart 90-seater, white with gold lettering exterior. Inside, very well decorated, cane chairs, plants, subdued lighting, upmarket, sophisticated. Named after its owner, Azizur (Aziz) Rahman, this restaurant is Oxford's best. Aziz is where you will find real Bangladeshi food. *'Our third visit this year and it just seems to get better. Service as usual, swift and polite. Popadoms and naans in handy size pieces. Keema Somasas superb. The sauces in the Chicken Patia and the King Prawns with*

Red Pumpkin and Green Chillies were wonderful. I rate the cooking here amongst the best anywhere and I can't recommend it enough. Suggest booking beforehand, it's so popular.' MS. *'My no 1 favourite.'* JCC. *'Excellent quality, charming service. Very comfortable and relaxing atmosphere.'* RT. *'Immediately impressed. Tables simply but elegantly set with crisp white linen. Good vegetarian selection on menu. Generous quantities and delicately flavoured. Emphasis on subtlety. A splendid meal.'* WC. *'Impressive reports confirmed. Mid-week the place was packed. Decor is upmarket and smart, the food well prepared and served in generous quantities. This is where the middle class, the academics and well-off students of Oxford eat and entertain. Service was slow but the place was very busy. Parking can be a problem.'* PAW. Arramba – to begin, Maach Bora, fish cake with potato, eggs and green chillies. Chott Pottie, chickpeas, egg and potatoes spiced with coriander. House Specialities: Murgh Jal Frajee, stir-fried chicken in batter, with fresh chillies – hot , Jerre Koligi, lamb livers with cummin. Chitol Bhuna, Bangladeshi fish rolled into Kofta, Galda Chineri Kodu, king prawns with red pumpkin and green chillies. Dimm Dal, eggs and red lentils with coconut milk. Takeaway: 15% discount. Sunday buffet Dimm Dal, eggs and red lentils with coconut milk. Takeaway: 15% discount. Sunday buffet 12-5.30, £7.50 per person, children £3.75. Hours: 12-2/6-11.30pm; Sun. 12-11.30pm; closed New Year's Day. High in our **TOP 100.**

CHUTNEYS — NEW ENTRANT

Oxford 01865 724241

'Modern, almost trendy decor. Arrived at 9.20pm, the place was packed. Struck by the breath of the menu, offered all usual favourites and many Specials eg: Kodu Gosht and lemon Murgh. Enormous vegetarian section. Settled on Aloo Nariyal. Food arrived fast, different tastes, quality very good indeed. Adequate portions, reasonable prices.' MD.

KASHMIR HALAL 

64 Cowley Road, Oxford 01865 250165

Opened in 1970 by Said Meah and seats 50 diners. A comprehensive menu listing all your favourite curries and accompaniments. Halal meat. Tandoori dishes a speciality of the house. *'Returned for the Chicken Tandoori Soup, which I never seen anywhere else and is absolutely delicious– basically chicken tandoori sauce made into a soup. Pleasant but unexceptional meal. Unlicensed but very good Mango Lassi.'* NP.

SHIMLA PINKS 

16 Turl Street, Oxford 01865 243783

Formerly the Taj Mahal which was established in 1937 on the first floor above Whites, making it Britain's third ever Indian restaurant.

RUTLAND

Britain's smallest county
Area: East Midlands
Population: 50,000
Adjacent Counties: Cambs, Leics, Lincs

Leicestershire's bureaucratic loss is Rutland's gain. Back again after decades of non-existence, it is once again Britain's smallest county – it is geographically smaller than the city of Birmingham.

Oakham

RUTLAND BALTI HOUSE 

18 Mill Street, Oakham 01572 757232

Owned/managed by Abdul Khalique, since '95. Formerly Oakham Tandoori, plain white artex walls and ceiling, seats a cosy 32 diners, serves Bangladeshi formula curries. *'Visited on my own, staying in hotel and getting the craving! Very pleasant staff, made me welcome. Prawn Puri, the best ever, tempted to cancel main dish and have two more! Garlic Chicken Balti, lovely flavour and tasted very fresh. Ice cold Cobra.'* JH. Takeaway: 15% discount. Hours: 5.30-2, Friday and Saturday to 12.30.

SHROPSHIRE

Area: Welsh Border
Population: 431,000
Adjacent Counties: Cheshire, Clwyd, Hereford, Powys, Staffs, Worcs

Newport

SHIMLA ©

22 St Mary's Street, Newport 01952 825322

Set takeaway meals are excellent value at Nurul Islam's restaurant. Balti includes Papadam with mint sauce and onion salad, Tandoori Mix Kebab, Chicken (or Lamb) Tikka Balti, Sag Aloo, Pullao Rice (half-portion) or Nan, and sweet or coffee. Minimum charge £10. Hours: 6-12am.

Shrewsbury

RAMNA BALTI HOUSE

33 Wyle Cup, Shrewsbury 01743 363170

'Situated in a scenic part of town, never yet have we had a bad meal there. Small, inviting and beautifully decorated. Baltis had rich, fiery sauces, liberally infused with meat and green chillies, naans enormous and absolute heaven. Generous portions and efficient service.' SW. Menu Extracts: Chicken Masala Dhal £1.80; Prawn Puri £2.25; Tandoori Butter Chicken £5.25; Keema Chilli Nan £1.45; Garlic Fried Rice £1.80. Minimum charge: £5. Delivery: 3 miles, Sunday to Thursday, 5.30-11, minimum charge £8.50. Delivery: 3 miles, £8.50 .Hours: 5.30-11.

SHERAZ NEW ENTRANT

79 Wyle Cop, Shrewsbury 01743 351744

'Onion Bhajia's size of brussel sprouts. Nan only about 6" diameter. Prawn Puri ok, Balti Garlic Chilli Puri, good, tasted very fresh, fantastic flavour.' JH. Delivery: 3 miles, £12 min, last order, 1/2 hour before closing. Takeaway: 15% discount, £12 min. Hours: 5.30-12, Fri/Sat-1.

SOMERSET

Area: West Country
Population: 493,000
Adjacent Counties: Bristol, Devon, Dorset, Glos, Wilts

Bath

THE EASTERN EYE TOP 100 © 10%

8a Quiet Street, Bath 01225 422323

140-seater, owned by Suhan Choudhury, pink and blue with most impressive Georgian interior, in one large room with three domes. *'Average high-street curry house it is not! It's a spectacular, huge and most impressive first-floor restaurant. Soft lighting, pink and blue colours, restful atmosphere. Tableclothes and cutlery are of good quality, even the hot towels are so thick they could almost have been squares of carpet! Stuffed pepper, whole green stuffed with spicy diced chicken, barbecued, nicely blackened, delicately spiced, interesting but filling starter. Onion Bhajia, two round bhajias, the best we have tasted for a long while, light, crispy and spicy. Prawn Puree – excellent, large succulent prawns, tangy sauce. Good, fresh and varied salad ganishes. Chicken Tikka Masala – most ordinary, standard offering. Chicken Mon Pasand, excellent, different, mild, yoghurt based sauce, very herby. Lamb Jalfrezi, large tender chunks of lamb, thick dark sauce, hotness hits you after first couple of mouthfulls. Vegetable Bhajee,good variety of diced vegetables, nicely spiced and enjoyable. Peshwari Nan and Pullao Rice were both good, nan not sickly and rice contained smattering of diced vegetables to make it interesting. Prices slightly above average, but for decor and type of restaurant, very reasonable. Service efficient and friendly. 10% CC discount. An excellent meal in an elegant restaurant.'* MW. Service charge: 10%. Specials include: Mon Pasand – slightly hot, enlivened with herbs and yoghurt £7.50, Shah Jahani – chicken breast, slightly spiced, shallow fried in ghee, blended with homemade cheese and cream £7.50, Sultan Puri Pilau – from Uttar Pradesh, spiced rice with lamb and cashew nuts, served with a gravy £8.95. Bangladeshi food nights, seafood buffet. Service 10%. Minimum charge: £9. Takeaway: 10% discount. Hours: 12-2.30/6-11.30. Highin our our **TOP 100**. *See page* 30.

Clevedon

MOGHULS TANDOORI ©

33 Old Church Road, Clevedon 01275 873695

'Started with Chicken Tikka, big, succulent. Followed by Tandoori King Prawn Masala, lovely sauce with cream. Excellent Pullao Rice with chopped almonds and fried onions. Delicious Mixed Vegetable Curry, green peppers, cauli, beans, onion and mange-tout.' MS. Hours: 12-2/6-12.

Midsomer Norton

SHAPLA ©

43 High Street, Midsomer Norton
01761 410479

Tiny, seats 24 diners, serves formula curries, CTM is most popular. *'I especially liked their Dandag (sic.) and had not previously heard of their Chicken, Lamb or Prawn Dim (sic..) – "cooked with egg in a sauce"'.* [Neither have we!] Takeaway 15% off. Delivery. Hours: 12-2/5.30-11.30. Branch: Tandoori Mahal, 13 Sadler Street, Wells. Next door is Shapla Indian Takeaway (tel. 01761 411887).

Wellington

TASTE OF INDIA ©

2 North Street, Wellington 01823 667051

Naz Choudhury's Taste is a cosy little a/c 30-seater, which serves, for example, 'home-style: Fish Kurma, Murgee Razzla, Vegetable Kebabs, Achar Gust, Pilaw, chutney and pickle for four £55'. Buffet £9.95. £7.20 wine, also have off-license for takeaway trade. Hours: 12-2/6-12. Tues. closed. Branch: Tandoori Spice, 12 Higher Street, Cullompton, Devon.

Weston-super-Mare

AVON TANDOORI ©

16 Waterloo Street, Weston-super-Mare
01934 622622

Opened in May '88, seats 49 diners, managed by A Hoque, formula and Balti dishes. Specials: Tandoori King Prawn Zalfarazai, lemon juice, capsicum, onion, hot green chillies £10.95. Minimum charge: £7 per person. Takeaway: 10% discount. Hours: 12-2/6-12.; Sat. 6-12.30; Sun. 6-11.30.

CURRY GARDEN 

69 Orchard Street, Weston-super-Mare
01934 624660

Seats 65, in two dining rooms, Bangladeshi curry house. Owned by Miah and Ali. Price check: *'Empty when we arrived at 7.30pm, seething by 8pm – book a table if you go, don't take a chance like we did. Chicken Tikka Masala was the best so far this year'.* MS. Takeaway: 10% discount. Minimum charge: £5. Hours: 12-2/6-12.

STAFFORDSHIRE

Area: North Midlands
Population: 1,066,000
Adjacent Counties:
Cheshire, Derbs,
Shrops,
W Mids, Worcs

Cannock

JASMINE BYO ©

125 Hednesford Road, Heath Hayes,
Cannock 01543 279620

N Islam's 50-seat Jasmine Balti Special. Prawn, King Prawn and Lobster is £9.75. BYO, no corkage. Minimum charge: £5. Takeaway: 15% discount. Delivery: £10 minimum, 3-mile radius. Hours: 5-12.30; Sat. 5.30-1am.

Hednesford

BENGAL BRASSERIE 

44 Market Street, Hednesford 01543 424769

Owner Kuti Miah's formula curry house seats 60. Specials: Chicken Keema Matter – succulent pieces of marinated chicken cooked in a spicy minced lamb sauce with chickpeas. Delivery: £15 minimum, 3-mile radius. Hours: 6-12. Branches:

Royal Indian Brasserie, Albion House, New Quay, Dyfed. Bay of Bengal, Crackwell Street, Tenby. Dilshad Brasserie, Whitford Street, Holywell, Clwyd.

Kingsley Holt

THORNBURY HALL RASOI

TOP 100

Lockwood Rd, Kingsley Holt 01538 750831

This unusual restaurant is approximately 10 miles east of Hanley (off the A52) in a renovated Grade II listed building, once a manor house. Since 1994 it has been owned and managed by Mr and Mrs Siddique, who have brought style and Pakistani food to this beautiful area. It has three public areas, including a conference room. The main restaurant leads from the bar and is decorated in gold and terracotta, ceramic floor, open fire for winter evenings. The Shalimar room, named after gardens in Pakistan, is decorated in green and gold, large windows and doors leading to garden. Dance floor, sparkling globe and sound system. Lahore dining room, large, elegant, richly decorated Georgian plaster ceiling, swagged curtains and a brass teapot, it nearly reached the ceiling! Pakistani delicacies are on the menu. *'Could be tricky to find, but my in-laws live close by. The main hall is very grand, but not always open. Other areas are elegant and comfortable. Service good, including some staff from the village in Pakistani dress. Excellent flavours and quality. Sensible portions.'* DRHM. *'Fantastic restaurant. Magnificent settings in a listed building. Kumbi Pullao Arasta Rice cooked with mushrooms was out of this world. Karahi Mogulai, pieces of lamb cooked with cream, egg, ground nuts, garnished with almonds, superb. Karahi Murgh Jalfrezi, cooked in green chilli, ginger, garlic, yoghurt and spices, the best my husband has ever tasted.'* MR&MRS C. We're pleased to retain it in our **TOP 100.** Hours: 12-2.30/6-11 (11.30 on Fri. & Sat.). Branch: 'Eastern Express' at Alton Towers,theme park *See Stoke-on-Trent, Staffs.*

Leek

BOLAKA SPICE NEW TO OUR TOP 100 ©

41 Stockwell Street, Leek 01538 373734

'Primarily a formula curry house, but two features make it stand out – the Haandis menu and a small specials board. Keema

Motor is an outstanding and rich mix of lamb, chick peas and spices. At Christmas, a divine Turkey Tikka Masala with vegetables. Aubergines in a Sweet Sauce is Wow! Service polite and efficient.' PK. *'Friendly and cosy, good welcome. Tables clean and ready with candles and flowers. Quality unbelievably good every time.'* ja. *'Have dined here many times, food always very fresh and tasty.'* rm. *'A friend gave me a hint that this place had a good reputation. Pickles and Popadoms offered as an appetiser were fresh and moorish. Starter, Chingri Begun and Mint Lamb Balti both impressed with flavours. Impeccable service.'* aeh. *'The best we have been too. Very friendly staff, clean tables, relaxing atmosphere and the best food – absolutely fabulous. Our favourite.'* ss. Welcome to our **TOP 100.**

PABNA ©

16-18 Ashbourne Road, Leek
01538 381156

Formerly India garden, Fazz Meah took over in March '98 and completely refurbished. Formula curry house, Rogan Josh most popular, seats 80. *'Average Prawn Bhuna, excellent Tarka Dall.'* PK. Takeaway: 15% discount. Hours: 5.30-12.

Lichfield

EASTERN EYE TOP 100 ©

19b Bird Street, Lichfield 01543 254399

Abdul Salam's venue represents a Swat valley house, right up in Pakistan's northern mountain ranges (just a nan nudge from Baltistan). It is famous for its forests and ornate wooden carved furniture, showing Buddhist influences going back 2,000 years. The beams, pillars and window are from Swat. The bar front is from neighbouring Afghanistan, the chairs are Rajasthani and the table tops are from 150-year-old elm. *'Count the rings,'* enthuses Mr Salam. The toilets are a 'must-see' on your list. The theme is Agra's Red Fort – probably India's best example of a Moghul residence. The food is well spoken of. Specials include Murgh with Apricot, marinated chicken with apricot yoghurt sauce, cream and fresh coriander. Rajasthani Paro Breast – pigeon. Michael Fabricant, MP, MCC (member of the *Curry Club*) continues regularly to take his seat at the Eye as a loyal local, rating it highly, as do so many other reports we get, e.g. *'From entering you know it'll be good. Decor reminded me of Putney's fine Ma Goa's (London sw). In a mild mood, had Murgh Special with apricot which was delicious. My friend loved his Eastern Eye Mixed Massala (king prawn, lamb and chicken).'* rl. *'Still my favourite. Mr Salam still very much in charge, evolving the menu and new dishes. Cooking excellent – far superior to average curry fare. Chicken and Banana, Chilli Chicken, Special tandoori Masala (inc chicken, lamb, king prawns) are all excellent. Amazingly light Naans. Wine list still consists of an armful of bottles placed on your table to take your pick from – a tradition I hope will remain and includes good examples from Spain and Australia. Deserves to be in the* **TOP 100.**' PJ. '*The food was unusual and beautifully presented on huge oval china plates. Will definitely try it again if we're ever in the area.'* K&ST. Discounts for CC Members on Sundays. Hours: 12-2.30 (Sat. only)/5-12.

LAL BAGU 

9 Bird Street, Lichfield 01543 262967

Formula curry house, seats 70, proprietor Masum Ahmed Chowdhury. Special: Shorti – chicken, lamb or prawn – cooked with chat masala, slight hot and sour, finely chopped green chillies and fenugreek. Delivery: £10 minimum. Sunday lunch £6.95. Takeaway over £20, free wine, papadam, salad and raita. Hours: 12.30-2.30 Sun. only/5.30-12 daily.

Newcastle-under-Lyme

BILASH 

22 Highland Keele Road, Newcastle-under-Lyme 01782 614549

Established by Mrs D Choudhury's curry house in 1988, seats 90 in three dining rooms. Specials: Bangladeshi Rezala. Keema and Garlic Nan. Takeaway: 20% discount. Hours: 5-12.30.

OSSIES BYO 

39 Ironmarket, Newcastle-under-Lyme
01782 662207

Formula (CTM is most popular) curry house seats 86 in two dining rooms. Formerly Ali Baba, taken over in late '96 by M Arshad. BYO no corkage. Hours: 6pm-1am (3am on Fri. & Sat.).

©	Curry Club Discount	U	Unlicensed
V	Vegetarian	ANP	Alcohol not permitted
e-a-m-a-y-l	Eat as much as you like	BYO	Bring your own alcohol

SAFFRON NEW ENTRANT

4-6 Pool Dam Newcastle 01782 661861

Mrs Aziz Bari's Saffron has cme to our attention on several occasions, and it is highly regarded. Behind its large frontage, you'l find a busy, bustling restaurantr serving high quality curries with allthe accompaniments. Credit cards accepted. Hours: 5.30-11.45, Friday and Saturday to 12.30.

Rugeley

BILASH ©

7 Horsefair, Rugeley 01889 584234

At Chowdhury, Rofique and Uddin's 90-seater: *'our favourite.'* N&GD (party room 48). The specials include Chilli Chicken Tikka, with red and green chillies, served with salad. Takeaway 10% off. Hours: 12-2.30/5.30-11.30.

Shenstone Woodend

THE LODGE BYO ©

Lodge Cottage, 24 Birmingham Rd, Shenstone W 01543 483334

Shenstone Woodend is a small green-belt village on the W Mids border, 4 miles north of Sutton Coldfield. Jamal and Imam Uddin's 70-seater Lodge, established in 1996, is beautifully appointed, with carpet and pine floors, simple chandeliers, white ceiling-roses, arches and cornices, and magnolia walls. *'My family eats as often as possible in this luxurious restaurant. Smart, efficient waiters remember customer names and preferences, and they adore children. Chef Shanur Ali excels with a wide variety of Indian cuisine.'* RLP. Parking in front for 32 cars, with CCTV. Takeaway: 15% discount. Delivery: £10 minimum, 4-mile radius. Hours: 5.30-12; Sat. & Sun. 12-2pm. Branch: Streetly Balti, 188 Chester Road, Sutton Coldfield

Stafford

CURRY KUTEER ©

231 Greengate St, Stafford 01785 253279

Established 1968. Seats 80. Specials: Hyderbadi Keema Masala £5.95 – minced lamb, green peas and potato. Vegetable tray £6.50 – three vegetable dishes of your choice (good value).Takeaway: 25% discount. Hours: 12-2/6-12. (Sat. to 1am).

SPICE DELIGHT NEW ENTRANT ©

5a Lichfield Road, Stafford 01785 245554

A popular curry takeaway serving all age groups. CC members will get a discount on Monday, their quiet night. Regular customers received free starters or popadoms. Set Lunch: Meal for One £4.95. Minimum charge: £6. Credit cards accepted. Why not email your order to: rumi@rahmed53.fsnet.co.uk

Stoke-on-Trent

(including Burslem and Hanley)

EASTERN PROMISE NEW ENTRANT

Alton Towers, Stoke-on-Trent 01538 702200

Parveen and Mohammed Siddique of Thornbury Hall Rasoi (*see Kingsley Holt, Staffs*) have opened a new restaurant serving Asian cuisine in a bold new venture at Alton Towers, Britain's favourite theme park. 'Eastern Express' is situated in the Merrie England area of the Park and serves freshly prepared meals using the highest quality ingredients and recipes carefully selected from the full Thornbury Hall menu. Open when the Park is open, ie in the summer.

ASHA TAKEAWAY ©

42 Broad Street, Hanley, Stoke 01782 213339

Where (I believe) Robbie Williams comes from. Established in 1991. Specials: Keema Chat £1.65. Tandoori Steak £7.50. Coriander Nan £1.50. Price check: Papadam 25p, CTM £4.80, Pullao Rice £1.30, Peshwari Nan £1.60. Hours: 5-12.

BOSTON CHICKEN & PIZZA HUT ©

42 Broad Street, Hanley, Stoke on Trent 01782 213339

Established in 1995. Good cheap and cheerful licensed curry house,. Hours: 7pm-3am.

MONZIL ©

44 Broad Street, Hanley Stoke 01782 280150

A Matin's Monzil's 1977, formula curry house, taken over by Mrs Chowdry in 1996 and seats 80. Chef's Special: chicken, meat, prawn, mushroom and tomato with spices and boiled egg. Takeaway: 10% off. Hours: 7pm-3am (2am on Sun.). Branch: Bilash, Newcastle, Staffs.

Uttoxeter

KOHI NOOR BYO ©

11 Queen Street, Uttoxeter 01889 562153

S Miah's 70-seater is *'difficult to find – it's at the back of Sketchley's Cleaners – and parking limited on site. Interesting decor. Food was good. Good value. It's never going to be a TOP 100 place but it is the archetypal English curry house – the backbone of curry houses in this country. Long may they live.'* PW. Specials include Chicken Sath, lemon flavoured vegetables (Shatkora), coriander, garlic herbs and spices. *'Interesting decor, early curry house style, red velvet chairs and '70's carpet. Food good. Good value.'* PAW. CC members in parties of 10 or more will get a percentage off the bill, so gather up friends and family! Allows BYO, no corkage. Delivery: £20 min, 3-mile radius. Hours: 5.30-12am (1am on Fri. & Sat.).

SUFFOLK

Area: East
Population: 675,000
Adjacent Counties:
Cambs, Essex,
Norfolk

Brandon

BRANDON TANDOORI ©

17 London Road, Brandon 01842 815874

Arjad Ali's 70-seater opened here in 1991, just a runway length from USAF Lakenheath. But the roar of the F111's is drowned out here by the roar of the tandoor, and the roar of approval from the locals. Our aero-med colonel pilot has retired back to the Midwest corn-bowl of America but still writes that he and his Suffolk wife miss their curries: *'I got my wings on Phantom jets, and again on the Brandon's Chicken Garlic Chilli, £6.10. It's hotter than my bird's jet pipe!'* [We don't think he's referring to his wife!] *'The food is always of a wonderful quality, quickly and cheerfully served, and you can always rely on it when taking friends from India. My mouth waters at the memory of the last Murghi Massala, marinated spring chicken, cooked with mincemeat, peas, potato and tomato. Book well in advance especially on Saturdays!'* RE. Takeaway: 10% off. Minimum charge: £10. Hours: 12-2/6-11.

TANDOORI HUT NEW ENTRANT

28 High Street, Brandon 01842 810808

A very popular takeaway. We have had a number of satisfied reports telling of a high level of care from arrival to departure, with *'excellent food'* ANON. This is as it should be, and it gets the Tandoori Hut into the *Guide*. Evenings only, every day, you

can get your currinary delights here. Credit cards accepted. Hours: *See below*

Bury-St-Edmonds

MUMTAZ INDIAN 

9 Risbygate Street, Bury 01284 752988

Formula curry house, seating 44, opened in 1974 by Syed Nurul Haque, who tells us that during the Falklands War, he was asked to cook curries for the soldiers. His food was flown out by military aircraft and he believes that because the troops ate his food they won the war! Who am I to argue? Special Set Thai dinner: Onion Bhajai, Vegetable Curry, Chana Masala, Tarka Dal, Pullao Rice, Puri and curry sauce. *'Good'* G&MP. Takeaway: 10% off. Minimum charge £6.50. Delivery: £10 minimum, 12-mile radius. Hours: 12-2.30/6-12. (12.30am on Sat.).

Felixstowe

BOMBAY NITE 

285 High Street, Walton, Felixstowe 01394 272131

Standard curry house, serving the formula. Owned and managed by Mahbub Alam. Seats 60 in three rooms, seating divided into booths. Decorated in cream and green. Takeaway: 15% discount. Hours: 12-2.30/6-11.30.

Halesworth

RUCHITA 

26 Market Place, Halesworth 01986 874524

E Miah and Z Allam run this 60-seater, with able assistance from John Gomez in the kitchen, whose handiwork is highly regarded. Try the King Prawn Re Jala, in cream with dry fruits, very mild spices £6.95 or the Chicken Patiwala, £6.95, diced chicken cooked with cheese, yoghurt, garlic, garnished with stuffed tomato and capsicum. Hours: 12-2.30/ 6-11.30.

Ipswich

TAJ MAHAL © 10%

40 Norwich Road, Ipswich 01473 257712

Established in 1964, making it Ipswich's first. Taken over by Syed Robbani in 1987. Seats 64. Serves formula curries, but *'anything can be arranged.'* Special: Achar Chicken Masala, with pickled spices. CC members will get 10% off the bill. Takeaway: 20% off. Hours: 12-2. (no lunch Fri.)/6-11.30.

Lowestoft

AHMED 

150 Bridge Road, Oulton Broad, Lowestoft 01502 501725

Boshor Ali's cute little restaurant has just 28 seats. *'Brilliant.'* says PJ. Hours: 12-2.30pm/6-11.30pm. Branch: Jorna Indian Takeaway, 29-33 Wherstead Road, Ipswich.

ROYAL BENGAL 

69 High Street, Lowestoft 01502 567070

Established in 1997. Seats 38. Specials include: Makari (chicken or lamb, two layers, the bottom cooked in tomatoey and slightly spicy sauce, and the top a mild creamy sauce), Dikush (a medium strength dish from the district of Sylhet, made with diced chicken/lamb, cooked in a special mosala sauce). Price check: Papadam 50p, CTM £6.50, Pullao Rice £1.70, Peshwari Nan £1.75, Lager £2.20 pint. Takeaway: 15% discount. Delivery: £12 minimum. Hours: 12-2/6-11.30.

SEETA 

176 High Street, Lowestoft 01502 574132

Seeta is the Indian goddess of beauty and love. Alternatively, the Sitar is the melodic Indian stringed instrument. Now you'll remember the name! Either way, you like the Seeta. It's a pretty restaurant, with dusky pink walls, white ceiling, ornate plaster cornice and ceiling rose. Ceiling fan and brass light fittings, green velvet chairs, napkins, white table linen. It has the usual curries and accompaniments on the menu including,

we're told, fresh scampi on request in the curries. But we think this is unique . . . You may order the 'Staff Curry' but please order the day before, so head chef Motin Uddin, can make extra portions.Takeaway: 10% discount. Hours: 12-1.30/6-11; closed Tues.

Stowmarket

ROYAL TANDOORI INTERNATIONAL ©

16 Tavern Street, Stowmarket 01449 674392

M Ahmed and S Miah's 60-seater is situated in a white Georgian building, in two blue and pink rooms with matching curtains and carpet. Formula curry house, seats 60. *'Waited fifteen minutes for our takeaway in well-lit restaurant. Good decor, pleasant ansd efficient service. Food excellent, generous portions and reasonable prices. The Maya Khalia Chicken was worth the extra cost, tasty and highly flavoured. Very comprehensive menu which we would like to work our way through.'* NDS. *'Food is gorgeous.'* PJ. 'Once I got used to the idea of curry gravy with Chicken Jalfrezi, it was decidedly delicious.' LG. Thursday: 10% discount in restaurant, 20% takeaway. Hours: 12-2.30/6-11.30.

SURREY

Area: Home Counties (south of London)
Population: 1,057,000
Adjacent Counties: Berks, Hants, Kent, London, Sussex

Parts of Surrey were absorbed by Greater London in 1965. We note affected towns/boroughs.

SONALI NEW ENTRANT

198, Station Road, Addlestone

'A takeaway only, but in a class of it's own. Knocks the competition into a cocked hat. Consistently good, never been disappointed. Deserves wide recognition. Seriously great'. D&DP.

Ashtead

MOGHUL DYNASTY 

1 Craddock Parade, Ashtead 01372 274810

Established in '86, managed by Adbul Mannan. Nicely decorated in cream with white pillars, table linen, green plants, wooden chairs with blue velvet seating, colonial fans. Formula curry house, CTM being most popular. Takeaway: orders over £12, 10% off. Minimum charge: £8.50. Hours: 12-2.30/5.30-11.

Byfleet

RED ROSE OF BYFLEET ©

148High Road, Byfleet 01932 355559

An attractively decorated restaurant, with plaster cornices and dado rails. Ivy and palms divide tables and chandeliers hang from the ceilings. King Prawn dishes are house specialities. Average prices. Managing partner, Shuel Miah, enjoys giving a red rose to the lady on departure. Hours: 12-2.30/6-11.30. Branches: Gaylord, Weybridge; Red Rose, of Surbiton, Red Rose of Chessington.

Camberley

DIWAN EE KHAS NEW ENTRANT

413 London Road Camberley 01276 23500

Licensed. Air conditioned. *'Quite simply the best in the area and certainly in the TOP 100 in the UK. I've had most things, including some not on the menu. Last time there, I had tandoori Duck as a starter followed by Duet of Tiger Prawns with lemon Rice and a Chilli Nan. Absolutely superb.'* PS. menu Extracts: Nawabi Chicken £2.50, minced chicken, pungent spices; Afgani Chicken £5.90, in yoghurt sauce; Keema Rice £2.80. Takeaway: 10% discount, £15 minimum. Delivery: £15 minimum. Credit cards accepted. Hours: 12-2/5.30-12.

FRIMLEY TAKEAWAY 

47 High S, Frimley, Camberley 01276 685537

Bengali takeaway established '85 by Hassan Ahmed (manager) and Hussain Ahmed (chef). *'As ever the service was impeccable. Vegetable Madras was beautifully spiced, naan bread was light and fluffy, sag aloo superb. I challenge you not to be delighted by your overall experience! If you are a vegetarian like I am, it is refreshing to have a restaurant who are willing to create a curry to your requirements. A restaurant which clearly values its customers' loyalty. To date I have received nothing but exemplary service coupled with outstanding food. Staff are always willing to tailor dishes to your palate, and as a vegetarian I find their helpfulness very refreshing. Nothing less than outstanding.'* WS. Popular lunch specials: Chicken Tikka Roll or Kebab Roll. Luncheon Vouchers accepted. Hours: 12-2/6-11.30.

MANZIL NEW ENTRANT

142 Frimley Road Camberley 01276 65588

'Fairly small, but extremely well appointed, laminated wooden flooring, air conditioning and starched linen – a sophisticated ambience. Very polite welcome. Tandoori Aloo, a revelation, potato scooped out and filled with a range of lentils and vegetables before being roasted. Robustly spiced Paneer Chilli Masala. Nan light and fluffy.' WS. Takeaway: 10%. Hours: 12 -2.30/6-11.

RAJPUR  10%

57d Mytchett Road, Mytchett, Camberley
01252 542063

Manager Abdul Motin tells us his 46-seater is *'plush with Bengali paintings, comfortable cushioned seating, and a bright interior.'* You tell us: *'Service and food is always of the highest standard. Quantities on large side. Comfort, decor, reception, service and ambience very good, thoroughly recommended. Best in area. CC Discount given even though we didn't ring before or book a table.'* RGB. *'Had the phone put down on me twice when trying to book. Never did succeed in booking! Turned up anyway to find the restaurant is one of five takeaways/restaurants/off licences all sharing a tight parking area immediately in front. Unable to find anywhere where I felt I could safely park, I went to Tariq's instead! I am sure the restaurant would have lived up to its Guide entry had I been able to enter!'* S&GM. *'Have tried to get in here, but parking a problem. Solved by going on Sunday lunchtime for buffet. Quite well patronised, buffet selection varied and frequently topped up. Chutneys and relishes fresh. Nice to see restaurant appealed to the older generation – which I think says a lot for its atmosphere and service. One criticism – food could have been hotter.'* SM. Special: Bangladesh Style Tandoori Masala, tandoori chicken, boneless, thick mild spicy sauce. Banquets Weds. evenings £9.95. CC members 10% discount. Takeaway: 10% off. Sunday buffet lunch £6.50, £3.95 kids. Hours: 12-3.30/6-11.

Carshalton (Greater London)

ROSE HILL TANDOORI 

320 Wrythe Lane, Rose Hill Carshalton
020 8644 9793

A wee 30-seater, est. 1982, owned by Salequr Rahman, manager Mr E Rahman, and unusually at a formula curry house, a lady chef, Mrs Rahman – a family business. And I bet if you ask she'll cook really authentic Bangladeshi food. I see Confederates' Coffee, made with Southern Comfort – nice one! Delivery: £12 minimum, 1½-mile radius. Hours: 12-2/5.30-12.

Cobham

SPICY CHIMNEY 

40 Portsmouth Road, Cobham
01932 863666

Abdul Alam and PH Choudhry's 72-seater is in two rooms of a quaint old building with lots of little alcoves, wooden beams decorated in peach and dusky apricot with rich damask tablecloths with matching napkins, and a fresh flower on each table. Chef Shaid Miah's *'menu is marvellous. Popadoms and relishes very good, one Popadom provided with the compliments of the waiter. King Prawn Suka, a large prawn pan-fried with a lovely thick, rich, slightly sweet and very oniony sauce. Onion Bhajias, four smallish spheres, very well spiced and not too stodgy. Butter Chicken, excellent. Pullao Rice, lovely texture. Nan, circular, quite light and deep. Salmon Kedgeree, unusual and good, very large plateful, spoiled by a large pile of inappropriate salad, served with thick lentil dhal. Brinjal Stuffed, two small aubergines, split, spread with spices and served in a rich creamy sauce, very good, not seen before. Service was absolutely first class, a very personable young waiter with a large smile, a full knowledge of the menu and competence added a great deal to the evening.'* HC. Sunday lunch £7.95. £8.95 wine. Delivery: £15 min order, 3-mile radius. Hours: 12-2.30/6-11.30.

Cranleigh

CURRY INN © 10%

214 High Street, Cranleigh 01483 273992

Bangladeshi formula curry restaurant, smart, bamboo chairs, palm trees, sugar pink table linen. Seats 93 diners, Bhel Puri dishes are most popular, well spiced with lemon, mint, bay leaves, methi (fenugreek) and dallcani (cinnamon), from £6. 16 car parking spaces at back of restaurant. Curry Club members: 10% discount. Sunday lunch £6.95. Hours: 12-3/6-11.30.

Croydon (Greater London)

(Includes Addington Hamsey Green, Selsdon and Shirley)

BANANA LEAF ©

27 ower Addiscombe Road, Croydon 020 8688 0297

Taken over in '97 by Mr D Sitha Raman. Masala Dosa is the most ordered dish. *'Not very familiar with South Indian food, decided to experiment. A small restaurant, tidy, clean and fresh. Friendly waiters. Pappadams, huge, crisp and fresh served with a variety of dips and onion salad. Bonda, hot, crisp, sensitively spiced with a small bowl of curry sauce. Onion Dosai ,freshly cooked with golden onions and fresh coconut chutney. King Prawn Fried, certainly had a good kick. I paid by credit card and when the slip was presented to me the bottom line had been filled in, pleased me tremendously!'* LH. We had a lovely meal – Idle, Masala Dosai and a Mushroom and Spinach Dry Masala but my partner decided to have a pint of draught Cobra with his meal. Foolishly we did not check the price and were astounded at £3.50.' JD. Hours: 12-2.30/6-11.

THE DEANS BYO

241 London Rd, Croydon 020 8665 9192

The Deans opened in 1993 and is named after its chef-owner Salam Ud Din and manager Zaka Ud Din. It is a massive, fully-licensed restaurant seating over 150 diners in two dining rooms, decorated in white with the 'sparkly' mosaic mirror Indian arches to be found in the Moghul palaces. It has a small but typically authentic Pakistani Punjabi menu, serving tandoori items and well-spiced curries. RE tells us of four visits: 1: *'A large busy restaurant favoured by Asians. Also does a very brisk takeaway. Apart from the papadoms (they are grilled which I don't like), the food is excellent. Lamb Nihari was "special" – very tender, quite hot with a distinctive ginger flavour. Lovely dish.'* 2. *'Happy to go back as I was in the area. Seekh Kebabs freshly cooked and spicy, Chicken Tikka fresh and moist. Service is efficient and friendly.'* 3. *'Third time is supposed to be lucky – not this time. Seekh Kebabs and Chicken Tikka were fine, but the Dhall Gosht, so good last time, was awful – undercooked meat in a pale, tasteless sauce. A chap on the next table was complaining that his curry was far too salty. A shame. I will (eventually) go back, but not for some time.'* 4, *'After a culinary disaster last time, I decided to give Deans on more try – Glad I did. Seekh Kebabs were great, in a hot iron plate with fried onions. Haandi Dhall Gosht – very good, hot, spicy, full of flavour and very tender meat. Service good and friendly, busy with families.'* RE. *'OK'* G&MP.Specials: Handi dishes, chicken £4.90, Methi Gosht £5. Handi Aloo Chana £3.50, Dhal-stuffed Karela (bitter gourd) £5. **BYO** no corkage. Delivery: £10 min, 3-miles. Hours: 12-2.30/6-11.30 (10.30 Sun.). '

KERELA BHAVAN NEW ENTRANT

16 London Road, W. Croydon 0181 668 6216

South Indian Restaurant right next to West Croydon Railway Station.. *'We were actually bound for The Deans, about 3/4 mile further along the London Road, but we made the mistake of stepping into the Fox & Hounds Pub opposite, where there was a very entertaining karaoke. Several pints and 2 hours later and we could not be bothered to walk to Deans. Anyway, Ray had often been tempted to try this South Indian Restaurant. The usual Indian background music was playing as we entered this pleasant restaurant. There were about 50 seats, set in alcoves, which gave a more intimate feel and was very nice. The waiter was very friendly and attentive. It was about half full. Ray headed for the toilet as he always does – two reasons: Firstly to wash his hands as he eats with his fingers; and secondly to include in his reports to you. He thinks the toilets often reflect the standard of hygiene throughout the establishment. These were fine– everything worked and there was plenty of soap etc. Poppadums came. They were nice and crispy and dry. Even I like poppadums. (Except some we had at Sheereen Kadah last week which were oily and tasted burnt I did not eat there, sorry to say I had a McDonalds burger and apple pie on the way home– Yum!!)'* [Yuk!! Ed] *'For a starter Ray had Parippu Vada (£1.95), which were two spicy fried lentil cakes. I tried a bit and said it tasted like a dry spicy bun. Ray said I was a Philistine, smothered his with onions, lime pickle and raitha and said I did not know what I was missing. Guess what I had? Yes, chicken kurma, £3.90'* [she only likes baby curry] *'and boiled rice, £1.60. The chicken was not too bad but the sauce was very watery. For his main course, Ray had Kerala Meat Chilli, £5.95. This consisted of quite hot cubes of very lean and tender lamb, which had been marinated in a sweet & sour marinade, then cooked with green chillis and capsicums. It was a dry dish, but very spicy. Ray enjoyed it and said he would recommend it. He also had a Karala Veesu Paratha ,£1.60, a sort of bread in strands. This was most unusual but a good accompaniment to the chilli meat. He also had a dall, which was very runny & bland. The bill was £22.90 and there was an added 10% service charge. Ray said he would recommend the Kerela Bhavan as a different type of Indian dining experience, but he prefers The Deans. So there you have it Dominique. If I'm honest I'm not very adventurous when it comes to food. Ray went to India with a Seekh friend some years ago. I declined to go too– I thought I might starve to death!! However, it is not all one sided. At home, Ray cooks me wonderful stews, chops, sausage toad and shepherds pie, so I'm happy.* She Who Only Likes Baby Curry (RUBY E).

PANAHAR 

316 Limpsfield Road, Hamsey Green, Croydon 020 8651 9663

First opened in 1999 with a fund raising dinner attended by over 100 guests, making over £6,500 for the Mayor of Croydon's charities. Seats 120. Takeaway: 10% discount. Hours: 12-2.30/6-11.

PLANET SPICE TOP 100

88 Selsdon Park, Addington, Croydon 020 8651 3300

This trendily named 90. seater opened in 1999 and, being owned by Emdad Rahman of London SE23's **TOP 100** Barbur, it has a lot going for it, especially with cooking by chef Kirti Rawat, ex chef to the President of India. A modern looking restaurant with bright, contemporary decor and furniture – not Indian at all. *'My first visit, I'm sold on it. Rivals the Tamasha on sheer quality and presentation of food. However, the Tamasha with it's decor and costumes adds that little extra. Staff were very pleasant and actually enjoyed playing with our two toddlers (13 months and 2 1/2 years). Harey Murgh Tikka, fabulous green colour, moist chicken and wow, the pureed coriander hand quite a kick. Mysore Chilli Chicken, great, quite hot from the shredded chili, lovely. Duck Curry, rich spicy with tender meat. Sali Jardaloo, lamb out of this world. Nan's hot, fresh and fluffy. Highly recommended.'* MPW. Regular food festivals (ie: Hyderabadi – tamarind, coriander, curry leaf, peanuts, sesame, mustard seeds, red chillies), organised by the talented Mr Rahman. Menu Extracts: Aloo Chaff £2.50, mashed potatoes and vegetables rolled in cashew nuts and fried golden, Patra £2.50, avari leaves layered with a spicy chick pea paste, steamed, sliced, deep-fried. Shugati Masala £5.95, chicken, spices, coconut, white poppy seeds, Podina Gosht £5.95, minted lamb, honey, lemon juice, Oonbaharui, banana, sweet potato, baby aubergine and shallots, lovage seeds, cumin seeds and asafoetida, Narial Chawal £2.25, basmati rice with shredded coconut. Live music with Graham Jones, Monday, Tuesday and Wednesday evenings. Sunday brunch – let their regular magician entertain the whole family. Takeaway: approximately 15% discount. Delivery: 2½ miles. Hours: 12.30-2.30p 6.30-11.30. Branch: Barbur, SE23.

RUPEES TAKEAWAY 

184 Wickham Road, Shirley, Croydon 020 8655 1866

Enamul Karim Khan and chef Chand Miah's takeaway offers a view of the clean, tidy, well organised open kitchen. Specials: Lamb Chop Bhuna. Chilli Nan. Delivery: £8 minimum, 4-mile radius. Hours: 5-11pm.

SHEESH MAHAL 

10 Lower Addiscombe Road, Croydon 020 8688 6239

Established in 1963. The current owner Mr Islam has been serving to three generations of customers. Head chef is an award winner of the Croydon Curry Chef of the Year Competition both in 1998 and 1999. Seats 32. Takeaway: 10% discount. Delivery: £9.50 minimum, 3-mile radius. Hours: 12-3/6 to late.

SURUCHI ©

120 Headley Drive, New Addington
01689 841998

Established in 1995. a/c.50-seater formula curry house, run by Aklis Miah, with manager Junel Ali. Specials: Lamb Shah Jahani £6.50 – thin slices of lamb seasoned with crushed pistachio nuts, onion and peppers. Chicken Tikka Nan £1.70. Set Dinner: £9. Sunday lunch £6.95. Delivery: £9 minimum, 3-mile radius. Hours: 5.30-11.30. Sun. 12-3/5.30-11.

Dorking

NEW CURRY GARDEN

41 South Street, Dorking 01306 889648

'Decor very striking, minimalist and modern, plain wood floor, bright walls and unusual squiggly light fittings. Food outstandingly good. Only one niggle, on main course did not come with the rest – caused manager great concern and much animated ticking-off of the staff. Excellent service – very enjoyable experience.' H&DRC.

East Molesey

GOLDEN CURRY ©

19 Hampton Court Parade, East Molesey
020 8979 4358

A Aziz's traditionally decorated 52-seater has been going since 1967. Three generations of regulars go for a stable, quality operation and friendly service, led by head waiter Abdul Karim. Sunday lunch £4.95. Minimum charge: £6. Takeaway: 10% off. Hours: 12-2.30/6-12.

PALACE INDIAN CUISINE 

20 Bridge Road, East Molesey
020 8979 1531

E Eshad's 60-seater is yards from Hampton Court Palace. DD. Chef's special: Murag Tikka Rajella, yoghurt based, spicy cooked with massala sauce and fresh garden mint. Minimum charge: £8. Takeaway: 10% discount. Delivery: £12 minimum, 2-mile radius. Hours: 12-2.30/6-11.30.

Epsom

EPSOM BALTI HOUSE

26 South Street, Epsom 01372 747425

Fully licensed and air conditioned. *'Restaurant excellent, nice decor and large round tables for four people. Attentive service without being annoying, traditional style Indian dishes – excellent. Popadoms crisp and hot. Shami Kebabs. small, nothing special. Prawn Puri and KP Butterfly – excellent. Main courses well presented. Meat Thali, superb. Colleagues spoke highly of Chicken Chilli Masala and Balti Chicken Shashlik. Food washed down with ice cold Cobra. Well worth a visit!'* DJL. Takeaway: 10% discount. Hours: 12- 2.30/6-12. (Sun. to 11.30).

LE RAJ TOP 100

211 Firtree Rd, Epsom Downs 01737 371371

Owner chef Enam Ali's 110 seater Le Raj is in outer Epsom (it's on the A240/A2022) in a line of shop fronts. *'One of my Asian colleagues and I had occasion to attend a training course at Surrey County Council's Highways House and we noticed that Le Raj was just down the road, so we gave it a try for lunch. It is a very different Asian restaurant– more like a Mediterranean Bistro than any Indian I have been in before. The presentation and style of the food is equally radical– as to whether it was chic will probably be a matter of individual taste. The place was deserted, and we were the only two customers. Our opinions on the food were frankly divided. My Kashmiri colleague thought it was well presented, but the food was tasteless. I thought it was absolutely not what you expect in your formula curry house, but I liked it, once I realised that it was aiming for a more sort of European / Asian fusion type of food than just a curry based fare. The decor of the place reflects this– all warm apricot walls and sun bleached yellows elsewhere. So what did we have: Kaathi Kebabs as a starter– minced meat roasted on a skewer in the kebab, my colleague Chingri Modu– KP's cooked with honey, fresh lime and tamarind sauce. The kebab was not as spicy as I expected, never the less it was tasty and I enjoyed it. For main course I had murg– e– mutazan, which was pieces of chicken cooked with cardamom and yoghurt, and gosht– e– jalali, which was described as 'spectacular dish of lamb, cooked with very strong spices' and had a two chillies sign against it. My friend for this was not justified, and that the dish was just about medium heat. I did try some, and I had to agree that it was not really as 'two chillies' as I would thought. However, it was very tender and tasty, even though it was not a 'fire eater!' We also had a Brinjal Bhajee and lime pickles, both of which were excellent, and a similar standard Akbori (chilli and mint) nan. I think if we ever crossed their threshold again, my colleague would request a more liberal hand with the chilli and methi etc. Although it was to my mind, and taste buds, not at all the norm for a curry house, I thought it was excellent, once I had got over the culture shock of going in a curry house that was not really one at all?? I celebrate diversity, so 'vive la difference' as far as Le Raj is concerned.'* MW. .Min charge: £15. Hours: 12-2.30/5.30-11.

Esher

PANAHAR TANDOORI NEW ENTRANT

124, High Street, Esher.

'Easily the best curry in the area, no mistake. Friendly service, atmosphere fine but always crowded, booking almost essential, not surprisingly.' D&DP.

Farnham

DARJEELING ©

25 South Street, Farnham 01252 714322

MA Rahman and S Islam's 46-seater is stylishly decorated, with mahogany wood panelling everywhere, brass plates decorate the walls and there is a large brass peacock in the window. *'Everything about this restaurant is good. The decor is subtle, low light, tropical fish. Good carpeting and sumptuous table linen and crockery. The menu is extensive. Service is very good. Waiters are friendly but unobtrusive. Food is excellent, subtly spiced, generous portions, excellent quality. Continues to be our favourite restaurant.'* JW. Special: Garlic Chilli Chicken. Takeaway: over £15, 10% off. Set dinner £26 for two. Minimum charge: £15. Hours: 12-2/6-11.30. Branches: Banaras, Farnham. Viceroy, Hartley Witney, Hants.

Fetcham

FETCHAM TANDOORI

248 Cobham Road, Fetcham 01372 374927

'What a lovely surprise. Good atmosphere, excellent and friendly service and really good food. Extensive menu, usual dishes, interesting vegetables. Full marks for fish curry being made with boal. All sensible portions, well cooked. Mango Sorbet, very good.' HJC.

©	Curry Club Discount	U	Unlicensed
V	Vegetarian	ANP	Alcohol not permitted
e-a-m-a-y-l	Eat as much as you like	BYO	Bring your own alcohol

GURKHA NEW ENTRANT

78, Bedfont Lane, Feltham.

'Best Nepali food for a long way, better than any in Aldershot. Some very unusual dishes, and wonderful service with cosy atmosphere. Near to Feltham Station and cinema'. D&DP.

Guildford

CINNAMONS

4 Chapel Street, Guildford 01483 300626

'Decor very open, light and modern, could be any cuisine. Menu very appealling. Good, friendly service, all young men dressed in identical blue shirts and trendy ties. Food outstandingly good, attractively served in white china dishes and in sensible rather than generous portions. Only grumble, delivery of food unacceptably slow. They did apologise and offered free liqueurs. Espresso coffee served with good quality chocolates. No Indian desserts. Definitely wish to return.' HC. Takeaway: 20% discount. Hours: 12-2.30/6-11.30.

BOMBAY SPICE NEW ENTRANT

17 Park Street Guildford 01483 454272

'Decor is light, modern and fairly sparse. Menu fairly large, a few unusual items, prices and portions good. Gulan Jamun a plus.' hc. Delivery: £10 min, 5-mile radius. Hours: 12-2.30/5.30-11.30.

Hampton Court

GOLDEN CURRY NEW ENTRANT

19, Hampton Court Parade, Hampton Court.

'Best by far out of a cluster in area, so take no substitutes and insist upon this place. Friendly service, just across the road from Hampton Court Station.' D&DP.

Horley

FORT RAJ BALTI 

74 Victoria Road, Horley 01293 822909

Established in 1995, Shah Ali Athar and Abdul Khan's Fort is a 74-seater (party room 32). Chef Ali Mokoddus's Specials include Balti Chicken or Lamb Tikka Shankapuri, whose sauce contains coconut and red wine, and Tava Murg (a light and healthy stirfried dish, delicately cooked with special herbs and spices, and flambéed with white wine) *'Portions large and well-presented. Service very friendly. Decor is tasteful.'* MR&MRS DNL. Minimum charge: £6.50. Takeaway: 15-20% discount. Delivery: £15 min, 3-mile radius. Hours: 12-2.30/6-12.

Kingston-upon-Thames (Greater London)

MONTYS TANDOORI 

53 Fife Road, Kingston 020 8546 1724

70-seater Nepalese restaurant, owned by Kishor Shrestha. South Indian face-masks decorate the white walls and hang from cream drapes. Hand-painted silk pictures of Indian scenes cover the walls, the floor is tiled. Specials: Nepalese Murgh Masala, chicken on the bone. 'Service is excellent, unobtrusive, polite and no mistakes. Food is plentiful and piping hot.' ST. Takeaway: 10% off. Hours: 12-2.30/6-12.

Lingfield

BENGAL VILLAGE NEW ENTRANT

Lingfield

A favourite curry house for MR & MRS RL, who reckon the food, care, decor, servoce waiters and the whole experience is simply as good as it gets. What more can we say?

Morden (Greater London)

INDIAN VILLAGE 

10 Morden Court Parade, London Road, Morden 020 8640 8556

44-seater, fully licensed and air conditioned, established in 1998, whose decor includes fruit trees and flowers. Specials: Salmon Samosas £2.95. Stuffed Coco Yam Leaves, patra leaves spread with a spicy paste, rolled and steamed, sliced and deep-fried (Pat particularly likes this dish). Boal, a fresh water fish marinated in coriander sauce. *'My wife and I took our four daughters for a special occasion night, owner treated us so very well. Food really cooked well and portions just right. £128 for six (inc Champagne)'* RL. Delivery: £15 minimum. Delivery: £15 min. Hours: 5.30-11.30; closed Mon.

Motspur Park (Greater London)

MOTSPUR TANDOORI 

365 West Rd, Motspur Park 020 8949 4595

Established in 1982. Seats 70. Plans to refurbish in 2001. Specials include: Machley Jhol £6.99 (fish cooked in an authentic style with fresh coriander and onions, and with a blend of light spices). Delivery: £12 min, 3-mile. Hours: 12-2/6-11.30.

New Malden (Greater London)

CHARLIE'S INDIAN CUISINE 

276 Burlington Rd, New Malden 020 8949 7476

Established in 1975, taken over by Mr Faruque and Mr Hoque in 1998. Previously called Shannon Tandoori. Seats 42. Air conditioned. Specials: Murgh Rezala, chicken with green chillies, hot. Peshwari Chicken, hot and fruity. Takeaway: 10-15% discount. Delivery: £12 min, 3-mile radius. Hours: 12-2.30/5.30-11; closed Mon.

Oxted

GURKHA KITCHEN AWARD WINNER AND TOP 100

111 Station Road, East Oxted 01883 722621

Oxted town is divided by the railway, like Woking, which is very irritating. We drove up and down Station Road West twice before we realised about the other Station Road, not so easily reached by car, on the other side of the tracks. We arrived at 8pm and our coats were taken immediately by the waiter, who sat us in the reception/waiting area. The floor is boarded, which makes it slightly noisy, but the whole look is very elegant. Beautiful hand-forged black steel chairs, the seat and back were wickered, the seat then covered in a small patterned carpet with a fringe on two sides. White linen tablecloths and napkins, large, fragile wine glasses, drinking receptacles for the connoisseur, their slender stems making a lovely bottle of Argentinian Norton red wine the more enjoyable. I asked our waiter if a lot get broken. *'Yes,'* he said proudly, *'and I break the most.'* At the back of the restaurant an area is decorated with a small roof as in a Nepalese village, fishing net and basket hanging from the wall. The food is perfectly cooked Nepalese fare. But it isn't earthy village food. It's slightly evolved *and modern, yet indisputably Nepalese. 'Yes, it's spot on. Extremely interesting menu with not one dish that appears on a standard high street curry house menu. We had first class starters: Bhutuwa (excellent melt-in-the-mouth chicken livers stir fried in a delicately spiced light sauce served in a small wafer basket), Vegetable Khaja (filo pastry wrapped up like spring roll, but not so thick with vegetable filling and mint and mustard dressing , . They were cut in half, diagonally, a small green salad with the dressing decorating the centre of the plate, the Khaja in four corners. Extremely mild, but tasty. Main dishes (Mooli Chicken, Piro Lamb and Hariyo Machha – monkfish wrapped in spinach prepared in a mild, dry fruit sauce) were all superb, with the flavouring of each being totally different and distinct from the others. Portions not large, but sufficient. Prices marginally higher than average. Waiter could have looked a bit happier.'* MW. *'Nepalese cuisine served here in sophisticated modern surroundings. A mystery into the unknown as nothing whatsoever on the menu was familiar. However, fortified by large bottles of Kathmandu beer, we chose dishes that sounded good. Couldn't remember what they all were, nicely spiced and tasty. Only the breads were disappointing but perhaps they were meant to be like that – who knows! Well worth a visit, helpful, friendly waiters. Only £60 for three – worth every penny!'* CS. *'Friends 40th birthday celebration. Large party of over 20 adults, plus 10 children. Sunday evening buffet. Food excellent as was ambience and service. Looked after our noisy group often and extremely well.'* SO. Palungo Sag, steamed spinach sautéed with fenugreek seeds; the spinach was fresh. Gurkha Aloo, diced delicately, prepared in turmeric and cummin seeds, mild potato cubes fried a little brown on the sides. Rashilo Bhat, rice cooked with bay leaf, cardamom, garnished with brown onion £1.95, light, fluffy and flavoursome. Joano Patre, bread with carom seed £2, just like a Nan really, quartered, very good. Golbeda Ko Achar, fresh tomato pickle, spicy, a good accompaniment to all dishes. Everything was delivered in seperate white china dishes, the plates hot. All the waiters are smartly dressed and polite. For the surroundings, food, aperitifs I was expecting a bill of something around £60, but I was pleasantly surprised at a total of £43.45, service not included . A **TOP 100** restaurant. No-smoking. Sunday buffet 1-10pm. Hours: 12-2.30/6-11 (11.30 on Fri. & Sat.).

Redhill

EXOTICA TANDOORI 

18 Cromwell Road, Redhill 01737 778624

Chef/owner Ali Shazid's 30-seater is decorated in dark cherry, matching carpet, green plants. Specials: Chicken Chat, small juicy pieces of chicken, cooked in a hot and spicy sauce. Passanda, sliced meat cooked in fresh cream, cultivated yoghurt and ground nuts. Minimum charge: £10. Delivery: 4-miles. Hours: 12-2.30/5.30-11.30 (12am on Fri. & Sat.).

Reigate

LAL AKASH NEW ENTRANT

27 Bell Street Reigate 01737 223773

'Met up with a old work mate, he recommended this restaurant. Very large dining area, looked bigger, it was quiet! Perused the menu with Popadoms and Kingfisher. Eight different chutneys – excellent. Started with excellent Sheek Kebab and Lamb Momo. Generous portions of beautifully cooked Nepal Kalio, Gosht e Laziz, Shest Rice, Tarka Dal and Keema Nan. Attentive service, drinks topped up regularly. Will visit again, I urge others too!' DL. Menu Extracts: Chingri Roshon £2.95, prawn, panfried, garlic, coriander; Nawabi Masala £6.50, chicken or lamb, onions,tomatoes, peppers, orange, carrots, mint, spinach; Shesto Rice £2.50, peas, egg, almond, sultanas and spices; Chana Bhajee £2.50, chickpeas.

VILLAGE BRASSERIE 

10 West Street, Reigate 01737 245695

40-seater fully licensed and air-conditioned curry house owned by MDA. Rashid. It has some South Indian specials, Mossala Dosi (sic.), pancake filled with delicious spicy vegetables, served with salad. Specials include: Bengal Chicken or Lamb, cooked with citrus lemon. Chicken or Lamb Rezala, cooked with mince. Green Kebab, spinach, cottage cheese, garlic and ginger cakes and Choti Poti, chickpeas, potato, egg, garnished with Bombay Mix. Sunday buffet, kids under

twelve,. Banquet Night: every Thursday evening £9.95. Delivery: 2-mile radius, £10 minimum. Takeaway: 10% discount. Hours: 5.30-11.30; Sun. 12.30-3.30/5.30-11.

Richmond-upon-Thames (Greater London)

ORIGIN ASIA NEW ENTRANT

100 Kew Road, Richmond 0208 9480509

Good site among the alfresco restaurants at the Richmond roundabout end of Kew Road. It was good when we went twice, but ownership changes at the time of writing may result in chef changes. Pity if that happens, because the Indian chef brigade are good at their job.

Staines

ANCIENT RAJ 

157 High Street, Staines 01784 457099

Owner-chef Syed Joynul's restaurant is *'appropriate for all occasions, from takeaways to family celebrations' A stylish setting. Moghul swordsmen decorate the walls. I tried a Wednesday evening when the full, standard menu is replaced by a slightly smaller banquet menu – fixed price for a starter, main course, side dish and rice or naan. Aloo chat was very tasty with a good balance of spices, jeera chicken excellent, matter paneer was disappointingly covered in a thick red-coloured sauce.'* RH. *'We are impressed with the consistently high standard of well-presented and hot food. Reasonably priced.'* SR. Hours: 12-2.30/6-11.30.

Surbiton (Greater London)

AGRA TANDOORI 

142 Ewell Road, Surbiton 020 8399 8854

Owner-manager HK Paul runs a good and reliable curry house, serving competent curries and their accompaniments. Hours: 12-2.30/6-12.

AJANTA 

114 Ewell Road, Surbiton 020 8399 1262

Rubel Ahmad will help you to find all your favourites. *'Set meal for four, looked good value and so it proved. Huge quantities, good selection of starters, sensitively spiced Lamb Dupioza.'* CJC. Hours: 12-2.30/6-12. Branches: Shapla, Bristol Road, Selly Oak, and Stratford Road, Shirley, Birmingham.

JOY

37 Brighton Road Surbiton 020 8390 3988

'We are lucky to have a large number of really good Indian restaurants within easy reach, but Joy will make them look to their laurels. Plain decor, modern but not stark, chairs upholstered and comfortable, table cloths white, glassware good quality and cutlery so attractive. Waiters all wear purple shirts and ties, professional and friendly. Menu slightly more expensive, but worth every penny. All dishes individual in appearance and taste with spicing on the hot side. Rice served in lidded casseroles. £198 (ex service) for ten.' HC. Menu Extracts: Paneer Tikka Kathi £3.50, rolled in gram flour pancake, served with spicy mint sauce; Raj Kachori £3.50, flffy whole wheat puri stffed with urid dal dumplings, potatoes, vermicelly topping with sweet and sour sauce and curd (yoghurt); Charra Aloo Masaledar £3.35, new baby potatoes, tossed with onion and tomato; Sikandari Raan £11.50, whole leg of lamb soaked overnight in run marinade, cooked in charcoal oven. www. joy-restaurant.co.uk e: info@joy-restaurant.co.uk Takeaway: 15% discount. Hours: 12 to 2.30 and 6 to 12.

RAJ 

163 Ewell Road, Surbiton 020 8390 0251

Aziz Miah's curry house seats 58 and 'offers the best value for money, excellent food, good-sized portions, attentive yet not overbearing waiter service and tasteful decor in clean and comfortable surroundings.' SH. Chef's Choice: Special Garlic Chicken, tikka cooked with garlic, onions, green peppers, in garlic sauce. Fully licensed and air conditioned. 'Looks very ordinary from the street, but highly rated by the locals. We were a group of fourteen at lunchtime, two waiters and chefs deserve praise for the service and food, delicious.' HC. Starters include: Kolijee Puri, lightly spiced chicken liver stir-fried, served on bread. Main courses: Chicken or Lamb Cashew Nut Tikka, cooked in a creamy sauce with cashew nuts. Chilli Nan. Takeaway: 10% discount. Sunday buffet. Takeaway: 10% discount. Delivery: £15 min. Hours: 12-2.30/6-12; Sun. 12-12.

Tolworth (Greater London)

JAIPUR 

90 The Broadway, Tolworth 020 8399 3619

The external decor makes this venue unmissable. Its huge pink stone pillars make it stand out, a fact not unnoticed by the local council, who in the early days spent a considerable amount of time, and presumably money, trying to force owner SU Ali to remove them. Fortunately bureaucracy lost, and the pillars remain; indeed, they continue inside, giving a very Indian feel to the interior. India's Jaipur is the pink city, where every building is made from pink sandstone. Naturally the Jaipur's theme is pink too, with *'an amazing sugar-pink decor, with friezes of dancing ladies seemingly sculpted out of the wall.'* DD. *'Thoroughly enjoyable.'* DRC. *'One of my regular haunts.'* PD.

Virginia Water

VICEROY OF INDIA 

4 Station Approach, Virginia Water
01344 843157

MS Ali's Viceroy remains *'a very popularcurry house with good atmosphere and friendly staff.'* CP. *Restaurant empty (Wednesday lunchtime). Brusque waiter. Chicken Chilli Masallah and Meat Madras – nice spicing, especially the rice. OK value at £25 for two.'* MG. *'This is a seriously excellent restaurant. Everyone I take there ABSOLUTELY REFUSES to go anywhere else and insists on going back. Chilli Chicken Masala ranks as historic and their Dhansak cannot be bettered.'* AF.

Walton-on-Thames

NEW RAJDOOT NEW ENTRANT

21 Moseley Rd, Waltony.

'Always consistent, wonderful flavours, friendly and attentive service, never been disappointed yet. Warm and welcoming atmosphere. Our personal second favourite.' D&DP.

ORIENTAL CURRY CENTRE 

13 Church Street, Walton 01932 222317

Established in 1968. Taken over by manager Asif Iqbal in 1999. Seats 70. Specials include: Balti and Bangladeshi special dishes. *'Long standing, well above high street curry. A good reliable fallback.'* D&DP. Delivery: 4-mile radius. Hours: 12-2.30/6-12.

Weybridge

GOLDEN CURRY 

132 Oatlands Drive, Weybridge 01932 846931

Good reports still received about owner Enayeth Khan's golden curries.

THE HUSSAIN 

47 Church Street, Weybridge
01932 844720

All reports speak well of the food and the service at M Suleman's Hussain. *'Garlic chicken was memorable, even next day, according to one wag.'* HC. Branch: The Curry Corner Tandoori, Hersham, Surrey.

Whyteleafe

CURRY GARDEN 

242 Godstone Rd, Whyteleafe 01883 627237

An effort is made at Akhlaqur Rahman and Moynoor Rashid's 54-seater air-conditioned restaurant. On the ground and first floor, it's decorated in light blue wallpaper, silk plants, with a superb bar. Special: Vegetable Malai Kofta, minced vegetables made into balls and cooked in cream. Sunday buffet 12-3. Minimum charge: £6. Service: 10%. Takeaway: 10% discount. Delivery: £13 minimum order, 3-miles. Hours: 12-3/6-12.

Woking

BUKHARA NEW ENTRANT

6–7, High Street, Woking.

'Unusual items: Crab Kolhapuri, Main courses: Bengal Fish Curry, delicious, very authentic, Raan e Guddaz marinated lamb shank. Very high quality, service and ambience, but quite pricey. Good for a special occasion.' D&DP.

JAIPUR TOP 100

49 Chertsey Road, Woking 01483 772626

This elegant 60-seater, established in 1993, is owned by Nizam Ali and his two delightful sisters, Reggi and Sophi, all of whom I met in their gorgeous Sylheti home, during a monsoon storm a few years ago. *'The ambience (of the restaurant) is smooth and peaceful. The bar on the right invites you to enjoy a relaxing drink, while the huge pillars in their subdued tones of pink make you feel you are in India. Service is superb headed by manager Shahab Uddin. The food is always an adventure, spiced with care and forethought by long-standing chef Rupa Kumar, who was crowned Woking Curry Chef of the Year, 1999. The whole meal was outstanding.'* DBAC. *'Basically traditional menu with a few interesting items. Food served with a smile. Chicken Dupiaza very light on onions. Could not fault the food but ordinary.'* MP. *'We started with King Prawn Butterfly and Meat Samosa (both excellent). We followed with Sali Boti (sliced lamb with apricots) which was mild and beautifully cooked. The Nan bread (slightly crispy and buttery on top) was sensational. Service was perfect and this is definitely a worthy* **TOP 100**.' AF. Minimum charge: £6.95. Business weekday self-serve buffet lunches, Sunday e-a-m-y-l buffet: £6.95 adult, £3.95 kids. Takeaway: 10% discount. Delivery: £10 min, 5-miles. Hours: 12-2.30/6-11.30.

KHYBER PASS 

18 The Broadway, Woking 01483 764710

It's a standard curry house, green decor and Hindi arches. *'Food is always good. Of particular interest to us is the lime pickle on the chutney tray.'* DRC. Manager Jafar Abdul Wahab promises to give a generous discount to Curry Club members. Branches: Khyber Pass, 12 Lower Guildford Road, Knaphill and 54 Terrace Road, Walton-on-Thames.

LOTUS OF BENGAL 

45 Goldsworth Road, Woking
01483 766226

Established in 1984, taken over by Mostaque Rahman in 1996. Seats 44. Parking at front of restaurant after 6pm. Banquets every Thurs. night. Takeaway: 10% discount. Delivery: £15 minimum, 3-mile radius. Hours: 12-2.30/6-11.30; Sun. 1-11.

SUSSEX

Area: South
Population: 1,487,000
Adjacent Counties: Hants, Kent, Surrey

For the purposes of this Guide we combine East and West Sussex.

Barnham

PASSAGE TO INDIA

15 The Square, Barnham 01243 555064

Set in a small village, Mr Muhammed Yousuf Islam's 58-seater is a well established, popular and competent curry house enjoyed by its locals. Service, customer care and food are all above average, without being over -priced. Special: Butter Chicken £5.70. Seats 58, ample parking for 60. Spacious, air-conditioned. Takeaway: 10% discount. Hours: 12-2.30/6-11.30. (12 -Fri/Sat.).

Bexhill-on-Sea

SHIPLU 

109 London Road, Bexhill 01424 219159

At Abdul Kalam Azad's Shiplu *'service couldn't be bettered, all dishes were well cooked and presented in adequate quantities.'* DJB. Hours: 12-2.30/6-12.

Bognor Regis

ANWARS NEW ENTRANT

43 Queensway Bognor 01243 842010

'Two companions and I stopped off on the way home. Chicken Bombay, potatoes, tomatoes and boiled egg – had a strong tomato base, quality and quantity fine. Overall a competent and enjoyable meal.' MK. Menu Extracts: Samosa £2.10, chicken, meat or vegetable; Corn Massala, medium, sweetcorn, butter with vegetable, chicken or lamb, from £3.05; Garlic Nan £1.65. Takeaway: 10% discount, £10 minimum. Licensed. Air conditioned. Hours: 12-2.30/6-12.

PASSAGE TO INDIA NEW ENTRANT

15 The Square Barnham Bognor Regis

'Ample parking 10 yards away. Noticed waiter accompanied an elderly woman to her table and pulled it out to ease her into a banquette. Many families with well-behaved children. Short wait for Popadoms and pickles. Long wait for food, but worth it. Food not only superb in quality but over generous in quantity. My husband, no mean trenchman, was unable to finish. Husband visit loo, said very clean.' JS-S.

Brighton

BALTI HUT

2 Coombe Terrace, Brighton 01273 681280

30-seater, est. '97 by Dost Mohammed, serving formula curries and Balti specials from £4.80. *'Informative menu, with plenty of unusual delights. I used my naan to mop up every last trace of my Tandoori Nowab, excellently cooked and very delicious. Forget location prejudice.'* N&D. Service 10%. Takeaway: 10% off. Delivery: £8 min, 3-miles. Hours: 6-11.30pm (12am on Sat.).

BAYLEAF

104 Western Road, Brighton 01273 773804

Established in 1998. Seats 87. *'Bingo, an oasis in the wilderness of mostly mediocre formula curry houses in Brighton. Bills itself as an Indian Brasserie and it's certainly different from yer average eaterie. Light airy room with tiled floor, polished wood tables and a cool blend of jazz and blues background music. Not a Balti, Pakora or Vindaloo in sight – about 12 starters and 12 mains, of mostly unusual dishes. The price for mains (about £6.90 per dish) was inclusive of side dishes of Dahl and Vegetable of the Day, so it was pretty good value. Food was uniformly excellent. Chicken Chaat gets a special recommendation – a really good interpretation of what is rapidly becoming in some places a very hackneyed (and oily- ugh!) dish.'* SM. *'An unusual and refreshing different menu, although for the unadventurous some standard curries are available. I had Chicken Chaat followed by a Bayleaf Khasi – fresh lamb pieces with onion and red chillies, which came with Dal and a Vegetable Curry. Good quantities and the quality of food was excellent. Offered a drink on the house.'* MK. Specials include: Chicken Nilgiri (chicken cooked with spinach and mint), Jeera Pullao (cumin flavoured basmati rice). Price check: CTM £6.95, Pullao Rice £1.45, Peshwari Nan £1.85, Lager £2.60 pint. Takeaway: 15% discount. Delivery: £10 minimum, 3-mile radius. Hours: 12-3pm/5.30-11.30pm; Sat. 12pm-12am.

NISHAT TAKEAWAY

58 Preston Street Brighton

'Without doubt, consistantly high quality food. Meat is tender, no fat or gristle. Service polite and quantities good.' JP.

POLASH BYO ALLOWED ©

19 York Place, Brighton 01273 626221

Formula 60-seater, owned and managed by Nosir Ullah. Licensed but BYO, no corkage. Takeaway: 10% off. Delivery: £10 min. Hours: 12-2/6-12.

Burgess Hill

SHAPLA

226 London Rd, Burgess Hill 01444 232493

'No airs and graces at this restaurant, but boy did the curry hit the spot. It was marvellous. Chicken Tikka Massala and Karai Chicken were exceptional.' N&D

Chichester

MEMORIES OF INDIA

Old Bridge Road (A259), Bosham Roundabout, Chichester 01243 572234

Abdul Jalil's formula curryhouse is nicely decorated, peach walls, tablecloths and napkins, and blue carpet. Separate bar, highly polished floor, cane chairs and tables, green plants. *'Had a takeaway and despite the decor which made us think it would be expensive we found it to be very reasonable. My only complaint, Sag Paneer was made with cheddar. Helpful staff, despite being busy.'* SW. Specials: Lamb Podina, thin lamb with garlic, fresh mint and coriander £6.95. Ayre Jalfrey, Bengali fish cooked with chillies, garlic, peppers in a hot spicy sauce £7.95. Takeaway: 15% off. Minimum charge: £13.50. Hours: 12-2.30/6-12.

SHAPLA TANDOORI

Eastgate Square, Chichester 01243 775978

Formerly The Peacock. *'On second floor above old swimming pool. Very functional feel with bright pink emulsion painted walls. Usual menu with handful of unusual dishes – King Prawns in Mustard Sauce. Food well spiced, good chunks of garlic, chilli and excellent Nan bread. Service was a bit "dump it all on the table and run". Still worth including.'* CC. *'Visited here twice before. Both times just before visiting the Festival Theatre for a Russian ballet performance. It is indeed painted in bright pink – but never mind, the food is typical curry house fayre but done passably well. I enjoyed their Chicken Dhansak (quite hot) and yes the Nan bread is excellent. Good value for money too.'* DC.

Crawley

BLUE INDIA — NEW ENTRANT

47 High Street Crawley 01293 446655

If the menu lives up to its description, this must be a lovely restaurant and Crawley is very lucky indeed, to have chef Kirti Rewart. Menu Extracts: Crab Masala £4.95, fresh white crab meat, spices, white wine, mango juice, topped with cheese, served in shell. Patra £3.50, avari leaves layered with spicy chickpea paste, steamed, sliced and deep-fried. Tangri Kebab £3.75, chicken wings marinated in green chilli, ginger, garlic, yoghurt and tamarind roasted in tandoor. Goan Fish Grill £7.50, lightly spiced, grilled with onions, tomatoes and capsicums. Red Lamb Lemongrass £7.95, sweet and sour, with lemongrass and shrimp paste. One of my favourites Chicken Chettinand £7.95, hot sauce, ginger, garlic, tomatoes, onions and coconut. Caldine £7.95, fish with jeera, tamarind, coriander, spicy piquant coconut milk sauce. Chingri Shatkari £12.95, king sized prawns cooked in calamansi juice, lemon leaf and naga chilli, crisp, hot and tangy. Hours: 12 -2.30/6-11.30.

RAJ TAKEAWAY 

8 Broadfield Barton, Crawley 01293 515425

SU Ahmed has a loyalty discount scheme: collect stars for a free meal. As well as the goodies, chef A Ali does curry sauce and chips, kids' favourite. Hours: 5.30-11.

RUBY MURRAY & CHILLI FUSION

4 Pegler Way Crawley 01293 417147

'Same Place, Different Menu.' There is nothing this place doesn't do. Fortuitous Crawley! Ruby Murray: Set Meal for Four: 4 x Popadoms, 2 x Nan, Chicken Tikka, Sheek Kebab, Chicken Tikka Masala, Chicken Korma, Meat Bhoona, Mixed Vegetable Korma, 2 x Pullao Rice, Onion Bhajee, Cauliflower Bhajee, Bombay Potato, 2 x Mint Sauce, 2 Mango Chutney and a bottle of wine (red/white) is cracking value at £34. Menu Extracts: Channa Chat Puri £2.95, Butter Chicken £7.95 (served with Pullao Rice); Peshwari, Keema or Garlic Nan £1.95. Chilli Fusion: Indian, Mexican, Thai and Lebanese. Absoluely everything is listed from Chilli Roghan Josh to Texas Tooth Picks, thin cuts of onion and mild Jalapenos cooked in a batter served with picante salsa, sour cream or guacamole – yummy! to Pad Thai, pan fried Thai noodles with shrimps, tofu, egg and bean sprouts (an absolute must when eating Thai) to Moutabel, baked aubergine, onions, crushed wheat, lemon juice and olive oil. Delivery: £7 minimum. Credit cards accepted.

Hours: 4-1, last orders 12.45.

ZARI

214, Ifield Drive, Ifield, Crawley
01293 553009

'The Zari is wonderfully different – up market, classy, clean, subtle light, dimmer switches, high back light wood chairs. Generous portions – two Rice and Sag Aloo £2.30 for three people. Although not advertised I often order a portion of masala sauce for my veggie daughter. Takeaway for four £39.95.' BW. Starters include : Machli Papeta na Pattice £2.95 – flakes of fish, mashed potato, herbs and spices. Murgh Tikka Mariali,spicy green chicken tikka. Main courses: Zari Jhalak Machli,crunchy pomfret on bed of crispy fried onions and aubergine salad, served with tangy sauce. Assorted Vegetable Tikka Chat, vegetable cutlets marinated in yoghurt and fresh spices then barbecued in the tandoor. Disabled access. Hours: 12-2.30/6-11.30.

Crowborough

ROSE OF BENGAL

2-3, Crowborough Hill, Crowborough
Crowborough 01892 662252

A favourite curry house for MR & MRS RL, who reckon the food, care, decor, servoce waiters and the whole experience is simply as good as it gets. What more can we say?

Eastbourne

INDIAN PARADISE 

166 Seaside, Eastbourne 01323 735408

A Khalique's bright restaurant has been serving competent curries and accompaniments to a local following for the last 15 years. Delivery. Hours: 12-2.30/6-12.

Hastings

SPICE OF INDIA 

177a Queens Road, Hastings 01424 439493

Formerly the Shiplu, it is *'tastefully decorated and clean. Service on the slow side but friendly. Pops warm and crisp, Onion B large, could not be beaten. Phall not on the menu but asked for it. Very hot as it should be.'* BP-D. *'Visited many times. Comfortable, unpretentious. Nothing very ambitious but always acceptable. Excellent Sag Gosht. Prices cheap.'* JR. *'We found the food excellent. My partner was particularly pleased with the Lamb Madras, claiming it as one of the best he has ever had.'* AK&KW. Hours: 12-2.30/6-12.

Haywards Heath

CURRY INN 

58 Commercial Square, Haywards Heath
01444 415414

At Abru Miah's 60-seater with blue and green marble effect bar, pillars, plants and chandelier lighting, Korma is the most popular dish. Hours: 12-2.30/6-11.30. (12am on Sat.).

Hove

ASHOKA 

95-97 Church Road, Hove 01273 734193

100-seater owned by Bashir Meah and Rafique Miah. *'Nice roomy restaurant, clean and comfortable. Onion Bhaji, small but good and tasty. Chicken Ceylon with Pilau Rice and Nan, hot, as it should be, nicely served and plenty of it! Bill allowed for 10% discount to Curry Club member, but offset by service charge.'* BP-D. Madras most popular. Service 10%. Sunday lunch: £6.95. Hours: 12-3/6-12. Branch: Bombay, Preston Street, Brighton.

GANGES 

93 Church Road, Hove 01273 728292

Established 1992 by Abdul (front) and Karim (kitchen) who run an attractive restaurant decorated in white and green. Seats 100. Specials: Brandy King Prawn, served with Pullao Rice. Takeaway: 10% discount. Hours: 12-2.30p/6-12.

IKARIM'S TANDOORI 

15 Blatchington Road, Hove 01273 739780

Formula curry house, traditionally decorated, seats 38. Balti dishes available. Minimum charge: £7.95. Service 10%. Delivery: £8 minimum order. Hours: 6-11.30. (12am on Sat.). Branch: Balti House, Coombe Terrace, Brighton.

KASHMIR ©

71 Old Shoreham Rd, Hove 01273 739677

Established way back in '78, by Subab Miah, who is a busy chap, being manager and head chef. Seats 45. Traditional decor, formula curries. *'The food is always delicious, the service courteous and friendly.'* HF. *'A consistently high standard of cooking and preparation.'* JHW. *'Mr Miah and family provide excellence at all expectations.' crc. 'I've been coming since it opened. The seating and bar are very pleasant. The curries are delicately spiced and individual.'* LH. Specials include Balti dishes. *'This restaurant being staunch supporters of Brighton Hove and Albion, saw that we were in a hurry to get to the match, and acted fast. Food excellent and good portions. Seemed au fait with the Guide coupon scheme and I got 10% discount.'* BP-D. Hours: 12-3/6-12.

Lewes

SHANAZ 

83 High Street, Lewes 01273 488038

Taken over in '97 by Mrs LB Salim, her 98-seater (party room 44) is decorated cottage-style with varnished wood panelling. *'Best in Lewes. Food consistent. Chicken Nababi – large quantities of chicken tikka and minced lamb in a spicy, rich sauce – yum! Vegetable Pasanda – sweet and boozy. A useful eating place.'* JR. *'On the way to watch football, my son remarked he could "murder a curry". I replied that I could slaughter one anytime, so we stopped at the Shanaz. What a surprise we got when we were led downstairs to a room resembling a jungle – tropical plants. Pleasant and relaxing ambience. Staff friendly and awake. Served food of excellent quality, quantities quite large. We would both like to come back and have a meal in the evening and enjoy the surroundings more.'* and *'Gorged on the best of Indian food – Lobster curry. Had to book a week in advance. Lobster obtained from nearby Newhaven, was presented to us in the form of Jalfrezi. One of the best curries we've ever had, big chunky wads of beautifully tasting lobster, hot spices accentuated the flavour. The meal, although, not cheap – what do you expect for REAL lobster – worth every penny. 10% CC Discount.'* BP-D. Hours: 12-2.30/6-12.

Newhaven

LAST VICEROY 

4 Bridge Street, Newhaven 01273 513308

AS Ahmed's 40-seater is divided into smoking and non-smoking zones and has a separate entrance for t/a customers and an off-licence – cigarettes can be delivered to your table! Specials: Garlic Duck Masala. King Prawn Zafrani. *'Our favourite, always offering good food and friendly service. Ample portions, very enjoyable.'* BJMCK. Kid's half-price menu. Sunday, free starters with main meal, eat-in only. Minimum charge: £10. Takeaway: 30% off. Delivery: £10 min. Hours: 12-2.30/6-11.30.

Nutbourne

TAMARIND AND MOONLIGHT EXPRESS

Main Road, Nutbourne 01243 573149

Set in this small village, in a freestanding building which could once nave been a pub, whose distinction is a brown and cream Pullman railway carriage standong folornly at the back of the yard. Ample parking puts one in the mood to enjoy the food. Inside aambieence is welcoming as are the staff. There is a wide range of chioces

©	Curry Club Discount	U	Unlicensed
V	Vegetarian	ANP	Alcohol not permitted
e-a-m-a-y-l	Eat as much as you like	BYO	Bring your own alcohol

on the menu, and cooking is as distinctive as the Pullman. We've had lots of contented reports on this one. Indeed some say this is a top100 contender. We feel it is nearly there, and would like your further reports to promote it. *'Our takeaway order was good, and we were very impressed with our subsequent dining-in. Extensive menu. My wife had Patrani Machli (salmon fillets with mild spices baked in foil), and she said it was among the best fish dishes she has ever had. I had the Goa Machli Curry also made with salmon and also excellent. Tarka Dhal and boiled rice were OK..'* RH

Portslade

EVEREST — **NEW ENTRANT**

244 Portland Road, Portslade.

D *'Dashain celebration– beer and wine courtesy of Cobra (many thanks). Over 100 people, 13 nations, traditional dress and music. Buffet was Rice Flakes, Lamb Choyrla, excellent garlic and ginger pickle, Soya Beans. Main included goat, Achar, Aloo Bodi Tarma (potato, beans and bamboo), Black Dhal and Spicy Chicken. A excellent evening all round. Worth being regulars! Everest now run by owner of Kumar, Worthing.'* CC.

Seaford

BENGAL PALACE 

30 Church Street, Seaford East
01323 899077

Air-conditioned, traditional decor, saris hang on walls, engraved glass screens divide tables. Managed by Eleas Hussain, formula curries, seats 48. Sunday lunch £7.95. Delivery: £10 minimum. Hours: 12-2.30pm/6pm-12pam.

Shoreham-by-Sea

MILLAN

Upper Shoreham Road, Shoreham-by-Sea
01273 440699

'Outside it doesn't look particularly attractive so the interior came as a very pleasant surprise. Pale green with etched glass panels, separating different areas. Good atmosphere, most tables occupied. Competent kitchen.' HC.

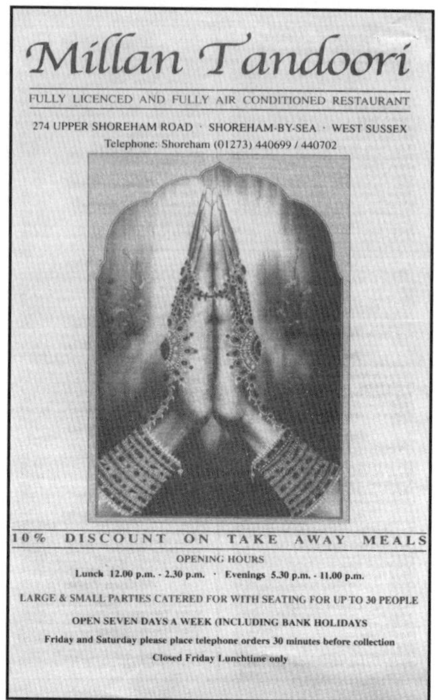

RAJAH — **NEW ENTRANT**

Windmill Parade Old Shoreham Road
Southwick 01273 593636

'Waiters looked a bit amazed when we arrived – Tuesday lunchtime, nevertheless made us welcome. Food wonderful. Tandoori King Prawns, excellent and very atractively served. Mushroom Rice and Brinjal Bhajee all well above average. A very pleasant lunch.' hc. *Hilary thoght it so good, she returned with Danny and friends. 'We had a good range of dishes, everybody choosing something different. We were all more than happy with all the food. Service unhurried and unobtrusive but also friendly.'* HC.

Worthing

INDIAN OCEAN TAKEAWAY

66, Teville Road, Worthing 01903 528888

Last time, Yusuf Khan was so keen to get into the Guide, he got all his customers to write to us, and he is not the only owner to do this. This time nowt. Next time out. Delivery. Hours: 5-11.

MA'HANN TOP 100 

179-181 Montague Street, Worthing
01903 205449

Established in 1984. Seats 150. Mahaan obviously cares about its regular clients very much, we hear nothing but praise for the host, A. Monnan, his able manager, Abdul Kadir and his staff. *'Food and standard of service has not faltered over the last five years. Waiters have a friendly attitude no matter how busy they are.'* PAH. *'I praise the consistent quality of food, menu choice and politeness of staff.'* RDL. *'Food always excellent, matched equally by Abdul's staff. Not the cheapest but one would expect to pay more for top quality cuisine. Simply the tops.'* M&S. Specials include: Murgh Sylhety, Chatga Prawns, Murgh Bhazzan, Murgh or Beef Sunam. Remains in our **TOP 100** as a formula curry house doing the job as well as it can be done. *'Decor too plain. Perfectly cooked food, nice and spicy.'* RL. Takeaway: 10% discount. Hours: 12-2.30/5.30-11.30.

SHAFIQUE'S 

42 Goring Road, Worthing 01903 504035

Shafique Uddin decribes his 48-seater as '30s colonial'. Special: Bangladeshi Mass, fish curry, hot. Takeaway: 10% discount. Delivery: £1, 3-mile radius. Hours: 12-2.30pm/5.30-11.30pm.

TASTE OF BENGAL TAKEAWAY 

203 Heene Road, Worthing 01903 238400

Owned by Faruk Kalam (chef) and Salik Miah since '84. Formula takeaway. Special: Murgi Mossallam, spring chicken cooked in mild spices, almonds, minced meat, fruit and eggs, served with saffron rice. Delivery: £7 min, 5-miles, charged at 95p! Hours: 12-2/5.30-12.

TYNE & WEAR

Area: North East
Population: 1,127,000
Adjacent Counties:
Durham,
Northumberland

Gateshead

(includes Bensham, Bill Quay, Low Fell and Shipcote)

BILL QUAY TAKEAWAY 

78 Station Road, Bill Quay, Gateshead
0191 495 0270

Est. '87 by Syed Amir Ali. Bangladeshi curry takeaway, CTM most popular. Price check: Papadam 35p, CTM £3.95, Pullao Rice £1.10. No credit cards. Hours: 6-12.

CURRY GARDEN TAKEAWAY ©

53 Coatsworth Road, Bensham, Gateshead
0191 478 3614

Owned by Abdul Malik Choudhury since 1996, *'splendid from decor to menu,'* serves formula curries. Special: Tandoori Bhuna Masala with Pullao Rice. Delivery: £5 minimum order, 3-mile radius, £1 charge. Hours: 12-2pm (Sun. closed)/6-12.

THE LAST DAYS OF THE RAJ ©

218 Durham Road, Shipcote, Gateshead
0191 477 2888

A takeaway-only serving Bangladeshi curry house food. Hours 12-2.30/6-12.

LAST DAYS OF THE MOGUL RAJ

565 Durham Road, Low Fell, Gateshead
0191 487 6282

Run by Ali and Ali. Formula curry house. Special: Raj Lamb and Cabbage. Hours: 12-2 (Sun. closed)/6-12am.

THE LAST DAYS OF THE RAJ
TOP 100 ©

168 Kells Lane, Low Fell, Gateshead
0191 482 6494

Athair Khan's up-market 100-seater has stylish decor – pure 30's Art Deco, complete with grand piano. Live music Thursdays. Crisp linen tablecloths laid on beautifully presented tables, brass light-fittings, ceiling-fans, trellis-climbing plants, and fresh flowers. Luxurious surroundings, with friendly and efficient waiters. The bar is spacious and well stocked. This restaurant must have one of the biggest and most comprehensive menus in the country; it is quite a delight. You will find all the regular formula curries with some regional and authentic dishes including recipes from the British Raj – Country Captain,, a dry dish cooked with chicken breast, onion, ghee, chillies, ginger, garlic, turmeric and salt. Raj Lamb and Cabbage is cooked with yoghurt, poppy seeds, lemon juice, green coriander, garlic, onion, fresh coconut, green chillies, ground coriander, ginger, cinnamon and cumin with ghee and chilli. You will also find on the menu a few dishes with an oriental flavour, such as Dim Sum, Oriental King Prawn Rolls and Butterfly Breaded Prawn, and there is a Pizza or two – quite fabulous, definitely a **TOP 100** restaurant. Hours: 12-2.30 (closed Sun.)/6-11.30. Branch: Last Days of the Raj, Durham Road, Low Fell, Gateshead.

Newcastle-upon-Tyne

(Includes Denton Burn, Forth Banks and West Jesmond)

LEELA'S NEW TO OUR TOP 100 ©

20 Dean Street, Central Newcastle 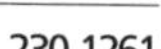 **0191 230 1261**

60-seater serving South Indian food, established in 1990, owned by Kuriakose and his wife Leela Paul. He cooks she serves. *'Leela welcomes you, takes your order, even makes your order for you if you'll give them a free hand. She suggested a vegetarian feast that was flawless. Food preparation is supervised by her husband Paul. Best treat in Newcastle, and is the best. Deserves to be extremely popular!'* WH.

'Leela is charismatic and ever present. Masal Dosa is herbaceous, Kathrika Chuttathu is orgasmic, and Kerala Meen superb. What a place!' TJ. Specials: Paper Dosa, lentil and rice pancake with savoury sauce. Chemmen, marinated prawns stir-fried with cashew nuts, Irachi Thoran, strips of lean lamb, soaked in almond sauce and stir-fried. Welcome to our t**OP 100**, not just because you are a rare asset outside the capital city, a south Indian, but because everyone says you deserve it. Hours: 6-11.

SACHINS TOP 100

Old Hawthorn Inn, Forth Banks, Central Newcastle 0191 261 9035

As ever, contented reports come in about Sachins. It stays comfortably on our **TOP 100**, for, as ever, being spot on, unpretentious, non-exhibitionist, and well above average. Among the popular starter and main course favourites is Paneer Pakora, curd cheese deep-fried in a gram flour batter, Murgh Pakora, chicken pieces deep-fried in a gram flour batter, Murgh Marchi Masala, like a Chicken Tikka Masala but with fresh green chillies to give it a bite. *'Thoroughly enjoyed my Muglai Akbari.'* FD. Scottish owner Liam Cunningham adds to the flair.

SHIKARA ©

52 St Andrew's Street, Central Newcastle 0191 233 0005

Established in 1992. Bodrul Haque's Shikara seats 100. Chef Tipu Sultan's specials include: Murg Tandoori Masala Panjabi Style, Mirchi Kurma Kashmiri Style, Jinga Goa Style. *'Great value for money.'* MS. *'Impressive menu.'* DC. Takeaway: 15% discount. Hours: 12-2 (except Sun.); 6-12; Sat. 6-12.30.

THE SPICE CUBE NEW ENTRANT

The Gate, Newgate St, Newcastle 01921 221 181

Newcastle's Gate Development area in the city centre has attracted a number of bars, pubs and restaurants and is home to Jalf Ali's Spice Cube restaurant. Design company, Cubit Design has created a modern looking interior with bright background colours, a dramatically high ceiling and sweeping central staircase. In addition to the restaurant, Spice Cube also has a designated bar area and operates as a cafe too. Reports please.

THALI 

44 Dean St, Central Newcastle 0191 230 2244

Established in 1995. Seats 52. Recently redeorated. Specials: Dahi Baigon, grilled aubergine stuffed with vegetables and topped with yoghurt. Dali Gosht, diced lamb with lentils, sweet and sour sauce. Murgh Zhal Roshun, spring chicken with garlic and green chillies. . Hours: 12-2/6-12.; Sun. 6-12.

VALLEY JUNCTION 397 TOP 100

397 The Old Station, Jesmond, Newcastle N 0191 281 6397

Daraz and his brother Locku have a penchant for purchasing old railway things and making money from them. First they spend a great deal to get the decor right. This one was formerly the Carriage Pub. The carriage in question was built for the Great Northern Railway at Doncaster in 1912. Numbered 397, it was a saloon for *'wealthy families to hire for their journeys'*. Now incorporated into the restaurant, it is decked out in greens and golds, and still earns its keep for the well-heeled. Like its sister restaurant, it has quickly earned a reputation for good food, indeed the menus are identical. Says RL: *'A delightful dining experience. (For those not familiar with the area, it is next to Jesmond Metro station, down a subway. Our table was in the old railway carriage – a tight squeeze, so a lot of 'scuse me's.) Chringri Moslai delicious, Chicken Kebab great too. One minor quibble would be the phone ringing, and the waiters calling through to the bar.'* RL.Chingri Varkee, grilled green pepper stuffed with spicy prawns. Tandoori Dhakna, chicken wings marinated in fresh herbs and spices, served with minty yoghurt sauce. Murgh e Khazana, breast of chicken cooked mainly with mild spices and honey, in a creamy sauce. Mangsho Pesta Ke Shadi, top side of beef cooked with a blend of mild spices and pistachio nuts.. Branch: The Valley, The Old Station House, Station Road, Corbridge, Northumberland. Safe bet **TOP 100.**

VUJON BEST IN THE NORTH EAST TOP 100 ©

29 Queen St, Central Newcastle 0191 221 0601

Stylish restaurant, seatsing 90 on two floors, with a party room for 40., established in 1990 on Newcastle's quayside, by the elegant Mr Matab Miah. Like its owner, Vujon exudes class, care and style. From the uniform to the decor, it's all just perfect. *'The waiters seem to smile all the time.'* RL. *'Comfortable, well-lit and very clean. No standard curries, but starter and main courses proved interesting and a good choice.'* KDF. *'Most luxurious surroundings in Newcastle. Excellent tandoori starter.'* T&KM The food is somewhat stylised and can disappoint those expecting the regular curryhouse experience. But stick with it and be open minded. For those with an inexhaustable appetite, try the Vhandaris Surprise, a ten course banquet. *'We had it and enjoyed it, but we dieted for a day per course – 10 days!'.* HEG. you love it so much that we are making Vujon our **BEST IN THE NORTH EAST AWARD.** Remains in our **TOP 100**. Hours: 11.30-2.30 (except Ssunday)/6.30-11.30.

South Shields

SAFFRON BALTI HOUSE ©

86 Ocean Rd, South Shields 0191 456 6098

Abdul Kadir's 56-seater has *'light modern decor with traditional pictures on the walls, comfortable seating with tables for 2 to 8 people.'* Sunday lunch £3.95. Takeaway: 15% off. Hours: 12-2.30 /6-12.30 (2am Fri. & Sat/12am Sun.).

STAR OF INDIA 

194 Ocean Rd, South Shields 0191 456 2210

The first curry house in South Shields, it opened in 1960, and was taken over by M Faruque in 1972. Seats 60, light gold and white wall coverings, burgundy seats, alcove seating on both sides of restaurant. *'Standard restaurant and menu in very competitive area. Good service, excellent food and extremely cheap. Great value for money, no frills, good portions, not spotlessly clean, but I'll be back.'* IB. Specials: Chicken Tikka Jalfrezi and Chilli Pilau. Takeaway: 15% off. Hours: 12-2.30 /5.30-12. Branches: Royal Bengal, Prince Regent Street, Stockton. Shapla, 192, Northgate, Darlington.

Sunderland

MOTIRAJ 

6 Church Lane, Sunderland 0191 565 6916

Established in 1974. Seats 90. Parking for 20-25 cars outside main entrance. Fully refurbished in their Silver Jubilee Year (1999). Specials: Gobi Musallum £2.05 – spicy cauliflower, coconut and cashew nuts. Takeaway: £1 off all main dishes. Hours: 6-12.

Whickham

JAMDANI 

3 The Square, Front Street, Whickham 0191 496 0820

Opened in 1988 by Mr A Miah. Try the Chicken Saffron or King Prawns – delicious. Hours: 12-2/6-11.30.

MOTI JHEEL TAKEAWAY 

9 Front Street, Whickham 0191 488 0851

First opened in 1982, taken over by MM Rahman in 1990. Specials: Bamboo Shoot Bhajee £1.80. King Prawn Bhajia £2.60. Great selection of rice dishes: Onion Pullao £1.80, Lamb Tikka Pullao £3.20, Aloo Pullao £1.80 and Chilli Pullao £1.80 to name just a few. Delivery: £1 within 2-mile radius. Hours: 12-2/6-11.30; Sat. & Sun. 6-12am.

Whitley Bay

HIMALAYA ©

33 Esplanade, Whitley Bay 0191 251 3629

Reliable curry house. Owner is Abdul Goffar. Hours: 12-2.30/5.30-12.

KISMET ©

177 Whitley Road, Whitley Bay 0191 297 2028

First opened in 1968, taken over in 1996 by Shohid Ahmed. Seats 45. Specials include: Chicken Tikka Massala Punjabi style, Lamb Shahi Tukra. *'The best Indian restaurant we have been to.'* KW. Takeaway: 10% discount. Hours: 12-2 (Fri. closed)/6-12.

SHAHENSHAH ©

187-189 Whitley Road, Whitley Bay
0191 297 0503

Established 1988 by Abu Taher, *'good-looking' decor. Bangladeshi formula curries cooked by A Hannan. 'Food first-class. Chicken Tikka terrific, full of flavour.'* MB. *'My local for a year.'* SN. *'We found the restaurant busy in a quiet and efficient way. Cobra the perfect accompaniment.'* PP. Hours: 12-2.30/6-12.

TAKDIR ©

11 East Parade, Whitley Bay
0191 253 0236

Majibur Rahman's reliable 70-seater. Minimum charge £10. Hours: 5.30pm-12am. Branches: Akash, 3 Tangier Street, Whitehaven, Cumbria; Al Mamun Takeaway, 5 John Street, Cullercoats T&W.

Winlaton

BALTI HOUSE  20%

18a The Garth, Front Street, Winlaton
0191 414 2223

Established in 1996. Seats 42. Specials include: King Prawn Peli Peli, King A 34-seater. Owner F.I. Khan continues to promises a takeaway discount of 20% for *Curry Club* members. You can't get fairer than that! Hours: 6-12. Branch: Balti House, Newcastle.

WARWICKSHIRE

Area: Midlands
Population: 506,000
Adjacent Counties: Derbys, Shrops, Staffs, W Mids, Worcs

Coleshill *B46*

POLASH BALTI CUISINE

85 High Street, Coleshill, B46
01675 462868

A chapatti throw from the NEC, and just inside the Warwickshire/W Mids border, is Coleshill. And much, it seems to the delight of the locals, is this 32 seater cosy curry house, first opened in 1997. Taken over by in 98 by Adbul Mannan, it is decorated in cream, blue velvet chairs and carpet, with engraved glass screens dividing the seating. Car parking for 30 to rear of restaurant. Chef Taj Ullah cooks up the curries. Special: Bengal Fish Masala, Bangladeshi fish on the bone, cooked with herbs, coriander, served with rice £8.95. *'What an experience! Such attention, such luxury, such choice and such cooking! Our congratulations and thanks to the Polash'.* HFC. Takeaway: 10% discount. Delivery: £15 minimum, 3-mile radius. Hours: 5.30-12.

Kenilworth

THE COCONUT LAGOON **TOP 100**
BEST UK RESTAURANT GROUP AWARD

149 Warwick Road, Kenilworth 01926 851156

Opened early 1999 within the Peacock Hotel, Kenilworth. In its previous incarnation, it was known as Balti Towers and Kenilworth Lodge Hotel, respectively. Coconut Lagoon is a superlative leisure resort in the town of Kumaragom, in India's deep south. It is an astonishingly good restaurant, as good as any in London and big surprise for the provinces, where genuinely "Indian" establishments are so few. Since our last Guide, three more Coconut Lagoons have been opened, see branches. Decorated in the vibrant spicy colours of southern India. Seats sixty. Here's what those lucky people of Kenilworth have to say about their local. *'Bright, clean, very pleasant surroundings. Very knowledgeable staff gave clear explanation of food, origin, preparation etc. So good we went back the next night!'* AD. [and why not] *'Our first visit, recommended by friends. Warm, courteous welcome. Excellent guidance to menu, food beautifully presented.'* JK. *'Reminded us of holidays in India.'* [I know just what you mean, just check out this menu.] Masalai Paniyaram £1.50, spongy and savoury crumpets served with tomato chutney. Karaikudi Cutlet £3.75, minced lamb cutlets with almonds and sultanas on a spicy sauce. Paneer Roti £5.75, pan fried crispy soft cheese with onions and tomatoes in a light and fluffy roti. Shakoothi £11.50, goan style chicken roasted with mild chilli, tamarind, mustard seeds and fenugreek in a thick sauce, served with mango rice and aviyal. Goanese Vindaloo £12.25, cooked with garlic, red wine and flavoured with cider vinegar and dried chillies, served with tamarind rice and lentils with snakegourd. Konkani Porial £11.50, crisp mangetout parcels of minced pork cooked in sherry and lightly steamed - mild and flavoursome. Accompanied with mango rice and stir-fried vegetables. Andra Shank £12.75, an absolute favourite of Pat and myself shank of lamb slow cooked in a delicate kuruma bringing out its full range of flavours, served with lemon rice and aviyal. Malabar Omelette £7.50, strips of Malabar coast omelette in a thick curry with lemon rice - a complete meal! Aviyal £4.50, poached aubergines, french beans, carrots, potatoes and green banana in a thick coconut sauce. Yum yum. *'Starters innovative, main courses small but well presented, excellent quality.'* GS. *'Food very tasty and South Indian dishes.'* NR. *'Food delicious, very different. Quite expensive.'* BP. *'Delightful decor. Wonderful Ghee Thosai £4.25, conical rice flour pancake, home-made chutneys. Unsual vegetable dishes - lentils and snake gourd. A pearl in the Stratford oyster.'* PO. *'Fresh and original food, served well. The best in the area, having been here for three weeks on business, I have visited most.'* CE. *'Different from any other we have visited, from internal decor to the ambience one experiences and most importantly the cuisine. Choice and quality of food that really is a world of difference. Well done!'* JEC. *'An elegant setting, exceptional food. A joy to the tastebuds.'* B&RF. *'Comfortable with discreet background music.'* IL. Pat and I can verify all of the above as we have visited several times and have stayed the night, which is a must - lovely colonial suite with everyhting you could possible want - recommended. Feast dinner £21.75, four courses. £2.00 pint lager, £8.95 bottle house wine. BYO allowed - corkage £7.50. Takeaway: 10% discount. e: kenilworth@coconutlagoon.com www.coconutlagoon.com Branches, EC1, Straford and Birmingham. (*See pages* 2 & 48).

RAFFLES TOP 100 BEST UK RESTAURANT GROUP AWARD

57 Warwick Road, Kenilworth 01926 864300

Under the same ownership as Coconut Langoon. *'As the name suggests, really a Malaysian restaurant, menu is made up of Malaysian Malay, Malaysian Indian and Malaysian Chinese. Very different range of dishes from each cultures, from starters to main courses. Style of restaurant redolent of old Empire and evokes a real feeling of being in Raffles Hotel in Singapore. Lighting and atmosphere good. Make the best Gin Slings I have ever tasted - including Singapore.'* [That, Clynt, wouldn't be difficult. The Singapore Slings at Raffles, Singapore are very poor indeed, however, I am pleased to say that the cocktails served here are fantastic. *'Caution: take great care if you go beyond three. Food is truly out of this world. Menu changes with new dishes being introduced every few months or so, but favourites have been retained. Claypot and Pandri Perratal are simply a must. Absolutely delighted.'* CRS. *'Have always found the food well prepared, clearly freshly cooked and with subtle spicing.'* KN. *'Our favourite restaurant. Unusual and imaginative menu, food superb, beautifully cooked and presented. Service impeccable. Toilet immaculate.'* IS. *'My first visit was a surprise 60th birthday - fantastic. The food, ambience, the courteous was we were all greeted and looked after. Delighted.'* VAB. *'Group of 60, pre-arranged banquet Malaysian menu. Greeted with a Singapore Sling , good start to evening, food served on platters, more than ample. Everyone has an enjoyable evening. Highly recommended.'* RD. *'First class.'* VB. *'Have been many times, also to sister restaurants Coconut Lagoon. Always a pleasant experience, although, a non-smoking area would be appreciated!'* TN. *'Superb Colonial decor, fine crustao glasses and crisp well laundered linen. Ikan Goreng - delicious, Udang Bakar Kerinc - sensational, Hianese Chicken - unforgetable - I could go on!! [I've eaten that - yes, I agree, really good] Exceptionally consistent - can't wait to return!'* BW. [Now I have a report from Graham and Melinda - who both know a thing or two about curry. Here is what they said...] *'Murtuabale - savoury Indian bread layered with minced beef, lightly toasted in a griddle - a light and crisp texture. Mysore Anda - slow cooked lamb served with Roti and Malaysian Coleslaw. Pandri Perratal - pan fried spicy pork in a uniquely blended rich sauce served with yoghurt rice, beetroot, a bundle of long green beans, coleslaw and Appatam - an exquisite dish given the contrasting spicy pork together with cool yoghurt rice. A superb experience, but at a price!'* [Luxury restaurants always have a price tag, but we are glad you enjoyed it.] Three course dinner £21.50, Four course dinner £23.50. www.rafflesmalaysian.com Hours: 12-2.30 and 6.30-12.30. Branches called Georgetown at SE1, and Stratford-upon-Avon. (*See pages* 2 & 48).

Leamington Spa

BOMBAY TANDOORI 

38 Regent Street, Leamington 01926 420521

Opened in 1990 by chef Anar Ahmed. Serves Bangladeshi and north Indian curries. House specials: Khata Masli (Bangladeshi fish steaks in tangy spicy sauce), Kooris Lamb (whole leg of spring lamb spiced, marinated for at least eight hours, roasted tandoori-style, garnished with mincemeat and served with Vegetable Bartha and Pillao Rice) £58.50 for four. Min order £5.50. Takeaway: 20% off. Delivery: £12 minimum, 3-mile radius. Hours: 6-1am (3am on Fri/Sat.).

KING BABA NEW ENTRANT

58 Bath Street, Leamington 01926 888869

All reorts lead to King Baba. It's many people's Leamington favourite. Baltis are done correctly in Balti pans, as in Brum, and the food is aromatic and tasty, as it should be. Staff are caring, and prices more than reasonable. Weekend hours for night-owls. Hours: 6-12, Tues-Thurs & Sun/6-2.30am, Fri & Sat. Closed Monday.

Nuneaton

RAJDHANI ©

1 Cambourne Drive, Horeston Grange, Nuneaton 01203 352254

Surat Miah's 56-seater. Opened in 1985. Unusual specials: Tikka Paneer Jalfrezi, cooked with tomatoes, onion and green chillies, £6.95. and Tandoori Quail or Trout. Minimum charge £12. Takeaway: 20% off. Hours: 5.30-11pm.

Rugby

TITASH INTERNATIONAL BALTI

65 Church Street, Rugby 01788 574433

'Rather more upmarket than traditional plastic chair/formica table/BYO Balti house, but is good value and serves excellent curries. Small reception area, friendly welcome, etched glass panels and marble-top tables. Service polite and efficient, high quality food. Particular favourites: Tandoori Mixed Kebab and Lamb Spare Ribs. Baltis are delivered to the table on a trolley and vigorously heated to serving temperature over a gas burner, aromas make for a mouthwatering experience. Chicken Tikka Chilli Masala is highly recommended. Wines have increased in price in short space of time. One of my favourite places for a tasty, no-nonsence curry experience.' PJ.

Stratford-upon-Avon

COCONUT LAGOON NEW ENTRANT AWARD

21 Sheep StreetStratford 01789 293546

This is the second-to-open branch of Coconut Lagooon, Kenilworth Warks, where you will find menu and other details. The restaurant is on two floors, with an interesting balcony overlooking the ground floor. Winner of our **BEST GROUP AWARD**.

LALBAGH BALTI ©

3 Greenhill Street, Stratford 01789 293563

Opened in 1989 by Abdul Aziz, who is also to be found in the kitchen as head chef. 46 seater, decorated in maroon with patterned wallpaper, green carpet and Bangladeshi pictures on the wall. Specials: Mushroom on Puri, and Fish Kebab. *'Conventional menu. Excellent comfort. Polite and reserved service. Papadoms served with delicious sauce and onion relish, very good. Lalbagh Special Chicken, large quantity, wholesome chicken, quality ingredients.'* GG&MP. Takeaway: 10% discount. Hours: 6-12.30; Fri/Sat. 6-1AM.

GEORGETOWN NEW ENTRANT AWARD

23 Sheep Street, Stratford 01789 204445

This is a Malaysian restaurant and a branch Raffles, Kenilworth Warks, where you will find menu and other details. The restaurant is a winner of our **BEST GROUP AWARD**.

USHA INDIAN CUISINE

28 Meer Street, Stratford 01789 297348

First opened 1968, taken over by Nazrul Isuam in 1995. Seats 56. *'With one and a half hours to kill before the theatre, we found this delightful restaurant by chance. Service and food first class. Popadoms crisp, mango chutney and lime pickle "simply wonderful". Starters: Chicken Pakora and Persian Tandoori Kebab – excellent portions and taste. Main courses: Chicken Sag Balti – breast and Special Mixed Balti – full of meat, prawns, sauce a little watery with Keema Nans – arrived already sliced, like pizza, a nice touch.'* DJL. Takeaway: 15% discount. Hours: 5-12 (Sat. to 12.30); Sun. 6-12.

WEST MIDLANDS

Area: Midlands
Population: 2,638,000
Adjacent Counties:
Staffs,
Warks, Worcs

West Midlands was introduced as a county in 1965 and contains the conurbations from the Black Country at its west, through to Coventry in the east. At its hub is Birmingham city.

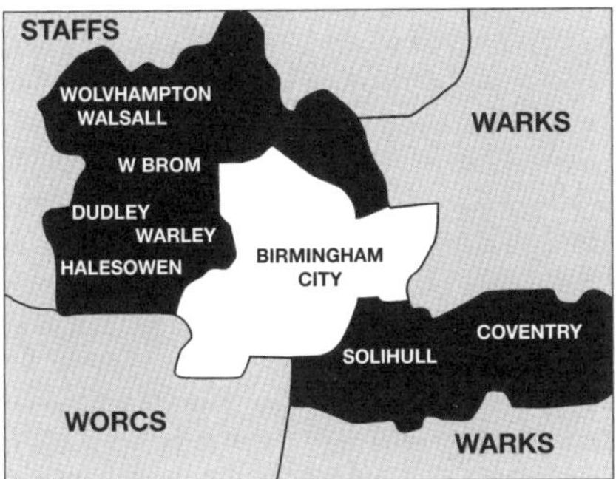

Birmingham City

Birmingham postcodes,
B1 to B46
Population – 1,018,000

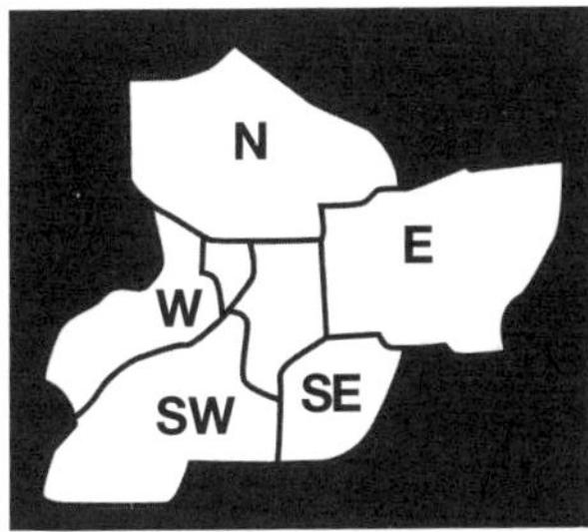

Unquestionably Britain's number two city, Brum has come vibrantly alive with investment in its infrastructure. For the purposes of this Directory, we divide the city into geographical areas, in which are grouped postcode zones B1 *to* B48 *although, as ever, there is no sequential logic to postcode numbering. They are frankly a jumble. But it is the system which exists, and to help narrow things down, we have divided the city, using major roads as our arbitrary boundaries. We start with Birmingham Central, then go south to the adjacent Balti Zone, next North of the city, then East, South East, South West, and West. Further* B *postcodes,* b62 *(Halesowen) to* B93 *(Solihull) follow, listed alphabetically by their suburb name.*

Birmingham Central

Postcodes B1 to B5

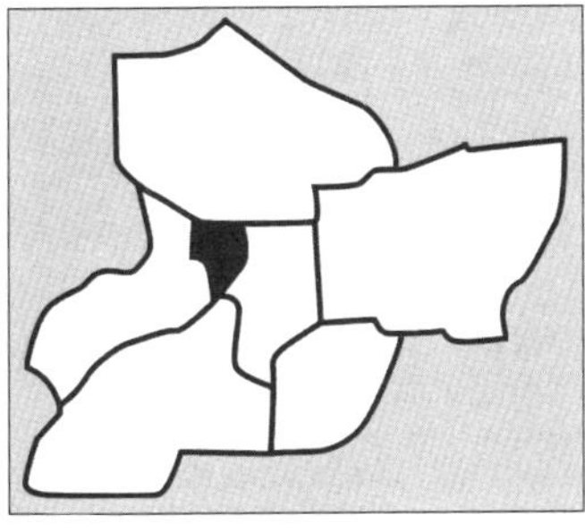

(restaurants listed in alphabetical order)

ALOKA

6 Bristol Street, Digbeth, Birmingham, B5
0121 622 2011

The Darjeeling, Steelhouse Lane, was Brum's first curry house. It opened c 1946, and has long-gone. The Shah Bag was next on Bristol Street, and had opened by 1957. I know because I always came here once a week on my day off, from as far afield as Coventry, where I lived and worked. Hard to believe now but Coventry had none then I don't know when it became the Aloka, but it is now. During the 1960s, the spread of the curry house was as prolific as the city's building. Now it's Birmingham 300, Coventry 43. So here's to the Aloka, a pioneer indeed.

BARAJEE NEW ENTRANT

265, Broad Street, 1st Floor, Birmingham, B1
0121 643 6700

Owned by successful restaurateur Moula Miah, of Rajnagar International Restaurant Group, (*see Solihul, West Midlands*) Barajee overlooks Brum's exciting canal system. Dishes on the menu include monkfish cooked in olive oil, garlic and bay leaves and simmered in spiced tomato sauce. Chefs: Abdul Rouf and Abdul Khalique have also developed set menus where prices start at £14.95 per head for a vegetarian meal and £18.95 for a meaty version. Lunch and dinner daily.

BUDHA LOUNGE NEW ENTRANT

The Mailbox, 116 Wharfside Street, Birmingham, B1 0121 643 7979

Café Lazeez (*see London sw7*) had a go here but pulled out after a year or so. Budha Lounge has only just moved in as we went to press. Reports please.

COCONUT LAGOON NEW ENTRANT BEST GROUP AWARD.

12 Bennetts Hill, Birmingham, B2 0121 643 3045

This is the fourth-to-open branch of Coconut Lagooon, Kenilworth Warks, where you will find menu and other details. The restaurant is on two floors, with an interesting balcony overlooking the ground floor. Winner of our **BEST GROUP AWARD**.

INDI NEW ENTRANT

Arcadian Centre, Hurst Street, B5 0121 622 4858

A good all-day waterhole in club and theatreland. Ideal for a quick snack (and try the Indian Tapas-type snacks, or a longer dwell-time for a full meal. Noon-2am/1230am Sun

LASAN NEW ENTRANT

3 Dakota Bldgs, James St, St Paul's B3
0121 212 3664

Lasan is in its second year and already has established itself as a top class venue. Manager Jabbar Khan and Aktar Islam, 24, restaurant managers at Lasan, St Pauls Square, Birmingham won the *Manager of Tomorrow Award of Excellence* from ther *Midlands Association of Restaurant Caterers and Hotels.* Chef Munayam Khan was a recent winner at *Hospitality Week's Authentic Foods of the World* competition. Sous chef is Ashutosh Bhardwaj. Between them they run a very good curry house.

MAHARAJAH
PREVIOUS AWARD WINNER AND TOP 100

23 Hurst St, Birmingham B5 0121 622 2641

N Bhatt's Maharajah is a small place (62 seats on two floors) and booking is recommended. The food is Indian, cooked by Gurmaj Kumar and Jaskarn Dhillon. The menu looks a little ordinary, bur the food is still always spot on. Ask about the Special Dish of the Day. I recall this restaurant serving Biriani topped with edible silver leaf (vark) when it first opened in 1971. It was the first time I'd seen it used in Britain, though traditionalists in India would not contemplate the dish without it. It was a Moghul fetish, of course, the emperor permitting a gold leaf garnish only on the food for himself and the chosen member of the harem (the dish of the day!), while his wives had to make do with silver leaf. They believed it to be an aphrodisiac. It is not for me to comment on the validity of this claim and, with the EU ban on vark (because of aluminium adulteration), neither can the Maharajah's diners – they no longer serve it, sadly. Service is mature and careful, and the place is often full to bursting. Waiting bookers are deftly dispatched to the downstairs bar. Such competence is rare and welcome. We continue to receive plentiful reports on the Maharajah, and just one snorter (from MRS JJB). Stays in our **TOP 100**. Hours: 12-2/6-1; closed Sun. & bank hols.

MILAN INDIAN CUISINE 

93 Newhall St, Birmingham B3 0121 236 0671

Dhirendra Patel's 120-seater, established in 1989, is decorated in pastel shades, giving it a light and airy feel. The bar area is typically Indian with beaten copper drinks tables and large coffee pots. Chef Balbir Malhi's menu features all the usual curry house favourites from Korma to Jalfrezi but there is also an extensive vegetarian section. Paneer Tikka £2.50, spicy paneer cooked in the tandoor. Stuffed peppers filled with coconut, potatoes and coriander £2. Reshmi Mattar Paneer £5, homemade cheese with herbs, spices, peas, cashews and corn. Hours: 12-2/6-12.; Sat. 6pm-12am; Sun. closed. Branches: 129 Stoney Lane, B11, 238 Soho Rd, Handsworth B21, and 296 Abel Street, Milpitas, nr San José, California, US.

MOKHAM'S OF DIGBETH U 

140 Digbeth High Street, Birmingham B5
0121 643 7375

Of Naz Khan's venue AM says *'Mokham's pride themselves on their cooking so you may have to wait as all the food is freshly prepared. Tandoori Sheeksh Kebab is certainly one of the best I have ever tasted. Balti Exotica is meat, chicken, prawns, mushroom and pasta, without doubt unique in my experience. A very substantial dish, served up in the traditional black bowl, it was beautifully spiced and the pasta blended superbly but when combined with my Nan bread it left me feeling like Pavarotti.'* And RW says: *'Small but smart genuine Balti house in the city centre. Very friendly, family run. Extensive menu. Fresh papadoms, light and well cooked chat, tender Lamb Tikka cuts in a mild to medium sauce. Light and fluffy naans buttered and pleasantly sweet.'* Hours: 12-2.30/6 to late.

Birmingham Balti Zone

Consists of B10 to B13

(restaurants listed in alphabetical order within postcode)

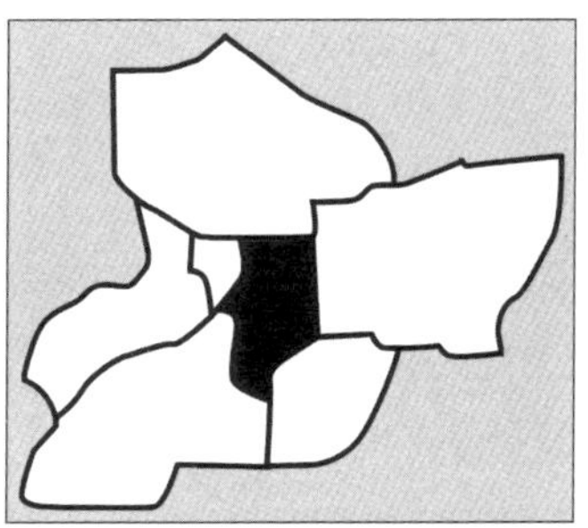

The Balti Zone starts about 2 miles south east of the city (follow the a34), and is thickly spread around the suburbs of Small Heath, Sparkhill, Sparkbrook and Moseley (b10 to b13). The population is largely north Pakistani, mostly from Kashmir's Mirpur, adjacent to which is the district of Baltistan, high up in the Pakistani mountains. You'll find recipes and more about this subject in my newly republished 'Balti Bible'. Those who doubt the existence of Baltistan should visit k2 Baltihouse, upon whose walls is the biggest map of the region that I've seen, and it is from there that Balti originated. But for those who prefer to say it did so in a bucket in Birmingham, you are certain to get the nation's best Baltis here. There have been innumerable changes here over the last two years. Too many venues has led to empty houses, even at the weekend, and subsequent closures. One result is the e-a-m-a-y-l buffets, which, whilst value for money, never, in our view compare in quality to individually cooked baltis. Here are the views of the lucky scribes who live there, and those who visit:

Birmingham B11

Sparkbrook, Sparkhill

ADIL 1

AWARD WINNER AND TOP 100 BYO 

148-150 Stoney Lane, Sparkbrook, B11
0121 449 0335

Mohammed Arif, Rashid and Abid Mahood opened here in 1975. Although they are not the first balti (it was a café called the Paris opened in 1973 by a Mr Ramzan, the former long-closed because the latter had retired back to native Baltistan before discovering that he had started an international cult). Arif is happy to claim to be first, and he is indisputably the longer at it. *'My grandfather'* he says, *'ran a restaurant in Kashmir decades ago, called Adil meaning Justice. Customers chose their own fresh raw ingredients, and watched the entire cooking process. Apart from that, our Sparkbrook restaurant is identical.'* Well, it was. There's been a sparkling modernisation recently, enlarging the place to 100 seats with 56 upstairs. The menu hasn't changed. It still offers 72 different Baltis, including their much-copied signature dish, meat 'chicken' mince with veg-dall-spi-chana. *'My birthday and what better, after a 7.30am champagne and Guinness breakfast in London's Smithfield Market, than to travel to Birmingham for a Balti at Adil's. After the initiation course of Green Chilli Bhajis 70p, we settled down to enjoy Balti Chicken Tikka Veg-Dall-Spi-Chana „ two massive Table Nans and two portions of rice . My colleague Ian (two puddings) Hunter could not contain himself, unable to decide between Rasmali, Barfi and Kulfi, and ate all three. Simple as abc – Adil's for Balti Curry.'* DB. *'If I'm anywhere near Birmingham I pilgrimage to Adil's. Oh! the Baltis! and so low a price. Avoid the starters, they are ordinary and the small portions make them poor value for money. Not licensed, but there is an off-licence next door run by his cousin. If you order a cab, the driver is another cousin! Family enterprise!'* CD. Adil's own car park opposite. Often pioneers are best: although Adil's took a dive in popularity and quality recently. I am happy to see it begin to thrive again in its second generation, same-family management. Remains in our **TOP 100.** Delivery: minimum £10. 3-mile radius. Hours: 12am-12am (Thurs.-Sat. to 1am).

DESI KHANA ANP

706 Stratford Rd, Sparkhill, B11 0121 778 4450

RE said last time: *'This is my favourite. Decidedly Asian – European customers are rare – strict Muslim. Glass top tables and a shortish menu, but the food is good.'* This time he says: *'Still great food. Sheeh Kebab freshly cooked on sizzling platter, excellent. Peshwari Gosht in a balti, had quality lamb pieces in a thick, tasty sauce. The price for one person was high by comparison with most others in the area, but the food is good.'* [On a subsequent visit Ray reports that it has had a facelift, and food is still very good.]

MILAN SWEET CENTRE V

191 Stoney Lane, Sparkbrook, B11
0121 449 1617

A branch of the Milan restaurant in 93 Newhall Street, Birmingham B3 (see entry above). This is a takeaway venue for Indian sweets, and savoury snacks. The selection is huge and satisfying, at prices too cheap to ignore. Sister t/a branch at 238 Soho Road, Handsworth, B21

ROYAL NAIM
AWARD WINNER TOP 100 BYO ©

417-419 Stratford Road, Sparkhill, B11
0121 766 7849

The Nazir brothers' restaurant is huge – 180 seats on two floors, yet it doesn't feel oversized. It's open all hours, of course it's BYO, and the prices are very reasonable. You can fill yourself for £5, and blow up for £10. You are made welcome and are served with prompt efficiency throughout. The portions are still huge, and more importantly, the food is as tasty as you can get in any style of 'Indo-Pak' restaurant. Order from the menu located under the glass table top. The selection is huge, with every Balti combination you can think of and some more. Then leave it to Chef Shaffique and his crew to get cooking, while your taste buds tingle. But before your choice arrives, get nibbling on a papadom, if for nothing else, to taste the lurid red delicious chutney that accompanies it. Unless your stomach is horse-sized, don't order more than one Balti, and don't eat too much before it arrives – it's a huge portion. Order rice if you must, but doing it the Pakistani way, with no cutlery, and huge naan breads to tear and scoop with is hugely satisfying. And then it arrives, served the Balti way, in 10" steel karahis (Balti pans) the food cooked in the pan, made black with thousands of

hours of cooking. It's more than filling and great fun. The Naim also produce deep frozen Baltis for retail outlets and local schools. *'No wonder Birmingham's education standards are starting to rise!'* AM. *'The atmosphere was building before we found the actual restaurant because of the community in which it is situated and the numerous other Balti restaurants surrounding it. The basic nature emphasized the excellent food. Owner very attentive and helpful. Returned a month later. Once you get the Balti in front of you and taste it you don't want it to end.'* SR. *'Visited on a busy Saturday night. Standard of service, choice, quality of food and value for money is very high. Party of eight, four adults, four children, plenty of choice for all. Our large Naan £3 covered the table. Washed down with a jug of Lassi. Ras Malai for pudding is hard to beat. My children insisted I make a detour two days later on our return from Kendal to Suffolk to revisit the Royal Naim.'* DB. Delivery: £10 minimum, 3-mile radius. Hours: 12pm-1am; Sat. 12pm-3am.

SHAHEHSHAH

326 Ladypool Road, Sparkbrook, B11
0121 449 6463

'Shami Kebabs £1.00 – excellent value for money. Very good and very spicy. Generous portion. Chicken Masala Balti – sauce a little bland, but chicken of good quality. Menu extremely wide, variable quality, generous quantities, service very good. But we were all agreed that our meals were much too salty and this was passed on to the management. Overall verdict: absolutely superb'. GG&MP.

TY'S JAZZ & SPICE

132 Stratford Road, Sparkhill, B11
0121 773 1632

Authentic Kashmiri cuisine here *'and excellent too'* AN. The clue's in the name. This place hums, literally with its emphasis on live jazz on certain days. Established in 1999. Formerly the Kashmir LodgeSeats 80. *'Very impressive decor, high ceilings, drape curtains, chandelier. Mixed Grill, Lamb Tikka, Chicken Tikka, Tandoori Fish, Sheesh Kebab, wonderful mixture of flavours. Very large quantities, top-quality ingredients. Service slow with starters but these were obviously freshly cooked, so understandable.'* GG&MP.Private car park for up to 30 cars with CCTV. Chic, modern decor.

Birmingham B12

Balsall Heath, Sparkbrook, Sparkhill

AL-FRASH BYO 

186 Ladypool Road, Sparkbrook, B12
0121 753 3120

Established in 1994, Mukhtar Ahmed's 180-seater is a *'Traditional curry house with old style decor. A little on the dark side perhaps. Customer care rating very high (they asked whether the person ordering the Meetha Ghosht was allergic to nuts). Succulent Mixed Grill, outstandingly melt-in-your-mouth Tandoori Fish, but undercooked Aloo Pakora and very poor Vegetable Samosas.'* GG&MP . Starters include Onion Rings, one of DBAC's favourites. It's one of Andy Munroe's Top 10: *'Starters to die for – the mushroom and aubergine Pakoras come highly recommended. For main course try the "white rose" house speciality which is not a steal from a Bradford curry house but a popular Lahore dish comprising chunks of chicken breast languishing in a cardamom flavoured sauce with cashew and cream. Alternatively try Meetha Gosht which is tender lamb in fried onions, sultanas, coconut and almonds, a great balance of a spicy back taste off-setting the sweetness. Mop it all up with voluptuous garlic Nan, although the coriander version takes some beating.'* AM. Smart decor with authentic Kashmiri furniture. Specials include: Meetha Ghusht. Hours: 5pm-1am.

ALI BABA U BYO 

250 Ladypool Road, Sparkbrook, B12
0121 449 4929

We like Mr Aslam's logo of a chap holding a sizzling Balti, sitting on a flying carpet (beats cars for home delivery?) *'Clean comfortable. BYO. Very good Sheek Kebab 70p, freshly cooked and spicy. Nice Roti. Lamb Bhuna, prepared with extra chilli, very accommodating.'* RE.

IMRAN'S BALTI HUT U BYO

264 Ladypool Road, Sparkbrook, B12
0121 449 1370

'Baltis, superb. Family Nan, unbelievable – 3 feet by 2 feet. BYO from "offy" next door. Excellent value for money.' RS. *'Claims to have been around at the time of the first-ever splitting of Balti bread in Brum. Spacious and includes in-view cooking for those who like to see a Sheeksh Kebab being cooked live. My main course Balti Chicken and Mushroom had an impressively spicy kick.*

Unusually you can also get a family Chapatti also Quail Balti (a dish which has now achieved almost protected status).' AM. *'Lamb Jalfrezi, meat tough and lacked depth of flavour. Chicken Korma – too hot for a Korma and for my wife.'* RE. Hours: 12pm-12am.

KASHMIR KEBAB HOUSE

141 Ladypool Rd, Sparkbrook, B12. 0121 BT do not have

'A cross between McDonalds and a wine bar. Thriving takeaway. Food is all on display in glass cabinet. Food is very good and exceptional value for money.' RE.

KASHMIR LODGE

132 Stratford Road, Sparkbrook, B12
0121 773 1632

'Housed in a former bank – the sort of grandiose building used before such establishments became virtually an excuse for a hole in the wall. Prices remain at a credible Street, level. There is a good range of Baltis including Balti Tinda (sweet potato) and Balti Karele (bitter gourd).' AM. Hours: 12-2.30/6-12.

KHYBER U BYO

365 Ladypool Road, Sparkbrook, B12
0121 449 5139

'Cosy family restaurant where the sign should read 'enjoy as much as you like'. Tasty Tikkas and no-nonsense Balti just like mom used to cook 'em. Lovingly prepared so expect to wait a little for a true taste of Birmingham's unique Balti experience'. AM.

KING'S PARADISE U BYO ©

321 Stratford Road, Sparkhill, B12 0121 753 2212

Owned by Mahboob Hussain. *'Balti Tandoori Butter Chicken, very smooth-tasting, in bright red sauce with some onion in there. Peshwari Naan, large, tasty with just a hint of syrup.'* GG&MP. Mushroom Naan sounds great! Hours: 12-2.30/5.30-12am. Private car parking.

KUSHI U BYO ©

58 Moseley Road, Birmingham B12 0121 449 7678

Messrs Mohammeda and Haydur's 62-seat *'Kushi appears to have picked up just about every cup apart from the Jules Rimet. However, never mind the awards, try the food. Kushi's Kebab is one of the best of its kind as are the sizzling Shashliks. Wide choice of main courses including Kushi's new and highly valued range of "saffron" dishes. Good selection of Nans from Keema to Kulcha'.* AM. *'All nine of us agreed that this was a magnificent Balti house.'* GG&MP. Delivery: £10 minimum. Hours: 5.30pm-1am (2am on Sat.); Sun. 6pm-12am.

LAHORE KARAHI U BYO

357-363 Ladypool Road, Sparkbrook, B12
0121 449 9007

One of the pioneers of the Balti Buffet, now available at so many of the 'Zone's venues. But this one is probably the best of the buffet bunch. RE is a frequent customer, and here is an amalgan of his views. *'A large self-service, always bustling busy restaurant, with space for 300 diners. Small car park at the rear, but otherwise can be difficult. Many Moslem and Seikh customers. E-a-m-a-y-l – amazing variety of food for £5.95. Sheekh kebabs good and tasty, roti not too thick, lamb dall superb, mixed dall nice consistency, spinach lamb, on the bone really tender meat.and delicious. Keema Peas – delightful. Great food and great value. The trouble with buffet style restaurants as good as Lahore is knowing when to stop eating. Having said that I then went for seconds! Highly recommended.'* RE. *'Everything qualifying for the top melt-in-the-mouth award. Highly recommended. Booking is advisable at weekends.'* MJB.

LAHORE KEBAB AND PAN HOUSE U

187 Ladypool Road, Sparkbrook, B12
0121 440 3264

'You can't go much more down market than this. Predominantly a takeaway offering just seekh kebabs, fish massala, samosas, pakoras, tikkas etc. In other words no main courses. However, what they do serve is freshly cooked and very good. Worth going for a cheap snack.' RE.

PLAZA TANDOORI U BYO 

278 Ladypool Road, Balsall Heath, B12
0121 449 4249

The food at this unlicensed (BYO welcome) 80-seater is more Southall than Sparkbrook or Balti Heath, since owners R Singh and GS Pank and chef Gurmit (1997 Birmingham Council Chef of the Year) are Sikhs who specialise in Northern

Indian Punjabi food. This adds a different flavour to the cooking. *'I enjoyed my first visit so much that I have been back twice. Seekh kebabs as good as before, spicy chicken wings great taste and hot.'* RE. Hours: 5-12.

POPULAR BALTI U BYO

139 Ladypool Road, Sparkbrook, B12
0121 440 0014

'Small, slightly scruffy restaurant. Sheeh Kebabs not quite so good as on my previous visit (I suspect they may have been 'Blue Peter' kebabs – here are some we prepared earlier). Lamb curry very good indeed. This cafe/restaurant rates one of the best for value.' and *'Redecorated since last visit, but the bright green striped wallpaper takes some getting used to! Service quick and friendly. Seekh Kebabs were fresh cooked and spicy. Very good value, good food.'* RE.

PUNJABI PARADISE BYO

377 Ladypool Road, Sparkbrook, B12
0121 449 4110

'Mohammed Shabaz's popular place. One of the Balti glitterati featured on more TV programmes than Ulrika Jonsson. However, the food backs up the image – fresh coriander laden Baltis, yeasty Nan breads with a frantic but friendly atmosphere. Their special chicken Kebabs are worth a stab. Even has its own garage for all its valued (and that's everybody) customers.' AM. *'Food very good.'* RE. Minimum charge £6. Hours: 5pm-1am.

ROYAL AL FAISAL U BYO

136-140 Stoney Lane, Balsall Heath, B12
0121 449 5695

Spelt Faisal, or Faisel, the other venerable Balti, contemporary with Adil's (1982) from whom it is a few doors away, is Mohammed Ajaib's smartly decorated restaurant in shades of green. Seats 150 diners, tables of four. This early leader is now following the buffet trend and is, we hear, as busy as ever. *'Celebrating a momentous victory for Northampton's Saints, away at Gloucester. On recommendation, pulled off* M42 *to visit Royal Al Faisal. 6.30pm – very busy. Now a Balti Buffet Restaurant. One price of £5.95 – all you can eat. Faced with a huge array of dishes. Starters: Tandoori Chicken, Onion Bhajia, Mushroom Bhajia, Sheek Kebabs with Popadoms and Chutneys plentiful. Main courses: wide range of Baltis, vegetarian and meat, Tarka Dal Balti – first class. Excellent value for money. Convenient shops nearby to purchase your own drinks.'* DL. *'Food is good but I think the Lahore Karahi Buffet has the edge. Twice in one week is OK in the name of serious research! Must return again soon.'* RE. Hours: 11.30am-12am.

SEVEN SPICE NEW ENTRANT BYO

53 Moseley Road Birmingham B12
0121 440 4408

Cooking is from the Punjab, so expect spicy but not necessarily hot curries. Menu Extracts: Popadoms a mere 25p – is this the cheapest? Samosas also a bargain at 55p,either meat or veg. Min charge: £7. Credit cards accepted. BYO. Secure car park at rear. Takeaway: 10% discount.

SHANDOR

353 Ladypool Road, Sparkbrook, B12
0121 449 5139

asas *'Very similar to Lahore Karahi Buffet next door, but on a smaller scale. Not so much choice, but what there was was excellent.'* re. *'Visited as result of write-up in Guide. Ethos has changed – to a buffet style – pay one price and e-a-m-a-y-l . Many other local restaurants have also changed to this style. A pleasant experience, none-the-less. My wife enjoyed it because she could try a bit of everything.'* MR&MRS T. *'Incidentally it is licensed and £4.50 for a bottle of Sparkbrook's finest Liebfraumilch must make every hour a happy one.'* AM. Private car parking. Hours: 12pm to late.

SHEREEN KADAH U BYO

543 Moseley Road, Balsall Heath, B12
0121 440 4641

asas *'Busy and cheerful. Large open barbecue by the window where the kebabs etc are freshly cooked to order. Sheeh Kebabs were excellent, balti meat superb. Unfortunately, my wife's Chicken Kurma was awful – too spicy and the sauce had curdled. To be fair they took it off the bill. Very good value.'* RE. On subsequent visits RE reports: *'Food was excellent, service was brisk and friendly, the clientele was largely Asian. Back to a good standard after my disappointing visit.'* RE. *'In the display cabinet is a selection of Kebabs on an array of sharp skewers which look like a Zulu armoury after an attack on Rourke's Drift.'* AM. BYO. Children welcome before 11.30pm, [that's way past their bed time!] Menu Extracts: Popadom 30p [wow] Family Nan £2.60. Chana Fried Rice £1.40, Tropical Biriani £8, Ras Malai £1, Barfu 45p, Jalebi 45p. Hours: 11am-12am.

Birmingham B13

Moseley

COSMOPOLITAN TANDOORI

U BYO

31 Woodbridge Road, Moseley, B13
0121 449 5793

Not a Balti, but a formula curry house which, for some, makes a pleasant change in Baltiland. Established in 1990. Seats 40. Specials: Ceylon Balti dishes with black pepper and lemon juice from, Malayan Balti dishes with coconut cream and pineapple, Chicken and Lamb Shashlick £3, Balti Mix Extras (King Prawn, Chicken, Lamb and Mushroom). Hours: 6-11.30 (Fri. & Sat. to 1am).

K2

107 Alcester Road, Moseley, B13 0121 449 3883

N Pasha and M Niam's 58-seater is named after the highest mountain in Pakistan, shown on the biggest map of Baltistan (to prove it exists to the doubters) on one wall. Peppered Chicken £3.10, is Chino-Tibetan (a Baltistan influence) with its sweet and sour chicken prepared with a mixture of black and green pepper, ginger, soya sauce, sugar and lime. Balti Chicken and Mushroom £5.50, Nan £1.20. The favourite venue of more than one BBC Pebble Mill crew, but not of RE. Access and Visa accepted. Hours: 6-11.30.

SPICE AVENUE

562-4 Moseley Road, Birmingham B13
0121 442 4936

In a corner-site on the fringe of the Zone, it's a smart licensed restaurant with rear car park *'which is handy. Attentive and friendly staff. Food OK. A bit overpriced [compared with the rest of the Zone].'* RE. *'The Balti Ginger Chicken is a straightforward but excellent combination. However, the lamb Shahan is an excellent exotic alternative with tender lamb cutlets stuffed with garlic mushrooms. Accompanying onion kulcha will make your eyes and mouth water.'* AM.

Birmingham North

Consists of B6, B7, B19 to B24, B35, B42 to B44

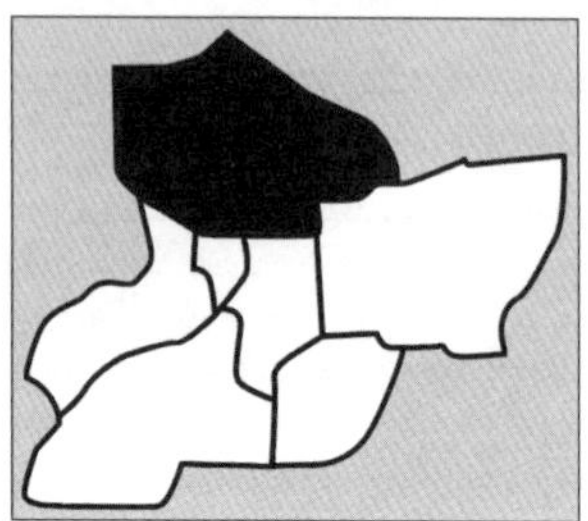

Birmingham B21

Handsworth

MILAN SWEET CENTRE V

238 Soho Road, Handsworth, B21 0121 551 5239

A branch of the Milan restaurant in 93 Newhall Street, Birmingham B3 (see entry). This is a takeaway venue for Indian sweets, and savoury snacks. The seletion is huge and satisfying, at prices too cheap to ignore. Sister t/a branch at 191 Stoney Lane, Sparkbrook, B11.

Birmingham B23

Erdington

EASTERN FLAVOUR NEW ENTRANT

15 Station Road Erdington Birmingham B23 0121 350 6382

'Quick and polite telephone manner, speedy delivery by clean looking drivers (ie: no dirty jeans/t-shirts). Good quality cuisine. Excellent value for money, usually with more Popadoms.' CL. *'I use this takeaway every week, travelling twelve miles each way...'* now, that's what I can customer loyalty! *'...Food consistently good.'* gc. *'Very pleased, with good food and staff.'* GY. *'The best I have tasted.'* GM. *'Well prepared food served by a very friendly and obliging staff.'* RM.

SAMRAT TANDOORI ©

710 Chester Road, Erdington, B23 0121 384 5900

Samrat means Emperor, established in '83, managed by Mr Dey, chef Mr Choudhury. Air-conditioned, seats 50, party room 30. Special: Spicy Fish £3.30. Kurzi lamb, served with Basmati rice £21 for two. Delivery: £6, 5-mile radius. Hours: 5pm-1am (2am on Fri. & Sat.).

STOCKLAND BALTI TAKEAWAY U BYO ©

332 Marsh Lane, Erdington, B23 0121 377 8789

Owned and managed by Mrs Amina Begum since '93 serving competent curries to a regular crowd. Delivery: £10. Hours: 5-12am (1am on Fri. & Sat.).

Birmingham B44

Great Barr

BALTI SPICE TAKEAWAY 

1240 Aldridge Road, Great Barr, B44 0121 366 6548

First opened in 1981, taken over by Nazrul Hussain in 1998. with Bilal Miah (manager) Chef Abdul Ahad's open kitchen allows customers to see their formula curries cooking. Coke, Fanta and mineral water available. Takeaway: 10% discount. Delivery: £8 minimum, 3-mile radius; £12 minimum, 4-mile radius. Hours: 4.30pm-12am; Sat. 4.30pm-1pm.

Birmingham East

Consists of B8, B9, B25, B26, B33, B34, B36, B37, and B40 (NEC)

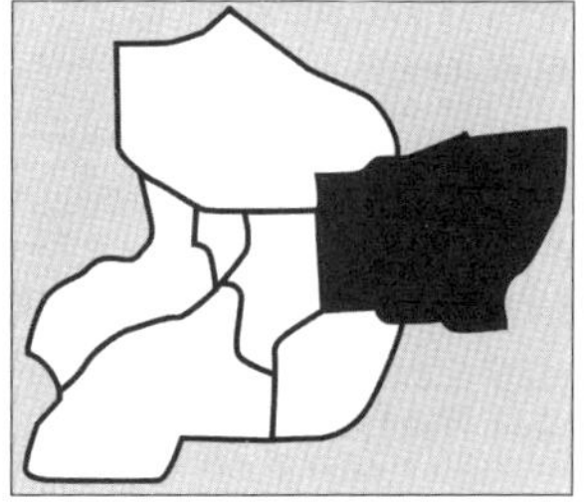

Birmingham B9

Small Heath

IIB NE GHANI U BYO 

264-266 Green Lane, Small Heath, B9 0121 772 8138

Competent curries and Baltis at Dawood Hussain's establishment. Hours: 5pm-1am; Fri. & Sat. 4pm-2am.

Birmingham B25

Yardley

YEW TREE COTTAGE 

43 Stoney Lane, Yardley, B25 0121 784 0707

Opened in 1979 by Jamal Chaudhuri, this 40-

seater curry house is in old cottage-style with oak beams has been refurbished. Takeaway services on the ground floor, restaurant on 1st floor. Gourmet Nights, four courses. Special starters: Tikka Sandwich, chicken tikka with nan, salad and dressing. Mixgrill Sandwich, chicken and lamb tikka, sheek kebab and Nan. Banana Chicken, medium spiced. Madras sauce. Vindaloo Sauce. Minimum charge: £15. Sunday buffet £9.95. Delivery: under £40, £2.50 charge, over £40, free, 3-mile radius. Hours: 5 (Sun. 6)-1am (Sat. 2am).

Birmingham B26

Sheldon

BENGAL FLAVA

2065 Coventry Rd, Sheldon, B26
0121 722 3205

'Impeccable service. I ate there on two consecutive nights. All menus accidentally binned! All I can say is it's in a road on the way out of Birmingham about half a mile from Harry Ramsden's fish shop and the cheap Travelodge my cheapskate employers put me in!!!' PM..

SHABAR TANDOORI ©

4 Arden Oak Road, Sheldon, B26
0121 742 0636

Angur Miah Qureshi and Mozamil Ali's Balti restaurant, seats 62. Special: Chicken or Lamb Zarzara and Table Naan. Spiced Banana in ghee. Sunday lunch: £5.95. Takeaway: 10% discount. Hours: 5.30-12am..

TITASH INTERNATIONAL

2278 Coventry Road, Sheldon, B26
0121 722 2080

Away from home? Have to endure the dreaded catering, dispensed expensively and with a straight face at the neighbouring NEC, railway station, airport, and hotels of varying pretensions? Want to know of an alternative close to hand? That's what this Guide is for. Titash is a good standard, formula curryhouse, with ample on-street parking.

Birmingham South East

Consists of B27 and B28

(Beyond this is Knowle and Solihull – see entries)

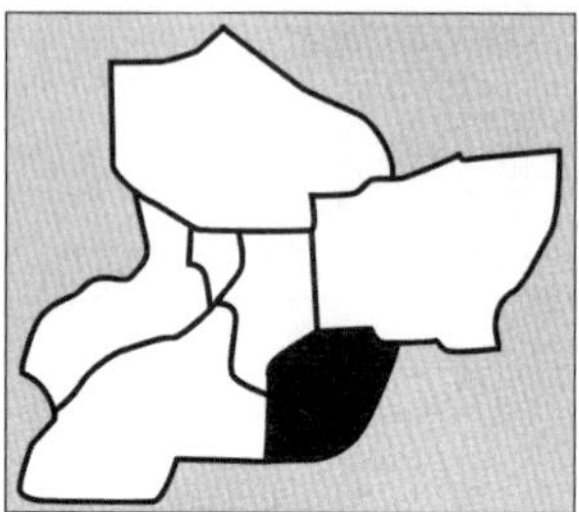

Birmingham B27

Acocks Green

DEVDOOT ©

1st Floor, 37 Westley Road, B27
0121 706 4842

Seats 46. Specials: Persian Chicken Biriani £5.15 – with omelette and Malayan Chicken Biriani £5.15 – with pineapple. Hours: 6-1am (Sat. to 2am).

MOGHUL ©

1184 Warwick Road, Acocks Green, B27
0121 707 6777

At Mr Hassan's mahogany and pink venue. Special starters: Tandoori Fish and Mushroom Garlic Fry. Takeaway: 20% discount. Minimum charge: £5. Hours: 5.30-12.30 (1am on Sat.). Branch: Diwan Balti, Alcester Road, Moseley, Birmingham.

Birmingham B28

Hall Green

MIZAN 

1347 Stratford Road, Hall Green, B28
0121 777 3185

Formerly J Jays, KA Rahman's curry house seats

66. Takeaway: 10% off. Minimum charge: £5. Special: Saag Kamal Kakri, spinach and lotus roots. Hours: 12-2pm/5.30-12 (12.30 on Fri. & Sat.).

Birmingham South West

Consists of B14, B29 to B31, B45, B47, B48, B60

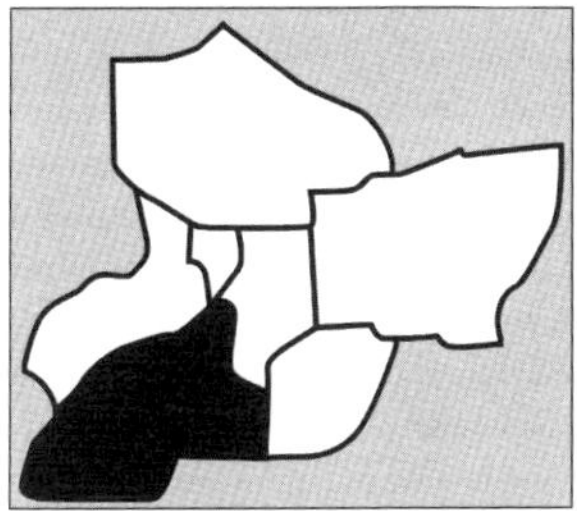

Birmingham B14

Hollywood, Kings Heath, Selly Oak

KINGS BALTI

13-15 York Rd, King's Heath, B14
0121 443 1114

Owned and managed by Salim Miah. Specials: Panir Tikka,curd cheese dipped in gram flour and fried £2.05. Balti Chicken Tikka Naryl, delicate coconut sauce. Balti Chicken Dan Gali, cashew, sultanas, almonds, pistachio, fresh banana. Delivery: £8, 2-miles. Takeaway: 10% off. Hours: 5.30-11.30.

Birmingham B29

Selly Oak

DILSHAD INTERNATIONAL

618 Bristol Rd, Selly Oak, B29 0121 472 5016

Established in 1978. Seats 80. Specials include: Achar Gosth £6.10, Champa Koli Bahar £7.95, Fish of Bengal £7.65. Takeaway: 10% discount. Delivery: min, 3-miles. Hours: 5.30pm to late.

Birmingham B30

Cotteridge, Stirchley

RAJPOOT 

1831-1833 Pershore Road, Cotteridge, B30
0121 458 5604

Watir Ali's 94-seater does all your favourites. 'A glitzy little place with friendly service. All the family use it regularly.' JAD. Hours: 6pm-2am.

YASSER TANDOORI BYO 

1268 Pershore Road, Stirchley, B30
0121 433 3023

A Hussain and Sarwar Khan's Yasser seats 80, and specialises in Pakistani and Kashmiri cooking. Special: Tandoori Fish. Balti Chef Special Tropical, prawn, chicken, meat, mushroom. Garlic Family Naan. BYO. Parking for 12 cars. Hours: 4pm-1am.

Birmingham West

Consists of B15 to B18 & B32

(Beyond this is Halesowen, Smethwick, Warley and West Bromwich – see entries)

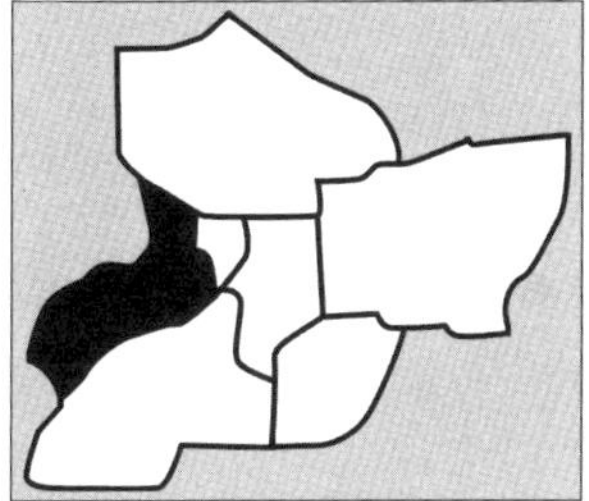

Birmingham B15

Edgbaston

SHIMLA PINKS

214 Broad Street, Birmingham B15 0121 633 0366

This was the first branch of a proposed franchise operation all over the UK led by Kal Dhaliwal's

Oriental Group. Just west of Central TV, this fully licensed, upmarket pricy pilot has established a formula which appeals to some, but not others. *'Nans the best I've had. Bhuna Chicken particularly good. Service courteous. Plenty of space. Strange decor.'* mjg. *'Minimalist decor. Food out of this world.'* sr&lg. *'Unusual modern decor in agreeable surroundings. An upmarket restaurant, with good food, which on the whole is mildly spiced.'* NR. *'A party from work attended and whoever was paying (not a curry regular) decided we would have one of their "banquets". I had been looking forward to the meal as I had heard a lot about it but I was very disappointed. Each dish tasted similar and the portions small. If that was a banquet I'm glad I didn't pop in for a quick snack! I'm glad that I wasn't paying as it came to over £350. All in all, very poor.'* CS. Branches: Shimla Pinks Manchester M3. Oxford, Johnstone Strathclyde, and London EC. Hours: 12-2.30, weekdays/6-11 every day.

Birmingham B16

Edgbaston

J JAYS

2 Edgbaston Shopping Centre, Five Ways, B16 0121 455 6871

Upmarket (Roman Villa) restaurant with marble everywhere, material tented ceiling. Serves north Indian curries and accompaniments.

Birmingham B32

Quinton

SOHO INDIA 

417 Hagley Road, West, Quinton, B32 0121 421 3242

Bangladeshi formula curry house, seats 50, established in 1985 by Mohammed Abdul Muquit. CC members will get 10% off their bill. Special: Village Special Soup £1.75. Lager £1.85 pint, one of the lowest prices in the guide. No takeaway. Minimum charge: £6.50. Hours: *5-12.*

Remainder of West Midlands

Coventry

BOMBAY PALACE

64 Earlsdon Street, Earlsdon, Coventry 024 7667 7851

'Good quality food, average quantity and service. Decor very pink. We rate this no 2 in the city.' GG&MP.

CAFE TAMARIND NEW ENTRANT

376 Kenilworth Road Balsall Common Coventry 01676 533308

Menu Extracts: Zaffrani Tikka £2.40 – chicken marinated in freshly ground garam masala, garlic and cheese. Fish Amritsari £2.85 – crispy fish nuggets, marinated in caron flavoured chick pea batter, shallow fried. Prawn Balu Chao £5.85 – very spicy, semi dry preparation using Goan red chillies. Mangsho Lal Kumro £5.75 – beef stew with sweet gourd, robust sauce simmered with garam masala and herbs. Chicken Santoor £5.75 – mild sauce with Simla chillies. Isn't that a contradiction? Khurkuri Bhindi £2.10 – crispy fried slices of okra tossed in tangy chat masala and fresh coriander. Cheese, Garlic and Coriander Nan £1.95 – *'a tasty combination , at a good venue'* HEG. Hours: 5-11.30, Friday and Saturday to 12.

HOLLY BUSH PUB

Holbrooks Lane, Coventry 024 7668 6923

'Nice relaxed pub atmosphere. I was amazed to be told it had been going for since 1995. Balti Chicken Tikka was tasty. Generally, the meat was good, but the vegetables had not been properly marinated and the peas were tinned. Prompt service, but rather impersonal.' GG&MP.

L'IMRANS EXPERIENCE

14 Butts Lane, Earlsdon, Coventry 024 7623 1699

'This was the first restaurant to open in Coventry which predominantly focusses on the buffet side of things. You have 2 hours to e-a-m-a-y-l for £7.95. We visited about three weeks after opening and were very impressed. There were fish, red meat, white meat and vegetarian alternatives for both starter and main courses. Air-conditioned and with a separate non-smoking section. Overall impression was an extremely favourable one.' GG&MP.

The time limit is a new twist, and I wonder what they'd do if you run overtime?

MONSOON TOP 100 

20-21 Far Gosford Street, Coventry
024 7622 9651

Owned by J Raj and G Judge, since 1996. 'Modern, zazzy music.' Pakistani curries, *'Recently refurbished with many paintings now decorating the wall. This has greatly improved the look of the restaurant. Firmly established as my favourite. We were given a very generous discount with the voucher from the CC Magazine. As superb as ever with an excellent Chana Masala starter. Balti Chilli Chicken Masala £3.95 was a feast, wonderfully spicy with sumptuous chicken, Balti Mince £3.95 with vegetables including okra, pepper, chana, tomatoes, potatoes and courgettes was mouthwateringly good. Peshwari Nan £2.10. The bees' knees for Balti houses. An incredible amount of vegetables in the meals. Free popadoms. Once again absolutely top quality food, served in huge quantities, and with magnificent service. I simply cannot fault it.* GG&MP. *'Pleasant decor, average service, standard menu. Good portion of tasty Chicken Tikka Masala and large Nan.'* IB. Remaians in our **TOP 100.** Takeaway 10% off. Delivery: £10 minimum, 4-mile radius. Hours: 6-12 (1am on Sat.).

QUICK STOP BALTI BYO

80 Far Gosford Street, Coventry
024 7663 2578

'Unlicensed and unpretentious restaurant. Fairly basic menu, service very good. Balti Chicken Jalfrezi, well marinated.' GG&MP.

ROYAL BENGAL

172 Albany Road, Coventry 024 7671 2345

Recommended by Biren and the gang at Cobra. Reports please.

RUPALI 

337 The Hill Lane, Coventry 024 7642 2500

Ashik Ali's huge 200-seater maintains its reputation for good food and good service. *'Raita was superbly fresh and seemed to fizz on your tongue, excellent. Lamb Stuffed Pepper very different, beautifully served, excellent. Special Chicken Jafrezi also excellent. Overall good food, biggish portions, slightly overpriced with polite, friendly service. Recommended.'* MPW. The personable Chef Rois Ali can cook, and we are glad to hear from several reporters that the Rupali has increased its portion size, though prices are still at the high end. *'Naan were excellent as were the Popadoms and pickle tray. Two lagers and two soda waters came to £7 – scandalous!'* DH. *'Good, but too posh!'* GG&MP. Curry Club members 10% off. Sunday lunch: £7.95. Minimum charge: £9.95. Hours:5.30-11.

SHAHI PALACE 

367 Foleshill Road, Coventry 024 7668 8719

It had a record four names in 10 years (Palace, Kashmir, Balti). Since 1995 it's been Iqbal Hussain's Shahi Palace, a licensed 90-seater, nicely decorated in greens. Special: slices of Bangladeshi boal fish in hot and tangy taste with green chilli and shatkora. Nawabi Murgh, pieces of chicken marinated cooked in mince lamb sauce and freshly garnished with chilli, coriander and egg . *'OK'* GG&MP.Daily banquets £5.95. Minimum charge £10. Service 10%. Delivery: £10 minimum, 4-mile radius. Hours: 5.30-12.30am.

SONARGAON

153 Daventry Road, Coventry
024 7650 4670

Recommended by Biren and the gang at Cobra. Reports please. *'Good'* GG&MP.

STANDARD SWEET CENTRE NEW ENTRANT

424-26 Foleshill Road Coventry

asas *'Cheap and cheerful Indian style cafe type venue with formica tables. Surly service, popular with locals.'* GP.

TURMERIC GOLD NEW ENTRANT

166 Medieval Spon Street, Coventry

Opened in 2001 and has been awarded Best Restaurant in Coventry and Warwickshire for two years running by the readers of Coventry Evening Telegraph, voted by people filling in forms from the papers. *'We will grately appreciate if you could tell us what qualities are required to be included in your Guide'.* P.S.

 Curry Club Discount
V Vegetarian
e-a-m-a-y-l Eat as much as you like
U Unlicensed
ANP Alcohol not permitted
BYO Bring your own alcohol

ZOOKA NEW ENTRANT

Coventry

Rois Ali's Bar. Located in a Grade One listed fire station it's scheduled to open after we go to press. reports please.. *See Rupali, Coventry, above.*

Dudley

BALTI 4 U BYO 

63 Halesowen Road, Netherton, Dudley 01384 240230

At R Khan's small restaurant we continue to hear of the Happy Hour special menu from 6-9pm Hours: 6pm-2am (3am at weekends).

Halesowen *B62, B63 & B65*

AMEENA 

192 Hagley Road, Hasbury, Halesowen, B63 0121 550 4317

Hiron Miah's 78-seater (est. 1974) *'I've only tried this restaurant once. The food was good standard, and while I was waiting regulars were warmly welcomed.'* NR. *'Have visited twice recently, on first occasion the food was exceptionally good – in particular the Chicken Tikka Buna and the fresh naan bread. Second visit was not so good, but still of a standard that I would choose to call again if in this area.'* RJP. *'Slightly downmarket feel to the place but not the food! Prawn Bhuna is delicious with the sauce adding a tasty extra. Chicken Jalfrezi with thin strips of ginger laid on top lattice work fashion. Enjoyed the Sag Aloo. Cobra a pleasant fix. Waiters cheerful and attentive. In the guide and deserves it.'* MS. Delivery service: 3 miles, £10 minimum, 5.30-10. Hours: 5.30-12. (Fri. & Sat. to 1am).

Kingswinford

(THE) BALTI BYO

847 High St, Kingswinford 01384 823111

Formerly Mr Daves. *'BYO, quite cheap, excellent standard of Balti. Chicken Pakora is the greatest we've ever had.'* SR&LG.

Knowle

BILASH 

1608 High Street, Knowle, B93 01564 773030

Mashud Uddin and Nowab Ali's Bangladeshi curry house seats 64, party room 40. Set in black and white surroundings, dating back to the 16th century. Special: Jeera Chicken Dilkush, spring chicken, coconut, jeera, tomato and mixed spices. *'Very good quality.'* J&MCL. Takeaway: 10% off. Hours: 5.30-12am. Branches: Bilash, 82-90 Priory Road, Kenilworth. Bejoy Takeaway, 763 Old Lode Lane, Solihull, West Midlands.

KNOWLE INDIAN BRASSERIE ©

1690 High Street, Knowle, B93 01564 776453

Established in 1995, Hossain Miah's air-conditioned Bangladeshi curry house seats 45. Nicely decorated in cream and pale pink, plaster cornices and velvet upholstered chairs. Special: Fish Bhuna Bengal Style, chunks Bangladeshi fish, cooked in medium sauce with spices, herbs and green chillies. *'Excellent. Good, helpful service. Food tasty, hot, prompt. Would definitely return and recommend.'* J. *'Malai Kebab, chicken marinated in cream with herbs and spices and baked in a clay oven – very tasty. Chicken Tikka Sylhet, boneless chicken with minced lamb and egg cooked with spices and herbs – unusual mixture of mince and chicken, very spicy with good texture and flavours. Bombay Aloo, well-marinated potato although not as spicy as they promised in the menu. Quantities – enormous. Not as expensive as one might expect. A top-quality restaurant.'* GG&MP. Takeaway: 10% discount. Delivery: £12 minimum, 3-mile radius. Hours: 5.30-11.30; Sun. 5.30-10.30.

LLOYDS NEW ENTRANT

7 Station Rd, Knowle, Solihull 01546 477 5777

Run by Hosoun Miah, Nanu Miah and Chef Ana Miah, it serves formula curry house food, and we have good reports about it. But we'd like more detailed ones please.

Lye

PEPPER AND SPICE BYO ©

204 - 205 High Street, Lye 01384 893933

At Sabber Iqbal's 40-seater you can get these intriguing specials: Pepper Chicken, capsicum stuffed with tandoori chicken. Fish chat, fish in a sweet and sour sauce. Balti Chicken and Mushroom, Naan. Licensed but BYO allowed. Credit cards not accepted. Delivery: £7 minimum. Hours: 6-12am.

Solihull *B90 to B93*

RAJNAGAR INTERNATIONAL
NEW TO OUR TOP 100

256 Lyndon Rd, Olton, Solihull, B92
0121 742 8140

'It really is exceptionally good.' MM. *'Interior decor, pale pink and cream walls, cream carpet – optimistic re spillages!, stylish tables and chairs with monogrammed linen exudes quality and class. Attentive service, swiftly delivered Popadoms, chunky pickles and cold lager. I chose Meat Samosas (spring roll style), Chicken Tikka Dupiaza, Pullao Rice and Nan – ALL SUPERB!'* TE. It is probably the best in the area, and we are happy to promote Rajnagar to our **TOP 100.**

Stourbridge

NEEL AKASH BALTI AND TANDOORI 

2F High Street, Wollaston, Stourbridge
01384 375919

Chef Mujibur Rahman's 60-seater. Bangladeshi formula curries including Bengal Masala and Bhoona Shashlik. Balti Chicken and Mushroom, Naan. Minimum charge: £5. Special: Acher Special, chicken, meat or prawn with pickles. Takeaway: 10% off. Delivery: £8 minimum, 3-mile radius. Hours: 5-12.

Sutton Coldfield *B72 to B76*

ASIAN GRILL

91 Park Road, Sutton Coldfield, B73
0121 354 7491

Opened way back in 1968. If you, or any other business for that matter, have survived that long, you must be good. Bangladeshi and formula

©	Curry Club Discount	U	Unlicensed
V	Vegetarian	ANP	Alcohol not permitted
e-a-m-a-y-l	Eat as much as you like	BYO	Bring your own alcohol

curries on the menu including Balti Chicken Tikka with Naan. Seats 76. Minimum charge £8. Hours: 5.30pm-12am (1am on Fri. & Sat.).

Walsall

EAST END ©

9 Hawes Close, Walsall 01922 614800

Muhibur Rahman is proud of his veteran 1967 curry house. Special is Green Chilli Chicken Tikka Masala. Balti Chicken and Mushroom, Naan. Hours: 5.30-12am.

GOLDEN MOMENTS

3 Ablewell Street, Walsall 01992 640363

Established in 1993. Seats 100. *'Having eaten Indian food for 25 years this establishment must rate as the one of the best. Staff, service, surroundings and food are excellent.'* BD. Specials: Betatawada,mashed potatoes with herbs and spices, battered and deep-fried. White Chicken Tikka, delicately spiced, wonderfully tender. Dhaba Gosht, small cubes of lamb,Tandoor-cooked, in a thick sauce. Takeaway: 15% discount. Hours: 6-12am.

KING BALTI BYO ©

89 Ablewell Street, Walsall 01922 620376

48-seater owned by Dudu Miah. Chicken Tikka Jalfrezi most popular. Takeaway: 10% discount. Delivery: £12 minimum, 3-mile radius. Hours: 6pm-1am; Sat. 6-1.30am.

SAFFRON ©

42-43 Bradford Street, Walsall 01922 627899

Fully licensed 105-seater, smart restaurant in two rooms, opened in 1963. New ownership. *'Superb genuine Balti house within easy (post meal) wobbling distance of the railway station. Excellent starter, Nargis Kebab, spicy Scotch egg style, crisp salad, yoghurt sauce plus Popadoms with usual chutney mix. Mixed Balti, lovely medium thick sauce with a well balanced and mouth watering blend of spices, sizable chunks of lamb and chicken, plus some small but juicy prawns, medium hot. Lovely light Chappatis £1.10 a little on the dear side. Good service, real tablecloths.'* RW. E-a-m-a-y-l buffet : £6.96 on Weds. & Thurs. evenings and Sun. lunch. Menu Extracts: Chicken Tikka £5.25, with orange or lemon sauce; Spice and Garlic Fish Fry £2.50; Salmon Samosas £2.25; Cheese Layered Crispy Paratha £1.90; Liver Puri £2.65 Prawn and Coconut Puri £2.75. *'All delicious!'* RL. Delivery: £8 minimum. Licensed. Hours: 5.30-12.30, Friday and Saturday - 1.30. Sunday 12.30-12.30.

Warley *B65 to B68*

AL MOUGHAL BYO ©

622 Bearwood Road, Smethwick, Warley, B66 0121 420 3987

100-seater managed by Mumtaz. Pakistani-style curries on the menu. *'Reasonably clean, down-market but cheap and cheerful. Chicken Karahi Tikka Massala Special and three Chapatis, waiter advised only two – spot on. Food competent and tasty. Tremendous value. If this place was a wine it would be a Blue Nun.'* PAW. [Yuk! Let's settle for a 'Brown Nan' -Ed] Balti Chicken Tikka Aloo Jalfrezi. Onion Nan. BYO. Delivery: £10 minimum, 3-mile radius. Hours: 6-12am.

STANDARD ©

2 High St, Blackheath, Rowley Regis, Warley, B65 0121 561 2048

Kazi Ashafuz and Kazi Wahiduz Zaman's tiny 30-seater (pretty, green wallpaper and wood-panelling) serves formula curries. Special: Chicken Jaipur, creamy, egg and nuts. BYO. Takeaway: 10% off. Delivery: £10 minimum. Hours: 6-1 (2am on Sat.).

Wolverhampton

inc: Albrighton, Compton, and Wednesfield

JIVANS BALTI

14 Broad St, Wolverhampton 01902 427289

Recommended by Biren and the gang at Cobra.

MOTHER INDIA

136 Tettenhall Road, Wolverhampton 01902 750755

Punjani cuisine. Specials: Chicken Tunda – deep-fried chicken with a lemon dipping sauce. Lamb Dhai – lamb with mint and yoghurt. *'Great samosas, followed by South Indian Garlic Chilli Chicken (tender chicken lumps, lashings of creamy spicy sauce), with enough rice to feed the Bengal Lancers. I loved it except the naan bread which was nearly as bad as the ones I try to cook. And not cheap. Other than this can recommend it.'* MS.

WILTSHIRE

Area: Mid West
Population: 608,000
Adjacent Counties: Berks, Dorset, Hants. Oxon

Chippenham

AKASH TANDOORI & BALTI ©

19 The Bridge, Chippenham 01249 653358

Established in '79 by Nurul Islam, an old friend of this *Guide*, having been in since our first edition. 46 seater, decorated in 'red dado and curtains with green plants and doors, incorporates framed pictures and tropical fish tank'. Special: Passanda, creamy fragrantly spiced dish £6.70. Specials include: Murgi Musala, for two (chicken marinated in the Chef's special recipe, roasted in the oven and served with an exotic sauce and special rice) £24.50.Takeaway: 10% discount. Hours: 12-2/6-12.

TAJ MAHAL 

51 Causeway, Chippenham 01249 653243

Established in 1989. Seats 40. *'Cosy little restaurant. Standard dishes, plus a number of lobster and duck variations. The only small criticism of the whole meal is that the Bhajias came without any accompanying salad, looking very bare and plain on the plate. Sag and cauliflower was the best I've had for a long while. Portions all plentiful, service efficient and friendly, prices about standard for the area.'* MW. Takeaway: 10% discount, £10 minimum. Delivery: £10 minimum, 8-mile radius. Hours: 12-2/6-12.

Ludgershall

MUGHAL 

33 Andover Road, Ludgershall 01264 790463

'Of Mrs Bushra Rahman's 44-seater's curries, Tikka and Balti are the most popular. Menu, both content and quality, excellent. Very welcoming. Lamb sheek kebab starter tender and juicy.' PA. Special: Jhingi Kodv. Delivery: £15 min, 3-mile radius. Hours: 12-2.30/6-12am.

Melksham

MELKSHAM TANDOORI 

26 Church Street, Melksham 01225 705242

Mr Mahammed Mayna's attractive Cotswold stone building is adjacent to a car park. Its bar/reception are in a long narrow room with 50 seats beyond. *'Chicken Tikka very well cooked, nice and succulent. Lovely mint sauce. Lamb Jalfrezi rich and loads of green chillies lurking in there for the unwary – I love 'em. Portions huge, cooking great and amazing value.'* MB.

Salisbury

ASIA

90 Fisherton Street, Salisbury
01722 327628

'Not the first time I have written about this thriving, always packed, splendid restaurant. Euphoria of our Friday evening family reunion curry has vigorously survived well into Saturday. House was full, glad we booked. Had variety of rich dishes – Patia, Dupazia, Madras, Butter Chicken, Chili Chicken and Balti. Curry sauces are smooth and rich, plenty of personality. Sag Bhaji was the best I've had – very spicy with guts and edge.' PE.

Swindon

BHAJI'S TAKEAWAY ©

76 Thames Avenue, Swindon 01793 533799

Owned by Iqbal Shishir. Special: Tandoori Garlic Chilli Chicken or Lamb, most popular. Established in 1997. Parking for 50 cars in front. Specials include: Tandoori Garlic Chilli Chicken or Lamb. Delivery: £10 minimum, 4-mile radius. Hours: 5pm-12am.

BIPLOB 

12 Wood Street, Swindon 01793 490265

Rokib Alo and Fozlur Rahman's 60-seater has a separate lounge/bar area seating 20. Well explained menu. House specials include Tandoori Duck Tikka (£9.95, but worth it for a treat), and Tandoori Duck Bonani (cooked with cream, cashews and brandy – £10.50) and Fish Buzon – Bangladeshi river fish (£7.95) and Begun Bahar – chicken in a herby gravy. £6.95. Minimum charge £10. Hours: 12-2.30/6-12am. Branch: Raja Takeaway, Cheltenham, Rajdoot, 35 Castle St Cirencester, Glos.

CURRY GARDEN  10%

90 Victoria Road, Swindon 01793 521114

R Khan's large restaurant was established as far back as 1969. It seats 80, and judging from reports, these are often filled, so it's popular. Chef specials: Tandoori King Prawn Jalfrezi, with green chillies. *'Good'* G&MP. *Curry Club* Members will get a 10% discount. Takeaway: 15% less. Hours: 12-2pm/5.30-12. Sundays & bank holidays 12-12.

GULSHAN 

122 Victoria Road, Old Town, Swindon
01793 522558

Owned and managed by Abdul Kahhar. Seats 80 on two floors connected by a spiral staircase. *'Very smart decor, pleasant attentive waiters. Extensive menu, mainly Bangladeshi. Muglai Paneer, cheese, mixed fruit, almond, sultanas, fresh cream in mild sauce served with Onion Bhajias and beer, cost £9.40. A nice idea was the revolving sweet tray with the bill.'* DS. Sunday all-day buffet £7.50. Takeaway: 15% discount. Hours: 12-2.30/6-12am;. Sat. 6-1am.

	Curry Club Discount	**U**	Unlicensed	
V	Vegetarian	**ANP**	Alcohol not permitted	
e-a-m-a-y-l	Eat as much as you like	**BYO**	Bring your own alcohol	

LALBAGH ©

171 Rodbourne Rd, Swindon 01793 535577

Established in 1997. Seats 60. Specials: Moonlight Chicken,with cauliflower, mushroom and brandy in medium sauce. Tarana Chicken, with potato, egg, green chilli and red wine in spicy hot sauce. Begana Lamb, with mixed fruit, cream, white wine in mild sauce. Spiced Nan, with garlic and chilli. Takeaway: 10% discount. Delivery: £10 minimum, 3-mile radius. Hours: 12-2.30/6-11.30.

PICKLE JOHNS NEW ENTRANT

25, Wood Street, Swindon. 01793 509921

Pickle Johns Pub & Restaurants are named after Indian gentlemen from the early part of the twentieth century, who was sent to this fair land to be educated in some of England's finest public schools (Eton, Harrow, Winchester). On their return to India they had adopted English manners.... and the English in turn perceived them as jovial and eccentric characters. In India, they were named *"PickleJohns"*. Most of the dishes are Indian cuisine but some are English and fusion. Hours: 12-2/6-11:30. Branches Popadom Express, Basingstoke and Southampton Hants.

RAFU'S TANDOORI TOP 100 

29-30 High Street, Highworth, Swindon 01793 765320

Opened in 1982 by Mr Rafu as the Biplob; renamed to prevent confusion. It remains popular. *'Very good'* G&MP. *'Menu large and varied choice. Complete satisfaction. Best Jalfrazi in the West. Good service, pleasant atmosphere, superb location. Everything nice except the prantha (too greasy).'* ZI. *'Menu had wide variety and choice. Quantity more than adequate. Service very courteous and polite. Atmosphere very convivial. Very good quality meal and good value.'* KS *'We visit weekly. Extensive and varied menu. Generous quantities. High quality. Outstanding service. Excellent Bangra. Hasina Chicken – best in Europe!'* IG&JN. *'The wine list is very good for an Indian restaurant. Whenever we go to Rafu's we know we are going to have a top-class meal, with friendly people, in pleasant surroundings.'* JS. Hours: 12-3pm/6pm-12am. Hours: 5pm to late. Remains in our **TOP 100.** *See previous page.*

SPICY AROMA 

144 Cricklade Road, Gorse Hill, Swindon 01793 488700

Established in 1996, Abdul Rouf Ali's Aroma now seats 64 in two dining rooms decorated with 'mahogany effect with cream background, with a classic wooden effect bar'. Specials: Scampi Chilli Masala, thick onion, ginger and garlic sauce. Takeaway menu reads please order by number – rather like a Chinese takeaway, is it a first for an Indian or before my time? Minimum charge: £6.95. Sunday lunch buffet: £7.95. Takeaway: 10% discount. Delivery: £12 minimum, 5-mile radius. Hours: 5-12.30am; Sat. 5-1.30am.

Wootton Bassett

MEMORIES OF INDIA

21 High Street, Wootton Bassett 01793 852365

Situated opposite the Curriers' Arms! Formerly Salik's. *'OK'* G&MP. *'Bhajia and Samosa freshly made, nicely presented and delicious! Fragrant, fluffy Pullao Rice. Lots of meat in Keema Nan. Massive portion of Chicken Biryani. Chicken Tikka Bhuna, lots of well-marinated breast meat.'* TE. *'This little gem deserves a mention. Extraordinary food, quality and service at a low price.'* AE. Delivery: free on orders over £10. Hours: 12-2.30/6-12am (1am on Fri. & Sat.).

WORCESTERSHIRE

Area: Midlands
Population: 476,000
Adjacent Counties: Glos, Hereford, Shrops, Warks, W Mids

Bewdley

THE RAJAH OF BEWDLEY 

8 Load Street, Bewdley 01299 400368

Anwar Uddin's 34-seater is in a grade 2 listed cottage with soft lighting and exposed beams.

'Food excellent, the people extremely friendly, offering a high standard of customer service.' SH. *'Good'* G&MP.Special: Tandoori Lobster. Takeaway: 10% off. Minimum charge: £4.95. Hours: 5-11.30pm.

Kidderminster

EURASIA TAKEAWAY 

Unit 1, 19, Stourbridge Road, Kidderminster 01562 825861

First opened in 97, taken over by Syed Hussain Ahmed in 99. Specials include: Jamuna (a hot dish cooked with chicken, meat, prawn and a selection of oriental spices, herbs and green chilli, garnished with an egg). Delivery: £10 minimum, 4-mile radius. Hours: 5-12am.

NEW SHER E PUNJAB 

48 George Street, Kidderminster 01562 740061

Evenings only at Puran Singh's restaurant which has been open a long time (since 1971).

Redditch

BALTI SPICE TAKEAWAY 

65 Popular Road, Batchley, Redditch 01527 596802

Opened in 1984, taken over in 1999 by Mastakin Miah. Previously called Pipasha Takeaway. Specials: Murghi Baburchi Walla,medium spicy, Tandoori Chicken, eggs and minced meat. Family Nan: from £2.40 to £3.00. Delivery: £8 minimum, 3-mile radius; £12 minimum, 4-mile radius. Hours: 5-12am; Sat. 5-1am.

Tenbury Wells

SHAMRAJ BALTI HOUSE 

28 Cross Street, Tenbury Wells 01584 819612

Owned by Mr Rahman, seats 60, party room 14, formula curries, marble-effect painted interior, light blue. Takeaway: 15% off. Hours: 12-2.30 (Sat. & Sun.)/5-12am.

Upton-on-Severn

PUNDITS

9 Old Street, Upton 01684 591119

'We booked the previous night, a good job, the place was very popular, despite being the most expensive in the area. A memorable place because the maitré greeted my wife with a kiss on the cheek and shook my hand even though it was our first visit. Enjoyed my Morche Roshun (garlic and chilli) Chicken Tikka, billed as hot, however, I may have been suffering from mouth numbness caused by my Chicken Vindaloo in Ilfracombe a few days previously. Good service.' T&MH. Menu Extracts: Chomothkar Talk Murgh Roti medium spiced, lemon chicken tikka on thin chapati bread; Podina Roshun (mint and garlic), mint sauce, whole roasted garlic cloves, roasted tomatoes and coriander with vegetables, chicken, lamb or prawns, from £5.45.

West Hagley

SHENAPUR

86 Worcester Rd, West Hagley 01562 884867

If you're in the area make a detour, I'm sure you won't be disappointed – the onion relish alone would be a good reason! This restaurant merits a **TOP 100** *position.'* MS. More reports could get it there.

Worcester

BOMBAY PALACE 

38 The Tything, Worcester 01905 613969

Abdul Rob tells us his 40-seater has 7 parking spaces at the back. Specials include: Kebabi Kofta, Chi Tik Pudina, Chicken Tikka Dhareswari and Tam Shami Moss. Generally good reports except one blaster from RJP. Takeaway: 10% off. Delivery: £10 min. Hours: 6-12am; Sat. 6-1am .

MONSOON TOP 100

35 Foregate Rd Worcester 01905 726333

White painted angled pillars and wooden stained concertina doors make this 120 seater restaurant stand out on Foregate Road. Established in 1999 by Rahman (manager), Choudhury and Choudhury. Reception has been painted in a creamy colour with comfortable sofa's upholstered in paprika. The retaurant has a light and airy feel, with bleached wooden flooring, paprika and cinnamon painted walls, original art hangs sparingly on the walls with matching chairs in paprika, cinnamon, turmeric and indigo. Natural wooden tables are economically laid with crisp white linen napkins and generous wine glasses. Specials: Tangri Kebab, drumstick marinated in cashew nuts, spices and served with tamarind chutney. Achar Wali Machi, salmon steak pickled in spices, served cold with salad. Parsi Jinga, tiger prawns in mint, turmeric, garlic and tamarind juice. Lamb Shikampuri, mince lamb balls stuffed with coriander, ginger, onion, raisins in curry gravy. Daal Panchmela, a mix of five varieties of lentils. Stays on our **TOP 100.** Takeaway: 10% discount. Hours: 6-12, Friday and Saturday to 1. Branch: Cheltenham Tandoori, 2 Great Norwood Street Cheltenham, Gloucs. Tel: 01242 227772.

SPICE CUISINE TOP 100 U BYO

39 Bromyard Road, Worcester 01905 429786

Hidden away behind Birmingham Midshires Building Society, just over the river bridge from Worcester Town, it has been owned by the same family for years, Muslims from Pakistan. *'Plain, simple and clean decor. Friendly and efficient service. Staff Curry - lamb on the bone in a thick, tasty, spicy sauce, cooked for hours with a thin rolled and crispy Nan. BYO welcome, they will chill and open. Manager - Iffty Shah (cousin of Masteen who manages the Kashmir in Birmingham) was very excited because they are now in the Guide for the first time.'* RE. [Well, Ray, I think that must be down to you, 'cos we have many reports from you singing their praises and here are some extracts from them]. *And extractw fro some of Ray's other visits: 'Toilets always clean with hot water, soap and dryer...' 'Chicken Korma £4.75 for Mrs E., which chef Ashar cooks just right for her and best of all, a large portion of staff curry with sauce to die for...' 'Brilliant as ever, freshly made Kebabs, spicy...' 'Father's Chicken Madras was entirely to his liking, chunks of tender chicken...' 'quality never varies...' 'Chicken on the bone and Aloo for me - excellent as usual...' 'My brother is also a curryholic - two portions of Sheek Kebab - excellent. Lamb on the bone for two - very tasty with side dish of thick dhal...' 'Keema with Peas and Aloo plus Pullao Rice - a change for me - was superb, fairly dry but spicy, minced lamb in a Balti with potato chunks. Apparently Keema is not a popular dish - much under-rated in my view.'* [You are quite right Ray, unfortunately us English don't think very much of minced meat, but Pat, like you, thinks it undeserved.] *'Lamb Chops, on the bone, which was the staff curry for the night. About six chops which had been cooking for hours so that the meat was falling off, served with a rich, quite hot sauce - superb. Roti to go with it, what else would you want for a Sunday dinner?' 'Washer-upper has been promoted to Tandoori Chef and made a very good start with Seekh Kebabs.. Unlicensed: BYO - they will chill and open it for you. Small card park with narrow entrance at the rear. Toilets always have hot water, soap and dryer. Non-smoking section.'* RE. Takeaway: 10% discount. Delivery: 3 miles, £10 minimum. Valued Customer Card: £25 p/a = 10% discount. Small car park at rear. Hours: 5.30 -11.30.

NORTH YORKSHIRE

Area: North
Population: 748,000
Adjacent Counties:
Cumbria, Durham,
Lancs, E & W Yorks

1997 *county changes returned 'Cleveland' south of the Tees, to North Yorks. At the same time, the changes created a 'new' Yorkshire county by transferring territory and towns from 'North Humbs' into East Yorkshire. This restored Yorkshire as Britain's biggest county. Because the area is so large, we deal with these four counties in their current administrative formats and in compass order,* N, E, S, W.

Bedale

TASTE OF INDIA NEW ENTRANT

32 Market Place Bedale

Established 1989. *'Plenty of free parking in market place. Smallish restaurant, quite long but narrow. Mixed Starters £3.80, very tasty, but not big enough for two. Main courses, absolutely gorgeous, each dish totally different. Jeera Chicken £6.10, very pleasant. Chicken Jalfrezi £6.60, excellent, fairly hot. We didn't leave a scrap despite portions being more than adequate.'* T&MH. Takeaway: 10% discount. Credit cards accepted. Hours: 6-11.30, Friday and Saturday to 12.

Bridlington

MAMONI NEW ENTRANT

106 St John Street Bridlington
01262 677088

asas *'Split into two, smoking and non-smoking. Nice decor, food very very good. Free Bombay Mix whilst waiting. My Chicken Jalfrezi came' a la vindaloo' with extra chillies. Nan disappointingly small. Prices a little on the expensive side of average. Waiters not very friendly.'* T&MH. That meal was a takeaway, wasn't it Tony? However, you and Monika decided to return to experience the sit down version. Were you impressed? *'Service was friendly...'* that's a change from last time. *'...but service was slow. Manager ran about organising everything and everyone, made up feel uncomfortable as he didn't walk anywhere. Tried the Deshi Bisato, a bit bland, although we cooked..'* It is a myth that Bangladeshi's all eat chilli hot food, they don't. I have check the menu and it is described as a home-style dish. Tony, you should have asked for a few chillies to be chopped up and combined in your curry, or you could have nicked a few chillies from Monika's Chilli Masala, I understand that her curry had some spare. *'...extremely reasonable bill.'* T&MH. Menu Extracts: Aloo Pakora £2.40; Deshi Bisato £6.60, mother's home cooking, lamb or chicken, heavy sauce, chunks of potato, mushrooms, green peppers and onions; Onion Fried Rice £1.90. Takeaway: 15% discount. Hours: 12-2/6-11.30, Friday and Saturday to 12.

SYLVIA DE SOUZA'S

Bridlington

'On holiday, we happened upon a real gem. Sylvia comes from a Goanese Roman Catholic background, hence pork and beef dishes. A short menu and, refreshingly, no CTM! We ordered a cold takeaway for our dinner, which we could reheat back home – while we waited (it was lunchtime) we all had freshly made Dosas – absolutely mouth watering. Started with Minced Beef Cutlets, Khati Rolls and Onion Bhajias, more like tempura, delicious. Main course of Fish Molee, Crab Puttu, Oxtail Vindaloo, Ox Tongues Pepper Fry, Coconut Rice, Dhal and Spinach. We were given Popadoms with the compliments of the house. Sylvia talked us into Lamb Biriani, she was right! it was unlike any other. Remains made an excellent lunch snack the next day! It's just a pity that we live in Aberdeen.' TC. All sounds absolutely fabulous, what a lucky find! More information please.

Harrogate

CINNAMON ROOM NEW ENTRANT

340 Oxford Street, Harrogate 01423 505600

Partners Tuah Ahmed, Suka Ullah and Zakariya have recently relocated from London, to open this modern 50 seater first floor restaurant. Full-length windows overlooking Oxford Street give an airy feel. Indian fusion food from head chef, Syed W Ahmed include Tandoori Trout, and a hybrid-sounding Szechuan Tofu Aloo. Ahmed's family owns Bombay Brasserie in Orpington and Black Fin in Kent.

RAJ RANI TAKEAWAY ©

235 Skipton Road, Harrogate 01423 529295

Ahad Miah, the proprietor of this takeaway only, is offering Monday and Tuesday CC customers 15% discount on collected takeaways over £15. Special Lamb Tikka, sliced lamb tikka, keema, peppers, onions, herbs and coriander. Delivery: £8.50, 4-miles. Hours: 5.30-11.30 (11 on Sat., 10.30 Sun.).

Malton

MALTON SPICE NEW ENTRANT

24 Castle Gate Malton 01653 691222

'Booked at table for Saturday at 8pm. It is relatively small, and on arriving it was buzzing. Given a table for four, we were only two. Lighting, very poor, had great difficulty reading menu. First mistake – don't order the Malton Special Sizzling Mix. It's gigantic! My first words were 'bloody hell' a table for four would probably manage it. Main courses were large – Nan could have been bigger, but I'm greedy, I couldn't eat everything that was put before me. The waiters, like policeman, look younger and younger. I still have trouble equating a Bangladeshi face with a strong Yorkshire accent.' T&MH. Menu Extracts: Chana Puri

£1.80; Garlic Mushroom £1.80; Malton Gosht £5.95, lamb, fresh garlic, ginger, capsicum, onions and a thick sauce; Lemon Rice £2. Delivery service available. Gourmet Night: four courses, £9.95 adult. Hours: 5-22.

RAJ TANDOORI ©

21 Church Street, Norton, Malton 01653 697337

S Islam's friendly 34-seater has dusky pink and petrol blue walls, white cornices, Indian art, pink and white linen and spotlights. Special: Akhini Chicken, pineapple, almond, sultanas, peas and rice, served with vegetable curry £6. *'Has been a satisfying experience following their progress, to what is now a very good restaurant.'* AT. *'Infamous for the serious flooding several years ago. Subdued green lighting on the outside doesn't feel very welcoming, but inside things change. Were given a window seat table next to the radiator. Pleasantly decorated. Enjoyable Sheek Kebab and Royal Mix Kebab. My favourite Chicken Jalfrezi at Madras level and Chicken Tikka Chilli – looked similar but tasted different, we enjoyed them both. Nan quite big, tasty and fluffy. Adequate and ample Mushroom Pullao. Portions just right, we returned nothing to the kitchen.'* T&MH. Menu Extracts: Paneer Pakora £2.10; Pickle Tray £1; Balti Steak Masala £8. Delivery: £2 charge. Takeaway: 20% off. Hours: lunch by appointment (clever) and 5.20-12. Closed Monday, except bank holidays.

Middlesborough

CLEVELAND TANDOORI 

289 Linthorpe Road, Middlesbrough
01642 242777

First opened in 1991, taken over by owner-chef Abid Hussain in 1996. His 32-seater serves formula curry, but there are some Pakistani gems: Shalgum Gosht is meat with turnip and Lahori Gosht, meat with okra. There is a range of Haandi dishes. For the yet-to-be-converted-to curry, try Abid's Anglo Indian Coronation Chicken, created in 1953 by London's Cordon Bleu school in honour of QEII's Coronation: diced chicken cooked with apricots in a creamy sauce. Abid is keen on his fund-raising for the MacMillan Cancer Relief fund in memory of his brother and father, who both died of cancer. Last year his customers raised £1088 in just one night at the restaurant. . E-a-m-a-y-l Sunday, Monday, Tuesday. Delivery: £6 minimum, 3-miles. Hours: 6-12am (2.30am on Fri./Sat.).

Northallerton

SPICE OF INDIA NEW ENTRANT

1a Friarage Street Northallerton
01609 777600

'Surrounding streets give ample parking even on a Saturday night. A window seat was found for the four of us. Generally good first impressions, bright, well decorated as well as clean. Plenty of smartly dressed waiters, service was prompt, courteous. Enjoyable Mixed Kebab, very tender Lamb Tikka. Very good Special Mixed Curry, Madras strength, plenty of it, rice and bread were extra. Monika's Chicken Achar, taste of pickle was very obvious. Very little was left, we did 'pig out'.' t&mh. A good time was had by all!

Ripon

MOTI RAJ 

18 High Skellgate, Ripon 01765 690348

I was hosting a cooking theatre at an ethnic exhibition, which William Hague officially opened (for posterity, when our great-grand children are reading yellowing, curry-stained copies of this tome, he was Tory opposition leader at this time). When I asked him if he liked curry *'er yes I do actually'* and when I asked where was his fav rest, he said *'er the Moti Raj Ripon'*. I quote the *'er'*, but he did say Moti Raj without hesitation, and he is more or less a local. Abdul Malik's restaurant is indeed a local to a good many scribes who inform me of its qualitites. Abdul's philosophy is: *'the only path to good food, like good wine, is time.'* And what he means is, relax and enjoy your evening. Special: Sliced Chicken Tikka with Keema. *'For main course I had Chicken Karahi, served in a proper cast iron karahi and piping hot. One of my friends had Prawn Bhuna, not on the menu, but not the slightest trouble for them to provide. Total bill (for 3) came to £24.'* JMFP. *'Very busy with locals, quite a bit of banter about the cricket team, some soccer banter too. Heavy use of takeaway service. Starters served promptly, then long wait for main courses. Food was really excellent, although I have had a bigger Nan...' [Tony, you and your Nan's!] '...waiter asked us if we had heard of Pat Chapman's Curry Club – they had a certificate. I produced my membership card, he brought us a f.o.c. drink. Tremendous value for money.'* T&MH. Menu Extracts: Moglai Pullao £1.60, egg, almonds and sultanas; Mas Biran £2.30, fish spiced and grilled, served with salad; Garlic Potato £1.55. Takeaway 10% off. Delivery: 3 miles, £8 minimum. Hours: 5.30-12, including Bank Holidays.

Settle

SETTLE TANDOORI ©

9 Commercial Courtyard, Duke Street, Settle 01729 823393

Established in 1998 by Abdul Rob. Seats 50. Palm trees in middle of restaurant. Specials: Garlic Chicken £4.70. Chicken Tikka Balti £6.50. Takeaway: 10% discount. Hours: 5.30-11.30

Skipton

AAGRAH TOP 100 ©

Devonshire Place, Keighley Road, Skipton01756 790807

Established in 1989 and managed by Mostafizur Rahman, this 52-seater is the third of seven very popular Aagrahs (so booking advisable) *(See Shipley, W Yorks for detailed comment.)*. Pakistani food, more gutsy and robust than the Bangla formula, sometimes attracts criticism (T&KM didn't like it, for example) but this doesn't mean it should be demoted from our **TOP 100**. Specials include: Achar, Hydrabady and Masala dishes. Takeaway: 10% discount. Hours: 6-12; Sun. 6-11.

Tadcaster

AAGRAH TOP 100 ©

York Road, Steeton, Tadcaster 01937 530888

Managed by Aagrah boss, Mohammed Aslam, this 120-seater, which opened in 1996, is the sixth of seven very popular Aagrahs. It's on the A64 near York, with easy parking. See Aagrah Skipton, above. *'Very large, pleasantly decorated and comfortable restaurant. A bit pricey, but good service, even when very busy on buffet night. Good portions and excellent Murgh Chana and Stuffed paratha.'* IB. Specials include: Achar, Hydrabady and Masala dishes. Takeaway: 10% discount. Hours: 6-11.30. Sun. 6-11. All the Aagrahs are rated with a collective **TOP 100** cachet. *(See Shipley, W Yorks, for fuller comment.)*

York

AKASH 

10 North Street, York 01904 633550

Established in 1983, chef/owner JU Ahmed hasn't upped his prices since our last *Guide*. His 38-seater does a set dinner for £9.50. Specials: Kabuli Chicken or Lamb, chickpeas, tomato and fresh coriander £6.20. Takeaway 20% off. Delivery: £8 min, 3-miles. Hours: 5-12.

BENGAL BRASSIERE

21 Goodramgate, York 01904 640066

Established in 1999 by Dobir Malik and Iqbal Chowdury, a 100-seater that is typical of the of the new style contemporary decor being applied by restaurants of all nationalities. Hard polished wooden floors, brightly coloured upholstered chairs, wrought iron stair casing, spot lighting, and white walls. The food is good here. Chef Mohan Miah was a finalist in the CIEH chef of the year contest in 2002. It's a caring restaurant. Takeaway: 20% discount. Hours: 5.30-11.30. Sat. 12-2.30/5.30-11.30; Sun. 12-10.30. Branch: Bengal Brasserie, York Business Park, Mifield Lane, Nether Poppleton, York. 01904 788808

JINNAH BALTI TOP 100 

105-107 Micklegate, York 01904 659999

Saleem Akhtar's chain of restaurants is growing, reflecting each branch's popularity, in an area which has previously not been known for currinary excellence. Decor, including conservatory extensions, smart logos, menus and staff, *'all contribute to a good experience, which is very different at lunch time to evening. We've been at both times of day, to all of Mr Akhtar's restaurants. Each has its own atmosphere, but you can tell they are in the same ownership'.* ED. *'I started with the Seekh Kebabs and thought I was going to be disappointed with the place as the Kebabs were of the red-colouring variety and possibly microwaved (the best I've tasted were at Bharat in Bradford). However, the main course, Jinnah Special Balti which was chicken, lamb, prawn and mushrooms was excellent.'* RC. However, JR found *'the Jinnah Special Biryani flavouring unadventurous, ditto the vegetable curry accompaniment, but everything else OK.'* JR. Stays on our **TOP100.** Hours: 12-2.30/6-12am. Branches: Jinnah, A64 Malton Road, Flaxton, York; Jinnah Balti, 105-107 Micklegate, York; Viceroy of India, 26 Monkgate, York; Jinnah, 845 York Road, Leeds; Jinnah Takeaway, 18 The Village, Haxby; Taj Mahal and Viceroy of India, York.

EAST YORKSHIRE

Area: North
Population: 800,000
Adjacent Counties:
Lincs,
N S & W Yorks

1997 *county changes created this 'new' Yorkshire county by transferring territory and towns here from 'North Humbs'.*

Beverley

NASEEB ©

9-10 Wednesday Market, Beverley
01482 861110

Established in 1988 by Abdul Muzir, seats 44 diners, Bangladeshi formula curries. Very pretty restaurant, Indian painting, white walls, arches, ceiling fans, blue tablecloths and napkins, velvet chairs and curtains. Roshoon Mirch Murgh, hot, thick sauce, fresh garlic, green chillies, green pepper, chopped tomatoes and fresh coriander leaves £6.10. Delivery only available to Nasseeb club members, ask for details. Takeaway: 10% discount. Hours: 6-11.30.

KHANS — NEW ENTRANT

Wylies Road, Beverley, 01482

'We frequent Khans. Food produced is excellent and service is second to none.' BU.

Hessle

LIGHT OF INDIA 

27 The Weir, Hessle 01482 649521

Saiful Islam Tarafdar's Light is under the shadow of the fabulous bridge, and does 'fabulous takeaways only' KY. Special: Indian Burger, pitta bread with spicy kebab and salad £1.90. Curry Sauce and Chips £1.90! Delivery: £7 minimum, Hessle area and £10 minimum local area, possibly small charge! Hours: 5-12 (12.30 on Sat.).

Hull

TANDOORI MAHAL 

589 Anlaby Road, Hull 01482 505653

Abu Maksud and Mizanur Tarafder's 64-seat restaurant is one of RKCfavourites. *'Have been regular customers for over three years. We have always received first class service and excellent food.'* PT. Kurzi Lamb £45. Set dinner £16.95. Hours: 6-12.

SOUTH YORKSHIRE

Area: North
Population: 1,306,000
Adjacent Counties:
Derbys, Lincs, Notts,
E & W Yorks

Barnsley

DIL RAJ — NEW ENTRANT

8-12 High Street Dodworth Barnsley
01226 202 606

Formerly the Horse and Jockey Pub. *Friendly service. Pleasant decor. Well spiced food, carefully cooked. Good quality breads. Clean loos.'* HL. Always interested in hearing about the loos, it says a lot about the management. Menu Extracts: Tandoori Platter £2.70; Chingri Sizzler £5.50, Bengal tiger prawns, stir-fried, onions, peppers, baby potatoes;Dahi Murgh £4.30, char-grilled chicken, sweet and sour sauce. Hours: 6-12.

JALSA ©

7 Pitt Street, Barnsley 01226 779114

Emdadur Rahman established his Jalsa in 1992. It is a comfortable, smart, 50-seater with a delightful reception area and bar. And we know it's popular. Specials include: Chrigri Sizzler £6.90 (Farons Bengal Tiger prawns steamed with baby tomatoes, mushrooms and stir fried, served with salad). Takeaway 15% off. Takeaway: 15% discount. Hours: 6-12.

K2 ©

5 Royal Street, Barnsley 01226 299230

Kashmiri Balti takeaway-only establishment. *'Excellent.'* TH. They don't do lunch and we're not surprised, owner/manager/chef Ditta must be exhausted with these hours! 10% off for students before 10.30pm. Hours: 6pm-3am (4am on Sat., 12.30am on Sun.).

Doncaster

AAGRAH TOP 100 AWARD WINNER 

Great North Road, Woodlands, Doncaster 01302 728888

Opened in 1995, the fifth of seven very popular (so booking advisable) Aagrahs. This 90-seater is a franchise run by cousin Liaquat Ali. Like its sisters, it is awarded a collective **TOP 100** cachet. *'I would put it at no. 1 in Doncaster, and there's a lot of competition.'* JF. *(See Shipley, W. Yorks for detailed comment.)* Specials include: Achar, Hydrabady and Masala dishes. Takeaway: 10% discount. Hours: 6-11.30pm; Fri. & Sat. 6-12; Sun. 6-11.

INDUS 

24 Silver Street, Doncaster 01302 810800

Long-established (1968) 175-seater, owned by Karim Din, with manager M Ilyas. Modern, upmarket Anglo/Indian decor. *'A sophisticated restaurant.'* DC. *'Is and always has been our favourite in Yorkshire.'* WHH. Takeaway: 10% discount. Delivery: £20. Sun. buffet £12. Hours: 12-2/6.30-11.30.

TAJ MAHAL 

32 Hallgate, Doncaster 01302 341218

Established in 1989. Seats 78. Specials include: Lahore King Prawns. Takeaway: 10% discount. Delivery: £ 10 minimum, 3-mile radius. Hours: 5.30-12.30am (Fri. & Sat. 5.30-1am).

Rotherham

MUGHAL CURRY CENTRE 

1 Bellows Road, Rawmarsh, Rotherham 01709 527084

Established in 1993. Seats 48. Karahi dishes are most popular. Monday, Tuesday and Thursday: two for one. Takeaway: 10% discount. Hours: 6pm to late; Sat. 6-3am.

Sheffield

ASHOKA TOP 100

307 Ecclesall Rd, Sheffield 0114 268 3029

Established in 1967 by Mrs M Ahmed, this 38-seater is managed by Kamal Ahmed. *'The best Indian restaurant we have been to, including many in the London area and Birmingham. We went back to it every night of the week [while attending a scientific meeting in Sheffield]. We cannot praise its delicate and distinct flavours too highly, and the friendly, efficient service.'* J&AF. Yours is one of many contented reports, so we are happy that this well-established and well run venue stays in the elite **TOP 100.** Most ordered dish Bhel Puri, (*see page* 50), Liver Puri – chicken livers, stir-fried in masala, served on bread. Takeaway: 10% off. Hours: 6 (Sun. 7)-11.30. *'One of the finest Indian restaurant in South Yorkshire. Diners are assured of excellent service, an amenable atmosphere and outstanding service. Comprehensive and high quality wine* *list. Book early to avoid disappointment.'* D&CS. *'Just wanted to send you a glowing report. Not only was the vegetarian curry superb, but the waiters were friendly'* KH. *See page 41.*

BENGAL SPICE 

457 Manchester Rd, Sheffield 0114 288 8666

Established in 1998. Specials: Musca, tikka with bananas, pineapple and fresh cream, fruity. Haryali Murgh, marinated chicken in sauce of spinach, mint and coriander leaf. Delivery: £10 minimum, 4-mile radius. Hours: 5-11/Sat. 5-11.30.

BILASH TAKEAWAY

347 Sharrow Vale Road, Sheffield
0114 266 1746

Established by chef Abdul Jahir in 1986. Specials: Chicken Tikka Jalfrezi, King Prawn Sag. Hours: 5.30-12, Sun to Thurs. To 1am, Fri/Sat.

DILSHAD 

96 The Dale, Sheffield 0114 255 5008

Established in 1995. Seats 48. Specials: Shahi Chicken or Lamb £4 – with mincemeat, eggs, onions, peppers and tomatoes, medium. Gatta Special £4 – chicken, meat, prawns and fruit, medium. Investigate the set meals – there is something for everyone. Takeaway: approximately 15%. Hours: 6-12; Sat. 6-12.30.

ELINAS 

282 Sharrow Rd, Sheffield 0114 267 9846

First opened in 1993, taken over by Mrs Reba Khan in 1999. Seats 40 in two-tone lime green marble effect walls. Specials: Chicken Shobuz Masala £4.40 – fresh coriander and green chillies, hot. Sag Tikka £4.30 – with spinach. Takeaway: 15% discount. Delivery: £10 minimum, 3-mile radius. Hours: 5.30-11.30; Sat. 5.30-12.

EVEREST TANDOORI 

59 Chesterield Rd, Sheffield 0114 258 2975

First opened in 1978, taken over by NM Raja in 1998. Seats 76. Specials: Bhattak Masalla £7.95 – duck, marinated, spices, fresh onion, tomato, rich masala sauce. Chicken or Lamb Razalla £5.95 – with onion, tomato, fresh green chillies, thick spicy sauce, very hot! Takeaway: 10% discount. Delivery: 2-mile radius. Hours: 6-1am; Thurs. 6-2am; Fri. & Sat. 6-3am.

IJAFLONG 

182 Northfield Road, Crookes, Sheffield
0114 266 1802

A cosy Bangladeshi formula curry house, seating just 36 diners. Balti dishes on the menu, from £3.50. Special: Jahangir Bhuna Prawn, medium, onions, tomatoes and mushrooms £4.20. Hours: 6-12am (1am on Fri. & Sat.).

NIRMAL'S TOP 100 

189 Glossop Rd, Sheffield 0114 272 4054

Mrs Nirmal Gupta is the owner chef, with the front going to Mr PL Gupta. But Nirmal is no retiring backstage person. She makes appearances on the restaurant floor and *'enjoys talking about food'* PM. She is a huge personality and has no hesitation in telling customers like William Hague and Jamie Lee Curtis such snippets as *'curry is an aphrodisiac'*. But not all her clients are stars. She opened in 1981 near the University *'to feed hungry students'*, indeed many of her regulars work and study there. Mrs Nirmal's has virtually doubled in size since we first reported on it, and now has a reception area, cocktail bar and 80 seats on two floors. Its famous Special Board, upon which are chalked the dishes of the day, fortunately remains. The technique would hardly merit a mention in 1001 bistros up and down the land, but it is rare in the world of curry. I mentioned this back in 1984, and I'm still waiting for the formula wallahs to cotton on! The menu is northern Indian with, on the face of it, just standard Tandoori, Tikkas, Kormas, Bhunas, Madrases, Vindaloos and the rest. *'But do not expect one-sauce cooking here.'* RS. *'All is cooked superbly, as at an Indian home.'* GA. Of those specials: *'Nirmal's Potato Chops £2.25, are amazing mashed potato rissoles with a central stuffing of spicy lentils topped with almond tikka. The vegetable dishes prove the point that this is exceptional cooking. The paneer is always light and fresh, and stuffed Bhindi (okra) is always the test of a good chef – they can so easily go sappy! I've not seen that happen here.'* BR. SG. Menu extracts: Papadam 45p, CTM £6.95, Pullao Rice £1.95. Tomato Paneer, £4.95. Parsnips with peppers and tomatoes £4.50. Aubergine Green Pepper £4.95. Gourmet Buffet night on Tuesday, £9.95 from 7.30-11pm. Sun. buffet £9.95. Service 10%. Nirmal's stays firmly in our **TOP 100.** Hours: 12-2.30/6-12am.

WEST YORKSHIRE

Area: North
Population: 2,125,000
Adjacent Counties:
G Man, Lincs,
N & S Yorks

Batley

BOMBAY PALACE BYO 

3 St James Street, Batley 01924 444440

Location: off the A652 Bradford Road from Dewsbury, easily accessed from M1 junction 40. Balti 74-seater in an old converted bakery, with many features still apparent, such as the dough mixers, opened in 1992 by G. Maniyar and Shahid Akudi. Brick walls display Moghal paintings, open fire. 'Upstairs with a light industrial theme, very pleasant surroundings which includes a separate family room. Popadoms are complimentary after giving your order. Food excellent, every dish has its own flavour. As the level of hotness tends to be gauged higher than most restaurants, this will suit the fire eaters. Portions are generous, one rice is enough for two. Staff extremely friendly and efficient.' PVI. 'My wife and I have been regulars since it opened. Our current favourites are Seekh Kebabs – beautifully spicy, not too hot, fresh and tasty. Nargis Kebabs – full of flavour with a velvety texture. For special occasions there are banquet menus, which again represent excellent value for money.' TN. Specials include: Shikari dish £6.90, Achari dish £6.90, and Palace Raan, whole leg of lamb, marinated for 24 hours in herbs, yoghurt, almonds and cashews, cut into slices, plenty for 4, £60. Price check: Papadam 20p, CTM £7.50, Pullao Rice £1.50, Peshwari Nan £1.70. Takeaway: approximately 10% discount. Delivery: £10 minimum, 3-mile radius, £6 minimum, 2-mile radius. Hours: 6-12.

SPICE GARDEN BYO 

**2 Market Place, Birstall, Batley
01924 471690**

Specials at Abrar Hussain's Pakistani 74-seater include the Grand-Slam – it's four different meats, vegetables, prawns, massive portion – so now you know! Takeaway: 10% off. Delivery: £7, 3-miles. BYO. Hours: 5-12.

Bradford

(inc: Baildon, Chapel Green, Great Horton, Idle, Manningham and Thornbury)

Bradford has a high pedigree curry background, with its very well-established, largely-Pakistani population. This means Halal meat and few veg at the many unlicensed cheap n' cheerful spit n' sawdust caffs. Since many are strict Moslems, not all welcome BYO. In such establishments, please check with the staff that you may BYO, and even if 'yes', always drink discretely and in moderation. The restaurants, sweet shops and cafés are much more widely spread around than, say, Southall. Curryholics must locate them, for their excellent, uncompromising ethnic food at real value-for-money prices.

ANAM'S — NEW ENTRANT

211 Great Horton Rd, Bradford. 01274 522626.

Mohammed Latif has launched this venue, and we hear of good food at good prces.

ASHA 

31 Cheapside, Central Bradford
01274 729358

Special Feast Night on Sundays and Thursdays at owner Abdul Anwar's Asha. Hours: 6-12.

BOMBAY BRASSERIE

1 Simes St, off Westgate, Central Bradford
01274 737564

Established in 1983. Taken over in 1998 by Ali Shan. The building was once a Presbyterian church and makes a fantastic venue, seating 150 in smoking and non-smoking areas. *'Great atmosphere, and food, indeed a memorable occasion, and something quite out of the Bradford norm.'* AN. Hours: 5.30-11.30pm; Fri. & Sat. 5.30-12.30; Sun. 12.30-11. Scores 8/10 DB.

INTERNATIONAL TANDOORI

40 Manville Terrace, off Morley Street, Central Bradford 01274 721449

'I have been eating at Bradford curry houses for over 20 years, and my favourite has been the Kashmir. However, having had a couple of disappointing meals there recently, I decided to try somewhere new. The International was recommended and I have returned on three occasions since. The food, while not being particularly sophisticated, is excellent. I'm not able to report on a wide range of dishes since I've tended to stick to classic curry house dishes, but I can vouch for old favourites like the Shami Kebabs and the Kemma Vindaloo. MB.

KARACHI

15-17 Neal Street, Central Bradford
01274 732015

Karachi claims to be the first Curry house in the UK. It wasn't. It's not even the first in Bradford. The Kashmir, (see next entry) opened in 1958, The Sweet Centre, Lumb Lane in 1964, and the Kashmir, third in 1965. Still, it's a long time in curry circkles. *'Limited menu but others dishes can be asked for, provided no long preparation is required. Proudly home-run with friendly and unflappable staff. Cheap, cheerful and excellent food. To round off a cracking meal I had a homemade Pistachio Kulfi, frozen solidly, but melting into a sweet and spicy mush.'* RW. *'Food is good quality, service is friendly. Decor reminded us of a school canteen, and the guide is correct – the toilets are dreadful. Goes without saying that in Bradford it came with three chapatis. However, this was its undoing, as they were too thick meaning that you left feeling bloated.'* HR.

KASHMIR

27 Morley Street, Central Bradford
01274 726513

The Kashmir has had a lot of national press recently, and it has made into a kind of superstar cult-café. It's always had cult-status, but since the press coverage, the trendies may have tried to make it their own. Anyway, we did get a spate of reports which found the Kashmir wanting. We did not recognise one reporter's name, so they went into the bin. We hope the Kashmir is keeping to its usual high standards, and believe it is. The restaurant holds about 200 on two floors, downstairs – formica tables, upstairs – carpeted, tablecloths. *'After sitting down it was some five or ten minutes before a member of staff approached our table – I had time to wonder if the management had over extended or perhaps the ordering system had changed and I was supposed to go to the counter. My wife's Chicken Kashmiri £3.90 and my Chicken Masala £3.60 looked very similar but the difference in taste was obvious. We both enjoyed our brief stop-off meal but left thinking that it wasn't as good as I remembered – rose tinted memories? A very popular restaurant with its local clientele.'* AT. *'Seekh Kebabs 60p very good flavour, Meat Roghan Josh £ 3.90 – not as spicy as other dishes but still good. Good service, pleasant staff.'* L&CH. Hours: 11am to 3am. Branch: Kashmir, 858 Leeds Road, Bradford Centre. 01274 664357 (near the hospital).

MUMTAZ PAAN HOUSE

386 Great Horton Road, Great Horton, Bradford SW 01274 571861

Says PS: *'Noted as being the place to go in Bradford; also as the place not to go if you like "Europeanised" curries because they serve only the real thing! With this in mind we went looking forward to a decent curry night out, but came away rather disappointed, not because of the food, but other things: patchy service, we were affected by smokers on surrounding tables, menu is not as extensive as in other restaurants, hard to check your bill due to payment method (the waiter leaves a copy of your order at the table inside a folder which you take to the cash desk, where codes are entered into the till, and you are uncertain whether service charge has been added). Despite all above, food was superb, and I shall return (better prepared!).'* PS. *'In my view and the view of many friends in Leeds, this is one of the finest curry houses in the country.'* AF.

PAZEEKAH BYO

1362 Leeds Road, Thornbury, Bradford E 01274 664943

Ex bus driver Mazhar-ul-Haq's tells us he likes to change the decor and the menu regularly, 'because that's what customers want to see.' Successful Pakistani restaurant, seats a considerable 130 diners. Chef/manager is son Mohammed Jamil. Hours: 4pm-12.30am (1.30am on Sat.). They also own an 18,000 sq ft Asian Superstore, selling Asian food, and utensils at 91 Edderthorpe Street, off Leeds Road, Bradford.

RAWAL BYO 

3 Wilton Street, off Morley Street, Central Bradford 01274 720030

Owner-Chef Abdul P Butt cooks Pakistani curries in his open kitchen, Mobin Iqbal manages the 50-seater and promised a 10% discount to CC members. Special: Grand Slam, mixture of meat, chicken, keema and fresh vegetables, served with Pullao Rice £5.70. Zam-Zam Special, meat, chicken, king prawns, and chick peas, served with Pullao Rice £5.70. Rawal claims *'Once tried never forgotten'.* DC says it is indeed true: *'Great price, great food'.* Takeaway: 10% off for students, 3 chappatis or boiled rice with each order. Hours: 5-2am (3am on Fri. & Sat.); closed Mon.

SHAH JEHAN 

30 Little Horton Lane, Central Bradford 01274 390777

Aka Ormar's Shajehan or just Omar's, after their owner/chef Omar Gulzar Khan. His three branches have identical menus. The Horton Lane branch seats 150 and is spread over three rooms. It is stylish and luxuriously decorated, with lovely leather sofas to relax on, while waiting for a takeaway, and pretty red chairs for your table. Goods comments on all three branches, usually: *'An extremely smart and well laid out restaurant with friendly service throughout. We had the whole leg of lamb ordered 24 hours in advance. Superb. Highly recommended.'* CT. *'Very, very, very good.'* LH. But one downer: *'Slightly disappointing – have had better meals here in the past. Has won several awards from various bodies, and it's possible that staff are not trying as hard as before the restaurant became "famous". But Meat Pathia very tasty.'* L&CH. Hours: 12-2.30/5.30-12am. Branches: 6 North Gate, Baildon, Bradford N; 726 Manchester Road, Chapel Green, Bradford S.

SHIRAZ BYO 

133 Oak Lane, Manningham, Bradford N 01274 490176

Owned by Mohammed Gulbahar, with Mohammed Aslam managing and Mohammed Afzal cooking competent Kashmiri curries and Baltis. Hours: 4pm-2am. Closed Christmas Day and for Muslim festivals.

SHISH MAHAL BYO 

6 St Thomas Road, Central Bradford 01274 723999

Mohammed Taj's 54-seater *'is next door to one of the best pubs in Britain, The New Beehive – tremendous real ale with genuine character. The food at this BYO restaurant is nothing short*

©	Curry Club Discount	U	Unlicensed
V	Vegetarian	ANP	Alcohol not permitted
e-a-m-a-y-l	Eat as much as you like	BYO	Bring your own alcohol

of marvellous. Flavour literally explodes in the mouth. Sensational garlic chicken. Friendly and informal service.' SL. Hours: 4pm-3am.

SWEET CENTRE

110 Lumb Lane, Central Bradford 01274 731735

The Sweet Centre opened in 1964, and was Bradford's second ccurry venue. At the counter you order savouries and sweets by the pound. I know because way back, I purchased 120 samosas here for a *Curry Club* function, and we all found the measuring process a wee bit complex. Eventually they settled for 15p each and the sams were worth the sum! The sit down's fun too: *'Unlicensed all-hours cafe, cutlery on request. Asian clientele. Food cheap.'* DC. *'Excellent. The service is good and the food very tasty.'* SL.

TASTE OF BENGAL 

79 Bradford Rd, Idle, Bradford N 01274 618308

First opened in 1980. Abdul Subhan took over '98 and it's a cosy restaurant, decorated in, 'simple, plain wallpaper, minty colour, Axminster carpet' has just 28 covers, so book at weekends, or be disappointed or have a takeaway. Abdul Qayum runs the front with Uddin Khan in the kitchen. Balti and Bengal Specialities feature on the menu with a Dine Bangladeshi-Sylhet Special – cooked in a thick blend of spicy sauce with king prawns, mixed vegetables and (more) prawns. Jaflong dishes, Niralee dishes, Sylhet special dishes. Takeaway: 10% discount. Hours: 6-12am; Sat. 6-12.30. Branches: Moghul, Horsforth, Leeds and Ilkley.

ZAM ZAM TAKEAWAY 

5 North Road, Ravensthorp, Dewsbury 01924 469677

First opened in 1980, taken over by Perwaiz Khan in 1994. Samosas and Shami Kebabs are great value at £1.30 for two. Main dishes are served with either three Chapatis, Rice or Chips. Pizzas also available from £2.80 for 12" thin crust and from £3.80 Large deep pan. Delivery: £5 minimum, 3-mile radius. Hours: 6-12.30am; Sat. 6-2.30; Sun. 6-1.

Garforth

AAGRAH TOP 100 

Aberford Road, Garforth 0113 287 6606

Nephew Wasim Aslam manages this 175-seater, opened in 1993, and the fourth of the very popular Aagrahs. *(See Shipley, W. Yorks for detailed comment.)* Car parking for 90. Specials include: Achar, Hydrabady and Masala dishes. 'Excellent' says PW. Takeaway: 10% off. Hours: 6-11.30; Fri. & Sat. 5.30-11.30.

Halifax

CROWN TANDOORI 

31 Crown Street, Halifax 01422 349270

Established in 1995. Seats 62. Onion Bhajia's and Samosas are great value at £1.30 each for two. Specials: Full Tandoori Chicken with Vegetable Curry £8. Chicken Tikka and Chips £4.25. Outrageous Pickle Tray £1.50. Delivery: £8 minimum, 3-mile radius. Hours: 6-1; Sat. 6-3.

Huddersfield

NAWAB,

35, Westgate, Huddersfield. 01484 422775

'The Nawab chain have a bit of a reputation, at least in West Yorkshire as being a bit high class. The building panders to this reputation as it used to be a bank. Busy Sunday evening. Interior smart enough. Menu is extensive. I expected a really classy, expensive meal but got a good but not particularly outstanding one at a reasonable price. The waiters didn't even wear ties.' T&MH. We agree with everything you say. Several years ago, Pat and I went to the Bradford Nawab. Yes, the building is fabulous and it was very busy with small and large parties all, apparently, having a good time. However, the service was too flippant and (I suspect that the chefs were having a hard time with the volume of custom) the food was very average. We were both very disappointed. Frankly, the Nawabs should be taken out of the Guide, but if we do that we get complaints and queries asking why. There is no doubt the

Nawabs have a huge, satisfied following, and it may just be that readers of this Guide see things differently. So we are continuing to give it a big, comprehensive entry. We sincerely look forward to receiving good reports from reportes we trust. Menu Extracts: Paneer Pakora £2.50; Aloo Chana on Puri £2.50; Butter Chicken £7.95; Achari Lamb £6.95; Gobi and Aloo Makhani £5.95; Keema Nan £2.20; Aloo Paratha £2.20. Branches: Nawab, 35 Westgate, Huddersfield. 01484 422775; Nawab, 47 Rochdale Road, Manchester. 0161 839 0601; Nawab, Avenida Joan Miro 309, San Agustin, Palma De Mallorca, Spain. 00 34 9 71 401 691, Nawab, Contralmirante Ferraout, 2 Magalluf, Majorca. 00 34 9 71 130 607; Nawab, Ibiza, 9 Bajo Loc, 2 Gemelos 4, 03500 Benidorm, Spain. 00 34 9 65 856 024; Nawab, Calya Pinada, 8 Local I, 07181, Toronova, Palma Nova, Majorca. 00 34 9 71 681 336; Nawab, Ramon De Moncada, 38 Santa Ponsa, Calvia, Majorca. 00 34 6 20 648 748.

SERENA ©

12 St Peters St, Huddersfield 01484 451991

Ihsan Elahi's *'modern and chic'* Pakistani formula curry house, established in 1993, seats 62, the party room, 40. Chef Khalid Hussain's specials include Balti and Karahi dishes, and Hawahan Muragh, chicken with pineapple, cream. 'Good quality, well prepared dishes. Value for money, service excellent.' JT. Service 10%. Takeaway: 15% discount. Hours: 6-11.30.

Ilkley

EXOTIC TANDOORI ©

10 Church Street, Ilkley 01943 607241

Shah Marshal Alom's traditionally decorated 50-seater has golden arches and hanging plants. Special: Boul Mas, Bangladeshi fish £7. Price check: Papadam 30p, CTM £5.95, Pullao Rice £1.40. House wine £3.95 half-litre. Takeaway: 10% off. Hours: 5.30-12.

SABERA © 10%

9 Wells Road, Ilkley01943 607104

This old friend of the *Guide* first opened in 1974. Taken over by Abdus Sattar in 1998, it is, we hear: *'A clean restaurant with pine panelling and 48 seats. I enjoyed my Kalajee Gurda Dil and will return to try some of their other dishes.'* DM. Specials include: Murgi Mossaala £10.95, Korahi dish £7.95. Delivery: £10 minimum, 2-mile radius. Hours: 5.30-12.

Keighley

KEIGHLEY TANDOORI 

Unit 3 Park Way House, Worthway, Keighley 01535 691818

Established in 1995 by Mohammad Hanif. Seats an intimate 24. Samosa Special £2.50 – served with chick pea curry. All main dishes are served with three Chappati, Boiled Rice or Chips – the choice is yours! Burgers from £2.20. Delivery: £7 minimum, 3-mile radius. Hours: 6-1.

SHIMLA SPICE BYO 

14 South Street, Keighley01535 602040

Opened in 1998 by Mohammed Ayub and his two brothers, who had their 70-seater built from scratch on a useful corner site. Interior is decorated beautifully, ornate plasterwork on ceiling and walls, colonial fans, large chandelier, 'Tiffany' lamps and cane furniture.*'We've become regulars. Staff are always polite and helpful, menu is excellent.'* BD&FH. *'I eat here at least once a week either on my own after working late, or with family or friends. Excellent quality of food, very friendly and prompt service, attractive decor. Extensive menu including a very wide choice of vegetarian meals. Portions generous, flavours well blended, dishes include a variety of fresh vegetables and herbs. The top of our list.'* JB. *'I eat here more than any other restaurant. Starters are excellent, especially the Shami Kebabs, Chicken Pakora and Fish Masala. Main course favourites are the Chicken and Meat and Chicken and Keema Balti dishes, the Tandoori Bemisaal and the Achari dishes. The price of such a good meal is surprisingly reasonable. I feel this is a restaurant on a par with many in your Top 100.'* MB. Specials include: Fish Masala, Murgh Jaipur, Achri Gosth, CTM, Murgh Makani, Lamb Jallfrazi. Takeaway: 10% discount. Delivery: £8 minimum. Hours: 6-12.15. (Sat. to 1.15am).

Knottingley

JEWEL IN THE CROWN 

110 Weeland Road, Knottingley
01977 607233

Pakistani curries at Manager Adnan Miraf's 40-seater. 'Excellent food at reasonable prices. Service friendly and efficient. Recommend the Punjabi (Tandoori) Mixed Grill.' IB. E-a-m-a-y-l £8. Takeaway: 20% off. Delivery: £8, 2-mile radius. Hours: 6pm-12am.

Leeds

(includes Headingley, Horsforth, Kirkstall, Oakwood, Morley and Stanningley)

AZRAM'S SHEESH MAHAL

348 Kirkstall Rd, Leeds NW 0113 230 4161

First opened in 1987, taken over by Azram Chaudhry in 1990. Seats 76 with a further room for 38. Up the road from YTV studios, Azram's as the locals know it, set on its prominent corner site, has recently been refurbished and expanded. Specials include: Kofta Special, Balti Murgh, Murgh Punchabi Masala. *'Highly recommend the food, service and ambience. All dishes reasonably priced. Azram is a first rate host, well liked by clients. Welcomes children and family groups.'* EP. Hours: 5-12am (open for lunches from Nov. to end Jan.).

CHIRAAG BALTI 

30 Chapel Hill, Morley, Leeds S 0113 253 5720

40-seater, taken over in February '97 by T Hussain. Fully licensed. *'Excellent Seekh Kebabs £1.60, Very tasty Balti Lamb Rogan Josh £4.95. Service good, staff very pleasant.'* L&CH. *'Consistently excellent spicy dishes.'* PW. Specials: Fish Pakora, Mushroom Pakora,Sweetcorn and Mushroom Biryani. Takeaway: 15% off. Delivery: £8, 3-mile radius. Hours: 6-12 (Fri. & Sat. to 1am); closed Tues.

DARBAR TOP 100

16 Kirkgate, Leeds Centre 0113 246 0381

A turbaned doorman welcomes you at *'a very ordinary street-level door, but upstairs the decor is a revelation.'*

©	Curry Club Discount	U	Unlicensed
V	Vegetarian	ANP	Alcohol not permitted
e-a-m-a-y-l	Eat as much as you like	BYO	Bring your own alcohol

HJC. It's exotic, with traditional Moghul paintings and an antique Hawali (palace) door, specially brought from India. *'Has a very impressive interior. Room is large and the decor promotes the Indian Palace feeling – spacious yet warm and elegant'.* AG *'Excellent restaurant, especially at lunchtime, self service buffet. Probably deserves* **TOP 100,** *although I am always slightly suspicious of Indians with grandiose decor.'* RC [You'd be suspicious of India then, Robert! -Ed]. *'Very good service and cooking. And, the decor is marvellous.'* SL. *'Overall this restaurant is superb and complements the Shabab very well. Indian food-lovers in Leeds are very fortunate to have two such restaurants.'* HJC. Special: Murgh Lahori, bone-off spring chicken, tangy spices, green coriander, cream, yoghurt, tomatoes and ginger. Daal Mash, white lentils cooked in butter with ginger, garlic and fried onion. Strawberry Lassi (large jug). Minimum charge: £16 eves. Lunch e-a-m-a-y-l £4.95. Hours: Mon.-Sat. 11.30-2.30/6-11.30 Sun. closed.

HANSA'S GUJARATI VEGETARIAN — V ©

72 North Street, Leeds — 0113 244 4408

Owned by Mr and Mrs Hansa Dabhi, this is a Gujarati (*see page 50*) vegetarian restaurant, staffed by women. *'I particularly enjoyed the crunchy, spicy flavour of the Shrikhand.'* DM. *'As a non-veg I went with an open mind. Food was fine but portions small.'* DB. *'Exquisite Lassi, portions small.'* DO'R. Hours: 12-2/6-11.

KASHMIR BYO 

162a Woodhouse Lane, Leeds N — 0113 245 3058

Unlicensed, 72-seater restaurant, managed by T Mahmood. Price check: Papadam 20p, CTM £4.60, Pullao Rice 95p. Hours: 12pm-3am.

POLASH — TOP 100 

103 Town Street, Stanningley, Leeds W 0113 256 0989

M Arif's huge 150-seater is popular, it seems. *'I had a family party at home and asked the Polash to cater for me. The resultant banquet was beyond praise.'* EF. *'Our daughter, 14, says that the Polash Chicken Korma is her favourite, even though she has tried others in many other Indian restaurants.'* BT. *'We were impressed. Food tasty. Service a little stretched at busy times.'* IEF-E. *'How much we enjoy our visits. Excellent food, courteous staff.'* MG. *'Always welcoming and courteous, high standard, always consistent, always start with Chicken Tikka followed by King Prawn Khass.'* JS. *'Combination of service and freshly cooked food, makes the Polash our favourite.'* MH-R. *'Very smart inside. Good mix of standard and unusual dishes – Chana Aloo Puri was superb. Friendly attentive service. Gold card scheme – £25 annual fee entitles you to 25% off all food including takeaways.'* M&SR. *'Excellent restaurant. Best starters we have tasted anywhere.'* MM. *'For several years we have been patrons of the Aagrah at Thornbury, but for nearly two years now changed to Polash. Standard of food and service is superb. Choice is tremendous, carefully prepared, garnished and served with a smile. Reasonably priced – half the cost of the Aagrah!'* MR&MRS DH. *'We tell all our friends of the Polash.'* MC. *'Spacious restaurant in dis-used Conservative Club. Tandoori Mixed Grill, an enormous plate full of Tandoori Chicken, Chicken and Lamb Tikka, Lamb Chops, Seekh Kebab, Liver and fresh salad with a Vegetable Curry (does anyone actually finish that lot?) Gold Card Scheme – £25 a year, member and up to five guests 20% discount (except on Saturday). Very popular facility.'* RW. *'Speciality curries are our firm favourites: Nagisi Kofti £7.95 (inc Mushroom Rice), Murgh Keema Aloo £7.25 (inc Lemon Rice) and Garlic Chicken Balti £8.20 (inc Pullao Rice) – truly excellent.'* DF. *'Proprietors are always on hand to oversee, spotless kitchen.'* pjs. *'Well presented, tasty, freshly prepared and served food. Meat is lean – important to us.'* DA. *'Good car park. Deceptively large restaurant, we had pre-booked. Seething on a Saturday night, much activity from waiters, slowish service. Vegetarian Platter, excellent value, very nicely presented and very tasty. Chilli Chicken Mushroom was not what I expected – chicken, grilled, Pullao Rice, Mushroom Curry, salad and mild Korma sauce – no room for anything else.'* T&MH. *'Spoke to manager, Mr Morid re usual Curry Club discount. He was unaware of it, so I showed him the Guide. He was very kind and courteous and gave me a discount to honour the agreement. Food, above average quality. Bit short on waiters, only two for full house.'* JL. Well done, John, for getting the discount, but the manager must be new or what, and you didn't follow the rules. See page 364. It almost cost this otherwise excellent restaurant its **TOP 100** rating. Menu Extracts: Smoked Chicken Raan £2.95; Prawn Pakora £2.95; Lamb Chops £2.80; Chicken Achar £7.95, served with Lemon Rice; Lamb Kaju £7.95, cashew nuts, served with Garlic Nan. So much praise – we'll keep the Polash in our **TOP 100.** Hours: 5.30-11.30 (Mon. & Sun. to 11).

RAJA'S NEW ENTRANT

186 Roundhay Road, Leeds 0113 274 0411

B.P Singh cooks Punjabi food here (see page 50) and it is well-liked in a city full of curryhouses. Hours: Weekdays: 11-2/5-10.30. Sat & Sun: 3.30-10.30.

SPICE OF OAKWOOD
NEW ENTRANT

633a Roundhay Road Leeds 0113 248 6660

'Quickly built up a loyal local following. Simply furnished, orange decor and spotlessly clean (even the toilet). Kebab and Tandoori brought to table sizzling and placed on fresh bed of salad by waiter. Main courses are presented in large korahi. Chicken Rogan Josh, made with fresh tomatoes £4.50; very creamy Chicken Tikka Masala £5.20; King Prawn Korai with large fresh prawns £7.90. Chef Amir also creates an excellent Fish Tikka Masala. Excellent restaurant.' RW.

TARIQ'S 

12-16 St Michaels Road, Headingley, Leeds 0113 275 1881

'Windies were playing England and it was stopped by rain. After waiting till early evening in hope, there was a stampede down to Tarriq's just round from the cricket ground. Got there first, luckily – they were queuing within minutes. Superb meal made up for a wet day.' IB. Owned and managed by Bobby Sharma, this Balti House seats 64. Special offer meal deal, Thursday and Sunday before 10pm. Dining in – free papadams and chutneys – nice touch. Price check: Papadam 20p, CTM £4.90, Pullao Rice £1.20. Lager £2 bottle, house wine £6.50. Delivery: £6, 3-mile radius. Hours: 5.30pm-2.30am (3am on Sat., 12.30am on Sun.). Two visits: Scores: 2/10 & 3/10 (Takeaway) DB. 'I recently had a great meal at Tariq's in Leeds Regards'. RG.

Pontefract

ROTI 

North Baileygate, Pontefract01977 703915

Arshad Mahmood's 110-seater (party room 40) is bright and airy with tented ceiling, beams, cream-with-green napkins, marble table tops, wicker furniture. Abdul Aziz's kitchen on view behind glass. Pakistani food. *'Excellent quality, bordering on the expensive.'* KH. Hours: 5-12.

VICEROY 

6 Front Street, Pontefract 01977 700007

First opened in 1990, taken over by Chef Akram Hussain Lohn in 1994. He cooks Pakistani food at his 60-seater, managed by Susan Ruckledge. Mushroom Pakora a speciality. Karai (including rice, chips or three chapatis).Takeaway: 30% discount. Delivery: £6 minimum. Hours: 5-1am.

Pudsey

AAGRAH TOP 100 AWARD WINNER 

483 Bradford Road, Pudsey01274 668818

Located midway between Bradford and Leeds, the second Aagrah is Head Office, as well as a 72-seater managed by Arshad Mahmood opened in 1986. Car parking for 25. Specials include: Achar, Hydrabady and Masala dishes. Takeaway: 10% discount. Hours: 6-11.30; Fri. & Sat. 6-12; Sun. 12.30-11.30.

Shipley

AAGRAH TOP 100 AWARD WINNER 

27 Westgate, Shipley01274 594660

Today there are seven Aagrahs, all in Yorkshire, and all **TOP 100**s in this guide. It was here in 1977, refurbished in 1999, that this 50-seater was opened by Mohammed Sabir. The notion to expand came from son Mohammed Aslam (then a London bus driver) assisted later by brother Zafar Iqbal, who now runs this one. It is notable for its Kashmiri-style decor with attractive block-print table linen and those fabulous hand-made, hand-painted colourful lacquered chairs with the cute tinkly bells, especially commissioned in Pakistan (£60 each). Gradually Aslam encouraged his extended family to join the enterprise as managers, staff and cooks. With increasing impetus the other branches have been brought on-stream, as stylish and up-market restaurants. We hear contentedly from many regulars who visit twice or more a week, and visitors from afar. Their average age is over 25 (no after-pub teenage louts here). Their average spend of £15 gives the chain a turnover of *c.*£2 million. The food is Pakistani, which self-taught cook Aslam has insisted that all family members also learn, training in both the kitchens and out front to NVQ level. This way the service and food in all the Aagrah restaurants is of equal standard. There is ample choice in the identical menus. Starters includeYahknee, spicy chicken soup, and Panir Pakora, Indian curd cheese fritter. Balti Liver, is a main-course dish, with garlic, ginger, chillies, tomatoes and coriander. There are many meat, chicken and fish dishes. Aslam's current *pièces de résistance* are Murgh Hydrabady, spring chicken, tangy spices, coriander, cream, yoghurt, tomatoes, ginger. Balti Bhindi Aloo Paneer, curd cheese, bhindi and potato, onions, ginger, garlic, coriander. Family Nan, Cheese and Onion Nan. Takeaway: rice and 3 chapattis free. Specials include: Achar, Hydrabady and Masala dishes. Takeaway: 10% discount. Hours: 6-12. Fri. & Sat. 6pm-1am. Branches: Garforth, Pudsey, Wakefield, W Yorks; Skipton Tadcaster, N Yorks; Doncaster, S Yorks.

Wakefield

AAGRAH TOP 100 

108 Barnsley Road, Sandal, Wakefield01974 242222

The seventh of seven Aagrahs, a 100-seater, opened in 1986. Parking for 40 cars. Like its sisters, it is justifiably very popular and good enough to be awarded a collective TOP 100 cachet. (See above entry for detailed comment.) The Aagrah is also able to offer accommodation – so don't drink and drive, just stay over at the Sandal Court Hotel. Specials include: Achar, Hydrabady and Masala dishes. Price check: Takeaway: 10% discount. Hours: 6-11.30; Fri. & Sat. 5.30-11.30; Sun. 6-11.

THE ISLES AND ISLANDS

When he failed to capture the British Isles, Napoleon dismissed us as a nation of shopkeepers. Were he around today, he might observe that we are now a nation of curry house keepers. Some isles, including Lundy, the Isles of Scilly, Uist, Mull, etc., have no curry houses but, for neatness, we group those that do together. For those who delight in collecting useless information, Lerwick, capital of the Shetland Isles, contains the nation's most northerly curry house (and still probably that of the whole globe). It is 600 miles from London and 800 miles from our most southerly curry house in St Helier, capital of Jersey.

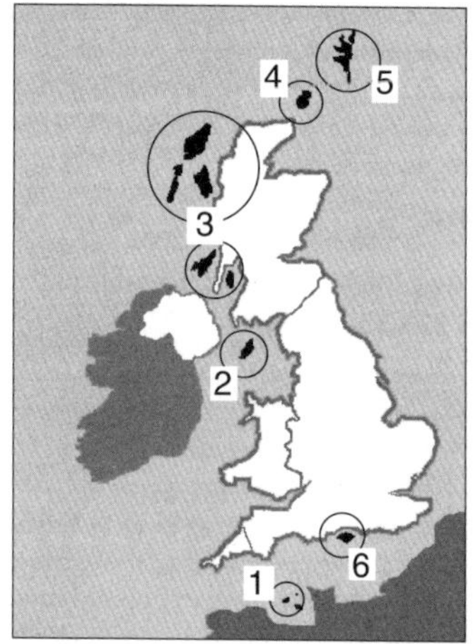

CHANNEL ISLANDS

1 on the map

ALDERNEY

NELLIE GRAYS INDIAN CUISINE

Victoria Street, Alderney 01481 823333

Established 1996, owned by Matin Miah (formerly the head chef of Jersey's Bombay Brasserie), and managed by Ashraf Makadur. Seats 50 in two dining rooms. Two parking spaces at rear of building. Jalfrezi most popular, chef's special Tarkari. Service: 10%. Hours: 6-11; Sun. 12-2.

Guernsey

L'Eree

TASTE OF INDIA

Sunset Cottage, St Peter, L'Eree 01481 264516

Owned and managed by Tony Fernandes, who is from Goa, since 1989. Pink stone wall design with maroom seating for 60 diners. Chef Paltu Bhattachajee holds court in the kitchen serving specialities such as Sardines on Puri £2.95, Tandoori Lobster and Bhuna – market price and subject to availability. Takeaway: 10% discount. Set lunch: £10.95 and £24.95 (for two). Pickle Tray a very expensive £1.50. Price check: Papadams 40p, CTM £8.95, Pullao Rice £2.50, Peshwari Nan £2.20, Lager £2.20 pint, House wine £9 bottle. Hours: 6-11pm; closed Mon. Branch: Taste of India, St Peter Port.

St Peter Port

TAJ MAHAL

North Esplanade, St Peter Port
01481 724008

Mujibul Hussain's 60-seater is located in the heart of St Peter Port opposite the main public car park. 'Beautifully decorated with tables in canopied booths. Charming and attentive staff. Interesting menu – imaginative main courses and unusual vegetable side-dishes (Uri Besi, mangetout and butter beans; Balar Aloo, mashed potatoes with garlic). Special main course vegetarian section including Baygoon (aubergine, spinach and chickpeas) which was sampled by non-veggies with some envy! Delicious Chicken Sholay arrived flamed in brandy. All food was fragrantly spicy with subtle differences between each dish.' CC. Hours: 12-2/6-11.30 (12am on Sat.).

TASTE OF INDIA

2, Mill Street, St Peter Port 01481 723730

Established in 1990. Seats 50. Owned and managed by Tony Fernandes. Decorated in maroon. Specials: Bamboo Shoot Masala – a dry curry. Takeaway: 10%. Hours: 6-11pm; closed Mon. Branch: Taste of India, L'Eree.

JERSEY

St Aubin

SHAPLA

Victoria Road, St Aubin 01534 746495

'Decor high standard with rich reds, golds and blues. Hasna Kebabs, lamb marinated in yoghurt, tandooried with onions, peppers and tomatoes, really tasty. Chicken Jalfrezi, aroma terrific. Simply perfect Lamb Rogan Gosht. Polite and helpful waiter.' MB. Hours: 12-2/6-12am.

St Brelade

BENGAL BRASSERIE

11 La Pulente, St Brelade 01534 490279

Formerly Taj Mahal. *'Menu has some very interesting and inventive dishes, including Fish Jalfrazi, salmon and even lobster curries. Favourite dish is the Chef's Balti – like no other – chicken, lamb, prawns, egg, kidney beans, mange tout, you name it. Portions more than adequate. Service best on the island, staff very friendly. Al fresco in the summer. Only 30 yards from St Ouens beach. Best place to see the sunset.'* GL. Hours: 12-2/6-11.30.

St Helier

NEW RAJ

8 Burlington Parade, St Saviours Road, St Helier 01534 874131

Owned and managed by Kass Malik since 1984. Decorated with tented ceiling. Seats 60 in two dining rooms. *'Onion Bhaji was good, Chicken Chat not so good, being insipid and needing some salt. Chicken Dhansak was well spiced, my wife's CTM was rated the best she has had for some time..'* MW. Beef currys on the menu from Korma to Pal. Takeaway: 7-10% discount. Hours: 12-2/6-12.

SHEZAN

53 Kensington Pl, St Helier 01534 22960

A small restaurant seating 40. *'Meal very good. A bit expensive, but worth it.'* SC. *'Owner, Shani Gill, is always the gentleman. His endeavours to satisfy all his customers have made him many friends.'* GDM.

TAJ MAHAL CENTRAL

La Motte Street, St Helier 01534 20147

'Classy and luxurious restaurant. You are surrounded by running water and tropical fish. Had best ever Tarka Dal.' TM.

ISLE OF MAN

2 on the map

Douglas

SAAGAR TANDOORI ©

1 South View, Queens Promenade, Douglas 01624 674939

Mr and Mrs Chowdhury and Mr Jaigirdar's 60-seater is *'the best I've been to.'* RR. *'One time we tried the special Kachee Biriani – 12 hours' notice is required to prepare it. It's partially cooked Basmati rice layered over meat marinated in spices, yoghurt and herbs then cooked in the oven – perfumed with saffron. £25 for two. Delicious. Next time we brought friends and tried Kurzi Lamb – 24 hours' notice is required for this extravaganza (£48 for four). We've yet to try £70 whole leg of lamb marinated in fresh ground spices with lamb mince meat cooked in the oven. Mixed starters, side dishes, rice and breads for four are also included.'* AN. Hours: 12-2/6-12am.

Ramsey

SPICE OF LIFE

8 Peel Street, Ramsey 01624 816534

We enjoyed the food, and would have done had it been in Manchester' GB. *'Bizarre note on the door, We do not serve drunks.'* DMcC.

SCOTTISH WESTERN ISLES

3 on the map

Isle of Bute

INDIAN PAVILION

7 Argyle Street, Rothesay, Isle of Bute 01700 504988

Est. 1993 by Bobby Mahey, 30-seater. Dave Mahey cooks north and south Indian and Goan food. Delivery charge 95p. Hours: 5pm-12.30am.

Isle of Lewis

STORNOWAY BALTI HOUSE

24 South Beech, Stornoway 01851 706116

First opened in 1991, taken over in 1996 by Abarok Ali. Previously called Ali's Takeaway. Seats 46. Specials include: Chicken Tikka Balti £7.50, Chicken Korma £5.95. Price check: Papadam 60p, CTM £6.95, Pullao Rice £1.90, Peshwari Nan £2.10, Lager £2 pint. Takeaway: 10% discount. Hours: 12-2/5-11.30;. Sat. & Sun. 5-11.30.

Isle of Skye

SPICE HUT INDIAN (NAME CHANGE)

Bayfield Road, Portree 01478 612681

Formerly the Ghandi. *'Difficult to find – at the rear of the big car and coach park near the Tourist Information Centre. A bizarre experience. We turned up at 1pm to find "Closed" on the door. However, we tried the door anyway and it opened. Two bored looking Asian teenagers were folding napkins, and one lethargically showed us to a table in the otherwise totally deserted restaurant. He took our order with his now customary lack of charm, and we prepared for the worst. However, the food arrived very promptly and was actually delicious. Vegetable Rowghon was fragrant and packed with fresh tomatoes. Garlic Chicken Tikka was equally good. It is an enormous shame that a clearly excellent chef is having his hard work marred by a front of house crew displaying such shameless amateurism.'* CC. *'Good.'* G&MP.

ORKNEY ISLANDS

4 on the map

Kirkwall

MUMTAZ

7 Bridge Street, Kirkwall 01856 873537

'Comfortable and modern restaurant. All food very tasty. Service good and efficient.' PAWW. Hours: 12-12am.

SHETLAND ISLANDS

5 on the map

Lerwick

RABA INDIAN

26 Commercial Rd, Lerwick 01595 695554

'Warm decor. Well-cooked Indian cuisine at reasonable prices. Samosas, Bhajia and Chicken Tikka Masala were all delicious.' AIE. Hours: 12-2/4.30pm-12am. Sunday buffet: 1pm -11pm. Adults £9.50/Kids £6 (à la carte also available).

ISLE OF WIGHT

6 on the map

Cowes

COWES TANDOORI 

40 High Street, Cowes 01983 296710

At Ashid Ali's 64-seater. DB *'loves the Podina Gusht and Garlic Chicken'* and L&CH found *'Tasty Sheek Kebabs'.* Hours: 12-2/6-12am.

Newport

NABAB PALACE 

84 Upper Street, James Street, Newport 01983 523276

'Jila Miah's 54-seater serves good, competent curries and accompaniments at reasonable island prices, eased by his offer to give a 10% discount to CC members. Well deserved place in Good Curry Guide. Nizami Chicken delicious.' L&CH. *'Pleasantly surprised. Decor clean and comfortable, service efficient. Starters: King Prawn – fresh and well cooked. Chana Puri – well spiced. No vegetarian main courses but prepared a Vegetable Dhansak without a problem and it was good. Tarka Dal very good. Garlic Nan – plenty of fresh garlic. Well worth the money. £30 for two.'* AG. Hours: 12-2pm/6pm-12am.

©	Curry Club Discount	U	Unlicensed
V	Vegetarian	ANP	Alcohol not permitted
e-a-m-a-y-l	Eat as much as you like	BYO	Bring your own alcohol

NORTHERN IRELAND

Population: 1,600,000

Curry still hasn't grabbed this part of the world in the way it has on the 'mainland'. We have just 25 establishments on our database all over the province. Compare this with Bradford W Yorks and you'll get the picture. There are fewer curry establishments per head of the population than in any other place in Britain (the ratio is 1:64000). However, the number of curry restaurants has more than doubled in the province in 3 years. That's a good statistic for the media. We'd dearly love more reports, please.

Belfast

ARCHANA

53 Dublin Road, Belfast 028 9032 3713

'Menu very comfortable. Vindaloo very hot, excellent. Balti Chicken Chilli, also excellent. Decor and comfort good. Value for money.' JP.

ASHOKA 

363 Lisburn Road, Belfast 028 9066 0362

Ravi and Ms Sonal Chawda's 130-seater is an elegant, pillared dining room (apparently the only Indian restaurant in Northern Ireland with an Indian chef – Ishtiaque Khan). Frequented by politicians and celebrities, including Ian Paisley, David Trimble, members of U2 and Liam Neeson. Specials: Lobster dishes. Baltis. Takeaway: 20% off. Hours: 5.30-11.30.

GHANDI

701c Lisburn Road, Belfast 028 9066 6833

'The food took a fairly long time to arrive, but this proved to be more of a case of care being taken with every dish than sloppy service. One immediately noticeable feature of the entire meal was the restrained use of ghee for which the chef is be commended. Each dish was fresh and light with its own distinctive taste well brought out. The top of my list of Belfast curry houses.' DMcD.

JHARNA

133 Lisburn Road, Belfast 028 9038 1299

Large a/c 110-seater. *'We found the Tandoori Crayfish superb and different £11.95.'* CD. Hours: 12-2/5.30-11.30. Branch: Tamarind, Carrickfergus; Bithika Takeaway, Belfast .

MOGHUL

62 Botanic Avenue, Belfast 028 9032 6677

Established 1984 and taken over in 1998 by H Sirpal. Formerly Maharaja. Seats 80 diners. Specials: Tikka Special £7.95 – marinated chicken, mild sauce with mangoes and banana. Pakora Curry £5.95 – fairly hot, with yoghurt, gramflour and Punjabi spices. Paneer Makhani £6.95 – chef's own paneer, mild buttery sauce. Kebabs (delivery only): Donner, Sheesh, Chicken Tikka etc available from £3 and Chicken Burger with salad . Delivery: £1 charge. Hours: 12-2/5-12.

SCOTLAND

In 1965, much to the Scots' disgust, the age-old mainland Scottish shires and counties were amalgamated into nine large counties (or regions). In 1997 new changes resulted in only three staying totally unchanged (D&G, Fife and Highland). Two others have the same boundaries but new names: Borders became Scottish Borders, while Central once again became Stirling. Tayside is no more, being split into two (Angus and Perth & Kinross). Part of Grampian has been retained, with its western part returning to Moray. Northern Strathclyde has become Argyll & Bute, while the rest of Strathclyde, and the whole of Lothian have been split into sixteen Unitary Authorities, administering the larger cities and surrounds. For the time being, and until Scotland itself takes all these changes for granted, we retain in this Guide, the nine former counties (listing their ancient shires and/or new names within them, as relevant). Scotland's population of just over 5 million (less than that of central London) occupies a land mass nearly half that of England, though most of her curry houses are in and around the large cities. We'd adore a huge postbag of Scottish reports for our next Guide please.

BORDERS

Now called Scottish Borders –

(Includes Peebles and Roxburgh)

Area: Southeast Scotland
Population: 107,000
Adjacent Counties:
D & G, Lothian, Northumberland, Strathclyde

Galashiels

SWAGAT

36 Market Street, Galashiels 01896 750100

'Well lit, comfortable little place. Service is good. Very tasty Jalfry.' GMcG. Helpful and polite waiter on telephone. Hours: 12-2/5-11.

Hawick

SHUGONDA BALTI HOUSE

4 Station Building, Dove Mount Place01450 373313

BM Talukder's 50-seater Bangladeshi curry house has 10 car parking spaces. Specials: Harsa Mossalla Chi, Masooru Dall Chi, Bengal Begun Mushroom Jal Hours: 12-2/6-11.30.

CENTRAL

Now called Stirling

i.e the former Stirlingshire

Area:
Mid Scotland
Population: 276,000
Adjacent Counties:
Lothian, Strathclyde, Tayside

Drymen

DRYMEN TANDOORI ©

5-7 Stirling Road, Drymen 01360 660099

Established in 1994 by Sohail Wahid. Seats 65. Car parking for 14 cars. Specials: Samosas, filling choice of vegetable, mince, cheese and potato. South Indian Garlic Chilli, fresh garlic, chilli sauce with coriander and a touch of crispy red chilli. Pizzas also available. *'Does quite a tasty little number of average curries, a tad on the expensive side and carry out staff at least are a little unfriendly and disinterested.'* T&KM. Takeaway: 10% discount. Delivery: £10 minimum, 5-mile radius. Hours: 12pm-12am.

DUMFRIES & GALLOWAY

Area: Southwest Scotland
Population: 148,000
Adjacent Counties:
Borders, Cumbria, Strathclyde

Dumfries

JEWEL IN THE CROWN ©

48-50 St Michael Street, Dumfries
01387 264183

Manager A Muhit. *'Attentive staff. Bombay Mix on the table as we perused menu. Pops & pics immediately ready. Good starters – Vegetable Pakora and Mix Kebab. Chicken Dhansak and Chicken Methi reasonable. Good value.'* AY. 'This is an excellent restaurant which has recently been extended due to demand. Specialise particularly in Tandoori, but menu wide ranging and quality of food and service is maintained at a high level. Clean restaurant as are the toilets. Adequate parking.' Anon. Hours: 12-2.30/6-11.

FIFE

Area: East Scotland
Population: 351,000
Adjacent Counties:
Lothian, Tayside

Glenrothes

NURJAHAN ©

Coslane, Woodside Road, Glenrothes
01592 630649

Manirul Islam's 110-seater. Decorated in pinks to a very high standard. Roomy carver-chairs at all the tables. Striking menu with photographs of spices, dishes of curry and breads. *'Truly magnificent meal. Decor tastefully outstanding and spotless. More than generous quantities. The best quality we have ever tasted. A superior restaurant in every aspect.'* MAJF. Waiters very polite and helpful. Hours: 12-2/5-11. (Fri. & Sat. to 12am); Sun. 4-11.

St Andrews

NEW BALAKA BANGLADESHI

TOP 100 PREVIOUS AWARD WINNER

3 Alexander Place, Market Street, St Andrews
01334 474825

Even before you enter Abdur Rouf's up-market and sophisticated 52-seater, note the frontage floral display. He has won awards for it. The unique feature is the huge kitchen garden at the rear, in which Mr Rouf grows all his own herbs and many vegetables. More foliage inside with palms dividing tables and hand stitched Bangladeshi tapestries on the walls. Unusual dishes on the menu include Mas Bangla – salmon marinated in lime, turmeric and chilli, fried in mustard oil, garlic, onion, tomato and aubergine. I had the privilege of being trained to cook this dish by chef Abdul Monem which I reproduced at a lecture at St Andrews University for the Chemical Soc and all of Mr Rouf's friends. I hope they enjoyed it as much as I did. We then moved on to the restaurant for a fabulous meal. Amazingly the restaurant has no tandoor, which is detectable in the flavours of the breads and tikkas. But that aside, Mr Rouf's team continues to provide outstanding food in superb surroundings. We have lots of contented customer reports. All show a friendly, caring patron, and here's proof: *'Is still excellent.'* M. *'We dined here with a large party of friends from the Netherlands and around the world. The evening was a tremendous success – wonderful food and service.'* TGM. *'Nice decor, good service. Good portion of wonderful Afghani Gosht. Over– priced Pickle Tray £2.20.'* ANON. *'Not bad curries.'* T&KM. It seems to me it's always busy, and if you are really lucky you might just see Sean Connery on the nearby golf course. Please book your table. *'Nice decor, good service. Good portion of wonderful Afghani Gosht. Over-priced Pickle Tray £2.20.'* ANON. *'Not bad curries.'* T&KM.. www.balaka.co.uk info@balaka.co.uk Delivery: 5 miles, £2 minimum Hours: Sun.-Thurs. 5pm-1am; Fri. & Sat. 12am-1am. Open Christmas Day. Comfortably in our **TOP 100**.

GRAMPIAN (& MORAY)

Inc: Aberdeenshire, Banff, Kincardine and Morayshire

Area:
North Scotland
Population: 537,000
Adjacent Counties:
Highland, Tayside

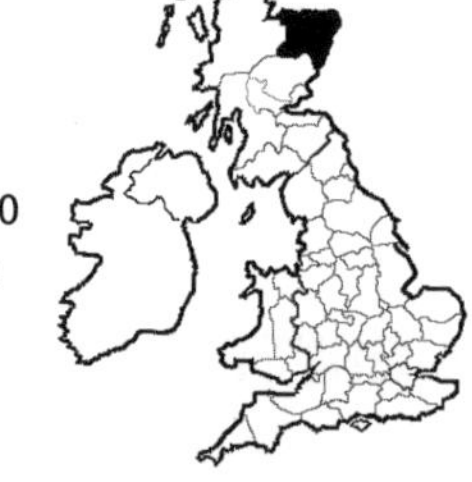

Aberdeen

KURY NEW ENTRANT

22King Street Aberdeen 01224 645015

Formerly Manzil. 'Booked for 8pm on Saturday night. Was asked "buffet or a la carte," asked for buffet – £15.95 each. On arrival, found very dangerous 10" step...' that is incredibly dangerous, how can the elderly and small children managed that? '...very smart, modern, new, all steel, chrome and glass. Split into two rooms, one a la carte (totally full), one buffet (half full)...' sounds sensible. 'Food fair. Starters, dry, Lamb Madras very good, melt in the mouth, but ran out and not refilled. Only Plain Nan and Brown Rice offered. Expensive.' nkc. Menu Extracts: Brie or Haggis Pakoras £2.95; Prawn Pardesi £6.95, spinach, shallow fried onions, mushrooms simmered in rich ginger, garlic, tarka base; Chicken Tikka Chasni £6.95, light, smooth, slightly sweet and sour creamy sauce; Lamb Himalayan Hot Pot £6.95, fresh garlic, ginger, green chillies, vegetables and lemon juice; Vegetable Paratha £1.95. Delivery: £12 minimum, 3 miles. Hours: 5-11, Friday and Saturday to 11.30. Sunday Brunch: 4- 7.

Elgin

QISMAT ©

202-204 High Street, Elgin 01343 541461

Established in 1987 by Liaquat Ali. Seats 100 diners in a modern and brightly decorated restaurant with wooden polished floor, palms, coloured seat pads and air-conditioning. Specials: Chicken Tikka Achari £8.40 – cooked with tangy pickle, fresh green chillies and coriander. Chicken Rice £2.60. Garlic and Green Chilli Nan £2.20. 'Not very impressed by the service. Waiters seemed very uninterested in the customers, they had mastered the art of throwing the meals onto the table whilst staring at the ceiling. On the plus side there was lots of chicken in the Dhansak and the service was the quickest I have ever had.' IW. Takeaway: 10% discount. Delivery: £10 minimum, within Elgin only. Hours: 12-2pm/5-11.30pm; Sun. evening only. Branch: Qismat, 1b Millburn Road, Inverness.

Ellon

NOSHEEN 

5 Bridge Street, Ellon 01358 724309

Established in 1989. Owned by Khalid Ahmed. Restaurant decorated rather lavishly in crimson ceiling and chairs, cream walls, green tablecloths and brass light fittings. Seats 92. Banquet A: £14.50 – Papadams and Spiced Onion, Pakora, Bhoona or Korma, Patia, Pullao Rice and Nan – for two. Takeaway: 10% discount. Delivery: £12 minimum in Ellon, £18 minimum outside Ellon. Hours: 5-11.30. (Sat. to 12am).

Inverurie

BANANA TANDOORI 

56 Market Place, Inverurie01467 624860

Formerly Alo Chaya. Remains a well-established restaurant, owned since it was opened in 1987 by Syed Mujibul Hoque. 'Waiters efficient and friendly. Buffet night is worth a visit.' AMCW. Open 12-2.30/5.30-11.30.

©	Curry Club Discount	U	Unlicensed
V	Vegetarian	ANP	Alcohol not permitted
e-a-m-a-y-l	Eat as much as you like	BYO	Bring your own alcohol

HIGHLAND

Inc: Caithness, Inverness, Nairn, Ross & Cromarty and Sutherland

Area: North Scotland
Population: 211,000
Adjacent Counties: Grampian, Strathclyde, Tayside

Inverness

QISMET TANDOORI ©

1b, Millburn Road, Inverness01463 716020

Established in 1998 by Liaquat Ali; your host is pictured on the takeaway menu. Restaurant seats 100 and is brightly decorated, polished wooden floor and chairs, white tablecloths, palm trees, spot lighting. Specials: Chicken Tikka Sonali £8.75 – with finely chopped ginger, green chillies and onion, medium hot. Mazedar £8.40 – lamb tikka with Worcestershire sauce, lemon juice, cream and cheese. Takeaway: 10% discount. Hours: 12-2/5-11.30.

Nairn

AL RAJ ©

25 Harbour Street, Nairn01667 455370

Mobarok Ali's 70-seater has built up a good reputation with helpful waiters. Even Nick Nairn himself has been seen here. Hours: 12-2/5-11.30p.

LOTHIAN

Area: Mid Eastern Scotland
Population: 774,000
Adjacent Counties: Borders, Central, Fife, Strathclyde

The region of Lothian has been disbanded, the larger cities and surrounds split into a number of Unitary Authorities. For the time being, we are sticking to the old Lothian in this Guide. *Our prolific Edinburgh reporter, Mr NK Campbell, tells us "there are about a dozen new Indo/Pak restaurants that have opened in the last year or so in Edinburgh. Reports indicate lots of empty tables, despite many promotions in the newspapers. He asks, are there too many new openings?" What are your views? Are there too many curry houses in the whole UK?*

ST JOHNS CURRY CLUB NEW ENTRANT

100 St Johns Rd Corstorphine 0800 587 2092

With every main dish, the restaurant has suggested a side dish, quick a novel idea for those you can never make up their mind! Menu Extracts: Mach Puree £2.95, sardines cooked with fresh herbs and spices wrapped in puffed fried pancake (puree), served with salad. Pune Palak Chicken £5.95, chicken with spinach, whole green herbs and spices, garnished with grated garlic and ginger, suggested side dish, Bombay Potato £2.65. Delivery service: 0800 587 2092.Buffet Lunch: 3 courses, Monday to Friday. Hours: 12-2/5- 11.30.

Edinburgh

(Includes Blackhall, Dalry, Greenhill, Roseburn, Stockbridge and Viewforth
(Leith is entered separately)

ADBULS TAKEAWAY NEW ENTRANT

22 Comiston Road Morningside Edinburgh 0131 447 4999

asas *'Very good as usual - one of the top 5 in Edinburgh. Busy night - delivery took 50 minutes, which was OK. Usual melt in the mouth Lamb Rogan Josh £4.95, very good marinated meat. Chicken Korma £5.95 and Chicken Tikka £5.25,wonderful.'* NKC. Other menu delights include: Green Bengal Chicken £4.95 - tender pieces of chicken in a spicy sauce cooked with green peppers, fresh coriander, garnished with spring onions and fresh ginger. Theeval Kootoo £3.80 - potato and peas in a sour and spicy sauce with coconut. Credit cards accepted. Hours: 5-11.

CITY SPICE NEW ENTRANT

88 Haymarket Tce Edinburgh 0131 476 1593

asas *'Very good first impressions, good smiley welcome, very clean. Plain white tablecloths and napkins. Expensive modern chairs - 48 covers. Dishes of Chutney on the tables. Huge menu. Fair quantities but tiny, thin Naans with no stuffing of Peshwari or Keema. Jalfrezi contained strips of stir-fried lamb, not melt in the mouth and the sauce was very very fiery, double or treble of a Vindaloo, really stupid. Chicken dishes OK. Good service. No Cobra but very good, nutty draught Lal Toofan @ £3 pint!!'* NKC. Some new interesting names for some regular dishes: Bengal Begoonnie £2.35, lightly seasoned baby aubergine, dipped into batter, then fried in oil. Jessorie Sabzi Singara £2.35, new potatoes, cauliflower, green peas and roasted peanuts, stewed then covered with flour pasties and deep-fried. Nahars Lamb Pista Korma £5.95, steam cooked lamb with sweet yoghurt, pistachio, nutmeg, mace, cream, cardamom and saffron. Decorated with butter fried onion, broken pistachio and gold sultanas. Hours: 12 -2/5.30-11.30.

CLAY OVEN NEW ENTRANT

88 Morningside Road 0131 447 9724

'Just back from holidays. Trumps again. Delivery for Mrs C and mother in law, in middle of call added Lamb Madras £3.95 for myself, not easy to get a good one in Edinburgh, this one came out 110%, as I expect from the best in Edinburgh. Usual huge, hot portions. I ate all mine, the others froze half for another day!' NKC. 'Credit card order for delivery. Big helpings, melt in the mouth, superb, not expensive. For a change ordered Lamb Biryani £5.95, excellent.' NKC. 'As before, the BEST. We all had done a 120 hour week and wanted a good, reliable takeaway with big portions at a reasonable cost, too tired to try a new (iffy?) place. Brilliant, huge as before. I took the Garlic Chicken £4.95 for a change and found it very good.' NKC. Normanl likes this place very much,. Menu extracts: Panir Cutlet £1.55, shallow fried, served with mint sauce. Chicken Puri £2.95, subtle sauce, fresh coriander, served with puffed fried bread and green salad. Aloo Gosht £4.95, tender lamb, potato cubes, green chilli. Delivery: 5 miles, £10 minimum. Hours: 12-2/5- 12.

FAR PAVILION TOP 100 

1-12 Craigleith Road, Stockbridge, Edinburgh W0131 332 3362

Est. 1987, this 85-seater in two rooms is 'no ordinary curry house. Owners Wasim and Aasim Chaudhry brought in Glasgow-based designers, Platform 9, to revamp the bar area of his Far Pavilions, to coincide with a new permanent exhibition called 'Art India'. The 125 seat restaurant has new menus from Chef Abdul Aziz and an award-winning wine list. *The Scotsman's* Gillian Glover says *'the walls bore dimpled panels of buttoned velvet. Even the staff were upholstered.'* The Chaudhrys say'. Remains in our TOP 100. The CC discount eases the bill as does the e-a-m-a-y-l Tuesday 6.30-10, £11.95 and lunchtime buffet. Takeaway: 10% off. Hours: 12-2 (weekdays)/5.30-12am; closed Sun. except December.

KEBAB MAHAL

7 Nicholson Sq Edinburgh 0131 667 5214

'Very good place, probably the 2nd oldest in Edinburgh. Have eaten in and had takeaway.' NKC. *'Recommended. Not upmarket or designer, but the food is extremely good and consistent and also quite cheap.'* DR DD. Menu Extracts: Fish Pakora £2.25; Chana Chat £1.75; Lamb Korma £4.35; Tinda Curry £2.65. Hours: 12-12, Friday and Saturday to 2 in the morning!

KHUKURI NEW ENTRANT

W Maitland St Edinburgh 0131 228 2085

Menu extracts: Bhenda Momo £2.95, steamed spicy minced lamb, Bara £2.75, thick lentil pancake, garlic, ginger, spices, both served with Nepali dip. Trisuli Poleko Machha £3.95, marinated baby fish, cooked in tandoor, served with green salad. Kukhura Hariyali £7.00, spicy yoghurt sauce, mint, coriander, green chillies. Solukhumbu Bhenda £7.25, from East Nepal, long slices of lamb stuffed with mint, in spicy sauce of onions, garlic, ginger, tomato. Aloo Tama Bodi £4.25, potato, bamboo shoots, black eyes beans. Hours: 12-2, Sunday closed and 5.30-1.30, Fri/Sat to 12, Sunday to 11.

KHUSHI'S BYO

16 Drummond Street, Central Edinburgh
0131 556 8996

Established 1947. *'Good and as busy as ever.'* NKC. *'Nice short menu, good helpings, very good meat, perfectly marinated. Fair service, nice Italian waiter. Clean, light-painted decor, very clean toilets. Good comfort on padded benches and formica tables. Excellent big starters. No alcohol, but most people brought big jugs (2-3 pints) of beer from the pub next door. Madras was now a Vindaloo; Bhuna and Korma could have been Madras.'* NC. Hours: 12-3/5-9. (Friday and Saturday 9.30) Closed Sundays except during Festival. Branch: Khushi's of West Lothian, Mid Calder.

LASANI NEW ENTRANT

44 South Clerk St Edinburgh 0131 667 0239

Formerly Curry Palace. 'Chef and owner of Chilli Connection at 47, South Clerk Street who have moved across the road to 44. They were good at 47, should be good at 44. Plans to extend the seating area.' nkc. Also serves kebabs, burgers and pizzas - something for everyone! Set Meal for One: Popadom, spiced onions, Sabzi Pakora, Lasani Classic Curry with Pullao Rice or Nan at £5.95 is good value. Delivery: £10 minimum. Hours: 5 to 1, Friday and Saturday to

LANCERS BRASSERIE TOP 100

5 Hamilton Pl, Edinburgh 0131 332 3444

70-seater opened in 1985 by Wali Udin JP, managed by Alok Saha, head chef Badrul Hussain. Beautifully decorated, stylish restaurant for business and special occasions. Pink suede on the walls, tiled floor, highly polished tables. *'Went for lunch. Very attractive decor. Papadoms were sadly not accompanied by pickles – so annoying that. I tried Sabzi Kofta Massallam, mixed vegetable balls in a mild, cream sauce. Tasty enough, but not something I'd have again too soon. Worth visiting.'* RL. *'Lovely food with courteous service.'* T&KM. Downstairs is a private dining room for 12 diners. Chippendale-style furniture, banquet-style Raj prints decorate the walls. A small but selective menu. Takeaway: 20% off. Delivery: £15, 4 miles. Hours: 12-2.30/5-11.30.

MYA NEW ENTRANT

9 Commercial Quay 92 Commercial Street
0131 553 4000

Formerly Saagar. Thai and Indian restaurant. Business Lunch £6.75 - two courses or £7.75 - three courses. Menu extracts: Thai Mixed Starters (min 2), mixed seafood in filo pastry, prawn wonton, hoisin duck, spring rolls, and seafood wrapped in rice flour skin. Seabass, a crispy pan fried fish, cooked with ginger, spring onions and oyster sauce; Roast Duck, stir-fried in a spicy and sweet sauce flavoured with honey and mustard. Hours: 12-2/6-10.45. Closed Monday.

PALKHI NEW ENTRANT

9 Brandon Terrace, Canonmills, Edinburgh

Formerly The Curry Club and no connection to us. *'Present owners have spent quite a bit of money, new light fittings, brass door furniture, chandeliers– all very nice and real heavy linen table cloths and napkins, new cutlery and crockery. Good to average quantities & service. , average comfort - was cold, no central heating just small electric heaters. Main courses, very good, came hot in steel, copper bottomed pot and were placed on hot dish warmers, hot plates delivered and two very good hot Nans, straight from the oven.'* NKC. Delivery: £10 min. Hours: 12-2.30/5-11.30.

SHAMIANA
TOP 100 PREVIOUS AWARD WINNER

14 Brougham St, Edinburgh 0131 228 2265

First opened in 1977, taken over in 1992 by co-owner brothers Nadim (manager) and Mohammed (head chef) Butt. Seats 37. Specialising in Pakistani Kashmiri cuisine. *'I have been a regular customer of your excellent restaurant for around seven years and have been consistently impressed by the quality of your food. I also appreciate the professional manner in which your restaurant is run, and that last orders are taken at 10pm, thus restricting clientele to genuine curry enthusiasts.'* TN. *'The food at Shamiana is excellent and the standard during the last ten years has been first class'* A& AM. *'Another excellent meal. My business colleagues look forward to further frequent visits now that our office headquarters are located around the corner'* TAS. *'Very good menu, set meal £12.95 a head. Strangely small quantities but excellent, top notch, melt in the mouth lamb. Very good Keema and*

Peshwari Nans. All food hot to the table.' NKC. *'We hadn't booked, it was midweek, it was packed, we got the penultimate table. Popadoms crispy, good chutney tray, but naughty, naughty – don't put tomato ketchup in the cachumber ever again! Samosa, was shaped like a spring roll, but tasted very good. Main course portions good. Pat ordered his beloved Methi Chaman Gosht, with spinach, fenugreek, fresh oriental herbs and hot spices – £4.95, and pronounced it authentic and delicious. I had the Pakistani equivalent of CTM – Kashmiri Chasni Tikka, spicy, and equally good. Rice and breads enormous.'* DBAC. Great to see Kulfi Pista, Gulab Jaman and Garjar Halwa on the dessert menu. Hours: 6-10.

SINGAPORA ©

69 North Castle Street, Central Edinburgh0131 538 7878

Malaysian-Singaporean 65-seater owned and managed by chef C Pang. Decor is *'dominant decorative wood and high ceiling reminiscent of colonial-style romance, the waitresses in national dress.'* AG. Satay: Chicken, Beef, King Prawn or Tofu, marinated, skewered and chargrilled, served with a delicious peanut sauce (five sticks). The Malay Kari – chicken, beef, or vegetables in a coconut base, and Redang Beef, the national dish curry. Takeaway: 10% off. Delivery. Hours: 12-2.30/6-10.30. Sun. closed winter.

SURUCHI 

14a Nicolson Street, Central Edinburgh 0131 556 6583

Unique at Herman Rodrigues' 70-seater is his careful selection of his own beautiful photographs of India which hang on the walls. Suruchi means, in most Indian languages, good taste, an apt name when considering the decor has been imported from India, and is clean and smart. Jaipur blue/turquoise tiles adorn the walls. Table linen is vegetable-dyed pink and tableware is beaten coppered brass. It serves real home-style Indian food. Well-situated for a pre-theatre (which is opposite) curry dinner. Regional Indian food festivals held monthly. *'Very tasty, I can highly recommend it.'* SK. Menu Extracts: Dalvada £2.50, crispy lentil and curry leaf fritter, Simla Chaat £3, chickpeas, potatoes, cucumber, coriander and banansa topped with tangy sauces; Nirvana £6, chicken, lemon grass, mustard seed, curry leaf, lemon and creamed coconut; Venison Maharaja £9.95, cubes of Scottish vension marinated with spices and baked in tandoor; Neeps and Tatties £3, ginger, cummin; Coriander Paratha £2.50. One of our correspondents has sent a menu, 'the translation of it's Indian dishes into Scots Language is hilarious, I can translate if you have trouble?' Lets see how we go: Chana Masala £7.50, *a rare trait fur yer taste buds. Sappie chick peas cookit wi spices in a rich tomatay an ingan sauce,* Tandoori Gobi £7.50, *moothfaes o caller cauliflooer, steepit in a tandoor sauce o ginger, garlic, yoghurt an spices,* Dakshni Murgh (medium) £8.75, *a curry wi teeth. Chucken cookit wi black pepper an aniseed in a reamy coconut base,* Aloo Palak £3.95, *tatties tossed wi spinach;* Vegetable Pullao £3, *rice steered wi s mister-maxter o vegetables;* Paneer Nan £2.95, *stappit (filled) wi caller (fresh) cheese.* Many thanks Stewart for the menu. Food festivals held regularly ie: Goan. Menu Extracts: Mussels, shallow fried with onions, ginger, vinegar, chillies; Mince Cutlets, mince, potato cutlets with fresh coriander; Aloo Tikki, potato dumplings, cashew nuts, coconut, spices; Chicken Shakuti, nutmeg, black pepper, coconut, spices; Lamb Chops, marinated with vinegar, chilli, black pepper, baked in tandoor; Smoked Aubergines, smooth curry, mashed aubergines, fennel seeds, two course £9.95. Takeaway: 33% discount. Hours: 5.30-10.30.

TIPPOO SAHIB 

129a Rose St, Edinburgh 0131 226 2862

A Pakistani restaurant opened in 1982 as the Shanaz by the Parvez family. In 1996 Anjam Parvez renamed the 60-seater. Tippoo Sultan ruled south India in the late 17th century. His battle collaborations with the French caused the British severe problems, but left Tippoo's name in legend. Tippoo's Tiger, his famous favourite mechanical 'toy', is now housed in the V&A Museum. His portrait by Sir David Wilkie is in the Scottish National Gallery. It was Edinburgh's Wild Macrea's regiment who defeated Tippoo. The colourful murals at the restaurant depict the story. *'Chicken Mancharry, tandoor-cooked, with freshly grated chilli, garlic and ginger, Chicken Nentara, cooked with onions and methi, and Massalidar Gosht, meat cooked with pickles, and*

Karella Gosht meat with bitter gourd. 'First class quality food, staff and atmosphere. Reasonable prices.' RC. Hours: 12-2/5-12am; Sat. 12-11.30; Sun. 5-11.30.

VERANDAH TOP 100 

17 Dalry Rd, Edinburgh 0131 337 5828

44-seater opened in 1981 by Wali Tasar Uddin, MBE, JP, and his nephew, Foysol Choudhury, who describes it as 'reassuringly low-key' serving northern Indian and Bangladeshi cuisine. It's a pretty, relaxing restaurant with cane chairs and bamboo-slatted wall blinds, a clever and effective illusion. We have had an overwhelming response from Verandah patrons, extolling the virtues of this long– established restaurant: Here are some: *'Perfect'* AM. *'Lovely food, esp murgh–e– ada'.* SM. *'Good beer, good curries, awesome curry'* CDN. *'Never let me down, first class food and service. Chicken Dhansak is my favourite - hot, sour, tangy taste.'* IH. *'Food and service, its usual high standard.'* WC. *'Pleasant warm and relaxing atmosphere, tables nicely set. Food served promptly.'* TS. *'Regular customers for the past 8 years. Perfect cleanliness, staff well turned out.'* GWM. *'Restaurant consistently full of people, all enjoying themselves.'* JAM. *'Have been coming here for 15 years, nothing is too much trouble.'* JB. *'Have tried most things on the menu and have found them all delicious.'* JM. *'Warm, friendly, welcome, have witnessed this over 21 years and will not go anywhere else.'* AF. The wine list is very much above average, and includes a drink-what-with-which-curry-guide. Delivery: £15. Hours: 12-2/5-12am.

ZEST NEW ENTRANT

15 North St Andrew St, Edinburgh

Pretty cafe– style restaurant, polished wooden floors, glass shelves, tubular steel chairs and pastel colours. *'For a dinner on Saturday, thought quantities were less than average. Good hot food on hot plates. Strange cold roti. Order drinks, gin and tonic and brandy and American - came ready poured and tasted of nothing much...'* very bad manners, should be poured at the table. *'...Fair comfort, place was warm. Decor let down by very poor / cheap cutlery. Good hot food on hot plates, but very strange Roti - cold.'* NKC. Set meals good value, Chicken Kebab, Green Herb Lamb, Aloo Gobi, Pullao Rice, Gulab Jamon £12.95. Delivery: £10 min. Hours: 12-2.30/5.30-11.30.

Leith

BRITANNIA SPICE ©

TOP 100 PREVIOUS AWARD WINNER

150 Commercial Street, Britannia Way, Leigh
0131 555 2255

A superb new venue (est. 1999) with a nautical theme from Wali Uddin, MBE. Seats a considerable 150 diners in a dining room with blue chairs, polished wooden tables and floors, brass railings and blinds that look like sails. A perfect stop-off after you have visited Ocean Terminal where the former Royal yacht *Britannia* is docked. The menu is divided by countries - Bangladeshi, Thai, Nepalese, North Indian and Europe. Menu delights from the starters include: Assorted Vegetable Pakora £2.25, Tom Kha Gai £3.75, chicken and coconut soup, Maccher Bhorta £3.95, baked fish, minced with mustard oil, onion, green chillies, and fresh coriander leaves, Prawn Sweet 'n' Sour Puri £3.95.*'What a great restaurant, lovely surroundings, great courteous service and the food is just up with the very best. We had Chicken Tikka Chasni Masala bit more spicy than your average CTM and Methi Murgh. The Aloo Jeera was simply divine, the Okra tasty, if a bit oily.* **TOP 100** *stuff no doubt, elegant.'* T&KM. *'Very, very tiny helpings - beautifully plated. Very, very expensive.'* NKC. *'Whilst on business, my colleague and I found ourselves staying at the Holiday Inn Express (adjacent to the restaurant). On checking-in, we were both offered vouchers for Britannia Spice - 10% off! We walked past the restaurant at 7pm - it was empty, deciding on a beer first. Returned at 8.30pm - it was packed, despite this we got a table! Excellent starters of Assorted Kebabs £4.95. Main courses: Northern Indian Garlic Chicken £7.95 - roaster chicken with hot sauce, Harrey Masaley Ka Gosht £7.95 - cubes lamb in green masala or coriander, mint, green chilli, curry leaves and spices, a superb, best ever tarka Dal. Very impressive, worthy of its guide entry. Will visit again!'* DL.If David's choice of dishes did not tempt you, why not try something from the Nepalese section: Himalaya Rui Khumbi £7.25, spicy trout roasted with fried mushrooms, tomatoes, green chilli, mustard seed and fresh herbs, Himalayan Momo £8.95, minced meat mixed with flour and cooked in the traditional mountain way You can mix and match from the Thai dishes: Goong Ob Mordin £9.95, steamed king prawn with black bean sauce, ginger and onions, Pad Ho Ra Pa Kub Nua £8.50, beef, stir-fried with Thai spices and basil. For the totally unadventurous there is a small choice of English dishes – steak, roast chicken etc. Buffet banquet lunches: Mon.-Fri. 12-2.15pm £7.95. Takeaway: 15% discount. Delivery: £50 minimum, 5-mile radius. Hours: 12-2.15/5-11.45. *See overleaf.*

GULNAR'S PASSAGE TO INDIA

TOP 100 ©

46 Queen Charlotte St, Leith, Edinburgh
0131 554 7520

Mohammad Ridha Saleh's 82-seater Passage, serves north Indian and Kashmiri food. *'Many are the nights I've spent there feeling like a desert king, being fed the most amazing food under the drapes that give the establishment the air of a Bedouin tent. One Arabic dish at Gulnar's especially emphasises this feeling: Helahil, chicken cooked with sweetcorn, onion, fresh coriander and chilli, served on a bed of rice with salad, a superb dish with a wonderful mix of flavours. Two new introductions are: Halabcha, spiced and roasted aubergine cooked in the tandoor with chicken, yoghurt, tomatoes, onions, garlic, chilli and coriander, a hot dish that tantalises the tastebuds; and Onion Sambal, combined with Chicken Tikka is an incredible edible experience.'* GR. *'Recommended by several people, but to be honest we thought it sounded a bit too good to be true. We soon realised that all that accolade was not exaggerated. We went for the atmosphere mainly, but were very thrilled with the variety and quality of the exotic food. A great cheer to a marvellous place which had given us one of the best nights out in the UK for a long, long time.'* FA. *'Free papadoms, nice dips. My dining partner thought the Chicken Tikka was the best she'd tasted, but my Jhal Frezie was not so good – too bland. Service was good and fast.'* GMcG. Specials include Aloobora – spicy potato balls filled with minced lamb £2.10. Potahari Sangam – minced lamb fried with fresh herbs and spices, garnished with coconut, wrapped in a puri. Rooflifter, lamb and chicken marinated, tandoor-cooked and prepared with mint, nuts and spices. Such delights keep Gulnar's in our ⅔ 100. Hours: 12-2/5.30-12. (1am on Sat.).

2004 COBRA GOOD CURRY GUIDE

County Index, see page 7. Town Index, see page 363.
A to Z of the Menu, page 52. Contributors Key, page 360.

Livingstone

ASHOKA SHAK NEW ENTRANT

Almondvale Ave, Livingston 0800 195 3195

Charan Gill, MBE, Managing Director, Harlequin Leisure Group Ltd, has opened a smart looking new restaurant in Livingston, West Lothian and will be launching branches in Coatbridge and Dundee in the coming months. Implementing a five year growth plan, it is anticipated that by the end of 2006 there will be around 25 Shaks nationwide. Chef Dhillon oversees kitchen operations and is responsible for standardising recipes for over a dozen restaurants in the group. Reasonably prices– Ashoka Shak offers a takeaway and home delivery service in addition to eat in facilities.

Musselburgh

SHISH MAHAL ©

63a, High St, Musselburgh 0131 665 3121

Established 1979, Idris Khan's and manager Shezad's 40 seater is decorated with original Pakistani wall hangings. Chef Tariq's specials include Shajaman Murgh, half barbecued chicken, on- or off-bone, in medium curry sauce,. Specials include: Shish Garlic and Chilli, Kashmiri Kebab Curry, Shish Kebab Murgh, Nawabi Bhindi Gosht – okra with lamb. Buffet Tuesday. *'The food is outstanding. I live 10 miles from Musselburgh but it is worth the trip as the food is always superb. My favourite in Scotland.'* LW. Takeaway: 10% discount. Delivery: £10 min. Hours: 5-12.

Penicuik

CLIPPERS

26 High Street, Penicuik 01968 679977

Clean lines and no clutter make for a smart restaurant to dine in. Crimson walls, highly polished wooden floor, chairs and tables. The menu tells the story of waht clippers were and did. Starters: Shammi Kebab £2.55, spiced minced patties, stuffed with lentils, diced onions, finely chopped green chillies coated with egg, accompanied by salad and mint sauce. Aloo Chapps £1.55, shallow fried vegetable fritters, potatoes, peas, coriander and medium, served with mint sauce. Very reasonably priced main courses: Podina Murgh Massallam £5.25, marinated chicken cutlets, charcoal grilled, cooked in a medium sauce with fresh mint, spring onions. Shahi Chasni £5.25, chicken kebabs cooked in a delicate sweet and sour sauce, a big favourite at the curryhouses of Scotland. Fangash Dupiaza £5.35, fish cooked with green beans and garnished with spring onions, herbs and garlic. Alo Chapps Massallam £3.75, mixed vegetable cutlets in a mild buttery sauce – sounds delicious! Hours: 12-2/5.30-11.30.

STRATHCLYDE

Inc the former counties of: Argyle, Ayrshire, Dunbartonshire, Lanarkshire and Renfrewshire

Area: Central west Scotland
Population: 2,255,000
Adjacent Counties: Borders, D & G, Central, Highland, Lothian

Note: For this edition we are continuing to use the old region of Strathclyde here, but we point out that Northern Strathclyde has become Argyll & Bute, while the rest of Strathclyde is divided into a number of Unitary Authorities, administering the larger cities and surrounds.

Coatbridge

PUNJAB EXPRESS 

22 West Canal Street, Coatbridge 01236 422522

Opened in 1993 by the Dhanda brothers, Kally and Tari. The Punjab Express is part of the former Coatbridge Central Station House. Built in 1899, the building still has many of the period features. The station was closed by Lord Beeching in 1963 and the restaurant is situated in what used to be the station master's accommodation. Downstairs, in the former ticket office, is the Pullman Lounge.

GLASGOW

(Includes BattlefieldFinnieston, Hillhead, Muirend, Nitshill, Pollockshields, Scotstoun, Townhead,)

Glaswegians are at pains to tell us that Glasgow curries are 'the real thing, the best anywhere'... 'everywhere else is a pale imitation, especially the pakoras', writes one person frequently. The reason is a largely Pakistani population, and this means gutsy, spicy Kashmiri/Punjab-style curries, as are found in Southall and Bradford, which are quite removed from the Bangladeshi curry house formula. Put another way, Glasgow's curries are the authentic thing, once tasted, never forgotten. The argument about whether Glasgow or Edinburgh is best for curry or the curry capital is fatuous. Glasgow has come a very long way since its tennement-block, 6pm pub-closing, Mars-bar-loutishness reputaion. Modern Glasgow is breathtaking. Its Indian restaurant scene is as good as it gets. Here are your favourites:

AMBALA SWEET CENTRE ANP ©

178 Maxwell Road, Pollockshields, Glasgow S0141 429 5620

This is a franchise operated by Mrs S Ahmad. (See Ambala, Drummond St, London, NW1.) As well as the counter takeaway sweets and snacks, chef Akmal cooks a small range of curries for the 26-seat restaurant. *'Lamb Bhoona is amazing!'* DF. BYO not allowed. No credit cards. Hours: 10am-10pm.

THE ASHOKA TOP 100

108 Elderslie Street, Central Glasgow 0141 221 1761

Originally opened 1968, it was taken over in 1995. Owned by brothers Bhpoinder and Parminder Purewal, who assure you that their Ashoka has no connection with the many other Ashokas in the area. Ashoka, incidentally, was an Indian emperor from centuries ago. Recently 110 seats in two dining rooms. Had a £250,000 facelift by

restaurant designer Harris Khan. Critics have described it as *'Baroque into fantasyland'* and *'rich opulence'*. You love chef Alexandré Paaeschi's cooking? The new menu has plenty of play on the words 'spark' and 'flame' (Old Flame for example are the old favourites like CTM). *'This restaurant oozes class, little wonder it was voted the Guide's* **BEST IN SCOTLAND.** *'The decor, service, presentation and food are excellent.'* MC. Takeaway: 10% off. Hours: 5-11./12-11.30; Sun.

ASHOKA AT THE MILL TOP 100

500 Corselet Road, Nitshill, Glasgow SW 0800 195 3195

There have been Ashoka restaraunts in Glasgow since 1968. Balbur Singh Sumal grew the number to six during the 1980s (including the original at Elderslie Street, noted abov,e which is one is no longer part of the group). The remainder, listed together here, are now part of Charan Gill's Harlequin Group of several Ashokas in and around Glasgow, and one in Johnstone. The menus are the same at each branch, and the service is, we hear: *'exemplary, the food as good as ever from the old days.'* IMcT. This Ashoka is novel, and the clue is in the name. It is indeed located in an old mill, and is now Charan Gill's flagship, containing 'head office'. The location is off the M77 at J3 – go west half a mile along the A726, turn left and follow the signs, and suddenly you've left industrial Glasgy behind. Gill had to do a huge refurb job on the premises, and he let his fantasy run a wee bit. There is a Scotland the Brave, neo-Medieval look to the place, with bare stone contrasting with plaster walls, boarded floor and silver/electric-blue decor. The chairs look a bit spindly, but probably cost a fortune, branded cattle ranch-style, with the letter 'A'. The large venue (225 seats) is not dwarfed by its central feature – a tree trunk painted blue (*'it was there so I used it'* said designer David Roulston). The tree continues on upstairs in the mezzanine section. Large windows ensure plenty of daylight. The food, according to IMcT: *'is not all Indian, but it's all at the Ashoka standard worth travelling for.'* Specials include Goanese fish and prawns, Kala Mirch Masala, sliced chicken breast in a peppery, tangy herbal sauce. Average spend is £15, and we welcome more reports. We are pleased to keep the Mill in our **TOP 100.** Branches: Ashoka Ashton Lane, 19 Ashton Lane, Hillhead, Glasgow, 0141 357 5904. Ashoka South Side, 268 Clarkston Road, Muirend, Glasgow. 0141 637 5904. Ashoka West End, 1284 Argyle Street, Central Glasgow 0141 339 0936. Kama Sutra, Murphy's Pakora Bar, Mr Singh's, Glasgow, Ashoka Johnstone.

CAFÉ INDIA

171 North St, Charing Cross, Central Glasgow
0141 248 4074

Described (by its owner Abdul Sattar) as *'Britain's first-ever designer buffet restaurant'.* It certainly has changed since it opened in 1979, its seating by 1999 having reached a monumental 500, and two years on 560. The ground floor is open-plan and bright. The seats are expensive high-backed pale wood with pink or blue upholstery, depending which zone you are in, and there are some alcove tables. The area called the galleries in the lower floor is moody, with darker reds and wrought iron. There is provision for self-service via a smart counter. Both floors have eye-catching artwork and light fittings. Suddenly this style of decor is already dated, being installed up and down Britain as fast as red flock in the 60s. Young clientèle love it though and their set meals, which are a speciality, and the Friday/Saturday e-a-m-a-y-ls (at £12.50). Sattar it seems is proud of the fact that he served 1160 diners in a single day. Takeaway: 10% off. Hours: 12-12; Sun. 3-12am.

CHAPATI I 

2017 Dumbarton Road, Glasgow W
0141 576 0118

Chain of 11 takeaways, est. 1983 by Iqbal S Gill each of which has its own personnel, but are overseen by Deepa Gill (service) and Harnak Singh (chef). Curries, Kebabs and Pizza. Prices are not cheap for takeaway: Onion Bhajia £2.25, Mango Chutney 70p, Potato and Cauiflower Curry £3.50. Most ordered dishes: Karahi Chicken and Chicken Jullander. Hours: Sun.-Thurs. 4pm-12.30am; Fri. & Sat. 4pm-1.30am. Branches: (All Glasgow area) Chapati 2, 1576 Dumbarton Rd, 0141 954 3154; Chapati 3, 339 Dumbarton Rd, Partick, 0141 337 1059; Chapati 4, 20 Byres Rd, 0141 334 4089; Chapati 5, 354 Paisley Rd W , 0141 427 6925; Chapati 6, 468 Dumbarton Rd, Dalmuir, 0141 952 9210; Chapati 7, 182 Paisley Rd W, Renfrew, 0141 885 2313; Chapati 8, 5 Lennox Dr, Faifley, 01389 879914; Chapati 9, 3 Greenock Rd, Bishopton, 01505 862 222; Chapati 10 39 Main St, Busby, 0141 644 1971; Sajjan, 2372 Dumbarton Rd, Yoker, 0141 951 1839. Neelim, 1590 Dumbarton Road, Glasgow, 0141 959 6265.

CHARGHA'S FOOD CLUB 

2, Glebe Street, Townhead, Central Glasgow
0141 886 5161

Established in 1996. Specials include: Tikka Masala, Chicken or Lamb Bohana and Korma. Price check: Papadam 50p, CTM £5.20, Pullao Rice £1.30, Peshwari Nan £1.95. Hours: 3.45pm-12am; Sat. 3pm-1am.

LA CREME DE LA CREME TOP 100

1071 Argyle Street, Finnieston, Central Glasgow0141 221 3222

Adbul Satar's restaurant seats 650, and boasts a public house license for 1,700, making it one of Glasgow's most popular venues for corporate events. Along from Central Station, it's in a former cinema aiming up-market, with former stalls and dress circle in use. No expense has been spared, creating a style reminiscent, in parts, of London's Bombay Brasserie. The recently revamped menu features modern Indian dishes such as South Indian Garlic Chilli Chicken, but Chicken Tikka Masala remains the firm favourite of customers. *'Service superb. Prices dear, but portions large.'* DMCK. *'Tried the buffet, my first experience of this type of spice inhalation. All reasonable.'* CW. Weekday lunch prices 20% off until 3pm. Balcony evening e-a-m-a-y-l buffet served 6-10pm, £8.95 weekdays, £11.95 weekends. Hours: 12-12. It stays in our **TOP 100.**

KOH I NOOR TOP 100 E-A-M-A-Y-L

235 North St, Charing Cross, Central Glasgow0141 204 1444

Glasgow's earliest Indo-Pak opened in 1961, and boasts to be the originator of the famous e-a-m-a-y-l buffet nights (Mon.-Fri. 7-9pm). Authentic Indian and Pakistani design with authentic Asian decor, with hanging rugs, arches etc. *'Fabulous decor.'* DBAC. Northern Indian formula curries. Its 150 seating is now small in comparison with other Glasgow venues, but is still big considering the national average of 50, and it's still very busy. *'Not only was the service friendly and helpful but the food arrived very promptly, considering the number of people there. The Chicken Dansak was excellent and the naan breads terrific'.* RA. *'Excellent. Samosas so filling, had to leave most of my main course!'* SF. *'Starters very impressive, quantities large. Garlic Nan not for the faint-hearted: beautiful. Chicken Tikka Chasini and Chicken Nentara memorable.'* HB. *'Absolutely superb. In a class of its own.'* BS. We have a difference of opinion here. *'Average, not Top 100, food not good enough.'* T&KM. *'Visited on thre consecutive nights, although had to pay a hefty £26 for Popadoms, starter, main course rice and Nan. Still think it currently the best Indian I've tried. Lamb Lyallipour - eyewatering hot, so succulent and tasty. Garlic Chilli Lamb -*

superb. Quick service, highly efficient, polite. My girlfriend Birgit - not a spice freak like me requested a mild curry. The waiter sensed that something was wrong, whisked here Okra Korma away and brought back a different one, declaring this would be palatable and indeed it was.' DP. Hours: 12-12. (Fri. & Sat. to 1am).

MOTHER INDIA

28 Westminster Tce, Glasgow 0141 221 1663

A well-known Glasgow landmark, Mother India opened its doors for business in 1992, and is run by Monir Mohammed. Famed for the Chilli Garlic Chicken and Lamb Musallam Curry with Okra, Mother India also does a brisk trade in hearty Chicken Biriani and Samosas. 'The jewel of Glasgow. Small unpretentious restaurant, Top 100 no doubt about it!' t&km.

MISTER SINGH'S INDIA TOP 100

149 Elderslie Street, Central Glasgow 0141 204 0186

Satty Singh owns this 90-seater restaurant, as its

eponymous title suggests, and like other Glasgow restaurants, as part of Charan Gill's Harlequin Group, it benefits from group marketing and purchasing muscle. Decor combines ethnic and traditional Scottish. Manager Jamil Ahmed, and the waiters wear kilts and the girls wear salwars; Younis Ahraf (who wears chef's whites, by the way) does curried Haggis! And we hear that there's a French influence at work in the kitchens too. '*Without question the best I have visited! Vast menu. Fantastic food, good portions. Booking essential, even mid-week. Brandy-drinkers beware. They have a 200-year-bottle of Napoleon's brandy at £35 a shot!*' GD. '*For me, it is a 'must' when I am travelling to Glasgow! The food is so good and tasty, particularly the Chilli Garlic Chicken.*' RA. Takeaway: 10% off. Hours: 12-3/5-11.30; Sun. 2.30-11.30.

MURPHY'S PAKORA BAR
TOP 100 

1287 Argyle S, Glasgow 0141 334 1550

Like Mr Singh's above, now part of Charan Gill's Harlequin Group, it still retains its owner Teresa Doherty, herself, with as much of an eye to sound bites as Charan. '*It was love at first bite! As we sank our baby teeth into our first chunk of pakora, there were loud karahis of more mum!*' [groan] '*The word Pakora, to a Scot, slips off the tongue as easily as haggis, neeps and tatties. It's one of those snacks that can be eaten at any time of day or night ... one bite is never enough. At Murphy's the chef's a Scot (R. McGregor) which is why there's Haggis Pakora. Beam me up, Scotty.*' CW. And there are 30 others including Chilli. Or there are Pizzas – traditional or with an Indian twist. Of course, it is a licensed bar, selling, well Murphy's of course! Takeway: 10% off. Hours: 12pm-12am (1am on Fri./Sat.).

VILLAGE CURRY — NEW ENTRANT

129 Nelson St Glasgow 0141 429 4610

'*Superb. Religious place, no alcohol, no BYO, must be Halal as 90% of customers of Asian appearance. Very good middle range menu, not short or too long. Good quantities, very good prompt service. Good comfort, amazing decor. We were taken upstairs to an excellent restaurant, all fitted out in dark, polished tables and chairs, nice stone coloured walls, huge red/yellow/gold paisley ceiling drapes to give a huge tent effect. Being a Friday night, we booked. Hive of industry - eating!*' NKC.

WEE CURRY SHOP — NEW ENTRANT

7 Buccleuch St Glasgow 0141 353 0777

Everything about this eatery is small, including the menu, smaller than a paperback book. '*Really good. Very wee indeed. Seats approximately 20 with one chef and one waiter. Vegetable side dishes seem to have low priority. My pal has been eating here for years.*' GG. The menu is also probably the smallest selection we have ever seen. However, as the saying goes, better to cook one dish well than ten badly. There are only four starters to choose from: Vegetable £2.60 or Chicken £3.60 Pakoras, Aubergine Fritters £3.20 and Mutter Paneer Puri £3.50. There are a few more mains to choose: six Chicken dishes, prices from £5.50 to £6.95; one Lamb, a Karahi dish at £6.50; four Vegetables eg: Aloo Sag, Black Eye Beans and Broccoli and one Dal, all at £5.50. To accompany your curries, there is Basmati Rice £1.50, Garlic Potatoes £1.75, Chappati 60p, Paratha £2.05 and Raitha £1.10. We agree: you don't need anything more!

ZEERA — NEW ENTRANT

181 Kirchintilloch Road, Bishopbriggs, Glasgow, G41 0141 772 9393

Toni Ghani and his father (both share the same name) have been designing and building Indian restaurants for well over a decade andhave recently taken up ownership of Zeera. Distinctive, with its expansive windows that look into a tasteful furniture – South African black marble floor tiles, black walls, and comfy leather chairs in the dining area.

Helensburgh

CAFE LAHORE — NEW ENTRANT

33 West Clyde St Helensburgh 01436 674971

'*Light, clean and simple decor. Helpful, cheerful and friendly service. Very varied menu, one of the biggest I've seen. I opted for the buffet, came with enormous starter of Mixed Pakroa, eight main dishes, two rices and bread. Nan disappointing, hard as leather. However, if you order fresh, you are in for a treat – small is the size of a moderate coffee table! Quite fantastic Lassi and Chai. Excellent Lal Toofan. Recommended.*' RT. Menu

Extracts: Fish or Paneer Pakora £2.85, Garlic Okra £2.25, Chicken lyallpuri £7.50, green chilli and coriander; Hasina £7.25, tender lamb, marinated, onions, capsicums, tomato, baked in tandoor, sauce, served on sizzler; Mix Hot Rice £6.60, fried rice, chicken, lamb, prawns, fresh green chillies, served on hot sizzler. Buffet Nights: 6-11, £8.95, children under 12 half price. Takeaway: 10% discount. Delivery: £15 minimum. Hours: 12-2.30/5-12, Fri/Sat to 12.

TAYSIDE

(Inc Angus, Kinross and Perthshire)

Area: East Scotland
Population: 394,000
Adjacent Counties:
Central, Fife,
Grampian,
Highland,
Strathclyde

Dundee

DIL SE

NEW ENTRANT TOP 100
BEST IN SCOTLAND AWARD 2004/5

99 Perth Road, Dundee 01382 221501

Abdour Rouf's the recently opened 150-seat Dil Se (pron dill see) restaurant was presented with the Dundee Civic Trust Award for its outstanding contribution to the improvement of the city. Billed as the largest Bangladeshi restaurant in Scotland it specialises in Bangladeshi, Indian and Thai cuisine. *'Dil Se, (Bangladeshi for from the heart) opened in 2003 on that stretch of Perth road near South Tay Street that's packed with boozers and eateries. Its sister restaurant, the Balaka in St Andrews, Fife has been thrilling curryholics, myself included, and winning prestigious Curry Club awards for 21 years. Decor is modern and minimalist and the toilets are like a fake leopard skin coat – absolutely spotless. The Dil Se menu is a carbon copy of The Balaka's and every last morsel of food is cooked to order. 'Please be patient,' says the blurb on the front page. 'Good food is like art and like at it takes time.' We kicked off with chilli pickle – careful, friends, this red hot stuff will seriously blow your tights off – and a pile of popadoms that were so fresh I'm surprised they didn't try to slip the haun. Then came the real starters – Chicken Tikka and a Shami Kebab. Simple Chicken Tikka is always a smart option if you want to judge any Indian – or, in this case, Bangladeshi restaurant. The Tikka at Dil Se was perfect. Every mouthful burst with flavour – particularly when smeared thickly with the awesome chilli pickle – and I loved the tasty little burnt bits. From the list of fifteen or so chef specials, I tried the Mas Bangla, salmon fillet, marinated in lime juice, turmeric, green chilli and several other spices then fried in mustard oil with garlic, onion, tomato and aubergine. Believe it or not, it tasted even better than it sounds, and special doesn't even begin to describe it. I said it before and I'll say it again, why can't more curry houses start using salmon? It always works well'.* Tam Cowan, Dundee Record. This is an outstanding, caring restaurant, and following the tradition of its sister, the Balaka in St Andrews, Fife, we have great pleasure in giving it our **BEST IN SCOTLAND AWARD 2004/5 AWARD.** Delivery: 5 miles, £2 minimum Hours: Sun.-Thurs. 5pm-1am; Fri. & Sat. 12am-1am. Open Christmas Day. *See page* 39.

Perth

MANZIL ©

13 York Place, Perth 01738 446222

Rana Ali's 85-seat curry house. The most popular dish: South Indian Garlic Chilli. Takeaway: 10% discount. Delivery: free local. Hours: 12-2pm/5-11.30pm. Branch: Tandoori Knights, Princess Street, Perth (takeaway only).

TANDOORI NIGHTS ©

12, Princes Street, Perth 01738 441277

Established in 1998. Seats 38. Indian Specialities: Chicken Nashedar £5.45 – barbecued chicken or lamb in a spiced cream based sauce with cashew nuts and flavoured with brandy. Lamb Tikka Achari £5.45 – strong, spicy dish, slightly sour, cooked with tangy pickle, fresh green chillies, lemon and fresh coriander. Menu also has Turkish kebabs, Italian Pizzas and European Dishes. Takeaway: 10% discount. Delivery: free in Perth. Hours: 5-12am. (Sat. to 1am).

WALES

As with England, the Guide runs alphabetically in county and town order. In 1997 a large number of Unitary Authorities replaced the six Welsh counties (regions) which had themselves replaced the age-old shires and smaller counties in 1965. To provide a convenient geographical division of Wales in this Guide, we retain the six former counties (listing their shires within them). With a population of under 3 million, (nearly matched by Greater Manchester alone) and only 270 curry restaurants in the whole of Wales, (there are more in London sw) we cannot say Cymru is big on the nation's favourite food. And we would very much welcome a plethora of Welsh reports for next time.

CLWYD

(Inc: Denbighshire, Flintshire and Wrexham)

Area: North Wales
Population: 421,000
Adjacent Counties: Cheshire, Gwynedd, Powys, Shrops

Deeside

BENGAL DYNASTY TOP 100 

106 Chester Road East, Shotton, Deeside 01244 830455

Opened in 1991 by Mohammed Monchab Ali, with Rico managing, seats 92 with an additional lounge area for 40, in air-conditioned, purpose-built, airy and elegant, luxurious surroundings. Chef Foyzur Rahman's north Indian and Bangladeshi specials include Kashir Rezala, £7.95, Chicken Bondhuk, £8.95, Satkora Gosth, £8.55, Bengal Fish Curry, £7.95. *'Truly exceptional place. The food was just the business. This restaurant is well worthy of its Best in North Wales rating.'* MW. *'Immense size of restaurant – huge. Politely greeted and guided to bar. Can see why this restaurant features so highly in the Guide.'* MW. *'Outstanding.'* WAJ. The Dynasty's Bangladeshi food festival in May was raved over by locals, as were the cookery demos from three of the industry's greatest chefs (Manzoor Ali from London's Tabaq, Mohammed Ali from Yorkshire's Agra, and Monchab himself) and the superb menus. Takeaway: 15% discount. Delivery: £10 minimum, 5-mile radius. Hours: 12-2.30/5.30-11.30; Sun. 12.30-11. Branch: Bengal Dynasty Northwich Cheshire and Llandudno Gwynedd.

PLAZA AMANTOLA 

Welsh Rd, Sealand, Deeside 01244 811383

Opened in 1997. A pretty restaurant decorated in reds and greens with soft, comfortable sofas to relax on while taking coffee and liquers after a satisfying spicy meal. Seats 300 diners in two rooms. 'Lunchtime and I'm not alone. Sat in bar with drink while perused the menu. Good varied menu, caters for English and Chinese. Imaginatively titled dishes include 'Dive in the Bay of Bengal' – haddock in spiced dhal and curry sauce, and 'Celony Thunder' – very hot, coconut, garlic, ginger, chilli. *'Went for lunchtime special – two Popadoms (at 70p each a bit pricey) with Chutney Tray, Onion Bhajia, Chicken Jalfrezi, Pullao Rice. Waiter took my drink to the table where the excelent Popadoms and largest choice of excellent Chutneys were waiting. Two Onion Bhajias arrived, size of tennis balls, nicely presented with salad, lemon. Nice, crisp, outside and in, one would have done. Good portion of Jalfrezi and rice. Chicken slightly dry, vegetables crisp, rich, hot sauce, plenty of green chillies. Pity I can't get there more often.'* DB. *'Arrived just after noon, shown to bar, served a drink. Ordered lunchtime special – Popadoms, Chicken Tikka, CTM with Pullau Rice .Popadoms took an age to arrive, but good selection of chutneys – Tandoori Chutney was excellent. CTM – sliced chicken, bright red, sweet and very rich sauce with a little kick. Really tasty but not good for my cholesterol. Good portion of nicely fluffy rice.'* DB. Takeaway: 10% discount. Delivery: 5-mile radius, minimum charge £15. Hours: 12-2/5.30-12.

RAJ BALTI BYO NEW ENTRANT

70 Chester St, Flint 01352 733633

'Chicken Phal is consistently good, as hot as a phal should be. Good portions, excellent takeaway and home delivery service, although the eating area is rather small. BYO.' SA&AP.

©	Curry Club Discount	U	Unlicensed
V	Vegetarian	ANP	Alcohol not permitted
e-a-m-a-y-l	Eat as much as you like	BYO	Bring your own alcohol

Llangollen

SPICE LOUNGE — NEW ENTRANT

36 Regent Street Llangollen 01978 861877

Formerly Sylhet. *'Table for four booked for 8.30pm. Restaurant busy and smokey. Service was polite, smart and efficent. Popadoms and pickles excellent. Started with Chicken Chat £2.75, excellent, succulent. Sheek Kebab £2.25 and Aloo Puri £2.45, good. Main courses: Chilli Masala £7.20 (inc PR), very red, very hot, superb flabour. Lamb Dhansak £4.60, good. Very tender Lamb Pasanda, but sauce was colour of CTM? House Special Balti £6.20, very filling, well worth the extra pence. Fresh, hot Pullao Rice and excellent, stinking of garlic, Garlic Nan £1.40. Hot towels and complimentary brandy's served. Overall a great meal. £59.95 for four.'* MPW. Garlic Nan sounds great! Takeaway: 15% discount. Hours: 12-2, Saturday and Sunday only and 6-12.

Wrexham

CHIRK TANDOORI — NEW ENTRANT

1 Station Ave Chirk Wrexham 01691 772499

Licensed. *'Appears smart and and well ordered, staff exceptionally polite, helpful and efficient. Meal for four was truly outstanding in every aspect. I ordered Prawn Phall (not on the menu) which was one of the best I have ever tasted – hugely prawned and no evidence of the dreaded Campbells Tomato Soup syndrome! My three shipmates were equally impressed with their choices.'* DC. Credit cards accepted. Menu Extracts: Aloo on Puri £1.95; Butter Chicken £4.45, tikka, hot sauce; Persian Kebab Special £6.15, chicken fillets, onions, garlic, ginger, served with Pullao Rice and Curry Sauce; Mushroom Pullao £1.40; Garlic Nan £1.30. Hours: 6- 11.30.

JAMUNA — NEW ENTRANT

18 Yorke Street Wrexham 01978 261142

'Service excellent, hot food, tasty good portions, although my husband would like more sauce with Jalfrezi. Plenty of chicken in Dhansak and Balti, well presented. Reasonabley priced house wine.' dv-w. Takeaway: 10% discount, minimum £13. 20% discount, minimum £17. Menu Extracts: Murghi Masala £11.20, half spring chicken, creamy sauce of minced meat; Chana Special £6.95, tomatoes, green peppers, onion, chick peas, bhuna sauce; Service: 10%.

DYFED

(Inc: Cardigan, Carmarthenshire & Pembrokeshire)

Area: West Wales
Population: 356,000
Adjacent Counties:
Glam, Powys, Gwynedd

Carmarthen

TAJ BALTI 

119 Priory St, Carmarthen 01267 221995

Opened in 1995 by Lias Miah. *'My husband and I always enjoy their fare. Elegant decor, service excellent and friendly, with superb food. Muted traditional music, intimacy of individual booths, a special atmosphere. Tandoori Mixed Grill declared the best ever.'* JF. Sun. e-a-m-a-y-l buffet. Hours: 6-12.

Llanelli

BENGAL LANCER 

43 Murray Street, Llanelli01554 749199

78-seater fully licensed restaurant opened by Ahmed Ali in 1986. Muzaffar heads the cooking brigade. It's a very popular venue serving Bangladeshi and North Indian Tandooris, Curries and Accompaniments. Minimum charge £12.50. Takeaway: 10% off. Hours: 12-2.30/6-12. Branch: Anarkali , Swansea.

VERANDAH 

20 Market Street, Llanelli 01554 759561

Opened in 1985 by Mr A Khalique. Restaurant seats 64 diners. The restaurant has bright turmeric walls, indigo carpet and shelving with chilli-red and orange chairs and sofas. Specials: Charga Mossalla (half spring-chicken, marinated, tomatoes, green peppers, red wine). Dinner for One: £7.95, Lamb or Chicken kebab, CTM, Bombay Aloo, Special Rice, Nan and vanilla ice cream. Chicken Roll £2.25, crispy rolled pasties filled with chicken tikka. Hours: 6-12. (Sat. -12.30).

BAY OF BENGAL

1 Crackenwell Street Tenby 01834 843331

'Tenby is a lovely place and has some excellent restaurants. Very good meal at The Bay of Bengal. Beautifully furnished, restaurant looks out to the sea, food matched the view. Chicken and Chickpea for Linda and King Prawn Bhuna for me - so many prawns!' MG.

GLAMORGAN

Inc: the former West, Mid & South Glam

Area: South Wales
Population: 1,346,000
Adjacent Counties: Dyfed, Gwent, Powys

Note, in 1997, the counties of West, Mid and South Glamorganshire were disbanded in favour of 11 Unitary Authorities to administrate the 11 large towns (incl Newport) in the area. For Guide convienence we have retained the fomer Glamorgan goegraphy. For Newport see Gwent.

Barry

SHAHI NOOR NEW ENTRANT

87 High Street, Barry 01446 735706

Maybur Rahman's Shahi Noor Indian Cuisine restaurant is one of Barry's most popular curry houses. It serves all the favourite Bangladeshi and Indian dishes, from Starters , Tandoori, Balti and Curries, Specials, and Accompaniments. Notjing is overlooked. And we hear of careful serive and cooking, and a well-respected venue by its many regulars. Hours: 12-2.30/6-12.

©	Curry Club Discount	U	Unlicensed
V	Vegetarian	ANP	Alcohol not permitted
e-a-m-a-y-l	Eat as much as you like	BYO	Bring your own alcohol

Cardiff

JUBORAJ 2 — TOP 100

10 Mill La, Hayes, Cardiff 029 2037 7668

Jubraj 2, 'Fairly large, comfortable restaurant, good reputation, very popular. Visited by Tom Jones [wow!] *'In my opinion, one of Cardiff's best. Another visit, and the food once again was excellent.'* JB. *'Food excellent, service not.'* G&MP. *'Celebrating Liverpool FC's nail biting penalty shoot out victory in the Worthington Cup, we took the Guide's advice and headed for this restaurant. Service initially prompt, but as the fans from both sides descended, things got a little hectic at times!. Popadoms and Kebabs (Shami and Sheek) both excellent. Main courses, Chicken Madras, Chicken Sagwalls accompanied by Pullao Rice, Nan and Tarka Dal, excellent! Food a little more expensive, guess that was a result of its town centre location! Will visit again – hopefully after the FA cup final!'* DL.Hours: 12-2/6-12am. Branch: Juboraj, 11 Heol-y-Deri, Rhiwbina, Glamorgan and Juboraj, Lakeside, below. Remains in our TOP 100.

JUBORAJ LAKESIDE

Lake Road West Lakeside 029 2045 5123

Love the chairs in this restaurant, made from cane with wicker and upholstered in a richly coloured paisley styled material and a scrolled back, really nice. Menu Extracts: Karahi Duck £10.95, duck pieces barbecued and tossed in medium spices with onion, tomatoes and green peppers. Sunday Buffet. Licensed: Cobra. Hours: 6-11.

SPICE MERCHANT — NEW ENTRANT

The Big Windsor, Stuart Street, Cardiff Bay 029 2049 8984

Mike Ahmed spent £450,000 to give the Windsor Hotel, an historic docklands pub, a new identity. Spice Merchant, is a modern ground and first floor 180 seater . The first floor lounge and restaurant seats up to 130. Ahmed is also actively involved in promoting the Indian Food festival – a yearly event, held in Aberystwyth. He says: *'Spice Merchant does not add any preservatives or additives to our food to enhance flavours and only use the finest ingredients. Customers are invited to see our kitchens and meet our chefs, who have been brought in from first class hotels in India to ensure authenticity.'*

Kenfig Hill

MUKTA MAHAL — NEW ENTRANT

104 Pisgah Street Kenfig Hill 01656 746000

'Once a Bingo Hall. Spacious layout with large water fountain. It is possible to have a Thai / Indian mixed meal - the only problem - what to choose! Quality of food very good indeed with excellent service, even on busy nights. Worth a detour off the M4 at junction 36. Highly recommended.' KN. Thai Specials: Tord Mun Pla £3.95, deep-fried spicy fish cakes with cucumber, salad, delicate sweet and sour peanut; Yum Woonsen £4.95, spicy glass noodle salad with prawns and chicken; Gaeng Mad Sa Man Gai £5.50, spicy Muslim chicken curry, sweet potatoes, coconut milk, peanuts; Pla Rad Prik £9.95, crispy fish fillet topped with a hot chilli and garlic sauce. Indian Specials: Chicken Pakora £3; Chicken Makhani £6.50, barbecued chicken tossed in butter, yoghurt, fresh cream, tomatoes and spices, Lamb Tikka Mahal £7.70, green chillies, garlic, coriander; Keema Rice £2.50; Egg Nan £2.00. Takeaway: 10% discount. Hours: 12-2.30/5.30-12, Friday and Saturday to 12.30. Sunday 12-12.

Neath

SIMLA — NEW ENTRANT

25 Alfred Street Neath 01639 630043

Formerly Bangladesh Tandoori. *'Pleasant decor, good service and relaxed atmosphere. Good, varied menu. Complimentary Popadoms. Excellent Lamb Kel Degsi, like a tomatoey Jalfrezi and Mushroom Rice. Decent portion. More expensive than other restaurants in town, but well worth it. Excellent.'* IB.

Swansea

ANARKALI

80 St Helen's Road, Swansea 01792 650549

Fully licensed and air-conditioned 60-seater established by A Rahman way back in 1978. Such long-standing gives it an assurance, experience and confidence with a long list of regulars. Menu Extracts: Crab Malabar £4, made from flaked fresh crab, sauteed with spices.Mahasha £3, cabbage leaves stuffed with lamb mince, rice and selected green herbs, sweet and sour flavour. Goan Lamb Vindaloo £6, marinated lamb with hot chilli, fresh green chilli, paprika, tomato puree, fenugreek and coriander. Sunday Buffet: £7.00 eat as much as you like. Hours: 5.30-12, Saturday to 2, Sunday 12-12.

BONOPHOL BANGLADESHI

TOP 100 ©

93 Sterry Road, Gowerton, Swansea
01792 875253

Owned by Mohammed Al Imran since 1990, its name change from Gowerton Tandoori in 1996 to Bonophol gives it a unique and pretty name, meaning 'forest flower'. The exterior is elegantly picked out in attractive tones of green and gilt, and this theme continues inside, with with chandilier, modern Bangladeshi art and forty cane chairs. For those who like to know these things, the logo on the menu is a map of Bangladesh, in the national flag colours. What you get at this 40-seater fully licensed restaurant is *'fine Bangladeshi*

©	Curry Club Discount	U	Unlicensed
V	Vegetarian	ANP	Alcohol not permitted
e-a-m-a-y-l	Eat as much as you like	BYO	Bring your own alcohol

Cuisine, with all my favourites, done conscientiously and very well.' EG. *'Managed by a well-known pleasant and cheerful person known to all as Abdul – he has been around for years. Quality of food is very good, service also good'.* CMJ. *'Excellent impression, very clean, glass of Sherry for every customer on the house. Reasonable prices, very big portions.'* JM. *'Small, well furnished and pleasant atmosphere. Laid back service with basic menu. Excellent Chicken Jalfrezi and Mushroom Rice, fair portion.'* IB. Takes part in regular Bangladeshi food festivals with other Swansea restaurants. Menu Extracts: Murg Nawabi £4.60, barbecued chicken, blended with fresh herbs and spices, garnished with chopped spiced egg. Sunday Buffet: 12-5, £5.95 adult, £3.95 children Starter for CC discount. Takeaway: 10% discount. Delivery: £10 minimum, 4-mile radius. Hours: 5.30-11.55 (Fri & Sat. to 12.25am); Sun. 12pm-11.55.

KARMA 3 — NEW ENTRANT

Victoria Road Swansea 01792 477848

Opposite Swansea Leisure Centre, Karma's frontage is very striking, decorated with blue mosiac, so you can't miss it. Furinture, wood and wrought iron, was specially imported. The restaurant is deceiving in size, infact it is quite big, with dining rooms upstairs and down. Licensed. Sunday Banquet, served between 12-10: adult £7, child £4.50. Monday to Saturday two course lunch a bargain at £4.95. Hours: 12-2/6-11.

LAL QUILA

480 Mumbles Rd, Mumbles, Swansea
01792 363520

Formerly Ocean View. *'Completely refurbished, now has very attractive decor, waiters wear smart uniforms. Probably Swansea's most upmarket restaurant. Everything is spotless with quick and friendly service. I particularly like the Chicken Methi with lots of fresh fenugreek. Food generally good.'* JD. *'Very stylish, airy atmosphere with wonderful views over Swansea Bay. Over-formal, but efficient service and excellent, unusual menu – ostrich and monkfish. Fair portion of Mangalorian Fish Curry and excellent Aloo Paratha. Quality and nice for a change.'* IB.

MOGHUL BRASSERIE — TOP 100

81 St Helen's Rd, Swansea 01792 475131

60-seater, opened in 1989 by Shazan Uddin, who is also the chef, managed by Ashik Rahman. Bangladeshi and Balti cuisine. *'Have been regulars for several years. Consistency is the key word for Mr Uddin. Efficient service in very pleasant surroundings. Excellent Chicken Tikka Karahi, Sali Boti and my favourite Pathia (prawn and chicken). Mr Uddin recently exhibited a wonderful Cockle Masala, at a Culinary Festival. Superb!'* A&AP. *'We have never come across anywhere that comes even close to the wonderful cuisine served at the Moghul.'* E&ME. *'Scores: 6/10.* DB. *'Varied menu, beautiful decor and excellent attentive service. Fair portion of Chicken Sali and Mushroom Rice. Everything about this restaurant was top notch. Fully deserves TOP 100 Award. Excellent.'* IB. Menu Extract: Shankar Thai £9, Pullao Rice, Bombay Aloo, Bhindi Masala, Niramish, Baigon Samosa. Sunday Buffet: £7.00. Set Dinner: £18.00 for two. . Takeaway: 10% off. Remains in our TOP 100. Hours: 12-2.30pm/5pm-12am (2am on Fri. & Sat.). Sunday 12-12.

GWENT

(Monmouthshire)

Area: Southwest Wales
Population:
454,000
Adjacent Counties:
Glamorgan, Gloucs, Herefordshire and Powys

In the 1997 reorganisation, Monmouthshire was partly restored, and though Newport is now an independent Unitary Authority, we retain it here.

Abergavenny

BAY LEAF — NEW ENTRANT

7 Market St, Abergavenny 01873 851212

'End of term 'do' for sixteen of us. Prawn Puri - good, Chilli Chicken - very good, lots of rich sauce and fresh chillies...' Are you by any chance, Peter, a chilli man? *'...an excellent meal, well cooked and presented. Indian beer flowed copiously. Decor is very clean.'* PH. Peter returned. *'Proof of highest quality with large portions. Vegetable Rice is the best I have tasted. Highly recommended.'* PH Hours: 6-11.30.

PUROBI — NEW ENTRANT

35 Frogmore St, Abergavenny 01873 854790

Formerly The Red Rose. *'Pleasant welcome. Lamb Pasanda and Prawn Puri, good quantities, excellent puri. Chicken Chilli Garlic Chamlai, a very nice sauce, rich taste, plenty of chicken and chillies. Chicken Biryani and Prawn Biryani, sauce a little mild. Paratha, Nan and Chapati, fresh. Tasteless Aloo Gobi. Average service.'* PH. Takeaway: 10% discount. Hours: 6-11.30, Fri/Saturday to 12.

SHAHI BALTI — NEW ENTRANT

5 Mill Street Abergavenny 01873 792011

'Having gone to visit friends, they chose the venue and booked a table – good job too – very popular with locals and those from out of town. Had a drink in the tiny bar, whilst table was readied. Chose a rather unimaginative Chicken and Potato Balti, pleasantly surprised, tasty indeed, good value at £6.50. Suggested a vegetable Thali for friend, who is unused to eating spicy food. Very impressed, a very appetising selection with ample portions. One other thing to note - Nan's, tasty, substantial.' MD.

RAJDOOT — NEW ENTRANT

17 Main Street Crumlin 01495 243032

'Feeling hungry on the way home from Newport one night. Have tried it a few times since, even though it is quite away from my home, about 10 miles. I particularly like the Roghan Gosht, which was rich and creamy with a good portion. The Rajpoot Thali was excellent with a very good fruit salad. £21 for two.' ph. Hours: 5.30-12, Friday and Saturday to 12.30.

Monmouth

MISBAH TANDOORI — TOP 100

9 Priory Street, Monmouth 01600 714940

D Miah opened his 80-seater restaurant in 1990. This comfortable venue exudes customer care. Mr Miah's Misbah attracts celebs, and he's delighted to tell you about them (ask him – each one has a tale). Chef A Rahman cooks such items as Bengal Fish Mossala (freshwater fish from Bangladesh cooked in tomato and onion, Zahan Special £6.95, medium, aubergines, spinach, potato, chicpea, mixed vegetables; Jamdani £7.95, mild, chicken cooked with cheese, cream. *'As good as all the reports I have read: clean, friendly, basic menu, good service. Strangely quiet for a Friday night though. Excellent Chicken Jalfrezi and Pullao Rice. Excellent.'* ib. *'Warm, personal welcome. Intimate friendly service. Appealingly presented tables. All senses catered for. Wonderful food, succulent meat, stupendous prawns - all flavours beautifully blended, a richly textured Tarka Dal. Fluffy and exotically flavoured Rice and above all FRESH Mango! Gastromonic excellent.'* gl & dt. *'Have visited for takeaways and sit-down meals for over five years. Consistently, exceptionally high standard. Feels like home.'* jt. *'Popadoms and chutneys arrived immediately. Exciting menu with authentic dishes. Clean toilets.'* s&dt. *'Food superb and promtly served.'* he. *'The quality of the food is a good mix between the comfort blanket of the traditional and the innovative and new.'* ar. *'Delicious, wonderful food, lots of lovely vegetarian dishes.'* j&ha. Super stuff. Restaurants like this are what this *Guide* is all about. Stays high in our **TOP 100**. Minimum charge: £10.00. Set dinner: £11.95 per person. Takeaway: 10% off. Hours: 12-2pm/6-11pm.

Newport

THE KOH I NOOR 

164 Chepstow Road, Maindee, Newport 01633 258028

Mrs L Khanan's venerable 60-seat Koh i Noor was established in 1978, and has appeared in most of our *Guides*. We've said before that nothing on the menu changes. Chef Tahir Ullah's curries are listed under such categories as mild, fruity, fairly hot, very hot, hottest and most favourite. In other words this is one of the early curry houses with its clutch of once-a-week regulars. Nothing wrong with that. Hours: 12-2.30/6-1am. Sun. 6-12.

Risca

JUBORAJ

84 Commercial Street 01633 262646

Air-conditioned. Good decor, classy, almost temple - ish, very clean and inviting. Welcoming, friendly staff, attentive. Good and pricey menu... got to pay for that refurbishment. *'...Very tasty, fresh Mixed Starter – onion bhajia, meat samosas and chicken pakora, small portion. Lamb and Prawn Madras with Pullao Rice and Aloo Gobi, very good portions with generous sauce, not at all oily, flavoursome. Delicious Chicken Tikka Masala. Special Fried Rice a bit disappointing, seemed very similar to Pullao Rice. All in all very good.'* PAH. Menu Extracts: Juboraj King Prawn £5.75, cooked in shell; Coriander Chicken £7.95, chicken fillets, ground coriander; Kohlapuri £8.75, hot and spicy chicken, turmeric, cumin, coriander, green chillies. Takeaway: discounted. Hours: 12-2/6-12.

GWYNEDD

Inc: Anglesey, Caernarvonshire, Conwy and Merioneth

Area: North Wales
Population: 240,000
Adjacent Counties:
Clwyd, Dyfed, Powys

Abersoch

EAST MEETS WEST

The High Street Abersoch 01758 713541

'Very new and modern establishment in heart of quaint North Wales village. Open, light and airy interior, subtly decorated. Run by young and friendly staff, service efficient and cheerful. Excellent Reshmi Kebab £2.75, single large succulent, well spiced kebab, topped with large, well cooked omelette. Nice, crisp salad, but yoghurt sauce would not have gone amiss. Superb Lamb Balti Rogan Josh £6.75, tangy, beautifully balanced sauce, plenty of tomatoes, well cooked onions and peppers. Stuffed with good cuts of tender lamb, though gristle and tough lumps were present. They take the translation of Balti literally, my curry was served in a copper plated stainless steel bucket! Very well cooked Chapati £1.50 for two, soft, moist but not doughy or salty. Very enjoyable, highly recommended. Up to Top 100 standard.' RW. Menu Extracts: Bengal King Prawns £9.95, hot with green chillies, bay leaves, cinnamon; Agni £9.95, Chicken or Lamb Tikka cooked with onions,

green peppers, cooked in brandy and set alight; Egg Nan £1.80; Keema Paratha £1.80. Hours: 6 to late.

Llandudno

BENGAL DYNASTY TOP 100 ©

1 North Parade, Llandudno 01492 878445

Llandudno is a really fabulous seaside town with gorgeous Georgian buildings running in an arch along the waterfront. Lewis Carroll wrote *Alice in Wonderland* in this seaside resort. Established in 1988, the 86-seat Bengal Dynasty is situated upstairs in one of these fine buildings. *'I was about to settle for fish & chips when I saw it, upstairs above a shoe shop. I had Lamb Tikka to start and then Chicken Bhuna, which was excellent.'* AG *'King Prawn Butterfly followed by my usual main courses. A very accomplished meal. Keema Nan was the highlight together with a homemade Kulfi. Gets my vote.'* JL. *'Service was welcoming, prompt and polite. Pops and chuts fresh and crisp. Main meals were large, everything was hot and well presented. An enjoyable experience, but not outstanding.'* SR. *'Menu was wide and varied. Papadoms and chutneys excellent. Raita exceptional. All meals were served piping hot with hot plates and the portions were satisfying. Waiters were very accommodating in making changes to dishes for our individual tastes. Smart, clean and tasteful surroundings. Highly recommended.'* NC. Specials: Chicken Bondhuk, Lamb Satkora Gost Macher Tarkari. Takeaway: 15% off. Hours: 12-2.30. (4.30 on Sun.)/6-11.30. Branches: Bengal Dynasty, Deeside, Clwyd and Northwich, Cheshire.

POWYS

Inc: Brecknock and Montgomery

Area: Central Eat Wales
Population: 124,000
Adjacent Counties: Clwyd, Dyfed, Glamorgan, Gwent, Gwynedd, Herefordshire, Shropshire

Llansantfraid

TANDOORI PLAICE 

Waterloo House, Llansantfraid 01691 828152

Established in 1994 by manager Shoakoth Ali. Black ash coffee table with red chairs for waiting customers. Takeaway only. Menu Extracts: Keema Chana Masala £5.25, minced lamb, chick peas, masala sauce; Pista Nan £1.40, pistachio nuts; Green Lamb Masala £5.25, lamb peices with peas, green herbs, touch of cream, butter. Credit cards not accepted. Hours: 5-11.30, Fri/ Sat to 12.

Newtown

SHILAM NEW ENTRANT

49 Broad Street Newtown 01686 625333

'I have been recommended to visit this restaurant and it certainly did not disappoint. Clean, fairly modern surroundings. Service very friendly and prompt. Good all round menu. Superbly presented, very good food, garnished platters rather than the traditional oval stainless dish. Tandoori Trout starter exceptional and Vindaloo had lots of bite. Loads of green chillies in very hot Jalfrezi. Most impressed.' KN. Menu Extracts: Bangol Maslee £6.75, spicy trout. Chicken Green Masala £5.75, tandoori chicken, freshly ground chili, coriander, onion, green pepper, garlic, ginger, spinach, lime, pickle flavoured sauce, served with salad. Delivery service. Hours: 5.30 -12, Fri/Sat to 2.

List of Contributors

This Guide is possible thanks to the many Curry Club members, and others, who have sent in reports on restaurants. Especial thanks to the following regular, prolific and reliable reporters (apologies for any errors, duplications, omissions, and for the tiny print necessitated by space considerations).

A: Martin Abbott, Gloucs; Colin Adam, Kilwinning; Ray Adams, Kimberley; Meena Ahamed, London; Paul Allen, Chatham; Tony and Lesley Allen, Rugby; MF Alsan, Rugby; G Amos, Wirral; Capt R Ancliffe, BFPO 12; Apryl Anderson, Ponteland; Karen Andras, Nottingham; Lisa Appadurai, Benfleet; Robin Arnott, Stafford; Mrs M Asher, Woodford Green; Dave Ashton, Warrington; Jo Ashton, Elland; Allan Ashworth, York; Berry Ashworth, Compton Bassett; Michelle Aspinal, Chester; Darius Astell, Southampton; Rachael Atkinson, Cheshire; Simon Atkinson, N5; Y Atkinson, IOM; Claire Austin, Stoke; Arman Aziz, N4.

B: Tom Bailey, Alresford; John Baker, Loughton; Mridula Baljekar, Camberley, Kim Baker, Hatfield; Mr & Mrs ML Banks, Enfield; Keith Bardwell, Hertford; Ian Barlex, Ilford; Trevor Barnard, Gravesend; Christopher Barnes, Ashton; Derek Barnett, Colchester; Tony Barrel, Hounslow; Joanne Bastock, Saltash; Mike Bates, Radcliffe; Shirley Bayley, Worthing; Karin and Angela, Rugby; Mr MJ Beard, Stafford; Joyce Bearpark, Murcia Spain; Dave Beazer, Cornwall; DJ Beer, Ross-on-Wye; Derick Behrens, Bucks; Ian Bell, Cheshire, Matt Bell, Derbys; P Bell, Carlisle; Sam Bell, Coventry; TW Bennett, Sherborne; Becky Benson, Worcs; John Bentley, Northampton; Ron Bergin, Gerrards Cross; Ian Berry, Goole; Martyn Berry, SE3; Kenneth Beswick, Lincoln; DJ Betts, Bexhill; Jonathan Bick, Cardiff; Brian and Anne Biffin, Fleet; Colin Bird, Welwyn Garden City; BH Birch, Hyde; Jim Birkumshaw, Derbys; James Birtles, Manchester; Chris Blackmore, Bristol; David Bolton, Lichfield; Mrs C Bone, Norfolk; A Boughton, SE27; L Le Bouochon, Jersey; Mrs I Bowman, Rochester; Robert Box, Knottingley; Alan Boxall, Burwash; Sean Boxall, Andover; F Boyd, Stranraer; Iain Boyd, Wealdstone; Roderick Braggins, Peebles; Amanda Bramwell, Sheffield; Dave Bridge, Wallasey; Michael E Bridgstock, Northants; Sandra Brighton, Nelson; Steve Broadfoot, Anfield; John and Susan Brockington, Sutton Coldfield; Paul Bromley, SE13; Robert Brook, London; Nigel John Brooks, Stoke on Trent; David Brown, Leeds; IA Brown, Fernhurst; Mark Brown, Scunthorpe; Steve Brown, Twickenham; DA Bryan, York; RC Bryant, Witney; Robert Bruce, Thornaby; Heather Buchanan, Inverness; Dr TM Buckenham, SW11; Mrs J Buffey, Sutton Coldfield; LG Burgess, Berkhamsted; DABurke, London, A Burton, Weston-super-Mare.

C: D Cadby, Swindon; Barry Caldwell, Chesterfield; David Caldwell, Brownhills; Stan Calland, Kingsley; Hugh Callaway, Cleethorpes; Duncan Cameron, Fordoun; Frank Cameron, Dundee; HS Cameron, Wirral; Alex Campbell, Ramsey Campbell, Wallasey; Hartley Wintney; Mrs E Campbell, Harrogate; N Campbell, Edinburgh; Josephine Capps, Romford; L Carroll, Huddersfield; James Casey, Wiltshire; Peter Cash, Liverpool; Mark Caunter, Guildford; TM Chandler, Farnborough; Desmond Carr, N8; J Carr, Birkenhead; TO Carr, Warrington; BR Carrick, Wakefield; DL Carter, Huntingdon; Mrs M Carter, Colchester; Madeline Castro, Bury St Edmunds; Dr WF Cavenagh, Norfolk; Neil Chantrell, Warrington; Hilary J Chapchal, Leatherhead; Mr & Mrs DR Chapchal, Leatherhead; John Chapman, Leics; Paul Chapman, Leighton Buzzard; Mr & Mrs Chatfield, Wimborne; Rajender Chatwal, Bicester; Dr GT Cheney, Salhouse; Paul Chester, Cuffley; Sqn Ldr PF Christopher, Ferndown; Alexis Ciusczak, Capistrano Beach, CA; Peter Clyne, SW11; VA Coak, Penzance; Louise Coben-Sutherland, Enfield; CH Coleman, Sussex; Robin Collier, Mid Calder; Chris Coles, Biggin Hill, Billy Collins, Wirral; Mrs J Collins, Portsmouth; CJ Comer, Basingstoke; Rhys Compton, Cheltenham; A Conroy, Durham; Joseph Coohil, Oxford; Neil Cook, Royston; Mr LW Coombes, Devon; Alan & Margaret Cooper, Llansteffan; Kim Cooper, Basildon; DW Cope, Whitchurch; Dr JC Coppola, Woodstock; Will Coppola, Oxford; Nigel Cornwell, Orpington; John Costa, Tunbridge Wells; MJ Cotterill, Bristol; Stephen Cowie, SW16; Steve Cowling, Shropshire; Julie Cozens, Oxon; Dr AM Croft, Cornwall; Roderick Cromar, Buckie; C Cross, Poole; Yasmin Cross, Huddersfield; Major & Mrs FJB Crosse, Salisbury; Robert Crossley, Huddersfield; Frank and Elizabeth Crozier, Redruth; R Cuthbertson, Southampton.

D: S Daglish, Scarborough; P Dalton, Wirral; Jan Daniel, Felpham; Mr & Mrs PE Dannat, Eastleigh; Martin Daubney, Hitchin; Gary Davey, W4; Alasdair Davidson, Heswall; Adrian Davies, NW3; Gwyn Davies, Wirral; Mrs JC Davies, Leeds; Josephine Davies, Swansea; Lucy Davies, Essex; Paul Davies, Chiddingfold; Mrs G Davies-Goff, Marlow; Colin Davis, Tatsfield; Ian Dawson, Mirfield; DM Day, Preston; Michael Day, West Bromwich; Peter Deane, Bath; Gary & Katy Debono, High Wycombe; David Dee, Ruislip; Elizabeth Defty, Co. Durham; Neil Denham, The Netherlands; R Dent, Bishop Auckland; Les Denton, Barnsley; Richard Develyn, St Leonards; Nigel Deville, Uttoxeter; Ken Dewsbury, Somerset; Richard Diamond, Romsey; RC Dilnot, Broadstairs; Graham Divers, Glasgow; James Dobson, Burscough; S Dolden, Rochester; R Dolley, W11; Clive Doody, Surrey; Keith Dorey, Barnet; Neil Downey, Worthing; Sarah Dowsett, Swindon; Anna Driscoll, Cape Province; Mrs J Driscoll, BFPO; Diane Duame, Wicklow; Eric Duhig, Hornchurch; Sheila Dunbar, Pinner; James Duncan, West Kilbride; Mark Dunn, E18; Rachael Dunn, Hemel, Robin Durant, Brighton; Martin Durrant, Chester; Avishek Dutt, London, Mr & Mrs JA Dywer, Birmingham.

E: A Edden-Jones, Bristol; Bruce Edwards, Norwich; Dave Edwards, Rugeley; CM Eeley, Witney; Rod Eglin, Whitehaven; Wendy Elkington; Ray Elliott, Worcester; Peter Ellis, London, PT Ellis, W'rtn; Mrs G Elston, Woodley; Tony Emmerton, Chorley; Mark Evans, Caersws; Mr & Mrs A Evans, Manchester; Brian Exford, Derbys.

F: Gary Fairbrother, Crosby; J.M.Fairhurst, Baldock; Hazel Fairley, Guildford; Chris Farrington, Cherry Hinton; Graham Faulkner, Dorking; John Fearson, Bucks; Denis Feeney, Glasgow; Kevin Fenner, Rothley; Bill and Laraine Field, Newcastle-upon-Lyme; Stephen Field, Norton; Mick Fielden, Glossop; AJ Finch, Enfield Wash; Duncan Finley, Glasgow; Maureen Fisher, Woodford Green; Bernard Fison, Holmrook; John Fitzgerald, Great Missenden; Merly Flashman, TN12; Colin & Toni Fleet, Dorset; Dr Cornel Fleming, N6; KD Flint, Kempsey; Fiona Floyd, Truro; Stephen & Elizabeth Foden, Lynton; Chris Fogarty, Enfield; Gareth Foley, Porthcawl; Neil Foley, Essex; IE Folkard-Evans, Manchester; SR Tracy Forster, Beds; Rod Fouracres, Glos.; Rosemary Fowler, Midhurst; John W Fox, Doncaster; Linda Foye, Barry; Theresa Frey, Fareham; Chris Frid, North Shields; Steve Frost, Kingston; Alan Furniss, Wraysbury; June Fyall, Bronwydd; Mrs MAJ Fyall, Dyfed.

G: Gail & Brendan, Orme; Stephen Gaines, Middlesex; MJ Gainsford, Burbage; Leo Gajsler, Geneva; Harry E Garner, London; Mrs FE Gaunt, Stonehouse; Phillip Gentry, Bexleyheath; Brian George, Wolverton; CM Gerry, Cyprus; G Gibb, SE21; Robert Giddings, Poole; Michael Gill, Leeds; Emma Gillingham, Huddersfield; Andrew Gillies, Edinburgh; AV Glanville, Windsor; Ms D Glass, Liverpool; A Glenford, Lincoln; Nick Goddard, Stevenage; Andrew Godfrey, Seer Green; Matthew Goldsmith, Burgess Hill; Mr & Mrs A. Goldthorp, Halstead; John Goleczka, Pensford; Michael Goodband, Perhore; Bryn Gooding, Corfu; Dr G Gordon, Kidlington; Mrs J Gorman, Strood; Ian Gosden, Woking; Bill Gosland, Camberley; David Gramagan, Formby; DC Grant, Enfield; Kathryn Grass, Wigan; Alan Gray, Erskine; DR Gray, SW11; A Greaves, Chesterfield; Andrew Greaves, Derbyshire; Rachel Greaves, Tavistock; Denise Gregory, Nottinghamshire; Jonathan Green, Cathays, Michael Green, Leicester; Nigel Green, Orpington; Richard Green, Gerrards Cross; Sheila Green, Barrow; A Gregor, Boston; Frank Gregori, NW10; Andrew Grendale, Ingatestone; A Griffiths, Milton Keynes; JK Greye, Bath; M Griffiths, Northampton; Dave Groves, Walsall; Lynda Gudgeon, Roopa Gulati, London; Willenhall, Louis Gunn, Chelmsford.

H: Karen Haley, Telford; John Hall, Cullercoats; Andrew Halling, Leigh; Stephen Hames, Bewdley; Alan Hamilton, Wakefield; Tina Hammond, Ipswich; Geoff & Janet Hampshire-Thomas, Kirkland; Neil Hancock, Derby; Ray Hancock, Chester; Dorothy Hankin, Fordingbridge; Sharon Hanson, Derby; Glynn Harby, Knaresborough; Martyn Harding, Powys; Roger Hargreaves, Stoke; J Harman, Brentwood; Gerald Harnden, Westcliff-on-Sea; Justin Harper, Hemel,; Dawn Harris, Dubley; Paul Harris, BFPO; David Harrison, Dursley; Patrick Harrison, Cambridge; David Harvey, SE24; S Harwood, Lewes; John K Hattam, York; Sally Haseman, Surbiton; Christopher & Linda Haw, Dewsbury; Ann & David Haynes, Bournemouth; John Haynes, Saffron Walden; DI Hazelgrove, West Byfleet; M Hearle, Tunbridge Wells; Kevin Hearn, Newcastle; Bernice Heath, Nottingham; Andy Hemingway, Leeds; Terry Herbat, Barnsley; Georgina Herridge, W9; T & M Hetherington, Preston; Victoria Heywood, Burton; Roger Hickman, N1; Pat & Paul Hickson, Chorley; Janet Higgins, Blackburn; Mrs S Higgins, Blackburn; Mrs B Higgs, Cotty; Dave Hignett, Newcastle-upon-Tyne; Alec Hill,

Wigan; Carolyn Hill, Nottingham; Stephen Hill, Chesterfield; Barry Hills, Surrey; David Hindle, W5; Bharti Hindocha, Richmond; Daniel Hinge, Bishop Auckland; Mrs MJ Hirst, Kent; SC Hodgon; Daniel Hodson, Abingdon; Peter Hoes, Bingley; Bernard Hofmiester, Berlin; P Hogkinson, Sheffield; Duncan Holloway, Windsor; Kevin Hooper, St Austell; Linda Horan, Wirral; Will H Horley, Barnsley; Peter Hornfleck, Farnborough; Jerry Horwood, Guildford; Dr MP Houghton, Rugby; Neil Houldsworth, Keighley; JK Howard, Enfield Wash; P Howard, Hornchurch; Mrs J Howarth, Oldham; Kathy Howe, Carlisle; Simon Howell, Gillingham; Bruce Howerd, Tongham; Lynn Howie, Sanderstead; Deh-Ta Hsiung, London; Jan Hudson, Hemel Hempstead; Tom Hudson, Jarrow; Chris Hughes, Wraysbury; Paul Hulley, Stockport; SP Hulley, Reddish; HL & S Humphreys, Stoke-on-Trent; AG Hunt, Southend-on-Sea; John & Frances Hunt, Langport; Paul Hunt, Essex; Roger Hunt, Sidmouth; Vince Hunt, Manchester; Penny Hunter, Brighton; Sheila Hunter, Dundee; Dr M Hutchinson, Gwynedd; Mrs V Hyland, Manchester.

I: DM Ibbotson, Sheffield; Nick & Mandy Idle, Ossett; Ken Ingram, Leeds; G Innocent, Dawlish; Mrs G Irving, Redditch; Robert Izzo, Horsham.

J: Dr AG James, Wigan; O Jarrett, Norwich; Sue Jayasekara, Essex; Sally Jeffries, Heathfield; L Jiggins, Dagenham; G John, Wirral; Maxine & Andrew Johnson, Leiden; Colin Johnson, Southall; Peter Johnson, Droitwich; Paul Jolliffe, Exeter; CML Jones, St Albans; Gareth Jones, Tonypandy; Kate Jones, Leiden; RW Jones, N9; Shirley Jones, SE13; WA Jones, Flints; Wendy Jones, Clwyd; Michael Lloyd Jones, Cardiff; Esther Juby, Norwich.

K: Tessa Kamara, W13; AD Kantes, Northants; Chris Keardey, Southampton; Anthony Kearns, Stafford; Russ Kelly, Seaforth; Prof. and Mrs Kemp, Royston; Mr & Mrs MJB Kendall, Hook; David Kerray, Akrotiri; John Kettle, Dover; JS Kettle, Banbury; Saul Keyworth, Essex; Stephen Kiely, N16; David King, Biggleswade; John & Jane Kingdom, Plymouth; Alyson Kingham, Oldham; Frances Kitchen, Langport; Peter Kitney, Banbury; J & P Klusiatis, Reading; Drs Heather & Mark Knight, Oxford; Drs MJ & A Krimholtz, SW14.

L: Caz Lack, Kent; Martin Lally, Chester; Alan Lathan, Chorley; Clive Lawrence, email; Cass Lawson, Swindon; Ronnie Laxton, London; Jonathan Lazenby, Mamhilad, Gwent; Gary Leatt, St. Brelade, Jersey; Andrew Lecomber, Durham; DH Lee, Waltham Abbey; Jackie Leek, Dartford; Simon Leng, Wakefield; David Leslie, Aberdeen; Russell D Lewin, NW2; A Lewis, Sherborne; Margaret Ann Lewis, Ashford; R Lewis, Rayleigh; Pat Lindsay, Hampshire; David Lloyd, Northampton; David Lloyd, Oswestry; Eleanor & Owen Lock, Geneva; Peter Long, Cheltenham; J Longman, Bodmin; John Loosemore, Orpington; DA Lord, Hove; Julia & Philip Lovell, Brighton; AP Lowe, Tolworth; Mr & Mrs DN Luckman, Horley; Jeremy Ludlow, Dorset; Mrs H Lundy, Wallasey; Graeme Lutman, Herts; Tim Lynch, Romford; Jamie Lyon, Burscough.

Mac/Mc: M Mcbryde, Watford; David Mackay, Twickenham; David Mackenzie, Darlington; Lin Macmillan, Lincoln; Deb McCarthy, E6; Patrick McCloy, N8; Vanessa McCrow, Teddington; David McCulloch, NW11; Michael McDonald, Ellesmere Port; David McDowell, Telford; BJ McKeown, Seaford; Ian McLean, Brighton; Dr and Mrs J McLelland, Mid Calder; Alan & Jean McLucas, Solihull; Dr FB McManus, Lincolnshire; Alan McWilliam, Inverurie.

M: Chris Mabey, Swindon; Rakesh Makhecha, Harrow; Richard Manley, Wirral; Cherry Manners, Hatfield; E Mansfield, Camberley; Clive Mantle; JF Marshall, Bedford; Geraldine Marson, Winsford; Colin Martin, Nuneaton; Derek Martin, Marlow; Jane Martin, SW19; PR Martin, Southend; DH Marston, Southport; DJ Mason, Cleveland; LJ Mason, Leeds; John Maundrell, Tunbridge Wells; Gilian May, Hayes; Peter F May, St Albans; Simon Mayo, Farnborough; Simon Meaton, Andover; John Medd, Nottingham; Tim Mee, Harrow; Sue & Alf Melor, Hanworth; Nigel Meredith, Huddersfield; Sujata Mia, Middlesex; H Middleton, Coventry; Simon Mighall, St Neots; PJL Mighell, Canterbury; Robert Miles, Hertfordshire; Catherine Millar, BFPO; DR Millichap, Horsham; BW Milligan; AJ Millington, Woodford; Sally Millington, N10; Mr & Mrs P Mills, Mold; Mary Mirfin, Leeds; Al Mitchell, Belfast; Jonathon Mitchell, Alton; F Moan, Cuddington; Sarah Moles, Buxton; Jon Molyneaux, Peterborough; Mrs SE Monk, Gisburn; AV Moody, Portsmouth; Christy Moore, Dublin; Christy Moore, London; DM Moreland, Willington; S Morgan, Feltham; Tim & Katherine Morgan, Scotland; Ian Morris, Gwynedd; Peter Morwood, Wicklow; A Moss, Colchester; Caroline Moss, Solihull; Mrs L Muirhead, Glasgow; David Muncaster, Stoke; Andy Munro, Birmingham; Joan Munro, Leyburn; Annette Murray, Thornton Cleveleys; JL Murray, Enfield; RG Murray, Carlisle; Drs Heather & Harry Mycook.

N: Simon Nash, Cheshire; Mrs PG Naylor, Salisbury; Hugh Neal, Kent; Jeff Neal, Bolton; Marcus Neal, Liss; A Nelson-Smith, Swansea; Liam Nevens, Stockton; Tony Newman, Margate; Rebecca Newman, Hayes; Clive Newton, Northwich; P & D Nixon, Basildon; Mrs DA Nowakowa, Tiverton; Robert Nugent, SE31; Canon Peter Nunn, Gloucestershire; Jody Lynn Nye, Illinois.

O: Beverley Oakes, Essex; AM O'Brien, Worthing; Eamon O'Brien, Holland; Pauline O'Brien, London; DC O'Donnell, Wetherby; Elise O'Donnell, Wolverhampton; Mary O'Hanlon, N Oliver, London; Helensburgh; Sheila Openshaw, Hampshire; David O'Regan, Leeds; Steve Osborne, Bucks; Jan Ostron, Felpham; Judith Owen, SW6; William & Sue Oxley, Southampton.

P: Trevor Pack, Rushden; RH Paczec, Newcastle; M Padina, Mattingley; Mr & Mrs GG Paine, Coventry; Keith Paine, Tilbury; GJ Palmer, Gainsborough; RS Palmer, Norfolk; Mrs A Parker, Birmingham; Mr GM Parker, Birmingham; John MF Parker, North Yorks; Philip Parker, Matlock; Bill Parkes-Davies, Tunbridge Wells; Angela Parkinson, Clitheroe; Nick Parrish; M Parsons, Fareham; Roy Parsons, Richmond; Donald Paterson, East Grinstead; GM Patrick, London; Mrs PA Pearson, Bristol; Mrs G Pedlow, Hitchin; David and Dandra Peet, Surrey; Mrs Barrie Penfold, Bourne End; J Penn, Southampton; Elaine & Martin Perrett, Dorchester; AJW Perry, Bristol; Graham Perry, Truro; Ian Perry, Essex; MJ Perry, E17; Ian Pettigrew, Edinburgh; Christopher Phelps, Gloucester; Adrian & Angela Phillips, Ammanford; Diane Phillips, Hyde; Jonathan Phillips, Saffron Walden; Steve Phillips, Wokingham; Colin Phipps, Scarborough; Sara Pickering, Northolt; Jack Pievsky, Pinner; Dirk Pilat, e-mail; Mike Plant, Essex; Susan Platt, Bury; D Pool, SE2; K Pool, Leyland; SR Poole, Runcorn; Tony Pope, Derbyshire; Steve Porter, Walsall; RL Power, Sutton Coldfield; Dave Prentice, Dartmouth; Steve Prentice, Devon; Tim Preston, Barrow; Alison Preuss, Glencarse; Jeff Price, Bristol; Mr J Priest, Sawbridgeworth; Dr John Priestman, Huddersfield; D Pulsford, Marford; Janet Purchon, Bradford; Steve Puttock, Chatham; Julie Pyne, County Down.

Q: Sheila Quince, E11.

R: Diane Radigan, Welling; Clive Ramsey, Edinburgh; Alison Ratcliff, Halstead; KJ Rayment, Hertford; RC Raynham, Chelmsford; CR Read, Epsom; Mark Read, Romford; Kim Reeder, South Shields; Debbie Reddy, W12; Francis Redgate, Nottingham; Steven Redknap, Ashford; I Reid, Fife; Lorraine Reid, Edinburgh; Duncan Renn, Dursley; Derek Richards, Bewdley; Sean Richards, Dover; Simon Richardson, Gainsborough; Mike Ridgway, Buxton; Mathew Riley, SE3; Lindsay Roberts, Lancaster; Margaret Roberts, Rubery; Peter Roberts, Shipston; Stewart & Anne Robertson, Leamington; Simon Roccason, Willenhall; Pat Roche, Chislehurst; J & P Rockery, Leicester; KG Rodwell, Harston; R Ronan, IOW; John Roscoe, Stalybridge; Brian Roston, Pontefract; John Rose, Hull; WJ Rowe; Steve Rowland, Matlock; Mrs EM Ruck, Darlington; DC Ruggins, Chalfont; JA Rumble, Rochford; Paul Rushton, Nottingham; K Ruth, W1; Bob Rutter, Blackpool; EJ Ryan, Effingham; N Ryer, Mansfield.

S: George and Mrs J Sadler, Thetford; MB Samson, Hertfordshire; Pauline Sapsford, Milton Keynes; MR Sargeant, Cornwall; Mark Sarjant, Guildford; GM Saville, Egremont; Mike Scotlock, Rayleigh; Mike Scott, Holmer Green; MJ Scott, SE26; Nicky & Don Scowen, Romford; Tim Sebensfield, Beeston; M Seefeld, W5; Patrick Sellar, Maidstone; Philip Senior, Liverpool; N Sennett, Hull; David Sewell, Aldershot; Mrs DA Seymour, Burnham-on-Sea; Richard Shackleton, Wakefield; Brian Shallon, Camberley; Jeane Sharp, St Albans; Howard & Mary Sherman, Upton-by-Chester; Mark Shaw, Swindon; Michelle Shaw, Ilford; Deborah Shent, Nottingham; Barrie Shepherd, Bishopston; Howard Sherman, Chester; Theresa Shilcock, Derbyshire; Ewan Sim, Leeds; Carolyn Simpson, SE13; Jennifer Singh, Enfield; Jeff Slater, E6; Joy Slater, Northum; William P Sloan, Camberley; Else & Harald Smaage, Sauvegny; David Smith, Norwich; David Smith, Swindon; Denis Smith, Swindon; EK Smith, Edinburgh; Gillian Smith, St Andrews; Hazel Smith, Llandrinio; Howard Smith, Cardiff; Jim Smith, Cork; LP & A Smith, Gibraltar; Mark Smith, Lancashire; Nora Smith, Cardiff; RB Smith, BFPO; Sue Smith, Northampton; Susan Smith, Devon; Colin Snowball, Cheltenham; Tim Softly, Leigh; Robert Solbe, Surrey; Peter Soloman, Middlesbrough; M Somerton- Rayner, Cranwell; Maurice Southwell, Aylesbury; Gill Sparks, Halifax; Andrew Speller, Harlow; GD Spencer, Stonehaven; Mrs P Spencer, Norwich; Andy Spiers, Brighton; R Spiers, Wolverhampton; CP Spinks, Church Langley; Chris Spinks, Ilford; John Spinks, Hainault; Martin Spooner, Wallsend; DJ Stacey, Cambridge; Mrs WL Stanley-Smith, Belper; Mr & Mrs M Stanworth, Haywards Heath; John Starley, Birdingbury; Nigel Steel, Carlisle; Avril Steele, Crossgar; Bob Stencill, Sheffield; John Stent, Liss; Ian Stewart, Potters Bar; Tim Stewart, Norfolk; Tina Stone, Illford; Barry Strange, Kent; Rob Struthers, Brighton; Mrs MB Such; FD Sunderland, Plympton; FC Sutton, Poole; Andrew Swain, Sudbury; Carolyn Swain, Leeds; Gary Swain, Coventry; DL Swann, Parbold; Frank Sweeney, Middlesbrough; Gill & Graham Swift, Beeston; MS Sykes, Dorrington.

T: Nigel & Gill Tancock, Newbury; Steve Tandy, Cleveleys; Bernard Tarpey, Failsworth; Andrew Tattersall, North Yorks; CB Taylor, Wolverhampton; Colin Taylor, Preston; Kevin Taylor, Sevenoaks; Ken Taylor, Sevenoaks; Peter Taylor, Kingston-upon-Hull; Philip & Vivien

Taylor, Cromer; Roger Taylor, Hamela; Len Teff, Whaddon; Mrs PF Terrazzano, Leigh-on-Sea; RL Terry, Kent; Michael Third, Nothum; Christopher & Niamh Thomas, Barnet; DG Thomas, Gloucestershire; DL Thomas, Peterborough; Mrs J Thomas, Cumbria; Mark Thomas, Exeter; Nigel Thomas, Lincoln; Dr DA & AHE Thombs, Slimbridge; Alan Thompson, Clwyd; David & Lisa Thompson, SE10; Richard Thompson, Rainham; Bill Thomson, Ramsgate; Paul Thomson, Salford; J Thorne, South Benfleet; Richard Tilbe, Wokingham; Mrs BM Clifton Timms, Chorley; Joan & Ken Timms, West Sussex; Mrs M Tindale, Beverley; Alan Tingle, Hayling Island; Graham Todd, Crawley; Joan Tongue, Huddersfield; Alex & Sarah Torrence, Cleveland; SR Tracey-Forster, Bronham; Bernard Train, Barton; Leigh Trevitt, Bishops Stortford; R Trinkwon, Ferring; Kevin & Sarah Troubridge, Chelmsford; Dr JG Tucker, SW17; Paul Tunnicliffe, Cleveland; Martin Turley, Belgium; Don Turnball, Geneva; Mrs SM Turner, Stroud; R Twiddy, Boston; S Twiggs, Lower Kingswood; Jeremey Twomey, Leamington; John Tyler, Romford.

V: David Valentine, Forfar; Alan & Lesley Vaughan, Paington; D Vaughan-Williams, Penyffordd; Puja Vedi, London; Mrs B Venton, Chipstead; Richard Vinnicombe, Camberley; Mr & Mrs T Vlismas, Crymyoh; Sarah Vokes, Dorking; Gordon Volke, Worthing.

W: Phil Wain, Merseyside; PM Waine, Manchester; R Waldron, Oxon; Alison Walker, Droitwich; Andrew Walker, Aklington; Katherine Walker, London; Dr JB Walker, Burnham; John Walker, Chorley; Dr PAW Walker, Wirral; William Wallace, West Kilbride; Alison Walton, North Shields; Mrs J Ward, Wakefield; Cathy Ward, Slough; Pamela Ward, Birmingham; Simon Ward, Croydon; John Warren, Lancs; Mrs G. Warrington, Hyde; Nicholas Watt, Houghton; RG Watt, Bromyard; Andy Webb, Aberdeen; Peter Webb, West Byfleet; TG Webb, Peterborough; Nick Webley, Llandeilo; Dave Webster, Gateshead; Harry and Marina Webster, Nottingham; Andrew Wegg, SW16; Michael Welch, Reading; J Weld, Eastleigh; Dave Weldon, Hale; John Wellings, Edinburgh; AD West, Leicestershire; Laurence West, Torquay; Dr PJ West, Warrington; Joyce Westrip, Perth, Australia; Sarah Wheatley, Leavesden; George Whilton, Huddersfield; Andy Whitehead, Swindon; Mr & Mrs DW Whitehouse, Redditch; George Whitton, Huddersfield; Peter Wickendon, East Tilbury; Jennette Wickes, Fleet; PM Wilce, Abingdon; Malcolm Wilkins, Gravesend; Chris Wilkinson, Cumbria; Geoffrey Wilkinson, Orpington; Babs Williams, Bristol; Mark P Williams, Bromley; P Williams, St Austell; Raoul Williams, Cambridge; Ted Williams, Norwich; David Williamson, NW3; David Williamson, Stamford; BP and J Willoughby, Devizes; Bob & Eve Wilson, NW2; Dr Michael Wilson, Crewe; Major Mike Wilson, BFPO 140; John Wirring, Swindon; Mrs AC Withrington, Hindhead; David Wolfe, SW1, W Wood, Hornsea; John Woolsgrove, Enfield; Geof Worthington, Handforth; Mrs C Wright, Glasgow; Mrs CF Wright, Stockport; Clive Wright, Halesowen; D Wright, Rotherham; John D Wright, St Ives; Georgina Wright, Nottingham; Lynn Wright, Newark; Mick Wright, Beds.

Y: Stephen Yarrow, NW11; EJ Yea, Cambridgeshire; Rev. Can. David Yerburgh, Stroud; Andrew Young, Cumbria; Andy Young, Penrith; Mrs B Young, Basildon; Carl Young, Nottingham; Mrs E Young, Ilmington.

What We Need to Know

We need to know everything there is to know about all curry restaurants in the UK. And there is no one better able to tell us than those who use them. We do not mind how many times we receive a report about a particular place, so please don't feel inhibited or that someone else would be better qualified. They aren't. Your opinion is every bit as important as the next person's. Ideally, we'd like a report from you every time you dine out – even on a humble takeaway. We realize this is hard work so we don't mind if your report is very short, and you are welcome to send in more than one report on the same place telling of different occasions. Please cut out the forms on the last page. Or you can even use the back of an envelope or a postcard, or we can supply you with more forms if you write in (with an S.A.E., please). If you can get hold of a menu (they usually have takeaway menus to give away) or visiting cards, they are useful to us too, as are newspaper cuttings, good and bad, and advertisements. So, please send anything along with your report. Most reports received will appear, in abbreviated form, in the Curry Magazine (the Curry Club members' regular publication). They are also used when preparing the next edition of this Guide. We do not pay for reports but our ever-increasing corps of regular correspondents receive the occasional perk from us. Why not join them? Please send us your report after your next restaurant curry. Thank you.

Pat Chapman
Founder, The Curry Club
PO Box 7
Haslemere
Surrey
GU27 IEP

Fax it to: 01428 645045

E-mail it to chapman.curry@virgin.net

Town Index

About the Author

Pat Chapman was born in London's Blitz, with an addiction to curry inherited from his family's six-generation connection with India, the story of which is told in Pat's book Pat Chapman's Taste of the Raj (see page 624?). Virtually weaned on his grandmother's curries, he was taken to his first curry houses – Veeraswamy in Piccadilly and Shafi's in Gerrard Street – at the age of six, at a time when there were only three such establishments in London, and six in the whole of the UK. Visits became a regular treat and confirmed in Pat a passion and a curiosity about the food of India. He was already a curryholic! Following education at Bedales and Cambridge, he did a short stint in the RAF, flying fast jets, then spent several years in industry.

He founded the now world-renowned Curry Club in 1982, at a time when the curry was just beginning to become nationally important, as a way of sharing information about recipes, restaurants and all things to do with spicy food. Soon a national network of curry restaurant reporters was established, whose voluntary contributions led to the publication of the first edition of this highly successful Good Curry Guide in 1984, and its prestigious awards to restaurants.

Assisted by his wife, Dominique, Pat frequently demonstrates at major food shows and appears on TV and radio, and they regularly stage cookery courses and events. His pioneering Gourmet Tours to India are now well-established holidays for aficionados.

With book sales exceeding 1.5 million, Pat is best known as a writer of easy-to-follow recipes. His succession of popular curry titles, , are published by Simon & Schuster, Hodder & Stoughton, Piatkus, Sainsbury's and the BBC.

CURRY CLUB MEMBERS'DISCOUNT VOUCHER SCHEME

SAVE POUNDS ON DINING!

To make big savings on your curry meals or takeaways, you must become a Curry Club member. It's easy: contact us at the address below. Members get our colourful Curry Club Magazine three times a year. In it are six vouchers, so you get eighteen vouchers a year.

Each voucher is valid at any one of the restaurants that have agreed to participate in this scheme. To identify them look for the © sign at the top right hand of the restaurant's entry.

The actual discount each restaurant is willing to give varies from restaurant to restaurant. Some will give a free bottle of wine, or free starters, others 5% off the bill, and some are offering as much as 10%, or even more.

We have agreed with the restaurant owners that these discounts are available at the discretion of the restaurant, at their quieter times, and that each Curry Club member will book in advance when using a discount voucher.

To find out how much discount you can get, and when they will give it to you, please PHONE THE MANAGER. (Where possible we have given the name of the individual owner or manager who has agreed to give the discount in the participating restaurant's entry.) Then please BOOK.

There is no limit to the number of people Curry Club members may take. One voucher is valid for a discount on one meal, and must be handed over when paying the bill.

REMEMBER, YOU MUST BE A MEMBER OF THE CURRY CLUB TO GET YOUR VOUCHERS. SO JOIN NOW TO SAVE POUNDS.

More information about the scheme and the Club from:
THE CURRY CLUB, PO BOX 7, HASLEMERE.. SURREY GU27 1EP
Please send an S.A.E.

RESTAURANT UPDATE INFORMATION

Even if you do not fill in a report overleaf, you may be able to give us vital information, such as that below. DO YOU KNOW OF ANY:

NEW CURRY RESTAURANT OPENINGS:

Restaurant name:

Street no and name:

Town: County:

Postcode: Telephone:

CURRY RESTAURANT CLOSURES OVER THE LAST FEW MONTHS,

Including any listed in this Guide

Restaurant name:

Street no and name:

Town: County:

Postcode: Telephone:

HYGIENE OR OTHER OFFENCES

Please back up with a local press cutting if possible

Restaurant name:

Street no and name:

Town: County:

Postcode: Telephone:

YOUR FAVOURITE RESTAURANT(S)

If possible, in descending order, best first

Restaurant name:

Street no and name:

Town: County:

Postcode: Telephone:

ANY OTHER CURRY RESTAURANT INFORMATION?

Please continue on separate sheets of paper if required

Please return your info to: The Curry Club, PO Box 7, Haslemere, Surrey. GU27 1EP

RESTAURANT REPORT FORM

Whenever you have an 'Indian' meal or takeaway, The Curry Club would like to have your opinion.

Restaurant name:

Street no and Streetname:

Town: County:

Postcode: Telephone: e.mail:

Date Visited

Your name, address & e-mails please:

Please continue on separate sheets of paper if required

Please return your info to: The Curry Club, PO Box 7, Haslemere, Surrey. GU27 IEP

Or e-mail it to pat@patchapman.co.uk

REPORT

Please tell us everything... your first impressions, the welcome, cleanliness, your table – was it appealing? Nice things waiting for you on it? the menu, quantities, quality, service, background music, comfort, decor. The food? How were the toilets? First visit? Been before? Would you go back/ recommend to friends? Overall was the restaurant good, bad or indifferent?